The Native Plant Primer

The Native

CAROLE OTTESEN

HARMONY BOOKS, NEW YORK

Plant Primer

Published by Harmony Books, a division of Crown Publishers, Inc., 201 East 50th Street, New York, New York 10022. Member of the Crown Publishing Group.

Random House, Inc. New York, Toronto, London, Sydney, Auckland

HARMONY and colophon are trademarks of Crown Publishers, Inc.

Manufactured in Hong Kong

Design by Kay Schuckhart

Library of Congress Cataloging-in-Publication Data
Ottesen, Carole, 1942–
  The native plant primer / Carole Ottesen.
  Includes bibliographical reference and index.
  1. Native plants for cultivation—United States.   2. Native plant gardening—United States.   I. Title.
  SB439.O88   1995
  635.9'517—dc20   94-19383

ISBN 0-517-59215-0

10 9 8 7 6 5 4 3 2 1

First Edition

To friends indeed

C o n t

ents

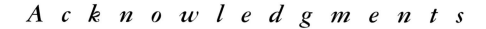

A c k n o w l e d g m e n t s

The contributors to this book, without whom it would have been impossible, include the following.

Betsy Clebsch, a charter member on the board of Yerba Buena Nursery, has a special interest in native plant communities—particularly those of northern California. She gardens on one and one-half acres in the mountains south of San Francisco, where she indulges her love of manzanitas and sages. The latter number over 150, making her garden a laboratory for her current undertaking, a book, *Sages,* to be published by Timber Press.

Eliza Earle has a background in ethnobotany—a B.A. in anthropology and an M.A. in landscape architecture. She is currently on the staff at the Theodore Payne Foundation, a nonprofit foundation dedicated to preserving California native plants by propagating, selling, and educating the public about them. She tends many natives in her home garden in the Hollywood hills. Eliza helped with the descriptions of California plants.

Sydney Eddison, a columnist for the *Litchfield Country Times,* has also written for *Fine Gardening, Horticulture, House Beautiful, HG,* and the *New York Times.* Her books *A Passion for Daylilies* and *A Patchwork Garden* were published by HarperCollins in 1992 and 1990, respectively. She tends what she describes as a "big disheveled country garden." Sydney made suggestions for native plants in the Northeast.

Jenny Fleming is a charter member of the California Native Plant Society— now thirty chapters strong—which plays a vital role in preserving rare plant species and communities. She is a past president of the East Bay chapter and has served on state and local boards. Her garden, in the hills of Berkeley overlooking the bay, makes use of microclimates to support various California communities: a north slope supports a north coastal redwood garden; a meadow on the east side is planted with native fescue, *Brodiaea* complex bulbs, and other wildflowers; the upper part of a steep hill supports chaparral plants. Jenny had suggestions for native plants in California and helped with descriptions.

Fred Galle, former director of horticulture at Callaway Gardens in Pine Mountain, Georgia, has written extensively on azaleas, including two books, *The Southern Living Book of Azaleas* (Oxmoor House, 1974) and *Azaleas* (Timber Press, 1987). Among his many awards are the Gold Medal from the Rhododendron Society and the Liberty Hyde Bailey Award from the American Horticultural Society. Fred was generous with advice on native azaleas.

Peggy Grier and her husband, Bill, began gardening with natives at a house in Seattle, where they tried "putting back the forest, only better than it was." Their current house in Lafayette, California, was purchased for the lot—an acre with a north-facing slope, oaks, and snowberries. Efforts to landscape this house with natives put them in contact with the East Bay chapter of the California Native Plant Society, for which Peggy has served for seven years as plant sale co-chairman and nursery manager, overseeing 10,000 plants of about 350 species. Peggy helped with descriptions of California natives.

Edward R. Hasselkus, a native of Wisconsin, is a professor in the Department of Horticulture and Landscape Architecture, University of Wisconsin–Madison, and curator of the Longenecker Gardens at the U.W.

Arboretum. Among his many awards is the University of Wisconsin–Madison Distinguished Teaching Award (1987). His publications include *A Guide to Selecting Landscape Plants for Wisconsin* (University of Wisconsin, 1991). Dr. Hasselkus made suggestions for the Midwest.

Gwen Moore Kelaidis, editor of the *Bulletin of the American Rock Garden Society,* is president of the American Penstemon Society and helped with the penstemon chart. She has written extensively on horticultural subjects. Among her publications are "Rock Gardens" and "Shady Gardens," which she co-authored with her husband, Panayoti Kelaidis, for *Taylor's Guide to Garden Design* (Houghton Mifflin, 1988). She owns and operates Rocky Mountain Rare Plants, a mail-order business in cushion and saxatile plants. Gwen helped with plant descriptions and, with her husband, suggested plants for the Mountain Region.

Panayoti Kelaidis is curator of the Rock Alpine Garden at the Denver Botanic Gardens, Denver, Colorado. A past president of the Rocky Mountain chapter of the American Rock Garden Society and the American Penstemon Society, he serves on, among others, the board of the American Rock Garden Society. He speaks frequently at conferences nationally and internationally and is the recipient of a number of awards, including the Edgar T. Wherry Award from the American Rock Garden Society. Panayoti suggested plants for the Mountain Region with his wife, Gwen.

Arthur R. Kruckeberg, professor emeritus at the University of Washington, was chairman of the Botany Department from 1971 to 1977. In addition to research and university teaching, he conducted adult education courses on Pacific Northwest natives. An avid gardener on four acres, Dr. Kruckeberg helped to found the Washington Native Plant Society, of which he was president from 1975 to 1983. Among his publications is *Gardening with Native Plants of the Pacific Northwest: An Illustrated Guide* (University of Washington Press, 1982). Dr. Kruckeberg suggested plants for the Pacific Northwest.

Sally Kurtz is owner and proprietor of Water Ways Nursery, Inc., a business specializing in native aquatic and herbaceous emergent plants. The 34-acre nursery is located in Lovettsville, Virginia, in historic Loudon County. Water Ways' display gardens, around the Federal-style John Ruse House, include water and bog plantings, perennials, woodland plants, and natives of the Mid-Atlantic and Southeast. Sally was consultant for the chapter on water plants.

Joe Lawson is an environmental horticulturist and landscape designer with extensive training and a special interest in native plants. He is landscape supervisor of the Palm Beach County School Board. He co-founded and oversees a 10-acre nursery of native plants that feed landscape replacements, nature areas, and trails at 140 schools. He currently serves on the board of directors of the Florida Native Plant Society. Joe made suggestions for Florida.

Doug Larson, who has lived his whole life in the desert, has always had an interest in desert natives. He was curator of gardens at the Living Desert Reserve in Palm Desert, California, and worked as a residential landscape consultant before joining the staff at Arizona–Sonora Desert Museum in Tucson. Doug had suggestions for the Southwest and helped with descriptions.

Bob McCartney, a native of southeastern Virginia, was horticulturist for the Colonial Williamsburg Foundation. One of the owners of Woodlanders, Inc.— whose goal is to introduce and make available fine plants that can be grown in the South and around the world—he is a modern-day plant explorer who combs the Southeast for plants to introduce into cultivation. He works closely

with federal, state, and private agencies and organizations to locate, monitor, and protect populations of rare and endangered plants throughout the South. Bob suggested and helped to describe woody plants for the South.

Jan Midgley was owner and operator of Wildflower, a wholesale and retail source of native herbaceous perennials before moving to Alabama. She has gardened with native plants for 23 years, concentrating on propagation of plants that are unavailable in the trade. Jan is the program chairman for the Cullowhee Conference and a frequent lecturer and writer on native, medicinal, and wildlife plants. She has written *Nursery Sources of Native Plants of the Southeastern United States* (Wildflower, 1993). Jan lent unstinting support throughout the years that this book was in the works and shared her vast knowledge of plant propagation.

Judy L. Mielke holds a bachelor of science in horticulture from Washington State University and completed a master's of environmental planning at Arizona State University. She was a horticulturist at Desert Botanical Garden in Phoenix for nearly nine years and now runs her own landscape design business, specializing in native landscapes. Her book, *Native Plants for Southwestern Landscapes* (University of Texas Press), was published in 1993. Judy listed and described suggestions for the Southwest.

Bart O'Brien is currently the horticultural director of Rancho Santa Ana Botanic Garden, an institution dedicated to California native plants and research in plant systematics and evolution. He has written two books, one dealing with newer and unusual drought-tolerant plants and the other on California native plant cultivars. He has served on the board of directors and has been very active in the California Native Plant Society, the Western Horticultural Society, and the Yerba Buena Nursery Foundation. Bart suggested California natives, helped with their descriptions, and helped compose the *Arctostaphylos* and *Ceanothus* charts.

Judith Phillips studied art, journalism, philosophy, and anthropology before finding that school was interrupting her education. She began her hands-on training in horticulture in Indiana. She divides her time between producing native and locally adapted plants at Bernardo Beach Native Plant Farm in Veguita, New Mexico, using these plants in landscape design, and writing about them. Her book *Southwestern Landscaping with Native Plants* (Museum of New Mexico Press) was published in 1987. She is currently at work on a sequel. Judith suggested plants for the Southwest and helped with descriptions.

Felder Rushing is a seventh-generation Mississippian, a horticulturist, and a garden writer whose columns, magazine articles, photographs, books, and radio and TV programs regularly feature native plants and wildflowers. His photographs have appeared on the covers of *Southern Living* and the *Wildflower Journal*.

He has also written a book with Steve Bender, *Passalong Plants* (University of North Carolina Press, 1993). He is a past president of the Mississippi Native Plant Society and serves on the steering committee for the Cullowhee Conference. Felder listed perennials for the South.

Benny J. Simpson earned a bachelor of science from Texas Tech. He is currently a research scientist at the Texas Agricultural Experiment Station in Dallas, where he helps to select native plants for the landscape trade. He has written over 120 technical and popular publications and one book, *A Field Guide to Texas Trees* (Gulf Publications, 1988). Benny listed plants for Texas's various climates.

Richard E. Weaver, Jr., earned an M.S. and a Ph.D. in plant taxonomy from Duke University before joining the staff at Harvard University's Arnold Arboretum, where he was horticultural taxonomist, assistant curator, acting director, editor of *Arnoldia,* and project director. He is currently a co-owner of We-Du Nurseries in Marion, North Carolina. Dr. Weaver composed the *Viola* chart.

These plant people gave me advice about gardening in their regions and helped me to select plants for each part of the country based upon garden-worthiness, beauty, and availability. Their suggestions are noted in the plant lists within the region chapters. Bear in mind that the farther a plant is taken from the conditions of its region of origin, the more heroic efforts must be just to keep it alive. For example, with unlimited water, many eastern natives will grow in California, but their survival depends on that constant irrigation.

To help in choosing plants that can survive without all manner of supports, regions of origin, hardiness zones, and cultural information are also included in the descriptions of individual plants found in the chapters on perennials, annuals, grasses, ferns, water plants, vines, shrubs, and trees.

In addition to the regional native plant experts who lent their considerable advice, I wish to thank others who opened gardens, answered questions, and gave advice, particularly Rick Darke of Longwood Gardens, Dr. Richard Lighty and Jean Frett of Mt. Cuba Center, Barbara Pryor of the New England Wild Flower Society, Charles Mann, Gail Haggard, Glen Snell, Lee Morrison, Kim Hawks, Meredith Clebsch, and many, many others.

A big thank-you to my agent, Sallie Gouverneur, who got me together with the dream team: Alison Acker and Peter Guzzardi (whose assistants, Sarah Hamlin and Karin Wood, handled a thousand details with grace and charm). And thank-you to production editor Camille Smith, designer Kay Schuckhart, and production manager Bill Peabody for giving this book its final form.

F o r e w o r d

I've always lived in the Northeast, and I like it. If asked just what it is about this part of the country I find so spellbinding, I might say it is the strength and individuality of the seasons, but the images that come quickly to mind are not simple changes in the weather. I may picture myriad translucent leaves filling in the forest canopy, building a new roof over the spring woods and bathing it in a lime glow. I might remember low-angled autumn rays projecting the stately silhouette of a bare black walnut against an old mill in the morning, or maybe the tracery of my birches moving against a stucco wall during a windy winter sunset. Sound and scent memories are equally compelling: the rustling of meadow grasses; the sweetness of spring breezes; autumn's pungency. All these dramas are part of the essential rhythm and ritual of the Northeast, and they are largely attributable to the plant life that is particular to the region.

My initial fondness for native plants and their habitats led me to a career in horticulture, and my professional travels have provided a fascinating overview of landscapes both domestic and foreign. As I've delighted in the different sights, sounds and smells of these places, I've also been dismayed by increasingly evident homogenization of everything from architecture to gardens. Economics may be behind the relentless march of uniform little boxes across our former forests and farmlands, but do we really want the same street trees planted from Portland to Philadelphia?

I'm no purist at home; I grow a number of exotics that either please my eye, have sentimental appeal, or are simply best adapted to a difficult spot in the "yard," as we Americans tend to call our personal landscapes. Overall, however, native plants predominate, and this is quite deliberate. I chose my home because it was located near a preserved piece of quintessential Pennsylvania: wooded rolling hills bordering a rocky creek valley. The garden is perhaps my greatest opportunity for self-expression—my "art." I want it to be pretty and I want it to be functional, yet I also want it to display a reverence for the adjacent native landscape that ultimately provides my sense of place. The native plants I nurture at home connect me intimately with the natural cycles of my part of the country.

Happily, the business of gardening with natives is getting easier. Native plants, responsibly propagated, are becoming ever more available thanks to a new wealth of specialty nurseries springing up around the nation. Regional seminars on native plants and books like this one of Carole's, written by an American gardener for American gardeners, provide sound advice and inspiration. I believe our awakening enthusiasm for native plants will be a powerful force in conserving and enhancing the regional diversity that is fundamental to the health and beauty of American landscapes.

Rick Darke
Curator of Plants,
Longwood Gardens,
Kennett Square, Pennsylvania

P r e f a c e

Reading a book like this should immediately bring adventurous gardeners to the realization that there is a wealth of horticultural treasures awaiting them. The gardener will be awestruck that many of these extraordinary plants are likely to be found growing nearby. After the long-established tradition of pursuing the most exotic plants from the far corners of the earth, we as gardeners are only beginning to appreciate, develop, and use our native flora. Our lack of familiarity has not bred contempt for our local natives, just ignorance. My good friend Gerda Isenberg, owner of Yerba Buena Nursery (a California native plant concern), recalls that her horticultural advisers in the 1950s had expressed shock and disdain that she would want to grow "those weeds." Now "those weeds" are playing an ever-expanding role in our horticultural world: natural gardens, appropriate horticulture, ecologically correct gardens, the biodiversity crisis, and restoration are entrenching a horticultural context for our native plants.

Nationally, there has been a strong horticultural history associated with the native flora of the eastern United States and, as a result, many eastern plants are widely accepted in gardens. Western natives have had a much more difficult time gaining a foothold, with the major exception of the large number of our annuals, which have found their way into gardens around the world. I find that the usual reason for this lack of respect (if you will) is due to the significantly different climate found in the West—so foreign to most settlers that they rejected it outright and set us on the path to the misguided, resource-intensive effort of bringing their familiar gardening traditions to an outright hostile environment. Fortunately, there has been an influence from the Mediterranean, particularly from Spain and Italy, that has given us guidance on using plants from dry climates to create beautiful gardens.

Still, with the overall interest in North America native flora growing with each passing year, it has become glaringly clear that there are few reference books to encourage the appropriate use of these plants. As gardeners, we all need to focus our collective energies toward experimenting with our native plants, trying unfamiliar species in our gardens, selecting the most vigorous and beautiful individuals for garden use, propagating, naming, and distributing them to others, and writing about our experiences. Carole Ottesen's book is a major step toward filling this need. With more demand for these plants from the gardening public, an additional and necessary benefit from Carole's and other authors' efforts will be that more nurseries will be encouraged to propagate garden-tolerant selections of our native plants.

Because of the diversity of climates and growing conditions across the nation, there have been few horticultural books that have adequately covered the native flora of this vast land. Carole's book is an excellent tribute to the horticultural potential of our flora.

Bart O'Brien,
Director of Horticulture,
Rancho Santa Ana Botanic Garden,
Claremont, California

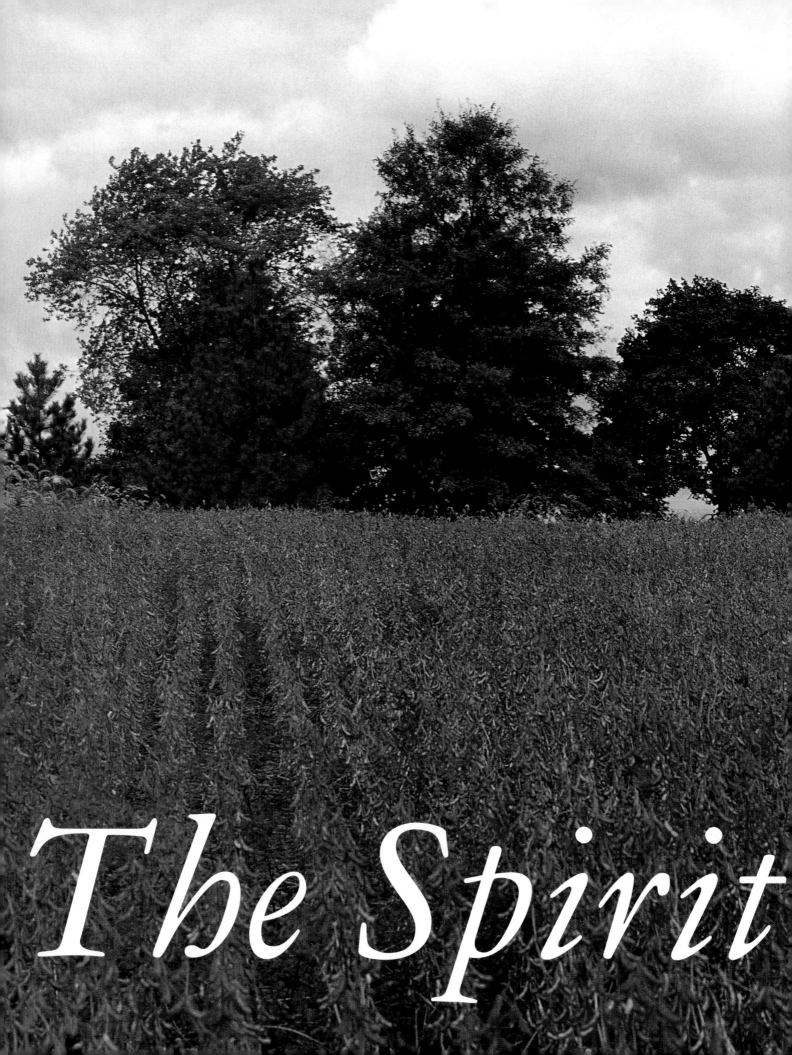

The Spirit

"I've gone to look for America"

SIMON AND GARFUNKEL

of the Land

Some YEARS AGO, ON A RAINY DAY IN EARLY SPRING, I GOT IN MY CAR AND SET OUT IN SEARCH OF THE AMERICAN GARDEN OR, RATHER, THE AMERICAN GARDEN AND THE AMERICAN GARDENER. MY PLAN WAS TO VISIT AS MANY GARDENS AND SEE AS MANY OF THIS VAST COUNTRY'S PLANTS AS I COULD. IN EACH PLACE, I HOPED TO MEET LOCAL GARDENERS AND DESIGNERS AND LEARN ABOUT THE PLANTS THAT GIVE EACH REGION AND ITS GARDENS THEIR SPECIAL CHARACTER.

DURING MY YEARS OF GARDENING, DE-SIGNING, AND WRITING, I GRADUALLY HAD COME TO THE CONCLUSION THAT IT WAS THE PLANTS THEMSELVES IN LOGICAL COMBINATIONS THAT GAVE A GARDEN WHAT THOUGHTFUL OBSERVERS SINCE ALEXANDER POPE HAVE CALLED "THE SPIRIT OF THE PLACE." COMING TO THIS REALIZATION WAS MORE LIKE A LONG JOURNEY FROM ONE MIND-SET TO ANOTHER. ALONG THE ROUTE, IN A FUNNY WAY, MY PROGRESS SEEMED TO PARALLEL THE HISTORY OF GARDENING.

OVERLEAF: *Church in Virginia*
ABOVE: *Boltonia and tithonia*

Oak leaf hydrangea

Many years ago, I passed an important milestone when I visited the Peradeniya Gardens in Sri Lanka. At that time, I had already experienced an initial infatuation with annuals, whose reliable blooms I count on over the hot summer months. And I had planted hundreds of bulbs, whose appearance out of the bare earth has never

New England asters

lost its magic. I had begun planting shrubs and trees around the house and was the proud owner of a perennial garden, which I fervently hoped resembled an English model. It was to have been crowned with delphiniums. This was in Washington, D.C., but I was young and determined to find the right food or spray to achieve my goal. Above all, I was optimistic that my delphiniums would reach man-height—just as they are shown in books depicting English gardens.

At the time, I felt that anything short of an English model would be failure. It seemed that all the world's great gardens were English and, I reasoned, to have a decent garden mine had to conform.

But then came Peradeniya. The first thing I wanted to see was its fabled spice garden. I followed the map and searched for it fruitlessly, finally going back to the entrance to ask for directions and being directed to exactly the same place. In frustration, I sat down on a bench to gather myself and the realization dawned: I

3

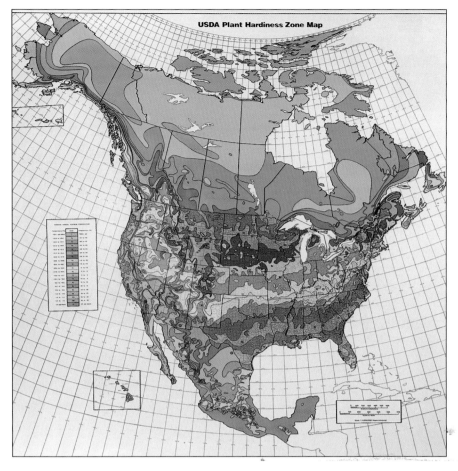

the flower garden. By that time, I had been primed for surprise, but what I saw stunned me. There was a place of honor, set off from all the other plants by a little white fence like a rare prize! I ran over to see what it was, and even as I recognized the plant, I searched for a label to prove it wasn't what I thought it was, a plant many Americans curse when it blooms, blaming it for hay fever (wrongly—the real culprit is ragweed). Here was a huge carpet of goldenrod (*Solidago*).

Working hard in my own garden, those goldenrods came often to mind. Somewhere along the line, I had picked up the idea that gardening ought to be difficult and plants had to be the limited few that show up in English borders. I pulled out the goldenrod seedlings that grew of their own accord.

"We often fail to remember that the treasures of our gardens are the weeds of other lands," wrote Vita Sackville-West. She understood well the relative value of plants when, in *A Joy of Gardening,* she described the reaction of some American visitors to Virginia bluebells growing at Sissinghurst: "For a moment, I thought they were going to show their helpfulness by pulling it up."

was indeed *in* the spice garden; it was only that my conception of what that garden should look like did not conform to the reality. I'd been looking for something low and patterned like the herb gardens I knew at home. This was the tropics and spices came from trees—large trees! My bench was located in the shade of nutmegs and cardamoms.

I set off to explore the rest of the garden. On the great lawn was an immense umbrella of a tree, spreading over 100 feet in diameter. Its botanical name read *Ficus benjamina*—the slender houseplant that grew in my window! I felt a little like Alice in Wonderland. This garden and its inhabitants in no way fit my stereotype of what a garden should be. Tropical plants in this tropical setting had a vibrant, rugged exuberance that didn't square with anything I'd seen in a garden book. And yet it was heart-stoppingly beautiful.

My last stop at Peradeniya was

The plants that survive in this protected courtyard would be houseplants elsewhere.
(Chris Friedrichs Design)

Like the American visitors, my initial reaction to the American plant in the foreign garden was negative, but it started some wheels turning. Vita Sackville-West possessed a clear-sightedness that transcended tradition, style, habit, and reputation. She saw a plant for what it was. So did William Robinson, the Victorian author of *The English Flower Garden,* who railed against the prevailing fashion of carpet bedding and chafed under the constraints of convention. He wanted "freedom to select from every source of beauty among hardy things."

And so I tried to see the goldenrods without blinders and came to the conclusion that they were actually pretty and certainly long lasting. In addition, there was really no care involved. They thrived along the roadsides without help from gardeners because they belonged there. They were the natives.

And I read Gertrude Jekyll: "To devise these living pictures from simple well-known flowers," she wrote in *Colour Schemes for the Flower Garden,* "seems to me the best thing to do in gardening." She had championed the cottage garden, with its simple, native flowers. But *her* simple flowers were not *my* simple flowers. If she had lived where goldenrods are native, would she have planted goldenrods? Probably.

Some time after I returned home, I took a long, hard look at my delphiniums. All the liquid fish in the world would not invigorate them. They were stunted and sad looking. What would William Robinson have done? "Throw . . . aside . . . plants that hate our soil and refuse to thrive in our flower garden." I put them out of their misery and have never looked back.

My journey to see the gardens of North America began in Maryland in early spring. I had divided the country into regions—the South, the Southwest, California, the Pacific Northwest, the Mountain Region, the Upper and Lower Midwest, the Northeast, and the Mid-Atlantic—based loosely upon the climates and the native plants that would be growing there. First, I would head to the warm South and then follow the good weather around the country. Rain followed me for the first 500 miles, but, even so, every time I stopped to eat, to gas up the car, or to sleep, the air outside felt a little warmer, a

Sun-loving scarlet sage blooms well into October at Monticello.

little balmier, and it struck me that I was experiencing the same information recorded on the weather charts I had pored over in preparation for the trip. I imagined myself driving across the bands of colored zones on the United States Department of Agriculture Hardiness Zone Map, that necessary guide that appears in every garden book, including this one (opposite).

From the car windows, I could see the progress of spring accelerated by my movement southward, and I thought of the weather chart that listed the first and last days of frost as they occurred across the country. How much more vivid was the reality: the morning I had left Maryland, the daffodils showed about six inches of green and only the witch hazels and forsythia were in bloom. Just south of Richmond, the daffodils were in full flower, and by the time I reached South Carolina, a few of the swollen buds on the Florida azaleas had opened.

OPPOSITE: *Pink and white garden phlox and pink roses create a delicate pastel effect in Ryan Gainey's Georgia garden.* ABOVE: *Hard-to-find Florida natives stand ready to go at a nursery for the Palm Beach public schools that horticulturist and designer Joe Lawson helped to found.*

THE SOUTH

My first stop in the South was Woodlanders Nursery in Aiken, South Carolina, to talk with Bob McCartney, who started this pioneering nursery "to seek out and propagate the beautiful but neglected plants of this region" with co-owners Julia and Robert Mackintosh in 1980. Since that time, some of the natives they rescued from obscurity have become better known and more widely available, among them fothergilla, cross vine, and *Baptisia alba*.

Bob has spent many years exploring the Southeast for garden-worthy native plants and had plenty of suggestions for southern gardens. Some, like magnolia and yaupon, have been used since Colonial times, but there were others—such as Georgia savory, *Stewartia malaco-*

dendron, and needle palm—that were new to me.

"Every southerner has his or her own idea of what the South is like," said Bob, "and each one is probably correct. The South is so large and so diverse that few can fully grasp the nature and character of the region. Just two states—Georgia and Alabama—are larger than all six New England states plus Ohio and Delaware!" With different climate and soil conditions and a diverse natural vegetation, it seemed at first that the South—or any other region, for that matter—was too diverse to categorize. However, there was one common characteristic shared in all parts: a long, hot summer.

Eventually we agreed that for this book the South should include the southeastern corner of Virginia, the eastern third of North Carolina, the eastern half of South Carolina, most of Georgia, Alabama, and Mississippi, the northern two-thirds of Florida, all of Louisiana, extreme southern Arkansas, and the five counties in Texas called the "pineywoods," known horticulturally as Zones 8 and 9, excluding tropical South Florida. Gardeners there are in Zones 10 and 11.

Before I left Aiken with Bob McCartney's list of plants for the South, we visited some gardens and I saw native live oaks, hollies, magnolias, sages, and wax myrtles. Used since Colonial times, these plants are an integral part of the southern gardening tradition, a gracious, formal style with strong ties to England. Ingenious and discriminating, southern colonists had substituted inkberry and yaupon for boxwood, and American holly for the English variety. And they adorned their gardens with treasures from the wild: fringe tree, bull bay and cucumber magnolias, and dogwood.

Moving south, these plants appear again and again until you come to South Florida. There, horticulturist and designer Joe Lawson showed me that South Florida has more in common with the Caribbean than with the northern part of the state.

My route took me through Georgia, where I saw cottage and woodland gardens in Atlanta that differed only slightly from the ones I knew at home. There were phloxes and Virginia bluebells, junipers and oak leaf

Virginia bluebells and dogtooth violets

hydrangeas—in bloom while their northern relatives were just breaking dormancy. And in the hills of North Carolina, where Richard E. Weaver co-owns We-Du Nursery, the Zone 7 climate is just slightly warmer than in my Zone 7 garden. Like an old-time plant explorer, Weaver botanizes on 30 acres and propagates southeastern natives (among other rare and unusual plants) that have been neglected by the gardening public.

Farther south, at Callaway Gardens in Pine Mountain, Georgia, I had taken Fred Galle's course on native azaleas and seen flame and sweet azaleas and red buckeyes. Now en route to Fred's woodland garden on a hillside in Pine Mountain, I smelled early-morning woodsmoke in the air, something that took me back to childhood summers in the North Woods. As I examined the woodland, it seemed a kinder, gentler, and definitely more luxuriant version of the woods I had roamed on vacations in Michigan and Minnesota. The South was indeed many faceted.

Next, I drove through the countryside around Jackson, Mississippi, and it too took me by surprise. I had expected something more along the lines of Spanish moss in grand old live oaks and big verandas. Instead, the flat, open farmland and the raw, cold, windy weather reminded me of my childhood home in Illinois!

It was not difficult, once I reached Jackson, to figure out which house belonged to Felder Rushing, seventh-generation Mississippian, extension agent, author with Steve Bender of *Passalong Plants* ("plants that friends insist on giving you, whether you want them or not"), and talk show host. Felder can expound on the fine line between "tacky" and "gaudy" and has taken the craft of making planters out of old tires to an art form. By his definition, the ones in his front garden were wonderfully gaudy.

Close companions Canada hemlock and sweet birch grew up together at Hillside Arboretum in North Carolina.

TOP: *Heat-loving pink moss phlox and rose verbena
bask in the heat around this house in Jackson, Mississippi.*
TOP RIGHT: *A "gaudy" tire planter in
Felder Rushing's garden*
ABOVE: *The rocker on this vine-festooned porch looks out over
a neat bed of colorful native perennials. (Kim Hawks photo)*
RIGHT: *Annuals enliven the vegetable
garden at this Virginia log cabin.*

The first thing Felder did was to set me straight about weather in the South. It seems that the relatively mild winters make it seem as if just about any kind of plant would grow there, but while appearing benign, the southern winter can be sneaky. The same plants that can tolerate prolonged temperatures of below zero elsewhere routinely suffer here. Weeks of mild, often sunny weather in midwinter cause plants to break dormancy. They are then utterly unprepared for even a relatively mild freeze. And there is never an insulating snow cover. In the South, most winter damage to landscape plants is usually not freeze damage, but desiccation during warm spells.

Instead of the quadrangle of lawn found at many colleges, the University of South Louisiana's heart is a cypress swamp, complete with alligators.

And then there's the summer—too long and too hot for many familiar garden plants to survive or perform well. Gardeners—particularly in Mississippi and Louisiana—have been heard to speak of plant "meltdown," the utter destruction of plants such as delphiniums or calendulas by heat.

Temperatures averaging in the upper 80s and striking into the 100s are daunting to plants and gardeners alike. And it doesn't cool down at night, depriving plants of evening rest. Worse, these high temperatures are not the record-breaking hot spells the rest of the country complains about, they are the norm: the annual period during which the mercury registers 90°F and above averages about 90 days throughout the South. Especially in the Gulf Coast states, high humidity adds to the discomfort level and can incubate diseases. High day and night temperatures, high humidity, and predictable summer droughts, broken only at long intervals by thunderstorms, make gardening with traditional exotic plants and large lawns impractical at best.

Nonetheless, Felder had plenty of suggestions for ornamental native plants, including mayhaw, parsley hawthorn, meadow beauty, silverbells, and Indian pink. Along with well-loved native vines, including trumpet honeysuckle and Carolina jessamine, these natives are gaining popularity as climate-adapted landscaping, he said. "In fact, it is unusual to find a garden that does not contain at least some native shrubs and trees as the year-round backbone, partly because they are attractive, partly for their adaptedness." Beautiful and tough, these plants are garden

As one heads west across Texas, succulents appear among the prairie grasses, foreshadowing the desert ahead.

mainstays that take the heat and fickle cold of the South.

It was that cold that made me drop down to the southernmost east-west route, Interstate 10, a road that begins in Jacksonville and ends in Los Angeles. To this day, I regret that I didn't have the wit to stop every hundred miles or so and take a photo. On this drive across the country, I witnessed the most vivid and dramatic scenes of the effect of decreasing rainfall on vegetation as I moved westward. This road skirts the Gulf of Mexico, the area of highest rainfall in the East, and branches down in Arizona to Interstate 8, which traverses bone-dry parts of the Sonoran Desert en route to San Diego.

At the start, it seems that water is everywhere. From Mobile to Baton Rouge, the road is frequently a bridge from which you can look down at the tops of trees or onto water. Land is low, vegetation is lush, and the air is thick with smells of rot and regeneration.

The Texas state line brought no appreciable difference in scenery; then the words of a plant scientist from the Texas Agricultural Experiment Station in Dallas, Benny J. Simpson, came to mind. "Gardeners in Brownsville, El Paso, Orange, Texarkana, and Texline, Texas, have one

Spanish moss overhangs a tiny pond, brimming with pickerelweed, lilies, and ferns, in R. J. Dykes's French Quarter garden in New Orleans.

TOP: *Sign at USL swamp*
ABOVE: *One of USL's resident alligators*

thing in common when they garden," he said. *"They have nothing in common."* What works in all of those places are natives. To this end, Benny Simpson has written more than 120 articles and a book, *A Field Guide to Texas Trees.* "Native plants," says Benny, "are beautiful and make such good sense."

Texas is huge and it is strategically placed between East and West, Midwest and Gulf Coast. It won't fit into any one region but has to join three: East Texas and the Gulf Coast go best into the South; southwest Texas belongs in the Southwest; and the high plains and Texas grasslands, north of U.S. 67, are grouped in the Lower Midwest.

Benny Simpson was absolutely right—as the miles passed, swamp and thicket gave way to forest. Trees shrank and became farther and farther apart, and then there was grassland, miles and miles of it. Somewhere near San Antonio, succulents appeared among the grasses, foreshadowing the desert ahead.

Plants for the South

Perennials

Amsonia hubrectii
willowleaf amsonia

*A. tabernaemontana**
amsonia

*Aquilegia canadensis**
columbine

A. c. 'Corbett'
Corbett columbine

Arisaema triphyllum
Jack-in-the-pulpit

Artemisia ludoviciana
sagebrush

*Asarum virginicum**
wild ginger

*A. shuttleworthii**
evergreen wild ginger

*Asclepias tuberosa**
butterfly weed

*Aster linearifolius**
savory-leaf, stiff-leaf aster

A. novae-angliae
New England aster

A. novi-belgii
New York aster

*Baptisia alba**
white false indigo

*B. australis**
blue false indigo

Boltonia asteroides
'Pink Beauty'*
pink boltonia

*B. a. 'Snowbank'**
white boltonia

*Chrysogonum virginianum**
green-and-gold

Chrysopsis mariana
Maryland golden aster

*Coreopsis auriculata 'Nana'**
dwarf-eared coreopsis

C. rosea
pink threadleaf coreopsis

C. verticillata and cultivars*
threadleaf coreopsis

*Dicentra eximia**
eastern wild bleeding heart

*Echinacea purpurea**
purple coneflower

E. p. 'White Swan'
white coneflower

Eryngium yuccifolium
rattlesnake master

Erythronium umbilicatum
(americanum)
dogtooth violet

Eupatorium capillifolium
dog fennel

*E. fistulosum**
Joe-Pye weed

Euphorbia corollata
flowering spurge

Filipendula rubra
queen-of-the-prairie

Gaura lindheimeri
gaura

*Geranium maculatum**
wild geranium

*Helianthus angustifolius**
swamp sunflower

H. tuberosus
Jerusalem artichoke

*Heuchera americana**
alum root

H. villosa
hairy alum root

*Hibiscus coccineus**
red mallow

*H. militaris**
smooth marsh mallow

*H. moscheutos**
rose mallow

Houstonia caerulea
Quaker ladies

*Iris brevicaulis**
zigzag iris

*I. fulva**
red flag iris

*I. giganticaerulea**
giant blue iris

*I. hexagona**
iris

*I. verna**
iris

*I. virginica**
Southern blue flag

Kosteletzkia virginica
marsh mallow

*Liatris microcephala**
small blazing star

L. spicata and cultivars
spike gayfeather

Lilium catesbaei
leopard lily

L. superbum
Turk's cap lily

*Lobelia cardinalis**
cardinal flower

*L. siphilitica**
great blue lobelia

Mertensia virginica
Virginia bluebells

*Mitchella repens**
partridgeberry

Monarda didyma
bee balm

*M. fistulosa**
bergamot

*Oenothera fruticosa**
sundrops

*O. missouriensis**
Missouri evening primrose

*O. speciosa**
pink evening primrose

*Pachysandra procumbens**
American pachysandra

Penstemon canescens
penstemon

Phlox divaricata
wild sweet william

P. d. 'Fuller's White'
white phlox

*P. maculata**
phlox

P. paniculata
garden phlox

P. stolonifera
creeping phlox

*P. subulata**
moss pink

Polygonatum biflorum
Solomon's seal

Rhexia virginica
meadow beauty

Rudbeckia fulgida 'Goldsturm'*
black-eyed Susan

*R. maxima**
giant rudbeckia

Ruellia humilis
wild petunia

Scutellaria incana
skullcap

S. serrata
showy skullcap

Shortia galacifolia
Oconee bells

Silene polypetala
silene

S. virginica
fire pink

Sisyrinchium angustifolium
blue-eyed grass

Smilacina racemosa
false Solomon's seal

*Solidago caesia**
wreath goldenrod

S. canadensis
Canada goldenrod

*S. flexicaulis**
zigzag goldenrod

*S. nemoralis**
gray goldenrod

*S. odora**
sweet goldenrod

*S. rigida**
stiff goldenrod

S. rugosa
rough-stemmed goldenrod

*S. sempervirens**
seaside goldenrod

S. speciosa
showy goldenrod

S. sphacelata
goldenrod

Spigelia marilandica
Indian pink

Stokesia laevis
Stokes' aster

Thermopsis villosa
Carolina bush pea

*Tiarella cordifolia**
running foamflower

*T. c. var. collina**
clumping foamflower

Tradescantia x *andersoniana*
spiderwort

Trillium species
wake robin, trillium

*Verbena canadensis**
rose verbena

12

V. tenuisecta
moss verbena

Viola species*
violet

Annuals

Coreopsis tinctoria
plains coreopsis

*Helianthus annuus**
sunflower

*Ipomopsis rubra**
standing cypress

Linum perenne
blue flax

*Phacelia bipinnatifida**
phacelia

Phlox drummondii
annual phlox

Grasses, Sedges, Rushes, and Reeds

*Andropogon glomeratus**
bushy bluestem

*A. virginicus**
broom sedge

*Carex austrocaroliniana**
sedge

*C. muskingumensis**
palm sedge

C. pensylvanica
Pennsylvania sedge

*Chasmanthium latifolium**
northern sea oats, river oats

Eragrostis spectabilis
purple lovegrass

Erianthus giganteus
sugarcane plume grass

Muhlenbergia capillaris
muhly grass (Florida)

M. dumosa
bamboo muhly

Panicum virgatum
switch grass

Phalaris arundinacea picta
gardener's garters, ribbon grass

Schizachyrium scoparium
little bluestem

Sorghastrum nutans
Indian grass

*Spartina bakeri**
sand cordgrass (Florida)

Sporobolus heterolepsis
prairie dropseed

Tripsacum dactyloides
Fakahatchee grass (Florida)

Ferns

Adiantum capillus-veneris
southern maidenhair fern

*Athyrium filix-femina**
lady fern

Onoclea sensibilis
sensitive fern

*Osmunda cinnamomea**
cinnamon fern

O. regalis var. *spectabilis**
royal fern

Polystichum acrostichoides
Christmas fern

Thelypteris hexagonoptera
broad beech fern

*T. kunthii**
southern shield fern

Woodwardia areolata
netted chain fern

Water Plants

Decodon verticillatus
swamp loosestrife

Equisetum hyemale
scouring rush

Iris fulva
red iris

I. versicolor
blue flag

Menyanthes trifoliata
bog bean

Nymphaea odorata
pond water lily

Orontium aquaticum
golden club

Peltandra virginiana
arrow arum

Pontederia cordata
pickerelweed

Saururus cernuus
lizard's tail

Typha angustifolia
narrow-leaf cattail

Vines

*Anisostichus capreolatus**
cross vine

*Aster carolinianus**
climbing aster

Campsis radicans
trumpet vine

Clematis viorna
leather flower

Decumaria barbara
climbing hydrangea

*Gelsemium sempervirens**
Carolina jessamine

Lonicera x *heckrottii*
red trumpet honeysuckle

*L. sempervirens**
trumpet honeysuckle

Parthenocissus quinquefolia
Virginia creeper

Wisteria frutescens
American wisteria

Shrubs

*Aesculus parviflora**
bottlebrush buckeye

*Agarista populifolia**
Florida leucothoe

Callicarpa americana
beautyberry

*Calycanthus floridus**
sweetshrub

Ceanothus americanus
New Jersey tea

Cephalanthus occidentalis
buttonbush

Clethra acuminata
cinnamon clethra

C. alnifolia 'Hummingbird'*
dwarf summersweet

C. a. 'Pinkspire', 'Rosea'*
summersweet

Clinopodium georgianum
Georgia savory

*Coccoloba uvifera**
seagrape (Florida, Gulf Coast)

Conradina canescens
conradina

C. verticillata
Cumberland rosemary

Cornus sericea
red-osier dogwood

Cotinus obovatus
American smoke tree

*Cyrilla racemiflora**
titi

*Eugenia foetida**
Spanish stopper (Florida)

*Euonymus americana**
hearts-a-bustin'

*Fothergilla gardenii**
dwarf fothergilla

F. g. 'Blue Mist'
Blue Mist fothergilla

F. major
large fothergilla

Hydrangea arborescens 'Annabelle'
wild hydrangea

*H. quercifolia**
oak leaf hydrangea

H. q. 'Snow Queen'
Snow Queen hydrangea

Hypericum frondosum 'Sunburst'
golden St. Johnswort

Ilex amelanchier
Sarvis holly

*I. decidua**
possum haw

*I. glabra**
inkberry

I. verticillata 'Winter Red'*
winterberry

I. v. 'Maryland Beauty'*
winterberry

*I. vomitoria**
yaupon

*Illicium floridanum**
anise tree

I. parviflorum
anise tree

Itea virginica 'Henry's Garnet'
sweetspire

Kalmia latifolia, many cultivars*
mountain laurel

Leucothoe axillaris
doghobble

*L. fontanesiana**
doghobble

Myrica cerifera 'Evergreen'*
wax myrtle

Pieris floribunda
fetterbush

*Rhapidophyllum hystrix**
needle palm

*Rhododendron alabamense**
Alabama azalea

R. arborescens and cultivars
sweet azalea

R. atlanticum
coast azalea

R. austrinum, many cultivars*
Florida azalea

R. bakeri
Cumberland azalea
R. calendulaceum, many cultivars
flame azalea
R. canescens and cultivars*
Piedmont azalea
*R. Chapmanii**
Chapman's rhododendron
R. flammeum (speciosum)
Oconee azalea
R. maximum
Rosebay rhododendron
*R. minus**
Piedmont rhododendron
*R. prunifolium**
plumleaf azalea
R. serrulatum
hammocksweet azalea
*Rhus aromatica**
fragrant sumac
R. copallina
shining sumac
R. glabra
smooth sumac

Serenoa repens
saw palmetto
Sophora tomentosa
necklace pod (Florida)
*Stewartia malacodendron**
silky camellia
Viburnum dentatum
arrowwood viburnum
V. lentago
nannyberry
*V. nudum**
possum haw
V. prunifolium
blackhaw
V. rufidulum
blackhaw
Yucca species
yucca
*Zamia pumila**
Coontie (Florida)
Zenobia pulverulenta
dusty zenobia

Trees
*Acer leucoderme**
chalk maple

Aesculus pavia
red buckeye
Amelanchier laevis
serviceberry
Asimina triloba
pawpaw
Betula nigra
river birch
B. nigra 'Heritage'
white river birch
*Cercis canadensis**
eastern redbud
*Chionanthus virginicus**
fringe tree
*Cladrastis kentukeya**
yellowwood
Cornus florida
eastern dogwood
*Franklinia alatamaha**
Franklin tree
Halesia carolina
Carolina silverbell
H. diptera 'Magniflora'*
Magniflora silverbell

*Ilex cassine**
Dahoon holly
I. opaca and cultivars
American holly
Juniperus virginiana
eastern red cedar
*Magnolia ashei**
Ashe magnolia
M. grandiflora and cultivars*
bull bay magnolia
M. virginiana
sweet bay magnolia
*Pinus palustris**
longleaf pine
*Quercus virginiana**
live oak
*Sabal palmetto**
sabal palm
*Taxodium ascendens**
pond cypress
*T. distichum**
bald cypress

*Recommended plants are starred.

Texas bluebonnets put on a colorful display along the roadsides in Texas every spring.

THE SOUTHWEST

All along the way, I gave thanks to Lady Bird Johnson and the Texas Highway Department, which began planting the roadsides with wildflowers over 50 years ago, something that has saved the taxpayers money spent on mowing, to say nothing of providing them with a popular and much anticipated annual event. Now there is nobody in Texas who couldn't identify a lupine. And no wonder! Lupines carpet the roadsides, sometimes in great blue sweeps and sometimes combining delightfully with orange-red Indian paintbrush, or with pale pink evening primrose, and sometimes with both.

Because the weather was still unsettled, my visits to the Dallas Arboretum and its new collection of Texas plants, as well as to the National Wildflower Research Center near Austin, had to be put off until later. But the San Antonio Botanical Center was right on my way. In a stroke of genius, the San Antonio Botanical Center has collected old Texas houses from around the state and transported them to the garden, where they have settled into a brilliant display that combines Texas history and Texas native plants. I sat on the worn steps of an old cabin and looked out across a field of gaura and penstemon and breathed in the grape Kool-Aid scent of Texas mountain laurel. It might have been a hundred years ago, it was so quiet. And then the sun started to set and it was time to move on.

Back on Interstate 10, from West Texas through New Mexico into Arizona, the vistas illustrated the Southwest's degrees of dryness and varieties of desert. Although it is true that deserts—the Mohave, Chihuahuan, and Sonoran—are found in the Southwest, the Southwest is not only desert. It is really a mosaic of different climate and vegetation zones—grassland, high plains, foothills, and mountains—all linked together by deserts. The region

OPPOSITE: *Parry's penstemon blazes hot pink at the Desert Botanical Garden in Phoenix.*
TOP LEFT: *An ocotillo and a stop sign provide color in the sere landscape at Big Bend National Park.*
MIDDLE LEFT: *The west is rich in yellow columbines.*
BOTTOM LEFT: *Nestled in cushioning winter-bleached Indian rice grass, a mullein basks in early spring sunshine in New Mexico.*
ABOVE: *A well-worn boot is recycled into a birdhouse.*

encompasses southeastern California, part of Nevada, much of Arizona, New Mexico, parts of northern Mexico, and West Texas.

What all of these places share is a climate of extremes of heat and cold, wind and drought, brilliant light and electric air. For a plant to adapt to life in the Southwest, it must be able to tolerate occasional below-freezing temperatures in winter and several months of scorching temperatures. (Summertime highs average in the 90s in the "cooler" desert areas and well over 100° in the hot spots, where daytime soil surface temperatures can reach 190°.) Plants have to live "on the economy," with a sparse amount of seasonal rainfall that often arrives in one or two drenching downpours. Flash flooding occurs

Dryland plants—prickly pear cactus, nolina, and mesquite—
landscape an adobe house and its outbuilding at the San Antonio Botanical Center.

frequently, except in drought years, when the rain evaporates before it reaches the ground.

It might seem that tropical plants—needle palm, necklace pod, and stoppers—would cope with the heat, but they need rain and can't tolerate the extremes of southwestern winters. On the other hand, many frost-hardy plants from northern latitudes, such as holly, myrtle, and viburnums, can't take the heat. But natives manage it all and thrive in the Southwest.

In New Mexico, I stopped in Santa Fe to visit Gail Haggard, owner of Plants of the Southwest, a business that originally had started modestly in her backyard, producing plants that could take the climate for gardens. Today, it is a large retail and mail-order nursery source of the ruggedly beautiful natives that give character and a sense of place to the demanding climate of the high desert.

Gail had come to Santa Fe as a student, fallen in love with the place, and never left it. She took time out from her hectic schedule to show me *her* Santa Fe, a generous gift I will always cherish. We visited the former Santa Fe estate of Georgia O'Keeffe, Sol y Sombre, where Ben Haggard showed us around. Even though it was still wintry on the high desert, I saw with her loving eyes the splendid, dazzling silvers and soft straw colors of dried chamisa, chollas, and Indian rice grass against the evergreens of yucca and dark mountain mahogany along the entrance drive.

Initiated into New Mexico's spare beauty by Gail, I was better prepared for a tour of gardens by Albuquerque designer, author, and nursery owner Judith Phillips at Bernardo Beach Native Plant Farm in Veguita. She produces native and locally adapted plants that she installs in designs that truly live on the economy—low-water-use gardens that age gracefully. She took me to several of her landscapes, where I was struck by their winter palette of silvers and tans against dark evergreens. Around one residence, drought-tolerant buffalo grass had been used for a seldom-mow lawn that had turned soft tan in the winter. Climate-adapted shrubs—lemonade berry, sage, and creosote bush—were beautiful but tough garden subjects.

TOP LEFT: *The silvers and tans of cholla, chamisa, and grasses contrast with deep green junipers at Sol y Sombre, the former Santa Fe estate of Georgia O'Keeffe.*

TOP RIGHT: *Autumn sage, Parry's penstemon, and white evening primrose bloom in a dryland border at the Freeder residence in Phoenix. (Christy Ten Eyck, The Planning Center Design)*

BOTTOM LEFT: *In landscaping as beautiful as it is educational, golden brittlebush, hot pink Parry's penstemon, and palo verdes lead customers through the parking lot to the Superstition Springs Shopping Center near Phoenix. (Christy Ten Eyck, The Planning Center Design)*

BOTTOM RIGHT: *The trunks of this foothills palo verde take over the job of photosynthesis when drought causes leaves to drop. Teddy bear cholla, armed with spines, grows at the tree's base.*

What I noticed about her designs was the way the combinations of junipers, chamisa, yucca, sumac, desert willow, and grasses blended the order of a garden with the colors and feel of the wild landscape.

With regret, I left the high sage and juniper-dotted plains of New Mexico and headed for the "other Southwest," the warm Sonoran Desert, where winters are mild enough for giant cacti like the saguaro, organ pipe, and senita, and the fascinating vegetation soon won my heart. Thanks to two rainy seasons, small trees such as palo verde and ironwood, along with a variety of shrubs and herbaceous perennials, are abundant in the Sonoran Desert, which has earned it the sobriquet "the lush desert."

My first stop was the Desert Botanical Garden in Phoenix, where I met with landscape architect and author Judy Mielke, who specializes in using natives in her designs. She provided me with suggestions of plants to use in southwestern gardens and talked about the softening effect of annuals and perennials around hard-surfaced desert plants such as aloe or agave. This in no way prepared me for the stunning first view of hundreds of brilliant penstemons blooming in bright pinks, reds, and

Chamisa, at home in the dry West, is a reliable and beautiful shrub, yellow in late spring, silver in winter. (Charles Mann photo)

center near Scottsdale, where Christy Ten Eyck of the Planning Center in Phoenix has designed a "canyon walk" to lead visitors from the parking lot to the mall through a garden of native penstemons, desert marigolds, and palo verdes. It is the kind of lush desert garden of creosote bush, cactus, penstemon, salvias, and verbena that designer Steve Martino used to surround the lovely Douglas residence.

After Phoenix, I had planned to visit the Arboretum at Flagstaff, but I learned that it was snowed in, so I headed south to Tucson and the Arizona-Sonora Desert Museum, where I met with staff member Doug Larson. In addition to working with plants, Doug had grown up in the desert and had his own well-considered ideas about what to add to the list of plants for the Southwest. Among his recommendations were mesquite, Texas ebony, mountain marigold (which he liked as a wall plant), and Texas mountain laurel, the same evergreen shrub with the grape Kool-Aid aroma that I had seen in San Antonio. He showed me around the garden, ablaze with brilliant penstemons and cheerful *Salvia gregii.*

I would have liked to have stayed at this beautiful garden for a month, but all too soon I was back on the interstate. In the Southwest, necessity has mothered an elegant, fashionable garden style that is as beautiful as it is durable. In the desert, foothills, grasslands, mountains, or plains of the Southwest, a harsh and erratic climate puts traditional garden plants at a disadvantage. Unique in color, distinct in shape, southwestern natives have a decided edge.

corals. Along with yellow desert marigold, these perennials were beautiful foils to the muted grays and greens of wax-coated, moisture-conserving desert plants such as agave and cactus.

Perhaps because Arizonans are water-conscious, perhaps because they are better educated about their unique desert flora, or perhaps for other reasons, using native plants in gardens in Phoenix is not merely accepted, it is regarded as garden design at the highest level. It is the type of landscaping one expects to find (and does) around a luxury hotel such as Westcourt in the Buttes, where palo verdes, ocotillo, and brittlebushes combine in elegant understatement. It is the type of landscaping implemented in Superstition Springs, an upscale shopping

I drove on. The driest place along the route came beyond Yuma in eastern California. In the evening light, my headlights picked up the sheen of bits of glass, the litter of decades, that lay along the road. It took me a while to realize that people here weren't any messier than elsewhere, it was the absence of any vegetation to cover it that made the litter noticeable. At the end of this seeming dead zone, soaptree yuccas and ocotillos appeared again and the car climbed to the Ocotillo Pass for the descent through forest to the California coast, a world away from the California desert, created in benevolent cooperation by ocean and mountain.

Plants for the Southwest

Perennials

*Allium cernuum**
nodding onion

Anemone cylindrica
thimbleweed

*Aquilegia caerulea**
Rocky Mountain
columbine

A. canadensis
columbine

*A. chrysantha**
yellow columbine

A. formosa
red columbine

Artemisia ludoviciana
sagebrush

Asclepias tuberosa
butterfly weed

*Berlandiera lyrata**
chocolate flower

*Callirhoë involucrata**
wine-cup

Camassia quamash
camas

Cassia species
senna

Castilleja species
Indian paintbrush

Chrysopsis villosa
golden aster

Coreopsis lanceolata
lanceleaf coreopsis

Dalea purpurea
purple prairie clover

Delphinium cardinale
scarlet larkspur

*Engelmannia pinnatifida**
Engelmann daisy

Epilobium angustifolium
fireweed

Erigeron species
seaside daisy

Eriogonum umbellatum
buckwheat

Gaillardia aristata
blanket flower

G. x *grandiflora*
blanket flower

Gaura lindheimeri
gaura

*Helianthus maximiliani**
Maximilian's sunflower

Iris missourensis
western blue flag

*Liatris punctata**
spotted gayfeather

L. spicata 'Kobold'
spike gayfeather

Lupinus species*
lupine

*Melampodium leucanthum**
Blackfoot daisy

*Mirabilis multiflora**
giant four-o'clock

*Oenothera caespitosa**
white evening primrose

O. missouriensis
Missouri evening primrose

*Penstemon ambiguus**
bush penstemon

P. barbatus
scarlet bugler

P. cobaea
white penstemon

*P. eatonii**
firecracker penstemon

P. grandiflorus
beardtongue

*P. parryi**
Parry's penstemon

*P. pinifolius**
pineleaf penstemon

*P. strictus**
Rocky Mountain
penstemon

*Ratibida columnifera**
Mexican hat

Rudbeckia hirta
gloriosa daisy

Salvia farinaceae
mealy-cup sage

*S. greggii**
autumn sage

Thermopsis montana
golden banner

*Zinnia grandiflora**
plains zinnia

Annuals

*Aster bigelovii**
purple aster

*A. tanacetifolius**
Tahoka daisy

*Baileya multiradiata**
desert marigold

Clarkia species
clarkia

*Cleome serrulata**
Rocky Mountain bee plant

Coreopsis tinctoria
plains coreopsis

Eschscholzia californica
California poppy

Helianthus annuus
sunflower

*Ipomopsis aggregata**
scarlet gilia

*Linum perenne**
blue flax

*Lupinus texensis**
Texas bluebonnet

Phacelia campanularia
California bluebells

Phlox drummondii
annual phlox

Grasses, Sedges, Rushes, and Reeds

*Bouteloua curtipendula**
sideoats

*B. gracilis**
blue grama

*Buchloe dactyloides**
buffalo grass

*Eragrostis trichoides**
sand lovegrass

Muhlenbergia dumosa
bamboo muhly

M. rigens
deer grass

Nolina microcarpa
bear grass

*Oryzopsis hymenoides**
Indian rice grass

Panicum virgatum
switch grass

*Schizachyrium scoparium**
little bluestem

Sorghastrum nutans
Indian grass

Water Plants

Equisetum hyemale
scouring rush

Iris missouriensis
blue flag

Typha angustifolia
narrow-leaf cattail

Vines

Lonicera x *heckrottii*
red trumpet honeysuckle

L. sempervirens
trumpet honeysuckle

Parthenocissus species
Virginia creeper

Shrubs

*Agave chrysantha**
century plant

*Amelanchier alnifolia**
serviceberry

*Amorpha fruticosa**
indigo bush

*Artemisia filifolia**
sand sage

*A. frigida**
fringed sage

*A. tridentata**
big sage

*Calliandra eriophylla**
fairy duster

*Cercocarpus ledifolius**
curl-leaf mahogany

*C. montanus**
mountain mahogany

*Chrysothamnus nauseosus**
chamisa

*Cowania neo-mexicana**
cliff rose

*Dalea greggii**
trailing indigo bush

D. pulchra
bush dalea

Dasylirion wheeleri
sotol

*Encelia farinosa**
brittlebush

*Fallugia paradoxa**
Apache plume

*Fendlera rupicola**
cliff fendlerbush

Forestiera segregata
wild olive

Fouquieria splendens*
ocotillo

Hesperaloe parviflora*
red hesperaloe

Holodiscus discolor
desert ocean spray

Juniperus species
juniper

Justicia californica*
chuparosa

Larrea tridentata*
creosote bush

Mahonia haematocarpa
mahonia

M. nevinii
Nevin's barberry

M. repens
creeping mahonia

Opuntia species*
prickly pear, cholla

Potentilla fruticosa
shrubby cinquefoil

Rhus aromatica*
fragrant sumac

R. trilobata*
threeleaf sumac

R. typhina
staghorn sumac

Ribes aureum
golden currant

Tagetes lemmoni*
mountain marigold

Viguiera stenoloba*
skeletonleaf goldeneye

Yucca species
yucca

Trees

Cercidium floridum*
blue palo verde

Chilopsis linearis*
desert willow

Forestiera neo-mexicana*
desert olive

Juniperus ashei
Ashe juniper

J. deppeana*
alligator juniper

J. flaccida
weeping juniper

J. monosperma*
one-seed juniper

J. scopulorum
Rocky Mountain juniper

Olneya tesota*
ironwood

Pinus edulis
piñon

P. monophylla
silvery-needled piñon

Pithecellobium flexicaule*
Texas ebony

Populus fremontii*
valley cottonwood

P. tremuloides*
quaking aspen

Prosopis glandulosa*
honey mesquite

Sophora secundiflora*
mescal bean

*Recommended plants are starred.

Giant-sized flowers top a large nolina.

CALIFORNIA

"California is not only distinctly different from all other parts of the country," said horticulturist Bart O'Brien, "it is, horticulturally speaking, a law unto itself." He proved his point as he drove me around Rancho Santa Ana's 85 acres, devoted to the flora of California's many communities, where we found desert, coastal, woodland, and riparian gardens and a great mesa of California wildflowers. From Bart, who has written books on drought-tolerant plants and California native plant cultivars, I learned that not only were the plants distinctly different, they had to be handled differently as well.

What is thought of in other parts of the country as "spring planting" could begin in late September in northern California and end in early March in the south to coincide with the rainy period of the year. The idea is to promote root growth during cool weather so that plants will be established before exuberant growth starts in spring. Planted later, plants often do not survive through the long hot, dry summer months. Because the majority of California's plants go fully or partially dormant during the summer months and prefer, or even require, summer drought and excellent drainage, neophyte native plant gardeners who compulsively water are courting disaster. California native plants are especially sensitive to crown rot, a condition best avoided by planting them slightly higher (about an inch) than the surrounding soil.

Establishing newly planted natives in California is tricky, too. A gardener must walk the fine line of careful watering in the summer months: too much water in this

ABOVE: *Ceanothus spills over a wall in Sidney Baumgartner's Santa Barbara garden.*
OPPOSITE: *Feltleaf ceanothus blooms in a field of Douglas iris in Jenny Fleming's Berkeley garden.*

season will cause the plants to die from water molds and fungi, too little water and the plants will dry up and die.

As with most plants, planting out smaller specimens is nearly always preferable to planting those of a larger size. Smaller plants are much more readily established into a garden's soil and will grow faster and perform much better than larger-sized specimens. Normally in California this means planting out one-gallon-sized plants, with an occasional five-gallon and a rare fifteen-gallon or larger-sized plant. Trees that are planted out in small sizes (one and five gallon) usually do not require staking. Many California natives grow extremely quickly

in containers and should have their root balls lightly feathered with a fork when they are planted. You could drive a truck over the root ball of *Ceanothus* and do no harm, while other plants (*Dendromecon, Romneya,* and others) have especially sensitive and fragile root systems that should be disturbed as little as possible when they are planted out.

At Rancho Santa Ana in Claremont and, later, when I visited the Theodore Payne Foundation in Sun Valley, I felt as if I were looking at plants from another continent—as if all the plants of my experience were horses, and the plants of California were kangaroos!

Theodore Payne, an English nurseryman who came to California in 1893, must have marveled at the strange and wonderful plants he saw growing around him. One of the first to understand and appreciate the native flora, he brought over 430 species of California native plants from the wild into gardens between 1903 and his retirement in 1961. Today, the foundation named after him provides information on natives and promotes their use in landscaping by making available some 600 species.

Eliza Earle of the Theodore Payne Foundation staff is a transplant to California who has fallen in love with her new state's natives. The first to snag her homesick heart was toyon, a red-berried evergreen that reminded her of the snowy scenes of her former home. Another of her favorites in the foundation's garden, where it forms a magnificent screen, is the white-flowered evergreen lemonade berry.

Californian Betsy Clebsch gardens in La Honda, where she indulges her love of manzanitas and sages. Betsy gardens an acre of her property, which houses over 150 sages, a living laboratory for her current undertaking, a book on sages. She also serves as a charter member of the board of Yerba Buena Nursery, another pioneering California native plant nursery in the hills of Woodside. Yerba Buena, started over 30 years ago by Gerda Isenberg, carries more than 500 varieties of California natives.

Savvy Californians have ever been in the vanguard of new thinking. And, thanks to native plant pioneers like Theodore Payne and Gerda Isenberg, innovative public gardens and arboreta like Rancho Santa Ana, the Santa Barbara Botanic Garden, and the University of California Botanic Garden, and a vibrant, active network of 30 chapters of the California Native Plant Society across the state, natives figure prominently and beautifully in sophisticated landscaping.

When I visited charter member Jenny Fleming, her Berkeley driveway was lined with containers for an upcoming native plant sale to be held at Tilden Park, a gem of a public garden that showcases natives in the hills above Berkeley. Jenny's own garden, the labor of over a quarter century, is a polished jewel. She has grouped plants from California's different communities into the microclimates of her garden. Braving the splendid vista of the Bay, with its attendant winds and fogs, are western azaleas. Manzanita and ceanothus clothe a sunny, fast-draining hillside above a tiny meadow of grasses and irises. And, on the shady front side of her garden, a red-

Red shanks' distinctive peeling bark adds textural interest to this drought-tolerant tree at Rancho Santa Ana Botanic Garden in Claremont, California.

Dwarf coyote bush and low-growing manzanitas tie the Grier garden to the surrounding hills. (Ron Lutsko Design)

Before I left the Bay area, I spent a long day at the University of California Botanic Garden in Berkeley. There, as I had at the Santa Barbara Botanic Garden, I spent hours wandering and taking photos, mesmerized by stunning California fescues, poppy fields, lupines, manzanitas, irises, ceanothus, and eriogonums, and wishing, by some miracle, that these would all grow in Maryland.

It was hard to leave, but I consoled myself with a farewell-to-California drive through the lovely Napa Valley and the Avenue of the Redwoods. North of Napa, the sky darkened, or, rather, I drove into what seemed like a low cloud and

wood community of western dogwood, *Smilacina stellata,* ferns, and sugar scoops revels in the moist shade.

Jenny urged me to visit the plant sale at Tilden Park, where I met Peggy Grier, co-chairperson of the sale, whose garden in Lafayette, only 20 minutes away by car, might have been in another world. On the hot side of hills that block mists from the Bay, the sun rules and summer temperatures vary between 80° and 100°F.

Before moving to California, the Griers had lived in a number of places at home and abroad and had developed an appreciation for the natural look of each place. They asked landscape architect Ron Lutsko, who also designed the native plant garden at Strybing Arboretum—complete with a spectacular California meadow—to limit himself to California natives in the landscaping of their home. Taking advantage of microclimates around the house, Lutsko grouped western azalea, vine maple, and trilliums on the cool side, added a meadow of native irises, and tied the whole garden together with *Ceanothus, Arctostaphylos,* and *Baccharis,* whose greens, in turn, link the garden to the surrounding hills. Among the *Ceanothus* are 'Julia Phelps', 'Concha', and 'Snow Flurry'.

I remembered from a chart of the average amount of precipitation in the United States that I was nearing Crescent City, California, a precipitation record holder, with over 100 inches of rain per year.

Poppies add a bright note to a subtle sweep of blue-eyed grass and lupines.

Perennials

Aquilegia chrysantha
yellow columbine

*A. formosa**
red columbine

*Armeria maritima**
thrift

Artemisia ludoviciana
sagebrush

*A. pycnocephala**
sand hill sage

Aruncus sylvester
goat's beard

*Asarum caudatum**
wild ginger

Asclepias tuberosa
butterfly weed

Berlandiera lyrata
chocolate flower

Callirhoë involucrata
wine-cup

*Camassia quamash**
camas

Castilleja species
Indian paintbrush

*Chrysopsis villosa**
golden aster

*Coreopsis gigantea**
tree coreopsis

*C. maritima**
sea daisy

*Delphinium cardinale**
scarlet larkspur

*Dicentra formosa**
western wild bleeding
heart

Dodecatheon species
shooting star

Epilobium angustifolium
fireweed

*Erigeron glaucus**
seaside daisy

Eriogonum species*
buckwheat

Gaillardia x *grandiflora*
blanket flower

*Helianthus californicus**
California sunflower

H. maximiliani
Maximilian's sunflower

H. tuberosus
Jerusalem artichoke

Heuchera maxima
island alum root

H. micrantha 'Martha Roderick'*
pale pink heuchera

*Iris douglasiana**
Douglas iris

I. innominata
golden iris

Liatris punctata
spotted gayfeather

L. spicata 'Kobold'*
spike gayfeather

Lilium species*
lily

*Lupinus albifrons**
silver bush lupine

*L. arboreus**
tree lupine

Oenothera caespitosa
white evening primrose

*Penstemon centranthifolius**
penstemon

*P. spectabilis**
penstemon

Polygonatum biflorum
Solomon's seal

*Romneya coulteri**
Matilija poppy

Rudbeckia species
black-eyed Susan

Salvia blepharophylla
sage

S. cacaliaefolia
sage

S. chaemaedryoides
Chihuahuan sage

*S. clevelandii**
blue sage

S. coccinea
scarlet sage

S. columbariae
Chia sage

S. confertiflora
sage

S. farinaceae
mealy-cup sage

S. greggii
autumn sage

S. involucrata
rosy leaf sage

S. leucantha
Mexican bush sage

S. leucophylla
purple sage

S. madrensis
forsythia sage

S. rutilans
pineapple sage

*S. sonomensis**
creeping sage

*S. spathacea**
pitcher sage

*Sedum spathulifolium**
stonecrop

Silene californica
California Indian pink

S. hookeri
Indian pink

*Sisyrinchium bellum**
blue-eyed grass

*S. californicum**
golden-eyed grass

Smilacina racemosa
false Solomon's seal

S. stellata
starry false Solomon's seal

Solidago californica
California goldenrod

*Tellima grandiflora**
fringe cup

Thermopsis montana
golden banner

*Tiarella unifoliata**
sugar scoop

Tolmiea menziesii
piggyback plant

Trillium species
wake robin, trillium

Vancouveria hexandra
vancouveria

*V. planipetala**
inside-out flower

Viola species
violet

*Zauschneria californica**
California fuchsia

*Z. septentrianalis**
California fuchsia

Annuals

Clarkia species
clarkia

*Eschscholzia californica**
California poppy

Helianthus annuus
sunflower

Ipomopsis aggregata
scarlet gilia

*Layia platyglossa**
tidy tips

*Linum perenne**
blue flax

*Phacelia campanularia**
California bluebells

Phlox drummondii
annual phlox

Grasses, Sedges, Rushes, and Reeds

Bouteloua curtipendula
sideoats

B. gracilis
blue grama

*Calamagrostis foliosa**
reedgrass

*Elymus condensatus**
giant wild rye

*Festuca californica**
California fescue

Millium effusum 'Aureum'
golden grass

Muhlenbergia capillaris
muhly grass

M. dumosa
bamboo muhly

*M. rigens**
deer grass

Oryzopsis hymenoides
Indian rice grass

Ferns

Adiantum pedatum var. *aleuticum**
five-finger fern

*Athyrium filix-femina**
lady fern

Blechnum spicant
deer fern

Osmunda claytonia
interrupted fern

O. regalis var. *spectabilis*
royal fern

*Polystichum munitum**
sword fern

Water Plants

Equisetum hyemale
scouring rush

Iris fulva
red iris

Iris missouriensis
blue flag

Menyanthes trifoliata
bog bean

Nymphaea odorata
pond water lily

Orontium aquaticum
golden club

Peltandra virginiana
arrow arum

Pontederia cordata
pickerelweed

Saururus cernuus
lizard's tail

Typha angustifolia
narrow-leaf cattail

Vines

Calystegia macrostegia
'Anacapa'*
wild morning glory

Lonicera x *heckrottii*
red trumpet honeysuckle

L. sempervirens
trumpet honeysuckle

Parthenocissus species
Virginia creeper

Shrubs

Agave chrysantha
century plant

Amelanchier alnifolia
serviceberry

Arctostaphylos edmundsii
var. *parvifolia**
manzanita

A. pajaroensis 'Warren
Roberts'* manzanita

*A. uva-ursi**
bearberry

Artemisia filifolia
sand sage

A. frigida
fringed sage

*A. tridentata**
big sage

*Baccharis pilularis**
dwarf coyote bush

Calliandra eriophylla
fairy duster

Ceanothus species*
ceanothus, California lilac

Cercocarpus ledifolius
curl-leaf mahogany

Chrysothamnus nauseosus
chamisa

*Cornus sericea**
red-osier dogwood

Dalea greggii
trailing indigo bush

Dasylirion wheeleri
sotol

Dendromecon harfordii
island bush poppy

Euonymous occidentalis
wahoo

Forestiera segregata
wild olive

Fouquieria splendens
ocotillo

*Fremontodendron califor-
nicum**
fremontia

*Garrya elliptica**
silk-tassel bush

*Gaultheria shallon**
salal

Hesperaloe parviflora
red hesperaloe

*Heteromeles arbutifolia**
toyon

Holodiscus discolor
ocean spray

Isomeris arborea
bladderpod

*Juniperus communis saxi-
talis**
mountain juniper

J. horizontalis
creeping juniper

Justicia californica
chuparosa

*Mahonia aquifolium**
Oregon grape holly

M. a. 'Golden Abundance'
Oregon grape holly

M. fremontii
Fremont mahonia

*M. nevinii**
Nevin's barberry

*M. repens**
creeping mahonia

Myrica californica
California wax myrtle

Paxistima canbyi
paxistima

Potentilla fruticosa
shrubby cinquefoil

*Rhamnus californica**
coffeeberry

Rhododendron occidentalis
western azalea

R. species
evergreen rhododendron

*Rhus integrifolia**
lemonade berry

*R. ovata**
sugarbush

*Ribes sanguineum**
red flowering currant

Rosa species
rose

*Trichostema lanatum**
woolly blue-curls

Vaccinium ovatum
evergreen huckleberry

Yucca species
yucca

Trees

*Acer circinatum**
vine maple

*Adenostoma sparsifolium**
red shanks

Amelanchier species
serviceberry

*Arbutus menziesii**
madrone

*Arctostaphylos manzanita**
manzanita

Ceanothus arboreus
feltleaf ceanothus

Cercidium floridum
blue palo verde

Cercis occidentalis
western redbud

Chilopsis linearis
desert willow

Cornus nuttallii
Pacific dogwood

Juniperus ashei
Ashe juniper

J. californica
California juniper

Picea engelmannii
Engelmann spruce

*Pinus edulis**
piñon

Populus fremontii
valley cottonwood

*P. tremuloides**
quaking aspen

Prosopis glandulosa
honey mesquite

*Prunus virginiana**
chokecherry

*Quercus agrifolia**
coast live oak

Q. chrysolepis
canyon live oak

Q. gambelli
Gambel's oak

Sophora secundiflora
mescal bean

*Recommended plants are starred.

OPPOSITE: *The Northwest begins in Northern California. Jenny Fleming has combined inside-out flower, wild ginger, and ferns in a Redwood Community garden.*
TOP LEFT: *Northwestern beauties: red flowering currant and Oregon grape holly are popular garden subjects the world over.* (Cynthia Woodyard photo)
TOP RIGHT: *Madrone bark peels away to expose the sinewy underbark.*

THE PACIFIC NORTHWEST

Northern California certainly fits the stereotype of the Pacific Northwest as a gentle place with a mild, wet "English" climate that never gets too hot or too cold. And when good gardeners die, aren't they given a choice of Portland, Seattle, or Vancouver in which to spend eternity? But, according to Dr. Arthur Kruckeberg of the University of Washington, there is far more to this vast, environmentally diverse region, which also includes Washington, Oregon, and Idaho, together with western Montana, southern British Columbia, and the coast of Alaska.

It seems that rugged mountains affect climate throughout the Pacific Northwest—the Cascades and the Olympics in Washington, the Cascades, the Wal-lowas, and the Blue Mountains in Oregon, the Klamath-Siskiyou mountain chain along the Oregon-California border, and the Rocky ranges in Idaho and Montana. The mountains tend to run north and south, blocking the climate-softening moist air from the Pacific Ocean. To oversimplify greatly, mountains divide the mild maritime west side, where there is plenty of rain, and the harsh, steppe-desert east side, where rain averages less than 20 inches per year.

No matter how much rain falls, Dr. Kruckeberg assured me, native plants abound on both sides of the mountainous weather barrier. In fact, some are old garden favorites, having been introduced to England in the 19th century, often by the intrepid David Douglas, who explored the Pacific Coast. Red flowering currant (*Ribes sanguineum*)—introduced by Douglas, but actually dis-

Solomon's seal, bleeding hearts, and uncurling sword ferns take part in the Northwest's spring celebration. (Cynthia Woodyard photo)

Not until my visit to the Berry Botanic Garden in Portland did the sun come out. This is the former home of Rae Selling Berry, and her collections of plants from around the world are a background to mahonias, salal, and flowering currant on the native plant trails. Since 1983, the garden has worked to restore rare and endangered plants of the Pacific Northwest. Among these are native lilies, as well as rare rock garden plants.

Even though Dr. Kruckeberg had prepared me for the east side of the Cascades, I never really gave up my mental picture of it as an extension of the kind of north woods one sees in Minnesota and Ontario. Driving due west out of Portland, I traveled the Columbia River Gorge, but as soon as the road left the river, I was astonished by the scenery. After the lush, moist coast, this high, dry sagebrush country was a veritable moonscape. And, yet, mock orange (*Philadelphus lewisii*), ocean spray (*Holodiscus discolor*), serviceberry (*Amelanchier alnifolia*), mountain balm (*Ceanothus velutinus*), Oregon box (*Pachistima myrsinites*), and Douglas (or Rocky Mountain) maple (*Acer glabrum*) inhabit the dry forests of the east side, and chamisa (*Chrysothamnus nauseosus*) dominates the sagebrush country with a smattering of annual grasses and perennials, including phloxes, penstemons, and Indian paintbrush, as well as sumacs, buckwheats, and serviceberries.

Perhaps nowhere else in the country is a region so dramatically divided as along the crests of the mountain chains of the Pacific Northwest. Or so I thought as I headed toward Denver.

covered by Archibald Menzies in 1793—and mock orange (*Philadelphus lewisii*), from the east side of the mountains, are familiar garden staples in Europe.

Dr. Kruckeberg gardens on the west side, north of Seattle, tending what he calls a four-acre arboretum. In addition to countless rock garden plants, including penstemons (he was a chairman of the Northwest Unit of the American Rock Garden Society), there are unusual trees and shrubs and Northwest natives—including madrone (he also helped found the Washington Native Plant Society, served as president, and edited *Douglasia,* its periodical). Not surprising for a man who was born into a family with a tradition of horticultural printing and publishing, Dr. Kruckeberg has, quite literally, written the book on Pacific Northwest natives, *Gardening with Native Plants of the Pacific Northwest,* as well as many articles.

On the west side of the Cascades where Dr. Kruckeberg gardens—in Seattle and farther south in Portland—gardeners can work all year in what seems like a heavenly climate—for plants, anyway. It was a good day for plants, raining in fine droplets (that the natives said were typical), the day I visited the late Jane Platt's paradisical garden in Portland, where native azaleas, wildflowers, fothergilla, and ferns combine with exotic azaleas, rhododendrons, and hundreds of others in pristine beds surrounded by emerald lawn. It was still raining when I visited Leach Botanical Garden, but the misty moisture seemed fitting in this lovely woodland garden, bordered by a creek. Along the trails, I saw vine maple, ocean spray, and mahonia, above an exquisite ground cover of trilliums, *Maianthemum,* and vancouverias.

The berries that follow Oregon grape holly's yellow flowers give this shrub its common name.

Plants for the Pacific Northwest

Perennials

Allium cernuum
nodding onion

*Aquilegia chrysantha**
yellow columbine

*A. formosa**
western columbine

*Armeria maritima**
thrift

Artemisia ludoviciana
sagebrush

A. pycnocephala
sand hill sage

*Aruncus sylvester**
goat's beard

Asarum caudatum
wild ginger

Asclepias tuberosa
butterfly weed

Aster species
aster

Callirhöe involucrata
wine-cup

*Camassia quamash**
camas

Castilleja species*
Indian paintbrush

*Chrysopsis villosa**
golden aster

Delphinium cardinale
scarlet larkspur

*Dicentra formosa**
western wild bleeding
heart

Dodecatheon meadia
eastern shooting star

D. pulchellum
western shooting star

Epilobium angustifolium
fireweed

Erigeron species
seaside daisy

Eriogonum species*
buckwheat

Erythronium albidum
fawn lily, dogtooth violet

*E. oregonum**
fawn lily, dogtooth violet

*E. revolutum**
fawn lily, dogtooth violet

Gaillardia x *grandiflora*
blanket flower

Gaura lindheimeri
gaura

Helianthus californicus
California sunflower

H. maximiliani
Maximilian's sunflower

H. x *multiflorus*
sunflower

H. occidentalis
western sunflower

H. salicifolius
willowleaf sunflower

H. tuberosus
Jerusalem artichoke

Heuchera maxima
island alum root

*H. micrantha**
alum root

Iris douglasiana
Douglas iris

*I. innominata**
golden iris

I. missouriensis
western blue flag

I. setosa
Alaska iris

*I. tenax**
grass iris

I. versicolor
blue flag

Liatris ligulistylus
Rocky Mountain blazing
star

L. punctata
spotted gayfeather

L. spicata 'Kobold'
spike gayfeather

Lilium species
lily

Lupinus arboreus
tree lupine

*L. polyphyllus**
lupine

Maianthemum dilitatum
false lily-of-the-valley

*Oenothera caespitosa**
white evening primrose

Penstemon species*
beardtongue

Phlox species
phlox

Polygonatum biflorum
Solomon's seal

Romneya coulteri
Matilija poppy

Rudbeckia fulgida 'Goldsturm'
black-eyed Susan

Salvia sonomensis
creeping sage

S. spathacea
pitcher sage

Sedum spathulifolium
stonecrop

Silene californica
California Indian pink

S. hookeri
Indian pink

Sisyrinchium bellum
blue-eyed grass

S. douglasii
grass widow

S. idahoense
blue-eyed grass

Smilacina racemosa
false Solomon's seal

*S. stellata**
starry false Solomon's seal

Solidago caesia
wreath goldenrod

S. californica
California goldenrod

S. canadensis
Canada goldenrod

*Tellima grandiflora**
fringe cup

Thermopsis montana
golden banner

*Tolmiea menziesii**
piggyback plant

Trillium species
wake robin, trillium

*Vancouveria hexandra**
vancouveria

V. planipetala
inside-out flower

Viola species
violet

Zauschneria californica
California fuchsia

Z. septentrianalis
California fuchsia

Annuals

Clarkia species*
clarkia

Cleome serrulata
Rocky Mountain bee plant

Coreopsis tinctoria
plains coreopsis

Eschscholzia californica
California poppy

Helianthus annuus
sunflower

Ipomopsis aggregata
scarlet gilia

Layia platyglossa
tidy tips

*Linum perenne**
blue flax

Lupinus texensis
Texas bluebonnet

Phacelia bipinnatifida
phacelia

P. campanularia
California bluebells

*Phlox drummondii**
annual phlox

**Grasses, Sedges,
Rushes, and Reeds**

Andropogon gerardii
big bluestem

*Aristida purpurea**
purple three-awn

*Bouteloua curtipendula**
sideoats

Buchloe dactyloides
buffalo grass

Calamagrostis foliosa
reedgrass

Carex pensylvanica
Pennsylvania sedge
Chasmanthium latifolium
northern sea oats, river oats
Deschampsia caespitosa
hairgrass
Elymus condensatus
giant wild rye
*Eragrostis trichoides**
sand lovegrass
Festuca californica
California fescue
Millium effusum 'Aureum'
golden grass
Muhlenbergia dumosa
bamboo muhly
*M. rigens**
deer grass
Oryzopsis hymenoides
Indian rice grass
Panicum virgatum
switch grass
Phalaris arundinacea picta
gardener's garters, ribbon grass
*Schizachyrium scoparium**
little bluestem

Ferns

Adiantum pedatum
northern maidenhair fern
Blechum spicant
deer fern
Polystichum munitum
sword fern

Water Plants

Equisetum hyemale
scouring rush
Iris fulva
red iris
I. missouriensis
western blue flag
Menyanthes trifoliata
bog bean
Nymphaea odorata
pond water lily
Orontium aquaticum
golden club
Peltandra virginiana
arrow arum
Pontederia cordata
pickerelweed

Saururus cernuus
lizard's tail
Typha angustifolia
narrow-leaf cattail

Vines

Calystegia macrostegia 'Anacapa'
wild morning glory
Campsis radicans
trumpet vine
Lonicera x *heckrottii*
red trumpet honeysuckle
L. sempervirens
trumpet honeysuckle
Parthenocissus species
Virginia creeper

Shrubs

*Amelanchier alnifolia**
serviceberry
Amorpha fruticosa
indigo bush
Arctostaphylos species
manzanita
A. uva-ursi
bearberry
Artemisia filifolia
sand sage
*A. frigida**
fringed sage
*A. tridentata**
big sage
Baccharis pilularis
dwarf coyote bush
Ceanothus species
ceanothus, California lilac
Cercocarpus species
mountain mahogany
*Chrysothamnus nauseosus**
chamisa
Cornus canadensis
bunchberry
C. sericea
red-osier dogwood
Dendromecon harfordii
island bush poppy
Fothergilla gardenii 'Blue Mist'
Blue Mist fothergilla
*Garrya elliptica**
silk-tassel bush
*Gaultheria shallon**
salal

Heteromeles arbutifolia
toyon
*Holodiscus discolor**
ocean spray
Hydrangea arborescens 'Annabelle'
wild hydrangea
H. quercifolia 'Snow Queen'
Snow Queen hydrangea
Isomeris arborea
bladderpod
Juniperus communis
juniper
J. horizontalis
creeping juniper
Justicia californica
chuparosa
*Mahonia aquifolium**
Oregon grape holly
M. fremontii
Fremont mahonia
M. hamaetocarpa
mahonia
M. x 'King's Ransom'
grape holly
M. nevinii
Nevin's barberry
M. repens
creeping mahonia
*Myrica californica**
California wax myrtle
Opuntia species
prickly pear, cholla
Paxistima canbyi
paxistima
*Philadelphus lewisii**
western mock orange
Potentilla fruticosa
shrubby cinquefoil
Rhamnus californica
coffeeberry
*Rhododendron occidentalis**
western azalea
R. prunifolium
plumleaf azalea
R. vaseyi
pinkshell azalea
R. viscosum
swamp azalea
Rhododendron species
evergreen rhododendron

Rhus aromatica
fragrant sumac
R. glabra
smooth sumac
R. integrifolia
lemonade berry
R. ovata
sugarbush
R. typhina
staghorn sumac
*Ribes sanguineum**
red flowering currant
Rosa species
rose
Sambucus canadensis
elderberry
Shepherdia species
buffalo berry
Vaccinium ovatum
evergreen huckleberry

Trees

*Acer circinatum**
vine maple
*A. glabrum**
Rocky Mountain maple
Amelanchier arborea
serviceberry
*Arbutus menziesii**
madrone
Arctostaphylos manzanita
manzanita
Ceanothus species
tree ceanothus
Cercis occidentalis
western redbud
Cornus nuttallii
Pacific dogwood
*Juniperus scopulorum**
Rocky Mountain juniper
*Picea engelmannii**
Engelmann spruce
Populus fremontii
valley cottonwood
*P. tremuloides**
quaking aspen
Quercus agrifolia
coast live oak
*Q. gambelli**
Gambel's oak

*Recommended plants are starred.

The spectacular natural scenery at Garden of the Gods in Colorado Springs, Colorado, simply can't be improved upon.

THE MOUNTAIN REGION

I f people in the Rocky Mountain West never gardened at all, contenting themselves with the natural splendor around them, it would surprise no one. Here, where the scenery is dramatic and ruggedly beautiful, there is a climate to match. And there is no gentle tradition of cottage gardens. Settled by hunters and miners, a magnet for those who love the outdoors, this region is, after Alaska, the least populated part of the United States. Vast, it includes Wyoming, Colorado, Utah, and northern New Mexico, as well as southern Idaho and northern Nevada.

Coloradans Gwen and Panayoti Kelaidis speak of their region's immense climatic diversity, citing a "fantastically corrugated topography" as but one factor that makes "horticultural generalizations" more or less meaningless. They ought to know. Internationally recognized, Panayoti Kelaidis is curator of the Rock Alpine Garden at the Denver Botanic Gardens in Denver, Colorado.

Gwen Kelaidis owns and operates Rocky Mountain Rare Plants, a mail-order business, in addition to editing the *Bulletin of the American Rock Garden Society* and serving as president of the American Penstemon Society.

Gwen and Panayoti Kelaidis know a thing or two about weather in the Mountain West. They explain: "Atop nearby mountains, frost-free summer may last only two weeks. And there are valleys in the northern, middle, and southern Rockies where rhododendrons form impenetrable thickets, where ferns and trilliums and orchids carpet the ground for miles, and annual precipitation approaches 100. But the great bulk of the West is sunny and dry, with as many as 325 days of sunshine and less than 20 inches of rain."

Searing sunshine is a given throughout the year, making transplanting risky. However, because of the cool evenings, transplanting can be accomplished nearly anytime in summer, as long as the plants are carefully shaded while they recover. There is so much sunshine—about as much as in Florida—that some plants that can take full sun elsewhere may need part shade here. "Western gardeners," say the Kelaidises, "learn to take

OPPOSITE: *Bluebonnets and roses embellish a rustic cottage in Colorado. (Charles Mann photo)*
ABOVE: *Chamisa and cattails grow effortlessly in this Rocky Mountain setting. (Charles Mann photo)*

advantage of rainy spells to plant out or move plants."

The upside of bountiful sunshine year-round is that gardens grow luxuriantly, and, of course, it's more fun to garden in sunny weather. The downside is drought. It is an ever-present specter. Like snow or rain, it can occur at any time of year, making it necessary to water new transplants even in the dead of winter or in spring, a chore that surprises gardeners from the East or West coasts.

Although some lucky souls garden at high elevations in acid soils where irrigation is not a problem, gardening in the Rocky Mountain West is more likely to involve heavy clay, sandy, or silty soils with

A hungry hummingbird couldn't miss this bright California fuchsia in the Kelaidis garden in Denver.

In the Rocky Mountains, erratic changes in weather are the norm, and snow is always a possibility; here, it frosts sumac at the Denver Botanic Gardens.

little humus content and, too often, a high pH. Even treated water can exceed pH 8.

Here, latitude has less to do with climate than do elevation and topography. For example, Laramie, Wyoming, at just over 7,000 feet, is Zone 3, while Casper, less than 150 miles to the northeast, is at Zone 5. Sheridan, 150 miles north, is a low pocket of genial Zone 5.

Elevation alone is a decisive factor in determining temperature. Above 5,000 feet, night temperatures usually drop below 70°F; at 8,000 feet, nights in midsummer will reach 40°, shortening the growing season significantly and limiting what can be grown.

The weather is nothing if not erratic. On any given day, it can rain, snow, or bake in blistering sunshine. Hailstorms can strip trees of their leaves; wet, heavy snow breaks off the branches of shrubs and trees. Fierce winds can blow up at any time. In some places, winds are continual. Temperatures can drop 30 to 50° in a few hours.

I arrived in Denver in a snowstorm and made plans to visit again in the fall. On my second trip the following October, it snowed again, but this time, it melted away, and though my shoes were damp as horticulturist Der-

mod Downes showed me around, my spirit wasn't. In fact, fall was a perfect time to visit Colorado. At the Denver Botanic Garden, sumacs and amelanchier were glowing scarlet and burnt orange. The cholla cactus bore deep maroon fruits, and a short grass prairie of buffalo grass was a pleasing tan.

Dermod also took me back to see Gwen and Panayoti Kelaidis's splendid rock gardens, where a zauschneria shone brilliant scarlet and dwarf chamisa and eriogonums added rich colors to a tapestry of rock garden subjects. It certainly is not surprising that this rugged climate is the center of rock gardening in the country. How clever of these tough, economical little plants to root deeply in rock crevices and to flatten themselves into indentations in the rocks for protection from wind and weather.

Where the climate is challenging, native plants survive where others falter. Rock garden plants and the same natives that cover the hills in wildflower displays—drought-tolerant irises, salvias, penstemons, columbines, and butterfly weeds—are plants of choice for the Mountain Region West. In their carefree splendor, they meet and match this region's rugged beauty and rugged climate.

Plants for the Mountain Region

Perennials

Actaea pachypoda
doll's eyes
A. rubra
red baneberry
Allium cernuum
nodding onion
*Aquilegia caerulea**
Rocky Mountain
columbine
A. canadensis
columbine
A. c. 'Corbett'
Corbett columbine
A. chrysantha
yellow columbine
A. formosa
red columbine
Armeria maritima
thrift
Artemisia ludoviciana
sagebrush
A. pycnocephala
sand hill sage
Asarum canadense
wild ginger
Asclepias tuberosa
butterfly weed
Aster laevis
smooth aster
A. novae-angliae
New England aster
Callirhoe involucrata
wine-cup
Camassia quamash
camas
Castilleja species*
Indian paintbrush
Coreopsis tripteris
tall coreopsis
Dicentra formosa
western wild bleeding
heart
Dodecatheon meadia
eastern shooting star
D. pulchellum
western shooting star
Epilobium angustifolium
fireweed

Erigeron species*
seaside daisy
Eriogonum species*
buckwheat
Eryngium yuccifolium
rattlesnake master
Erythronium species
fawn lily, dogtooth violet
Eupatorium maculatum
Joe-Pye weed
Gaillardia aristata
blanket flower
G. x grandiflora
blanket flower
G. pulchella
Indian blanket
Gaura lindheimeri
gaura
Geum triflorum
prairie smoke
Helianthus maximiliani
Maximilian's sunflower
H. mollis
downy sunflower
H. occidentalis
western sunflower
H. salicifolius
willowleaf sunflower
H. tuberosus
Jerusalem artichoke
Heuchera micrantha
alum root
H. sanguinea
coral bells
Iris setosa
Alaska iris
Liatris aspera
rough blazing star
L. ligulistylus
Rocky Mountain blazing
star
L. punctata
spotted gayfeather
L. pycnostachya
prairie blazing star
*Melampodium leucanthum**
Blackfoot daisy
Mirabilis multiflora
giant four-o'clock

Oenothera caespitosa
white evening primrose
O. fruticosa
sundrops
O. missourensis
Missouri evening primrose
*Penstemon ambiguus**
bush penstemon
*P. eatonii**
firecracker penstemon
*P. pinifolius**
pineleaf penstemon
P. strictus
Rocky Mountain penste-
mon
*Phlox nana**
Santa Fe phlox
Physostegia virginiana
obedient plant
Ratibida columnifera
Mexican hat
*Rudbeckia fulgida 'Gold-
sturm'*
black-eyed Susan
R. subtomentosa
sweet black-eyed Susan
Silphium integrifolium
rosinweed
Solidago caesia
wreath goldenrod
S. canadensis
Canada goldenrod
S. multiradiata
alpine goldenrod
S. rigida
stiff goldenrod
Thermopsis montana
golden banner
Trillium species
wake robin, trillium
Vancouveria hexandra
vancouveria
V. planipetala
inside-out flower
*Verbena canadensis**
rose verbena
Viola species
violet

*Zauschneria californica**
California fuchsia
Z. septentrianalis
California fuchsia
*Zinnia grandiflora**
plains zinnia

Annuals

*Aster bigelovii**
purple aster
*A. tanacetifolius**
Tahoka daisy
*Cleome serrulata**
Rocky Mountain bee plant
*Coreopsis tinctoria**
plains coreopsis
Helianthus annuus
sunflower
Ipomopsis aggregata
scarlet gilia
Linum perenne
blue flax
Lupinus texensis
Texas bluebonnet
Phlox drummondii
annual phlox

Grasses, Sedges, Rushes, and Reeds

Aristida purpurea
purple three-awn
*Bouteloua curtipendula**
sideoats
*B. gracilis**
blue grama
Buchloe dactyloides
buffalo grass
*Deschampsia caespitosa**
hairgrass
Eragrostis trichoides
sand lovegrass
Muhlenbergia dumosa
bamboo muhly
M. rigens
deer grass
Oryzopsis hymenoides
Indian rice grass
*Panicum virgatum**
switch grass

Phalaris arundinacea picta
gardener's garters, ribbon grass
*Schizachyrium scoparium**
little bluestem
Sporobolus heterolepsis
prairie dropseed

Ferns

Matteuccia pensylvanica
ostrich fern
Osmunda claytonia
interrupted fern

Water Plants

Equisetum hyemale
scouring rush
Iris versicolor
blue flag
Menyanthes trifoliata
bog bean
Nymphaea odorata
pond water lily
Orontium aquaticum
golden club
Peltandra virginiana
arrow arum
Pontederia cordata
pickerelweed
Typha angustifolia
narrow-leaf cattail

Vines

Campsis radicans
trumpet vine
Decumaria barbara
climbing hydrangea
Lonicera x *heckrottii*
red trumpet honeysuckle

L. sempervirens
trumpet honeysuckle
Parthenocissus species
Virginia creeper

Shrubs

Amelanchier alnifolia
serviceberry
Amorpha canescens
leadplant
A. fruticosa
indigo bush
Aralia spinosa
devil's walkingstick
Arctosphylos uva-ursi
bearberry
Artemisia filifolia
sand sage
*A. frigida**
fringed sage
A. tridentata
big sage
*Cercocarpus ledifolius**
curl-leaf mahogany
Chrysothamnus nauseosus
chamisa
Cornus sericea
red-osier dogwood
*Cowania neo-mexicana**
cliff rose
Dalea greggii
trailing indigo bush
Dasylirion wheeleri
sotol
Fallugia paradoxa
Apache plume

Fendlera rupicola
cliff fendlerbush
Forestiera segregata
wild olive
Hesperaloe parviflora
red hesperaloe
*Holodiscus discolor**
ocean spray
*H. dumosus**
desert ocean spray
Juniperus communis
juniper
J. horizontalis
creeping juniper
Mahonia aquifolium
Oregon grape holly
*M. fremontii**
Fremont mahonia
*M. hamaetocarpa**
mahonia
M. x 'King's Ransom'
King's Ransom mahonia
M. repens
creeping mahonia
*M. trifoliata**
agarita
Paxistima canbyi
paxistima
*Philadelphus lewisii**
western mock orange
Potentilla fruticosa
shrubby cinquefoil
Rhus aromatica
fragrant sumac

R. glabra
smooth sumac
R. typhina
staghorn sumac
Sambucus canadensis
elderberry
Yucca species
yucca

Trees

Betula fontinalis
birch
Chilopsis linearis
desert willow
Forestiera neo-mexicana
desert olive
Juniperus deppeana
alligator juniper
J. monosperma
one-seed juniper
J. scopulorum
Rocky Mountain juniper
Olneya tesota
ironwood
Oxydendrum arboreum
sourwood, sorrel tree
Pinus edulis
piñon
P. monophylla
single-leaf piñon
Populus fremontii
valley cottonwood
P. tremuloides
quaking aspen
Quercus gambelii
Gambel oak

*Recommended plants are starred.

Miles and miles of sunflowers stretch as far as the eye can see along the interstate through Kansas.

THE MIDWEST

From Denver, Interstate 70 dips southward and then shoots straight across Kansas. So did I, and as I crossed Kansas, I thought that everybody seems to have a story about driving through the Midwest—how flat it is, how he or she spent a whole day going through Kansas and saw nothing, *nothing*, but corn. For me, Kansas's infinite vista provoked the amazing sensation of being on a planet that was moving through the universe. But it was Willa Cather who truly understood the subtle beauty of the Midwest. She knew that the midwestern prairie's dominant characteristic, its vastness, was too big to be seen. It had to be understood. In *My Ántonia,* she wrote, "As I looked about me I felt that the grass was the country, as the water is the sea."

Stretching between the Rockies in the West and the Appalachians in the East, the Midwest is a region that is vast but unified in its continental climate, characterized by great extremes—cold winters, hot summers, and winds that sweep over the flat country with amazing force. In this vigorous climate, every farmer's wife soon learns how to shelter roses on the side of the house out of the wind and to tuck the kitchen garden between the outbuildings.

With the exception of the Great Lakes, which soften the extremes in their immediate vicinity, the Midwest has no climatic barriers. For this reason, latitude has the last word in determining the severity of heat and cold. The farther north one gardens, the earlier and colder the winter. The farther south one gardens, the longer the hot summer weather. For this reason, I divided the Midwest into Upper and Lower sections.

The Upper Midwest

The Upper Midwest is notorious for the length and depth of its winter. The first frost comes early and fall is brief, but glorious—in a good year, half of September

OPPOSITE: At first, Lorrie Otto's prairie landscaping drew skeptical glances. Seeing its beauty, neighbors eventually followed suit and the result is country in the suburbs.
TOP: This goldenrod prairie does not cause hay fever.
ABOVE: Silphium, black-eyed Susans, purple coneflowers, and prairie grasses turn this suburban yard into a country field.
RIGHT: Goldenrods, blazing stars, and coneflowers bloom in a field of Indian grass.

and October. Spring is shorter (May) and is sometimes lost between winter and summer. The gardening season, when the temperature stays above freezing, is only about 150 days in northern Illinois, Nebraska, Iowa, Indiana, and Ohio and fewer than 145 days in southern Manitoba, southern Ontario, North Dakota, South Dakota, Nebraska, Minnesota, Wisconsin, and most of Michigan.

Extremes of winter temperatures, from −60°F in North Dakota, −30°F in Wisconsin and Minnesota, and −20°F everywhere else, are not uncommon. Nor are summer temperatures that skyrocket to over 100°F anytime between early May and late September. (The same

While I was there, I met with Edward R. Hasselkus, a Wisconsin native, professor of horticulture at the University of Wisconsin in Madison and curator of the Longenecker Gardens at the U.W. Arboretum. He urged me to visit the Curtis Prairie, 60 acres of native prairie plants, a restoration that was begun in the 1930s with the support of conservationist Aldo Leopold. Undertaken as pure science, its aim was the preservation of the complex prairie ecosystem that included both plants and animals. If you choose to walk one of the paths *through* the prairie, bordered on both sides with six-foot turkeyfoot

Tall silphiums and goldenrods brighten the Curtis Prairie at the University of Wisconsin's Arboretum.

county in North Dakota that records −60°F in winter might record a summer temperature of 112°F). Only the toughest plants stand up to these extremes of heat and cold. I visited the University of Wisconsin's Arboretum to see what these were.

and ten-foot silphiums, you will have the unmistakable sense of being *inside* a great organism. But it is the beauty of the prairie that stays with you. There's a raised deck overlooking it, and on a sunny fall day, the plumes of Indian grass mesmerize in their undulations. I doubt

TOP: *A shady Milwaukee front yard is home to red baneberry, doll's eyes, and pink obedient plant.*
TOP RIGHT: *Elderberry, a shrub with an immense range, produces the berries that helped stock pioneer larders with jam.*
BOTTOM: *Prairie natives, growing in a strip against a house in this Minneapolis garden, compose a climate-proof perennial border.*
(C. Colston Burrell Design)
BOTTOM LEFT: *Bright yellow goldenrods bloom behind an Amish buggy, paused on a Wisconsin road.*

Memphis designer Tom Pellett counts on natives in the rigorous Lower Midwest.
Here, foamflowers line a dry streambed. (Karen Struthard photo)

if even Aldo Leopold could have realized what an impact this subtle beauty has had on the thousands who have since visited it.

One man who was inspired by the Curtis Prairie is Neil Diboll of Prairie Nursery in Westfield, Wisconsin, who grows a selection of prairie natives and also provides advice and expertise in establishing prairies. When I visited his nursery in August, I stepped out of my car into a cloud of aroma. I thought at first it was cilantro, but, no, Neil said that it was the scent of the flowers of prairie dropseed, a beautiful clumping grass.

No wonder midwesterners are turning to the perfectly adapted and perfectly beautiful plants of the prairie for their gardens. Frustrated perhaps by the performance of exotics in this vigorous climate, designers from Minneapolis to Chicago are designing with prairie and its utterly reliable inhabitants—plants like sweet black-eyed Susan (*Rudbeckia subtomentosa*) and prairie baby's breath (*Euphorbia corollata*) that stand up to heat and drought and make it through the winter.

Lorrie Otto, who lives north of Milwaukee, struggled with traditional garden plants for a few years before turning to beautiful and tough natives, and eventually planted part of her garden in tall grass prairie. She was the first in her neighborhood to have a prairie "lawn," but she is by no means the last. After some initial skepticism, a number of her neighbors have followed suit; the result is a suburban neighborhood that looks and feels like the country. In August, the houses are framed by the golds and yellows of silphiums, goldenrods, and sunflowers.

Mrs. Otto took me to some city gardens in Milwaukee that have used prairie in small doses—a little strip as a barrier along the road, a tiny patch along a fence—to splendid effect. I saw this same technique in Minneapolis, where, in a narrow strip between house and walk, landscape architect Cole Burrell had planted an exuberant perennial border of prairie natives: Joe-Pye weed, turkeyfoot, liatris, and silphium.

The handsome shrubs that grow on the edges of prairie—sumac, elderberry, chokecherry, and gray dogwood—are not only climate-proof, they are bird plants. In a challenging region like the Upper Midwest, choosing from among natives long acclimated to the vicissitudes of weather makes beautiful sense in the garden.

The Lower Midwest

If the Upper Midwest is known for its rigorous winters, the Lower Midwest is equally infamous for the rigor of its summers. States that share the sultry summer of the Lower Midwest, situated roughly below 40° of latitude, include Kansas, Missouri, southern Illinois, southern Indiana, the southernmost part of Ohio, Kentucky, western Tennessee, Arkansas, Oklahoma, and part of northern Texas.

Summers here are like those of the South, only more so, because in the Lower Midwest they are not softened by the moderating effects of the sea. There are more days over 90°F in Little Rock than in Miami, and approximately two and a half times as many as in Chicago! Summers are long and hot and, like the winters in the Upper Midwest, go on and on, sometimes with violent tornadoes, thunderstorms, and hailstorms.

Summer can hang on for so long that fall sometimes gets lost. This makes for a very long gardening season that averages more than 200 days a year and, of course, a correspondingly shorter winter that is also warmer than in the Upper Midwest—although it, too, can plunge to occasional but inevitable lows that kill the camellias. Spring comes early in the sunny Lower Midwest—usually—and much of the region enjoys about the same amount of sunshine as central Florida.

Memphis designer Tom Pellett counts on native plants for graceful, durable combinations. A favorite for a woodland border is foamflower in the foreground, Christmas fern and, perhaps, the exotic Lenten rose in the middle, backed by giant Solomon's seal. Behind these perennials, he suggests a shrub layer that might include oak leaf hydrangea, nannyberry, or red buckeye.

Sweet bay magnolia and bald cypress are some of the trees Tom uses. And amsonias and false indigos are perennials that mask their toughness with gracious good looks.

The Lower Midwest shares with the Upper Midwest a continental climate of great extremes. Because of its latitude, heat rather than cold is the rule, but extremes of cold are an occasional inevitable. Like its northern counterpart, the Lower Midwest is a challenging climate for plants.

Goldenrods at the edge of this shady garden take the heat and deep freezes of the Lower Midwest with ease.

Plants for the Upper Midwest

Perennials

Actaea species
baneberry

*Allium cernuum**
nodding onion

Anemone canadensis
Canada anemone

A. cylindrica
thimbleweed

*Aquilegia canadensis**
columbine

Artemisia ludoviciana
sagebrush

Asarum canadense
wild ginger

*Asclepias tuberosa**
butterfly weed

*Aster azureus**
sky blue aster

*Aster cordifolius**
heartleaf aster

*Aster ericoides**
heath aster

*A. novae-angliae**
New England aster

A. patens
wood aster

Baptisia species
false indigo

Callirhoë species
wine-cup

Cassia hebecarpa
wild senna

Castilleja species
Indian paintbrush

Caulophyllum thalictroides
blue cohosh

*Chelone glabra**
white turtlehead

Coreopsis tripteris
tall coreopsis

Dalea purpurea
purple prairie clover

*Dodecatheon meadia**
eastern shooting star

Echinacea species
coneflower

Epilobium angustifolium
fireweed

*Eryngium yuccifolium**
rattlesnake master

Eupatorium maculatum
Joe-Pye weed

E. perfoliatum
boneset

E. purpureum
Joe-Pye weed

*Euphorbia corollata**
flowering spurge

Filipendula rubra
queen-of-the-prairie

*Gentiana andrewsii**
bottle gentian

Geranium maculatum
wild geranium

Geum triflorum
prairie smoke

Helianthus mollis
downy sunflower

H. occidentalis
western sunflower

H. tuberosus
Jerusalem artichoke

Heuchera richardsonii
prairie alum root

Iris brevicaulis
zigzag iris

*Liatris aspera**
rough blazing star

L. ligulistylus
Rocky Mountain blazing star

L. punctata
spotted gayfeather

*L. pycnostachya**
prairie blazing star

L. spicata 'Kobold'
spike gayfeather

Lilium canadense
Canada lily

L. michiganense
Michigan lily

L. philadelphicum
wood lily

L. superbum
Turk's cap lily

Lobelia species
lobelia

Lupinus perennis
lupine

Monarda fistulosa
bergamot

Parthenium integrifolium
wild quinine

Penstemon gracilis
penstemon

P. grandiflorus
beardtongue

Phlox pilosa
prairie phlox

P. subulata
moss pink

*Physostegia virginiana**
obedient plant

Polygonatum species
Solomon's seal

*Ratibida pinnata**
prairie coneflower

Ruellia humilus
wild petunia

Rudbeckia species
black-eyed Susan

Sedum ternatum
sedum

Silene regia
royal catchfly

Silphium species
silphium

Sisyrinchium angustifolium
blue-eyed grass

S. idahoense
blue-eyed grass

Smilacina racemosa
false Solomon's seal

Solidago caesia
wreath goldenrod

S. canadensis
Canada goldenrod

S. flexicaulis
zigzag goldenrod

*S. nemoralis**
gray goldenrod

S. ohiensis
Ohio goldenrod

S. puberula
downy goldenrod

*S. rigida**
stiff goldenrod

S. rugosa
rough-stemmed goldenrod

S. sempervirens
seaside goldenrod

S. speciosa
showy goldenrod

Tradescantia x *andersoniana*
spiderwort

Trillium grandiflorum
great trillium

Vernonia species
ironweed

*Veronicastrum virginicum**
Culver's root

Viola species
violet

Annuals

*Coreopsis tinctoria**
plains coreopsis

*Helianthus annuus**
sunflower

*Linum perenne**
blue flax

*Phlox drummondii**
annual phlox

Grasses, Sedges, Rushes, and Reeds

*Andropogon gerardii**
big bluestem

*Bouteloua curtipendula**
sideoats

*B. gracilis**
blue grama

Carex pensylvanica
Pennsylvania sedge

Chasmanthium latifolium
northern sea oats, river oats

*Panicum virgatum**
switch grass

Phalaris arundinacea picta
gardener's garters, ribbon grass

*Schizachyrium scoparium**
little bluestem

Sorghastrum nutans
Indian grass

48

Sporobolus heterolepis*
prairie dropseed

Ferns

Adiantum pedatum*
northern maidenhair fern

Athyrium filix-femina
lady fern

Dryopteris carthusiana
florist's fern

D. marginalis
marginal wood fern

Matteuccia pensylvanica*
ostrich fern

Onoclea sensibilis
sensitive fern

Osmunda cinnamomea*
cinnamon fern

O. claytonia*
interrupted fern

O. regalis var. *spectabilis**
royal fern

Water Plants

Equisetum hyemale
scouring rush

Iris versicolor
blue flag

Orontium aquaticum
golden club

Peltandra virginiana
arrow arum

Pontederia cordata
pickerelweed

Typha angustifolia
narrow-leaf cattail

Vines

Campsis radicans
trumpet vine

Decumaria barbara
climbing hydrangea

Lonicera x *heckrottii**
red trumpet honeysuckle

L. sempervirens
trumpet honeysuckle

Parthenocissus quinquefolia*
Virginia creeper

Shrubs

Aesculus parviflora*
bottlebrush buckeye

Amelanchier alnifolia
serviceberry

A. stolonifera*
running serviceberry

Amorpha canescens
leadplant

A. fruticosa
indigo bush

Aralia spinosa*
devil's walkingstick

Aronia arbutifolia
'Brilliantissima'*
red chokeberry

Calycanthus floridus
sweetshrub

Cephalanthus occidentalis*
buttonbush

Clethra alnifolia
'Hummingbird'
dwarf summersweet

C. a. 'Pinkspire', 'Rosea'
summersweet

Comptonia peregrina
sweet fern

Cornus species
dogwood

C. canadensis
bunchberry

Hydrangea arborescens
'Annabelle'
wild hydrangea

H. quercifolia
oak leaf hydrangea

H. q. 'Snow Queen'
Snow Queen hydrangea

Ilex verticillata
winterberry

Juniperus communis
juniper

J. horizontalis
creeping juniper

Mahonia aquifolium
Oregon grape holly

Myrica pensylvanica*
bayberry

Paxistima canbyi*
paxistima

Potentilla fruticosa*
shrubby cinquefoil

Prunus americanus
American plum

Rhododendron x 'Rosy
Lights'*
azalea

R. x 'White Lights'*
azalea

Rhus aromatica*
fragrant sumac

R. glabra*
smooth sumac

R. typhina*
staghorn sumac

Rosa setigera*
prairie rose

Sambucus canadensis
elderberry

Viburnum dentatum*
arrowwood viburnum

V. lentago*
nannyberry

V. prunifolium*
blackhaw

V. trilobum*
American cranberry

Trees

Amelanchier species*
serviceberry

Betula nigra 'Heritage'*
white river birch

B. papyrifera*
canoe birch

Cercis canadensis*
eastern redbud

Chionanthus virginicus
fringe tree

Cladrastis kentukeya*
yellowwood

Hamamelis virginiana*
witch hazel

Juniperus virginiana*
eastern red cedar

Magnolia acuminata*
cucumber tree

Populus tremuloides
quaking aspen

Taxodium species*
bald cypress

*Recommended plants are starred.

Perennials

*Allium cernuum**
nodding onion

*Amsonia tabernaemontana**
amsonia

Anemone canadensis
Canada anemone

A. cylindrica
thimbleweed

*Anemonella thalictroides**
rue anemone

*Aquilegia canadensis**
columbine

Asarum species
wild ginger

*Asclepias tuberosa**
butterfly weed

Aster azureus
sky blue aster

*A. cordifolius**
heartleaf aster

*A. divaricatus**
white wood aster

*A. ericoides**
heath aster

*A. novi-angliae**
New England aster

Baptisia species*
false indigo

Callirhoë species
wine-cup

Cassia hebecarpa
wild senna

Castilleja species
Indian paintbrush

*Chelone lyonii**
pink turtlehead

Coreopsis tripteris
tall coreopsis

*C. verticillata**
threadleaf coreopsis

*Dodecatheon meadia**
eastern shooting star

Echinacea species*
coneflower

Eryngium yuccifolium
rattlesnake master

Erythronium albidum
fawn lily, dogtooth violet

E. umbilicatum
(*americanum*)
fawn lily, dogtooth violet

Eupatorium species
eupatorium

*Euphorbia corollata**
flowering spurge

Gaura lindheimeri
gaura

Geranium maculatum
wild geranium

*Helianthus hirsutus**
hairy sunflower

H. maximiliani
Maximilian's sunflower

H. tuberosus
Jerusalem artichoke

*Heuchera americana**
alum root

H. villosa
hairy alum root

Houstonia caerulea
Quaker ladies

Iris species
iris

Liatris punctata
spotted gayfeather

*L. pycnostachya**
prairie blazing star

L. spicata 'Kobold'*
spike gayfeather

*Lilium superbum**
Turk's cap lily

Lobelia species
lobelia

Lupinus perennis
lupine

*Mertensia virginica**
Virginia bluebells

Mitchella repens
partridgeberry

Monarda species
monarda

Oenothera fruticosa
sundrops

*O. missouriensis**
Missouri evening primrose

O. speciosa
pink evening primrose

Pachysandra procumbens
American pachysandra

Penstemon gracilis
penstemon

P. grandiflorus
beardtongue

*Phlox amoena**
chalice phlox

P. paniculata
garden phlox

*P. pilosa**
prairie phlox

P. subulata
moss pink

*Physostegia virginiana**
obedient plant

Polygonatum biflorum
Solomon's seal

Porteranthus trifoliatus
Bowman's root

*Ratibida pinnata**
prairie coneflower

Ruellia humilus
wild petunia

Rudbeckia fulgida
'Goldsturm'
black-eyed Susan

R. laciniata
green-headed coneflower

*R. subtomentosa**
sweet black-eyed Susan

R. triloba
branched coneflower

Sedum ternatum
sedum

Shortia galacifolia
Oconee bells

Silene polypetela
silene

*S. regia**
royal catchfly

S. virginica
fire pink

Silphium species
silphium

*Sisyrinchium angustifolium**
blue-eyed grass

*Smilacina racemosa**
false Solomon's seal

Solidago species*
goldenrod

Tiarella species
foamflower

Tradescantia x *andersoniana*
spiderwort

Trillium grandiflorum
great trillium

Vernonia species
ironweed

*Veronicastrum virginicum**
Culver's root

Viola species
violet

Annuals

*Coreopsis tinctoria**
plains coreopsis

*Helianthus annuus**
sunflower

*Linum perenne**
blue flax

*Phlox drummondii**
annual phlox

Grasses, Sedges, Rushes, and Reeds

Andropogon gerardii
big bluestem

Bouteloua curtipendula
sideoats

B. gracilis
blue grama

*Carex muskingumensis**
palm sedge

C. pensylvanica
Pennsylvania sedge

*Chasmanthium latifolium**
northern sea oats, river oats

Panicum virgatum
switch grass

Phalaris arundinacea picta
gardener's garters, ribbon grass

*Schizachyrium scoparium**
little bluestem

Sorghastrum nutans
Indian grass

*Sporobolus heterolepsis**
prairie dropseed

Ferns

*Adiantum pedatum**
northern maidenhair fern

*Athyrium filix-femina**
lady fern

*Dennstaedtia punctilobula**
hay-scented fern

Onoclea sensibilis
sensitive fern

*Osmunda cinnamomea**
cinnamon fern

*O. claytonia**
interrupted fern

O. regalis var. *spectabilis**
royal fern

*Woodwardia areolata**
netted chain fern

Water Plants

Equisetum hyemale
scouring rush

Iris species
iris

Menyanthes trifoliata
bog bean

Nymphaea odorata
pond water lily

Orontium aquaticum
golden club

Peltandra virginiana
arrow arum

Pontederia cordata
pickerelweed

Saururus cernuus
lizard's tail

Typha species
cattail

Vines

Anisostichus capreolatus
cross vine

Aster carolinianus
climbing aster

Campsis radicans
trumpet vine

Clematis viorna
leather flower

Decumaria barbara
climbing hydrangea

Lonicera x *heckrottii*
red trumpet honeysuckle

*L. sempervirens**
trumpet honeysuckle

*Parthenocissus quinquefolia**
Virginia creeper

Wisteria frutescens
American wisteria

Shrubs

*Aesculus parviflora**
bottlebrush buckeye

*Agarista populfolia**
Florida leucothoe

Amelanchier alnifolia
serviceberry

Amorpha canescens
leadplant

A. fruticosa
indigo bush

Aralia spinosa
devil's walkingstick

Aronia arbutifolia
'Brilliantissima'
red chokeberry

Artemisia filifolia
sand sage

*Callicarpa americana**
beautyberry

Calycanthus floridus
sweetshrub

*Ceanothus americanus**
New Jersey tea

Cephalanthus occidentalis
buttonbush

Clethra acuminata
cinnamon clethra

C. alnifolia
'Hummingbird'
dwarf summersweet

C. a. 'Pinkspire', 'Rosea'
summersweet

*Conradina verticillata**
Cumberland rosemary

Cornus alternifolia
pagoda dogwood

C. amomum
silky dogwood

C. sericea
red-osier dogwood

Cotinus obovatus
American smoke tree

*Cyrilla racemiflora**
titi

*Euonymous americana**
hearts-a-bustin'

Fothergilla gardenii
dwarf fothergilla

F. g. 'Blue Mist'
Blue Mist fothergilla

F. major
large fothergilla

Hydrangea arborescens
'Annabelle'
wild hydrangea

*Hydrangea quercifolia**
oak leaf hydrangea

H. q. 'Snow Queen'
Snow Queen hydrangea

Hypericum frondosum 'Sunburst'
golden St. Johnswort

Ilex decidua
possum haw

I. glabra
inkberry

I. verticillata 'Winter Red'
winterberry

I. v. 'Maryland Beauty'
winterberry

*Illicium floridanum**
anise tree

*I. parviflorum**
anise tree

Itea virginica
'Henry's Garnet'
sweetspire

Juniperus communis saxitalis
mountain juniper

J. horizontalis
creeping juniper

Kalmia latifolia,
many cultivars
mountain laurel

Leucothoe axillaris
doghobble

*L. fontanesiana**
doghobble

Mahonia aquifolium
Oregon grape holly

Myrica pensylvanica
bayberry

*Paxistima canbyi**
paxistima

Potentilla fruticosa
shrubby cinquefoil

Rhododendron arborescens
and cultivars
sweet azalea

*R. bakeri**
Cumberland azalea

R. calendulaceum, many
cultivars
flame azalea

R. canescens and cultivars*
Piedmont azalea

R. carolinianum
Carolina rhododendron

R. catawbiense
Catawba rhododendron

*R. Chapmanii**
Chapman's rhododendron

R. maximum
rosebay rhododendron

*R. minus**
Piedmont rhododendron

*R. periclymenoides**
pinxter azalea

*R. prinophyllum**
roseshell azalea

R. vaseyi
pinkshell azalea

*Rhus aromatica**
fragrant sumac

R. typhina
staghorn sumac

Rosa setigera
prairie rose

Sambucus canadensis
elderberry

*Stewartia malcodendron**
silky camellia

*Viburnum cassinoides**
withe rod viburnum

*V. dentatum**
arrowwood viburnum

V. lentago
nannyberry

*V. nudum**
possum haw

Yucca species
yucca

Zenobia pulverulenta
dusty zenobia

Trees

*Acer leucoderme**
chalk maple

*Aesculus pavia**
red buckeye

*Amelanchier laevis**
serviceberry

Asimina triloba
pawpaw

Betula nigra
river birch

B. n. 'Heritage'
white river birch

*Cercis canadensis** eastern redbud	*Halesia carolina** Carolina silverbell	*Magnolia acuminata* cucumber tree	*M. tripetela* umbrella magnolia
Chionanthus virginicus fringe tree	*H. diptera* 'Magniflora' Magniflora silverbell	*M. ashei** Ashe magnolia	*M. virginiana** sweet bay magnolia
*Cladrastis kentukeya** yellowwood	*Hamamelis virginiana* witch hazel	*M. cordata* yellow cucumber tree	*Oxydendrum arboreum** sourwood, sorrel tree
Cornus florida eastern dogwood	*Ilex opaca* and cultivars American holly	*M. grandiflora* cultivars bull bay magnolia	*Taxodium ascendens* pond cypress
Crataegus viridis hawthorn	*Juniperus virginiana* eastern red cedar	*M. macrophylla* bigleaf magnolia	*T. distichum* bald cypress

*Recommended plants are starred.

Rocks, rocky soil, and the nearness of the sea influence gardening in New England.

THE NORTHEAST

After the ruggedness of the Rockies and the vastness of the Great Plains, the eastern mountains appear positively gentle and the Northeast seems conveniently condensed: a rich patchwork of scenic landforms that fits compactly into a relatively small region. There are meadows and forests of hardwood and dark conifers; there are lakes and rivers and river valleys; there are gentle hills and rugged mountains—including Maine's Mount Katahdin, a substantial 5,258 feet. And there are thousands of miles of coast. Part of Quebec, part of New Brunswick, and Nova Scotia in Canada, together with Maine, New York, northeastern Pennsylvania, Vermont, New Hampshire, Massachusetts, Connecticut, and Rhode Island make up the Northeast region. If they have one thing in common—besides cold winters—it is rock.

Rocky soil may have driven farmers from New England and, according to Connecticut writer and gardener Sydney Eddison, "still tries the gardener's soul," but from what I could see, gardening is alive and well in the Northeast and nowhere more than in Sydney's wonderful Connecticut garden.

It was a hot day in August when I visited, and the Northeast had been suffering a long drought. The daylily buds had shriveled and dropped. That's how dry it was. We agreed to meet for lunch. Over lunch, happily, she gave me a tour. At its worst, her garden was lovely.

Its heart is a perennial border that looks to be about 100 feet long. It is a vivacious mix of natives and exotics. In addition to Sydney's great exotic passion, daylilies, there are natives: blue flax in the front border and Carolina lupine for early yellow, a smashing companion to blue false indigo. On the day I visited, the coneflowers, blazing stars, sunflowers, and Joe-Pye weed were holding forth bravely in the heat. Later on, boltonia 'Snowbank', which Sydney says is the only tall plant in the border that she doesn't stake, overlaps with willowleaf sunflower.

I asked Sydney if she had any advice for gardeners in the Northeast. Besides protecting plants from cold dam-

53

OPPOSITE: *Hay-scented ferns cover the ground around a clove-scented rose azalea behind this shady bench at the Connecticut College Arboretum in New London.*
ABOVE: *A rock wall and a pedimented arch define this New England perennial border.*

age, she says that the trick to gardening in the Northeast lies in "understanding the soil." Because soils are rocky and shallow-rooted trees compete with understory plants for water and nutrients, so "generous lashings of moisture-retentive humus at planting time and an organic mulch applied after the plants have been installed are the *sine qua non* of gardening in the vicinity of mature trees."

Sydney actually thinks of the Northeast as two zones. In the warm zone in the south and along the coast, frequent fogs and mists provide plenty of moisture and the temperature is moderated by the sea. On the coast of Maine, the first frost may not arrive until late October, while inland, some areas can see frost in early September.

Inland, temperatures are more extreme. Depending upon location, winter lows vary from cold ($-10°$) to deep-freeze ($-50°F$). Latitude and elevation divide the region into a generally northern cold section and a warm section from Saratoga, New York, southward, and including the coastline of Maine.

In the cold section of New England, says Sydney, "winter and summer are the long seasons." Aroostook County in northern Maine, in Zone 2, enjoys only three or four months of frost-free weather. Spring is an April thaw, followed by the mud season, when superficial water can't escape because the ground beneath remains frozen. "Northern summers arrive almost without warning and depart as suddenly," she concludes. When summer ends, snow can be expected at any time.

Fairfield County, Connecticut, in the warm section, enjoys 180 frost-free days and a USDA rating of Zone 6. Although spring here is short, fall is a generous season of sunshine and blue skies with an intoxicating nip in the air. While people in Fairfield County are planting bulbs, those in Aroostook County often find themselves shoveling snow.

One thing both cold and warm sections of the Northeast share is abundant rain—about 40 inches each year, fairly evenly distributed around the year. Some of the precipitation falls as snow.

Having lived in the Northeast for some years and having spent my childhood in Illinois, I recognize the euphoria in the air on the first really warm day of spring. In the Boston area, this usually happens in mid-May. Instead of plunging headlong down the street, heads bowed against the wind, people amble unhurriedly. Hungry for the sun, they smile and stroll about in what soon becomes a spontaneous street fest. It was on such a day that I visited Garden in the Woods outside Boston.

Owned and operated by the New England Wild Flower Society, Garden in the Woods promotes the conservation of temperate North American plants, offering courses, propagating rare and endangered natives, and maintaining a spectacular 45-acre garden. It was in their nursery that I saw (and still regret not buying) a double trillium.

By amazing good luck, when I got there, the flowering of spring-blooming perennials, shrubs, and trees had been telescoped into one grand, amazing spectacle: phlox, false Solomon's seal, Virginia bluebells, shooting stars, *Baptisia leucophaea, Tiarella, Maianthemum,* trilliums, azaleas, Carolina rhododendrons, amsonias, magnolias, and rue anemones all crowded the paths and filled the air with their sweet perfumes. I wandered until my feet ached, but I didn't leave until I used up all my film.

The next day held another rare treat at the Connecticut College Arboretum. When I think back on that day, the pictures in my mind are always colored the bright apple green of new hay-scented ferns and the vibrant pink of clove-scented rose azaleas. There were plenty of other natives in bloom as well: viburnums, *Maianthemum,* and leucothoes, hung with white bell flowers.

En route home, my head swam with visions of spring's explosion in the Northeast. Cold has its uses. It allows for such treasures as white paper birch and bunchberry and the exquisite rhodora azalea, plants that grow poorly if at all farther south. The Northeast's long, cold winter concentrates the spring show into one slambang, grand extravaganza to start off the growing season. And if cold and rocky soils combine to make gardening a challenge, northeastern natives meet the challenge gloriously and fit into the many landscapes of this richly varied region.

TOP: *Carolina rhododendron under a dogwood at Garden in the Woods in Framingham, Massachusetts.*
CENTER: *Sydney Eddison's garden blends together sturdy natives and exotics such as ornamental grasses and daylilies.*
BOTTOM: *Yucca serves as a shrubby accent under a pine grove.*

Perennials

Actaea pachypoda
doll's eyes

*A. rubra**
red baneberry

*Amsonia tabernaemontana**
amsonia

Aquilegia canadensis
columbine

Aruncus sylvester
goat's beard

Asarum canadense
wild ginger

Asclepias incarnata
swamp milkweed

A. tuberosa
butterfly weed

*Aster cordifolius**
heartleaf aster

*A. divaricatus**
white wood aster

A. laevis
smooth aster

*A. novae-angliae**
New England aster

A. novi-belgii
New York aster

Baptisia alba
white false indigo

*B. australis**
blue false indigo

B. leucophaea
cream false indigo

Boltonia asteroides cultivars*
boltonia

*Caulophyllum thalictroides**
blue cohosh

Chelone glabra
white turtlehead

*C. lyonii**
pink turtlehead

C. obliqua
rose turtlehead

*Chrysogonum virginianum**
green-and-gold

*Chrysopsis mariana**
Maryland golden aster

*Coreopsis rosea**
pink threadleaf coreopsis

C. verticillata and cultivars
threadleaf coreopsis

*Echinacea purpurea**
purple coneflower

E. p. 'White Swan'
white coneflower

Eryngium yuccifolium
rattlesnake master

*Erythronium umbilicatum
(americanum)*
dogtooth violet

Eupatorium purpureum
Joe-Pye weed

*Geranium maculatum**
wild geranium

Helianthus angustifolius
swamp sunflower

H. hirsutus
hairy sunflower

H. maximiliani
Maximilian's sunflower

H. mollis
downy sunflower

H. x multiflorus
sunflower

H. salicifolius
willowleaf sunflower

H. tuberosus
Jerusalem artichoke

Houstonia caerulea
Quaker ladies

Iris crestata
crested iris

I. versicolor
blue flag

Liatris aspera
rough blazing star

L. pycnostachya
prairie blazing star

L. spicata 'Kobold'
spike gayfeather

Lilium canadense
Canada lily

L. superbum
Turk's cap lily

*Lobelia cardinalis**
cardinal flower

*L. siphilitica**
great blue lobelia

Lupinus perennis
lupine

Monarda didyma
bee balm

M. fistulosa
bergamot

Oenothera fruticosa
sundrops

O. missouriensis
Missouri evening primrose

Penstemon digitalis
foxglove penstemon

P. pallida
white penstemon

Phlox divaricata
wild sweet william

P. d. 'Fuller's White'
white phlox

P. paniculata
garden phlox

P. stolonifera
creeping phlox

P. subulata
moss pink

Physostegia virginiana
obedient plant

Polygonatum biflorum
Solomon's seal

Porteranthus trifoliatus
Bowman's root

*Rudbeckia fulgida 'Gold-
sturm'*
black-eyed Susan

R. subtomentosa
sweet black-eyed Susan

Ruellia humilis
wild petunia

Sanguinaria canadensis
bloodroot

Scutellaria incana
skullcap

S. serrata
showy skullcap

Silphium integrifolium
rosinweed

S. laciniatum
compass plant

S. perfoliatum
cup plant

S. terebinthinaceum
prairie dock

Smilacina racemosa
false Solomon's seal

*Solidago caesia**
wreath goldenrod

*S. canadensis**
Canada goldenrod

S. flexicaulis
zigzag goldenrod

*S. nemoralis**
gray goldenrod

*S. odora**
sweet goldenrod

S. ohiensis
Ohio goldenrod

S. rugosa
rough-stemmed goldenrod

*S. sempervirens**
seaside goldenrod

S. spathulata
goldenrod

S. speciosa
showy goldenrod

*Stokesia laevis**
Stokes' aster

Stylophorum diphyllum
wood poppy

*Thermopsis villosa**
Carolina bush pea

Tiarella cordifolia
running foamflower

Trillium species
wake robin, trillium

Uvularia grandiflora
great merrybells

Vernonia noveboracensis
ironweed

Veronicastrum virginicum
Culver's root

Viola species
violet

Annuals

Coreopsis tinctoria
plains coreopsis

Helianthus annuus
sunflower

Linum perenne
blue flax

Phacelia bipinnatifida
phacelia
Phlox drummondii
annual phlox

Grasses, Sedges, Rushes, and Reeds
Andropogon virginicus
broom sedge
Carex muskingumensis
palm sedge
C. pensylvanica
Pennsylvania sedge
Chasmanthium latifolium
northern sea oats, river oats
Cymophyllus fraseri
Fraser's sedge
*Deschampsia caespitosa**
hairgrass
Panicum virgatum
switch grass
*Phalaris arundinacea picta**
gardener's garters, ribbon grass
Schizachyrium scoparium
little bluestem
Sorghastrum nutans
Indian grass

Ferns
Adiantum pedatum
northern maidenhair fern
Athyrium filix-femina
lady fern
Dennstaedtia punctilobula
hay-scented fern
*Dryopteris marginalis**
marginal wood fern
*Matteuccia pensylvanica**
ostrich fern
*Onoclea sensibilis**
sensitive fern
*Osmunda cinnamomea**
cinnamon fern
O. claytonia
interrupted fern
O. regalis var. *spectabilis**
royal fern
*Polystichum acrostichoides**
Christmas fern

Thelypteris noveboracensis
New York fern

Water Plants
Equisetum hyemale
scouring rush
Iris versicolor
blue flag
Nymphaea odorata
pond water lily
Orontium aquaticum
golden club
Peltandra virginiana
arrow arum
Pontederia cordata
pickerelweed
Typha angustifolia
narrow-leaf cattail

Vines
*Campsis radicans**
trumpet vine
Clematis viorna
leather flower
Lonicera sempervirens
trumpet honeysuckle
*Parthenocissus quinquefolia**
Virginia creeper

Shrubs
Arctostaphylos uva-ursi
bearberry
Aronia arbutifolia 'Brilliantissima'
red chokeberry
Calycanthus floridus
sweetshrub
Ceanothus americanus
New Jersey tea
Clethra acuminata
cinnamon clethra
C. alnifolia 'Hummingbird'
dwarf summersweet
C. a. 'Pinkspire', 'Rosea'*
summersweet
*Comptonia peregrina**
sweet fern
*Cornus alternifolia**
pagoda dogwood
C. canadensis
bunchberry

*C. sericea**
red-osier dogwood
*Fothergilla gardenii**
dwarf fothergilla
F. g. 'Blue Mist'
Blue Mist fothergilla
Hydrangea quercifolia
oak leaf hydrangea
H. quercifolia 'Snowqueen'
Snow Queen hydrangea
Ilex glabra
inkberry
I. verticillata 'Winter Red'
winterberry
I. v. 'Red Sprite'
winterberry
Juniperus horizontalis
creeping juniper
Kalmia latifolia, many cultivars*
mountain laurel
*Myrica pensylvanica**
bayberry
Paxistima canbyi
paxistima
Potentilla fruticosa
shrubby cinquefoil
*Prunus maritima**
beach plum
Rhododendron canadense
rhodora azalea
R. carolinianum
Carolina rhododendron
*R. catawbiense**
Catawba rhododendron
*R. maximum**
rosebay rhododendron
R. periclymenoides
Pinxter azalea
R. prinophyllum
roseshell azalea
*R. vaseyi**
pinkshell azalea
*R. viscosum**
swamp azalea
Rhus aromatica
fragrant sumac

R. typhina
staghorn sumac
Viburnum acerifolium
maple leaf viburnum
V. alnifolium
moose ears viburnum
V. dentatum
arrowwood
V. trilobum
American cranberry

Trees
Amelanchier laevis
serviceberry
Asimina triloba
pawpaw
Betula nigra
river birch
B. n. 'Heritage'
white river birch
B. papyrifera
canoe birch
*Cercis canadensis**
eastern redbud
*Chionanthus virginicus**
fringe tree
*Cornus florida**
eastern dogwood
Crataegus viridis
hawthorn
Franklinia alatamaha
Franklin tree
*Halesia carolina**
Carolina silverbell
*Hamamelis virginiana**
witch hazel
Ilex opaca and cultivars*
American holly
*Juniperus virginiana**
Eastern red cedar
*Magnolia acuminata**
cucumber tree
M. macrophylla
bigleaf magnolia
*M. tripetela**
umbrella magnolia
Populus tremuloides
quaking aspen

*Recommended plants are starred.

Dogwoods are one of the delights of spring in the Mid-Atlantic.

THE MID-ATLANTIC

I returned home in late spring with a head full of memories, a station wagon full of plants, and a grateful heart. In the past, I've had a regrettable tendency toward gardening envy, the bewailing of my climate's shortcomings—the humidity, the heat, etc., etc. After listening to the trials of gardeners elsewhere around the country, I began to look at my gardening glass as being half full. All things considered, the Mid-Atlantic is a pleasant place to garden, with an immense range of native ornamentals from which to choose. It is a climate of the proverbial four seasons, roughly equal in length. Although summers are hot and humid, with prolific, almost tropical growth, they are shorter and cooler than in the South. Winters are just cold and snowy enough to qualify as real winter, but lack the bite and deep-freeze conditions of the North. (Still, the Philadelphia Flower Show, when it comes in March, re-

ceives a warm welcome.) Spring and fall are not just a few moderate days, but real seasons that stretch on for months with the accompaniment of a long sequence of awakening wildflowers in spring and the bright color of turning leaves in the fall. Even the topography compromises in a most civilized manner: the landscape is flat at the coast and steep as it rises to the Piedmont, but is mostly gently rolling with a mixture of woodland and meadow.

New Jersey, southeastern Pennsylvania, Delaware, Maryland, and inland Virginia sit squarely in the center of the region. Western North Carolina and the northernmost parts of South Carolina and Georgia, by virtue of the cooler temperatures of higher altitudes, also belong to the Mid-Atlantic region climatically. Likewise, a narrow strip of northern coastline insulated by the ocean, which includes Long Island, a bit of coastal Connecticut, Rhode Island, and part of Cape Cod, enjoys the Mid-Atlantic climate.

Spring begins in March, when raw, wet winds usher in the growing season. Typically, the last frost and a general settling of weather occur in mid-April. As long as it is

Spikes of liatris bask in the hot summer sun at Water Ways Nursery in Lovettsville, Virginia

cool—the latter part of March, April, and early May—planting and transplanting are simple. The ground stays wet until the weather turns warm, and plants thrive in the even moisture. Early May brings a peak of delicate, lacy bloom with native azaleas, dogwoods, and many woodland wildlings flowering in concert. As successive waves of herbaceous plants—Virginia bluebells, phloxes, star grasses—bloom in spring, the landscape fills with lush green.

Sometime in June, summer arrives with tropical heat and humidity. August is usually the hottest month, with occasional days on which the temperature may reach 95° to 100°F in the hotter parts of the region. Thunderstorms dump almost a foot of rain. The other 30-odd inches fall regularly around the year.

This combination of heat, humidity, and abundant rainfall supports a lush kind of vegetation. Every inch of soil, every nook and cranny, brims with plant life. From tiny creepers that rise from cracks in rocks to the giant trees of field and forest, plentiful rainfall ensures that grasses, perennials, shrubs, and small trees fill in all the layers between to form dense walls of vegetation. By the end of July, the landscape is virtually filled with layer upon layer of plant life.

This climate lends itself to gardens, and gardens abound. Ever since Colonial days, when John Bartram and his son William hunted plants in the wilderness, Philadelphia has been a hotbed of horticulture, the center of sophisticated gardening in the East.

Gardens here have long memories and mature specimens. The greater Philadelphia area is generously endowed with places to see what your magnolia, American holly, azaleas, fothergilla, or franklinia will look like in 50 years or more. Scott Arboretum in Swarthmore, Morris Arboretum in Chestnut Hill, the Arboretum of the Barnes Foundation in Merion Station, and Bartram's own garden in Philadelphia—"America's Oldest Surviving Botanic Garden"—include magnificent old specimens.

The queen of Pennsylvania gardens is Longwood in Kennett Square—1,000 acres, of which 3½ are under glass! In this garden of superlatives, the attractions are so numerous it's hard to concentrate, but I think my favorite place is one that the curator of plants Rick Darke showed me: a quiet lawn adjacent to the Peirce–du Pont House under soaring old trees, including a magnificent *Magnolia acuminata,* planted by the Peirce family in the 1700s.

As if Longwood by itself weren't garden enough for one region, there are Winterthur and Nemours in nearby Delaware. But it is in Greenville, Delaware, at Mt. Cuba Center for the Study of Piedmont Flora, that Dr. Richard Lighty and his staff oversee a garden now dedicated exclusively to natives. Owned and designed by Mrs. Lammot du Pont Copeland, Mt. Cuba is not yet open to the general public and the number of visitors is extremely limited, but horticultural groups may apply (try at least a year or more in advance) for a tour from April to June. Just seeing the grove of serviceberries in bloom is definitely worth the wait.

Farther south, in the Washington, D.C., area, there is more: excellent public gardens such as the National Arboretum, and Brookside Gardens in Wheaton, Maryland, where native azaleas, hollies, and magnolias mingle with exotics.

Bartholdi Park—across Independence Avenue from the Conservatory at the U.S. Botanic Garden in Washington, D.C.—boasts a garden of ornamental natives that was begun in the fall of 1993. It features native ornamental grasses *Panicum* and *Sporobolus,* bold silphiums, and winterberries for bright color in the gray Washington winter.

Gaillardia and wild ageratum flank a birdbath in this Mid-Atlantic garden.

In addition to displaying plants, the congenial climate makes the Mid-Atlantic a good place to produce them as well. Water Ways Nursery in Lovettsville, Virginia (not far from Harpers Ferry), propagates native perennials and wetland plants. Proprietor Sally Kurtz, who gave generously of her no-nonsense advice on the selection and care of water garden plants for this book, can usually be found standing up to her hips in one of her ponds, examining golden club or harvesting lotus roots—no easy task! Sally's knowledge of water plants—including their culinary uses—is truly astounding (and she is the only person I have ever met who has performed successful surgery on a goldfish). Water Ways Nursery is one of many excellent nurseries that produce climate-appropriate plants for gardens in the Mid-Atlantic.

Sadly, another great native plant nursery, Wildflower, owned and operated by Jan Midgley, is moving to Birmingham, Alabama. Jan is a wizard at propagating natives that no one else can grow. She has spent the last 11 years propagating natives that are unavailable in the trade. The Mid-Atlantic's loss will be the South's gain.

Many of the plants that Jan grew here in the Mid-Atlantic will also grow in the South. One of the things that make this region's gardens so lush and richly varied is the overlapping of the northern and southernmost boundaries of many species. Natives that are at home in cold climates, like serviceberry, winterberry, nannyberry, aronia, and sweet fern, mingle with the more tender bull bay magnolia, showy stewartias, Florida azalea, and evergreen American holly. The plant palette is tremendous and tremendously varied. On the map as in the garden, many things come together and mix in the Mid-Atlantic region.

Searching for the new American garden put almost 13,000 miles on my car's odometer. When I look back on it, I visited only about two dozen gardens in all of those miles. And although these glow like small, bright lights in my memory, the far greater number of hours spent simply driving from one garden to the next was an exercise in comprehending the vastness of this continent. In the long stretches between gardens, there was plenty of time to look out the window and observe the continually changing

The fringe tree, a favorite of Thomas Jefferson, blooms at azalea time.

scenery, and after a while, I could begin to read in telltale native plants the stories of rainfall and wind and temperature. Chamisa spoke of dry cold and wind while saguaro told of dry warmth. Southern live oak indicated warmth and abundant moisture, while its western counterpart, the coast live oak of California, demanded summer drought. Madrones, which became taller up the Pacific Coast, thrive on perfectly drained soil and ocean mists. Short grass prairie meant less than 25 inches of precipitation per year.

As the miles flew by, plants appeared, grouped and regrouped, and then disappeared to be replaced by others in each new place, better suited to the particular mixture of soil, moisture, altitude, wind, warmth, and cold. And every group of plants, or, as the horticulturists say, every community, was both a product and an identifying signature of its region.

In this great country, although we may speak the same language and watch the same television programs and read the same magazines, we really live in very different climates. How could our gardens ever be the same?

This is the sort of truth we have probably always known, but have not really felt or addressed. The first time I felt it in my bones was in Arizona. I had been driving through desert and had seen nothing for many miles. Suddenly ahead, I saw a road into what would soon be a new housing development. Although there were no houses, there was a grand entrance that made me do a double take and grind to a halt. Here was landscape kitsch of the worst order. In the middle of a sere gray-green and tan world were two strips of garish emerald lawn that would have been subtle in Seattle. Towering above this shocking green were noble, stately saguaro cacti—each perhaps 100 years old. I looked at them sadly, then drove on, wondering how long it would take for the irrigation system to kill them.

Two dozen outstanding gardens of native plants and 13,000 miles of scenery had been powerful inspiration, but it was a horticultural oxymoron on the Arizona desert that made me realize how profoundly my concept of garden beauty had been altered. Beauty truly is in the eye of the beholder, and now my eye demanded that a garden make climatic sense, that it fit into the natural landscape around it, that it embody the spirit of its place.

Perennials

Actaea pachypoda
doll's eyes

*Allium cernuum**
nodding onion

Amsonia hubrectii
willowleaf amsonia

A. tabernaemontana
amsonia

Anemone canadensis
Canada anemone

Anemonella thalictroides
rue anemone

*Aquilegia canadensis**
columbine

A. c. 'Corbett'
Corbett columbine

A. chrysantha
yellow columbine

Arisaema triphyllum
Jack-in-the-pulpit

Armeria maritima
thrift

Artemisia ludoviciana
sagebrush

Aruncus sylvester
goat's beard

*Asarum canadense**
wild ginger

A. shuttleworthii
evergreen wild ginger

Asclepias incarnata
swamp milkweed

*A. tuberosa**
butterfly weed

Aster azureus
sky blue aster

A. cordifolius
heartleaf aster

*A. divaricatus**
white wood aster

A. laevis
smooth aster

A. linariifolius
savory-leaf, stiff-leaf aster

A. novae-angliae
New England aster

A. novi-belgii
New York aster

*Baptisia alba**
white false indigo

*B. australis**
blue false indigo

Boltonia asteroides 'Pink
Beauty'*
pink boltonia

B. a. 'Snowbank'*
white boltonia

Camassia quamash
camas

Cassia hebecarpa
wild senna

Caulophyllum thalictroides
blue cohosh

Chelone glabra
white turtlehead

C. lyonii
pink turtlehead

*C. obliqua**
rose turtlehead

*Chrysogonum virginianum**
green-and-gold

*Chrysopsis mariana**
Maryland golden aster

Cimicifuga americana
summer cohosh

*C. racemosa**
bugbane

Coreopsis auriculata 'Nana'
dwarf-eared coreopsis

C. rosea
pink threadleaf coreopsis

*C. verticillata**
threadleaf coreopsis

C. v. 'Moonbeam'
threadleaf coreopsis

*Dicentra eximia**
eastern wild bleeding
heart

*Echinacea purpurea**
purple coneflower

E. p. 'White Swan'
white coneflower

Eryngium yuccifolium
rattlesnake master

*Erythronium umbilicatum
(americanum)**
dogtooth violet

Eupatorium fistulosum
Joe-Pye weed

Euphorbia corollata
flowering spurge

*Filipendula rubra**
queen-of-the-prairie

Gaura lindheimeri
gaura

Gentiana andrewsii
bottle gentian

*Geranium maculatum**
wild geranium

Helianthus angustifolius
swamp sunflower

H. maximiliani
Maximilian's daisy

*H. salicifolius**
willowleaf sunflower

H. tuberosus
Jerusalem artichoke

Heuchera americana
alum root

*H. villosa**
hairy alum root

Hibiscus coccineus
red mallow

H. militaris
smooth marsh mallow

*Houstonia caerulea**
Quaker ladies

Iris brevicaulis
zigzag iris

*I. cristata**
crested iris

I. fulva
red flag iris

I. giganticaerulea
giant blue iris

*I. hexagona**
iris

I. verna
iris

*I. versicolor**
blue flag

Kosteletzkya virginica
marsh mallow

Liatris aspera
rough blazing star

*L. microcephala**
small blazing star

*L. pycnostachya**
prairie blazing star

L. spicata 'Kobold'
spike gayfeather

Lilium superbum
Turk's cap lily

*Lobelia cardinalis**
cardinal flower

*L. siphilitica**
great blue lobelia

*Mertensia virginica**
Virginia bluebells

*Mitchella repens**
partridgeberry

Monarda didyma
bee balm

*M. fistulosa**
bergamot

Oenothera fruticosa
sundrops

*O. missouriensis**
Missouri evening primrose

Pachysandra procumbens
American pachysandra

Parthenium integrifolium
wild quinine

Penstemon pallida
white penstemon

Phlox divaricata
wild sweet william

P. d. 'Fuller's White'
white phlox

P. glaberrima
phlox

P. maculata
phlox

P. paniculata
garden phlox

*P. stolonifera**
creeping phlox

*P. subulata**
moss pink

Physostegia virginiana
obedient plant

Polygonatum biflorum
Solomon's seal

*Porteranthus trifoliatus**
Bowman's root

Ratibida pinnata
prairie coneflower

Rhexia virginica
meadow beauty
Rudbeckia fulgida 'Gold-sturm'*
black-eyed Susan
*R. maxima**
giant rudbeckia
*R. subtomentosa**
sweet black-eyed Susan
Ruellia humilis
wild petunia
Scutellaria incana
skullcap
*S. serrata**
showy skullcap
*Sedum ternatum**
sedum
Shortia galacifolia
Oconee bells
Silene polypetala
silene
S. virginica
fire pink
S. laciniatum
compass plant
S. perfoliatum
cup plant
*S. terebinthinaceum**
prairie dock
Sisyrinchium angustifolium
blue-eyed grass
*Smilacina racemosa**
false Solomon's seal
Solidago caesia
wreath goldenrod
S. canadensis
Canada goldenrod
S. flexicaulis
zigzag goldenrod
S. nemoralis
gray goldenrod
S. odora
sweet goldenrod
S. rigida
stiff goldenrod
S. rugosa
rough-stemmed goldenrod
S. sempervirens
seaside goldenrod
S. speciosa
showy goldenrod
Spigelia marilandica
Indian pink

Stokesia laevis
Stokes' aster
*Stylophorum diphyllum**
wood poppy
Tellima grandiflora
fringe cup
Thermopsis villosa
Carolina bush pea
*Tiarella cordifolia**
running foamflower
T. c. var. *collina**
clumping foamflower
Tradescantia x *andersoniana*
spiderwort
Trillium species*
wake robin, trillium
Uvularia grandiflora
great merrybells
*U. perfoliata**
merrybells
*Vernonia noveboracensis**
ironweed
Veronicastrum virginicum
Culver's root
Viola species
violet
Zizia aptera
heartleaf golden Alexander

Annuals

Coreopsis tinctoria
plains coreopsis
*Helianthus annuus**
sunflower
Linum perenne
blue flax
*Phacelia bipinnatifida**
phacelia
Phlox drummondii
annual phlox

Grasses, Sedges, Rushes, and Reeds

Andropogon gerardii
big bluestem
*A. glomeratus**
bushy bluestem
*A. virginicus**
broom sedge
Bouteloua gracilis
blue grama
Carex albursina
white bear sedge
*C. austrocaroliniana**
sedge

*C. muskingumensis**
palm sedge
C. pensylvanica
Pennsylvania sedge
*Chasmanthium latifolium**
northern sea oats, river oats
Deschampsia caespitosa
hairgrass
Eragrostis spectabilis
purple lovegrass
Erianthus contortus
bent-awn plume grass
E. giganteus
sugarcane plume grass
*Panicum virgatum**
switch grass
Phalaris arundinacea picta
gardener's garters, ribbon grass
Schizachyrium scoparium
little bluestem
Sorghastrum nutans
Indian grass
*Sporobolus heterolepis**
prairie dropseed

Ferns

*Adiantum pedatum**
northern maidenhair fern
*Athyrium filix-femina**
lady fern
Dennstaedtia punctilobula
hay-scented fern
*Dryopteris carthusiana**
florist's fern
D. marginalis
marginal wood fern
*Matteuccia pensylvanica**
ostrich fern
Onoclea sensibilis
sensitive fern
Osmunda cinnamomea
cinnamon fern
*O. claytonia**
interrupted fern
O. regalis var. *spectabilis*
royal fern
*Polystichum acrostichoides**
Christmas fern

Water Plants

Decodon verticillatus
swamp loosestrife
Equisetum hyemale
scouring rush

Iris fulva
red iris
I. versicolor
blue flag
Menyanthes trifoliata
bog bean
*Nymphaea odorata**
pond water lily
*Orontium aquaticum**
golden club
Peltandra virginiana
arrow arum
Pontederia cordata
pickerelweed
Saururus cernuus
lizard's tail
*Thalia dealbata**
hardy water canna
Typha angustifolia
narrow-leaf cattail

Vines

Anisostichus capreolatus
cross vine
Campsis radicans
trumpet vine
Clematis viorna
leather flower
*Decumaria barbara**
climbing hydrangea
Lonicera x *heckrottii*
red trumpet honeysuckle
L. sempervirens
trumpet honeysuckle
*Parthenocissus quinquefolia**
Virginia creeper
Wisteria frutescens
American wisteria

Shrubs

*Aesculus parviflora**
bottlebrush buckeye
A. Pavia
red buckeye
Aralia spinosa
devil's walkingstick
Arctostaphylos uva-ursi
bearberry
Aronia arbutifolia 'Brilliantissima'*
red chokeberry
Callicarpa americana
beautyberry
*Calycanthus floridus**
sweetshrub

Ceanothus americanus
New Jersey tea

Cephalanthus occidentalis
buttonbush

Clethra acuminata
cinnemon clethra

C. alnifolia
'Hummingbird'*
dwarf summersweet

C. a. 'Pinkspire', 'Rosea'
summersweet

Clinopodium georgianum
Georgia savory

Conradina verticillata
Cumberland rosemary

Cornus alternifolia
pagoda dogwood

C. amomum
silky dogwood

C. sericea
red-osier dogwood

Cyrilla racemiflora
titi

*Euonymous americana**
hearts-a-bustin'

*Fothergilla gardenii**
dwarf fothergilla

F. g. 'Blue Mist'
Blue Mist fothergilla

F. major
large fothergilla

Hydrangea arborescens
'Annabelle'
wild hydrangea

*Hydrangea quercifolia**
oak leaf hydrangea

H. q. 'Snow Queen'
Snow Queen hydrangea

Hypericum frondosum
'Sunburst'
golden St. Johnswort

*Ilex decidua**
possum haw

*I. glabra**
inkberry

I. verticillata 'Winter
Red'*
winterberry

I. v. 'Maryland Beauty'
winterberry

Illicium floridanum
anise tree

Itea virginica 'Henry's
Garnet'
sweetspire

*J. horizontalis**
creeping juniper

Kalmia latifolia, many
cultivars
mountain laurel

*Leucothoe fontanesiana**
doghobble

Mahonia aquifolium
Oregon grape holly

M. x 'King's Ransom'*
King's Ransom mahonia

*Myrica pensylvanica**
bayberry

Paxistima canbyi
paxistima

Pieris floribunda
fetterbush

Potentilla fruticosa
shrubby cinquefoil

Rhapidophyllum hystrix
needle palm

Rhododendron alabamense
Alabama azalea

R. arborescens and cultivars
sweet azalea

*R. atlanticum**
coast azalea

R. austrinum, many
cultivars
Florida azalea

R. bakeri
Cumberland azalea

R. calendulaceum, many
cultivars
flame azalea

R. canescens and cultivars*
Piedmont azalea

R. carolinianum
Carolina rhododendron

*R. catawbiense**
Catawba rhododendron

R. Chapmanii
Chapman's rhododendron

R. maximum
rosebay rhododendron

*R. minus**
Piedmont rhododendron

R. periclymenoides
pinxter azalea

*R. prinophyllum**
roseshell azalea

R. prunifolium
plumleaf azalea

R. serrulatum
hammocksweet azalea

*R. vaseyi**
pinkshell azalea

R. viscosum
swamp azalea

Rhus aromatica
fragrant sumac

R. typhina
staghorn sumac

Rosa virginiana
Virginia rose

Sambucus canadensis
elderberry

*Stewartia malcodendron**
silky camellia

Viburnum acerifolium
maple leaf viburnum

V. dentatum
arrowwood

V. lentago
nannyberry

*V. nudum**
possum haw

*V. trilobum**
American cranberry

Yucca species*
yucca

Zenobia pulverulenta
dusty zenobia

Trees

Aesculus pavia
red buckeye

*Amelanchier laevis**
serviceberry

Asimina triloba
pawpaw

Betula nigra
river birch

B. n. 'Heritage'*
white river birch

*Cercis canadensis**
eastern redbud

*Chionanthus virginicus**
fringe tree

*Cladrastis kentukeya**
yellowwood

*Cornus florida**
eastern dogwood

Crataegus viridis
hawthorn

*Franklinia alatamaha**
Franklin tree

Halesia carolina
Carolina silverbell

H. diptera 'Magniflora'*
Magniflora silverbell

*Ilex opaca**
American holly

*Juniperus virginiana**
eastern red cedar

Magnolia acuminata
cucumber tree

*M. ashei**
Ashe magnolia

M. cordata
yellow cucumber tree

M. grandiflora and
cultivars*
bull bay magnolia

M. macrophylla
bigleaf magnolia

M. tripetela
umbrella magnolia

*M. virginiana**
sweet bay magnolia

Taxodium ascendens
pond cypress

T. distichum
bald cypress

Recommended plants are starred.

Peren

nials

If

WOODY PLANTS DEFINE A GARDEN'S STRUCTURE, PERENNIALS ARE THE GARDEN'S FURNISHINGS. THEY ARE THE SOFTENERS, THE HARBINGERS OF SEASONAL CHANGE, AND THE SOURCES OF COLOR. FOR MANY GARDENERS, GROWING PERENNIALS IS WHAT GARDENING IS ALL ABOUT.

UNLIKE ANNUALS, WHICH MAKE UP FOR THEIR SHORT, SINGLE-GROWING-SEASON LIVES BY BLOOMING NONSTOP ALL SUMMER, PERENNIALS LIVE FOR THREE YEARS OR MORE, OFTEN TAKING TWO OR THREE YEARS TO MATURE. THEY HAVE DISTINCT BLOOMING PERIODS EACH YEAR THAT MAY BE AS SHORT AS A WEEK OR AS LONG AS TWO MONTHS. THE ART OF USING PERENNIALS COMES WITH KNOWING WHEN A PARTICULAR FLOWER WILL APPEAR AND WHAT COMPANIONS WILL COMPLEMENT IT.

KNOWING THESE THINGS ALLOWS GARDENERS TO CHANGE THEIR GARDEN'S COLOR SCHEME SEVERAL

OVERLEAF: *Low hedges and artfully placed shrubs are the bones of Ryan Gainey's garden; perennials are its delightful furnishings.*
ABOVE: *This exuberant combination of prairie plants blooms together in a climate-proof Minnesota border.*
(*C. Colston Burrell Design*)

times over the growing season. For example, around a little pool in one part of my garden, the May bloomers are all pink, mauve, lavender, or blue: pink thrift, pink peonies, dark blue flag irises in the pool, blue columbines, mauve alliums, and baby blue German irises. Once these perennials have passed through their period of bloom, the garden changes color and personality. The early pastel, pinky "boudoir" effect gives way to a period of elegant reserve (which I think of as the garden's Federal period), dominated by yellows and blues: yellow Carolina lupine, blue false indigo, blue tradescantia, yellow yarrow, blue Stokes' aster. Then, in late July, the palette heats up. The sunny golds of coreopsis and black-eyed Susans and the fiery oranges of Turk's cap lilies and butterfly weed vie with the temperature. Then comes fall, a season of mad flamboyance: purple asters and golden sunflowers and goldenrods dominate, while the turning of leaves and ornamental grasses adds a backdrop of oranges, crimsons, and tans.

Gardens are still gardens in winter, but the mood is more somber. A few perennials are evergreen and others retain a rosette of foliage, but most die down to the roots or, as horticulturists say, go dormant. In places where rain is seasonal—for example, in parts of California—plants might go dormant in summer when there has been no rain. Whatever the reason for dormancy, the top fleshy or "herbaceous" part of the plant withers when conditions are not favorable. Under the ground, the roots stay snug and alive, waiting for the return of either moisture or warm weather to spring back into active growth again.

The following section on perennials, the largest in the book, includes plants suitable for every region of the United States and Canada. Each listing describes its place of origin and suggests regions where the plant will thrive as well as suggested hardiness zones. The culture and landscape use of each plant are given, too, to help you site it within your garden's microclimates; they may include places that are shady, windswept, sunny, pro-

Perennials mix with annuals in the garden of this Connecticut farmhouse.
(Sue Coe Design)

tected, moist, dry, or wet. Sometimes, a species may be totally unsuitable for your area, but the general description may list better related species under the heading "Species" or "Cultivars."

With the many choices in this section, you probably can find enough plants for at least a dozen color schemes. All the plants I've included were chosen for their good looks and availability. In most cases, you will be able to buy plants, but a few species are available only as seed. The source list in the back of this book includes growers large and small to help you locate your choices.

Baneberry (Actaea) *blooms with trillium.*

ACTAEA PACHYPODA Doll's eyes, white baneberry
RANUNCULACEAE Buttercup family

Carefree plants for lushness in a woodland garden, white baneberries are miniature look-alikes of their relatives the bugbanes (*Cimicifuga*) without the tall flower wands of the latter. Instead, their flowers are frothy white balls on shortish stems in early spring that look very pretty close up but are easy to pass by in a season of abundant bloom. The berries—white with a black dot—aren't really bigger but always command more attention, perhaps because they come in summer when there is less visual competition.

I like to think that little pioneer girls plucked doll's eyes berries and attached them to homemade dolls, but it is unlikely. The tiny eyeballs don't last. Like many common garden plants, including foxgloves, rhododendrons, and wisteria, baneberries are poisonous. While the others have poisonous leaves, the toxic parts of these plants are their alluring berries—attractive to small children. I would wait to grow them until children achieve reason. Intriguing as the berries are, doll's eyes is above all a foliage plant for a woodland garden.

In my garden, doll's eyes serves as a lovely step-down layer between evergreen azaleas and a low ground cover of wild ginger that takes up the space Virginia bluebells and cohosh dominate in the spring. As soon as the Virginia bluebells turn yellow, I remove their leaves and

take great pleasure in the baneberries' fresh presence. Later on in the summer, when the cohosh fades away, the baneberries are still fresh and clean looking.

Origin: Uplands of Nova Scotia, south to Georgia, and west to Minnesota and Missouri

Flower: Frothy balls of small white flowers appear just after the plant leafs out in May. Doll's eyes' white-dotted

Doll's eyes (Actaea pachypoda)

black fruit, which follows in summer, is poisonous.

Foliage: Compound leaves resembling those of astilbe

Hardiness: Zones 4 to 8

Height: 1 to 2 feet

Regions: Northeast, Mid-Atlantic, South, Midwest

Landscape use: Woodland garden

Culture: Part to full shade, medium to moist soil with a high humus content

Species: *Actaea rubra* (red baneberry, coral baneberry) has red berries.

Propagation: Seed

ALLIUM CERNUUM Nodding pink onion
LILIACEAE Lily family

The first year I grew nodding pink onion, it was a big disappointment: a few flowers bloomed like pale fireworks caught in midexplosion on tall (15-inch), thin, chivelike foliage. They were effective from a foot away. From farther away, not only was there not enough color or substance for the plant to hold its own, it also was too tall and upright for the edge of the bed where I had placed it. Then, on one of those fine,

Nodding onion
(Allium cernuum)

golden fall days when garden madness hit and all things seemed possible, I began moving plants around like furniture. I popped nodding onion in willy-nilly in some gaps between low-growing lavender and santolina. The new sites behind low-growing plants, but mostly nodding onion's ability to reproduce itself, have made all the difference. Masses of nodding onion are indeed what is needed and just what you get, if you wait. The story goes that the city of Chicago, a corruption of the Algonquin name for this plant, was named for great fields of nodding onion that once grew there. After hearing that story, Chicago's skyscrapers, arcing along Lake Michigan, will rise forever in my mind's eye out of thousands upon thousands of nodding pink onions.

Origin: Nodding onion is found on dry, rocky slopes from New York and South Carolina to British Columbia and California.

Flower: A drooping white onion flower that turns lavender-pink as it ages; it blooms in June and July.

Foliage: Flat, slightly fleshy leaves are long, narrow, and a delicate pale green.

Hardiness: Zones 4 to 8

Height: 15 to 18 inches

Regions: Very adaptable. Northeast, Upper and Lower Midwest, South, Mid-Atlantic, Pacific Northwest, Mountains, and, probably, Northern California.

Landscape use: Nodding onion will make headway as a meadow plant; border plant.

Culture: Sun, good drainage, but this is not a fussy plant and it tolerates drought.

Propagation: Bulbs multiply all by themselves, but nodding onion may be started from seed.

AMSONIA HUBRECTII Willowleaf amsonia, Arkansas amsonia

APOCYNACEAE Dogbane family

Compared with *A. tabernaemontana* (below), willowleaf amsonia has longer, far-narrower leaves, whorled around the stems. Its flower petals are narrower, too. It is extraordinarily attractive after blooming, when its long, narrow leaves turn yellow, as if the leaves themselves were great yellow flowers. Willowleaf amsonia is less hardy than the others.

Origin: Alaska to the Lower Midwest

Flower: Sky blue in May

Foliage: Very thin, ¼-inch leaves whorled around stem turn yellow, then orange, in fall.

Hardiness: Zones 6 to 8

Height: 3 to 4 feet

Regions: Parts of the Northeast, Mid-Atlantic, South, Lower Midwest

Landscape use: Great in a border, willowleaf's contrasting postbloom color is a good foil for shrubs.

Culture: Sun, part shade

AMSONIA TABERNAEMONTANA Blue star, amsonia

APOCYNACEAE Dogbane family

The White Flower Farm catalog describes amsonia as "the Lillian Gish of perennials"—inspired, perhaps, by its understated grace, the restrained blue of its flowers, and its ability to grow old gracefully. Certainly, amsonia will never be called "Mae West." *Amsonia tabernaemontana* grows into a clump, topped with light, steely blue (sometimes white) flower clusters in May that have the effect of white flowers rather than of blue. To bring out the blueness, pair amsonia with the blue-and-white Rocky Mountain columbine (*Aquilegia caerulea*) in a low ground cover of brunnera or forget-me-nots. The best thing about amsonia is its bushiness. It gives the plant trim substance well into the fall, when the foliage turns a very attractive yellow-peach.

Origin: Moist, humusy margins of woodland from Virginia to Missouri and south to Texas and Georgia

Blue star (Amsonia tabernaemontana) *forms a low, bushy hedge in Mary Painter's garden.*

The pale green leaves of willowleaf amsonia (A. hubrechtii) turn slowly to yellow.

Flower: Pale, steel blue clusters in May; white forms are also available.

Foliage: Slender leaves are a clean, matte green, turning banana yellow to peach in fall.

Hardiness: Zones 3 to 8

Height: 3 feet tall

Regions: Northeast, Upper and Lower Midwest, Mid-Atlantic, South, Mountain, Pacific Northwest, Northern California

Landscape use: Amsonia makes a nice short hedge, as well as being a shade-tolerant subject for the flower garden.

Culture: If grown in half to full shade (in warm areas), with adequate moisture, amsonia is tough and unbothered by insects or disease; shear right after flowering to keep it compact. Amsonia is late to break dormancy.

Species/cultivars: *Amsonia tabernaemontana* var. *montana* is shorter and more compact, growing only about 2 feet high with slightly darker flowers.

Propagation: Dry seed, clip end, soak 24 to 48 hours.

ANEMONE CANADENSIS Canada anemone
RANUNCULACEAE Buttercup family

Canada anemone is a real survivor that spreads rapidly by rhizomes in its preferred rich, moist soil, in sun or part shade. Its kinship with buttercups is evident in late spring and early summer, when the plant is covered with fresh, up-facing white flowers that are great for bouquets. The leaves, too, are good for arrangements, being deeply cut and a nice dark green. In my garden, Canada anemone stands about a foot tall (though the actual stems are longer, they rest on the ground) and is swiftly becoming a ground cover in a low spot around a grove of river birches that is moist in spring and winter. Its fellow inhabitants in this place are cinnamon fern, lurid sedge, and an uninvited carpet of smartweed.

Origin: Quebec to British Columbia and south to Maryland, Missouri, and New Mexico

Flower: White buttercup flowers around a rich yellow center, in spring

Foliage: Deeply cut green leaves are pierced by leaf and flower stalks.

Hardiness: Probably Zones 2 to 7

Height: 12 inches

Regions: Quebec to Alberta and south to Colorado and West Virginia

Landscape use: Wild garden; moist meadow; ground cover in low, moist area

Culture: Canada anemone is invasive. Grow it in a place where it is challenged and where it will not overcome

Thimbleweed (Anemone virginiana)

Rue anemone (Anemonella thalictroides)

when you come upon it after a long winter, because it is proof positive that spring has finally arrived.

Origin: Woodlands and streamsides in eastern North America west to Oklahoma

Flower: White to pink single petals around an ornate center measure ½ inch across on thin, wiry stems in spring, with a few sporadic blooms throughout summer.

Foliage: Like that of a tiny meadow rue, light green rounded, compound leaves, airy and delicate

Hardiness: Zones 4 to 8

Height: 8 inches

Region: Eastern North America

Landscape use: Woodland, shady rock garden

Culture: Half to full shade, moist to medium soil

Species/cultivars: There is a double white form and a cultivar 'Schoaf's Double Pink' that looks more like a cross between a rose and a chrysanthemum.

less robust plants: in the ditch next to the driveway, behind the garage. It prefers a moist soil, but will grow rampantly in good garden soil. Full sun in the North; part to full shade in the southern part of its range.

Species/cultivars: *Anemone cylindrica* and *Anemone virginiana*. Two other thimbleweeds are taller than their cousin the Canada anemone. *A. cylindrica,* from the Midwest, grows to about 30 inches and is at home in a drier site. Once established, it is extremely drought-tolerant. *A. virginiana,* from dry and open woods, is aggressive, but if you have room in an out-of-the-way place, it is an excellent source of cut flowers that are stiff stemmed and slightly greenish, followed by thimblelike seed heads.

Propagation: Seed and root cuttings

ANEMONELLA THALICTROIDES Rue anemone
RANUNCULACEAE Buttercup family

It's hard to imagine that a plant as delicate looking and diminutive as rue anemone could be so tough, seemingly impervious to cold and heat. I have seen it growing in moist, acid humus near a stream, but in my garden it is contentedly forming colonies in half shade that is somewhat dry in the summer. When closely observed, each plant is a perfect tussie-mussie, tiny flowers in a lace ring of blue-green leaves.

A true survivor, rue anemone spreads easily; a few plants become a great colony in five years. And no matter where it sows itself, it never seems out of place. The little tuberous roots can be transplanted easily even while the plant is blooming. To make a show, you need several dozen plants, but even a single flower is a treat

AQUILEGIA Columbine
RANUNCULACEAE Buttercup family

Of the 30 species of *Aquilegia* on the American continent, the showiest have long been grown in gardens. Nurseryman and gardener to Charles I, John Tradescant listed American columbine (*A. canadense*) along with 39 other American natives in his 1634 list of merchandise. Easily started from seed, American columbine will bloom the second year and self-sow forever after—although seedlings are never troublesome. Volunteers in my garden have formed a handsome colony in the dry shade between a huge silver maple and a great wall of leatherleaf viburnum.

One reads that American columbine is short-lived, but to be honest, I've never noticed which older plants die out. Each year, I move a few volunteer seedlings around to keep plants evenly spaced (about 15 inches apart) and to extend the colony. I've always thought of them as shade plants of moist woodland, but their taproots allow them to inhabit surprisingly dry sites—especially those that are spring moist and summer dry. They grow well in rock gardens.

The summer-blooming red columbine (*A. formosa*) from the West Coast is similar in appearance to American columbine, with nodding red flowers and lacy, waxy gray, dissected leaves. It blooms, starting in May and throughout the summer, in moist soil in sun to partial shade—for example, in a place with morning sun.

The West is rich in columbines. From the Rockies comes the spectacular *A. caerulea* in shades of blue and purple with long spurs and attractive gray-green foliage.

73

Aquilegia

Name	Origin	Flower	Foliage	Zones	Height	Regions	Landscape Use
Aquilegia caerulea Rocky mountain columbine	Mountains of Idaho, Nevada, Nebraska, Wyoming, Utah, Colorado	Large, spurred, sky blue/purple and white	Ferny, gray-green leaves in threes	3 to 9	1 to 2 ft	Mountain, but very adaptable	Border, wild garden
Aquilegia canadense American columbine	Nova Scotia to Florida, Minnesota, Tennessee	Red and yellow flowers with long spurs in May and June	Matte green above, pale below, three lobes, wiry stems	4 to 9	To 30 in	Eastern North America	Woodland garden, border
Aquilegia chrysantha Golden columbine	Arizona, New Mexico, Mexico	Yellow with long, narrow spurs, fragrant!	Bushy habit with hairy undersides	3 to 9	To 3 ft	Southwest, Southern California	Border, wild garden
Aquilegia flavescens Columbine	Mountains of Washington, Oregon	Cream/yellow	Flowering stems arise from clump	3 to 7	To 2 ft	Northwest, Upper Midwest, Northeast	Border, wild garden
Aquilegia formosa Red columbine, Western columbine	Alaska to North Carolina, west to Montana, Utah	Red, yellow, long spur, summer	Loose, open habit, leaves	4 to 8	2 to 3 ft	North America	Border, wild garden
Aquilegia longissima Long spur columbine	West Texas, Mexico	Yellow with spurs 3 to 5 in, May	Semi to evergreen, long flowering stalks above bushy clump	6 to 10	2 to 3 ft	Southwest	Border, wild garden

The elegant blooms always remind me of flying flowers with birds' tails when they appear in late spring and early summer.

Also from the West are the wonderful yellows: *A. chrysantha, A. flavescens, A. hinckleyi,* and *A. longissima.* With the exception of *A. flavescens,* these are dry-climate plants: some water will keep them from going dormant; too much will cause crown rot.

All columbines may be started from seeds to bloom the second year. Plant them in fall or cold stratify for one month. In the garden, they will volunteer—often among rocks—and different species will cross. Most require some protection from the hot summer sun and do best in high, filtered shade. They are, however, surprisingly tolerant of dry conditions after their flowering period is over. They make good cut flowers if they are picked when half open. (See *Aquilegia* chart, above.)

ARISAEMA TRIPHYLLUM Jack-in-the-pulpit, Indian turnip, dragonroot

ARACEAE Arum family

The next time you are plagued by clouds of gnats, remember that the same gnat whose bite swells your eye or ear may also have pollinated your Jack-in-the-pulpit. Gnats must be hard workers, because once you have one Jack in a moist, shady spot, it isn't long before a colony forms.

After eight years, a single Jack-in-the-pulpit I had planted in ordinary, shaded soil downslope from a large sycamore became a great, unruly colony in various stages of development. Roots are filled with the same chemical (calcium oxalate) as dumb cane, which keeps small mammals away.

Jack-in-the-pulpit is a plant that is routinely dug from the wild rather than propagated from seed. One reason for this is that it takes five years from seed to flowering. Another reason is Jack-in-the-pulpit's bizarre sexuality. Jacks begin life as males and become hermaphroditic with age. About 10 percent of a colony are well

Yellow columbine (Aquilegia)

Culture	Propagate	Comment
Moist soil, sun, filtered shade	Seed	Colorado state flower, lovely bi-color, neutral soil
Part shade, medium to moist soil	Seed	Self-sows, lures hummingbirds, full sun with moisture, will tolerate dry shade when established. Cultivar: 'Corbett', yellow, 6 to 8 in.
Part shade, moist, good drainage	Seed	Nice cut flower. Cultivar: 'Silver Queen' is an outstanding white
Moist, sunny spot	Seed	Needs cool summer climate
Filtered shade, summer water	Seed	Attracts hummingbirds, similar species: *A. eximia* from California
Require good drainage, filtered shade	Seed	Very showy, longest spurs, tolerates limestone. Cultivar: 'Maxistar,' a good white.

Jack-in-the-pulpit (Arisaema triphyllum)

enough developed to be what are more accurately called "Jack and Jills," individuals with both male and female parts. The male Jacks are ephemeral; the female Jack and Jills remain and grow throughout summer, consort with gnats, and are the only ones that reproduce by means of orange berries. Be sure you aren't buying a collected plant; buy yours from native plant societies or arboreta that have started plants from seed.

In spring, a colony of Jack-in-the-pulpit, like organ pipes of graduated sizes rising from the ground, is a magical sight. By midsummer, the males vanish and only mature, hermaphroditic Jack and Jills remain to produce lovely red berries. For me, the berry stalks often flop over instead of standing tall the way they do in garden catalog photos. This will not matter if you provide some summer cover like a low-growing creeping phlox or a tiny hosta to keep the spot from looking bare.

My biggest Jacks never grow much taller than 18 inches, but I have seen them close to 3 feet tall. Besides age, the difference in this plant's ultimate size and fall performance depend upon the moisture and nutrients in rich, humusy soil: the more richness and moisture, the better.

Origin: Swamps and rich, moist soil from New Brunswick and Nova Scotia to Minnesota and south to Florida and Texas

Flower: Green to purple striped hooded "pulpit" petals around a fleshy spadix "Jack"

Foliage: Dark green, three leaflets

Hardiness: Zones 4 to 9

Height: 18 inches to 3 feet

Region: Eastern North America

Landscape use: Woodland garden, streamside, bog garden

Culture: Shade, wet to medium soils. Mature plants are difficult to move, but young ones can be handled easily.

Species/cultivars: *A. t.* subsp. *Stewardsonii* has an all-green flower; *A. quinatum* has a green flower and five leaflets; *A. draconitum* is viper green with a hood and "tongue."

Propagation: Dry seed with fleshy coat; six-week stratification; bulbs

Columbine (Aquilegia canadense)

*Thrift (*Armeria maritima*) in the Grier garden*

ARMERIA MARITIMA Thrift, sea pink
PLUMBAGINACEAE Leadwort family

There are over 30 cultivars of this popular species that occur naturally around the world and on the Pacific Coast of North America. However, it is very easy to grow thrift from seed started indoors on the windowsill. Plants that bloom modestly the first year can be had in as few as 12 weeks. And the variety of colors that comes from seed—pink to hot pink with an occasional white—never seems to clash. I did this over 10 years ago and have had a small, thriving colony of thrift in a sunny rock garden ever since. The first flowering is so heavy, deadheading is a chore I never mind. That first burst of thrift comes in concert with deep blue pond iris (*I. versicolor*), the big purple balls of Persian alliums, and the baby blue of bearded iris.

Origin: Europe, Asia Minor, North Africa, Pacific Coast of North America

Flower: A burst of bloom: round heads of pink, lavender, sometimes white flowers in May and intermittently throughout summer and fall

Foliage: Dark green grasslike clumps

Hardiness: Zones 4 to 8

Height: 12 inches (in flower)

Regions: Coastal areas of California, Northwest, Northeast, Mid-Atlantic, South, Midwest, Mountain

Landscape use: Front border, ground cover, rock garden

Culture: Sun; clay-tolerant with good drainage; needs water in dry climates

Cultivars: Many cultivars exist, and if you want a particular flower color, buying a cultivar will guarantee it.

Propagation: Blooms the first year from seed; division.

ARTEMISIA LUDOVICIANA Artemisia, southernwood, sagebrush
COMPOSITAE Sunflower family

Spreading by rhizomes where you do and where you don't want it, artemisia needs no introduction. I don't mind its spreading tendencies because its silver-gray foliage is so useful in bouquets. In fall, I uproot errant plants and then wind them into wreaths to store until the holidays.

An invaluable plant for southwestern gardens, southernwood thrives anywhere it has sun and good drainage. I use the cultivar 'Valerie Finnis' as an edger along my stone patio. It is especially dramatic at dusk, when it glows, a feature that is beautiful along paths and edges.

Origin: Michigan to Washington, south to Arkansas, Texas, and Mexico

Flower: Inconspicuous

Foliage: Silver-white

Hardiness: Zones 4 to 9

Height: To 3 feet

Region: Grows anywhere

Landscape use: Border, cutting garden

Culture: Sun, well-drained soil

Cultivars: 'Silver King' (bushy, nice foliage); 'Valerie Finnis' (with broader, whiter leaves; supposedly noninvasive and said to be derived from *A. ludoviciana*)

ARTEMISIA PYCNOCEPHALA 'David's Choice' Sand hill sage
COMPOSITAE Sunflower family

For California gardens, Bart O'Brien of Rancho Santa Ana recommends the cultivar of *A. pycnocephala* 'David's Choice', which he finds superior to the species. 'David's Choice' is a low, dense-growing selection with finely divided silvery foliage. Wider than tall, it produces 6- to 12-inch spikes of silver-gray. 'David's Choice' is easy to grow, but Bart O'Brien cautions against overhead watering—especially during warm weather. To keep plants dense and good-looking, remove inflorescences as they develop.

Origin: Point Reyes, Marin County, California

Flower: 6- to 12-inch silver-gray flower spikes in summer

Foliage: Finely divided, silvery, hairy, dense foliage on plants broader than tall

Hardiness: Zones 9 to 10

Height: 1 foot by 2 feet wide

Region: California

Landscape use: Mixed border, edging, rock gardens

Culture: Full sun to light shade; easily grown in most

Southernwood (Artemisia ludoviciana) *in Jane MacLeish's garden*

gardens; avoid overhead watering in warm weather; remove inflorescences to promote dense growth; best with good drainage

ARUNCUS SYLVESTER Goat's beard
ROSACEAE Rose family

Goat's beard is a plant for the background, the edge of woodland, the shady backside of a border between lower-growing perennials and shrubs. In my garden, it stands tall behind a ground cover of astilbes, which it resembles in both leaf and flower. In June, this robust perennial bears huge clusters of tiny creamy white flowers. Pacific Northwest native plant expert Arthur Kruckeberg recommends goat's beard for his region and comments that although male plants are showier, females in fruit make fine dried bouquet material.

Origin: North America
Flower: Creamy white, astilbe-like plume in June
Foliage: Graceful compound leaves with a ferny appearance
Hardiness: Zones 5 to 8
Height: To 4 feet
Region: North America
Landscape use: Shady back of border, woodland garden
Culture: Sun to part shade, humusy, medium to moist soil
Propagation: Easy from seed

ASARUM (HEXASTYLIS) Wild ginger
ARISTOLOCHIACEAE Birthwort family

Anyone who has ever walked under the giant redwoods will remember long-tailed ginger, along with redwood sorrel, as the two plants that form a cool, green ground cover in forests of the Pacific Coast. Vigorously rhizomatous, long-tailed ginger is at home in deep to high filtered shade. It takes its name from the long-tailed petals on curious flowers that hide under the leaves. Evergreen except during extreme cold, it is also both water tolerant and a good subject for dry shade, in which situation its growth rate is slow. It will die without any summer water.

In my garden, wild ginger (*A. canadense*) is a real workhorse plant. It is tough, enduring, and a great spreader that gives a finished look—fast—to odd corners and edges in shade. This wild ginger spreads energetically but is easy enough to pull up where it isn't wanted. Leaves are coarse and rounded and are carried on short stems about six inches above the ground. Flowers bloom in spring, but—as with all gingers—you have to get down on your knees and peer under the leaves to see the strange, brownish purple, bell-shaped blooms. Its great misfortune is that it is deciduous and therefore invisible in winter.

A number of wild gingers are evergreen—some with plain leathery leaves and others with leaves veined and mottled. In the wild, gingers are variable, so there are

Goat's beard (Aruncus) *in Bob Dash's garden*

many good selections for gardeners. Cyclamen-leaved ginger (*A. hartwegii*) from the West is an evergreen ginger with beautiful silver markings along the veins. Heart-leaf wild ginger (*A. arifolium*) has a decidedly different, heart-shaped leaf. And while deciduous wild ginger (*A. canadense*) or Pacific Coast native wild ginger (*A. caudatum*)

Asarum

Name	Origin	Flower	Foliage	Zones	Height	Regions	Landscape Use
Asarum arifolium (*Hexastylis arifolia*) Heart-leaf wild ginger, little brown jugs	Virginia south to Alabama, Florida	Little brown jugs in spring	Glossy, sometimes mottled, heart-shaped, evergreen	6(?) to 9	6 in	South, Mid-Atlantic	Ground cover, woodland garden
Asarum canadense Wild ginger	New Brunswick to North Carolina, Missouri	Little brown jugs in spring	Matte green, large, round leaf	3 to 8	6 in	Eastern, Midwestern North America	Ground cover, woodland garden
Asarum caudatum Long-tailed ginger	British Columbia to California	Little brown flowers have "tails"	Round, evergreen	6(?) to 8	6 in	Northwest, California	Ground cover, woodland garden
Asarum hartwegii Cyclamen-leaf ginger	Oregon and California	Long-tailed flower, spring	Heart-shaped, silver veins, evergreen	6 to 8	6 in	Northwest, California	Ground cover, woodland garden
Asarum shuttleworthii (*Hexastylis shuttleworthii*) Wild ginger	Virginia to Georgia, Alabama	Little brown jugs	Round, mottled, evergreen	7 to 8	4 in	South, Mid-Atlantic	Ground cover, woodland garden
Asarum virginicum Wild ginger	Virginia to South Carolina, Tennessee	Little brown jugs	Mottled, evergreen leaves	6(?) to 8	6 in	South, Lower Midwest	Ground cover, woodland garden

makes swift headway in the garden, evergreen gingers are slower to spread. In my garden, two of these, *A. shuttleworthii* and *A. virginicum,* will not cover in their lifetime what *Asarum canadense* covers in two seasons. Of the evergreen gingers I grow, the one that covers ground fastest (even though its leaves are smaller than others) is a cultivar of *Hexastylis shuttleworthii* called 'Callaway', named for Callaway Gardens in Pine Mountain, Georgia, where Fred Galle selected it. 'Callaway' has very attractive silver mottling on the dark green leaves.

None of the wild gingers belongs to the real ginger (Zingiberaceae) family. Because of a slightly gingery aroma when the leaves are crushed, as well as the fact that Native Americans used wild ginger for seasoning, colonists named them for the tropical spice. All gingers

*Wild ginger (*Asarum shuttleworthii*)*

grow best in woodland conditions—humusy soil and part to full shade. (See *Asarum* chart, above.)

ASCLEPIAS INCARNATA Swamp milkweed
ASCLEPIADACEAE Milkweed family

While butterfly weed (*A. tuberosa*) withstands drought, swamp milkweed thrives in a moist or swampy soil and is a good plant for a moist meadow or pond side. It adjusts nicely to average garden soil. Up close, the flowers are two-tone, soft red and white, but the effect in the garden is a soft rose. Not as striking as the bright oranges and reds of butterfly weed, it is excellent in bouquets and very pretty in masses in the garden.

*Wild ginger (*Asarum canadense*)*

Culture	Propagate	Comment
Moist, humusy soil, part to full shade	Seed, division	Slow grower
Moist, humusy soil, part to full shade	Division, seed	Fast coverage, deciduous
Moisture in summer, shade	Division, seed	Quick spreader, does not tolerate drought
Moist, humusy soil, part to full shade	Division, seed	Cultivar: 'Silver Heart'
Moist, humusy soil, part to full shade	Division, seed	Variable. Cultivar: 'Callaway' (mottled, vigorous, small leaves).
Moist, humusy soil, part to full shade	Seed	Stays in place

Like butterfly weed, it is also a caterpillar and butterfly plant. Swamp milkweed thrives in the same moist soil as queen-of-the-prairie (*Filipendula rubra*), with its cotton-candy pink plumes.

Origin: Swamp milkweed is found growing in wet places from Nova Scotia to Florida and west to Utah.

Flower: Old rose, red, pink, white flower umbels on erect stems in July

Foliage: Very upright stems with broad, elliptical, opposite, green leaves

*Long-tailed ginger (*Asarum caudatum*)*

Hardiness: Zones 4 to 8
Height: To 4 feet
Regions: Northeast, Mid-Atlantic, South, Midwest, Mountain
Landscape use: Meadow, border
Culture: Sun and average to very moist soil
Species/cultivars: 'Alba' 'Ice Ballet' (white)
Propagation: Seed

*Butterfly weed (*Asclepias tuberosa*)*

ASCLEPIAS TUBEROSA Butterfly weed, pleurisy root
ASCLEPIADACEAE Milkweed family

Butterfly weed came by its name honestly. Dianas, coral hairstreaks, fritillaries, crescents, and monarch butterflies take nectar from the vivid, flat flower umbels. Queens and monarch caterpillars feed on the foliage. With one of the widest ranges of any native perennial and very little help, butterfly weed will grow just about anywhere in the United States or southern Canada. It is a real survivor—cold-hardy, heat-tolerant, drought-tolerant, and tolerating a pH from 5 to 7. Best of all, it blooms—riveting orange at a time when you really need it—in the heat of midsummer, when other, less sturdy flowers have withered. Late to break dormancy in spring, butterfly weed's location should be marked to avoid digging into the root. Plant it in and around early bloomers like *Oenothera* species to avoid empty spots in the early summer. Because butterfly weed is tap-rooted, mature plants must be moved with great care.

Origin: Butterfly weed is found in dry, open fields and roadsides from Maine to Florida and west to the northern Rockies and Arizona.

Flower: Typically bright orange, but also red and yellow

Foliage: A compact, bushy plant with long, dark green leaves on stiff stems

Hardiness: Zones 3 to 9

Height: 24 to 30 inches

Region: North America

Landscape use: Border, wild garden, meadow

Culture: Butterfly weed grows best in full sun but will tolerate light shade. It requires good drainage.

Species: *A. rubra; A. curassavica* (similar, red-orange bicolored flowers on showy 5-foot plants are not as hardy—probably Zone 9); *A. exaltata* (5 feet, white)

Cultivars: Gay butterflies are butterfly weeds with a wide variety of color. At the time of this printing, there are rumors about of wondrous colors—cream, raspberry, rose—in the breeding, but, so far, anyway, no named sources. Keep your eyes open.

Propagation: I am told that if you grow butterfly weed from seed, you will get colors that vary from golden yellows to reds. I've tried starting butterfly weed from seed several times and have always failed. Thompson & Morgan suggests pretreating seed by freezing it in damp sand. Nurserywoman Jan Midgley says that she had trouble germinating butterfly weed until she began gathering her own seed, which she stores, dry, in the refrigerator. A mature root can be broken into 4-inch pieces and planted to produce new plants. Plant the root pieces so that the stem end is up and root end is down.

Scarlet milkweed (Asclepias curassavica)

ASTER Michaelmas daisy, frost flower, aster
COMPOSITAE Sunflower family

Once you begin to grow asters, you'll find that they will quickly replace chrysanthemums as the flower you associate with autumn. And every garden has a place for at least four. There are more than 600 species of aster, most from America, and they come from every sort of cultural niche.

New England (*A. novae-angliae*) and New York asters (*A. novi-belgii*) have long been garden staples both in the United States and abroad. In England, where they were introduced over 250 years ago and are called "Michaelmas daisies" because they are in bloom for the feast of St. Michael, dozens of aster selections and cultivars have been made.

Asters also hybridize in the wild, sometimes making it impossible to tell them apart. However, the classic, straight, unimproved species New England aster is generally fast growing and tall—it can reach 6 feet—with 1-inch purple flowers and orange centers. Wonderful as this is in the fields, its height and general bushiness can overpower companion plants in the garden. Much smaller are the new and choice cultivars of *A. novae-angliae* such as 'Purple Dome'—about 2 feet tall and covered with purple flowers in September. Dr. Richard Lighty of the Mt. Cuba Center for the Study of Piedmont Flora spotted this low, broad plant growing in a Pennsylvania field (never, never drive behind a horticulturist—particularly one with an interest in native plants!). Dr. Lighty procured the plant, tested it, and introduced it in 1990. 'Alma Potschke', another great new cultivar, blooms a really different salmon-magenta color with a rounded 3- to 4-foot habit.

Like New England asters, New York asters (*A. novi-belgii*) need no introduction. The usually 4-foot, rhizomatous, straight species with lavender blue flowers has yielded many cultivars. There are pure whites like 'Snow Flurry', crimsons like 'Alert', and, of course, blues like 'Marie Ballard'.

When all of the cultivars are added together, just these two species offer a bewildering array of choices. And there are many, many more. In this immense genus of over 600 species—most native to North America—there are asters of every height and description. Many provide food for the caterpillars of butterflies such as the crescentspots and checkerspots.

For woodland gardens, there is the (usually) blue heart-leafed aster (*A. cordifolius*), the white wood aster (*A. divaricatus*), and the spreading aster (*A. patens*). Before I knew what white wood aster could do, I used to pull it up, thinking it a nondescript little weed of no ornamental merit. Good strong light makes the most difference. This little aster will grow to a bushy 2 feet, covering itself with 1-inch white star flowers with yellow eyes; it spreads quickly by rhizomes *and* self-sows! Leaves are a deep green and stems of the best forms are "black"—actually, a dark purple. It is the perfect transition plant to use between a woodland or shrubs and lawn. Just three plants set out three years ago on a shady slope around a ground cover of Christmas fern have become a great colony that spills down a hill between a planting of rose shell azaleas and my driveway, the white flowers dazzling in September and October.

Spreading aster (*A. patens*) has lavender-blue flowers with yellow eyes on airy sprays that are wonderful at the shady edge of woodland. Mine share a space in light shade with columbine.

The stiff- or savory-leaf aster (*A. linariifolius*) is unique among asters for its tightly radiating habit and its preference for a hot, dry spot with perfect drainage. Its foliage is stiff, dark green, and leathery.

Many asters are fairly forgiving about site conditions, performing just about anywhere there is sun. One of these, the heath aster (*A. ericoides*), inhabits a hot, dry spot in my garden. Just as white boltonia begins its yearly show, heath aster bursts into three weeks of synchronous, but smaller (and shorter), bloom with hundreds of tiny, yellow-centered, white ray flowers so heavy that the long, bushy, horizontal branches never stand more than 2 feet high. Heath

Aster novae-angliae *'Alma Potschke'*

aster, a tough customer, spreads vigorously and will hold its own with grasses in a meadow planting.

Both sky blue aster (*A. azureus*) and smooth aster (*A. laevis*) bloom at the same time—early fall. Both are tough, hardy prairie plants with a vast native range.

Calico aster (*A. lateriflorus* 'Horizontalis') came into my garden after a visit to the Lichterman Nature Center in Memphis, Tennessee, where, past bloom, a large specimen sparkled in the October sunshine: hundreds of tiny seed heads had gone a silvery white. I brought it back only to discover that it grows in great abundance along the C&O Canal—only a mile or two from my home. (See *Aster* chart on pages 82–83.)

An aster bouquet includes, clockwise from left, Aster azureus, Aster novae-angliae *'Richard's Purple', pink boltonia, white* Aster ericoides, Aster laevis, *and bright salmon-rose 'Alma Potschke'.*

*White wood aster (*Aster divaricatus*)*

Aster

Name	Origin	Flower	Foliage	Zones	Height	Regions	Landscape Use
Aster azureus Sky blue aster	Southern Ontario, New York, Minnesota, south to Texas, Alabama	⅞ in, lavender/ blue with yellow eye in airy spray, in fall	Slightly blue-green arrow-shaped leaves in rosette	4 to 8	To 5 ft	Rockies to East Coast	Border, meadow, wild garden
Aster cordifolius Heart-leaf aster, blue wood aster	Nova Scotia to Minnesota to Georgia, Missouri	¾ in, lavender/ blue, loose spray, September	Toothed, heart-shaped leaves in clump	4 to 7	To 3 ft	Eastern North America	Woodland garden
Aster divaricatus White wood aster	Woodlands of New Hampshire, Ohio to Georgia, Alabama	⅞ in, white with yellow eye, in fall	Dark green on (preferably) black stem	5 to 8	To 3 ft	Eastern United States	Woodland garden
Aster ericoides Heath aster	Maine to South Dakota, south to New Mexico and Mexico	½ in, white with yellow eye in profusion, September; faintly fragrant	Stiff, short, needle-like leaves on bowing stems	4 to 9	To 4 ft	Rockies to East Coast	Border, slope
Aster laevis Smooth aster	Yukon, Oregon to Maine, south to New Mexico, Georgia	1 in, lavender/ blue, yellow eye, in fall	Medium to blue-green in basal cluster, long flower stalks	2 to 8	To 4 ft	North America	Border, meadow, wild garden
Aster lateriflorus 'Horizontalis' Calico aster	Southeastern Canada to Minnesota south to Florida, Missouri, Texas	½ in, white/pink, raspberry eye, September, October	Tiny, dull green leaves blush mahogany	4 to 9	3 ft	Eastern North America, mid-western North America	Border, rock garden
Aster linarifolius Stiff aster, savory-leaf aster	Quebec, Maine to Wisconsin, Missouri, Texas	¾ in, lavender/ blue with yellow eye, September, October	Leathery, flat, savory leaf	4 to 7	18 in	Eastern, mid-western North America	Rock garden, border
Aster macrophyllus Large-leaf aster	Quebec to Michigan south to Georgia, Tennessee, Illinois	1 in, lavender/blue in flat corymbs	Coarse, deep green, sandpapery texture	4 to 7	To 4 ft	Eastern, mid-western North America	Ground cover, border
Aster novi-angliae New England aster, Michaelmas daisy	Vermont to Wyoming south to New Mexico, Alabama	1½ in, purple/ lavender, September/October aromatic	Long leaf	4 to 8	To 6 ft	North America	Border, meadow
Aster novi-belgii New York aster, Michaelmas daisy	Newfoundland along the coast to Georgia	1 in, lavender/ blue, September, October	Long, narrow, dark green leaf	4 to 9	To 4 ft	Eastern North America	Border, meadow
Aster oblongifolius Aromatic aster	Midwest, Minnesota south to Texas	1-plus in, lavender blue, yellow eye, October	Fragrant, pale green, stiff, sprawling stems	4 to 8	To 2 ft	Midwestern North America	Border, meadow, low hedge
Aster patens Spreading aster	New Hampshire and Maine to Georgia, Alabama, Missouri	⅞ in, lavender, aromatic, in September, October	Velvety basal leaves, wiry stems	4 to 8	To 5 ft	Eastern, mid-western North America	Woodland garden

BAPTISIA ALBA White false indigo, white wild indigo

LEGUMINOSAE Pea family

There has been some wild name-calling among the *Baptisia*s and (if I have it right) what used to be called *B. pendula* had its name changed first to *B. lactea* and then to *B. alba*. This is what it is like: each spring, it pops out of the ground and shoots up, asparagus fashion, in a few days. When it unfurls its leaves, they are oval, slightly waxy, and blue-green in color. Although it is swift to go from dormancy to growth, white wild indigo is actually extremely slow growing, taking four or five years to reach maturity. When it finally gets there, you'll have an absolutely eye-popping bloomer. Imagine wisteria flowers that don't hang, but are held upright. Imagine them white, contrasting with dark purple stems held above low, shrubby, attractive foliage, and you'll have the right idea. After the big bloom in May, distinctive seed-

Culture	Propagate	Comment
Sun, medium to moist site	Seed	Delicate sprays arch over neighbors, may need staking, lovely color
Part shade, moderate to moist soil	Division, seed	Tall, very late blooms, use for edge of woodland, rhizomatous. Cultivar: 'Ideal' (2 in)
Part to full shade, moderately moist soil	Division, seed	Connecticut roadside plant, best with good light, variable, seek out dark-stemmed forms, rhizomatous
Sun, moderate to dry soil	Division	Sturdy, adaptable, pleasantly aromatic, vigorously rhizomatous. Cultivars: 'Esther' (pink), 'Blue Star', 'Silver Star' (white).
Sun, moist or dry soil	Seed	Very adaptable; rigid stem needs staking or supportive neighbors
Sun, moderate to dry soil	Division, cuttings	Tough, tolerates poor soil, rigid cantilevered stems, army green after frost
Sun, dry soil, good drainage	Seed, cuttings	Pinch back in early summer to promote heavier flowering
Sun to part shade, moderate to moist soil	Division	Aggressively rhizomatous
Sun, moderate to moist soil	Division, cuttings	Easy, carefree, many great cultivars: 'Alma Potschke' (luminous rose), 'Purple Dome' (2 ft), 'Treasure' (early), 'Hella Lacy' (3 ft)
Sun, moderate to moist soil	Division, cuttings	Variable, easy, rhizomatous, many good cultivars: 'Snow Flurry' (white), 'Mary Ballard' (pale blue)
Sun, average to dry lean soils, tolerates neutral pH	Seed, division	Large, purple, aster flowers mid- to late October; pruning keeps it compact
Part shade, moderate to moist soil	Division, seed	Lovely loose sprays of flowers, rhizomatous

False indigo (Baptisia alba)

lished, but it will be forevermore a thing of beauty and a source of joy.

Origin: Ohio to Minnesota, south to Mississippi and Texas

Flower: 10-inch raceme of white pea flowers in May

Foliage: Blue-green, oval, waxy leaves in bushy habit

Hardiness: Zones 5 to 8

Height: To 4 feet

Region: Eastern North America, where it is hardy

Landscape use: Border

Culture: Sun to part shade, good drainage

Species: *B. alba minor* (shorter); *B. villosa* (yellow flowers)

Propagation: Seed, division

BAPTISIA AUSTRALIS False indigo
LEGUMINOSAE Pea family

False indigo is a beautiful, long-lived source of blue in the late spring–early summer garden, when long racemes of indigo contrast with the petal pinks and ruby reds of peonies or the whites, yellows, and pinks of irises. False indigo's flowers are held above dense, shrubby plants whose bright blue-green, oval leaves reveal pea family kinship. After a month of flowering, dark, hanging pods decorate neat foliage that is shrubby and attractive all through the growing season. False indigo will thrive just about anywhere it has full sun. What it cannot stand is wet feet. Very heat- and drought-tolerant, false indigo makes a good substitute for lupines, which won't tolerate the heat of the South. It attracts butterflies.

Origin: Places in which other plants have difficulty growing: clay hardpans, prairies, and rocky soil from

pods form. And there is much to be said for a plant that gets better every year. White wild indigo tolerates a wide variety of soils, from moist to moderately dry. It also tolerates partial shade, although it does best in full sun. In my garden, it grows in the front of a border, flanked by threadleaf coreopsis—the unimproved species *C. verticillata,* not the shorter cultivars.

White wild indigo is a garden must. It may take a while longer than other perennials to become estab-

Pennsylvania to North Carolina and Tennessee
Flower: Indigo blue pea flowers on showy racemes in May
Foliage: Clean, blue-green oval leaves
Hardiness: Zones 3 to 8
Height: Once established, the plants grow to 5 feet in flower.
Region: Eastern North America
Landscape use: Border
Culture: Full sun, good drainage. It is initially slow to develop.
Cultivars: *B. a.* 'Alba' (white)
Propagation: Seed (soak for 24 hours before planting); cuttings

False indigo (Baptisia australis)

BAPTISIA LEUCOPHAEA Cream false indigo
LEGUMINOSAE Pea family

Slow growing, long lived, cream false indigo blooms just ahead (early May) of white false indigo. This is a stunning plant. It is shorter growing—to a bit more than 2 feet. Instead of white, the flowers are a lovely creamy yellow, and both flowers and foliage are more drooping. Nurseryman Larry Lowman says that cream false indigo thrives in the heat of Arkansas where it "looks great through the stress of summer and takes western sun and a hot, dry place."

It can share a bed with showy primrose (*Oenothera speciosa*), late-to-show summer-blooming butterfly weed (*Asclepias tuberosa*), behind dianthus or moss phlox (*Phlox subulata*).
Origin: Michigan west to Minnesota and south to Arkansas and Texas
Flower: Creamy yellow pea blooms in a long raceme
Foliage: Blue-green, waxy, lax stems
Hardiness: Zones 4 to 8
Height: To 2-plus feet
Region: Eastern North America, where hardy

Landscape use: Border
Culture: Sun, well-drained soil. Cream false indigo does not transplant easily.
Propagation: Seed

BERLANDIERA LYRATA Chocolate flower, broach flower
COMPOSITAE Sunflower family

Chocolate flower reminds me of the song (and place) "Oleana," where "land is free . . . the cows and goats, they milk themselves, the hens lay eggs ten times a day while on the bed you rest yourself." Chocolate flower is too good to be true: not only do these flowers fill the morning garden with the smell of chocolate, you can dry the flowers for arrangements as well.

Give chocolate flower decent soil and it gets leggy and flops over. It does its absolute best in poor, dry soils, where it develops into a compact, handsome clump. If you garden in dry country, grow this plant!
Origin: Kansas west to Colorado and south over Arizona into Mexico
Flower: A 2-inch yellow daisy flower around a green center with fuzzy maroon disc flowers, blooming in a big burst in spring and sporadically through fall
Foliage: Light green with a rosette in winter
Hardiness: Probably Zones 6 to 9
Height: To 4 feet
Regions: Dry parts of the Lower Midwest, Southwest, West Texas
Landscape use: Dry border, meadow
Culture: Sun, unimproved soil, good drainage
Species: *B. texana* and *B. pumila* are similar.
Propagation: Easily from seed, sown anytime.

Cream false indigo (Baptisia leucophaea)

BOLTONIA ASTEROIDES 'Pink Beauty'
COMPOSITAE Sunflower family

Boltonia asteroides 'Pink Beauty' was a chance pink seedling found by designer Edith Eddleman in Powell's Nursery in North Carolina. Edith shared it with Montrose Nursery, who propagated it, and today it is widely available. In my garden, it developed more slowly than 'Snowbank' (below) with a more relaxed habit and far less profuse growth. However, these attributes were perfect in juxtaposition with the mass of a big *Miscanthus sinensis* and the stolidness of *Sedum fulgida* 'Autumn Joy'. 'Pink Beauty' seemed to float around these two companions with hundreds of starry pink flowers that started in July and rebloomed on short stems *behind* spent blooms through September.

Origin: A cultivar of *B. asteroides*

Flower: 1-inch pink aster flower from July through September

Foliage: More lax and a lighter, grayer green than the species

Hardiness: Zones 4 to 9

Height: 5- to 6-foot-long stems bow under the weight of flowers to 3 to 4 feet.

Regions: Midwest, South, Mid-Atlantic, Northeast, Northwest, Mountain

Landscape use: Border, where it mixes well with 'Autumn Joy' sedums in their pink phase; herb garden

Culture: Sun, average to moist soil

Propagation: Division

BOLTONIA ASTEROIDES 'Snowbank'
COMPOSITAE Sunflower family

If I were allowed only five perennials in my garden, *Boltonia asteroides* 'Snowbank' would be one of them. There is no other plant that is as dependably showy—even after the hottest and driest of summers. As I write this on September 18, I am observing 'Snowbank' through the window after a scorching summer. It is in the high 90s today. Three plants, put in about five years ago, unfazed by heat and drought, stand straight and dominate an all-white garden on a southwest slope that also is home to Missouri primrose, wild quinine, and white false indigo. For the last month, each has been a 5-foot upright mound of white, 1-inch asterlike flowers. Although they were originally set about five feet apart, they have very nearly grown together.

These boltonia seem oblivious to site conditions. In one spot, they grow in soil that is poor and dry—filled with builder's trash. Elsewhere, they perform equally well in light shade and moist clay.

Relaxed Boltonia asteroides *'Pink Beauty' next to upright* Boltonia asteroides *'Snowbank'*

Origin: Fields of Missouri, Kansas, and Oklahoma

Flower: 1-inch white aster flower around a yellow center, August to October

Foliage: Narrow, elliptical leaves, widely spaced on densely packed upright stems

Hardiness: Zones 4 to 9

Height: 4 to 6 feet with a vertical habit

Regions: Midwest, South, Mid-Atlantic, Northeast, Northwest, Mountain

Landscape use: Border, tall meadow plant

Culture: Growing in full sun to high shade, ordinary to poor soil, boltonia is not a fussy plant. It spreads wider each year. Dig it up and divide it in fall or early spring when it outgrows its space. Give some to a friend.

Cultivars: 'Nana' is shorter (around 24 inches).

Propagation: Division

CALLIRHOË INVOLUCRATA Wine-cup, poppy mallow, buffalo rose
MALVACEAE Mallow family

Wine-cup is the common name that fits these western wildflowers best because they are cup-shaped and their color is a deep magenta—the color, perhaps, of a Bordeaux with sunshine streaming through it. If you've traveled back roads in Texas during the spring, you've probably seen wine-cups, often by themselves in bright colonies, but also in the company of other Texas treasures such as showy primrose and lupines. Good plants for sun and dry soil, taprooted wine-cups' long, trailing stems stand only about 6 inches high, but spread out along the ground in a loose mat. For this reason, it is a good plant for a rock garden or to train over a wall.

Origin: North Dakota west to Wyoming, south to Missouri, Texas

Flower: Flowers are silky, deep magenta with five petals forming a floppy cup that fades white in the center.

Foliage: Hairy, medium-green, goose-foot leaves on procumbent stems

Hardiness: Zones 4 (possibly 3b) to 8

Height: To 1 foot

Regions: Northeast, Midwest, Mid-Atlantic, South, Northwest

Landscape use: Rock garden, meadow, wall garden

Culture: Full sun, good drainage, dry soil, dislikes transplanting

Species: *C. digitata,* a taller (18-inch) Texas species, often blooms with lupines.

Propagation: Seed or cuttings

Wine-cups (Callirhoë involucrata) *(Charles Mann photo)*

CAMASSIA QUAMASH Camas
LILIACEAE Lily family

I like to imagine that the Lewis and Clark party came upon fields of blue-violet camas in the spring-wet meadows of the Northwest. Native plant expert Dr. Arthur Kruckeberg says that camas was a mainstay food for Plains Indians and a supplemental vegetable for coastal tribes. Whether or not Lewis and Clark dined upon them, it is Rafinesque, the French naturalist, who is credited with their "discovery" and introduction.

So strong, however, is the northwestern association of camas for me that it came as a shock to see it growing lustily at Bowman's Hill Wildflower Preserve in Washington Crossing, Pennsylvania. There it was growing with ostrich and sensitive ferns in a naturalistic setting, a combination that might easily be adapted to a more formal garden. All three plants tolerate a wet situation, but all three fare just fine in soil that is very moist in early spring—even if it dries out later. Since this description fits most of my garden, I tried them.

They are lovely! Tall, willowy stems and grasslike leaves reveal their kinship with the lilies. In bud, the flowers look a little like svelte hyacinths, but when they open, they are blue stars studded with golden anthers.

Origin: British Columbia to Montana, Idaho, and Oregon

Flower: Blue-violet saucer-shaped flowers in spring

Foliage: Long, narrow leaves

Hardiness: Zones 4 (possibly 3) to 6

Height: To 2 feet

Regions: Pacific Northwest, Mountain, places that are very moist in late winter and spring

Landscape use: With perennials, bulb garden

Culture: Abundant moisture in spring, well drained to dry in summer; more adaptable than native lilies

Species: *C. cucksii* (from Oregon), *C. scilloides* (Mississippi River to Appalachians)

CASSIA HEBECARPA Wild senna
LEGUMINOSAE Pea family

Wild senna is a bold perennial that adapts to a wide variety of climatic factors with ease. Very cold-hardy, it doesn't mind heat and adapts to dry or moist soils—be they alkaline or acidic. It grows to a big background plant or shrub with rather upright, irregular stalks and soft green, feathery foliage. With this plant, you get a lot of green, rather than the yellow of flowers that reveal their pea family kinship.

Origin: New England to Wisconsin and south to North Carolina and Tennessee

Flower: Yellow pea flowers in late summer, followed by long seed pods

Foliage: Feathery, light green leaflets on upright stalks

Hardiness: Probably Zones 3 to 8

Height: To 6 feet

Regions: Midwest, Mountain, Northeast, Mid-Atlantic, South

Camas (Camassia)

Wild senna (Cassia) and teasel at
Wave Hill, New York City

Landscape use: Wild garden, edge of woodland, field, stream bank

Culture: Very adaptable, sun to part shade, moist to dry; self-sows; cut back in fall

Species: *C. marilandica* is similar but smaller.

Propagation: Seed

CASTILLEJA INTEGRA Chihuahuan paintbrush, Indian paintbrush

SCROPHULARIACEAE Figwort family

It is a great disappointment to have seen this plant growing, effortlessly, along roadsides of the West and to know I cannot grow it in Maryland. I confess to a bit of *Schadenfreuheit* upon learning that even westerners have difficulty with Indian paintbrushes. While they grow by the thousands on their own, they can be obstinate about showing up where they have been seeded. It seems that the young plants are parasitic on the roots of other plants and need to grow in company. Even knowing this doesn't guarantee success. Some paintbrushes are easier to grow than others.

Gwen Kelaidis, editor of the *Bulletin of the American Rock Garden Society,* says that the pale salmon-flowered Chihuahuan paintbrush, a native of the southern Great Plains and northern Chihuahuan desert, is "possibly the most successful perennial paintbrush in cultivation." She adds, "This species has a soft orange color that is not as vivid, but every bit as beautiful as the more westerly species." She recommends establishing Chihuahuan paintbrush alongside *Bouteloua gracilis,* either from seed or as a young transplant.

Origin: Northern Colorado to northern Chihuahua, Texas, and eastern New Mexico

Flower: Pale orange to deep salmon, blooming from April to autumn frost in typically moist garden conditions and in the summer rainfall belt

Foliage: 4 to 10 inches tall, pale green and somewhat hairy

Hardiness: Zones 4 to 7

Height: 5 to 12 inches

Regions: Best on the Great Plains or warm Mountain environments

Landscape use: Best naturalized among half-wild grasses such as gramma grass or mosquito grass.

Culture: Some summer irrigation during droughts; otherwise, leave it alone

Propagation: From seed. Seems to do better with company: either two seedlings to a pot or grow with artemisia or grasses.

CAULOPHYLLUM THALICTROIDES Blue cohosh

BERBERIDACEAE Barberry family

Slow to reach maturity, blue cohosh is long lived and carefree. Site it in rich, moist, organic soil and you'll be rewarded each spring with the bluest new growth in the garden. As blue cohosh leafs out, the deep, smoky blue color fades a bit. Lacy foliage is a great knee-

Chelone

Name	Origin	Flower	Foliage	Zones	Height	Regions	Landscape Use
Chelone glabra White turtlehead	Low, moist places, Newfoundland to Ontario, south to Georgia, Missouri	White snapping turtle heads in fat spikes	Toothed leaves held horizontally	3 to 8	To 5 ft	Eastern and mid-western North America	Pond edges, stream side, moist border, woodland edge
Chelone lyonii Pink turtlehead	Smoky Mountains	Pink turtle lowers	Stiff, erect stems, toothed leaves	3 to 8	To 4 ft	Eastern United States	Pond edges, stream side, moist border, woodland edge
Chelone obliqua Rose turtlehead	Tennessee, Maryland, south to Florida	Pink turtle flowers	Stiffly held leaves on erect stems	4 to 10	To 4 ft	Eastern United States	Pond edges, stream side, moist border, woodland edge

high layer between shrubs and lower plants like the wild bleeding hearts or the ephemeral dicentras, Dutchman's breeches, and squirrel corn. Blue cohosh flowers are tiny and inconspicuous, but the blue berries are knockouts in the autumn garden.

Origin: Eastern North America

Indian paintbrush (Castilleja) *and bluebonnets on a Texas roadside*

Flower: Small panicles of starry yellow and brown flowers appear in spring, last for two weeks, and are followed by beautiful blue berries in fall.

Foliage: Emerges a wonderful smoky blue, fades to bluish gray-green, fades in late summer.

Hardiness: Zones 3 to 8

Height: 1 to 2 feet

Region: Eastern North America

Landscape use: Shady woodland garden

Culture: Rich, moist, organic soil that is neutral to slightly acid

Propagation: Seed

CHELONE Turtlehead

SCROPHULARIACEAE Figwort family

Members of the same family as the snapdragons, in profile, *Chelone* flowers look not like dragons, but like little turtles. And, yes, children can pinch their flowers for the snapdragon effect. Not only does pinching open their mouths, it exposes tiny, curved fangs!

The turtleheads hail from marshes and wet thickets in the wild, making them wonderful for those deadly, poorly drained, shady areas that often go unplanted. With adequate moisture, turtleheads will also take more sun. Their late summer blooms overlap attractively with both cardinal flower and blue *Lobelia siphilitica,* with which they can share a site comfortably. Stiffly erect foliage stays crisp and dark green well into October where there is adequate moisture.

There are three turtleheads that make good garden plants: *C. glabra,* a tall, white one, *C. lyonii* (pink), and *C. obliqua* (called "rose turtlehead," but also pink). A little nipping at the tips in late spring will keep them to a nice, bushy 2 to 3 feet. Propagate by seed or division.

Turtleheads are good butterfly plants. The larvae of the

Culture	Propagate	Comment
Part shade, moist to wet soil	Seed, division	Pinch back in June for more compact growth. Cultivar: 'Ninja White' (18 to 24 in).
Part shade, moist to wet soil	Seed, division	Earliest to bloom, needs plentiful moisture
Part shade, moist soil	Seed, division	Tougher plant, takes more sun. Cultivar: 'Alba' (white).

Pink turtlehead (Chelone lyonii)

Baltimore checkerspot feed on them, and other butterflies come for their nectar. In a bird and butterfly garden at the Chicago Botanic Garden in August, pink turtlehead combined beautifully with two other wildlife plants, *Physostegia virginiana* and *Lonicera sempervirens.*

Chelones can be started from seed that has been stratified for two months. They can also be started from cuttings. (See *Chelone* chart, above.)

CHRYSOGONUM VIRGINIANUM Goldenstar, green-and-gold

COMPOSITAE Sunflower family

Hordes of what botanists call "damned yellow composites," or simply "DYCs," are common in the sunny fields of late summer, but goldenstar is different. It is a woodland plant that begins flowering in a burst around the end of April, continues for more than a month, and blooms on and off until hard frost. One of its other common names, "green-and-gold," is a perfect description of the way its golden yellow flowers contrast with its deep green foliage.

I first grew this plant in moist organic soil that was overhung with trees and grass, and it barely bloomed at all. I have transplanted it to a brighter place, a slope along a path in high shade, and the plant has lived up to its reputation. Not only does it produce cheerful flowers, it also has made great strides as a ground cover around stepping stones in the path. Green-and-gold frames the little *Aquilegia* 'Corbett', otherwise (I find) a difficult plant to place.

Origin: Woodlands from Pennsylvania to Florida and Louisiana

Flower: A burst of golden 1-inch daisies in spring is followed by sporadic blooms throughout the growing season. In the lower South, goldenstar blooms for nine months!

Foliage: Crinkled, deep green above, lighter green below, ground-hugging leaves on short stems that grow into dense, green mats

Hardiness: Zones 6 to 8

Height: To 5 inches

Regions: Northeast, Mid-Atlantic, South, Lower Midwest

Landscape use: Ground cover, slope plant, shady rock garden

Culture: Part shade in humusy soil with good drainage

Varieties/cultivars: There is a lot of variability in wild populations. I have read about, but never found, a true clump-forming plant. Everything I plant spreads. 'Allen Bush' is an excellent cultivar.

Propagation: Cold-stratify seed or divide the plants in spring or fall.

Goldenstar (Chrysogonum virginianum)

89

Maryland golden aster (Chrysopsis mariana)

CHRYSOPSIS MARIANA (HETEROTHECA MARI-ANA) Maryland golden aster
COMPOSITAE Sunflower family

Except for the goldenrod-yellow coloring of its profuse daisy flowers, Maryland golden aster could pass for an aster, but despite its name it is not an aster. A plant for dry, sandy soil that has excellent drainage, Maryland golden aster is carefree when established in the kind of dry, poor soil in which other plants fail. It might share a bed with other tough perennials: Missouri primrose, butterfly weed, and prairie baby's breath. It has the edge in this kind of place, but in richer soil, other plants outcompete.

Origin: Barren, sandy soils and pinewoods from New York west to Ohio and south to Florida and East Texas
Flower: 1- to 1½-inch golden yellow daisy with a golden yellow eye in loose heads in September
Foliage: A rosette of long, dark green leaves with long white hairs sends up fairly upright stems.
Hardiness: Zones 6 to 8
Height: 1 to 3 feet
Regions: Eastern coastal plain; dry, sandy soils east to Ohio
Landscape use: Border, bank planting
Culture: Sun to light shade, poor to average soil that is dry to moderately dry and well drained
Species: Silkgrass (*C. graminifolia*), with yellow flowers,

has silvery, grassy leaves and is drought-tolerant.
Propagation: Seed (a layer of grit will ensure perfect drainage)

CHRYSOPSIS VILLOSA 'San Bruno Mountain'
COMPOSITAE Sunflower family

Bart O'Brien, a California gardener and plant expert, convinced me that 'San Bruno Mountain' had to be in this book, so here, thanks to him, it is. A useful plant for hot, dry gardens, 'San Bruno Mountain' produces a steady crop of golden yellow daisylike flowers on low, broad plants with finely hirsute, light green leaves. The selection 'San Bruno Mountain' was chosen for its small stature, its handsome foliage, and its free-flowering tendency. Grow 'San Bruno Mountain' in full sun or light shade. Heat-tolerant, it looks best with some summer watering and regular deadheading (which can be done with a weed whip).

Origin: California
Flower: 1-inch, golden yellow daisies on nearly ever-blooming plants
Foliage: Light green, oval, dense, covered with fine white hairs
Hardiness: Zones 9 (possibly 8) to 10
Height: 4 to 8 inches tall, spreading 1 to 2 feet wide
Regions: California, Southwest
Landscape use: Mixed border, edging, rock gardens
Culture: Full sun to light shade; easily grown in most gardens; avoid overhead watering. Tolerates heat; best appearance with some summer watering.
Propagation: Cuttings

CIMICIFUGA RACEMOSA Bugbane, snakeroot
RANUNCULACEAE Buttercup family

This is a plant that would make the right sort of backdrop for a production of *Midsummer Night's Dream*. It ought to be called fairy candles, or something more descriptive of its subtle, ethereal presence when its white wand flowers uncurl in July. Its attraction begins in spring, when compound leaves unfold a lovely wine color before turning green—not unlike those of a very large astilbe. They are most effective against a dark background of something like rhododendrons or mountain laurel or conifers. After bloom, pealike seedpods sometimes weigh down the stems clumsily. If this bothers you, cut them off. Or leave one to self-sow. The foliage, handsome all by itself, is a tall ground cover that persists until hard frost.

Bugbane (Cimicifuga racemosa)

Origin: Rich, moist, deep humus of woodland from Ontario to Georgia and west to Missouri

Flower: Flowers are white, opening from bottom to top on wands or candles on 6- foot (or taller!) inflorescences in July

Foliage: Cut leaves in handsome 2½-foot clumps; look good all season long

Hardiness: Zones 4 to 7

Height: 6 feet

Regions: Northeast, Midwest, Mid-Atlantic, South, Northwest

Landscape use: Most effective in groups of six or eight plants in the shady part of a border or on the edge of woods

Culture: *Cimicifuga* grows happily in moist half shade to moist sun. Keep vines and aggressive plants away from bugbane or they will overwhelm it.

Species/cultivars: I have been trying for years to find a source for the (reputedly) smaller, later-blooming *C. americana,* but have never found one.

Propagation: Seeds require double dormancy; division.

COREOPSIS Tickseed
COMPOSITAE Sunflower family

It's hard to choose from among the more than 100 species of (mostly golden yellow) *Coreopsis.* Of the perennials, several stand out from the crowd. Because of the smart contrast of its dark, yellow-green foliage with small rosy pink flowers and its tolerance of moist clays, *Coreopsis rosea* is unique and useful.

Two other species I know of have thin, threadlike leaves: *C. pulchra, C. verticillata,* and its cultivars are true survivors—tough, extremely hardy—that bloom through the hot summer.

Dwarf-eared coreopsis, *C. auriculata* 'Nana', is hard to find but worth the effort. Its ground-hugging, 3- to 5-inch-high, very dark green foliage and golden flowers on 8-inch stems are early—April to June.

Most other species have long stems, which makes them good cut flower plants. All are sun loving, and most do better with good drainage. (See *Coreopsis* chart on pages 92–93.)

DALEA PURPUREA (PETALOSTEMUM PURPUREUM) Purple prairie clover
LEGUMINOSAE Pea family

Purple prairie clovers display their small, round, violet flowers in early summer. Resembling roadside clovers, the flowers open in a spiral along cylindrical cones held on wiry stems. Like clover, they are best in masses. The tough plants have taproots of turmeric yellow that help them bloom for as long as two months in the heat and drought of summer. C. Colston Burrell, a landscape architect in Minneapolis, likes them in prairies where "they make a dazzling show with golden Alexanders, mountain mint, prairie phlox, and bergamot amongst the bright green clumps of young grasses." In gardens, he combines them with yar-rows, phlox, and purple coneflowers. The only difficulty with this plant is that rabbits gnaw off the new buds. Chestnut burrs piled around the emerging growth will probably help. The

Pink tickseed (Coreopsis rosea)

Coreopsis

Name	Origin	Flower	Foliage	Zones	Height	Regions	Landscape Use
Coreopsis auriculata 'Nana' Dwarf-eared coreopsis	Woodland edges and open places of the Southeast	Toothed, 1- to 2-in, yellow, on 8-in stem in April, May	Dark green, lobed leaves in 2- to 4-in rosettes	5 to 8	2 to 10 in	Southeastern U.S.	Ground cover, edger, rock garden
Coreopsis gigantea Tree coreopsis	Coastal Southern California	Profuse, golden yellow, April/May	Elegant, ferny leaves on a stout "tree"	8 to 10	4 ft	California	Back border, accent, early specimen
Coreopsis grandiflora Big-flowered coreopsis	Midwest to Florida and New Mexico	Golden yellow, late May and June	Long, narrow leaves, wiry stems	5 to 8	3 ft	Southwest, South, Midwest	Border, accent, cut flower
Coreopsis lanceolata Lance coreopsis	Sunny, dry soils, Midwest to Florida and New Mexico	Golden yellow, long stems, April to June	Narrow leaves in a large, loose rosette	4 to 9	18 in	North America	Border, accent, cut flower, meadow
Coreopsis maritima Sea daisy	Coast, islands of Southern California	Bright yellow daisies, long stems in spring	Yellow-green, ferny leaves	8 to 10	2 ft	California	Border, accent, cut flower, seaside
Coreopsis nudata Swamp coreopsis	Deep South	Pink, cosmoslike flowers	Medium green leaves, long stems	8 to 10	2 to 3 ft	South	Meadow, border, cutting
Coreopsis palmata Stiff coreopsis	Prairies of the Great Plains	Bright yellow, July	Upright, fine foliage	3 to 8	2 to 3 ft	Midwest, Mountain	Prairies, border, cutting
Coreopsis pulchra Tickseed	Southeastern United States	Profuse, large, gold flowers with a red eye!, summer	Fine, wispy foliage forms an airy clump	6 to 8	30 in	Southeastern U.S.	Border, accent
Coreopsis rosea Pink tickseed	Moist places from Nova Scotia to Georgia	1-in pink flowers, yellow eyes, June to August	Rich green, needle-thin leaves in running climps	3 to 9	12 to 15 in	North America	Front border, edging, ground cover
Coreopsis tripteris Tall coreopsis	Medium to moist soils from Ontario to Louisiana and Kansas	Shiny yellow in July/August	Long, narrow leaves on lanky stems	4 to 8	6 ft	Eastern North America to mountains	Back border, accent, good with grasses
Coreopsis verticillata Threadleaf coreopsis	Open, sunny places from Maryland to Arkansas, Florida	1-in gold flowers from June to August	Upright, airy, nice-ly shaped clump, thin, thread leaves	3 to 9	3 ft	North America	Ground cover, edger, front border

Threadleaf coreopsis (C. verticillata), right, and its lemon yellow cultivar, C. verticillata 'Moonbeam'

dried charcoal gray seed heads are attractive in the winter garden.

Origin: Prairies and open woods from Indiana and Kentucky west to Manitoba and New Mexico

Flower: Red-violet to purple cloverlike flowers with protruding stamens in tight, cylindrical heads from mid-June through July

Foliage: The $\frac{1}{4}$- to $\frac{1}{2}$-inch leaves have three to five narrowly oval leaflets that densely clothe thin, wiry stems.

Hardiness: Zones 3 to 8

Height: 1 to 3 feet

Regions: Eastern North America, Midwest, Southwest

Landscape use: Formal borders, meadows, prairies, and rock gardens

Culture: Full sun to light shade, moist sandy

Culture	Propagate	Comment
Full sun to part shade; tough, not fussy	Seed	Long, early bloom, nice with small bulbs
Full sun, summer water, fall rest, frost tender	Seeds, cuttings	Loses leaves, but will survive a dry summer, needs camouflage
Full sun, infertile, well-drained soil	Seed	After burst of bloom, sporadic flowers through summer. Cultivars: 'Rotkelchen' (10-in yellow with red center), 'Early Sunrise' (18-in semi-double yellow).
Full sun, poor soil, well-drained	Seed	Self-sows, burst of bloom followed by sporadic flowers, tolerates very dry places
Full sun, sandy soil, summer water	Seed	Long blooming period (spring–summer), great cut flowers
Sun, moist, acid soil	Seed	Good plant for damp places
Medium to dry soil or even sand	Division, seed	Tolerates extremely dry soil, easy to grow, spreads by rhizomes
Sun, good drainage	Seed	Red-eyed flowers, threadleaf foliage
Sun, moist, tolerates clay	Division	Floriferous, good foliage, spreads by rhizomes, grows in clay. Cultivar: 'Alba'.
Sun, medium to moist soil	Seed	Fast growing, good with other oversized plants
Sun, medium to dry soil	Division, seed	Very neat, fine foliage in an airy clump, long bloom. Cultivars: 'Moonbeam' (lemon yellow, 15 in), 'Zagreb' (gold, 15 in).

Tree coreopsis (Coreopsis gigantea) *at Santa Barbara Botanic Garden*

Purple prairie clover (Dalea purpurea) *(Jessie Harris photo)*

or loamy soils. Drought-tolerant once established because of deep, thickened roots.

Species: Two other garden-worthy species are available: white prairie clover (*D. candida*), with larger flower heads, blooms in July and August and is extremely drought-tolerant; and silky prairie clover (*D. villosa*), with rose-purple, pink, or white flowers, grows best in well-drained to dry sandy soil.

DELPHINIUM CARDINALE Scarlet larkspur
RANUNCULACEAE Buttercup family

For a dry perennial border in California, scarlet larkspur is a graceful choice. A short-lived perennial that is easy to grow from seed, scarlet larkspur's flowers are cardinal red and appear in early summer. Occasionally, you see one that's yellow. Because of its delicate appearance, five or more plants are needed in a group to make a show. Hummingbirds like it.

Origin: Coastal southern California from Monterey County south into Baja

Scarlet larkspur (**Delphinium cardinale**) *(Charles Mann photo)*

Flower: Cardinal red flowers appear in early summer.
Foliage: Leaves are divided and delicate.
Hardiness: Probably Zones 9 to 10
Height: 3 to 6 feet
Regions: Coastal areas of California into Oregon
Landscape use: In groups in the border and with shrubs
Culture: Full sun to part shade, excellent drainage, no additional water.
Propagation: From seed.

DICENTRA Wild bleeding heart
FUMARIACEAE Bleeding heart family

The bleeding heart family has members that delight and fascinate children of all ages. Ephemeral Dutchman's breeches *(D. cucullaria)* look like old-fashioned bloomers hung on a line. And the flowers of both the native and exotic bleeding hearts look like little dangling hearts with a single drop of blood about to drop from the pointed end.

Wild bleeding hearts are smaller in stature, with lacier leaves, than *D. spectabalis,* the exotic bleeding heart. Both the eastern (*D. eximia*) and western (*D. formosa*) native species are plants whose performance is directly related to the richness of the soil, the presence of adequate moisture, and the right amount of sun. With high, light shade or full morning sun and deep, moist, loose, humusy soil, wild bleeding heart's pink or pale red flowers and mound of elegantly cut, gray or blue-green

foliage will persist until hard frost (unlike that of the exotic *D. spectabilis,* which disappears in midsummer). Afternoon sun (especially in the South) may turn foliage yellow. Near-neutral conditions with good drainage are ideal. Ants disseminate the seeds.

Dicentra cucullaria Dutchman's breeches
Origin: North America
Flower: White, upside-down, bloomer-shaped flower with yellow sexual parts at the "waistband"
Foliage: Blue-green, deeply cut with a lacy effect
Hardiness: Zones 3 to 7
Height: To 10 inches
Region: Northern North America to Zone 7
Landscape use: A lovely spring ephemeral, Dutchman's breeches is charming along a woodland path, followed by ferns.
Culture: Loose, humusy soil that is moist and partly shaded
Species: Squirrel corn (*D. canadensis*) has a very similar, more heart-shaped flower that is often all white. It gets its name from the yellow, corn-kernel-like little tuber. It is slightly smaller, growing only about 6 to 8 inches tall.
Propagation: Divide the little clusters of tubers in early spring or summer.

Dicentra eximia Eastern wild bleeding heart
Origin: New York to the mountains of Tennessee and North Carolina
Flower: Pink (also white) heart-shaped flowers on arching stems in spring and sporadically in summer
Foliage: Deeply cut, gray-green
Hardiness: Zones 3 to 8
Height: 18 inches
Regions: Grows well outside of its range: Northeast, Mid-Atlantic, South, Midwest, parts of the Southwest
Landscape use: Border, woodland garden, streamside
Culture: Rich, moist soil; part shade
Cultivars: 'Alba' (white)
Propagation: Divide rootstock with a sharp knife in early spring or collect self-sown seedlings.

Dicentra formosa Western wild bleeding heart
Origin: Mountain woodland from British Columbia to California
Flower: Pink to pale red and sometimes white heart-shaped flowers in June and July
Foliage: A mound of deeply cut, blue-green ferny leaves
Hardiness: Zones 6 to 7
Height: 15 to 18 inches

Regions: Northwest, California, Mountain
Landscape use: Leaves are so attractive that wild bleeding heart is a good plant for massing as a ground cover.
Culture: Full sun to high shade; rich, humusy, moist soil
Species/cultivars: *Dicentra formosa* ssp. *oregana,* with white to yellow flowers, has yielded a number of excellent cultivars: 'Luxuriant' (happier in my garden in full sun), 'Adrian Bloom' (dark pink); and 'Spring Morning' (pale pink).
Propagation: By seed or division

DODECATHEON MEADIA Shooting star
PRIMULACEAE Primrose family

Neil Diboll, who operates Prairie Nursery in Westfield, Wisconsin, and installs bits of prairie around the country, has honed his nursery's offerings to a choice few. One of his recommendations for gardens in the Midwest is shooting star. Typically, a single stem bearing a ring of dangling flowers that do indeed resemble shooting stars rises above a basal rosette. Shooting stars prefer a near-neutral soil (and are tolerant of soil alkalinity) and do best with fall transplanting.

Shooting stars are so beautiful, it is all you can do not to pick them and gather them into magical bouquets. I think this is the reason that a shooting star is the symbol of the American Rock Garden Society. Rock gardeners look at their whole gardens as bouquets. Of the many beautiful shooting stars native to North America, the following are readily available.

Origin: Pennsylvania west to Wisconsin and south to Texas and Alabama
Flower: Variable—magenta, lavender, or white petals are

Western bloodroot (Dicentra formosa) with Solomon's seal and oxalis (Cynthia Woodyard photo)

strongly reflexed around a banded, pointed center. As many as 20 flowers dangle on short stems that radiate out from a tall, central stem in May and June.
Foliage: Smooth, broad leaves in a flat rosette, disappearing in late summer
Hardiness: Zones 3 to 8
Height: 18 inches
Regions: Northeast, Mid-Atlantic, Midwest, South, Mountain, Northwest
Landscape use: Shady border, rock garden
Culture: Light shade; moist, well-drained soil that is nearly neutral
Species: *D. pulchellum* (Western shooting star) to 12 inches, pink or red flowers, from Northwest
Cultivars: 'Pink Comets' (pink with dark stems), 'Alba' (white flowers)
Propagation: Seed (stratify two months)

ECHINACEA Coneflower
COMPOSITAE Sunflower family

Tough, undemanding, beloved of birds and butterflies and of gardeners who have made their acquaintance, coneflowers begin to bloom in late June and continue through the heat of summer into late August and, sporadically, through September.

None of the three species listed here, black Sampson (*E. angustifolia*), pale purple coneflower (*E. pallida*), or purple coneflower (*E. purpurea*), is a thirsty plant. All thrive on available rainfall, and sun and heat won't faze them. Pale purple coneflower, from a little farther west, with pale pink, thinner, spidery flowers, is taprooted,

Dutchman's breeches (Dicentra cucullaria)

Echinacea

Name	Origin	Flower	Foliage	Zones	Height	Regions	Landscape Use
Echinacea angustifolia Black sampson	Dry prairies of Minnesota, Saskatchewan to Texas	2½- to 3-in pale pink ray flowers, flat cone	Narrow leaves, hairy stem	3	10 to 24 in	Midwest	Border, prairie, wild garden
Echinacea pallida Pale purple coneflower	Dry prairies, barrens, Michigan, Montana to Georgia, Texas	3- to 6-in pale pink reflexed flowers, flat cone	Medium oblong leaves, hairy stem	3	To 4 ft	Midwest, Mountain, South, Southwest	Border, prairie, wild garden
Echinacea purpurea Purple coneflower	Prairies, open woods of Ohio, Iowa to Louisiana, Georgia	4- to 6-in flat, bright purple-pink flowers, large orange cone	Dark green, oval, hairy leaves, stem	4	To 5 ft	Eastern North America	Border, prairie, wild garden

Shooting star (Dodecatheon meadia)

drought-tolerant, and reputed to be longer lived than the purple coneflower. At last reckoning, it was considered a threatened plant, but it is propagated and available from reliable nurseries.

The purple coneflower (*E. purpurea*) responds to site conditions. With full sun, rich soil, and moderate moisture, it will produce plants up to 5 feet tall. In ordinary soil, it stays about 3 feet tall. I have read that purple coneflower prefers a neutral soil, but in the acid (pH 5.5 or thereabouts) clay soil of my garden, it has outdone itself with only compost as an amendment. Robust plants of purple coneflower produce dozens of huge—up to 6 inches across—flowers with ray petals held stiffly around a prominent orange cone. As cut flowers, they last weeks,

and three or more plants grouped together will provide bouquets and attract clouds of hovering butterflies all summer long.

After a season of bloom, the coneflower patch begins to look rather worn out, and just at the moment one resolves to go out and cut it back, treeloads of birds appear, wanting the seeds, and the show goes on. But purple coneflower still self-sows lustily and produces plants that bloom modestly the next year from the leftover seed.

All three species may be started from seed, divisions, or root cuttings. Another attractive coneflower, *E. laevigata,* is worth growing if you can find it.

Although the straight species is enormously satisfactory, there are cultivars of purple coneflower to be had. 'Bright Star' is supposed to be stockier. There are also white forms. One of these, 'White Swan', comes true from seed. (See *Echinacea* chart, above.)

ENGELMANNIA PINNATIFIDA Engelmann daisy, cutleaf daisy

COMPOSITAE Sunflower family

Drive through Texas on a May morning and chances are you'll see "bushes" covered with hundreds of bright yellow Engelmann daisies on the roadsides. Like evening primroses, Engelmann daisies open in the cool of the evening and remain open until the heat of the following day. After a long, hot day, their fresh yellow blooms are a delight in the first cool of the evening. In the garden, where they don't have to compete with other roadside plants, they grow to be quite bushy. Engelmann daisy's taproot sees it through the driest summers undaunted.

Origin: Dry soils from Kansas and Colorado over Texas to Louisiana and New Mexico

Flower: Abundant 2-inch lemon yellow daisy flow-

Culture	Propagate	Comment
Sun, well-drained, medium to dry soil	Seed, division	Drought-tolerant, endangered, bird, butterfly plant
Sun, well-drained, medium to dry soil	Seed, division	Spidery flower; bird, butterfly plant; very showy
Sun, well-drained, medium soil	Seed	Wonderful in masses! Showy, flat flowers, good cut flower, some fragrant

ers from February until fall, peak bloom in April–May, clustered at the tips of stems. Flowers close in high heat.

Foliage: Evergreen rosette sends up deeply cut, hirsute leaves that resemble thick, hairy ferns.

Hardiness: Probably Zone 7 to 9

Height: To 3 feet

Regions: Texas, Southwest

Landscape use: Back border, meadow

Culture: Sun to part shade, excellent drainage, drought-tolerant, neutral soil, tolerant of lime, caliche

Propagation: Seed

EPILOBIUM ANGUSTIFOLIUM Fireweed, French willow, willow herb

ONAGRACEAE Evening primrose family

Bold and beautiful, fireweed—so called because it is one of the first plants to appear on scorched ground after a fire—has seeds that may lie dormant for years. After a fire destroys trees, fireweed

Purple coneflower (Echinacea purpurea)
at Brookside Gardens, Wheaton, Maryland

White purple coneflower (Echinacea purpurea 'White Swan')

springs up in the bright, new light conditions, affirming life and making up for loss with its wild beauty. In nature, the life cycle continues and trees will eventually come up again to shade the fireweed out. In a garden, with no curbs, its running rhizomes, and a tendency to self-sow, fireweed can take over. Use a shovel to reduce the clump and remove errant plants in spring or fall.

Origin: In northern places around the world

Flower: Striking spires of bright magenta or white flowers open from bottom to top

Foliage: Long, narrow, coarse willow leaves on reddish stems

Hardiness: Zones 3 to 6

Height: To 6 feet

Region: Northern North America

Landscape use: Wild garden, woodland's edge, back border with vigilance

Culture: Sun, average soil

Propagation: Seed

ERIGERON GLAUCUS Seaside daisy, beach daisy

COMPOSITAE Sunflower family

Seaside daisy, a fine perennial with pale, blue-green leaves that remain in good condition all year, bears daisylike lavender flowers that come and go

Eriogonum

Name	Origin	Flower	Foliage	Zones	Height	Regions	Landscape Use
Eriogonum arborescens Island buckwheat	Santa Catalina islands	Ivory pink flower clusters, late summer	Gray-green	8 to 10	4 ft	Southern California	Banks, borders
Eriogonum corymbosum	Colorado desert, Utah, Colorado, (Wyoming, Idaho)	Cream, aging buff, pink, brown, from August to October	Gray-white, oval, hairy leaves, usually with wavy margins	At least 4 to 8	28 in	Mountain, California, Southwest	Dry border, large, dry rock garden, banks
Eriogonum crocatum Conejo buckwheat	Rocky hills of California	Flat, sulphur yellow heads, April–July	Gray-white, thick, felty leaves	8 to 10	2 ft	California	Rock garden, ground cover
Eriogonum fasciculatum California buckwheat	Central and Southern California	White-pink flower heads, summer–fall	Variable, narrow, gray-green leaves	8 to 10	3 ft	California	Ground cover, erosion control
Eriogonum giganteum St. Catherine's lace	Santa Catalina islands	Cream-colored flower clusters to 24 in, late summer	Whitish, gray felted leaves	8 to 10	6 ft	California	Sculptural accent, naturalized
Eriogonum jamesii	Arizona, New Mexico, Colorado, Wyoming, Utah	Chartreuse aging orange, or cream aging brown	Bun of gray-green, felted leaves	3 to 7	12 to 18 in	Southwest, Mountain	Banks, dry low border, rock garden
Eriogonum latifolium Coast buckwheat	Central coast of California	Heads of beige-rust flowers	Evergreen foliage, densely hairy, whitish gray	8 to 10	6 in by 6 in	California	Ground cover
Eriogonum niveum	Eastern Washington, Oregon	Snowy white aging buff	White felted leaves at base	At least 7 to 8	26 in	Northwest, California, Southwest	Dry border, bank or large, dry rockery
Eriogonum umbellatum Sulphur buckwheat	Interior California	Clear yellow, June–August	Small, round, matte green leaves with white undersides	7 to 8	2 ft	California, Southwest	Dry border, rockery

throughout the summer. It is a reliable presence for the front of the border and excellent in containers, where it is a substantial partner to delicate annuals such as baby blue eyes (*Nemophila menziesii*), *Clarkia elegans,* or *C. pulchella*.

Origin: Coastal areas of California from Santa Barbara north to southern Oregon

Flower: Lavender, pale purple, or white

Foliage: Coarse, blue-green leaves

Hardiness: Seaside daisy will probably survive 20° weather for short periods. Probably Zones 8b to 10.

Height: Multiple branches of flowers to 2 feet

Region: California

Landscape use: Borders and containers

Culture: No hot sun, good light, good drainage, little water.

Species: *E. caespitosus,* with large white or pale pink daisies and plump gray leaves, for a dry garden; quick from seed. *E. compositus,* a white or lavender-flowered daisy with cut leaves, comes in good but also ugly forms; self-sows. *E. chrysopsidis* var. *brevifolius* 'Grand Ridge', a sterile form that blooms all summer with dainty yellow

Fireweed (Epilobium angustifolium) *(Charles Mann photo)*

Culture	Propagate	Comment
Good drainage, full sun, little or no water	Seed	Easy from seed, good dry flower
Full sun, little to no water, clay okay if sloped	Seed	Fantastic for late summer color. Cut back to 4 in to achieve rounded ball effect.
Excellent drainage, full sun, drought-tolerant	Seed	Dazzling silver-white foliage and yellow flowers
Drought-tolerant, sun, excellent drainage	Seed	Grows fast, good source of green, flowers dry to a rust color. Cultivars: 'Theodore Payne' (low), 'Dana Point' (vigorous, deep green leaves).
Good drainage, full sun, little or no water	Seed	Spectacular in bloom and after, good dried flowers
Full sun, good drainage, little or no water	Seed	July bloom, long color season, easy!
Good drainage, full sun, little or no water	Seed	Grown for foliage, flowers are not handsome
Full sun, drought-tolerant	Seed	Dazzling white in August. Excellent contrast with *Zauschnerias*. Forms round ball; cut back as for *E. corymbosum*.
Good drainage, full sun, little or no water	Seed	Long season of bloom, compact habit

Erigeron *and cactus*

ERIOGONUM Wild buckwheat
POLYGONACEAE Buckwheat family

Among the many, many wild buckwheats native to California and the West are annuals, shrubby perennials, and shrubs. Most often the flower clusters are flat, and dry on the plants to attractive after-bloom shades of pink or brown. They also make good cut flowers.

Buckwheats make up a part of the native chaparral plant community in California. Like sagebrush and chamisa, over time, buckwheat produces litter that will fuel fires if allowed to accumulate. For safety, remove litter from time to time.

Some buckwheats are old garden standbys. Others, beautiful strangers, are new to gardens. There is a handsome candidate for every garden.

Often broader than high, buckwheats range in size and character from tiny coast buckwheat to the statuesque St. Catherine's lace. Many have the hairy, silver-colored foliage of dryland plants and will go without summer water when established. All require good drainage. The chart above mixes annuals, perennials, and shrubs, but includes a smattering of garden-worthy species of these dryland plants.

ERYNGIUM YUCCIFOLIUM Rattlesnake master
UMBELLIFERAE Carrot family

If you ever look upon a well-grown rattlesnake master, you'll spend the next six months trying to find the perfect place for it. This side of the Sonoran Desert, there's nothing like it. Rattlesnake master is a dramatic, sculptural plant with blue-green leaves simi-

daisies and soft gray leaves; propagate by cuttings.
Cultivars: 'Wayne Roderick', a low-growing form, 6 to 10 inches and 3 feet wide; hardy from −10° to 115°F. 'Cape Sebastian', compact, 4 to 6 inches high, spreads 2 to 3 feet, pale lavender flowers.
Propagation: Cuttings, division

Silvery buckwheat (Eriogonum) *under shrubs*
(Sidney Baumgartner Design)

Erythronium

Name	Origin	Flower	Foliage	Zones	Height	Regions	Landscape Use
Erythronium albidum White dogtooth violet	Ontario, Minnesota to Kansas, Arkansas, Texas	Pendant white bell, spring	Maroon, green and gray	3 to 8	10 in	Eastern, mid-western North America	Woodland garden, shady rock garden
Erythronium oregonum Fawn lily, dogtooth violet	British Columbia to Oregon	2 in, white, pink	Mottled leaves	6(?) to 8	1 ft	Northwest	Woodland garden, shady rock garden
Erythronium revolutum Fawn lily, dogtooth violet	Vancouver to Northern California	1½ in, rosy pink, lavender	Mottled green and brown	6(?) to 8	15 in	Northwest, Northern California	Woodland garden, shady rock garden
Erythronium umbilica-tum (E. americanum) Trout lily, dogtooth violet	Nova Scotia to Minnesota, Florida, Alabama	2 in, pendant, yellow with brown shading	Maroon mottling	4 to 9	10 in	Eastern, mid-western North America	Woodland garden, shady rock garden

lar to those of a yucca and pale green flowers that look like the spike-studded iron balls that were used as weapons in the Middle Ages. I would love to see rattlesnake master rising out of a cloud of pink evening primrose or softened by white prairie baby's breath, both of which could share a hot, dry place.

In the wild, rattlesnake master is found growing in sandy soil and open woodland. It is taprooted. From sad experience I know that while not fussy about other things, rattlesnake master needs good drainage. Its common name refers to use of the brewed root as an antidote to rattlesnake venom.

Origin: Its appearance suggests the Southwest, but its range is from the Atlantic Coast to the Great Plains and south to Florida.

Flower: Greenish white, spiky balls that appear on stout stems in July and August

Foliage: Flat, light gray-green, straplike, slightly spiny leaves

Hardiness: Zones 3 to 8

Height: 2-foot foliage, 4 feet in flower

Regions: Eastern Canada and Eastern United States

Landscape use: A striking accent, nice with other gray foliage plants

Culture: Sun, air, and excellent drainage. Taprooted, so avoid unnecessary moves!

Propagation: Seed

ERYTHRONIUM Trout lily, fawn lily, dogtooth violet
LILIACEAE Lily family

Among the great delights of a shady garden or a walk in the spring woods, trout lilies are, all by themselves, reason enough not to bother with lawn in shady places. Though tiny, the lemon yellow trout lilies' waxy perfection of bloom upstages even taller, flowery companions like Virginia bluebells. Both are spring ephemerals. When their sky blue and lemon yellow collaboration begins to fade, fall-blooming white wood asters or ferns take over neatly.

Trout lilies grow from tiny corms that work their way ever deeper into the soil. Some gardeners grow them over a buried rock to stop the downward progression of the corms and keep them within easy digging. Trout lilies grow all winter and flower in spring. In summer they are dormant. The common names "trout lily" and "fawn lily" refer to the mottling on their leaves, while the epithet "dogtooth" is a description of the corms—yellowish and curved like fangs.

Of about 18 species of *Erythronium* in North America,

Eriogonum jamesii ssp. flavescens, *at right, with rusty brown flower heads, next to a dwarf yellow chamisa in the Kelaidis garden, Denver*

Culture	Propagate	Comment
Moist, humusy shade	Seed, corms	Propagate from seed or corms if available, will eventually produce colonies
Moist, rich, well-drained soil, shade	Seed, corms	Easy from seed, flowers take two to three years, but eventually form colonies
Moist, rich, well-drained soil, shade	Seed, corms	Easy from seed, flowers take two to three years, but eventually form colonies
Moist, rich, well-drained soil, shade	Seed, corms	Long bloom, showier each year as corms mature

*Dogtooth violets (***Erythronium umbilicatum americanum***)*

the showiest come from the West. The spectacular glacier and avalanche lilies (*E. montanum, E. grandiflorum*) grow in subalpine climates from British Columbia to Oregon. Far too demanding for a low-altitude garden, they are to be enjoyed in the wild. Trout lilies from lowland woods are easier to establish in a shady garden, if very hard to find. Because it takes about five years from seed to flowering plant, when you do find them, expect plants to be costly. If they are not, they have probably been collected from the wild, unless sold by native plant societies or botanic gardens. (See *Erythronium* chart, above.)

EUPATORIUM

COMPOSITAE Sunflower family

The genus *Eupatorium* contains a number of underused species from eastern North America that make excellent heat-tolerant, summer-blooming

garden subjects. Most familiar of these is Joe-Pye weed, the common name for *E. dubium, E. fistulosum, E. maculatum,* and *E. purpureum,* four species of rather similar plants named for a medicine showman of the 19th century. Once you've seen a Joe-Pye weed, you'll never forget it: a great big, bold, multistemmed specimen, topped with rounded clusters of mauve, lavender, or white flowers that may reach 12 inches across and be held 10 feet in the air. When you buy *E. fistulosum,* observe the stem color. Very dark stems indicate the richly colored flowers to come.

In addition to the Joe-Pye weeds, other eupatoriums such as white snakeroot and hardy ageratum are great for cutting. The dried roots of white snakeroot were used to treat snakebite—whether successfully or not, I can't say. This tall fall bloomer is weedy, but just the right thing for a filler on the shady edge of woodland.

The strange and wonderful dog fennel (*E. capillifolium*), a common roadside weed from Maryland south, is in a class by itself. I first saw dog fennel featured in the North Carolina State Arboretum's perennial border, designed by Edith Eddleman. There, in the back of the quite elegant July border, flanked by Carolina lupine and Culver's root, was what looked like a stunning, 10-foot, bright green, swaying asparagus plant! The second time I saw it used in a garden was at Niche Gardens, a nursery in Chapel Hill, North Carolina, owned by Kim and Bruce Hawks. What Kim did was to plant dog fennel all by itself as a specimen. The effect was brilliant. This imposing plant, towering 12 feet tall and perhaps 4 feet wide, has fine grassy foliage that moves and sways with the lightest of air currents—like a piece of kinetic sculpture.

*Rattlesnake master (***Eryngium yuccifolium***)*
at Montrose Nursery in Hillsborough, North Carolina

Eupatorium

Name	Origin	Flower	Foliage	Zones	Height	Regions	Landscape Use
Eupatorium capillifolium Dog fennel	Southeast woodland edges, disturbed places	Fragrant, but inconspicuous	Fine, feathery, bright green	7 to 9	8 to 12 ft	South	Specimen, back border, screen
Eupatorium coelestinum Mistflower, hardy ageratum	New Jersey, Texas to Florida, West Indies	Flat clusters of lavender, August and September	Hairy, heart-shaped, saw-toothed leaves	4 to 10	2 to 3 ft	Southeastern United States	Border, meadows, woodland edges
Eupatorium fistulosum Spotted Joe-Pye weed	Eastern United States	Honey scented, 12 to 20 in, mauve, August	Green or spotted, hollow stem, coarse leaves	4 to 8	7 to 10 ft	Eastern United States	Specimen, back border, cut flower
Eupatorium hyssopifolium	Eastern North America	White, yarrowlike flower, July	Fine, threadlike leaves, whorled around stem	4 to 8	3 ft	Eastern, mid-western North America	Border, cut flower
Eupatorium maculatum Joe-Pye weed	Damp, calcareous soils of eastern North America	Flat, purplish-rose clusters	Very narrow leaves, rough, spotted stem	4 to 8	6 ft	Eastern North America	Specimen, back border, cut flower, wild garden
Eupatorium perfoliatum Boneset	Moist, wet places, eastern North America	Large, flat, white flower heads	Gray-green, felted leaves, joined at base	3 to 8	5 ft	Eastern North America	Wild garden, meadow, woodland edge
Eupatorium purpureum Joe-Pye weed	Eastern North America	Fleshy mauve/pink	Solid green stem, coarse leaves, vanilla scent	3 to 8	6 to 10 ft	Eastern, mid-western North America	Wild garden, meadow, back border, cutting
Eupatorium rugosum White snakeroot	Dry uplands of eastern North America	White flower heads	Broadly oval, serrated leaf	3 to 8	3 to 4 ft	Eastern North America	Wild garden, border, cutting, shade garden

Dog fennel (Eupatorium capillifolium)

Eupatoriums can be started from seed that has been stratified for one month or from cuttings. (See *Eupatorium* chart, above.)

EUPHORBIA COROLLATA Flowering spurge, prairie baby's breath

EUPHORBIACEAE Spurge family

The flowers of *Euphorbia corollata,* dainty and white like baby's breath, can be seen growing on grassy roadsides from Florida all the way up into Canada. I have seen it in July in the Smokies and in early August blooming in the Curtis Prairie restoration at the University of Wisconsin's Arboretum. There, it is called "prairie baby's breath," and, like baby's breath (*Gypsophila*), it is wonderful for cutting.

In my garden, it begins blooming in June. It follows tulips in a space shared by purple *Liatris spicata,* with which it consorts charmingly.

Origin: Ontario to Florida, Texas

Flower: Airy sprays of small, white, profuse flowers on fine, wiry stems from May to August

Foliage: Widely spaced, almost perfectly elliptical, matte green leaves with a contrasting pale green midrib and stem

Culture	Propagate	Comment
Full sun, part shade; tough, not fussy	Seed	Spectacular plant, bouquets, dramatic, green spot screen
Full sun, part shade, moist, but well-drained soil	Seed, cuttings	Great cut flower; contain rampant rhizomes. Cultivars: 'Cori' (bright, clear blue), 'Wayside' (long-flowering, violet blue).
Full sun, moist soil	Seed, cuttings	To control height, cut back in late June. White-flowered form: 'Bartered Bride'.
Full sun, dry to medium soil	Seed, cuttings	Drought-tolerant
Full sun, moist soil, tolerates neutral soils	Seed, cuttings	'Gateway' (purple stems, purplish flowers). Similar: *E. dubium* (grows on acid soils, eastern coastal plain).
Sun, part shade, adaptable	Seed, division	Striking in fall, fresh or dry
Part shade, sun, medium to dry soil	Seed, cuttings	Cut back in late June to control height; tolerates dry soil
Part shade, sun, moist/average soil	Seed, division	Blooms in shade, nice with asters

'Gateway' Joe-Pye weed (Eupatorium maculatum)

Hardiness: Zones 3 to 8

Height: 2 to 3 feet

Regions: Northeast, Mid-Atlantic, South, Upper and Lower Midwest

Landscape use: Nice in border, as cut flowers, in meadows and prairies

Culture: Although it appears delicate, it is tough. Takes cold, heat, wind; best in full sun with good drainage.

Propagation: Seed, cuttings

FILIPENDULA RUBRA Queen-of-the-prairie
ROSACEAE Rose family

Majestic in its proportions, queen-of-the-prairie functions as a deep green foliage plant, a perennial "shrub," that blooms true cotton-candy pink. Queen-of-the-prairie combines boldly in my garden with big purple *Buddleia* and a group of stocky magenta coneflowers. Someday, I'll try the same combination with white *Buddleia* and white coneflowers. With plenty of space—at least eight square feet—and adequate moisture, queen-of-the-prairie is easy to grow.

Origin: Midwest east to Pennsylvania and south to Georgia and Kentucky

Flower: Cotton-candy pink plume in July

Foliage: Dark green, deeply cut, six-fingered leaves

Hardiness: Zones 3 to 9

Height: 6 feet

Regions: Upper and Lower Midwest, Northeast, Mid-Atlantic, South

Landscape use: Bold accent, specimen, hedge, back-of-border plant

Culture: Queen-of-the-prairie thrives in a rich, moist soil and tolerates wet soil. Give it full sun. Although it is not invasive, it spreads by stolons to form sizable clumps.

Cultivars: 'Venusta', a deep rose

Propagation: Seed

GAILLARDIA Blanket flower, Indian blanket
COMPOSITAE Sunflower family

Blanket flowers like full sun and don't mind fast-draining soil, making them perfect for gardens near the beach. Although they come in solid colors, the common name refers to the typically striped petals in the same reds and golds as Indian blankets. The threadleaf coreopsis 'Golden Showers', with its golden flowers, and the smaller eared coreopsis are good companion plants.

The blanket flower most frequently seen in garden

Gaillardia

Name	Origin	Flower	Foliage	Zones	Height	Regions	Landscape Use
Gaillardia aristata Firewheel, blanket flower	North Dakota to Colorado, south-western Canada, Oregon	Red and yellow daisy flower with yellow tips	Light green, velvety	3 to 10	2 ft	Northwest, Canada, Mountain, Southwest, California, Midwest	Border, meadow, cutting
Gaillardia x *grandiflora* Indian blanket, blanket flower	Hybrid	Red, yellow, orange, maroon variations	Light green	3 to 10	10 in to 2 ft	Grows anywhere with fast-draining soil, sun	Edger, front border, meadow, cutting
Gaillardia pulchella Indian blanket, firewheel	Florida, Virginia to New Mexico, north to Colorado, Missouri	Yellow, red with yellow tips	Light green	annual	12 to 20 in	Grows in sunny, well-drained soil	Border, meadow, cutting

Prairie baby's breath (Euphorbia corollata)

centers is *Gaillardia* x *grandiflora,* very vigorous and easy to grow, a cross that in the wild occurs between two native species, G. *aristata* and the annual G. *pulchella.*

As with many garden-worthy native American species, controlled breeding of *Gaillardia* has been done abroad. Crosses yielded cold-tolerant plants with defined colors such as 'Burgundy' (all wine red) or 'Golden Goblin' (all golden yellow).

What has never been bred into blanket flowers is damp-tolerance. Although with excellent drainage and full sun this western native will bloom from May to September, it dies in cold, wet clay—without fail, in my garden. The problem is winter's cold dampness. For those with sun-baked, fast-draining, sandy soil or places at the beach, this is a great, colorful, floriferous plant that self-sows in an auspicious place. Others would do better to grow it in containers or to plant the annual *Gaillardia.* (See *Gaillardia* chart, above.)

GAURA LINDHEIMERI Gaura
ONAGRACEAE Evening primrose family

The first season I grew gaura, I couldn't figure out what all the fuss was about. The flowers were pretty enough close up, but that first year, their habit looked hopeless: gangly, with the small white flowers carried along long stems that flopped on the ground. The problem, as it turned out, was not with the gaura, but with

Queen-of-the-prairie (Filipendula rubra) *with purple butterfly bush and white Culver's root*

Culture	Propagate	Comment
Sun, excellent drainage, light soil	Seed	Drought-tolerant when established; cutting flowers lengthens bloom; thrives in hot, dry places, sandy soil
Sun, excellent drainage, light soil	Seed, cuttings	Needs light soil to survive in winter. Many cultivars with different colors, sizes: 'Burgundy' (red), 'Tangerine' (orange), 'Baby Cole' (red, yellow, 6 in), Goblin' (red, yellow, 12 in), etc.
Sun, excellent drainage, light soil	Seed, cuttings	Very floriferous, thrives in hot spots. The cultivar 'Lorenziana' has frilly pom-pom flowers.

Indian blanket (Gaillardia) in the front border

the place I had put it. I now grow it on a slight incline in a well-drained position with full sun where it looks good and produces an endless supply of white flowers that gradually turn pink as they age. Its airy sprays arch and lean and weave over and around its neighbors—for months! It does the same thing with great charm in bouquets or in a (dry-ish) meadow with more voluminous neighbors.

Origin: Louisiana, Texas, and Mexico

Flower: White to pink, June to October

Foliage: Light green

Hardiness: Zones 6 to 9

Height: 24 to 30 inches

Regions: Northeast, Mid-Atlantic, South, Lower Midwest, parts of Southwest

Landscape use: Borders, meadows

Culture: Full sun, good drainage. Gaura tolerates a dry spot. Cut it back after flowering to keep order.

Cultivar: 'Whirling Butterflies'

Propagation: Seed

GENTIANA ANDREWSII Bottle gentian
GENTIANACEAE Gentian family

My first gentian plant came in a box from Prairie Nursery in Westfield, Wisconsin. It was the bottle gentian, *G. andrewsii,* a "closed" gentian that always looks like a big bud that's about to open, but never does. Before it bloomed, I thought that the name "bottle gentian" referred to its shape, but the minute I saw the flower, I knew that it was a description of the bluest flower I had ever seen, the color of a cobalt bottle held up to the light.

Plant bottle gentian in moist soil where it will receive some sunlight. It doesn't bloom until late summer or early autumn, a treat worth waiting for.

Origin: Throughout eastern North America

Flower: A flower that looks, in August/September, as if it is just about to open, but never does. It is a deep blue that is, according to the late horticulturist Hal Bruce, "the mother of blueness itself, the primal, original, very source of blue."

Foliage: Handsome, clean, glossy green lance-shaped leaves whorled about 1-foot stems

Hardiness: Zones 3 to 7

Height: 12 to 15 inches

Regions: Coastal Northwest, Upper and Lower Midwest, eastern Canada, Northeast, Mid-Atlantic

Landscape use: Wild garden, sun-dappled edge of woodland

Culture: Bottle gentian requires acid soil, some sun, and moisture—just about the same conditions required for cardinal flower.

Species/cultivars: There are many. Closed, bottle, or blind gentian (*G. clausa*), from Maine to Minnesota south to North Carolina and Missouri, resembles *G. andrewsii* but is smaller. *G. saponaria* is similar, but pale violet. *G. flavida* is a closed flower that is cream colored.

Gaura (Gaura lindheimeri)

GERANIUM MACULATUM Wild geranium
GERANIACEAE Geranium family

Tough and adaptable, wild geranium will grow just about anywhere in North America. Curiously, my first experience with scented geraniums was in a hill station in South India. The cottage I had rented there had once housed vacationing missionaries in the days of the British Raj. Wild geranium of a species I did not know had taken over the beds and scented the air after the monsoon rains.

With that hill station in mind, I planted *G. maculatum* on a shady hill and (perhaps because of lack of visual competition) it draws attention in fall and early winter, when cold weather brings out the red-purple hues in the stems and leaves, which turn brilliant rose. Otherwise, it's a clean, flower-dotted, aromatic, green ground cover that smothers weeds. Although it spreads too quickly to stay in its place in a flower border, it is the nicest way of keeping a bit of garden weed-free and under control until you have the time and inspiration to do something else with it. And it smells wonderful after a rain.

Origin: North America
Flower: 1½-inch pink in May and sporadically until frost; also white
Foliage: Deeply cut, 4-inch leaves are downy and medium green above, pale green below, fragrant. Semievergreen; leaves turn burgundy/red over winter.
Hardiness: Zones 2 to 8

Height: To 15 inches
Region: North America
Landscape use: Fragrant ground cover
Culture: Grow in humusy soil, moist to dry, shade to full sun. When well established, wild geranium will spread and smother weedy competition.
Propagation: By root division; plant roots 2 inches below the ground in fall. Also by seed.

GEUM TRIFLORUM Prairie smoke
ROSACEAE Rose family

Tough and adaptable, prairie smoke is deceptively delicate in appearance, especially when its deeply cut, hairy leaves emerge in the earliest of cold northern springs. It gets its common name from its silvery pink, feathery seed heads, showier than the rosy flowers, reminiscent of upside-down medieval foolscaps. In the wild, prairie smoke, which spreads by rhizomes to form great drifts, does indeed appear to be a low cloud of smoke. The botanical epithet "triflorum" refers to the flowers' appearance in groups of three. In the garden, prairie smoke's small stature and long season of showiness make it ideal for a low ground cover, perhaps in place of lawn, mixed with tiny bulbs and one of the short, ever-

Bottle gentian (Gentiana andrewsii)

green sedges that are being tried as lawn substitutes.

Prairie smoke's seeds require cold stratification, and plants develop slowly. Division is easier, faster.
Origin: Alberta and British Columbia south to Washington and New Mexico
Flower: Rosy balls with long, prominent bracts in threes

Wild geranium (Geranium maculatum)

Foliage: Attractive, deeply cut, hairy green leaves are handsome as a ground cover and turn shades of red and mahogany in fall.

Hardiness: Zones 1 to 6

Height: To 1 foot

Regions: Central Canada, Upper Midwest, cold parts of the Southwest, Mountain

Landscape use: Distinctive and handsome ground cover, wild garden, low prairie

Culture: Medium to dry soil, good drainage; transplant in fall or very early spring

Propagation: Seed

HELIANTHUS Sunflower
COMPOSITAE Sunflower family

When most people think of a sunflower, the one that comes to mind is the familiar annual one, beloved of children and squirrels, *Helianthus annuus.* It, along with about 150 other species, belongs to a large New World family with members in every state and every cultural niche. With so many pretty representatives, it seems odd that only Kansas had the good sense to take the sunflower as its official state flower.

Many of the sunflower species are potentially excellent perennial garden plants just waiting to be discovered. True to their name, they all require sun and thrive in the high temperatures of North American summers. Most are late bloomers that provide welcome seeds for birds (children, squirrels) in the fall.

Very often, they grow so tall, they flop over. Dogs, children, thunderstorms, can beat them down. It was ever so. "It is needefull that it leane to some thynge, where it groweth, or elles it will bee alwaies falling," wrote Nicholas Monardes of a sunflower in *Joyfull Newes out of the Newe Founde Worlde* (1577). To avoid flopping and to encourage shrubby growth, cut one-third to one-half of the sunflower plant back in late June (May for early bloomers).

There are so many good sunflowers, it's hard to choose. In my garden, Maximilian's sunflower *(H. maximiliani),* one of the tallest members of a tall family, is part of a back-of-the-border screen with some large ornamental grasses. It would also serve brilliantly all by itself on a lawn as a big, warm-season shrub that blooms from late August until frost. Big yellow flowers and attractive light green seedpods form, hollyhock fashion, all along its stalk, making instant arrangements.

Why drought-tolerant willowleaf sunflower (*H. salicifolius*), from dry limestone areas of the West, performs so well in my Mid-Atlantic, acid, moist, Zone 7 garden is a great mystery for which I am profoundly grateful. This plant is valuable for its bushy, leathery, dark green foliage alone—especially in the dog days, when it looks refreshingly green and unscathed by all of the terrible things that attack plants when they are the least bit stressed. It's a little like having a beautiful, deep green shrub come up from the roots each year. Flowers are nothing if not prolific, and they come by the dozen from September until hard frost. Combined with red, berried dogweed branches, the seed heads of the ornamental grasses northern sea oats and *Miscanthus sinensis,* and the copper red flowers of sedum 'Autumn Joy', willowleaf sunflower's bright golden daisy flowers make striking autumn arrangements.

Prairie smoke's (Geum triflorum) *foliage turns color in fall.*

Perennials

Helianthus

Name	Origin	Flower	Foliage	Zones	Height	Regions	Landscape Use
Helianthus angustifolius Swamp sunflower	Acid bogs, Florida to Texas, New York to Indiana	2 to 3 in, yellow with a maroon center, in October	Long, narrow, glossy, attractive	6 to 9	6 to 8 ft	Eastern, mid-western United States	Back border, specimen
Helianthus californicus California sunflower	California, riparian settings	2 in, yellow, from July into fall	Rough, medium green	7 to 8	6 to 8 ft	California	Back border, with large shrubs, perennials
Helianthus debilis Beach sunflower	Florida dunes, Gulf Coast	3 in, golden yellow with brown center, annual	Rough, dark green on recumbent stems	7 to 8	2 to 6 ft	South, beach gardens	Ground cover, accent
Helianthus giganteus Giant sunflower	Maine to Georgia, Minnesota, Illinois	3 in, deep yellow, in October	Narrow leaves taper at the ends	4 to 8	12 ft	Eastern, mid-western United States	Against walls, specimen
Helianthus hirsutus Hairy sunflower	Southeastern United States	3 in, pale yellow, in July, August	Velvety, medium green leaves	5 to 8	3 to 5 ft	Southeastern United States	Border
Helianthus maximiliani Maximilian's sunflower	Dry sites, British Columbia, east to Texas, Missouri	3 in, rich yellow, August to hard frost	Pale green, long, narrow leaves	3 to 8	7 to 10 ft	Western North America, but very adaptable	Specimen, border
Helianthus mollis Downy sunflower	Prairies, Massachusetts, Wisconsin, Kansas, Oklahoma, Texas	3 in, butter yellow, in August, September	Hairy, medium green leaves	4 to 7	3 to 5 ft	Midwest	Specimen, border
Helianthus occidentalis Western sunflower	Western United States	4 in, dark gold disk, in July, August	Clumping	4 to 8	4 ft	Western United States	Cutting, border, accent
Helianthus x multiflorus 'Loddon Gold'	*H. annuus* x *H. decapetalus*	2 in, double, gold, July to September	Bushy, dark green	4 to 9	4 ft	Adaptable	Cutting, border, summer hedge
Helianthus x multiflorus 'Flora Pleno'	*H. annuus* x *H. decapetalus*	2 in, double, yellow, July to September	Bushy, dark green	4 to 9	6 ft	Adaptable	Cutting, border, summer hedge
Helianthus salicifolius Willowleaf sunflower	Dry, limestone areas, Missouri, Kansas, Oklahoma, Texas	3 in, yellow, September until frost	Very narrow, dark green, leathery, drooping leaves	3 to 8	5 to 8 ft	Lower Midwest, but very adaptable	Hedge, cutting, border
Helianthus tuberosus Jerusalem artichoke	Nova Scotia to Florida, west to Texas	3 in, yellow, August, September	Medium green, broad, rough leaves	3 to 8	6 to 10 ft	North America	Back border, edible

"Hairy sunflower" (*H. hirsutus*) is an unappealing name for an outstanding, fuss-free plant. Small, pale yellow flowers work well with other border plants. The airy, flower-studded stems weave over and around the solid forms of ironweed and maiden grass. Swamp sunflower (*H. angustifolius*), a fall bloomer, is a 7-foot beauty that quickly forms a handsome clump.

The hybrid 'Loddon Gold' can grow to 5 or 6 feet, topped with golden yellow, chrysanthemum-shaped flowers. To keep it an erect, shrubby 4 feet, cut it back in June. It is an easy-to-grow plant, needing only full sun for a long season of long-lasting flowers and great volume. 'Flora Pleno' is the slightly taller, yellow-flowered version. It spreads lustily. Dig up and give away the excess in spring.

Tough, drought-resistant, rhizomatous western sunflower (*H. occidentalis*) holds its large, golden flowers on

Hairy sunflower (Helianthus hirsutus) leans over pink boltonia.

Culture	Propagate	Comment
Lean soil; cut back in June	Seed, cuttings	Stunning, late
Summer water, space; cut back in fall	Seed, cuttings, division	Glorious at peak, spreads politely
Dry sandy soil	Seed, cuttings	Good with grasses
Moist soil	Seed, cuttings	Majestic, late
Adaptable	Seed, cuttings	Good blender with other perennials
Drought-tolerant	Seed	Great for flower arrangers
Poor, dry soil	Seed	Unique flowers, good in prairies
Dry soil; spreads	Seed, division	Tolerates drought, good for cutting
Adaptable	Division	Very bushy, heavy flowering, mildew
Adaptable	Division	Very bushy, floriferous
Adaptable	Seed, cuttings	Outstanding, blooms until hard frost
Rich, moist soil	Tubers	Harvesting the tubers keeps the plant in bounds; aggressive!

*Just a sprig of Maximilian's sunflower (*Helianthus maximiliani*) becomes an instant arrangement.*

leafless stalks, making it a good source of cut flowers. Jerusalem artichoke (*H. tuberosus*) is an aggressive sunflower that can be curbed by harvesting its edible roots after frost has "sweetened" them. Leave them in the ground all winter (under mulch) to dig as needed. Those not harvested by spring will begin to grow again. (See *Helianthus* chart, above.)

HEUCHERA Coral bells, alum root
SAXIFRAGACEAE Saxifrage family

Coral bells (*Heuchera sanguinea*), with their "bright coral bells upon a slender stalk," have been garden favorites for over a century. More recently, other native alum roots are sharing the limelight, valued for their attractive foliage rather than their flowers.

All alum roots have roughly the same habit. Stalks of diffuse, often whitish, flowers rise above a ruffled rosette of handsome, overlapping leaves. These leaves—with variable color, marbling, and winter hues—are causing the current excitement over this genus. A deep red leaf cross, *Heuchera micrantha* var. *diversifolia* 'Palace Purple', is a brilliant example of an American native who returns from abroad to thunderous applause: on its return to American soil in 1991, reputedly from the Royal Botanic Gardens at Kew, 'Palace Purple' was named Plant of the Year by the Perennial Plant Association. No one seems absolutely sure of its parentage, but *H. micrantha* and *H. villosa* are being tossed around as possible progenitors.

California gardener Jenny Fleming enjoys the straight species of *H. micrantha,* which she mixes with other partial-shade plants such as iris, oxalis, vancouverias, and ferns. Normally, she says, their flowers are quite lovely—tiny, white, and elegant. Another of her favorites is the cultivar 'Martha Roderick' (sometimes called 'Weott'), a beautiful shade of pink with a lacy appearance and a long period of bloom in late spring.

Another "new" alum root is *H. americana* 'Dale's Strain', named for Dale Hendricks of North Creek Nurseries, who collected seed from a specimen in the

Heuchera

Name	Origin	Flower	Foliage	Zones	Height	Regions	Landscape Use
Heuchera americana Alum root, rock geranium	Ontario to Georgia, Louisiana, Missouri	White clusters on tall, 18-in stalk, early summer	Mottled, hairy leaves turn red with cold	3 to 8	12- to 15-in clump	Eastern North America	Rock garden, ground cover, wild garden, front border, edger
Heuchera maxima Island alum root	Islands off the California coast	Many white, pink flowers on 2-ft stalks, February to April	Round, heart-shaped, dark, large to 7 in, glossy green	8 to 10	18-in clump	California	Accent, ground cover, wild garden, border
Heuchera micrantha Alum root	British Columbia to Southern California, swales, moist places	Small, diffuse, white, pink flowers on 2-ft stems in spring	Low, bold rosette, long stalked leaves, often mottled	4 to 9	9- to 12-in clump	West Coast	Ground cover, border, edger, rock garden, massing
Heuchera 'Palace Purple'	Hybrid	Many 18-in stalks, white flowers, July	Deep maroon, maple-shaped leaves	5 to 9	3- by 3-ft clump	North America	Ground cover, border, edger, massing
Heuchera richardsonii Prairie alum root	Saskatchewan, Manitoba to Minnesota, Indiana west to Rockies	Small greenish white bells on 24-in stalks, May, June	Deeply veined, lush spring foliage	3 to 7	12- to 15-in clump	Eastern, mid-western North America	Ground cover, border, edger, wild garden
Heuchera sanguinea Coral bells	New Mexico to Arizona, Mexico	Coral, white, pink, red flowers on 15-in stalks in spring	Flat rosettes with rounded leaves	4 to 9	6- to 8-in clump	Southwest	Edger, front border, rock garden
Heuchera villosa Hairy alum root	Virginia and Tennessee to Georgia	White flowers from August to September	Light green, velvety leaves in dense rosette	6 to 8	1 ft	Mid-Atlantic, South, Lower Midwest	Massing, front border, rock garden, wild garden

The roots of this yellow sunflower (Helianthus tuberosus) *are edible Jerusalem artichokes.*

wild that had silver mottled leaves. Grown from seeds, the resulting plants are variably marked in foliage. The May-blooming straight species is usually a medium green. I like it as a somewhat taller substitute for Japanese pachysandra and have it as an edging in partial shade between azaleas and lawn.

Taking full sun in the North, but part to full shade in the South, alum roots demand nothing but good drainage, and once established, they manage very well as ground covers in dry shade. Partly to fully evergreen, they change leaf color with the amount of sun or cold to which they are exposed. (See *Heuchera* chart, above.)

HIBISCUS Mallow, rose mallow
MALVACEAE Mallow family

Easy and colorful, mallows need first of all moisture and then sun to provide plenty of color and flowers during a marvelously long flowering season from late June through September. The tropical-looking flowers grow from 5 to 12 inches across—with a feathery, prominent proboscis of reproductive organs that is almost as showy as the large, floppy petals. In gardens with adequate moisture (mulching helps to conserve it), rich soil, and no competition, *Hibiscus* grow

Culture	Propagate	Comment
Full sun/shade, good drainage	Division, seed	Great ground cover, drought-tolerant when established. Selection: 'Dale's Strain'.
Part shade; established plants need little water	Seed, division	Bold, dramatic plant, needs occasional water
Full sun/shade; moist soil, easy, water or drought-tolerant	Division, seed	Outstanding garden plant, cut flowers, occasional water, tolerates drought under oaks. Cultivars include: 'Martha Roderick' (rose), 'Wendy' (pink), 'Santa Ana Cardinal' (riveting red).
Sun/part shade, average to dry soil	Division	Striking deep maroon foliage, contrasting flowers, very adaptable
Sun/part shade, average to dry soil	Seed, division	Very hardy; rich soil produces the best plants
Sun/part shade, good drainage	Seed, division	Cut flower. Cultivars include x *brizoides* 'Coral Cloud', 'Pretty 'Polly' (pink), 'Firebird' (red, 2 ft).
Sun/part shade, adaptable	Seed, division	Bright green foliage is an attractive contrast, nice in shade. Cultivar: 'Purpurea' has velvety purple leaves.

Heuchera *'Wendy'*

Alum root (Heuchera maxima) *under a coast live oak*

bigger and bushier than in the wild. With the exception of willowy *H. coccineus,* with its bobbing scarlet pinwheel flowers, the mallows look and act more like flowering shrubs than the perennials they are. They also make great container plants one can't possibly overwater. Started from seed in very early spring (indoors), they will bloom lightly the first year and copiously thereafter.

They can also be started from cuttings. (See *Hibiscus* chart on pages 112–113.)

HOUSTONIA CAERULEA Quaker ladies, bluets
RUBIACEAE Madder family

Quaker ladies are so tiny, one doesn't really think of their having an ordinary function in the garden. Words like "ground cover" or "accent" are far too clumsy for them. They would be better classed with dew-bejeweled spiderwebs and speckled robin's eggs. Quaker ladies are wonderful sown into moss for a flowery cover in late spring.

Origin: Nova Scotia, Quebec west to Wisconsin, south to Georgia, Alaska

Flower: Dozens of 1/8-inch blue, violet, or white flowers on 5- to 6-inch stems, from April to July.

Foliage: Small, grassy, 2- to 4-inch clumps

Hardiness: Zones 3 to 8

Height: 3 to 5 inches

Regions: Eastern United States and Canada

Heuchera *'Palace Purple'*

Hibiscus

Name	Origin	Flower	Foliage	Zones	Height	Regions	Landscape Use
Hibiscus coccineus Scarlet hibiscus, red mallow	Ditches, marshes of coastal plain, Alabama, Georgia, Florida	Scarlet, July–September, also pink, purple, white, 6 in	Tall stalk, elegant, large, cut leaves	7 to 10	To 10 ft	South	Accent, back border, pond edge
Hibiscus militaris Smooth marsh mallow	Swamps, marshes, Ontario and Minnesota to Texas, Florida	White, pink, 4 to 6 in, July–September	Dark green, heart/dagger-shaped	4 to 10	To 6 ft	Eastern, mid-western North America	Shrub, back border, pond edge
Hibiscus moscheutos Wild cotton, rose mallow	Marshes, Maine to Florida	White, cream, 8 to 12 in wide, July–September	Oval heart shape, toothed leaves, green above, white below, red stems	5 to 10	3 to 8 ft	Eastern United States	Shrub, border, pond edge

Landscape use: Fine tuning, a small detail

Culture: Sun to part shade, well-drained soil around the roots of trees, in the cracks of paving, rock garden

Species/cultivars: Creeping bluets (*H. michauxii*) are taller and spreading.

Propagation: Seed and division

IRIS

IRIDACEAE Iris family

Although irises hail from all over the American continent, some states get more excited about their native irises than others. Louisianans are high on their state flowers, the Louisiana irises. These native species have been crossed into a whole race of lovely irises. Before they were hybridized—indeed even before they were "discovered" in 1926 by Dr. J. K. Small, a curator of the New York Botanical Garden— early Louisiana native plant enthusiast Caroline Dormon sang their praises. In 1920, she wrote, "I think I may safely state that never before was so gorgeous a flower brought straight from the wilds to gardens." A quarter century later, author and nurseryman William Fontenot, from Prairie Basse, Louisiana, had this to say: "Sadly, breeders have neglected to make our 'straight' native species available, opting instead to sell the 'prettier' (certainly subject to debate) hybrids." Whether you grow the species or the hybrids, Louisiana irises are terrific for hot, muggy climates where they are hardy—which may be into Canada! Reports from Sioux Falls, South Dakota, Kansas, and Illinois indicate that earlier fears that they were delicate, cold-shy southerners are unfounded.

California is another state rich in species of beautiful irises that also have been crossed to create the Pacific Coast hybrids. Hybrids of both the Pacific Coast hybrids and the Louisiana irises are plentiful and easy to buy. Only some of

Scarlet hibiscus (Hibiscus coccineus)

an abundance are included in the chart on pages 114–115.

So popular, in fact, are the hybrids that some of the straight species are harder to find. Yet, their admirers find the species more desirable. Berkeley, California, gardener Jenny Fleming, whose garden clings to a windswept slope that overlooks the Bay, says of the Douglas iris; "Many hybrids are floppy and less vigorous. I much prefer the clean, crisp lines of the species flower."

Douglas iris, says Jenny Fleming, "is both a star and a workhorse in a California garden." She adds that "it does well with no summer water on the coast and occasional water (every two weeks) inland, but overhead watering can cause rust spot problems." They come easily from seed, and some I acquired that way have passed through two (very wet) winters in my Zone 7 garden.

Generally speaking, irises fall into two categories:

Culture	Propagate	Comment
Moist soil, sun	Seed, cuttings	Does well in moist sites in the garden; mulch to conserve moisture; tropical looking
Moist soil, sun, easy from seed	Seed, cuttings	Attractive red stems contrast with foliage, floriferous, cross with *H. moscheutos* 'Blue River' (white flower)
Sun, moist, need wind protection	Seed, cuttings	Salad-plate-sized flowers, showy. Many cultivars: 'Disco Belle' (shorter), 'Lord Baltimore' (red).

Wild cotton (Hibiscus moscheutos) *in a container*

those that need good drainage and those that don't. In the former camp are the dwarf crested iris, the similar, but uncrested, deep blue to purple *I. verna,* which takes more sun, and most of the West Coast irises. These do well with moist, humusy, but well-drained soil during the growing season (late winter through spring). Thereafter, they tolerate dryness in varying degrees.

Among the irises that take to wet places are the Louisiana irises and the blue flag irises (*I. versicolor* and *I. virginiana*). I have grown a container full of blue flag irises in a little garden pool for years, letting it stay submerged over winter, often under several inches of ice. It wasn't until recently I learned that these same *I. versicolor* will do just fine in the ordinary soil next to my garden pool (that's where I have some of the exotic yellow flag irises [*I. pseudacorus*], a plant that will also grow in standing water).

My guess is that those that prefer drainage won't sur-

vive being submerged, or even prolonged wetness, but those that can live in water are capable of making it through a period of drought as long as they are moist during their late winter–early spring growing season until flowering time.

Irises grow from bulbous roots that are most successfully divided very early in spring. These divisions will produce plants identical to the original. Growing them

Quaker ladies (Houstonia caerulea) *in a mossy rock garden*
(Kim Hawks Design)

Iris hexagona, *one of the Louisiana irises*

Iris

Name	Origin	Flower	Foliage	Zones	Height	Regions	Landscape Use
Iris brevicaulis Zigzag iris, Lamance iris, short-stemmed iris	Moist areas of Alabama, Texas, Louisiana, Ohio, Kansas	5 in, blue to lavender, May/June	Lengthens after bloom	6 to 9	To 10 in	South, Mid-Atlantic, Midwest	Water garden, border, pond side
Iris cristata Dwarf crested iris	Woodland from Maryland to Georgia, Missouri	3 to 4 in, lavender-blue flowers with crested petals	Neat, pale green, disappears mid-summer if too dry	3 to 8	6 in	Eastern, mid-western North America	Rock garden, edger
Iris douglasiana Douglas iris	Coastal grasslands, open woods of Oregon, California	Lavender-blue, yellow, rarely white, January/February	Deep green above, pale underside, in neat fans, russet when old	7 to 8	6 to 18 in	Northwest, California	Border, erosion control on slopes, massing, rock gardens, naturalizing
Iris fulva Red flag iris, copper iris	Wet, low places from Louisiana, Georgia to Illinois, Missouri, Texas	Brick red to red	Long, narrow, blue green	6 to 9	2 to 3 ft	South, Lower Midwest	Water garden, border, pond side
Iris giganticaerulea Giant blue iris, blue flag iris	Freshwater marshes, Louisiana, Texas	7 in, blue-purple, April/May	Long, narrow, light green, straight stalk	8 to 9	5 ft	South, Lower Midwest	Water garden, border, pond side
Iris hexagona	Swamps, Louisiana, Texas, South Carolina, Florida	3 to 4 in, blue to lavender, May/June	Neat fan of light green leaves	7 to 9	2 ft	South, Mid-Atlantic	Water garden, border, pond side
Iris innominata Golden iris	Open woodland, Oregon, California	Gold to yellow, also lavender, purple	Relaxed, narrow, grasslike clumps, evergreen	6 to 8	12 in	Northwest, California	Border, naturalizing, rock garden
Iris missouriensis Rocky Mountain iris, Western blue flag	British Columbia, South Dakota to California, Arizona, Mexico	Lavender, blue with purple veins	Blue green	5 to 9	2 ft	Western North America	Border, stream or pond side
Iris setosa Alaska iris	Alaska, Asia	Blue, red-purple	Sword-shaped	5 to 7	8 to 12 in	Northwest	Rock garden
Iris tenax Grass iris, tough-leaf iris	Oregon and Washington	Pink, lavender	Fibrous, very narrow	6(?) to 8	2 ft	Northwest	Border, naturalized
Iris verna	Pennsylvania to Kentucky, Georgia	3 in, blue, lilac, April/May	Glossy evergreen	5 to 8	6 to 8 in	Eastern United States	Rock garden, ground cover
Iris versicolor Blue flag	Eastern Canada to Pennsylvania, Minnesota	3 in, blue-purple flowers in May	Very narrow, medium green	4 to 8	30 to 36 in	Eastern, mid-western North America	Water garden, pond side
Iris virginica (*I. caroliniana*) Southern blue flag	Coastal plain, Virginia to Texas	3 in, lavender, May/June	Bold, semi-evergreen	7 to 10	30 in	South	Water garden, pond side

from seed is slower but easy, and produces great variety in plants that bloom the second year. Different species of iris may also cross on their own.

Irises, as elegant as cattleya orchids, are carefree, requiring only division when they get too crowded. They carry their large, shapely blooms above neat foliage that maintains its presence in the garden long after the flowers have faded. Iris flowers are variable, most often shades of blue or purple, and marked with attractive lines and white and yellow blotches that both delight gardeners and serve as nectar guides for bees. Tiger swallowtails are some of the butterflies that partake of the nectar. (See *Iris* chart, above.)

KOSTELETZKYA VIRGINICA Marsh mallow, seashore mallow
MALVACEAE Mallow family

In the wild, marsh mallow is found on the wet edges of marshland. However, like the hibiscus cousins it resembles, it is quite adaptable and will thrive in average garden soil and doesn't mind the salt air of beach

Culture	Propagate	Comment
Pool, bog, or moist garden soil, full sun	Offsets, seed	Wet soil or soil that is moist during growing season, Louisiana Iris parent, butterfly plant
Well-drained soil in part shade	Division, seed	Short period of bloom, but handsome foliage throughout growing season, spreads rapidly, tolerates dry shade
Dry soil, sun to part shade; transplants well, spreads; cut back September	Division, offsets, seed	Bombproof in California, showy, variable, many hybrids, butterfly plant, good foliage, no overhead water, cut back in September
Pool, bog, or moist garden soil, full sun to part shade	Offsets, seed	Unusual color, small flowers, wet or ordinary soil, Louisiana iris parent, butterfly plant
Pond, marsh plant	Offsets, seed	Bold iris with lightly scented flowers, Louisiana iris parent
Pool, bog plant, or ordinary garden	Offsets, seed	Wet or ordinary soil, easy from seed, butterfly plant, vigorous!
Sun, part shade, good drainage	Offsets, seed	Minimal water in summer; light, rich soil; excellent drainage
Moist to wet soil, full sun	Division, seed	Tolerates summer dry if moist/wet during growing season, rhizomatous
Moist soil, sun	Division, seed	Delicate flowers. Variety: *canadensis* (dwarf, very hardy)
Medium moist soil, sun	Offsets, seed	Nice in meadow. Variety: *gormanii*, (pale yellow flowers).
Well-drained soil, sun	Division, seed	Similar to *I. cristata,* but takes more sun, spreads more slowly. Variety: *smalliana* (4 to 6 in).
Pool, bog, or garden soil, full sun	Division	Wet or ordinary garden soil, spreads vigorously
Pool, bog, or garden soil, full sun	Division, seed	Southern form of *I. versicolor,* wet or ordinary garden soil, spreads, big, vigorous, varies. Cultivar: 'Contraband Girl'.

Iris douglasiana, *Douglas iris*

Iris cristata alba, *a white form of the crested iris*

gardens. In my garden, at this moment, it creates a pink event with *Sedum* 'Autumn Joy' in its pink phase and *Boltonia* 'Pink Beauty'. It would be nice, also, edged with the deep pink *Coreopsis rosea*. The marsh mallow is covered with pink "hollyhock" flowers, each with a prominent yellow proboscis. After a flower fades, it is eclipsed by new growth and new flowers. In this manner, the marsh mallow grows quickly to a broad pyramid that will need plenty of space, perhaps 5 feet, when it is mature. Propagate marsh mallow by seeds or cuttings.

Origin: Coastal marshes from New York to Louisiana

Flower: Pink, June to September
Foliage: Matte green, roughly triangular, wider at the base
Hardiness: Zone 7
Height: To 5 feet

Liatris

Name	Origin	Flower	Foliage	Zones	Height	Regions	Landscape Use
Liatris aspera Rough blazing star	Ontario, Ohio to South Dakota, Texas, South Carolina	Bright magenta flowers, widely spaced on 3-ft stalk	Lance-shaped in clump, narrow on stem	3 to 8	To 6 ft	Midwestern North America	Border, meadow, wild garden
Liatris cylindracea Dwarf blazing star	Ontario, Minnesota to Arkansas	Rosy purple spike, many ½-in flowers, July/August	10-in clump of narrow leaves	3 to 7	8 in to 2 ft	Midwestern North America	Rock garden, front border
Liatris ligulistylis Rocky Mountain blazing star	Wisconsin, Alberta to Colorado, New Mexico	Multiple bright purple spikes in July/August	Narrow, dark green clump, leaves on stem	3 to 9	To 3 ft	Midwest, Southwest	Border, meadow, wild garden
Liatris microcephala Small-headed blazing star	Tennessee, Mississippi	Lavender spikes in August/September	10-in clump of grasslike leaves	6 to 8	To 2 ft	Midwest	Ground cover, front border, wild garden
Liatris mucronata Gayfeather	Nebraska to Mexico	Rose-purple spikes in fall	15-in grassy clump	4 to 9	To 3 ft	Midwest	Border, meadow, wild garden
Liatris punctata Spotted gayfeather	Alberta, Manitoba, Iowa, New Mexico	Bright purple flower spikes, July/August	Low clump of medium green, short leaves along stem	3 to 6	To 3 ft	Midwestern, southwestern North America	Border, meadow, wild garden
Liatris pycnostachya Prairie blazing star, gayfeather	South Dakota to Florida, Louisiana, Texas	Tightly packed magenta flower spikes, August	Narrow, dark green leaves along stalk	4 to 9	4 to 6 ft	Eastern, midwestern, southern North America	Border, meadow
Liatris scariosa Scaly blazing star	Mountains of Pennsylvania, South Carolina, Georgia	Lavender flowers, summer	Narrow, green	5 to 8	2 to 3 ft	Eastern North America	Border, meadow
Liatris spicata Spike gayfeather	New York, Michigan to Florida, Louisiana	Magenta flower spikes, July/August	Dark green, narrow leaves along stem	3 to 9	To 5 ft	Eastern, midwestern North America	Border, meadow, wild garden
Liatris tenuifolia Blazing star	Gulf Coast	Long, narrow, rose-purple spikes, August–October	2-ft clump of grassy leaves	7 to 8	To 6 ft	South	Border, meadow

Seashore or marsh mallow (Kosteletzkya virginica)

(Jessie Harris photo)

Regions: Mid-Atlantic, South
Landscape use: Back border, seashore plant
Culture: Full sun, moist to wet soil
Propagation: Seed

LIATRIS Gayfeather, blazing star
COMPOSITAE Sunflower family

Of the 40 species of *Liatris,* a wholly North American genus, there is certain to be one for every garden from the Rockies to the Atlantic Coast. The best-known species, spike gayfeather (*L. spicata*), is widely known and grown. Tightly packed along rigid stalks, the ciliate rose-purple to magenta flowers open from top to bottom, lending new spikes the aspect of feathery, pink baseball bats. They are terrific cut flowers and dry beautifully, keeping their rosy color. Prairie blazing star or button snakeroot (*L. pycnostachya*) is similar, but taller and requires more moisture.

Culture	Propagate	Comment
Full sun, well-drained soil	Seed, division	Striking flower, drought-tolerant when established
Full sun, dry; drought-resistant when established	Seed, division	Good for dry soils, very small plant
Sun, rich soil	Seed, division	Showy, good wildlife plant, attracts finches
Sun, medium to dry, average to infertile soil	Seed, division	Nice small size, tolerates poor soil, drought-tolerant
Sun, thin, well-drained soil	Seed, division	Tolerates limestone, dry soil
Sandy, limestone soil, excellent drainage	Seed	Taprooted, hard to transplant, very drought-tolerant
Rich, moist soil, full sun	Seed, division	Showy, but immense in flower; use with large scale plants; good cut flower, dries well
Full sun, dry soil, good drainage	Seed, division	Showy, drought-tolerant when established. Cultivar: 'White Spire'.
Sun, moist but well-drained soil	Seed, division	Showy, good cut flower, dries well, see-through plant. Cultivars: 'Kobald' (dwarf), 'Alba', 'Floristan White'.
Sun, excellent drainage, thin soil	Seed, division	Dramatic, elegant flower

White blazing star (Liatris *'Floristan White'*)

Bright purple blazing stars are the heart of this perennial border at White Flower Farm, Litchfield, Connecticut.

In my garden, clumps of grasslike, medium to dark green foliage took more than two years before they developed into big, showy plants. But once they did, they became stars of the late summer garden. "Liatris," says designer Edith Eddleman, "is one of the best plants for vertical accent in the garden." After the flowers fade, the seeds are a big hit with the birds—notably finches.

Not all of the species of *Liatris* are as bold and buxom as prairie blazing star or spike gayfeather. *L. tenuifolia*, a denizen of dry, sandy sites along the Gulf coastal plain, bears elegant, thin spikes of lavender-rose flowers up to 18 inches long on stalks that rise to 6 feet. *Liatris elegans*, a species that inhabits sandy soils from Texas to South Carolina, bears ghostly spikes of spidery pale pink flowers, sometimes accented a deep rose. *Liatris microcephala*, with short, grassy foliage and correspondingly small flowers, grows only 1 to 2 feet tall.

All *Liatris*es need full sun and good drainage. Most are drought-tolerant once established. Some—notably *L. punctata* and *L. mucronata*—grow happily in exceedingly dry sites. Most grow easily from seed, although at least one—*L. punctata*—may benefit from moist stratification. A faster, easier way to multiply plants is to dig up the

Lilium

Name	Origin	Flower	Foliage	Zones	Height	Regions	Landscape Use
Lilium canadense Canada lily	Damp woods, thickets of Quebec, Minnesota to uplands of Virginia, Alabama	Yellow, orange, or red, spotted, bell-shaped, summer	Narrow, green on stout stalk	3 to 6	To 7 ft	Eastern North America	Woodland garden
Lilium catesbaei Leopard lily, pine lily	Bogs, swamps, pinewoods, Florida, Louisiana to Illinois, Virginia	Red-orange, spotted flower, in summer	Narrow, grassy leaves	6 to 8	To 3 ft	Eastern United States	Bog garden, low spots
Lilium columbianum Tiger lily, Columbia lily	Meadows, coniferous woods, British Columbia to Northern California coast ranges	Yellow-orange or maroon, in summer	3-in leaves, whorled or scattered	6 to 9	To 4 ft	Northwestern North America	Dry border
Lilium michiganense Michigan lily	Moist woods, thickets of Ontario, Manitoba south to Tennessee, Arkansas and Kansas	Orange with cinnamon freckles, loosely reflexed petals	Whorls of dark green, sword-shaped leaves	3 to 7	3 to 6 ft	Northeastern and midwestern North America	Moist border, edge of woodland
Lilium michauxii Carolina lily	Open places, high stream banks, Virginia to Florida	Orange-spotted flower	Whorls of sword leaves	7 to 10	To 4 ft	South	Pond edges, moist border
Lilium pardalinum Leopard lily, Panther lily	Coastal ranges and foothills, Sierra Nevada, California to Oregon	Orange with maroon spots, yellow throat	Long stems	6 to 10	To 7 ft	California, Northwest	Moist garden bed, edge of woods
Lilium philadelphicum Wood lily	Dry, open, acid woods, British Columbia to Maine, uplands from Arizona to North Carolina	Yellow, orange or red, up-facing flower	Whorled leaves	4 to 8	To 3 ft	North America	Dry bed, slope garden
Lilium pitkinense Pitkin marsh lily	Pitkin Marsh, Sonoma County, California	Orange-red, with black spots in umbels	Widely spaced leaves on tall stalk	7(?) to 10	To 5 ft	California	Border, woodland edge
Lilium superbum Turk's cap lily	Moist, swampy places, New Hampshire to New York, Alabama, Georgia	Candelabras of orange spotted maroon, green throat	Whorls of dark green leaves	4 to 8	To 8 ft	Eastern United States	Moist border, edge of woodland

dormant clumps in very early spring and divide the corms. The squirrels find them tasty, but, fortunately, there are plenty to share. Having worked their way up to the soil surface, these corms are often visible around established plants. (See *Liatris* chart, pages 116–117.)

LILIUM Lilies
LILIACEAE Lily family

The American continent is rich in lilies—some 25 species. With a few exceptions, all are spotted and display orange to red-orange multiple flowers carried on tall stems with whorled leaves. Some flowers are bell shaped and others have petals that recurve to form Turk's caps.

Native lilies are often considered difficult to grow. This is probably because most lilies thrive in what is in many gardens a rare combination: cool, moist, well-drained spots, rich soil, and enough sunshine to encourage bloom.

Saying "A soil could not possibly be too rich for them," Lee Morrison, of Lamtree Farm Nursery, confessed to using nearly straight, well-rotted horse manure to grow the Turk's cap lilies (*Lilium superbum*) he sells. They are perhaps the easiest to grow of the eastern lilies. Although Turk's cap lilies require plenty of moisture, they also need excellent drainage. A place where the plant will receive sunlight, but where the roots are in humusy, shaded, and cool ground, is ideal. "If you have a heavy soil, [dig a hole that is] deeper and wider," cautions Morrison, so that water will drain away. The bulbs will rot if water stands in the hole.

Because lilies are particular about their sites, it's best to try those native to your area that have been propagated locally. You may find you succeed with a lily few others can grow. The Canada and Pitkin lilies need a steady

Culture	Propagate	Comment
Moist, rich soil, part sun	Seeds, bulbs	Hanging bell flowers on reddish stems
Very moist, rich soil, part sun	Seeds, bulbs	Up-facing, single, large flower
Dry, organic soil, sun, part sun	Seeds, bulbs	Cultivar: 'Ingramii' (deep orange, relatively easy)
Rich, moist soil, part sun	Seeds, bulbs	Runners
Moist, but well-drained, sandy soil	Seeds, scales, bulbs	Similar to *L. superbum*, but more delicate in all parts
Moist all year	Seeds, bulbs	Easiest of California native lilies, variable in height, color
Sun to part sun, good drainage, dry acid soil	Seeds, scales, bulbs	Spaces between petals allow for drainage!
Sun, part sun, moisture all year	Seeds, bulbs	Small native range, easy
Part sun, moist, very rich soil	Seeds, scales, bulbs	Easier than other eastern lilies

Turk's cap lily (Lilium superbum)

supply of moisture. The wood lily prefers dry, open, acid woodland and has developed adaptations for staying dry; when it rains, gaps in the skyward-pointing flowers allow water to escape and anthers curl shut.

Growing a particular type takes not only ideal circumstances for the type, but also time. In my garden, most of a group of monstrously large bulbs of Turk's cap lilies disappeared for a year after transplanting. I assumed they had been eaten by voles. Three years later, nearly all have reappeared, towering 5 feet above a cooling canopy of 2-foot grasses and forbs; their wonderful candelabras of maroon-spotted golden orange blossoms open in July.

In a swale that is moist all year, Michigan lily (*Lilium michiganense*), roughly similar to Turk's cap lily, has done well for me without the disappearing act.

Luck as well as careful siting seems to be a factor in growing lilies, because they are not without destructive

admirers. Deer eat the tops. Voles eat the bulbs. Cavorting dogs can destroy an entire plant in moments. But should they survive, they are truly spectacular, long lived, and worth the effort.

Perhaps the hardest thing about growing native lilies is finding a source for plants that have not been collected from the wild. The lily bulbs will not be cheap, but consider them an investment. Good sources are out there, but they have to be tracked down. Begin with the listings in the back of this book, and check out your local native plant society. Some societies hold sales for members. So do arboreta with native plant collections. The Pitkin lily, a species that has almost disappeared from its natural habitat, is being propagated and sold by, among others, the UC–Berkeley Botanical Garden. The species listed on page 118 are the smattering of native lilies that have been offered for sale by reputable nurseries, arboreta, or native plant societies. They have been propagated from seed or scales, a process that takes time—about three to five years—but is not difficult.

Grower Lee Morrison offers the following advice for increasing Turk's cap lilies, which may be applied to others: Should you wish to increase your Turk's cap lily population, remove the outer two rows of scales and plant them

Cardinal flower (Lobelia cardinalis)

Height: 30 to 40 inches

Regions: Northeast, Mid-Atlantic, Midwest, South, Northwest

Landscape use: Border, meadow, wild garden

Culture: In cold climates, mulch lightly with a non-packing substance such as straw or pine straw, but remove the mulch in late winter to avoid crown rot. Cardinal flower is not exceptionally long lived; it lives about three years, but reseeds where conditions are right.

Cultivars: 'Heather' (peach-pink) from Niche Gardens, Chapel Hill, North Carolina, 'Alba' (white), 'Ruby Slippers' (a gorgeous wine color), 'Pink Flamingo' (dark pink)

Propagation: Seed, cuttings

like seeds about two inches deep around the rim of the hole prepared for the "mother" bulb—and forget about them. Most should develop into "real" bulbs and surprise you with blooms in about three years. Somehow, as the scales grow and develop, they crawl deeper into the soil, so transplanting is not an issue. (See *Lilium* chart, pages 118–119.)

LOBELIA CARDINALIS Cardinal flower
LOBELIACEAE Lobelia family

Whoever said "Lobelia is more loved than grown" had a point. People look forward to the mid- to late summer, when its blazing red, 30-inch spikes and the attendant hummingbirds and butterflies appear—in the wild. There, cardinal flower finds the kind of site it prefers: in sun, along streams and in wet meadows. In the garden, that elusive combination of abundant moisture and full sun ideal for its growth is rare. Fortunately, cardinal flower will adapt to garden soil that is consistently moist, and there its brilliant flowers will not disappoint. In warmer parts of its range, it is better to site it in high shade that has constantly moist, rich soil than in a spot that is sunny but may dry out. Using a mulch or a low ground cover to shade the soil helps conserve moisture and protect the plant over winter in northern gardens, but leaving mulch on in the spring will rot the emerging plants. I can vouch for this.

Origin: New Brunswick west to Minnesota and south to Texas and Florida

Flower: Scarlet in July/August; there are white, pink, and dark red forms.

Foliage: Medium green rosette sends up flower stalks in July/August.

Hardiness: Zones 2 to 8

LOBELIA SIPHILITICA Great blue lobelia
LOBELIACEAE Lobelia family

Blue lovers, here is a source of late summer blueness! Easier to grow than its red-flowered cousin, the cardinal flower, great blue lobelia adapts

Great blue lobelia (Lobelia siphilitica)

readily to good garden soil and will grow in full sun to half shade. Flowering overlaps with that of cardinal flower for a stunning combination. Having a foil—red cardinal flower, yellow goldenrod, or pink phlox— brings out an otherwise quiet blue. Even though it isn't red or orange, great blue lobelia attracts hummingbirds.

Origin: Rich, moist soils from Maine to South Dakota and south to Kansas and North Carolina

Flower: Blue, from August into fall

Foliage: Stems arise from a medium green rosette of velvety leaves.

Hardiness: Zone 4

Height: 30 inches

Regions: Northeast, Mid-Atlantic, South, Midwest, Northwest

Landscape use: Border, wild garden, moist meadow

Culture: Rich, moist soil ensures long flowering.

Cultivars: Some crosses with *Lobelia cardinalis* exist, including *Lobelia* x *vedrariensis,* named for the French nursery where this cross between *L. cardinalis* and *L. siphilitica* was made. Flowers are a brilliant purple held on 30-inch spikes and bloom for two months.

Propagation: Seed

LUPINUS Bluebonnet, lupine
LEGUMINOSAE Pea family

Wherever lupines grow naturally—unfortunately, not in the heavy clay soil of my garden—they have their admirers, both human and insect. Humans who can't grow them can see them in the wild in the kinds of places they prefer: usually light, acid soil with excellent drainage. Along the highways of Texas (Texans certainly have the right idea about what to plant along the highways) and the back roads of Arizona, one can see bluebonnets in mid- to late April (usually), and on the coast of California a spectacular sight, the tree lupine. Most native lupines hail from the West. One showy exception is *Lupinus perennis.*

Lupines not only need specific rhizobium in the soil to grow, but they are pollinated by insects that read directions on where to go to pick up pollen by flower coloration. White spots in the fresh, new flowers are like "This Way" signs to the insect pollinators; red spots on already pollinated flowers render the flowers invisible to their insect admirers. Although lupines have an attractive, sweet smell, they have no nectar.

Nitrogen-fixing plants, lupines grow wild in poor, sandy soils that are well drained. Too much water may cause rampant growth, root rot, and death. Particularly susceptible is

White lupines (Lupinus) *(Rosa Finsley Design)*

the tree lupine (*Lupinus arboreus*).

The lupines generally offered for sale, the Russell hybrids, were bred in England. I've had no luck with them, either. Of uncertain parentage, they may or may not have American blood.

Betsy Clebsch, sage fanatic and lupine lover, contributed to the lupine chart on pages 122–123, which includes a few of many native lupines.

MAIANTHEMUM False lily-of-the-valley
LILIACEAE Lily family

Aggressive, but handsome as a carpeter in shade, false lily-of-the-valley isn't for everyone and everywhere. Both the eastern form, *M. canadense,* and the western one, *M. dilitatum,* spread by rhizomes to form dense masses of glossy green foliage. Both prefer cooler

Lupinus

Name	Origin	Flower	Foliage	Zones	Height	Regions	Landscape Use
Lupinus albifrons Silver bush lupine	California	Blue/purple with white, April/June	Pale green	Probably 8 to 10	Varies, to 3 ft	California	Border
Lupinus arboreus Tree lupine	California	Fragrant, butter yellow, for 1+ month, early summer	Gray-green, evergreen	8b to 10	4 to 5 ft	California	Back border
Lupinus neomexicanus Silver lupine	New Mexico	Lavender flowers, early summer	Silver gray	6(?) to 8	2 ft	Southwest	Border
Lupinus perennis Wild lupine, sundial lupine	Maine to Florida	Sky blue flowers, May	Dark green	4 to 9	2 ft	Sandy soils of the eastern United States	Meadow, border
Lupinus texensis Texas bluebonnet	Texas	Dark blue/white flowers, April	Light green	Annual	12 in	Texas, Southwest	Meadow, border

*False lily-of-the-valley (*Maianthemum dilitatum*),
Connecticut College Arboretum*

summers than are found in the South. Places where its spreading tendency is an advantage—like shady slopes or dark, woodsy corners—exist in most landscapes.

Maianthemum canadense False lily-of-the-valley

Origin: Newfoundland to British Columbia, south to Georgia and Tennessee

Flower: Fragrant, white 2-inch racemes in early summer, followed by a cluster of small, pale red berries in fall

Foliage: Glossy, deep green, 4 inches long

Hardiness: Zones 3 to 7

Height: 3 to 6 inches

Regions: Northeast, Midwest, Mid-Atlantic

Landscape use: Ground cover in shade

Culture: Moist, rich, humusy shade

Propagation: Division

Maianthemum dilitatum (M. kamtschaticum) False lily-of-the-valley

Origin: Alaska, British Columbia to Idaho, northern California

Flower: 2-inch raceme of white flowers in early summer, followed by fall berries

Foliage: Glossy, heart-shaped leaves to 6 inches

Hardiness: Zones 3 to 6

Height: 4 to 6 inches

*Creeping mint (*Meehania cordata*) (Jessie Harris photo)*

Culture	Propagate	Comment
Full sun, good drainage, no summer water	Seed	A shrub, drought-tolerant
Good drainage, loose soil, full sun, water once every two to three weeks	Seed	Good cut flower, easy from seed. Variety: *L. a. eximius* (inland form, not as robust, pale yellow flowers), rampant with more water.
Sow in fall; poor, sandy, well-drained soil; hard to transplant	Seed	Silvery foliage, heat-tolerant, drought-tolerant
Sun, good drainage, sandy loam to dry sandy soil, no clay!	Seed	Easy from seed, carefree in sandy, well-drained soil
Full sun; well-drained, poor, sandy soil; annual, sow in place	Seed	Excellent cut flower. Species: *L. subcarnosus* (similar).

Regions: Alaska, Northwest, northern California
Landscape use: Ground cover for shade
Culture: Moist, humusy shade
Propagation: Division

MEEHANIA CORDATA Creeping mint
LABIATAE Mint family

Richard E. Weaver, Jr., one of the two owner/operators of We-Du Nursery in Marion, North Carolina, scours the wilds for beautiful and garden-worthy native flowers, most of which are still unknown to gardeners. (For this reason, my We-Du catalog becomes dog-eared within days of its arrival.) He calls creeping mint a prime example of such a plant. Low-growing and reminiscent of an ajuga, but with much larger flowers, creeping mint forms a loose mat that Mr. Weaver describes as a pefect underplanting for taller woodland plants such as trilliums or Solomon's seal, or for those that go dormant early such as trout lilies or Virginia bluebells. He adds that the bright flowers appear at an opportune time, just as the riot of color in the springtime garden begins to fade.

Named to honor Thomas Meehan, distinguished botanist and horticulturist of Philadelphia in the 1800s, creeping mint's only close relatives are found in Japan. This rare plant deserves a wider audience.

Origin: Rich woods in the Appalachians from Pennsylvania to North Carolina.
Flower: 1½ inches, bright lilac, in short spikes; blooms in late spring

Blackfoot daisy (Melampodium leucanthum)

Foliage: Creeping stems with heart-shaped, semievergreen leaves
Hardiness: Probably Zones 5 to 8
Height: 2 to 4 inches
Region: Eastern United States
Landscape use: Loose ground cover in the shade garden
Culture: Shade, humus-rich soil
Propagation: Division

MELAMPODIUM LEUCANTHUM Blackfoot daisy
COMPOSITAE Sunflower family

Once established, its deep roots allow lime-loving Blackfoot daisy to survive in dry climates without watering. While intermittent deep watering in summer will increase its flowering, too much water, especially in winter, is lethal. Handsome, low-growing, Blackfoot daisy's gray-green foliage is almost evergreen, and it blooms as a mound of white daisies throughout the summer. Blackfoot daisy is difficult to propagate from seed. Buy plants.

Origin: Dry plains, limestone canyons, and rocky slopes from Kansas and Arizona to Mexico
Flower: White daisy flowers from March to November
Foliage: Glaucous, evergreen, fine, narrow, hairy leaves on a compact plant (especially if it receives no supplemental water)
Hardiness: Probably Zones 5 to 9
Height: 6 to 15 inches and more broad than tall
Regions: Southwest, dry parts of Midwest, California
Landscape use: Rock garden, edger, dry garden
Culture: Full sun, excellent drainage, tolerant of lime; prune during the warm months to discourage woodiness.
Propagation: Seed

Virginia bluebells (Mertensia virginica)
with 'Apricot Beauty' tulips

MERTENSIA VIRGINICA Virginia bluebells
BORAGINACEAE Borage family

The first time I saw a great colony of Virginia bluebells in bloom was in the backyard of a rental house in Bethesda, Maryland. Even at the height of summer, the shade from huge trees—oaks and tulip poplars—supported only a bit of anemic grass in this yard. It was astonishing, then, to see it in spring with hundreds of Virginia bluebells crowding what was usually bare ground scored by the roots of the giant trees. Now I realize that had the occupants of the house limed the soil in an attempt to raise the pH to support lawn, the Virginia bluebells would not have found the place so congenial. If they had applied a preemergent weed killer, the Virginia bluebells would have died.

The books all say Virginia bluebells need moist soil, but I think that is only during the growing season (March to May). Thereafter, the plants go dormant, so if the soil is sucked dry by large trees, it won't matter. My robustly expanding colony thrives under a chestnut in soil that dries out in summer. As they self-sow, and the hard, black tuberous roots continue to extend, every year they put on a bigger show in April, along with the daffodils. Like daffodils, Virginia bluebells do not age gracefully before disappearing for the summer. The broad, bright green leaves that are so fresh and fine in April grow coarse and turn a hard-to-ignore yellowish tan after bloom. In my garden, I foolishly allowed them to naturalize very close to a path. It is wonderful to walk the path in April, but by late May, ungainly, fading, fleshy leaves flop over the stepping stones. It would have been much better to have kept them well behind something that is pretty when they are not, like astilbe, ferns, or wild ginger. The fall-blooming white wood aster would be another excellent follow-up plant.

Origin: New York west to Kansas and south to Alabama
Flower: Pale blue, fading to pink in April
Foliage: Soft, pale green from March through April, motley yellow as it fades
Hardiness: Zones 4 to 8
Height: 18 inches
Regions: Northeast, Mid-Atlantic, South, Midwest, Northwest
Landscape use: Best used in a wild garden with another, later-developing plant to mask the after-bloom foliage
Culture: Shade to part shade, moist soil in spring
Species/cultivars: There are a number of western species of bluebells, including *M. cana* and *M. viridis,* alpines.
Propagation: Seed (stratify two months)

MIRABILIS MULTIFLORA Giant four-o'clock
NYCTAGINACEAE Four-o'clock family

For dry-climate gardens, giant four o'clock is a fast-growing, showy southwestern native perennial that covers the ground like a low shrub with bright green leaves and hundreds of magenta blossoms. Once established, the deep and extensive root system allows plants to survive with only rainfall, but they will drop leaves in a drought, as they do in winter. Giant four-o'clock stays green and flowers best if watered periodically. Its tubular flowers attract hawk moths and hummingbirds. Since the stems break off cleanly at ground level in fall, cleanup is easy.

Origin: Southern Colorado to Mexico and west to California at elevations to 8,000 feet, often under piñon

Giant four-o'clock (Mirabilis multiflora) *(Charles Mann photo)*

*Partridgeberry (*Mitchella repens*)*

and junipers, but also in open grassland

Flower: Magenta trumpet flowers in late spring and through summer if water is available

Foliage: Smooth leaves on multibranched plant that is wider than tall

Hardiness: Zones 5 to 9

Height: 1 to 2 feet

Regions: Southwest, dry parts of Midwest, southern California

Landscape use: Summer shrub, ground cover, erosion control. Because it produces lush foliage on stems 1 foot high and spreading to 3 feet, it is attractive draping retaining walls and as a ground cover in full sun or part shade.

Culture: Full sun, excellent drainage, sandy soil, but adaptable; it will flower better if not fertilized or watered to excess. If kept too wet in winter, particularly in heavy soils, the top portion of the root may rot and die back, delaying growth the following year.

Propagation: Seed that has been stratified

MITCHELLA REPENS Partridgeberry
RUBIACEAE Madder family

Partridgeberry doesn't grow even an inch tall, but it will creep, rooting as it goes, to form deep green patches that can spread to 3 feet across, if given enough time and the right conditions. The tiny, rounded leaves are a dark, shiny green with raised veins. They form a mat, studded in spring with twin tiny white flowers and in winter with bright red berries. *Hortus Third,* the mammoth reference work that sooner or later finds its way onto all gardeners' bookshelves, states that the berries are "insipid, but edible." I have never eaten

one and am not really tempted to do so.

People may think that, because of its small size, it will take too long to cover the ground, but a well-rooted pint of partridgeberry will grow to 1 foot in diameter in a year and is a wonderful plant for fine-tuning a shady planting—especially when the neighboring plants are small in scale. Mine grows around a rough stepping-stone staircase with crested iris and ebony spleenwort, moss, and, here and there, rue anemone. The setting western sun hits one portion of this planting for about an hour each summer day, and it is there that partridgeberry grows thickest and most vigorously. Holly Shimizu of the United States Botanic Garden recommends partridgeberry as one of the best ground covers for dry shade.

Origin: Humusy, acid soil from Nova Scotia to Ontario and Minnesota and south to Florida, East Texas, and eastern Mexico

Flower: Tiny, ¼-inch pinkish white flowers appear in pairs in June.

Fruit: Pairs of red berries in winter

Foliage: Dark green, leathery, veined grayish white

Hardiness: Zones 3 to 8

Height: 1 inch

Region: North America from the East Coast to Texas

Landscape use: A great finisher for shade under trees and around stepping stones; will survive light traffic

Culture: Acid soil, shade or dappled sun, drought-tolerant once established

Propagation: Hardwood cuttings

MONARDA DIDYMA Bee balm, Oswego tea
LABIATAE Mint family

A rainbow of bee balm—'Snow White', 'Cambridge Scarlet', 'Prairie Night' (purple), and 'Croftway Pink'—has been delighting gardeners, butterflies, and hummingbirds for years. Recently, a new maroon, 'Mahogany', appeared, adding a luscious and useful color to the palette. A member of the mint family, bee balm bears a bold rather than dainty flower on coarse, aromatic plants that, like all mints, are square of stem. Bee balm can be rambunctious, especially in rich soil with plenty of moisture, and this scares gardeners. Planting it in a drier, thinner soil will slow it down, but after seeing miles of it growing at the edge of woodland in Pisgah National Forest, I think the best way to use it is to find a place where its coarseness and energy work to one's advantage: at the edge of woods, on the garden side of shrubs, in a moist meadow, or in a low spot along a drive or road. There, the more bee balm

Bee balm (Monarda didyma)

Wild bergamot (Monarda fistulosa)

spreads, the bigger the show. Wherever you grow it, bear in mind the flowers face the sun (or if there is a building or large shrub on the south side, the greater light). Position it so that the shaggy flowers will face you. Incidentally, the petals (if they have been grown without chemicals) are edible and look pretty in salads.

Origin: Rich woods from southern Canada and New England south to Georgia and west to Tennessee

Flower: Scarlet, resembling a circular cockscomb, but also pink, purple, white, and maroon

Foliage: Upright showing stem between coarse, widely spaced, downy leaves that measure up to 5 inches long, with a minty fragrance

Hardiness: Zones 4 to 7

Height: 3 feet

Regions: Northeast, Mid-Atlantic, Midwest, South

Landscape use: Woodland's edge, border

Culture: Sun to part shade; prone to mildew

Cultivars: Listed above and 'Marshall's Delight', a recent introduction from Manitoba that is a great fuchsia color and reputed to be mildew-resistant. So, they say, is 'Gardenview Scarlet'.

Propagation: Cuttings, seed

MONARDA FISTULOSA Wild bergamot
LABIATAE Mint family

To my eye, wild bergamot's foliage always looks neater than that of bee balm, and it is allowed to consort with golden coreopsis in a bed close to the house, while its devil-may-care cousin runs rampant under a grove of river birch out by the barn. It is taller—up to 5 feet—lighter in color, velvety, and the leaves are smaller and more closely spaced, giving the plant a bushier look. New leaves and buds are a light green and contrast with older foliage. Flowers are tighter, but similar to those of bee balm. They appear in late June and continue blooming into August. The straight species is usually a bright lavender-pink, but there are variations. Be choosy and shop while they are blooming to find a pretty flower color and deliciously scented leaves.

Origin: Eastern North America

Flower: Violet-purple, late June to September

Foliage: Bushy, pale green

Hardiness: Zones 4 to 8

Height: To 5 feet

Region: Eastern North America

Landscape use: Border, woodland's edge

Culture: Sun, moist to medium soil

Cultivars: 'Violet Queen', deep purple flowers

Propagation: Cuttings, seed

OENOTHERA Evening primrose
ONAGRACEAE Evening primrose family

Missouri evening primrose (*O. missouriensis*) was my first evening primrose; it came into my garden about 10 years ago via the American Horticultural Society's seed exchange. At the time, I had no idea what I was getting, and was doubly delighted when the seeds germinated easily and bloomed the second season—sparsely, but the two or three lemon yellow flowers were big, perhaps 5 inches across, and borne on floppy stems that gave them a charming, coltish air. It wasn't until they'd been in place for about three years that the clump spread nicely. Nothing in spring is as

White evening primrose (Oenothera caespitosa)

Missouri evening primrose (Oenothera missouriensis)

fresh and fragile looking as those first pale, lemon yellow flowers on narrow, glossy green foliage. Looks deceive; this delicate-looking plant, like most *Oenotheras*, has proven a true survivor. Although it is said to be a lime lover, it has done well in my generally acid soil because it grows in full, baking sun at the edge of a homemade stone terrace in which the cement is continually chipping and washing away. Pale green, pointed buds that are speckled red, and the golden orange of spent blooms, join the yellow blossoms for a really colorful effect. Deadhead it to prolong bloom, making sure that you remove the seed capsule—located at the *base* of the flower stalk!

White evening primrose (*O. caespitosa*) is a western plant. I have seen it at the edge of a terrace in Phoenix, Arizona, where a seemingly endless supply of big, white, sweet-scented flowers on low plants opens late in the day and can be appreciated during the evening hours. In dry climates, it will flower throughout the summer if it is irrigated.

Pink evening primrose (*O. speciosa*) will grow just about anywhere it has full sun and good drainage, but to me, it will always be a symbol of Texas in the spring, where it grows on the roadsides and in open, grassy places, blooming by day from April through June. Because it takes over gardens, some people think it should be restricted to highway median strips. Its vigor does allow people to grow it in meadows (or even lawns!), where the competition doesn't seem to bother it and where its somewhat gangly stems have some cover.

Sundrops (*O. fruticosa*), more upright than the Missouri and white evening primroses, have been a popular ornamental for over a century. In his 1883 classic,

The English Flower Garden, William Robinson named them "amongst the finest of hardy perennials." (See *Oenothera* chart, pages 128–129.)

PACHYSANDRA PROCUMBENS American pachysandra, Allegheny spurge
BUXACEAE Boxwood family

The first time I ever noticed an American pachysandra was at the home of Dr. Richard Lighty, director of the Mt. Cuba Center for the Study of Piedmont Flora. He had a patch of it as a ground cover in shade. The matte green leaves looked familiar enough to call to mind the same old Japanese *Pachysandra terminalis* that everybody has, but they were broader, downy to the touch, and more relaxed in habit.

In addition to differences in appearance, Allegheny spurge behaves differently from Japanese pachysandra.

Pink evening primrose (Oenothera speciosa)

Oenothera

Name	Origin	Flower	Foliage	Zones	Height	Regions	Landscape Use
Oenothera caespitosa White evening primrose	Rocky slopes of Washington, California to Colorado, New Mexico	3-in white flowers, afternoon, evening, spring	Downy, red, in spring, fall	5 to 9	8 to 10 in by 24 in wide	Southwest	Edger, ground cover, rock garden
Oenothera fruticosa Sundrops	Woodland edges, Nova Scotia, Michigan to Mississippi, South Carolina	2-in golden yellow, June, July	Upright, medium green	4 to 8	1 to 2 ft	Eastern, midwestern North America	Border, woodland edge
Oenothera missouriensis ssp. *incana* Missouri evening primrose	Missouri, Kansas to Texas	To 5 in, lemon yellow, afternoon, evening May/June	Slight gloss, medium green, 5-in leaves	5 to 8	To 15 in by 30 in wide	Midwestern United States	Rock garden, edger, ground cover
Oenothera speciosa Pink evening primrose	Kansas, Texas	2 to 3 in, pink around yellow-white center, April–July	Long, wiry stems; medium green, 3-in leaves; sprawls	5 to 8	1 to 2 ft	Midwest, Southwest	Meadow, container, border
Oenothera texensis Rose evening primrose	Southern United States, South America	Rose, ½ to ¾ in, summer	Red stems, small medium green leaves	7	4 to 6 in by 20 in wide	South, Southwest	Rock garden, edger

Allegheny spurge (Pachysandra procumbens)

Wild quinine (Parthenium integrifolium)

Not only is it anything but an aggressive spreader, it also demands moist, humusy soil in part to full shade. Only in such a situation will it take root and spread—slowly. In winter, leaves turn a greenish black with silver mottling, but severe exposure will either tatter them or cause them to drop.

A good use for Allegheny spurge would be as an edger along a shady path, where its beautiful coloration can be appreciated and where more robust ground covers such as wild ginger (*Asarum canadense*) would be too invasive.
Origin: Kentucky to Louisiana and Florida
Flower: White, fragrant, *Tiarella*-like flowers in April

Culture	Propagate	Comment
Sun, good drainage beneath	Seed	Very fragrant, floriferous, wider than tall
Sun	Seed, division	Evergreen rosette in warm climates
Sun; tolerates lime, caliche; needs good drainage	Seed, division	Wider than tall, spreads, easy from seed, drought-tolerant. Cultivar: 'Greencourt Lemon' (large, lemon yellow flower).
Sun, good drainage, not fussy	Seed, division	Aggressive spreader, good cut flower, drought-tolerant
Sun, adaptable	Seed	Good finishing plant, very low, wide, easy from seed

*Scarlet firecracker (*Penstemon eatonii*) and bright pink Parry's penstemon (*Penstemon parryi*), Freeder garden*
(Christy Ten Eyck, The Planning Center Design)

Foliage: Matte green in summer, silvery variegation in winter
Hardiness: Zones 4 to 7
Height: 6 to 9 inches
Regions: Northeast, Mid-Atlantic, South, Midwest
Landscape use: Ground cover in shade
Culture: Moist shade, rich soil, little competition
Propagation: Division, seed

PARTHENIUM INTEGRIFOLIUM Wild quinine
COMPOSITAE Sunflower family

Nothing fazes wild quinine, a survivor of heat and cold, sun and wind. For over a month, it has been blooming happily in my garden, despite temperatures that have hovered in the high 90s. My only complaint is that it is too tall and upright for the place where I put it. It belongs behind something mounding, like aster 'Purple Dome' or chrysanthemum 'Silver and Gold'. Flowers that look a bit like big, loose, cotton-white yarrows are carried on sturdy, no-nonsense stems that rise 30 to 40 inches above a ruff of coarse, 7- to 10-inch-long leaves. They last forever on the plant and in bouquets.
Origin: Massachusetts, Minnesota to Georgia, and Alaska
Flower: Long-lasting, white corymb, about 8 inches across, in June and July. Flowers are faintly fragrant but have a medicinal smell when bruised. Seeds are aromatic. They are carried on stiff, upright stems.
Foliage: Leaves 7 to 10 inches long with toothed, wavy margins, no stems; grow in an attractive basal clump.

Hardiness: Zone 4
Height: To 40 inches
Regions: Northwest, Mid-Atlantic, Midwest, South, Mountain
Landscape use: Midborder, prairie, cutting garden
Culture: Sun; fertile, well-drained soil
Species/cultivars: *Parthenium argentatum,* a smaller, bushier plant with silvery flowers, comes from Texas and Mexico.
Propagation: Seed

PENSTEMON Beardtongue, penstemon, wild snapdragon
SCROPHULARIACEAE Snapdragon family

Over 200 species of penstemon are native to North America, but, without doubt, the most colorful ones come from the West. It wasn't until I visited the Desert Botanic Garden in Phoenix that I became aware of the flamboyant characters in the penstemon family. At the time of my visit, hot pink Parry's penstemon was blooming with wild abandon, accompanied by the firecracker penstemon (blazing scarlet) and *P. pseudospectabilis* (riveting pink-red).

Penstemon

Name	Origin	Flower	Foliage	Zones	Height	Regions	Landscape Use
Penstemon ambiguus Bush, sand, pink plains penstemon	Sandy mesas, grasslands of Texas panhandle, Kansas, Colorado, New Mexico, Utah into California	White to pale pink or lavender, June to September	Symmetrical mound or woody bush	5 to 8	2 to 4 ft	Southwest, adaptable in dry places	Massed in beds, borders, meadows
Penstemon barbatus Shark's head penstemon, scarlet bugler	Utah to Mexico	Scarlet, in May, June	Evergreen rosettes with purple tinge	5 to 9	2 to 4 ft	Southwest, adaptable	Mid-border, prairie
Penstemon centranthifolius	Lake County to Baja California	Long, narrow, bright orange flowers	Gray, glaucous, 1 to 3 in long, basal	8 to 10	3 to 5 ft by 2 to 3 ft wide	California	Mixed dry border
Penstemon clevelandii	San Bernardino County to Baja California	Magenta tubular flowers	Dark green to glaucous, basal	8 to 10	12 to 18 in	California	Mixed dry border
Penstemon cobaea White wild snapdragon	Southeast Nebraska to Texas	White snapdragon flowers in June, clustered at top ¼ of stems	Attractive rosette of leathery, green leaves	5 to 9	24 to 30 in	Southwest, South, very adaptable	Border, meadow
Penstemon digitalis Foxglove penstemon	Maine to South Dakota, south to Texas	Plump white flowers with fine purple veins	Finely toothed, glossy leaf	3 to 8	2 to 4 in	Eastern, midwestern United States, adaptable	Border, meadow
Penstemon eatonii Firecracker penstemon	Rocky slopes, dry plains of southern California to Arizona, Nevada, Utah	Red, April–June	Oblong green leaves	4 to 10	2 ft	Southwest, southern California, adaptable	Massed in beds, borders
Penstemon fruticosus Shrubby penstemon	Rocky Mountains to Cascades, British Columbia to Oregon	Large, purplish tube flowers	Glossy, evergreen	4 to 7	18 in	Mountain, Northwest	Rock garden, low shrub
Penstemon heterophyllus Foothill penstemon	Coast ranges of California from Humboldt to San Diego counties	Electric blue, in late spring	Glossy green leaves, woody base	Probably 8 to 10	12 to 18 in	California hills	Filler in border, good in pots
Penstemon grandiflorus Beardtongue	Prairies of Illinois, North Dakota to Wyoming, Texas	Large lavender (pink, white) flowers in May	Deep green rosette	4 to 8	2 ft	Midwest, adaptable	Borders, prairies
Penstemon parryi Parry's penstemon	Desert slopes, washes, arroyos in southern Arizona and Sonora, Mexico	Hot pink, large tube flowers, March–April	Deep green basal rosette of shiny wavy-edge leaves perfoliate on stem	6 to 10	2 ft	Southwest	Border, wonderful dryland "softener"
Penstemon pinifolius Pineleaf penstemon	Rocky slopes, ridges of southwest Arizona to Mexico	Small, scarlet tube flowers, gold throat, May–September	Small, needle-thin evergreen leaves in irregular mound, wiry stems	5 to 10	6 to 12 in high by 18 to 24 in wide	Southwest, Mountain, adaptable	Ground cover, front border, rock garden
Penstemon spectabilis	Los Angeles County to northern Baja California	Lavender blue, wide-mouth flower	Bright green, 1 to 4 in, toothed	8 to 10	3 to 5 ft by 2 to 3 ft wide	Southwest, southern California	Mixed dry border, desert gardens
Penstemon strictus Rocky Mountain penstemon	Pine forests, rocky slopes, open meadows of Colorado, New Mexico	Blue-purple flowers, in May/June	Attractive, glossy, evergreen foliage	5 to 7	18 to 30 in	Mountain, high desert, adaptable	Ground cover in small areas, borders, meadows
Penstemon tenuis Gulf Coast penstemon	Low, wet prairies of Louisiana, Texas, Arkansas	Many small pink, purple tube flowers, March–May	Bright green, perfoliate leaves	Probably 9	1 to 2 ft	South	Evergreen ground cover (with water), massed in border

Culture	Propagate	Comment
Thrives in hot, dry, sun, well-drained site, prefers sand	Seed	Very long-lived; store seed cool and dry for 1 year before sowing
Full sun/part shade, well-drained soil, weekly water in dry climates	Seed, division	Long-lived, tolerates hot, cool sites; lax stems need propping; sow in fall. Cultivars: 'Schooly's Yellow', 'Prairie Fire' (red-orange), 'Rose Elf' (rose).
Excellent air circulation, full sun, good drainage	Seed	Hummingbird plant, very adaptable, may be short lived
Requires excellent air circulation, full sun, good drainage	Seed	Hummingbird plant, very adaptable, may be short lived, unhappy in cool shade
Full sun, well-drained soil, very drought-tolerant	Seed	Large flowers, subspecies *purpureus* has deep purple flowers, tolerates lime
Medium soils in sun or light shade	Seed, cuttings	Bumblebee flower, nearly evergreen rosette. Cultivar: 'Husker Red' (red leaves with cool weather, red stems, veins).
Sun, well-drained soil	Seed	Spectacular color, hummingbird plant; very drought-tolerant, good soft foil with cacti, succulents
Sun, dry, well-drained soil	Seed	Shrub, showy flowers
Full sun, fast drainage, little water	Cuttings	Fast growing, sow seed in fall for next season's flowers; self-sows. Cultivar: 'Blue Bedder'.
Light, well-drained soil	Seed, cuttings	Transplant in fall. Threatened or endangered in some midwestern states; buy nursery propagated plants!
Excellent drainage, sun	Seed, cuttings	Spectacular in masses! Hummingbird plant, heat-, drought-tolerant.
Well-drained soil, full sun	Seed, division	There are two forms: a short, 6-in, dense, compact one and a larger (12-in) one. Attracts hummingbirds, needs sun to bloom in the East.
Requires excellent air circulation, full sun, good drainage	Seed	Sometimes considered a bit coarse, but beautiful in bloom; may be short lived
Though tolerant of heavier soils, good drainage in wet climates	Seed	Long-lived (6 to 7 years) on well-drained sites; high humidity causes mildew. Cultivar: 'Bandera'.
Sun, part-shade, tolerates a wet place	Seed	A winner! Loaded with blooms.

Sand penstemon (Penstemon ambiguus) *(Charles Mann photo)*

Prior to that visit, my impression of penstemons as sweet and rather gentle flowers was based upon my experience with those species that come from the East and survive the heavy soil of my garden: white *P. digitalis,* white *P. grandiflorus,* and white *P. smallii.* These pretty flowers will always have a place in my garden, but the dazzling western penstemons will have a special place in memory.

It is a good idea to grow only those penstemons suited to your garden and your region. I bought the pineleaf penstemon, a southwestern native, because it is reputed to be adaptable and forgiving in moist eastern gardens. To compensate for the climate, I gave it the hottest, driest spot in the garden. After several years, the foliage looks okay, but I've seen only two little scarlet flowers. It is only fair to note that others have had better luck, but I'm equally sure that still others have killed it here in soggy Maryland.

White wild snapdragon (Penstemon cobaea)

A garden phlox (Phlox paniculata) *at Wave Hill*

Gwen Kelaidis, an expert on penstemons who gardens in Denver, points out that the pineleaf penstemon is not truly a desert plant. She finds it "likes some leafmold and food here in Colorado."

Although there are exceptions, most penstemons need excellent drainage, and some are exceptionally drought-tolerant. Virtually all red ones attract hummingbirds.

Gwen Kelaidis and many others helped with the chart on pages 130–131.

PHLOX

POLEMONIACEAE Phlox family

In a genus as rich and widely grown as *Phlox,* with around 60 native species, deciding what to include and where to start might have caused problems if I gardened in more phlox-friendly soil. Unfortunately, in a Zone 7 garden with hot, miserably humid summers, pleasant autumns, icy winters, and soggy springs, climate and nature take precedence. Powdery mildew, fungus, disease, and insects take their toll on some phloxes here.

In this climate, creeping phlox (*Phlox stolonifera*) is easily first on the list as a survivor that keeps its good looks throughout the summer. It is a creeper that rapidly covers shady, woodsy ground with a mat of evergreen foliage.

In late April and most of May, creeping phlox blooms with blue to violet flower umbels held above the plants on 6-inch stems. If you were to see this plant in flower in a garden center next to a blooming wild sweet william (*P. divaricata*), you would find it pretty, but might be tempted to buy the latter for its marginally showier flowers on taller stems. However, at summer's end, after every insect in the garden has taken a bite out of wild sweet

william (and all of its cultivars!), you would choose fresh, clean, green creeping phlox hands down.

I have irreverently lumped all of the other phloxes into three categories on the basis of how they perform in this unwholesome climate. Bear in mind my bias.

First come the sun-loving creepers that perform well with sun and good drainage, including the western species: *P. amoena, P. bifida,* and *P. douglasii,* and the moss pink (*P. subulata*), unjustly despised because it is the plant luridly illustrated in ads on the back pages of Sunday supplements. A superb plant if only for its evergreen, apple green foliage, it is a great edger and ground cover and will flow prettily over a wall. *Phlox* x *procumbens* 'Variegata' is a hybrid species from a cross between *P. subulata* and *P. stolonifera,* with flowers that resemble the latter.

The other phloxes I lump into two groups: those that have all manner of foliage problems and those with good foliage that take over the garden. In the former category are wild sweet william (*P. divaricata*), *Phlox glaberrima,* and *Phlox maculata.* In my garden, these get eaten by insects, fail to thrive, or get powdery mildew. *Phlox maculata,* with earlier bloom and glossier foliage, seems somewhat more resistant to mildew. 'Omega' is a nice

Wedding phlox (Phlox carolina) *around the steps to a Texas Hill Country ranch house* (Rosa Finsley Design)

*Creeping phlox (*Phlox stolonifera*), foreground,
and blue wood phlox*

*Obedient plant (*Physostegia virginiana*), left,
with pink turtlehead*

white that will bloom in the shade.

Among the aggressives are *Phlox pilosa,* with outstanding foliage but truly frightening powers of regeneration. Some Chattahoochee-type phloxes with a wonderful red-eyed blue flower are reputed to have *pilosa* blood, but they do not spread at all and (in my garden) their foliage suffers almost as much as that of *P. divaricata.* Garden phlox (*P. paniculata*) straddles both categories. The straight species has good, healthy foliage but multiplies with a vengeance. On the other hand, its cultivars are not invasive but often suffer mildew. Farther north, in cooler, drier places, this is less of a problem. Happily, one cultivar of garden phlox has proven itself: phlox 'David', a fragrant white flower with lovely, clean, dark green leaves that—knock on wood—don't get powdery mildew. Dr. Richard Lighty, director of the Mt. Cuba Center, was alerted by native plant lover F. M. Mooberry that there was an outstanding phlox growing in the parking lot garden at the Brandywine Conservatory in Pennsylvania. It was propagated vegetatively, tested, and named for Mrs. Mooberry's

Phlox stolonifera *'Bruce's White' with grape hyacinths*
(Kim Hawks Design)

husband, David. (See *Phlox* chart, pages 134–135.)

PHYSOSTEGIA VIRGINIANA Obedient plant, false dragonhead

LABIATAE Mint family

Obedient plant has many virtues and one fault. On the good side are its long, generous bloom, distinctive vertical habit, and long-lasting pink or white flower spikes for cutting. It is also a late-summer-into-fall bloomer that is even attractive after light frosts, when its buds turn maroon. Only its aggressiveness tilts the scales in the other direction. And it *is* aggressive. The cure for this could be handled as yearly maintenance. After the first two years in the garden, lift one-half of the clump and compost it or give it to a friend, with a caveat. Repeat this every subsequent year, overcoming that strong urge to replant the excess in the thrifty way of gardeners. Recycle it instead.

Origin: New Brunswick to Minnesota and south to Missouri and South Carolina

Flower: Flower spikes of dragonhead flowers open from the bottom up, giving a triangular aspect to each spike.

Foliage: Upright stems hold leaves at right angles.

Hardiness: Zones 3 to 8

Height: To 3 feet

Regions: Northeast, Mid-Atlantic, Midwest, South

Landscape use: Border, cutting

Culture: Sun; ordinary garden soil

Cultivars: 'Summer Snow' (white), 'Vivid' (dwarf 2-foot plant, big pink flowers), 'Variegata' (rose pink flowers, variegated foliage)

Propagation: Division, seed, cuttings

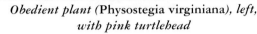

Phlox

Name	Origin	Flower	Foliage	Zones	Height	Regions	Landscape Use
Phlox amoena Chalice phlox	Rocky, sandy hills, Kentucky to Florida	Big rose-purple balls, May	Finely hirsute evergreen leaves, ⅓ in wide, blush red in winter	7 to 9	4 to 10 in	Eastern, midwestern United States	Rock garden, ground cover
Phlox bifida Sand phlox, cleft phlox	Michigan to Tennessee, Kansas, Arkansas	Lavender-blue, star flowers	Leaves like evergreen needles on low, spreading clump	2 to 9	4 to 6 in	Eastern, midwestern United States	Rock garden, ground cover
Phlox carolina (*P. suffruticosa*) Wedding phlox	North Carolina, Missouri to Florida, Mississippi	Purple, pink, sometimes white, elongated heads, in June, July	Medium green, evenly spaced leaves on upright stems	4 to 8	To 4 ft	Eastern, midwestern United States	Border, cutting
Phlox divaricata (*P. candensis*) Wood phlox, timber phlox, wild sweet william	Quebec to Michigan, south to Georgia, Alabama	Lavender, blue, white, variable, some with notched petals, April/May	Narrow leaves, variable	3 to 9	10 to 12 in	Eastern, midwestern North America	Woodland garden, shady front border
Phlox douglasii	Washington, Oregon, Montana	Pink, red, all summer	Intense green, mossy cushion	4 to 8	4 to 6 in	Western North America	Rock, scree, trough garden
Phlox glaberrima ssp. *triflora*	Maryland, Georgia to Indiana, Alabama	Large rosy, lilac heads, in May	Smooth green leaves, lax prostrate stems	3 to 10	To 2 in	Eastern, midwestern United States	Front border
Phlox nana Santa Fe phlox	New Mexico to Texas, Arizona, Mexico	Bright pink, spring, fall	Narrow, hairy leaves	5 to 10	8 to 12 in	Southwest	Ground cover, rock garden, edger
Phlox paniculata (*P. decussata*) Garden phlox	New York to Georgia, west to Illinois, Arkansas	Round heads of pink (cultivars: red, orange, purple, white), July–September	Smooth, green, lance-shaped leaves	3 to 8	3 to 6 ft	Eastern, midwestern United States	Border, wild garden
Phlox pilosa Prairie phlox, downy phlox	Michigan, North Dakota to Illinois, Kansas	Soft to bright pink	Handsome, narrow, hairy green leaves in a clump	5 to 7	To 18 in	Sandy pinelands, dry roadsides, Midwest	Front border, rock
Phlox stolonifera Creeping phlox	Pennsylvania to Georgia	Lavender, blue, pink, white, carpet, April/May	Dark evergreen round leaves creep, root along ground fall	3 to 8	2 to 6 in	Eastern United States	Great ground cover for woodland edge, part to full shade
Phlox subulata Moss phlox	New York, south to Maryland, west to Michigan	Seamless carpet, white, blue, rose, lavender flowers, May	Bright green, dense needle-thin leaves on horizontally spreading stems, evergreen	3 to 9	2 to 6 in	Eastern, midwestern United States	Ground cover, edger, wall plant, rock garden

POLYGONATUM BIFLORUM Solomon's seal
LILIACEAE Lily family

A mass of Solomon's seal's arching stems is a stately, graceful accent in a woodland garden, especially when it rises out of a low cloud of a baby blue carpeting of creeping phlox or the pure white froth of foamflower. Though Solomon seal's white-tinged green pairs of dangling bell flowers are very pretty when they bloom in May, this plant is really grown for the leaves, and the bigger they are, the better.

Rich, humusy soil with plenty of moisture and at least two hours of sun each day will grow you splendid 4-foot specimens in time. But pretty as these are in May, amid drifts of the bright golden yellow wood poppy and maidenhair ferns, they can go downhill fast in fall. In the best circumstances, they turn a lovely orangy tan. In the worst, they turn the same color but look shredded and slug-eaten. In both cases, it's nice to have something nearby to carry on until Solomon's seal returns in the spring. Fall-blooming wood aster or white snakeroot draws attention and provides cover at such a time.

Origin: Woodland from Connecticut west to Ontario

Culture	Propagate	Comment
Full sun, good drainage; to renew foliage, cut back after bloom	Cuttings	A low-grower with attractive, light green, broad leaves, nice winter color
Sun, excellent drainage	Cuttings	Very hardy, drought-tolerant; cut back yellowed foliage when new growth appears. Cultivars: 'Betty Blake', 'Starbrite' (dwarf).
Sun, part shade, moderately moist soil, cut back for rebloom	Cuttings	June bloom, more resistant to mildew than garden phlox. Grand old cultivar: 'Miss Lingard' (2 ft, white, fairly mildew-resistant).
Part shade, rich, humusy soil	Seed, cuttings	Spring carpet of flowers, good with bulbs. Cultivar: 'Laphami' (blue, fragrant). Hybrids: 'Chattahoochee', 'Eco Blue Moon' (blue with red eye).
Sun, excellent drainage	Cuttings	Plenty of good cultivars: 'Boothman's Variety' (deep mauve), 'Rose Cushion' (rose dwarf), 'Snow Queen' (white)
Sun, light shade, moist soil	Cuttings	Big lilac rose flowers on a short, prostrate plant
Full sun, dry site, excellent drainage	Seed	Long blooming, self-sows, drought-tolerant
Species tolerates shade; cultivars do best in sun; cut for rebloom	Cuttings	Space for air circulation to avoid powdery mildew; species is invasive. Many cultivars: 'Brite Eyes' (pink with dark eye), 'David' (white, mildew-resistant).
Full sun, part shade; for rebloom, cut back; average to dry soil	Division	Great foliage, can be invasive, stoloniferous. Variety: *ozarkana* (short, 15 in). Cultivar: 'Moody Blue' (blue with red eye).
Part shade, rich humusy soil; remove litter in winter	Division	1990 PPA Plant of the Year; litter can smother plants. Cultivars: 'Blue Ridge' (soft blue), 'Bruce's White' (good white).
Full sun, good drainage	Division	Deserves its popularity. Good new cultivars: 'Millstream Daphne' (pink with a yellow eye), 'Ice Mountain' (dwarf, white). *P. nivalis* is a similar species.

Solomon's seal (Polygonatum) *arches over sweet woodruff in Joanna Reed's garden.*

Culture: Moist, humusy soil in light to deep shade

Species: Great Solomon's seal (*P. commutatum*) grows to 6 feet.

Cultivars: German horticulturists have crossed species from around the world to produce hybrids like 'Weihenstephan' (early blooming, vigorous).

Propagation: Root cuttings

PORTERANTHUS TRIFOLIATUS (GILLENIA TRIFOLIATA) Bowman's root, Indian physic
ROSACEAE Rose family

The common names "Bowman's root" or "Indian physic," not the sort of enticing names that make a gardener's blood run hot, refer to this plant's having been brewed into a laxative and mashed into a poultice. Its garden potential was ignored on this side of the Atlantic, but of course in England, it has been known and grown—first mistakenly as a *Spirea*—since the early 18th century. William Robinson wrote about it in The *English Flower Garden* (1883), praising it as "graceful."

Graceful it is. Bowman's root looks like a very tidy, dwarf blackberry bush with neatly cut trios of narrow,

and Nebraska, south to Florida, Texas

Flower: Greenish white, narrow bell flowers hang, evenly spaced, below arching stems in May. These are followed by deep blue berries.

Foliage: 3- to 5-foot-long stems arch toward the greatest source of light. Pairs of smooth, medium green leaves are held parallel to the ground.

Hardiness: Probably Zones 3 to 9

Height: 3 to 4 feet

Regions: Northeast, Mid-Atlantic, South, Midwest

Landscape use: Accent or ground cover in a shady garden

toothed, crinkled leaves. Fine in June, Bowman's root frames the ponderous blossoms of such companions as peonies and clematis with clouds of spidery white flowers.

Origin: Ontario to Michigan, south to Alabama and Georgia

Flower: Small, white, starry flowers in loose panicles on wiry stems in June; reddish calyxes and fruit are apparent later.

Foliage: Toothed, textured foliage is abundant; orange-yellow in fall.

Hardiness: Zones 5 (possibly 4) to 8

Height: To 4 feet

Regions: Northeast, Mid-Atlantic, South, Midwest

Landscape use: Border; good in contrast with big, bold flowers

Culture: Light shade; moist to medium; rich garden soil; said to be "deerproof"

Species: American ipecac, *P. stipulata,* has smaller flowers.

Propagation: Seed (stratify 2 to 3 months)

RATIBIDA PINNATA Prairie coneflower
COMPOSITAE Sunflower family

Like freesias and crooked puppy smiles, there is something sweetly naïve about the flowers of prairie coneflower, whose effect is the antithesis of the neat regimentation of a stiff, upright *Rudbeckia* 'Goldsturm.' Prairie coneflowers are borne above the plant on thin, branched stems that bow under their weight.

Flower production seems cheerfully disorganized. At all times, it seems, there are old flowers with drooping, pale gold petals around brown cones, new ones with pale green cones, and future ones, held increasingly higher above the plants. It is said that concentrating upon certain paintings—for example, Cézanne landscapes—leads to a breakthrough in understanding art. I think that concentrating upon prairie coneflowers leads to an understanding of gardening.

Origin: Prairie coneflower is found across a huge stretch—from Ontario south to Georgia and west to Minnesota and Oklahoma.

Flower: Pale gold petals around prominant cones that start out green and turn brown

Foliage: Intricately divided leaves on lanky stems form a loose shrub.

Hardiness: Zones 3 to 8

Height: 3 to 5 feet

Regions: Midwest, Northeast, Mid-Atlantic, South

Landscape use: Back border, prairie

Culture: Full sun on medium to dry soils

Species: Mexican hat, *R. columnifer,* mahogany and gold, from Southwest Canada to Mexico, well-drained soil, Zones 4–9

Propagation: Seed

RHEXIA VIRGINICA Meadow beauty, deer grass
MELASTOMATACEAE Meadow beauty family

Meadow beauty's hot pink flowers always remind me of a child's drawing of the way a flower should look. It is a simple arrangement: there are four uneven, loopy petals around a center that can only be described as "fancy," with its disproportionately large yellow anthers. A plant for pond edges and wet meadows, meadow beauty flowers drop their petals within eight hours. However, a seemingly endless supply of more flowers keeps the plant colorful. As a single specimen, meadow beauty cannot compete with other garden-worthy natives, but in a naturalized mass, it is stunning. In a low, very moist meadow, it might be combined with the moisture-loving palm sedge, the pink swamp milkweed, cinnamon and royal ferns, and swamp azalea. *Rhexia virginica* is the most common of a number of species in the eastern United States, including: *R. mariana, R. aristosa, R. interior, R. ventricosa,* and *R. petiolata.*

Origin: Wet meadows, bogs, ditches throughout the eastern United States

Flower: 1-inch, lopsided, magenta-pink petals around yellow stamens in clusters

Foliage: Hairy stems with thin wings; ovate, opposite, toothed light green leaves are 1 to 2 inches long; grows into loose, bushy clumps.

Hardiness: Probably Zones 4 to 9

Bowman's root (**Porteranthus trifoliatus**) *(Jan Midgley photo)*

Height: 1 to 2 feet
Region: Eastern North America
Landscape use: Naturalized on the edge of ponds, in wet meadows
Culture: Moist, sandy, acid soil in part to full sun
Species: Texas extension agent Benny J. Simpson recommends *R. mariana,* with white to rose morning flowers, for Texas.
Propagation: By tuber division, stem cuttings, or seed first stored at room temperature, then stratified for two to three months. Seed needs light. Small plants grow slowly, bloom the second year.

ROMNEYA COULTERI Matilija poppy
PAPAVERACEAE Poppy family

First described by the Irishman William Henry Harvey around 1850, Matilija poppy quickly became a popular garden plant on both sides of the Atlantic. And no wonder! Imagine poppy flowers with sweet, floppy, crepe-paper petals around golden centers that measure up to 9 inches across! Picture them growing not singly on stems, but appearing in groups, continuously, on a showy subshrub.

Best treated as a perennial, Matilija poppy spreads vigorously from underground runners. Its wandering rhizomes are terrific for holding soil on hillsides, but in any but a very large garden they will need vigilant containment. Dig around the plant to remove unwanted excess growth.

Origin: Dry canyons of Southern California and Baja
Flower: Large, fragrant—up to 9 inches across—poppy flowers with floppy white petals around prominent yellow stamens from April to July
Foliage: Small, cleanly cut, blue-green leaves
Hardiness: Possibly Zone 7 (with winter mulch) to 10
Height: 5 to 8 feet
Regions: California, Southwest
Landscape use: Because of its size and tendency to spread, Matilija poppy is best for large-scale plantings, banks, roadsides, or large gardens.
Culture: Provide full sun and well-drained soil. Although an occasional summer watering may keep the plant looking good, Matilija poppy is best grouped with drought-tolerant plants and kept dry in summer. Cut it back to 2- to 3-inch stubs in winter, when it is dormant, to encourage fresh, new growth and promote better flowering. Matilija poppy resents transplanting.
Cultivars: The cross between Ventura Matilija (*R. trichocalyx),* a very similar species, with *R. coulteri* yielded

Prairie coneflower (Ratibida pinnata)

'White Cloud', a bushier 4 to 5 feet with enormous (8-inch) white flowers. 'Butterfly' has large flowers.
Propagation: Take winter cuttings of lateral roots.

RUDBECKIA Black-eyed Susan
COMPOSITAE Sunflower family

The black-eyed Susan hardly needs introduction. It comes from a wholly North American plant genus, *Rudbeckia,* whose representatives grow from Quebec to Florida and from New England to California. Although all of its members have ray (daisy-type) flowers, not all have gold petals and black "eyes." Some are yellow, others light gold with green eyes.

Known and grown for centuries, *Rudbeckia*s have been extensively hybridized. The English plantsman John Tradescant listed tall (to 9 feet), yellow-flowered *Rudbeckia laciniata* on his 1634 list. Among its modern hybrids is 'Gold Drop' ('Goldquelle'), a cultivar with double flowers on 30-inch stems.

Another good garden plant is *Rudbeckia fulgida* 'Goldsturm', a very upright, bushy 24-inch-tall plant that is terrific used in masses. Typically, black-eyed Susan flowers cover the top of the plant completely. When plants are spaced two feet apart, this characteristic provides a seamless blanket of flowers—for two months. The chief drawback of 'Goldsturm' is that it is thirstier than many other rudbeckias. Those mass plantings in hot summer

Rudbeckia

Name	Origin	Flower	Foliage	Zones	Height	Regions	Landscape Use
Rudbeckia fulgida 'Goldsturm'	New Jersey west to Illinois	Deep gold, dark brown cone, July–September	Dark, coarse, very upright, semievergreen rosette	4 to 8	30 in	Eastern, midwestern United States, adaptable	Border, ground cover
Rudbeckia hirta Gloriosa daisy	Maine south to Georgia, west to Illinois	Gold, orange, sometimes red, dark center, June–August	Hairy, toothed leaves	4 to 8	30 in	Eastern, midwestern United States, adaptable	Border, meadow, prairie
Rudbeckia laciniata Greenheaded cone-flower	Quebec to Florida	4 in, yellow, green cone	Deeply cut, smooth leaves	Probably 3 to 9	To 10 ft	North America	Back border, wild garden
Rudbeckia maxima	Missouri to Louisiana, Texas	Yellow-gold, long cone, very tall stems, July	1 ft, gray-green, smooth "cabbage" leaves in rosette	6 to 9	To 8 ft	Mid-Atlantic, Midwest, South, Northeast, adaptable	Accent, border
Rudbeckia nitida 'Herbstsonne'	Species comes from Georgia, Florida, Texas	4 in, yellow, August/September	Smooth, medium green, study upright stems	Probably 3 to 9	To 8 ft	North America	Back border, wild garden
Rudbeckia subtomentosa Sweet black-eyed Susan	Wisconsin to Louisiana, Texas	4 in, yellow-gold, round dark brown cone, August/September	Rough, dark green, three-part leaves, lax stems	Probably 3 to 9	To 5 ft	Eastern, midwestern United States	Mid-border, prairie garden

areas one sees in photos probably look wonderful because an irrigation system keeps them lush. Mulching helps to keep the roots moist, which extends the period of bloom, and it also keeps down unwanted seedlings.

The only time I have ever seen *Rudbeckia nitida* for sale is in cultivar form, and I bought one. *Rudbeckia nitida* 'Herbstsonne', freely available, is a great, loosely bushy 5

to 6 feet, topped with bright golden yellow flowers measuring 3 to 4 inches across, whose petals radiate around prominent cones. Some people think that it is a cultivar of *R. laciniata*. Flowers are produced lavishly from July through September. This is a large, cheerful, carefree addition to a border in full sun.

So vastly different is it from other rudbeckias, one suspects cabbage in the lineage of *Rudbeckia maxima*. It has up to 2-foot-long, dusty gray-green leaves (the color of lamb's ears without the fuzz) in a basal clump that sends up tall, thin flower stalks that may reach 9 feet! Like Mexican hats, the flowers are yellow, with drooping petals and prominent, elongated brown cones.

Neil Diboll, owner of Prairie Nursery in Westfield, Wisconsin, has a passion for prairie natives and a favorite rudbeckia: sweet black-eyed Susan (*Rudbeckia subtomentosa*), a non-stoloniferous one he recommends for the Upper Midwest. Judging from its range (Wisconsin south to Louisiana and Texas), it would probably do as well in the Lower Midwest. Flowers begin opening in August and continue for more than a month. Sweet black-eyed Susan is definitely more drought-tolerant than 'Goldsturm'. In my garden, in a place with more sun and less water, sweet black-eyed Susan bloomed nonstop for two months, while 'Goldsturm' sulked in the heat and drought of a particularly merciless summer. (See *Rudbeckia* chart, above.)

Meadow beauty (Rhexia virginica)

Culture	Propagate	Comment
Sun to part shade, plentiful moisture	Division, seed	Showy, seamless bloom when massed, intolerant of drought, invasive, self-sows
Easy from seed, sun to part shade, moist to average	Seed	May be annual, biennial, or short-lived perennial, 'Gloriosa' strain blooms first year from seed; great cut flower
Sun, moist to medium soil, tall plants	Division	Needs staking, great yellow late flower, good for cutting. Cultivar: 'Golden Glow', 30 in tall
Moist to average soil, sun	Seed	Tall flower stalks on 20-in plant, needs air circulation, careful placement; tolerates very moist places; unusual, self-sows
Moist to average soil, sun, cut back July/August for more bloom	Division	Showy, long bloom period, good cut flower, best in full sun
Sun, average soil	Seed	Floriferous late bloomer, more drought-tolerant than others, care-free

Matilija poppy (**Romneya coulteri**) *(Chris Andrews photo)*

RUELLIA HUMILIS Wild petunia, hairy petunia
ACANTHACEAE Acanthus family

Wild petunia is another example of a pretty native that is taking the leap from fields and field guides to gardens and garden books. Wild petunias resemble, but are not related to, annual bedding petunias. Each delicate, flaring trumpet flower lasts only a day or two, but the overall bloom period is four to six weeks, providing continuous floral display. Jan Midgley, who grows *Ruellia* at her nursery, says that the least weedy-appearing species of the various wild petunias is *R. humilis,* a species that grows from branching stems that form a mat, studded with small lavender tubular flowers.

Jan Midgely finds mass planting of *Ruellia* most effective, but says that individual plants would thrive in crevices in a semishady rock garden. She suggests placing wild petunia near a patio, a walk, or steps to get the most pleasure from the small blooms.

Origin: Open woods, clearings, dry slopes from Pennsylvania to Nebraska and south to Florida and Texas
Flower: Tubular, lavender trumpet with five flaring lobes in leaf axils
Foliage: Leaves are olive green, sessile, oblong, opposite, and hairy on hairy stems. Stems are erect, but the plant appears loose due to reclining branches.
Hardiness: Zones 4 to 9
Height: 1 to 2 feet

Regions: Midwest, Mid-Atlantic, South
Landscape use: Wild garden, rock garden; Neil Diboll suggests planting with short grasses in a dry prairie garden.
Culture: Dry soil, good drainage, full to part sun
Species: Many others, including: *R. strepens, R. caroliniensis, R. ciliosa,* etc.
Propagation: Seed

SALVIA Salvia, sage
LABIATAE Mint family

The flaming red, summer bedding salvia (*S. splendens*) we love to hate has 750 cousins—none of whom is quite as hard to take. Of these, so many hail from the New World that it was hard for sage expert Betsy Clebsch, who made up the chart on pages 142–143, to draw the line. In the end, the boundary was dropped to Mexico. This made it possible to include the lovely yellow forsythia sage from the Sierra Madres.

In my opinion, the recent surge of interest in sages is a sign of a growing sophistication in garden plants. Where once bedding out something as big and red and obvious as *Salvia splendens* fulfilled the gardening urge, today's gardener appreciates the tantalizing ratio of specks of riveting, scintillating color to the great billowing mass of calm foliage. Late bloom and a host of colors and sizes are further enticements to grow, collect, and even propagate these delightful plants.

Bushy sweet black-eyed Susan (Rudbeckia subtomentosa) in Sue Coe's garden

Northern gardeners now go to great lengths to take cuttings and overwinter these warm-climate, southern plants that rarely persist above Zone 7 outdoors. Members of the mint family, sages frequently prefer hot, dry places. Where frost kills them, however, they can be grown as annuals.

SANGUINARIA CANADENSIS Bloodroot, red puccoon
PAPAVERACEAE Poppy family

Bloodroot is a fragile, fleeting blossom on a persistent plant that will gradually self-sow to form large, lovely colonies. Actually, seeds of blood-

Rudbeckia maxima flowers top tall, blue-green stems in Bartholdi Park, Washington, D.C.

root have little protuberances called "elaiosomes"—delicious to the ants who pick up the seeds and carry them a few feet away year after year until colonies form. In the wild, one often sees whole hillsides of bloodroot in places that receive sun only in early spring and are then shaded later in the year.

Because of its ephemeral nature and its eccentric mode of spreading, bloodroot is a natural for a wild garden, where these tendencies will reward the gardener with an ever-larger, albeit fleeting, show each spring.

Bloodroot's name comes from a bright red sap in the roots, once used as war paint by Native Americans, that contains sanguinerine, now used in toothpaste. Fortunately for the supply of bloodroot in the wild, the

'Goldsturm' black-eyed Susan (Rudbeckia fulgida 'Goldsturm')

same substance is also found in the endlessly reproducing plume poppy (*Macleaya*).

Bloodroot is a plant that is sometimes wild collected, but it is also nursery propagated. Take care when purchasing!

Origin: Moist, well-drained, neutral to slightly acid soil; eastern North America west to Manitoba and Oklahoma south to Florida

Flower: Easily shattered white flowers bloom for about a week in March–May.

Foliage: Variable, a blue-green emerging leaf wrapped around the flower stalk, opens to round, leathery, irregular lobes. On large, established plants leaves persist until frost.

Hardiness: Probably Zones 3 to 8

Height: 8 to 12 inches

Region: Eastern North America

Landscape use: Wild, woodland garden

Culture: Part to full shade; rich, moist soil. Divide in spring or late summer by cutting rootstock just as the leaves go yellow and dormant.

Wild petunia (Ruellia humilis)

Autumn sage (Salvia greggii) at the Arizona–Sonora Desert Museum, Tucson

Cultivars: There is a lovely, sterile, double form sometimes called 'Multiplex' that resembles a peony.

Propagation: Division, wet seed (double dormancy), root division

SCUTELLARIA INCANA Skullcap
LABIATAE Mint family

Members of the mint family, native skullcaps are still pretty much in the experimental stage as garden plants—at least in the United States—and are usually grown only by specialty nurseries. The most widely grown at home and abroad seems to be *S. incana.*

At a loss to describe my very favorable opinion of the balance of flowers to foliage, I read a perfect synopsis by Kim Hawks in the Niche Gardens 1992 fall catalog: "There are some perennials whose role is to be a mixer and tie different plants together. . . . If all plants were sumptuous specimens, there would be no contrasts, our senses would be overloaded and we would miss the point of it all. To my eyes, skullcaps all by themselves are pretty simple plants, but when nestled among other perennials, they make pleasing compositions which are much better than the sum of the parts."

Origin: Ontario south to Virginia, west to Missouri

Flower: Hooded pale blue to dark purple-blue snapdragon flowers in racemes, bloom from July until frost

Foliage: Minty oval, toothed leaves, may turn reddish in full sun

Hardiness: Zones 5(?) to 6

Height: 30 inches

Regions: Northwest, Midwest, Mid-Atlantic, South

Landscape use: Border, naturalizing

Culture: Sun, part shade, in ordinary garden soil

Species: *S. serrata.* Wildflower Nursery owner Jan Midgley grows *S. incana,* but prefers "superior" *S. serrata* (more compact, flowers are dark blue).

Propagation: Cuttings, seed

SEDUM SPATHULIFOLIUM Stonecrop
CRASSULACEAE Orpine family

A West Coast native, this stonecrop is a perennial with great variations in leaf shape and color. Its leaves can be green, white, or red-purple and have different edgings. It is remarkably tolerant of moisture and will grow just about anywhere. The kinds of situations that many other plants love—with constant

Salvia *'Indigo Spires' at Niche Gardens*

Salvia

Name	Origin	Flower	Foliage	Zones	Height	Regions	Landscape Use
Salvia blepharophylla	Mexico	Orange/red, summer/fall	Lanceolate leaf, smooth above and below, "eyelashes" on edges	7 to 9	1 ft	Southwest, California	Front border, ground cover
Salvia cacaliaefolia	Mexico	True blue, spring/summer	Triangular leaves	7 to 9	3 ft	Southwest, California	Border
Salvia chaemaedryoides Wall germander, Chichuahuan sage	Mexico	Blue flowers, in summer	Small, gray leaves	8 to 10	2 ft	Southwest, California	Rock garden, ground cover
Salvia clevelandii Blue sage	Chaparral slopes, Southern California, Baja	Lavender flowers, in summer	Ash gray leaves	8 to 10	4 ft	Southwest, California	Border, accent, shrub
Salvia coccinea Texas sage, scarlet sage	South Carolina, Florida Texas, Mexico, West Indies	Red flowers, summer/fall	Hairy, triangular leaves on fine stems	8 to 10	30 in	South, Southwest	Border
Salvia columbariae Chia sage	California to Baja, Utah, Arizona	Purple flowers, in spring	Narrow, oval leaves	Annual	18 in	Southwest, California	Border
Salvia confertiflora	Mexico	Red flowers, in fall	Large leaves on floppy stems	7 to 10	To 5 ft	Southwest, California	Back border, accent
Salvia farinacea Mealy-cup sage	New Mexico, Texas	Blue/white, in summer, fall	Oval, gray leaves	7 to 10	2 ft	Southwest	Border, massed
Salvia greggii Autumn sage	Texas, Mexico	Red, orange, pink, salmon, in summer/fall	Dense, green leaves	7 to 10	30 in	Southwest, California	Edger, border, massed
Salvia involucrata Rosy leaf sage	Mexico, Central America	Pink, in late summer, fall	Smooth with red, pink bracts, stems	7 to 10	To 5 ft	South, Southwest	Back border, accent
Salvia leucantha Mexican bush sage	Mexico	Purple flowers, in summer/fall	Hairy, gray-green, shrubby	7 to 10	4 ft	Southwest, California	Back border, accent
Salvia leucophylla Purple sage	Coastal ranges of California	Pale purple flowers, early summer	Silvery, broad mound	8 to 10(?)	4 to 5 ft	California	Back border, hedge
Salvia madrensis Forsythia sage	Mexico	Yellow flowers, in fall	Heart-shaped leaves, large clump	7 to 9	To 7 ft	Southwest, California	Back border
Salvia rutilans Pineapple sage	Mexico	Red, in summer, fall	Bright green leaves	7 to 10	To 4 ft	Southwest, California	Border
Salvia sonomensis Creeping sage	California	Lavender/blue, in spring	Grayish white leaves	7 to 10	1 ft	California	Ground cover
Salvia spathacea Pitcher sage	California	Magenta flowers, in summer	Arrow shaped, pale green above, gray below	7 to 10	1 ft	California	Ground cover

Culture	Propagate	Comment
Part shade, moderate moisture, good garden soil, will spread under good conditions	Cuttings, seed, division	Perennial, good cut flowers, spreads under ideal conditions
Part shade, moisture, good garden soil	Cuttings, seed	Perennial, good cut flowers
Full sun, dry, average soil, will take extra water	Cuttings, seed	Shrub, small gray foliage of interest year around, cut flower
Full sun, dry (with occasional water) average soil	Cuttings, seed	Shrub, good cut flower, first-rate plant, foliage may be used in cooking, very drought-tolerant, almost no summer water. Cultivar: 'Whirly Blue' (54 in by 6 ft wide, Zone 9).
Full sun, moderately moist, good garden soil	Cuttings, seed	Perennial, treat as annual, overwinter cuttings, develops rapidly, great, white form. Cultivar: 'Brenthurst' (pink).
Full sun, dry (with occasional water) average soil	Seed	Sow early in spring for early summer bloom; good cut flower
Full sun, moderately moist soil, average soil	Cuttings, seed	Perennial, needs staking but worth the trouble, good cut flower
Full sun, moderately moist, good garden soil	Cuttings, seed	Perennial, nice with roses or shrubs. Cultivars: 'White Bedder' (white, 30 in), 'Victoria' (purple, 18 in), 'Indigo Spires' (indigo blue, 4 ft).
Full sun / part shade, moderate moisture, good garden soil	Cuttings, seed	Woody subshrub, cut flowers, cut back old wood in early spring
Full sun / part shade, moderately moist, good garden soil	Cuttings, seed	Perennial, dramatic, deep pink flowers and stems, cut flowers, pinch back for bushier growth
Full sun / part shade, moderately moist, good garden soil	Cuttings, seed	Shrub, nice hairy gray-green foliage, pinch back to keep compact, extremely drought–tolerant
Full sun, dry soil, withstands heat, drops its leaves in drought	Cuttings, seed	Silvery foliage, grows as broad as tall. Cultivar: 'Allen Chickering' (x with S. clevelandii, has mounding habit, rich blue/purple flowers).
Full sun / part shade, moderately moist, good garden soil	Cuttings, seed	Perennial, huge square stems and attractive heart-shaped foliage, makes a large clump, stoloniferous
Part shade, moderately moist, good garden soil	Cuttings, seed	Perennial, outstanding foliage, good cut flower, fruit scented. Cultivar: 'Honeymelon' (red, about 6 in).
Part shade, dry, average soil	Cuttings, seed	Perennial, nice foliage, good for dry, shady banks. Cultivar: 'Dara's Choice' (vigorous).
Sun, part shade, moderately moist, good garden soil	Cuttings, seed, division	Perennial, will spread and form a large patch, good cut flower

moisture, rich soil, and respite from the sun—allow this stonecrop to grow lush, lanky, and an uninteresting green from too much good living. Without mollycoddling, when it is exposed to the elements, it is at its trimmest, most colorful best. Clusters of yellow, starlike flowers are borne in early summer. With its many forms, this is a great plant for collectors, rock gardens, and stone troughs.

Origin: Mountains of California to 7,000 feet from Santa Cruz County north to British Columbia

Flower: Bright yellow, starlike flowers in May/June

Foliage: Varies greatly. Near the seashore, leaves are chalky white to a pale purplish gray. Inland, they can be red-purple or red-purple edged with white.

Hardiness: Probably Zones 6 to 8

Height: 4 to 6 inches

Regions: California, Northwest, South, Lower Midwest, Mid-Atlantic

Landscape use: Rock gardens, stone troughs, pots

Culture: Gritty, fast-draining soil

Cultivars: Many, including 'Cape Blanco' (silver-blue), var. *purpureum* (purple, red in winter), and 'Roseum' (teal blue–rose)

SEDUM TERNATUM

CRASSULACEAE Orpine family

Like most sedums, *S. ternatum* spreads quickly to form large mats. Unlike most other sedums, it does so in the shade. I have it growing on a shady slope, adjacent to a stone path. Although my sedum is not in contact with the stones of the path and is growing in highly acidic soil (pH 4.5 to 5), it appreciates, I have

Bloodroot (Sanguinaria canadensis)

read, lime. In May, it is covered with starry white flowers along arching branches. At other times of the year, whorls of small, round, pale green new leaves contrast with older, darker, dull green ones.

Origin: *S. ternatum* is found on rocky places in the eastern United States

Flower: Flowers are fleshy, off-white, star-shaped with contrasting black dots.

Foliage: Each leaf is like an elongated, flat scallop shell whorled around the stem. New leaves are smaller and lighter, brighter green.

Hardiness: Probably Zone 5

Height: 2 to 5 inches

Regions: Northeast, Mid-Atlantic, South, Midwest

Landscape use: Ground cover in shade, trough, pot

Culture: Full to part shade; moist, rich soil with good drainage

Species: *S. nevii* is similar, but tiny.

Propagation: Division, seed, cuttings

SHORTIA GALACIFOLIA Oconee bells
DIAPENSIACEAE Diapensia family

Poor Oconee bells! After André Michaux found and preserved a herbarium specimen of Oconee bells in 1787, it wasn't found again in the wild for nearly 100 years. This shy plant with delicate pale pink to white bell flowers is found only in a few isolated populations in the Carolinas and Georgia and has been classified as a federally endangered species. It is, therefore, a crime to buy or sell collected plants. Happily, a few growers are producing Oconee bells. If you have a place in your garden where this plant can survive, it is worth tracking down a legitimate source of it. Several are listed in Appendix 1 in the back of the book.

I have always seen Oconee bells in the company of moss. David Benner, the Pennsylvania gardener who has opened our eyes to the beauty and practicality of a moss lawn, explains that his current population of about 500 Oconee bells has naturalized over the years from just 12 plants, purchased in 1962. He feels that the moss is the perfect nurse plant for *Shortia*, and today, with his large colony thriving, he harvests the ripe seed and scatters it in other parts of the garden.

Against the velvety, bright green of moss, *Shortia*'s flat, glossy rosette of green, blushed red and maroon, is a lovely contrast in both texture and color. Otherwise, Oconee bells is as shy in the garden as it is in the wild and only really noticeable in spring, when the delicate, fringed flowers appear. Coming upon Oconee bells blooming in a spring garden, like a glimpse of a nest of robin's eggs, is a rare pleasure.

Origin: Mountains of Virginia, North and South Carolina, and Georgia

Flower: Pale pink to white petals with a pinked edge, borne on reddish stems

Foliage: Glossy, round, evergreen leaves with prominent veining; turn red-bronze with cold

Hardiness: Zones 6 to 7

Height: 6 inches

Regions: Mid-Atlantic, South

Landscape use: Streamside or woodland garden

Culture: Moist, well-drained, acid soil in light shade

Propagation: Seed

SILENE Campion, catchfly, wild pink, fire pink, moss pink
CARYOPHYLLACEAE Pink family

Best-known among the native silenes, moss campion, *Silene acaulis,* is a plant that is popular with rock gardeners around the world. If it never bloomed at all, it would be worth growing for its dense mats of glossy green foliage that seem to glide gracefully over rocks and stones. But it does bloom, sprinkling the mossy cushions with pink flowers of five petals—each tipped with a notch that is a common characteristic of this genus.

Not quite as familiar as moss campion—and of very different cultural needs—are some of the eastern silenes. The fire pink (*Silene virginica*), with fiery scarlet blooms, and its similarly bright relative, the midwestern royal catchfly (*Silene regia*), with flowers of deep red, are plants of open woods and prairies. When their star flowers appear, it

Skullcap (Scutellaria serrata)

Stonecrop (Sedum spathulifolium) *(Jessie Harris photo)*

seems to me they have a wide-open, surprised look.

The petals of some silenes are notched so deeply that they appear fringed. The white starry campion (*Silene stellata*) is one of these. There are also fringed forms of the exotic, but naturalized, pink *Silene armeria,* and the beautiful *Silene polypetala* has soft pink, fringed flowers. Fred Galle, whose *Azaleas* is the final word on that subject, gardens a wooded slope in Pine Mountain, Georgia, where *Silene polypetala* is a carefree, if not downright vigorous, grower. He explained that it was listed as endangered in Georgia, but not in his woodsy garden. *Silene polypetala* has been crossed with *Silene virginica* to yield a short plant with coral pink flowers, available from some specialty nurseries. It may be labeled 'Jim Ault', after its originator.

Two beautiful westerners are both called "Indian pink," scarlet *S. californica* and satiny pink *S. hookeri.* Indian pinks, like most silenes, are particular about sites and will not grow well outside their native range. (See *Silene* chart, on pages 146–147.)

SILPHIUM

COMPOSITAE Daisy family

"Silphium," wrote the conservationist Aldo Leopold in *A Sand County Almanac* (1949), "first became a personality to me when I tried to dig one up to move to my farm. . . . After half an hour of hot grimy labor the root was still enlarging, like a great vertical sweet-potato. . . . I learned by what elaborate underground stratagems it contrives to weather the prairie drouths." In *The English Flower Garden* (1883), William Robinson doesn't mention *Silphium*'s magnificent root, but comments on its "stout stem," adding that *Silphium* was one of the first perennials that suggested the idea of the "wild garden" to him, a style he and, later, Gertrude Jekyll pursued with great passion.

Four species of *Silphium*—all well rooted—hail from the prairies of Canada and the Midwest. Not a plant for the timid, prairie dock (*S. terebinthinaceum*), slow to develop aboveground, spends a good five years in root development, but when it comes into its own, it will delight those with a taste for the dramatic. It is a spectacular specimen. Great, lime green elephant-ear leaves remain close to the ground, while the flower stalks, bearing bouquets of yellow-gold, shoot up 10 feet in the air.

Compass plant's (*Silphium laciniatum*) large cut leaves remind me of the oversized houseplant *Monstera.* Up and down the 8-foot stalks, they align themselves between north and south, a stratagem, horticulturists believe, to protect large leaf surfaces from the sun.

Both prairie dock and compass plant do well on heavy soils. Because of their unique leaves and tall flower stalks, they are striking accents against the fine foliage of prairie grasses, either in gardens or in the wild. As specimen plants in gardens, without surrounding grasses for support, especially in rich soil, the flower stalks may require staking.

Cup plant (*Silphium perfoliatum*) grows to an imposing 10 feet where and when conditions are right. Prairie Nursery's Neil Diboll suggests planting cup plants two feet apart for "a nearly impenetrable summertime fence."

Sedum (Sedum ternatum)

Silene

Name	Origin	Flower	Foliage	Zones	Height	Regions	Landscape Use
Silene acaulis Moss campion	Arctic, mountains of Northwest, Eurasia	Lavender-pink, May	Bright green, tight cushion	4	1 in	Mountain	Rock, scree, trough garden
Silene californica Indian pink	Foothills of Oregon, California	Scarlet, double-notched, 1-in flowers	Sticky, dark green, multistemmed	7	12 in	Mountain, Northwest, California	Rock garden, slopes, border
Silene hookeri Indian pink	Rocky slopes of Oregon	White to pink, fringed, summer	Gray-green, fuzzy foliage	7	6 in	Mountain, Northwest	Rock garden, slope
Silene polypetala	Southern Appalachians	Fringed, pale pink, June	Dark blue-green, spoon-shaped leaves	7(?)	6 in	Eastern United States	Woodland garden
Silene regia Royal catchfly	Prairies, open fields from Ohio and Missouri south to Alabama, Georgia	Crimson, notched flower, June	Long, smooth leaves	5(?) to 6	3 ft	Eastern, midwestern United States	Border, prairie garden
Silene stellata Starry campion	Woods, openings, Maine to Minnesota, Georgia to Oklahoma, Texas	White, frilly, fringed petals, in July	Long, velvety leaves	3	18 in	Eastern, midwestern United States	Woodland garden, partly shaded border
Silene virginica Fire pink	Open woods, fields, New Jersey south to Minnesota, Georgia, Oklahoma	2-in scarlet stars, May, June	Dark green, evergreen rosette	3	To 15 in	Eastern, midwestern United States	Rock garden, border

Oconee bells (Shortia galacifolia) *(Jessie Harris photo)*

It's an attractive way to keep dogs and children out of the vegetable garden or to screen the compost heap. The strong stems are square, piercing the fused leaves to form small cups that can hold rainwater for days. These create hospitable oases with a soothing increase in humidity for the cup plant and a miniature watering hole for insects, who are joined in August and September, when the yellow flowers top the stalks, by hummingbirds and butterflies. Fittingly, cup plant is the thirstiest of the *Silphium*s. Plant it in a low, moist spot in sun.

Rosinweed (*Silphium integrifolium*), the most drought-tolerant of the *Silphium*s listed here, is also the shortest (only 5 to 6 feet) and the quickest to mature. Rosinweed grows multiple stems of fine dark green leaves topped with clusters of yellow daisy flowers. In the garden, it serves as a nice, small, dark green shrub that blooms in July. (See *Silphium* chart, pages 148–149.)

SISYRINCHIUM Blue-eyed grass
IRIDACEAE Iris family

From a distance, blue-eyed grass clumps look just like grass. But look more closely at this member of the iris family and you'll find yourself thinking of irises. The leaves are flat blue-green blades, and its starry, open flowers, which bloom in spring, are typically

Culture	Propagate	Comment
An alpine, rich scree, sun, perfect drainage	Seed	Foliage outstanding, may bloom sparsely. Variety: *pedunculata* (floriferous).
Light shade, rich soil, summer dry	Seed	Start from fresh seed, summer dormant, hummingbird plant, stems may flop, taprooted
Part shade, perfect drainage, summer dry	Seed	Particular about site, taprooted, many forms, start from seed
Part shade, moist, humusy soil	Seed, root, cuttings	Particular about site, grows vigorously where happy
Full sun, good drainage	Seed, root, cuttings	Somewhat rare, but offered by specialty growers, hummingbird plant
Part shade, moist, rich soil	Seed, root, cuttings	Particular about site, grows well where needs are met
Sun, part shade, moist with perfect drainage	Seed, root, cuttings	Long display, more flowers in sun, hummingbird plant. Cultivar: x 'Longwood' (compact, evergreen).

blue as in the eastern species, *S. angustifolium.* Trouble-free, blue-eyed grass makes a good edger or informal ground cover. I would love to see it combined in a low, no-mow flowery "lawn" along with the dwarf-eared coreopsis, *Carex pensylvanica,* dainty yellow 'Corbett' columbine, and little bulbs like *Crocus tomasianus* and the autumn-flowering *C. sativus* and *C. speciosus.* It volunteers with almost, but not quite, annoying frequency in my garden—always in moist semi to full shade. Interestingly, two of the biggest, healthiest clumps are transplants that I moved to moist, full sun, so I conclude that this plant doesn't need shade. The flowers of my local population are charming close up, but fleeting and altogether quieter than the showy blue-eyed grasses I remember from California.

One of them, *S. bellum,* produces tufts of grasslike foliage in the winter and early spring, and its spring bloom creates beautiful drifts on coastal California hillsides. In gardens, Californians like Betsy Clebsch—who contributed to this description and to the chart—grow them and the yellow *S. californicum* in large patches in shaded rock gardens and in containers.

Many species of blue-eyed grass from most parts of North and South America are easily propagated from seed or division. (See *Sisyrinchium* chart, pages 150–151.)

Fire pink (Silene virginica)

SMILACINA RACEMOSA False Solomon's seal
LILIACEAE Lily family

False Solomon's seal is a plant for a woodland or edge-of-woodland garden. Grouped with the purple flowers of (exotic) hesperus and the airy fronds of maidenhair fern, it is spectacular in springtime, when frothy, creamy white flowers bloom on the ends of its leaves and arch toward the light. In summer, red berries replace the flowers. However, if the plant doesn't get enough moisture in summer (as mine—under a sycamore—do not), the leaves mottle and dry. A spot that is moist year-round would probably keep Solomon's seal attractive longer.

Origin: North America

Flower: White panicles in May, followed by red (sometimes with purple spots) berries in late summer

Foliage: 3- to 4-inch-wide leaves on arching stems resembling those of Solomon's seal, contrasting dark stems

Hardiness: Zones 3 to 8

Silene polypetala

147

Silphium

Name	Origin	Flower	Foliage	Zones	Height	Regions	Landscape Use
Silphium integrifolium Rosinweed	Ohio, Minnesota to Mississippi, Oklahoma	Yellow, daisy flowers in July	Multistem, dark green, coarse leaves	4 to 8	5 to 6 ft	North America	Back border, accent
Silphium laciniatum Compass plant	Ohio, South Dakota to Alabama, Texas	Hundreds of yellow on tall stalks, July/August	Huge, glossy, deeply cut leaves in 3-ft cluster	4 to 8	To 10 ft	North America	Bold accent, back border
Silphium perfoliatum Cup plant	Moist prairies from Ontario, South Dakota to Georgia, Oklahoma	Yellow on tall stalks, in July/August	Large leaves join around square stems to hold water	3 to 7	7 to 10 ft	Northern North America	Specimen, back border, summer fence
Silphium terebinthinaceum Prairie dock	Praries of Ontario, Minnesota, Georgia, Louisiana, Missouri	Yellow daisy-flowers on sky-rocket stalks, in July/August	Huge, light green, elephant ears in 3-ft clump	3 to 8	To 10 ft	Northeastern North America	Bold accent, back border, prairie planting

Height: 3 feet

Region: North America

Landscape use: Woodland garden

Culture: Moist, humusy soil

Species: Starry false Solomon's seal (*Smilacina stellata*) is only a foot high, with white flowers followed by blackish berries; it spreads by underground stems. Fat Solomon, *S. racemosa* var. *amplexicaulis,* comes from the West.

Propagation: Root division, seed

SOLIDAGO Goldenrod

COMPOSITAE Sunflower family

My (very) old edition of the *World Book Encyclopaedia* lists goldenrod as the official state flower of both Kentucky and Alabama, but in other parts of their native land, it seems that goldenrods go unappreciated. They are even falsely accused of causing hay fever. Elsewhere in the world, they are valued for their beauty and durability. But American gardeners are only just beginning to appreciate the merits of this largely American genus.

Goldenrod's bright flowers add their hues to fall's final floral tapestry. Canada goldenrod (*S. canadensis*), a familiar plant of old fields and meadows, epitomizes this genus, but there are goldenrods of every shape and size.

The gray goldenrod (*S. nemoralis*), an excellent small to medium-sized goldenrod for the garden, starts producing rich yellow flowers with one-sided plumes in July.

The stiff goldenrod (*Solidago rigida*) is one heartily recommended by nurseryman Neil Diboll for the Midwest. Remarkably adaptable as to moisture, Diboll says it "tolerates anything from dry to semi-damp soil." It is topped with flat clusters of radiant yellow flowers.

In the future, we are likely to see more cultivars of goldenrods developed. Already, 'Golden Fleece', a cultivar from a plant found in a North Carolina garden by Dr. Richard Lighty, director of Mt. Cuba, shows promise as a garden staple. This plant grows in an attractive rosette of round leaves that swiftly becomes a thick clump about 12 inches high. Beginning in late August or early September, flowers appear in lateral branches along the stems. After a big flush of bloom in mid- to late September, flowers continue to appear as the stems elongate throughout October. In the Washington, D.C., area, bloom persists modestly into November.

'Cloth of Gold' is another low-growing cultivar. Its long, narrow leaves are whorled in tight succession around 18-inch stems that are topped with primrose yel-

Compass plant (Silphium laciniatum)

Culture	Propagate	Comment
Full sun, part shade, moderate moisture	Seed (cool, stratify 2 months)	Matures fast, adaptable, butterfly, bird plant
Full sun, moderately moist to dry soil	Seed (cool, stratify 2 months)	Slow to mature, hundreds of flowers, bird plant, leaves align north and south
Full sun, moist soil	Seed (cool, stratify 2 months)	Attracts hummingbirds, cups formed where leaves join around stems hold water, butterfly plant
Full sun, moderately moist to moderately dry soil	Seed (cool, stratify 2 months)	Slow to develop, five years to flower, dramatic foliage, rocketship flower, butterfly plant

low flowers from August through September. Friends (with shadier gardens) have grown this plant successfully for a year or two and then lost it—possibly because it requires full sun and good drainage.

Minnesota landscape architect Cole Burrell did most of the work on the chart, on pages 152–153.

SPIGELIA MARILANDICA Indian pink, worm grass
LOGANIACEAE Logania family

There are true pink Indian pinks, but *S. marilandica* is not one of them. Its flower is a bright crimson tube that when closed looks a little like a red bottle gentian, and opened reveals a yellow lining that always reminds me of the lined sleeve on a medieval

Sisyrinchium '*Quaint and Queer*', a beauty of uncertain parentage

*Blue-eyed grass (*Sisyrinchium bellum*) with lupines, University of California Botanic Garden*

gown. The unflattering common name "worm grass," rarely heard, probably refers to this plant's former medicinal use to expel worms. This species is one of the more northern members of a genus that extends all the way into South America.

It is a plant for the edge between sun and shade—the kind of place that people living in old, established neighborhoods often complain about because the trees have grown so tall, their gardens no longer produce decent tomatoes or zinnias. In such a place, Indian pink will develop into a deep green clump that produces little groups of cheery flowers at the tips of the branches.

Origin: South Carolina, Florida, and Texas
Flower: 2½-inch orange-red tube that opens to a yellow star
Foliage: Leaves are held at stiff right angles to stems. They are not bothered by insects and stay clean and dark green until frost.
Hardiness: Probably Zones 6 to 9
Height: 18 to 24 inches
Regions: Mid-Atlantic, South, parts of Lower Midwest
Landscape use: Place Indian pink where you can see it—along a path or near a doorway. Also woodland garden.
Culture: Morning sun; moist, humusy soil
Species: *S. gentianoides* is really pink.

Sisyrinchium

Name	Origin	Flower	Foliage	Zones	Height	Regions	Landscape Use
Sisyrinchium angustifolium Blue-eyed grass	Eastern North America	Blue with yellow eye, May	Narrow, green blades	3 to 8	To 12 in	Eastern North America	Edger, woodland garden, rock garden
Sisyrinchium bellum Blue-eyed grass	California	Blue/yellow center, in April/May	Glaucous green, flat blades	7 to 8	To 12 in	California	Edger, container, meadow, rock garden
Sisyrinchium bermudiana Blue-eyed grass	Bermuda	Violet-blue with yellow center, spring	Green, flat blades	6 to 8	To 12 in	South	Edger, rock garden
Sisyrinchium californicum Golden-eyed grass	Marsh, grasslands of coastal plain, northern California	Golden yellow, spring through summer	Small, flat, green leaves	7 to 8	6 to 8 in	California, Northwest	Edger, rock garden
Sisyrinchium campestre Blue-eyed grass	Sandy places, Manitoba to Illinois, Louisiana Texas	Light blue or white flowers, in May/June	Narrow, flat, green leaves	4 to 8	To 12 in	South, Midwest	Edger, prairie, rock garden
Sisyrinchium douglasii Grass widow	Savannahs, woods of Northwest	Purple, magenta nodding bells, early spring	Narrow, flat leaves	4 to 7	8 in	Northwest, northern California	Edger, rock garden, meadow
Sisyrinchium idahoense	Montana to British Columbia, Idaho, Oregon	Dark violet with a yellow eye, spring	Narrow, light glaucous green	3 to 8	To 12 in	Mountain, Northwest	Edger, rock garden
Sisyrinchium mucronatum 'Album'	Maine west to Wisconsin (species)	White flowers	Very narrow leaves	4 to 7	To 12 in	Eastern, midwestern North America	Edger, rock garden

STOKESIA LAEVIS Stokes' aster

COMPOSITAE Sunflower family

Stokes' asters, with their large, ruffled aster blossoms, have been grown in gardens both here and abroad long enough for there to be some outstanding cultivars. One of the newest, named by Allen Bush of Holbrook Farm in Fletcher, North Carolina, is 'Klaus Jelitto', honoring Allen's friend, an outstanding German seedsman. Ironically, Klaus Jelitto the seedsman will never sell seeds for 'Klaus Jelitto' the cultivar because, as such, it must be vegetatively propagated!

The cultivar has great big blue flowers—just under 3 inches across. Perfect contrasting companions for its June flowers are the catmint cultivar 'Dropmore', which has billowing silvery white foliage and pale blue flowers, or lemon yellow 'Moonbeam' coreopsis. 'Klaus Jelitto' and other Stokes' asters are long lasting in bouquets.

Origin: North and South Carolina, Louisiana, and Florida.

Flower: Reminiscent of a large, lavender blue cornflower, Stokes' aster has fringed petals (the ray florets) around a pom-pom center (the disk florets) of the same color. These measure about 2 inches across in the straight species.

Foliage: Radiating out of a basal clump, leaves are a smooth, medium green and lance shaped.

Hardiness: Zones 5 to 9

Height: 12 to 18 inches high

Regions: Mid-Atlantic, Northeast, South, parts of the Midwest

Landscape use: Border, cut flower

Culture: Sun, excellent drainage in winter

Cultivars: 'Klaus Jelitto', 'Blue Danube' (blue), 'Mary Gregory' (yellow!)

Propagation: Seed, root cuttings

STYLOPHORUM DIPHYLLUM Wood poppy, celandine poppy

PAPAVERACEAE Poppy family

If you have one golden wood poppy that likes the place where you've planted it, you'll soon have colonies. Like mice, there's no such thing as just one. In moist, open shade, this is a plant that will give even honesty (*Lunaria*) a run for its money. I have watched these two, gold and purple, vie for attention in a woodland garden that was, in a far less interesting phase, my

Culture	Propagate	Comment
Shade, sun, moist with good drainage	Seed, division	Will form thick clumps, flowers on end of leaves
Sun, light shade, humusy soil	Seed, division	Showy, summer dry or some water, easy from seed, self-sows, blooms first year from seed. Cultivar: 'Nana' (dwarf).
Full sun, good drainage	Seed, division	Has survived winters in Zone 6, showy
Full sun, light shade, moisture, regular water	Seed, division	Showy, needs moisture, hardy to 15°F.
Full sun, medium to dry, well-drained soil, plant in early spring or fall	Seed, division	Needs good drainage
Sun, part shade, plant in spring, good drainage	Seed, division	Needs to be moist in spring, tolerates summer dry, loses leaves
Sun, part shade, good drainage	Seed, division	Large-flowered, showy
Sun, part shade, moist	Seed, division	White-flowered cultivar of a species similar to *S. angustifolium*

*False Solomon's seal (*Smilacina racemosa*)*

TELLIMA GRANDIFLORA Fringe cups
SAXIFRAGACEAE Saxifrage family

Bill Johnson, the gardener at Hillwood, the former estate of Marjorie Merriweather Post in Washington, D.C., first introduced me to fringe cups, kin to woodland saxifrage, widespread in lowlands west of the Cascades. It is an acquaintance that grew rapidly into friendship. This charming Northwest native is an easy garden plant, perfectly at home edging a moss path in bright shade in my Maryland garden. It looks a little like a foamflower, with deeply rippled, evergreen leaves, but it blooms like an alum root, with tall white fringed flowers.

Origin: Woodlands of lowland Northwest
Flower: Racemes of creamy yellow on 2-foot stalks in spring, aging to pink

*Goldenrod (*Solidago*) in an autumn bouquet with black-eyed Susans and asters*

front lawn. Like honesty, wood poppy is easy enough to pull out where it isn't wanted, and also like honesty, it puts on a terrific show at peak bloom. Each fall, I transplant some young plants to light up unadorned shady places the following spring.

Too aggressive for a border, wood poppy is just the thing for a woodland garden that is home to other plants that can hold their own: frothy, white foamflower (*Tiarella*) and lady ferns (*Athyrium filix-femina*) with their red and lettuce green stems.

Origin: Eastern United States
Flower: 2-inch flowers with four floppy, yellow gold petals around a matching pom-pom center, blooming in spring with a very few sporadic blooms in early summer
Foliage: Leaves are gray-green and lobed.
Hardiness: Zones 4 to 8
Height: 18 inches
Regions: Eastern North America where it is hardy
Landscape use: Woodland, wild garden
Culture: Wood poppy seems to need moist soil above all. It will grow in light to full shade and will tolerate a wide range of soil pH.
Propagation: Seed

Solidago

Name	Origin	Flower	Foliage	Zones	Height	Regions	Landscape Use
Solidago caesia Wreath goldenrod, Blue-stemmed goldenrod	Open woods, Nova Scotia to Florida, west to Wisconsin, Texas	Open, wand flowers in August, September	Smooth, blue-green, lance-shaped, toothed edge	5(4?) to 9	1 to 3 ft	Eastern, midwestern North America	Accent plant or tall ground cover in shade, woodland
Solidago canadensis Canada goldenrod	Foothills and shores, open places, California to Oregon, west of of mountains	Club-flowered, dense, showy, July–October	Basal leaves often felted, oval to lance-shaped, toothed	7 to 9	1 to 4 ft	California, Northwest	Borders, with shrubs, open areas
Solidago californica California goldenrod	Open woods, meadows, prairies, roadsides throughout North America	Showy plumes, variable, July–October	Soft, hairy, lance-shaped, toothed leaves	3(2?) to 8	1 to 5 ft	North America	Borders, meadows, prairies
Solidago flexicaulis Zigzag goldenrod	Open woods, Nova Scotia to Georgia, west to North Dakota, Arkansas	Open, wandlike clusters, August–September	Broadly oval to rounded, toothed	3 to 8	1 to 3 ft	Eastern, midwestern North America	Shade gardens, specimens, woodland
Solidago juncea Early goldenrod	Meadows, fields, wood edges from Nova Scotia to South Carolina, west to Minnesota, Missouri	Open, plume flower like fireworks, July, August	Oval, toothed to lance-shaped leaves	3 to 8	12 to 42 in	Eastern, midwestern North America	Borders, dry banks, meadows
Solidago multiradiata Alpine goldenrod	High mountain meadows, slopes, Cascades, Sierra and Rocky Mountains	Flat-topped clusters of showy flowers, June–September	Spatula-shaped, hairy leaves in clump, variable	probably 2 to 5, 6 to 7 in west	2 to 15 in	Mountain	Rock, alpine gardens, troughs
Solidago nemoralis Gray goldenrod, One-sided goldenrod	Dry fields, prairies, wood edges, Nova Scotia to Florida, west to Alberta, Texas	One-sided, curved plumes, July–November	Oval to lance-shaped basal leaves, velvety, gray-green	3 to 8	6 to 36 in	North America	Borders, rock gardens, dry banks
Solidago odora Sweet goldenrod	Sandy, open woods, fields, Vermont to Florida, west to Ontario, Texas	Open, one-sided plumelike cluster, July–September	Narrow, lance-shaped, vanilla-scented leaves	5 to 8	2 to 4 ft	Eastern, midwestern North America	Informal gardens, meadows
Solidago ohiensis Ohio goldenrod	Bogs, wet meadows, prairies, Ontario to New York, west to Minnesota, Missouri	Dense, flat-topped clusters, August–September	Narrow, lance-shaped, shiny basal leaves	3 to 8	2 to 3 ft	Eastern, midwestern North America	Formal, informal gardens, meadows
Solidago puberula Downy goldenrod	Open woods, shores, mostly along coast, St. Lawrence to Florida, on sandstone	Slender, wandlike, August–October	Oval to broadly lance-shaped foliage	5(4?) to 8	18 to 36 in	Eastern North Almerica	Borders, dry banks, rock gardens, seaside
Solidago rigida Stiff goldenrod, Hard-leaved goldenrod	Moist or dry prairies, meadows, open woods, Maryland, Georgia west to Alberta, New Mexico	Dense, domed clusters of large, showy flowers, August–October	Soft, hairy, broad, lance-shaped basal leaves	3 to 8	1 to 5 ft	North America	Borders, informal plantings, prairies
Solidago rugosa Rough-stemmed goldenrod	Fields, meadows, wood edges, Newfoundland to Florida, west to Michigan, Texas	Open, plumelike clusters like yellow fireworks, July–October	Pointed, oval to lance-shaped leaves with sharp teeth	4 to 8	1 to 7 ft	Eastern, midwestern North America	Mass plantings, borders, informal gardens, meadows, shrub borders
Solidago sempervirens Seaside goldenrod	Coastal dunes, wood edges, Newfoundland to Florida, south to tropical America	One-sided wand, plume flowers, August–November	Smooth, fleshy, broad lance-shaped leaves	4 to 10	2 to 8 ft	Eastern North America	Dry soil, seaside gardens and dunes
Solidago spathulata	Rock crevices, dunes, mountain meadows, Nova Scotia to Virginia, west to British Columbia, California, Indiana	Wand or clublike flowers, July–October	Spatula or oval leaves in a basal cluster	3 to 8	6 to 24 in	North America	Rock gardens, walls, banks, informal gardens
Solidago speciosa Showy goldenrod	Open woods, fields, prairies, sandy soils, Massachusetts, Georgia west to Minnesota, Texas	Showy, tightly packed club flowers, July–September	Broadly oval, toothed basal leaves, red stems	3 to 8	1 to 3 ft	Eastern, midwestern North America	Borders, rock gardens, prairies, meadows
Solidago sphacelata	Open woods, Virginia to Georgia, west to Indiana, Alabama	Sparse, plume flower clusters like fireworks, September, November	Oval to heart-shaped leaves in clump	4 to 8	12 to 30 in	Eastern, midwestern North America	Borders, ground cover plantings, good under shrubs

Culture	Propagate	Comment
Part to full shade, moist or dry loamy soil	Seed	Best growth in open shade with rich soil, but flowers in deep, dry woods. Species: *S. curtisii* (similar, more southerly in distribution).
Sun, average moist soil	Seed	Easy, give some summer water, long blooming period
Sun or light shade, average to rich, moist to dry soil	Division	Rhizomatous, may be invasive; choose a named selection for the border
Full to part shade, average to rich, moist soil	Seed	Stems bend at angles between nodes, giving a zigzag appearance
Sun, average to poor soil, moist to dry	Seed	Prefers lean, sandy soil; flops in rich, moist soils
Full to part sun, moist, well-drained humus to rocky soil	Seed	Requires cool summers with low humidity
Sun, average to poor, well-drained to dry soil	Seed, division	Quite variable depending on moisture and soil fertility; always neat in the garden
Full sun to light shade, average to poor, moist to dry soil	Division	Open habit, creeping stems render plants unsuitable for formal gardens
Full to part sun, average to rich, moist soil	Seed, division	*S. riddellii* is similar with narrower, keeled leaves
Full sun to part shade, average to rich, moist to dry soil	Seed, division	*S. hispida* and *S. erecta* are similar; *S. bicolor* has white flowers.
Sun, average to rich, moist soil	Seed, division	A stately goldenrod of excellent garden merit. Lovely in bud, bloom, seed. Rose-pink fall color.
Sun or part shade, average, moist or dry soil	Division	A creeping species that forms spectacular clumps. Cultivar: 'Fireworks' (pendant flowers).
Sun, well-drained, sandy soil. Tolerates heat, seaside conditions	Seed, division	Grows too tall and flops in rich soil
Full sun to light shade, gravelly, humus-rich or sandy soil	Seed, division	A variable species with an extensive range. Eastern plants are larger, more robust. Western, mountain plants dwarf even in cultivation.
Full sun to light shade, sandy or loamy, moist to dry soil	Seed, division	Variable bloom depends on region and, perhaps, soil
Average to rich, moist soil	Cuttings	Cultivar: 'Golden Fleece' (floriferous, 2-ft selection from Mt. Cuba Center)

Solidago 'Fireworks' at Niche Gardens, Chapel Hill, North Carolina

Foliage: Rippled, hairy leaves, green above, pale below, evergreen

Hardiness: Zones 4 to 9

Height: 6- to 8-inch clump, 24 inches in bloom

Regions: Northwest, northern California, Mountain, Midwest, South, Northeast, Mid-Atlantic

Landscape use: Ground cover, edger in moist sun to shade

Culture: Sun to part shade, moist soil, good drainage

Propagation: Division, seeds; self-sows

THERMOPSIS VILLOSA (*T. CAROLINIANA*)
Carolina bush pea, false lupine
LEGUMINOSAE Pea family

Big, showy Carolina bush pea blooms between spring and summer like a giant, lemon yellow lupine. Flowers last for about two weeks, but the foliage, valuable for its early fullness, stays clean and attractive all summer long. Although Carolina bush pea is slow to develop, it eventually becomes a bushy 4 feet and functions somewhat like a spring-blooming shrub.

Although found on the edges of woodland in the wild, Carolina bush pea does best in absolute full sun and well-drained soil. It is drought-resistant.

Origin: North Carolina to Georgia

Flower: Lemon yellow pea flowers on very erect racemes to 10 inches long, followed by interesting seedpods

Foliage: Attractive, bright green leaflets, downy below, growing into upright, bushy 4- to 5-foot clumps

Hardiness: Zones 3 to 8

Height: 4 to 5 feet

Regions: Northeast, Midwest, Mid-Atlantic, South

Landscape use: Border, accent

Indian pink (Spigelia marilandica)

Culture: Full sun; average to somewhat dry, well-drained soil

Species: There are a number of western species. Of these, golden banner (*Thermopsis montana*) from the Great Basin area is available. It grows to only about 2 feet, with foliage and flowers similar to that of *T. villosa.*

Propagation: Dry seed (boiling-water soak), sown in spring or fall; or by division

TIARELLA CORDIFOLIA AND T. CORDIFOLIA VAR. COLLINA Foamflower
SAXIFRAGACEAE Saxifrage family

There was a time when people who cared about things like this knew—or thought they knew—that there were two foamflowers: a runner, *Tiarella cordifolia,* and a clumper, *Tiarella wherryi,* now correctly *Tiarella cordifolia* var. *collina.* The runner was great for rapidly covering ground in humusy shade and made a splendid show when its tight little buds on 12-inch stems opened to frothy white flowers that lasted about three weeks in late April and early May. The clumper stayed in place, had slightly pinkish blooms, and put its energy into a terrific show for two whole months. Although the flowers of both are quite different from those of coral bells, the leaves of both reveal a kinship. Nearly evergreen (in my Zone 7 garden), foamflower foliage turns a leathery cordovan after frost. A clumping cultivar, 'Oakleaf', also evergreen, spends winter on an exposed slope plastered to the ground as flat as if a steamroller had run over it.

Suddenly, along with a lot of interest in foamflowers, there are many more to choose from. Because different populations in the wild have enormous variation, the permutations are endless and always delightful. I haven't seen an unattractive one yet! Great was and is the temptation for nurserypeople to find lovely plants and introduce new cultivars. There are many to choose from, but 'Oakleaf' remains a favorite for its handsome ruff of foliage.

Origin: Eastern North America

Flower: White to pink feathery wand that lasts longer on the clumping foamflower, in April–May.

Foliage: Evergreen in warm climates, often with maroon coloration

Hardiness: Both are hardy in Zones 3 to 8

Height: 12 inches

Regions: Eastern North America

Landscape use: The running foamflowers make great ground covers for wooded areas. Clumpers are good edgers.

Culture: Moist, humusy soil, sun to part shade

Species/cultivars: 'Slick Rock' (a vigorous runner with shorter, fragrant flowers), 'Oakleaf' (a floriferous clumper

Stokesia *'Klaus Jelitto'*

Wood poppy (Stylophorum diphyllum)

with handsome, plain green, oak-shaped leaves), 'Rambling Tapestry' (runner, burgundy veins). Foamflowers, like coral bells (*Heuchera*), are members of the saxifrage family. *Heucherella* is the result of a cross between these two species.

Propagation: Fresh seed with light; division

TOLMIEA MENZIESII Piggyback plant, youth-on-age

SAXIFRAGACEAE Saxifrage family

A florist's favorite familiar houseplant, piggyback plant is hardly a tender tropical. It is a common carpeter on the forest floor from northern California to British Columbia and even up to southern Alaska. Its coarsely toothed, rounded leaves often produce baby plantlets at the juncture of leaf and stalk—thus, its common names. The several 1-foot flowering stalks are tipped with rather modest nodding flowers of an unusual chocolate color, dotted with yellow pollen sacs. Dr. Arthur R. Kruckeberg, an expert on the flora of the Pacific Northwest, writes that this and fringe cup (*Tellima grandiflora*) infrequently hybridize in the wild; such a cross should produce a good woodlander.

Origin: Woodlands of western North America

Flower: Small brown flowers on 1-foot stalks in spring

Foliage: Hairy, lobed, rounded leaves grow new plantlets at leaf and stalk junctures

Hardiness: Zones 7 to 10

Height: To 15 inches

Regions: Northwest

Landscape use: Woodland ground cover, hanging baskets

Culture: Moist, cool shade

Propagation: Division, plantlets on leaf/stem junctures

TRADESCANTIA X ANDERSONIANA (T. VIRGINIANA) Spiderwort

COMMELINACEAE Spiderwort family

People sing spiderwort's praises because it blooms in the shade, is hardy and undemanding, and flowers over a long period. For a long time, I was not one of those people. It looked like such a *messy* plant. Then I saw it blooming in a great mass, and what had previously looked unkempt had the spiky, uneven charm of an ornamental grass with the extra allure of flowers. The blue flowers are enhanced by red companions. It would thrive in the same moist soil and sun or light shade as cardinal flower, but spiderwort is also adaptable

*Fringe cups (*Tellima grandiflora*)*

enough to serve as a companion to pineapple sage or big red zinnias.

Origin: A hybrid of several species

Flower: Purple/blue, red, white

Foliage: Long, narrow, glaucous green leaves

Hardiness: Zones 4 to 9

Height: To 18 inches

Regions: Eastern North America

Landscape use: Shady border, wild garden, pot plant

Culture: Probably best in rather lean soil because they fall over as the growing season progresses when in moist, rich soil

Cultivars: There are many, including 'Major' (double flowers) and 'Red Cloud' (small plant, red flowers)

TRILLIUM

LILIACEAE Lily family

It is easy to see why the province of Ontario chose the trillium as its official flower. It is also easy to see why trilliums are officially endangered in the wild in the United States. It takes about seven years for a trillium to

Carolina bush pea (**Thermopsis villosa**)

grow from seed to flowering size. This represents a huge amount of work and time for nurserypeople, so the temptation to buy plants collected from the wild is a shortcut that is sometimes irresistible even to large, well-established firms because collectors typically charge very little for the plants they steal from the wild. When buying trilliums, *carefully* check your sources. Seek out those few growers and nurseries that have taken the trouble to propagate these slow-growing plants, and reward them with your business. In so doing, you will do this plant a double service: you will support a thriving wild population simply by leaving it alone, and you will also contribute to its overall population by adding this lovely plant to your own garden.

About 12 years ago, I bought some little tubers of the great trillium (*T. grandiflorum*) from the New England Wildflower Society and placed them expectantly on a moist but well-drained slope in bright shade that used to be the front lawn. It took, I believe, about three years before they bloomed, but then they formed a colony that is healthy and growing. What a pleasure it is in spring to walk the path to the front door and see these woodland treasures sparkling white and then fading to soft pink against the deep green of Christmas ferns!

Trilliums don't seem fussy at all—just slow. Immature three-leaved plants are popping up everywhere in that shady garden. Not at all like a pink lady-slipper that cannot adapt to conditions away from its site

in the wild, this trillium needs only standard woodland conditions to thrive. It will take many more years, probably, than I have left to have the kind of vast colony one reads about, but in the hopes that someone will be around to enjoy it, I open the mature seed capsules and shake them over un-trilliumed spots for future viewers.

There are many trilliums around the country. From the West Coast comes what I egocentrically think of as the western counterpart to the great trillium, one called *T. chloropetalum*. Its generally white flowers are large like those of the great trillium, but stemless on mottled leaves. Siskiyou Rare Plant Nursery offers *T. chloropetalum giganteum,* a form with maroon flowers. There is also a double, or at least double-looking, cultivar called *T. grandiflorum* 'Flore Pleno', the propagation of which is, I am told, a carefully guarded mystery.

Fairly common in eastern woodlands are both the nodding trillium (*T. cernuum*), whose agreeable white flowers really do seem to nod under the three-leaf canopy, and stinking Benjamin (*T. erectum*), a muted mahogany with a faint odor of beefsteak that attracts carrion insects as pollinators. Reputedly easy to grow is the eastern yellow *T. luteum*.

All trilliums come from moist, rich, well-drained woodland soils in part to full shade. They bloom for nearly a month in spring, then disappear—first the flowers and finally the foliage—in summer. Even the western forms are quite hardy—probably Zone 4. Plant all trilliums in fall. (See *Trillium* chart, pages 158–159.)

Foamflower (**Tiarella cordifolia**)

*Piggyback plant (*Tolmiea menziesii*)*

UVULARIA GRANDIFLORA Great merrybells, bellwort

LILIACEAE Lily family

Larger and showier than merrybells (*U. perfoliata*), great merrybells won't grow for me the way I have seen it in photos. It is said that this plant likes lime and my soil is acidic, but I also think it prefers a somewhat cooler climate than muggy Washington. At Garden in the Woods in Massachusetts, and at Mt. Cuba in Delaware, it looks wonderful with other delights of the spring woodland like white *Phlox stolonifera* and uncurling fern fronds. It would be spectacular massed.

Origin: Quebec west to Minnesota and south to Oklahoma and Tennessee

Flower: Lemon yellow, elongated bell flower in May

Foliage: Leaves are long, blue-green, ridged, and pierced by stems.

Hardiness: Zone 3

Height: To 24 inches

Regions: Northeast, Midwest, cooler parts of Mid-Atlantic, Northwest

Landscape use: Woodland garden

Culture: Moist, loose, humusy soil (with some lime) in part shade. Spreads by rhizomes. Plant in fall.

Species: Merrybells, *U. perfoliata,* smaller with persistent, perfoliate foliage, from Eastern United States, Zones 3–9. Wild oats, *U. sessilifolia,* with small, cream-yellow flowers, is similar, although its leaves are not pierced by stems and grow in a zigzag fashion.

Propagation: Seed; rhizome division

VANCOUVERIA HEXANDRA Inside-out flower

BERBERIDACEAE Barberry family

A sweet little woodland carpeter, inside-out flower has tiny, light green duckfoot leaves and dainty sprays of white flowers that look like they got dressed backward. A popular ground cover in sun or shade, it occurs in open woods from northern California to southern Puget Sound country (Washington). Unlike its rarer kin, *V. chrysantha* and *V. planipetala, V. hexandra* loses its leaves in winter. It is easy to increase your holdings by dividing and transplanting pieces of its sod.

Origin: Coastal Washington to California

Flower: Small, hanging white flowers in April/May appear to be turned "inside out."

Foliage: Light apple green, geometrically shaped compound leaves on thin, wiry stems

Hardiness: Zones 6(?) to 7

Height: To 15 inches

Region: Northwest

Landscape use: Ground cover

Culture: Moist, well-drained soil in light shade

Propagation: Division

*Spiderwort (*Tradescantia*) at Monticello*

Trillium

Name	Origin	Flower	Foliage	Zones	Height	Regions	Landscape Use
Trillium cernuum Nodding trillium	Newfoundland to Georgia	Nodding white flower fades to pink	Green leaves hide shy flower	3 to 8	9 in	Eastern North America	Woodland garden, rock garden
Trillium chloropetalum Wake robin	California	Large white, cream, maroon in spring	Attractive mottled leaves	6 to 8	1 ft	Northwest, California	Woodland garden, rock garden
Trillium erectum Stinking Benjamin, wet dog trillium	Eastern North America	Muted maroon flowers with narrow petals, green bracts	Neat green leaves in a large clump	3 to 8	2 ft	Eastern North America	Woodland garden, rock garden
Trillium grandiflorum Grand trillium, wake robin	Eastern North America	Large white flowers fade to pink	Clean green foliage in a large clump	3 to 8	18 in	Eastern North America	Woodland garden, rock garden
Trillium luteum Wood trillium	Kentucky, Georgia to South Carolina, Florida	Lemon-yellow stemless spring flowers, fragrant	Mottled leaves on 1-in plants	3 to 8	1 ft	Northeast, Mid-Atlantic, South	Woodland garden, rock garden
Trillium ovatum Coast trillium	British Columbia to California	Large white flowers fade to pink, spring	Clump of green leaves, 1 ft	6 to 8	1 ft	Northwestern North America, California	Woodland garden, rock garden
Trillium rivale Snow trillium, dwarf white trillium	Pennsylvania, Midwest	White, curved petals, some purple markings, spring	Flowers held above very small (6-in) green clump	3 to 8	6 in	Northeast, Midwest	Woodland garden, rock garden

VANCOUVERIA PLANIPETALA Inside-out flower
BERBERIDACEAE Barberry family

This inside-out flower is a redwood understory plant in Jenny Fleming's intriguing Berkeley, California, garden composed of different California plant communities. It shares the kind of shady microclimate one would find under the giant redwoods with redwood sorrel, wild ginger, and *Trillium ovatum*. Jenny Fleming much prefers the species *planipetala* to *V. hexandra,* which has a comparatively inconspicuous flower and, in her garden, starts looking shabby by midsummer. *V. planipetala* spreads slowly but steadily and is not aggressive.

Origin: Coniferous forests, Oregon to California
Flower: Tiny white flowers with swept-back petals on tall stems.
Foliage: Delicate foliage is glossy green, evergreen, beautiful!
Hardiness: Zones 7(?) to 9
Height: 4 to 16 inches (taller in shade; shorter in part sun)
Region: Cool woodland gardens of the West Coast
Landscape use: Ground cover in shade and part shade; nice with azaleas
Culture: Prefers loose acid soil, some summer moisture, mulch; grows, but burns badly, in sun. Takes deep shade. Once well established is very persistent; will grow in cracks between rocks.

Propagation: Division is best and easy, but divide in fall so that roots will be well established before spring growth.

Double trillium on sale at Garden in the Woods, Framingham, Massachusetts

Culture	Propagate	Comment
Easy, shade, humusy soil	Seed	Flowers are hard to see
Part shade, humusy soil	Seed, division of tuberous roots	Attractive, spreading plant
Part shade, humusy soil	Seed, division	The common name maligns a delightful plant, odor is not noticeable; prolific seeder
Part shade, humusy soil	Seed, division of tuberous roots	Worth waiting for its seedlings to bloom; self-sows
Part shade, humusy soil	Seed, division	Unusual, fragrant flowers
Part shade, humusy soil	Seed, division	Very easy, very showy
Part shade, humusy soil	Seed, division	Nice habit

VERBENA CANADENSIS Rose verbena, purple verbena

VERBENACEAE Vervain family

People use the words "rose" or "purple" to distinguish this verbena from the red one from South America, which is not hardy and is grown as an annual. In the North, where rose verbena is not hardy, it, too, is grown as an annual. In the Southeast, rose verbena has been a garden favorite for generations. Dense, crinkly green foliage creeps out over walks and paths, blurring boundaries; rose-purple flower heads are produced all summer. In the sunny, somewhat dry position it prefers, rose verbena is vigorous and can overpower neighbors, so I contain it in pots that can be nestled into the border or allowed to hold their own on deck and doorstep.

Origin: Pennsylvania to Florida, west to Iowa, Colorado, and Mexico

Flower: Rose-violet flowers in umbels all summer

Foliage: Low, spreading purple stems contrast with medium green, lobed, crinkly leaves.

Hardiness: Zones 6 to 7

Height: 8 to 12 inches

Region: Southeast

Landscape use: Edger, pot plant, rock garden

Wood trillium (Trillium luteum)

Culture: Sun, medium to dry soil, good drainage. I've lost plants in wet clay in winter.

Species: Moss verbena (*V. tenuisecta*) is a low-growing species with ferny leaves and purple flowers, *V. bipinnatifida* is a glorious everblooming native perennial or ground cover with neatly incised leaves that makes a mat 1 to 2 feet across. Flowering begins in May, with flushes of bloom until frost. Long lived and adaptable.

Forms/cultivars: Light, dark purple, white, pink; 'Appleblossom' (large pink flowers); 'Homestead Purple' (deep purple, resistant to mildew, extremely vigorous, and evergreen in the South); 'Silver Anne' (pink, from Christopher Lloyd's garden in England)

Propagation: Seed, cuttings

VERNONIA NOVEBORACENSIS Ironweed

COMPOSITAE Sunflower family

Ironweed is the source of that marvelous, riveting, deep magenta we have enjoyed on roadsides in late summer from Massachusetts to Mississippi. New to gardens, it is a great anchor plant that will give depth and substance to a planting. I like the way it is used as a companion to purple beauty berry in the perennial border at Brookside Gardens in Wheaton, Maryland. Catalogs generally list its potential height as 4 to 6 feet, but it is also responsive to soil conditions, and in a very rich site it may reach up to 8 feet! The "iron" in its common name comes hon-

Great merrybells (**Uvularia grandiflora**)

estly. Divide roots with an axe or chainsaw.

Origin: It is found in the wild from Massachusetts to Mississippi, and I have seen it blooming lustily along the interstate in northern Ohio in August.

Flower: Deep purple

Foliage: Coarse leaves

Hardiness: Zones 5 to 8

Height: 4 to 8 feet

Region: Eastern United States

Landscape use: Back border, specimen

Culture: Sun, medium to moist soil. If you wish, cut back ironweed in June for a more manageable size.

Species: The coastal ironweed, *Vernonia acaulis,* is generally shorter in clump but sends up wonderful airy flowers that can reach 7 feet. Unfortunately, it is almost impossible to acquire. *V. missurica,* a western species, grows to 6 feet.

Cultivar: 'Purple Haze' (deep violet flower)

Propagation: Seed (sow heavily)

VERONICASTRUM VIRGINICUM (VERONICA VIRGINICA) Culver's root

SCROPHULARIACEAE Figwort family

In the snake oil days of time gone by, Culver's root served as a useful, if unglamorous, liver tonic and laxative. That was then. Now it is coming into its own as an ornamental as elegantly understated as a white-on-white room. But it shows its subtle colors only if massed in groups of four or more. A thoroughly vertical plant, Culver's root is much taller than it is wide, with flowers held upright like narrow candelabras. In a group, this uprightness is enhanced through repetition, and the subtle white flowers are intriguing en masse.

Stories about where *Veronicastrum* is found in the wild conflict. Reputable observers swear it occurs on upland prairies; others have found it in wet meadows. For me, it performs in a good, moist soil.

Origin: Massachusetts to Manitoba, Florida to Texas

Flower: Tiny white flowers held in upright racemes, in June

Foliage: Narrow leaves whorled around erect stems

Hardiness: Zones 3 to 8

Height: Grows to 6 feet but is usually about 40 inches tall and only something over a foot wide

Regions: Everywhere conditions are moist enough

Landscape use: Perennial border

Culture: Rich, moist soil and sun in the North, but half shade in hot climates; spreads by stolons, but not invasive

Cultivar: 'Rosea' (pink flowers)

Propagation: Root division, stem cuttings, seed

VIOLA Violet

VIOLACEAE Violet family

New Brunswick, Prince Edward Island, Delaware, and New Jersey honor the violet as their official flower. And no wonder! Violets are second only to roses in their rich history and garden lore. In the language of flowers, they were symbols of faithfulness. In my memory, they will forever be associated with the first warm, fine afternoons of late spring, when, as children, we would gather them into thick fistfuls or sit on the new, green grass and work them into fragile chains.

Inside-out flower (**Vancouveria hexandra**)

Rose verbena (Verbena canadensis)

Much later, when I had young children of my own, I remember a violet harvesting expedition. One fine Easter Saturday, cousins, aunts, and uncles set out with baskets to pick some hundreds of the thousands of the gray-violet Confederate violets (*V. papilonacea*) in our yard, which we cooked into violet syrup for pancakes. After the last pancake had soaked up the last of that sweet, flowery syrup, I remember thinking that we had tasted the essence of spring.

Violets that haven't been subjected to herbicides or pesticides are edible. The flowers make a lovely garnish whether fresh or candied (dipped first into loose meringue and then into sugar).

Over 70 species of violets are native to North America, and nearly as many species come from other parts of the world. Some, like the bird's foot violet, are shy and solitary. Others, like the Labrador violet, are more gregarious, and some, like the Confederate violet, are downright aggressive.

So efficiently do some members of this genus reproduce themselves that people can grow violets without even trying. But there are places even outside of the kitchen where this kind of vigor is a boon. Shady places between buildings and odd corners where the lawn-

mower won't reach are perfect for violets.

Violets are not always violet in color. They come in whites, grays, yellows, and purples. Good wildlife plants, they attract fritillary butterflies that lay their eggs on or near the violets, which later serve as caterpillar food. Birds also take violet seeds, and rabbits eat the leaves.

The chart on pages 164–165 by Richard Weaver, whose We-Du Nursery in Marion, North Carolina, carries many species, includes some of the most ornamental violets for garden use.

ZAUSCHNERIA CALIFORNICA California fuchsia
ONAGRACEAE Evening primrose family

When I think of California fuchsia, it is the bright scarlet-flowered kind that comes to mind. I first saw it not in California, as its name might suggest, but in a Denver rock garden, where it was a blaze of red in October. There it dominated a show that also included buckwheat and kinnikinnick.

This species seems infinitely variable. Flowers can be big or smallish, scarlet or pink, and the leaves may be green, gray, narrow, or elliptical. The archetypal type has velvety gray-green leaves on a low-spreading plant.

Ironweed (Vernonia noveboracensis)

Brilliant scarlet trumpet flowers, about 1½ inches long, bloom from July until frost on the ends of the many branches. Clumps grow steadily outward.

Bart O'Brien of Rancho Santa Ana in Claremont, California, has the following suggestions for growing California fuchsia: In colder climates (Zone 6 and colder), he says, "It is a good idea to overwinter cuttings or small plants in a protected area." Try growing new plants from sections of these underground runners. To keep the plant looking good, "cut plants to half-inch stubs in late fall or early winter. If you find that your plants still seem to have a ratty appearance when they bloom, treat them as follows: cut them again in late fall or early winter and a third time in June."

Origin: Dry, rocky places throughout California

Flower: Bright red trumpets borne profusely from late summer into fall; there are also pink and white forms

Foliage: Narrow pale green to gray-green leaves covered with a fine down

Hardiness: Zones 4 to 10

Height: Plus or minus 1 foot

Region: A much wider range than its name suggests. I have seen spectacular specimens in Denver.

Landscape use: A ground cover in combination with other plants for dry places, rock gardens, banks, and edges. When established, it is tough and drought-tolerant and will take or do without summer water.

Culture: Lean, rocky, gravelly soil and drought keep its tendency to invade under control. Impervious to heat, it spreads outward by underground runners. Give it excellent drainage. Expect hummingbirds when it blooms. Most zauschnerias give their best performance when cut back to ½-inch stubs in late fall or early winter.

Species/cultivars: 'Evert's Choice' (scarlet, 4 to 6 inches), 'U.C. Hybrid' (bright orange-red, 2 feet), 'Cloverdale' (pale orangy red, 6 inches by 3 feet). *Z. californica* subsp. *latifolia* grows to 2 feet.

Propagation: Seed (blooms within two years), tip cuttings, rooted runners

ZAUSCHNERIA SEPTENTRIANALIS 'Mattole'
California fuchsia, hummingbird flower
ONAGRACEAE Evening primrose family

Dearly loved by hummingbirds are zauschneria's beautiful red flowers that open like narrow trumpets. There are also rare pale pink forms, but Jenny Fleming, whose garden overlooks San Francisco Bay, reports that they do better with inland heat in California and poorly on the coast. Leaves vary. About 1 inch long, some are narrow and some are oblong, and they come in a lovely range from light greens to soft gray forms.

From experience and observation, Jenny Fleming prefers the silvery gray 'Mattole'. Unlike most forms of zauschneria that are very invasive, 'Mattole' tends to be well behaved and spreads outward as a clump. 'Brilliant Smith' is another cultivar she rates as superior. It is similar but has green leaves. These cultivars are more handsome than many zauschnerias that become rangy, dry, brown, and rather unattractive about the time of flowering.

Origin: Near the Mattole River in California

Flower: Bloom from late summer or September, until winter cold arrives.

Foliage: Silvery gray leaf, broader than that of *Z. californica* and very attractive

Hardiness: Zones 7 to 10

Culver's root (Veronicastrum virginicum)
at White Flower Farm

Bird's foot violet (Viola pedata)

Viola pubescens

Height: 1 to 2 feet, but usually lower. Mine are not above 6 inches tall.

Region: California

Landscape use: Ground cover, rock garden, dry garden

Culture: Does very well in the summer without moisture; can tolerate any garden condition except shade, but it does fine in partial shade; likes gravelly soil.

Species: *Z. arizonica* has fantastic bright red flowers on 3-foot herbaceous plants with midgreen, thin leaves. It attracts hummingbirds and provides excellent late summer color from August until frost. It will not bloom well without strong sun. Deep roots don't withstand long pot culture. Plant by midsummer to establish before frost. Self-sows when happy. Very hardy. Zone 5.

Propagation: Easy by division in late fall; also easy by cuttings in July

ZINNIA GRANDIFLORA Plains zinnia, desert zinnia, prairie zinnia

COMPOSITAE Sunflower family

A Little Big Plant, plains zinnia grows only 6 to 8 inches high, but this tough, drought- and heat-tolerant perennial covers roadsides and fields with bright yellow flowers all summer. Gail Haggard, whose company, Plants of the Southwest, sells seeds of it, writes, "We've seen Prairie Zinnia on almost vertical hillsides."

The bright golden petals around orange eyes are held on branched stems that rise from a little, ground-hugging cushion that spreads wider than it is tall. Prairie zinnia is best grown from seed in a site that enjoys full sun and good drainage. It is not fussy and will tolerate calcareous soil. As I write this, I have convinced myself to try this in hanging baskets next summer!

Origin: Southwestern United States, Colorado, Kansas, into Mexico

Flower: Bright yellow petals

Foliage: Low mound of ferny foliage

Hardiness: Probably Zones 4 to 9

Height: To 6 inches

Regions: Southwest, parts of Midwest and Mountain regions

Violet foliage as a charming impromptu ground cover in Joanna Reed's garden

Viola

Name	Origin	Flower	Foliage	Zones	Height	Regions	Landscape Use
Viola appalachiensis	Pennsylvania to West Virginia	Pale to deep violet	Mat-forming, leaves small, round	4 to 7	2 to 3 in	Northeast, Mid-Atlantic, higher elevations in the South	Ground cover for small areas
Viola canadensis	Newfoundland to Alberta to South Carolina, Arizona	White, tinged purple outside	Large, heart-shaped leaves on tall stems	3 to 10	10 to 15 in	North America	Wild garden
Viola labradorica	Labrador to Alaska, south to New York, Michigan	Deep violet, white eye	Young leaves red-purple; mature leaves purplish	2 to 6	4 to 6 in	Northeastern North America	Accent in shade garden, rockery
Viola palmata	Maine to Minnesota, south to Mississippi, Florida	Deep violet, white eye	Leaves palmately lobed, tinged purple when young	3 to 8	6 to 10 in	Eastern, midwestern North America	Wild garden, Edging, ground cover
Viola papilionacea Confederate violet	Maine to Minnesota, south to Georgia, Oklahoma	Deep violet, white eye	Leaves large, heart-shaped, bright green	3 to 8	4 to 6 in	Eastern, midwestern North America	Edging, ground cover, wild garden
Viola pedata Bird's foot violet	Maine to Minnesota, south to Florida, Texas	Large, pale to deep lavender; bright orange stamens	Leaves deeply divided into many narrow segments	3 to 9	3 to 5 in	Eastern, midwestern North America	Rockery
Viola primulifolia	Quebec to Minnesota, south to Florida, Texas	Small, white with black in center	Stoloniferous; leaves pale green, oblong	4 to 9	2 to 4 in	Eastern, midwestern North America	Ground cover
Viola pubescens	Nova Scotia to North Dakota, south to North Carolina, Oklahoma	Yellow; dark lines in center	Tall stems with hairy leaves	4 to 7	10 to 12 in	Eastern, midwestern North America	Wild garden
Viola rostrata	Quebec to Wisconsin, south to Georgia, Alabama	Long-spurred, pale blue with dark center	Semierect stems; small, heart-shaped leaves	4 to 8	4 to 5 in	Eastern, midwestern North America	Wild garden
Viola striata	New York to Minnesota, south to Georgia, Missouri	Cream-colored; dark lines in center	Semierect stems; small, heart-shaped leaves	4 to 7	6 to 8 in	Eastern, midwestern North America	Wild garden
Viola walteri	Ohio south to North Carolina, Texas	Blue-violet; paler in center	Trailing stems; small heart-shaped leaves	4 to 8	6 to 8 in	Midwest, South	Wild garden

California fuchsia (Zauschneria californica)

Landscape use: Ground cover, rock garden, front border
Culture: Perfect drainage
Cultivars: None that are an improvement
Propagation: Seed

ZIZIA APTERA Heartleaf golden Alexander
UMBELLIFERAE Parsley family

The first time I laid eyes on a heartleaf golden Alexander was at Garden in the Woods in Framingham, Massachusetts, where it was in full bloom in May. One look at the wispy, yellow flowers that looked like lacy, see-through yarrows and the leaves that

Culture	Propagate	Comment
Shade; humus-rich soil	Seed, division	Makes a dense mat
Shade; humus-rich soil	Division, seed	Tall, stoloniferous species; spreads vigorously
Shade; humus-rich soil	Seed	Beautiful plant, outstanding for its dark foliage
Sun or shade; loamy soil	Seed, division	Not as invasive as *V. papilionacea*
Sun or shade; loamy soil	Seed	Seeds in profusely; 'Confederate' has gray-blue flowers
Sun or light shade; good drainage	Seed	Beautiful plant but not as easy as others; *V. bicolor* has deep velvety purple upper petals
Sun or light shade; likes moisture	Division, seed	Spreads rapidly, making a dense mat
Shade; loamy soil	Division, seed	Tall, stoloniferous species; spreads rapidly
Shade; humus-rich soil	Seed, division	One of the showiest violets
Shade; humus-rich soil	Seed, division	Unusual color; easy and vigorous
Shade; humus-rich soil	Seed, division	Rare in cultivation

Heartleaf golden Alexander (Zizia aptera)

emerged from between rocks like big, waxy ruffles, and I knew I had to have this plant. Heartleaf golden Alexander is very hard (but not impossible) to find, and I can't really think why because it is such a neat, pretty plant. Prairie Moon Nursery in Winona, Minnesota, Prairie Nursery in Westfield, Wisconsin, and We-Du Nursery in Marion, North Carolina, are some mail-order sources.

Heartleaf golden Alexander's leaves grow out of a circular clump and are attractive all by themselves. Semievergreen, they resemble the foliage of the common violet in shape, but are outlined by a zigzag edging of yellow teeth; in texture, they have the feel of leathery hellebore leaves. They stand up in a lovely ruffled collar around delicate yellow flower umbels held on 12-inch stems in May and June.

Origin: North America

Flower: Yellow flower umbels that look like lacy yarrows, in May and June

Foliage: Semievergreen, waxy, medium green leaves shaped like those of the common violet

Hardiness: Probably Zones 3 to 8

Height: 10 inches in clump, 20 inches in flower

Region: North America

Landscape use: Rock garden, woodland garden, shady border

Culture: Moist, humusy soil; part sun

Species: Golden Alexander (*A. aurea*) has similar flowers but divided leaves; it will take an even wetter site and blooms longer, but is reputed to be somewhat weedy.

Propagation: Seed

Desert zinnia (Zinnia grandiflora) *(Charles Mann photo)*

What

WOULD SPRING BE WITHOUT THE DELIGHTFUL RITUAL OF GROWING OR BUYING ANNUALS TO MARK THE FINAL PASSING OF COLD WEATHER? THESE ARE THE MIRACLE PLANTS THAT GROW FROM SEED TO FLOWER TO SEED IN A SINGLE GROWING SEASON. QUICK TO DEVELOP, THEY SPEND THEIR SHORT LIVES IN FULL BLOOM. THEY ARE THE FINISHING PLANTS, THE COLORFUL COMPLEMENTS TO THE GARDEN'S OTHER, MORE PERMANENT INHABITANTS.

THERE IS NO EASIER WAY TO SAMPLE NATIVES THAN BY PLANTING ANNUALS. AND WHETHER YOU LIVE ON THE 20TH FLOOR OF AN APARTMENT HOUSE IN NEW YORK CITY OR ON A RANCH IN IDAHO, YOU CAN GROW THESE OBLIGING PLANTS BECAUSE THEY TAKE TO WINDOW BOXES WITH THE SAME ENTHUSIASM AS THEY GROW IN THE FIELDS.

IF YOU'VE EVER SEEN A DRIFT OF CALIFORNIA POP-

OVERLEAF: *Each year, lucky Californians are treated to the sight of thousands of California poppies, blooming in the fields and on the hills.* ABOVE: *Texas bluebonnets, spectacular along roadsides in Texas, bloom where they are sown—here, in a container at the San Antonio Botanical Center.*

pies or Texas bluebonnets along a roadside, you know that their beauty is all the more poignant because, like youth, it passes in a season.

This chapter includes only a very small, token number of native American annual plants, as well as short-lived or tender perennials, plants that are perennial in warm climates but are killed by cold north of their range. Also included are biennials, plants that usually live for two years. What all of these plants share is a relatively short life span. They make up for what they lack in time with copious bloom. Some reseed generously.

ABRONIA VILLOSA Sand verbena
NYCTAGINACEAE Four-o'clock family

Playing prominent roles in yearly wild-flower shows, annual sand verbenas bloom on the heels of winter and spring rains in the deserts and sandy prairies of the West. Their perennial cousins bloom up and down the Pacific Coast throughout the year. Sand verbenas are not true verbenas; they are dryland plants that tolerate heat and drought but will also tolerate some summer water. In the garden, they serve as fast-growing, showy ground covers for hot, dry place.

Ranging in height from about 8 inches to about 2 feet, sand verbena's typically sticky, sprawling stems grow wider than high. They have thick, fleshy leaves and many tiny tubular flowers held in 2-inch clusters. They require perfect drainage and are not particularly hardy. Generally treated as annuals, they are started anew from seed sown in place each year in fall or early spring. Plant sand verbena after scraping off the seed's papery envelope.

Origin: Western North America
Flower: 2-inch umbel of pink or white flowers
Foliage: Light green, smooth or hairy, pairs of widely spaced leaves
Height: To 2 feet
Regions: Southwest, California
Landscape use: Ground cover
Culture: Sow where plants are to grow; in mild climates sow in fall; sun, good drainage. Perennials are often treated as annuals.
Species: *A. latifolia* (yellow), *A. maritima* (red), *A. umbellata* (pink, perennial)

Purple aster (Aster bigelovii) *(Charles Mann photo)*

ASTER BIGELOVII Purple aster
COMPOSITAE Sunflower family

Before flowering, biennial purple aster grows to a stout 15-inch mound. Then, in fall, its mound of neutral gray-green foliage covers itself with very showy aster flowers that can be any shade from pale purple to wine-colored. For dazzling color contrast, combine purple aster with chrome yellow chamisa.

Origin: Montana to Arizona, Texas
Flower: 2-inch lavender-purple aster flower in early fall
Foliage: Gray-green foliage on recumbent stems
Hardiness: Zones 3 to 6
Height: To 15 to 36 inches
Regions: Southwest, Mountain West
Landscape use: Border, large wild garden, accent, ground cover

Desert marigold (Baileya multiradiata)

Culture: Plant in fall or very early spring in average soil and sun. Cut back in early summer for lower, more compact bloom.

ASTER TANACETIFOLIUS Tahoka daisy
COMPOSITAE Sunflower family

Stunning Tahoka daisy becomes a solid mound of bright purple when it blooms from late summer into fall, a short lived but stunning plant. Because it is low—about 20 inches—it has a neat effect in the front border or as a ground cover. The finely dissected foliage adds to Tahoka daisy's charms.

Origin: Dakotas to Texas
Flower: 2-inch glowing lavender flowers
Foliage: Finely dissected foliage, attractive by itself
Hardiness: Zones 3 to 7
Height: 20 inches
Regions: Dry prairie gardens, Southwest, Midwest, Mountain West
Landscape use: Border, wild garden
Culture: Full sun, sandy soil or dry loam

BAILEYA MULTIRADIATA Desert marigold
COMPOSITAE Sunflower family

A native of the western deserts, in the low desert, desert marigold flowers nearly all year, slowing only in cold weather. Arizona landscape architect Judy Mielke likes it for the softness it adds to plantings of other dryland natives and the seemingly endless supply of cheerful yellow flowers. Its low water requirement makes it compatible with cactus plantings and naturalized desert landscapes. Desert marigold's handsome gray foliage blends with the colors of cacti, while its bright golden yellow flowers add smart contrast.

Origin: Southwestern United States, Mexico, on dry plains, rocky slopes and mesas
Flower: Golden yellow, 1- to 1½-inch flowers with double petals around a golden eye
Foliage: Leaves are fuzzy, silver-gray, in a basal rosette.
Height: 1 foot high by 1 foot wide
Regions: Southwest, southern California
Landscape use: Meadow, softener with cacti, border
Culture: Sow in place. Keep moist until seedlings appear, then decrease water gradually. Full sun, excellent drainage. Drought-tolerant.

CLARKIA PULCHELLA Clarkia
ONAGRACEAE Evening primrose family

Named for Captain William Clark of the Lewis and Clark expedition, clarkias are natives of western regions, where they thrive in sun, cool night temperatures, and sandy, well-drained soils. Typically about 12 to 18 inches tall with pink (to lavender) flowers along the stem, clarkia has been in the nursery trade long enough for there to be a number of garden forms—including white and double forms that look a little like small hollyhocks. For a very pretty, instant cot-

Spider flower (Cleome serrulata) *(Charles Mann photo)*

tage-garden effect, combine them with cornflowers and sweet alyssum.

Origin: Sandy, open ground from Washington to Oregon and east to Montana

Flower: Typically four widely spaced three-lobed pink petals on a 2-inch flower, but there are many forms, including doubles and colors ranging from white to lavender

Foliage: Smooth, very long, narrow leaves widely spaced on a hairy stem

Height: To 24 inches

Regions: Rocky Mountain, high plains, California, Northwest

Landscape use: Border, meadow

Culture: Thrives in cool weather. Scatter seed on prepared bed in fall or as early in spring as the ground can be worked.

Species: Farewell-to-spring, *C. amoena,* from the north

Pacific Coast, grows to 3 feet and has a cup of joined petals in rose or pink, often blotched. Red ribbons, *C. concinna,* from the Northwest and northern California, has vivid rose petals that are deeply cut. *C. unguiculata* (formerly *C. elegans*), from California, grows to 3 feet, and has widely separated triangular petals in shades of lilac to purple as well as salmon pink.

CLEOME SERRULATA Spider flower, Rocky Mountain bee plant, stinking clover

CAPPARACEAE Caper family

The popular spider flower from tropical America, *Cleome spinosa,* has a northern cousin, Rocky Mountain bee plant, *C. serrulata.* Growing to 3 feet, Rocky Mountain bee plant blooms in a ball of pinky purple flowers with elegantly protruding spidery stamens. A good meadow plant, it is also useful as an all-summer bloomer in borders. Rocky Mountain bee plant has been used as a dye plant.

Origin: Northern United States and southern Canada from Illinois westward

Flower: 4- to 5-inch ball of pinky purple (sometimes white) flowers with spidery stamens

Foliage: Leaves are divided into three narrow leaflets, held along very upright stems.

Height: To 3 feet

Regions: Midwest, Northwest, Rocky Mountain, plains

Landscape use: Meadows, borders

Culture: Sow on a prepared bed in fall or early in spring.

Species: Yellow bee plant, *C. lutea,* ranges from Nebraska to Washington, California, and New Mexico; grows to 4 feet with yellow flowers.

COREOPSIS TINCTORIA Plains coreopsis

COMPOSITAE Sunflower family

One of the easiest annuals to grow anywhere, plains coreopsis blooms generously with dozens of maroon-banded yellow or simply yellow daisy flowers held on

Plains coreopsis (Coreopsis tinctoria) *(Charles Mann photo)*

California poppy (Eschscholzia californica)

rather airy stems. Just a few plants yield a richness of flowers in midborder, and it's a great source of cut flowers.

Plains coreopsis is still used as a dye plant. With an alum mordant, it yields a rich yellow color, and with chrome, an orange.

Origin: Western North America, but naturalized in the East

Flower: Typically a 1½-inch golden daisy flower with dark maroon banding, but also solid gold or gold/brown

Foliage: Very thin leaves, widely spaced on the stem, give an airy effect.

Height: To 3 to 4 feet

Region: North America

Landscape use: Meadow, border

Culture: Sow in spring

Species: Douglas's coreopsis, *C. douglasii,* from California, a solid yellow daisy flower, grows to about 10 inches tall. Stillman's coreopsis, *C. stillmanii,* from California, bears orangy yellow daisy flowers on delicate 12-inch plants.

ESCHSCHOLZIA CALIFORNICA California poppy
PAPAVERACEAE Poppy family

California poppies light up California meadows and hillsides in spring with their golden orange flowers. In the garden, they are hard to misplace. A single plant or a smattering throughout the border never looks wrong—perhaps because the leaves are so delicate and the flowers so winsome.

Short-lived perennials, they are often grown as annu-als that thrive, thanks to their taproots, where other plants fail—in dry, poor soil in windy, exposed locations. The taproot makes them difficult to transplant, but they are easily started from seed in place and will bloom 6 to 8 weeks later.

Origin: Vancouver Island through Southern California into Baja California

Flower: Typically bright orange, but also rose, terra-cotta, pink, red, white, or yellow 2- to 3-inch flower

Foliage: Handsome, lacy, gray-green clumps

Hardiness: Zone 4

Height: 12 inches

Regions: California, Southwest, Northwest, other places as an annual

Landscape use: Wild garden, low meadow

Indian blanket (Gaillardia)

Culture: Full sun, good drainage. Drought-tolerant, but in dry climates, supplemental water will keep plants flourishing. Deadhead for heavier, longer bloom. If plants are cut to the ground before they have gone to seed, then watered, they will reappear and flower fully again (although flowers will typically be a bit smaller and more yellow).

Species/cultivars: *Eschscholzia mexicana,* with yellow flowers, is very similar.

Propagation: Seed

Sunflower (Helianthus annuus)

nial. *G.* x *grandiflora* is a cross between the annual and perennial species and is the most commonly available. *G. pinnatafida* is a yellow-flowered species that comes from short grass prairies of the West.

HELIANTHUS ANNUUS Sunflower
COMPOSITAE Sunflower family

Annual sunflower is a familiar garden plant that is freely available in a variety of forms. Children (of all ages) and birds love the giant kinds that shoot as far as 9 feet high with huge flower heads composed of a ring of golden petals around a circle of beautifully patterned, tightly packed edible seeds. Commercially grown for these nutritious seeds, sunflowers are the source of an oil that is high in vitamin E.

Annual sunflower was one of the first

GAILLARDIA PULCHELLA Indian blanket
COMPOSITAE Sunflower family

Annual gaillardia is one of the plants that put on so splendid a spring show along roadsides—especially in Texas. In the garden, Indian blanket is a nonstop source of hot color in even the hottest weather. Banded red, orange, and gold, the big 3-inch daisy flowers grow about 18 inches tall, tolerating dry soil and unmitigated sun. They are fine in combination with threadleaf coreopsis. There is a perennial gaillardia, but in places with clay soil that is wet in winter, it usually dies, making the annual the plant of preference.

Origin: Florida to Colorado and south to Mexico
Flower: 2- to 3-inch daisylike flower around a prominent red-brown center. Flower is usually banded, orange, red, and/or gold. There are also cream-colored forms, solids, and doubles that resemble chrysanthemums.
Foliage: Long, narrow, downy leaves on a fuzzy stem
Height: To about 20 inches
Region: Hot, sunny spots anywhere
Landscape use: Cut flower, border, dry meadow
Culture: Sow in early spring. Plants bloom within six weeks.
Species/cultivars: Firewheel, *G. aristata,* is a peren-

Beach sunflower (Helianthus debilis)

plants brought from the New World to the Old, where it must have been a sensational symbol of botanical riches to come. It spread throughout Europe and is today a common annual both in England and on the Continent. In Russia, the edible seeds are cherished.

Origin: North America, from Canada into Mexico

Flower: Flower heads are about a foot across, with a ring of golden petals around a large seed head.

Foliage: Light green, 1-foot leaves are alternate along an upright stem.

Height: To 10 feet

Region: North America

Landscape use: Back border, wildlife plant

Culture: Full sun. Plant when the weather is settled and frost is no longer expected.

Cultivars: Lower-growing kinds are more useful in the flower border. Among these, 'Italian White', growing to 4 feet with creamy white petals, is attractive. 'Sunspot' grows to only 2 feet.

HELIANTHUS DEBILIS Beach sunflower
COMPOSITAE Sunflower family

Beach sunflower, a dune plant that has earned the respect of gardeners and landscapers in Florida for its fuss-free long bloom, bears golden yellow flowers with a brown eye that measure only 2 to 3 inches across. They are borne on long, floppy stems that do not stand upright, but bend over and weave around com-

Blue flax (Linum perenne)

panion plants. It is especially handsome in combination with dwarf Fakahatchee grass and muhly grass.

Origin: Along the coast from South Carolina to Florida and Texas

Flower: Small, 2- to 3-inch golden yellow flower with a brown eye

Foliage: Leaves are elongated heart shapes that appear smooth, but feel rough to the touch.

Height: Stems measure from 2 or 3 to 7 feet, but do not stand upright.

Region: Dunes, coastal gardens of the South

Landscape use: Nice with grasses, beach landscaping

Culture: Full sun; dry, sandy soil

IPOMOPSIS RUBRA (GILIA) Standing cypress, skyrocket
POLEMONIACEAE Phlox family

Standing cypress, a biennial, spends its first year as a ferny rosette less than a foot tall. By midsummer of its second year, it is a dazzling 6 feet, topped by a dozen scarlet trumpets lining the stalks. As soon as they bloom, hummingbirds arrive. Extremely difficult to transplant, standing cypress should be sown in place;

A golden form of Layia *with tidy tips look-alike*
Limnanthes *and* Nemophila (*white*)

thereafter, if its site is suitable, it will self-sow into a colony. It could share a site and a hot color combination with showy golden eye.

Origin: Dry, sandy soils of the Gulf Coast, Texas, and the Carolinas

Flower: Scarlet trumpets line the top of stalks

Foliage: An unbranched stalk with fine, ferny leaves

Hardiness: Zones 7 to 8

Height: 3 to 6 feet

Regions: Southwest, Gulf Coast, South

Landscape use: Accent, back border, a great hummingbird plant

Culture: Full sun; dry, well-drained soil

Species/cultivars: *Ipomopsis aggregata,* with a range from the high meadows of British Columbia over Montana to southern California, with multiple stems, is similar but shorter and often yellow.

Propagation: Seed

LAYIA PLATYGLOSSA Tidy tips
COMPOSITAE Sunflower family

Well named, tidy tips are a clean, clear yellow with white tips on the outer ends of the notched petals. Tidy tips and at least a dozen other *Layia* species are natives of California—splendid in early spring, when they bloom in great masses. Members of this genus are pretty anywhere, by ones and twos or by the dozen.

Origin: California

Flower: 2-inch clear yellow flower with white-tipped notched petals and black anthers in a yellow center

Foliage: Leaves are narrow, long, on loose stems.

Height: 12 to 18 inches

Region: California

Landscape use: Meadow, front border

Culture: Sow in early spring; thin to 4 to 6 inches apart

Species: *Layia glandulosa,* a dryland plant, has 1½-inch all-white or yellow flowers with notched petals.

LINUM PERENNE Blue flax
LINACEAE Flax family

Blue flax is one western plant that thrives just about anywhere. Delicate in appearance, its needle-shaped, evergreen leaves are tinted gray and are soft to the touch. A short-lived perennial that blooms for a long six weeks, it is related to the flax of commerce, *L. usitatissimum,* that provides both fiber and seeds for linseed oil.

Blue flax is a wispy, understated plant that is best placed where it can be observed close up. Otherwise, to be effective, it needs company. After seeing it blooming en masse in nursery rows, where the repetition of the fine, feathery leaves and the pale blue flowers is nothing

Texas bluebonnets (Lupinus texensis) *with pink evening primrose* (Oenothera speciosa)

Drummond's phlox (Phlox drummondii)

Scorpionweed (Phacelia bipinnatifida)

short of spectacular, I've tried it in small drifts of four plants among more substantial plants like conradina, lavender, and candytuft. One way to have a mass is suggested in the 1993 Holbrook Farm catalog. They cut the plant back in July, "stripping the seed onto the ground, and raking it into a light layer of mulch." This produces "dozens of new plants" the following spring.

Origin: Prairies and open woodland east of the Cascades
Flower: Small, sky blue, May into July
Foliage: Very fine, pale blue-green, upright
Hardiness: Zones 5 to 10
Height: 15 inches
Regions: Northeast and Midwest where hardy, Mid-Atlantic, South, Northwest, California, Southwest
Landscape use: Border, meadow
Culture: Sun, well-drained soil; short-lived perennial
Propagation: Dry seed (stratify 2 to 3 months)

LUPINUS TEXENSIS Texas bluebonnet
LEGUMINOSAE Pea family

A symbol of Texas, bluebonnets grow with wild abandon along the roadsides, but they are a little more difficult to establish in a garden. They do not transplant well, so should be sown in place in the fall. The Texas Highway Department, which is to be commended for its service to mankind by planting wild-flowers along roadsides, cuts back the previous year's growth and then spreads the seed-laden material where next year's wildflowers are to grow.

Lupines are legumes that fix nitrogen and can thrive in very poor, sandy soil. They require full sun and excellent drainage.

Origin: Texas

Flower: Spike of dark blue, white-eyed pea flowers that open from bottom to a whitish top. White eyes turn red after pollination.

Foliage: Light green, starry leaves with five leaflets

Height: To 1 foot

Regions: Texas, Southwest

Landscape use: Meadow, front border

Culture: Sow in place in fall where winters stay above 0°F. If available, use treated seed, and water after planting.

Species: Big Bend bluebonnet, *L. havardii,* is taller—about 3 feet—and at home in Arizona and on dry, stony hills along the Rio Grande.

PHACELIA BIPINNATIFIDA Phacelia, scorpion-weed

HYDROPHYLLACEAE Waterleaf family

Biennial *Phacelia* forms a very neat, 8-inch mound of hairy, mottled, dark, evergreen leaves that is attractive throughout the winter before bloom. In May, stems of light green compound leaves shoot up to a bushy 2 feet. These are tipped with sprays of small, ½-inch, pale lavender flowers around a greenish white eye. The individual flowers are not showy, but the bushy masses add great volume to the spring wildflower garden. Biennial *Phacelia* blooms longer than the annual *P. purshii.*

Origin: West Virginia, west to Illinois and Arkansas and south to Georgia

Flower: ½-inch pale lavender flowers in loose inflorescences at the tips of branches

Foliage: Neat, dark green, mottled mounds, evergreen, shooting up light green in spring

Height: To 2 feet

Regions: Mid-Atlantic, South, Northeast

Landscape use: Woodland garden, shade border

Culture: Sow or transplant into semishade in fall. *Phacelia* self-sows.

Species: Annual phacelia, *P. purshii,* grows in semishade to a bushy 2 feet with flowers almost identical in color to its biennial cousin. Close examination reveals that the petals are daintily fringed. Annual phacelia self-sows with gusto.

PHACELIA CAMPANULARIA California bluebells

HYDROPHYLLACEAE Waterleaf family

From the deserts of southern California comes a showy, drought-tolerant annual that has bright blue bell-shaped flowers with yellow anthers. California bluebells do best in places with hot, dry days and cool nights. Under ideal conditions, they can bloom for as long as three months.

Origin: Desert areas of southern California

Flower: Bright blue bells, about an inch across, borne on loose stems

Foliage: Broad, toothed, hairy leaves; may provoke an allergic reaction in susceptible people

Height: To 2 feet

Regions: Southern California, Southwest

Landscape use: Massing, dry border

Culture: Sow California bluebells in a dry, sunny bed in late spring. Flowers take about six weeks to bloom.

PHLOX DRUMMONDII Drummond's phlox, annual phlox

POLEMONIACEAE Phlox family

Annual phlox is probably better known than many native phloxes because its seeds were collected and sent to England by Thomas Drummond just a year before his death in 1835. In England, it was grown and admired at Kew Gardens and soon became firmly established as a garden plant. As such, it made the return trip into American gardens. All the while its stay-at-home relatives continued to paint Texas fields and roadsides with brilliant shades of hot to pale pink, red, lavender, and white. Today, seeds are freely available.

Close up, the flowers are flat and five-sided, giving them a geometric look. This is reinforced in some flowers by red or white stripes around the central yellow eye. Annual phlox thrives where summers are hot. There are tall and short forms of this phlox. The former reaches about 18 inches and the latter only about 8 inches. They will self-sow.

Origin: Grasslands of Texas

Flower: Clusters of 1-inch phlox flowers in shades of pink, red, lavender, and white, in spring

Foliage: Long, medium green, hairy, sticky leaves

Height: To 8 or 18 inches, depending upon type

Regions: Texas, Southwest, well-drained soils

Landscape use: Ground cover, front border

Culture: Sow seed in place in fall or transplant in very early spring.

Gra

Growing

EVERYWHERE EXCEPT IN THE SEA, GRASSES, SEDGES, AND RUSHES CARPET THE EARTH LIKE FINE DOWN. THEY ARE SO MUCH A PART OF EVERY NATURAL LANDSCAPE THAT THE GREAT GERMAN NURSERYMAN KARL FOERSTER CALLED THEM "MOTHER EARTH'S HAIR." THEIR PRESENCE IS CONSTANT, FRIENDLY, AND FAMILIAR.

IN FACT, IN THEIR CONSTANCY, WE SOMETIMES FAIL TO NOTICE THEM. THEY CERTAINLY DON'T GET THE CREDIT THEY DESERVE.

WHEN GARDENERS LOOK AT A MEADOW, WE FREQUENTLY COMMENT ON THE FLOWERS GROWING IN IT.

OFTEN TOTALLY IGNORED, THE MATRIX OF THAT MEADOW AND WHAT GIVES IT ITS FORM — ITS "MEAD-OWNESS" — ARE THE GRASSES. YET, IN CERTAIN SLANTS OF LIGHT, GRASSES GLOW LIKE A SHIMMERING HALO. WITH THIS QUALITY OF DAZZLE — NOT IN COLOR, BUT IN THE SPECTACULAR PLAY OF LIGHT UPON THEIR

OVERLEAF: *The histories of humankind and grasses are intertwined. Grass family members wheat and rye have nourished people for millennia and continue to do so today. Here, wheat surrounds a seaside farmhouse on Prince Edward Island.*
ABOVE: *"As I looked about me I felt that the grass was the country, as the water is the sea. . . . And there was so much motion in it; the whole country seemed, somehow, to be running."*
Willa Cather, My Ántonia

flowers—grasses add a new dimension to the garden.

Because grasses grow everywhere, there is a grass for every region and a grass for every purpose. In the garden, big ones provide background, volume, and drama; small ones add accent and texture. Many bloom late to extend the garden season; many are handsome in winter, when the foliage has dried and turned shades of almond and rust. Some like wet feet; some love a good drought; some are sun worshipers; others settle comfortably in the shade. All add movement and sound, swaying and rustling in the faintest breezes.

The care of grasses is easy. Choose one suited to your soil, region, and site. Care for it until it is established, then leave it alone. Grasses that are killed by frost or drought are still beautiful in their dry state. Cut them down before next year's growth starts—in late winter or whenever they start looking tired—and they'll spring back to life next year.

The extensive root systems developed by prairie grasses allow them to withstand extremes of climate. Newly sown grasses put energy into developing this root system, while the aboveground plant remains small for the first year or so. But then it will take off aboveground, with its tough roots below ready for difficult times.

Because grasses are relatively new to gardens, we tend to respond to them differently from the way we do to other plants. In the concentrated, highly cultivated spaces of our gardens, even a single grass—like an elegant bonsai placed on a table—has the power to evoke something larger. Grasses bring into gardens a sense of the uncultivated and the wild.

Dangling, deep purple turkeyfoot (Andropogon gerardii) *adds color and texture to this border of prairie plants, including* Silphium, *blazing star, and Joe-Pye weed.* (C. Colston Burrell Design)

ANDROPOGON GERARDII Big bluestem, turkeyfoot
GRAMINEAE Grass family

Once a predominant part of the sea of grass that covered the Great Plains, big bluestem can still be found in wild places from Maryland to Mexico. Clumping and strongly vertical, big bluestem gets one of its common names from the deep blue, sometimes silver-blue color of its stem. The smoky purple three-pronged seed heads give this grass its other common name, turkeyfoot.

As a garden specimen, this grass looks distinctly wild.

Minnesota landscape designer C. Colston Burrell used it brilliantly in a perennial border that joins the spontaneity of prairie with traditional form. He combined it with other prairie plants—blazing star, goldenrod, sunflowers, and Joe-Pye weed—in an easy-care, wildlife-friendly natural garden.

Other *Andropogons* and little bluestem (now *Schizachyrium,* formerly *A. scoparius*) have the same stiffly upright habit, but are much smaller—usually about 28 inches tall.

Origin: Eastern North America west to Arizona and Mexico

Flower: Purple flower spikes in August/September, followed by the "turkeyfoot" seed head

Foliage: A clumping grass with light green to blue-green blades, turning rich orangy brown in fall.

Hardiness: Zones 4 to 10
Height: Variable with moisture and soil fertility: 3 to 7 feet
Regions: Eastern North America, Midwest, parts of the Southwest, Mountain states
Landscape use: Prairies, tall ground cover, specimen
Culture: Sun; medium to dry soil with good drainage. In dry places, big bluestem will be shorter. Cut back in late winter/early spring.
Propagation: Division in early spring, or fresh seed sown in a cold frame in autumn

ANDROPOGON GLOMERATUS Bushy bluestem
GRAMINEAE Grass family

Before it blooms, bushy bluestem looks a bit like some of its near relatives, broom sedge and little bluestem—although it is likely to be found growing wild in places that are far more moist. It is a good plant for a low spot that doesn't drain well, but it will also take a place in ordinary soil with ease. In bloom, bushy bluestem is unmistakable. Its flowers, clustered on the upper part of the stem, dwarf those of its relatives. Dramatic in arrangements, the large, cottony flowers catch the light and sparkle in the garden.

Origin: Eastern United States where hardy
Flower: Showy, fluffy seed heads that shimmer in sunlight are its distinguishing characteristic, in late summer, fall.
Foliage: Light to medium blue-green summer foliage,

Broom sedge (Andropogon virginicus)

which turns a warm, handsome russet in fall
Hardiness: Zones 5 to 10
Height: To 4 feet
Region: Eastern United States where it is hardy
Landscape use: Moist meadows, accent, pond side, cutting garden
Culture: Full sun to very light shade; rich, moist soil
Propagation: Seed or division

ANDROPOGON VIRGINICUS Broom sedge
GRAMINEAE Grass family

Similar in habit to little bluestem, broom sedge is a common plant of neglected farm fields, frequently seen growing in the company of eastern red cedar (*Juniperus virginicus*). In the wild, it isn't very noticeable in summer, but in fall and winter, when its foliage turns orange, it is unmistakable. Some of the best wild stands I've seen have been along disturbed roadsides and in the center of a highway exit in Tyson's Corner, Virginia.

In a garden, broom sedge is stunning in fall in the company of chrysanthemums or late sunflowers like willowleaf sunflower or Maximilian's sunflower.

A few growers are selling broom sedge now. Norm Hooven of Limerock Ornamental Grasses feels it may be shorter lived than other *Andropogon*s.

Origin: Old fields, disturbed areas, dunes from New England to Kansas, south into Mexico
Flower: Stems unroll to reveal silvery flowers in September.

Bushy bluestem (Andropogon glomeratus)

Foliage: Light green, sometimes blue-green
Hardiness: Zones 5(?) to 8
Height: Clumps grow to 1 foot; in flower, they reach 36 to 40 inches
Regions: Northeast, Mid-Atlantic, Midwest, South, Southwest
Landscape use: Naturalized, ground cover, erosion control
Culture: Full sun, good drainage, average to poor soil
Propagation: Spring division or seed

ARISTIDA PURPUREA Purple three-awn
GRAMINEAE Grass family

Wispy and soft, purple three-awn contrasts with the dense forms of other desert plants like cholla or prickly pear cactus. To their stolidity it adds movement, says Arizona landscape architect Judy Mielke, who loves the way the slightest breeze sets its purple-hued heads swaying. The purple color of this perennial bunch grass is most intense in late spring and early summer, after which time the heads turn a light straw color. Purple three-awn occurs from southern California as far east as Arkansas, and south to northern Mexico, typically on plains and rocky slopes. Availability is limited, so if you see one, snap it up and treat it like an honored guest in your garden. Better yet, buy three. John Greenlee Nursery in Pomona, California, carries it.

Origin: Dry, rocky slopes, plains from southern California, east into Arkansas and south to northern Mexico

*Purple three-awn (*Aristida purpurea*) (Jessie Harris photo)*

*A blue grama grass (*Bouteloua gracilis*) lawn*
(Charles Mann photo)

Flower: Wispy, purple flowers, turning straw-colored
Foliage: Fine blades in a narrow clump
Hardiness: Zones 8 to 10
Height: 18 inches
Regions: Southwest, Lower Midwest, southern California
Landscape use: Good contrast to desert plants
Culture: Sun, dry soil, good drainage

BOUTELOUA GRACILIS Blue grama, grama grass, mosquito grass
GRAMINEAE Grass family

Native to the high prairies of the West and Midwest, blue grama is extremely drought-tolerant but, thanks to a sturdy constitution, can hold its own in wetter places if good drainage is provided. It has been used brilliantly with roses at Brookside Gardens in Maryland, where its softness and airy bloom mitigate the effect of spiky, thorny canes. In my garden, its wonderful lightness contrasts with yucca and prickly pear cactus.

Its fine texture, low height, and drought-tolerance have made it a favorite lawn grass alternative in dry climates, where it is often combined with buffalo grass (*Buchloë dactyloides*). When used as lawn, blue grama may or may not be mowed. It is clump forming, but mowing causes it to sprout out at the base, for a denser effect.

Origin: Wisconsin to Manitoba, south to California, Mexico, and Arkansas
Flower: Seed heads resembling eyelashes form on wiry 18-inch stems, mid- to late summer.
Foliage: Fine, thin blades are blue-green. Blue grama

Grasses

greens up in response to soil warming in spring and turns a bleached tan when not actively growing, that is, after freezes in autumn and/or under drought conditions. Blue grama forms a sod.

Hardiness: Zones 3 (purchase seed from fairly local sources, as there could be considerable difference in cold hardiness by region) to 9

Height: 12- to 18-inch clump

Regions: California, Southwest, Mountain West, Midwest

Landscape use: Drought-tolerant lawn, accent, ground cover, as filler in short grass/wildflower meadows

Culture: Sun, good drainage. Blue grama tolerates poor soil.

Species: Sideoats grama (*B. curtipendula*), slightly taller (to 2 feet) with double rows of flowers on one side of the stalk, turns a lovely orange color as summer fades into fall. Sideoats is useful for banks and meadows, where it forms a sod.

Cultivars: 'Hachita' and 'Lovington' are southwestern cultivars

Propagation: A warm-season grass, it requires warmth to germinate; as a modified bunchgrass, it should be seeded heavily (four pounds per 1,000 square feet) to ensure a thick sod.

BUCHLOË DACTYLOIDES Buffalo grass
GRAMINEAE Grass family

Once used to build sod houses on the prairie, buffalo grass is being put to a new use in dry climates: lawn. It is valued for its drought-resistance, freedom from disease and insect pests, and general toughness and durability. Instead of the short, clipped, stiff look typical of most lawn grasses, a buffalo grass lawn is fine textured, sage green, feathery, and it grows slowly. Because it attains only a 4- to 6-inch height, it doesn't really need mowing, but is generally trimmed one or two times during the growing season. With some summer water during periods of drought, buffalo grass will stay green. Otherwise, it turns a soft tan until the rains return.

Origin: Drier areas in the Great Plains and arid plains of the Southwest from 3,000 to 7,000 feet in elevation

Flower: Comb-shaped male flowers are inconspicuous; seeds mid- to late summer

Foliage: Very thin blades create a fine, dense texture; green up in late March in the South, mid-April to May in the North, in response to warming soil; cure to a bleached tan color after autumn frost and under drought conditions. Buffalo grass is a sod former.

A buffalo grass (Buchloë dactyloides) *lawn in Santa Fe*
(Charles Mann photo)

Hardiness: Zone 4 (and probably Zone 3) to 9

Height: 4 to 6 inches

Regions: Mountain, Southwest, dry parts of Midwest

Landscape use: Lawn, bank stabilizer

Culture: Irrigate when starting buffalo grass. It germinates best in the heat of summer; treated seed should be used, since germination of untreated seed may take two years; takes a season to form sod; seeding rate is four to six pounds per 1,000 square feet; once it is established, too much water and fertilizer will promote weak growth.

Cultivars: New cultivars for lawn use are being developed but were unavailable at the time of publication.

Propagation: Can be started from seed, plugs (10 to 12 inches apart), or sod

CALAMAGROSTIS FOLIOSA Reedgrass
GRAMINEAE Grass family

California designer Ron Lutsko, Jr., included reedgrass in his design for a California meadow at Strybing Arboretum and Botanical Gardens in Golden Gate Park. In April, when it blooms—wonderful, silky rabbit's foot flowers on lush clumps of cascading foliage—it is unforgettable.

At Rancho Santa Ana, where it grows among other California natives, horticulturist Bart O'Brien notes that it seems to take one of two forms, either of which is an admirable addition to the garden: It can be an erect spreading clump with upright to arching inflorescences; or it grows into a clump that looks as if it has been comfortably sat on, and the inflorescences radiate out from the center.

Fairly new to horticulture, reedgrass is catching on with Californians. Berkeley gardener Jenny Fleming describes it as "a truly elegant grass, attractive throughout the summer, with a lovely, soft, pale, dense, golden flower head." Reedgrass is a low, compact grass on a scale suitable for small gardens.

Origin: Coastal northern California: Sonoma to Humboldt counties

Flower: Dense, attractive, somewhat reminiscent of a miniature *Pennisetum setaceum*

Foliage: Light gray-green, often tinted with red or bronzy tones; crowded toward the base, radiates outward

Hardiness: Zones 8 to 10(?); hasn't been tested much yet

Height: 1 to 2 feet and about the same width

Regions: Pacific states (and possibly the Southwest)

Landscape use: Accent, small-scale ground cover, meadow, dry border, rock garden, path edging, foreground

Culture: Very easy, adaptable; plants tolerate heat; needs adequate supplemental deep watering in hot areas, occasional water elsewhere; needs room; light to clay soil; full sun on the coast, part shade inland.

Propagation: Division, seed

CAREX ALBURSINA White bear sedge
CYPERACEAE Sedge family

This handsome, evergreen sedge came into my garden after I saw it for the first time for sale in Meredith Clebsch's Native Gardens booth at the

White bear sedge (Carex albursina)

1990 Cullowhee Conference. What a satisfying purchase it has been! White bear sedge's broad, blue-green leaves are striking in contrast to a very dark, leathery *Leucothoe* neighbor, which turns a deep purple in winter. White bear sedge has trebled its size in a shady place with humusy, consistently moist soil. It has also self-sown: little sedges are growing out of a rotting log retaining wall.

A good plant to use around ephemerals such as Dutchman's breeches, it will carry on and add substance through the winter in a woodland garden.

Origin: Canada south to Tennessee and South Carolina in rich woods, calcareous soil.

Flower: 1-inch creamy yellow heads in ornamental sprays in midspring; after flowering, seeds develop along the stem

Foliage: Broad blades (to ³⁄₄ inch) are a matte green, dusted gray, evergreen.

Hardiness: Probably zones 3 to 8

Height: 4 to 6 inches

Region: Southeast

Landscape use: Edging, woodland garden

Culture: Part to full shade; moist, well-drained, humus

Propagation: Divide in fall or let it self-sow.

Reedgrass (Calamagrostis foliosa)

CAREX AUSTROCAROLINIANA
CYPERACEAE Sedge family

This sedge sounded interesting in the We-Du catalog, so I ordered one a couple of years ago and have been delighted as it matures to a handsome plant. Evergreen, its bright, yellow-green foliage is just a little darker than hosta 'August Moon'. Mine has formed a broad, low clump—now over 15 inches across—in semishade and humusy soil that is moist except in late summer. *Carex austrocaroliniana* is a wonderful foil for other evergreen plants such as Christmas fern, and it is hard to imagine a more striking woodland ground cover. It seems to me that it has looked fresh from early last spring through summer and deep into winter.

Last summer, I had a pleasant surprise: I began finding little bright green seedlings downhill from this plant that certainly look like *Carex* offspring. I hope they are.

Origin: Mountains of North Carolina

Flower: Tiny cream yellow bottlebrush flowers in spring, followed by seeds that develop partway down the stem and are hung from fine, threadlike stems

Foliage: Broader than tall clump of bright yellow-green

Hardiness: Zones 7 (possibly hardier) to 8

Height: To 12 inches

Regions: Mid-Atlantic, cool parts of the South, Lower Midwest

Landscape use: Woodland garden, ground cover in shade, accent

Carex austrocaroliniana *and Christmas fern*

Palm sedge (Carex muskingumensis)

Culture: Part shade; moist, humusy soil with good drainage

Propagation: By division, seed

CAREX MUSKINGUMENSIS Palm sedge
CYPERACEAE Sedge family

Named for the palmlike way its narrow leaves are held on upright stems, palm sedge doesn't have the flat blades growing from a central clump typical of a sedge. Instead, bright green blades, like the ribs of an umbrella, rotate around the stem. This grass is a sleeper: at first glance, it doesn't have the pizzazz of some of the bigger ornamental grasses, but once you grow it, it grows on you.

In my garden, palm sedge is a feathery ground cover in semishade with Catawba rhododendrons and rose azaleas in a place that is somewhat dry in summer and fall. The colony always looks better—greener, denser, more feathery, taller—in spring, when the soil is quite moist. By fall, if the weather has been dry, it looks tired and flops. No wonder! Grass nurseryman John Greenlee writes that it will grow in three to four inches of standing water! Clearly, this plant tolerates a wide range of conditions. Less than robust in a less than ideal site, my colony grows only to about 20 inches tall. In the rich, moist soil it prefers, palm sedge would grow taller and thicker and look lush and lovely until frost turns it apricot.

Origin: Moist soil from Ohio to Arkansas and north into Canada

Flower: Flowers are borne in May on long, tan stems that attract more notice than the flowers.

Foliage: Three tiers of 5- to 8-inch narrow, bright green blades radiate around an upright stem.
Hardiness: Zones 4 to 9
Height: To 3 feet
Regions: Upper Midwest, Mid-Atlantic, Northeast, Upper South, Northwest
Landscape use: Ground cover, stream and pond edges
Culture: Moist soil, sun to part shade
Cultivar: 'Wachtposten' (more upright, shade-tolerant)
Propagation: Seed or division

CAREX PENSYLVANICA Pennsylvania sedge
CYPERACEAE Sedge family

Pennsylvania sedge stays under 8 inches or so, never needs mowing, and tolerates the dry shade under trees. For these reasons, this semievergreen little sedge is gaining popularity as a soft, dark green lawn substitute in shady places where lawn grasses won't grow or where it is too difficult to mow grass. Because it is a clumper rather than a sod former (although it appears to send out short stolons that produce new clumps), the in-between spaces can be filled with the rapidly spreading *Crocus tomasianus* or with fall-blooming crocuses.
Origin: Eastern United States
Flower: I've never noticed bloom.
Foliage: Dark green, fine textured, from a clump
Hardiness: Probably Zones 4 to 9
Height: To 8 inches
Regions: Northeast, Midwest, Mid-Atlantic
Landscape use: Ground cover under trees
Culture: Part to full shade, good drainage
Propagation: Division

The dangling seed heads of northern sea oats (Chasmanthium latifolium) *in a fall bouquet with sweet black-eyed Susan, pokeweed, dogwood leaves, and* Miscanthus *flowers.*

CHASMANTHIUM LATIFOLIUM (UNIOLA LATIFOLIA) Northern sea oats, river oats
GRAMINEAE Grass family

Besides being the single most aggressive self-sowing grass in my garden, northern sea oats is also one of the most accommodating. It will grow happily in the dry shade of a large silver maple, but attains great girth much faster in rich soil. In both cases, its seedlings are legion and grip the ground with a tenacity that doesn't yield to a casual pull. Removing one always necessitates a trowel. I suspect northern sea oats is far less prolific in drier places, or it would cover the world.

Its fecundity aside, this is a beautiful and unique grass that grows waist-high with broad, 1-inch blades and lovely dangling seeds. In summer, it looks a little like a small bamboo. In fall, the foliage turns a bright yellow before darkening to muted orange.
Origin: Woodlands from Pennsylvania to Florida, New Mexico, and Mexico. It grows along the Potomac River in places that are occasionally flooded.
Flower: Dangling green flowers in August become brown, oatlike seed heads that are attractive in arrangements.
Foliage: Blades are broad and light green on delicate, but strong, wiry stems.
Hardiness: Zones 5 to 9
Height: 30 inches
Regions: Eastern North America where hardy, west to the Rockies
Landscape use: Ground cover, woodland plant, dry shade
Culture: Northern sea oats grows best in rich, moist soil in semishade, but it is so vigorous, it will adapt to almost anything else.
Propagation: Seed

CYMOPHYLLUS FRASERI Fraser's sedge
CYPERACEAE Sedge family

A plant of rich, cool, woodland soils, Fraser's sedge has broad, straplike, evergreen leaves and rather showy little white sedge flowers. Perhaps because the blades are rather coarse or because the plant sends out short stolons to form new clumps, the effect of a large clump seems tousled and informal. Bold, deep green leaves are a nice foil for moss and the delicate flowers of plants like Dutchman's breeches or trout lilies that also prefer rich woodland.
Origin: Moist woods from Pennsylvania to South Carolina
Flower: Oblong, pointed pom-pom of white petals

Fraser's sedge (Cymophyllus fraseri)

Foliage: Evergreen, deep green, broad, straplike blades from a clump; exposed leaves turn red in winter
Hardiness: Zones 5 to 9
Height: To 1 foot
Regions: Northeast, Mid-Atlantic, cooler elevations in the South
Landscape use: Woodland garden, especially nice with ephemerals
Culture: Moist, cool woodland soil with good drainage, part to full shade
Propagation: Division

DESCHAMPSIA CAESPITOSA Hairgrass
GRAMINEAE Grass family

Judging from all the attention this grass has received from European—especially German—hybridizers, my guess is that it is a better choice for cool-summer climates. Just the names given to cultivars suggest something far more glamorous and showy than what I have observed of its behavior in my hazy, hot, and humid summer garden: 'Goldgehaenge' ('Gold Drop'), 'Goldstaub' ('Gold Dust'), 'Bronzeschleier' ('Bronze Veil').

Where summers are hot, hairgrass seems to get a second wind in autumn. The fine, flat, deep blue-green blades are a good evergreen substitute for grass in shady places. And unlike lawn grass, hairgrass sports a respectable haze of inflorescences that turns creamy after frost.

Origin: Bogs and wet places in North America south to North Carolina and California, Eurasia
Flower: Airy panicles of little spikes, sometimes purplish
Foliage: Clump of dark green, fine, narrow blades
Hardiness: Zones 4 (probably 3) to 8
Height: To 3 feet
Regions: North America

Landscape use: Ground cover in semishade
Culture: Medium to moist soil, semishade
Cutivars: Many, including the above and 'Tautrager' (delicate inflorescence)
Propagation: Seed or division

ELYMUS CONDENSATUS Giant wild rye
GRAMINEAE Grass family

Giant wild rye, a native Californian, can take the long, dry California summer but is at its best with deep, infrequent watering in the summer months. Bart O'Brien of Rancho Santa Ana in Claremont suggests light fertilizer in late fall to early winter along with an annual trim. He cuts back ratty-looking clumps to stubs.

He reports that the giant wild rye on the market is a clone that rarely blooms, introduced by the Santa Barbara Botanic Garden. Clones have been reproduced vegetatively to preserve outstanding qualities, as opposed to seed-sown individuals that, like children, are unpredictable because they combine genetic material from two parents.

Like other members of the genus *Elymus,* giant wild rye is extremely vigorous and spreads by underground runners to form large colonies. This makes it an excellent choice for erosion control.

Origin: Santa Barbara Botanic Garden introduction
Flower: This clone does not bloom very often.
Foliage: ½-inch-wide, steel blue, fairly stiff blades

A field of hairgrass (Deschampsia caespitosa)

Hardiness: Zones 8 to 10(?); still untested
Height: 3 feet plus; in flower, the culms reach 5 feet
Region: Pacific states
Landscape use: Dry border, erosion control, massing, specimen
Culture: Sun to light shade; deep, infrequent water in the summer months; easy!
Propagation: Division

ERAGROSTIS SPECTABILIS Purple lovegrass
GRAMINEAE Grass family

No, purple lovegrass is not an aphrodisiac or the nom de plume of a romance writer. It is a small grass whose July flowers look like clouds of rose-purple rolling along the ground. On close examination, the clouds are not beads of raspberry vapor at all but fine, fine flower clusters on delicate threads of stems. Hung with dew in the early morning, the flowers glow quicksilver.

Purple lovegrass would be splendid massed in a broad edging with sedum 'Ruby Glow', a contrast in form and a complement in color. Kim Hawks of Niche Gardens Nursery in Chapel Hill, North Carolina, who grows it in masses in her display garden, recommends placing it "where it subtly appears rather than as a focal point."
Origin: Dry, poor soils of eastern North America
Flower: Panicles of fine rose flowers on delicate stems
Foliage: Medium green clump
Hardiness: Zones 6 to 9

Purple lovegrass (Eragrostis spectabilis)

Height: 20 inches
Regions: South, Mid-Atlantic, Midwest where hardy
Landscape use: Ground cover
Culture: Full sun; will tolerate poor soil; self-sows
Propagation: Seed or division

ERAGROSTIS TRICHOIDES Sand lovegrass
GRAMINEAE Grass family

While its name may conjure up teenagers on the beach, graceful sand lovegrass is simply a drought-tolerant native of sandy plains. With its red-purple-tinged leaf tips, fine-textured seed heads, and arching stems, it is a good accent in clumps for textural interest or in borders. Sand lovegrass will tolerate light watering or survive a rainless period.
Origin: Sandy plains of Nebraska, Oklahoma, Texas, and New Mexico
Flower: Fine-textured flower/seed heads to 3 feet are held above the clump in August/September; seed heads persist until weathered by winter.
Foliage: Fairly bright green leaves turn a buff-russet in fall and winter.
Hardiness: Zones 5 to 9
Height: 12- to 18-inch clump
Region: Southwest
Landscape use: Accent, border, individual specimen, tall ground cover in light shade in warmer desert areas
Culture: Sun, sandy soil; it will adapt to most soils if not overwatered.

ERIANTHUS CONTORTUS Bent-awn plume grass
GRAMINEAE Grass family

Although this plume grass stays shorter in clump than *Erianthus giganteus* (below) and far more vertical in clump than the exotic *Erianthus ravennae,* it sends up flowers that are just as showy and dramatic as its two relatives, making it the best of the three for even a town-house garden. The foliage of this grass stays quite low—20 to perhaps 30 inches—but the flower stalks shoot up 6 to 8 feet, giving it big grass drama in a tiny space.
Origin: Southeastern United States west to Oklahoma
Flower: Plumes emerge magenta and lighten with age in fall; they turn an almond color over winter. They can reach 10 feet.
Foliage: Rather coarse, slightly blue-green, taking on tints of magenta and orange in fall
Hardiness: Zones 6 (probably) to 10

Height: Clump 20 to 30 inches
Regions: South, Mid-Atlantic, Lower Midwest
Landscape use: Accent
Culture: Sun, average soil; cut back in early spring or whenever the plant ceases to be attractive.
Propagation: Division, seed

ERIANTHUS GIGANTEUS Sugarcane plume grass
GRAMINEAE Grass family

At home in moist soil, sugarcane plume grass tolerates seasonally wet places. It is the largest native listed here. It has been slow to develop in ordinary garden soil in a very exposed, well-drained place in my Zones 7 garden (in the teeth of the north wind), blooming feebly for the second year in a row. Reports from warmer places suggest that this plant can grow, bloom lustily, self-sow, and even become a pest if it is warm and moist enough. I have seen great wild colonies of it or, possibly, its narrow relative *E. strictus* along I-81 in Tennessee—usually in ditches. An ideal background plant for an earthen pond, it also thrives in low, wet spots that don't drain.

Origin: Moist soils along the East Coast from New York to Florida and west to Kentucky, south to Texas
Flower: Red in September, turns cottony buff on a very tall stem. Very showy!
Foliage: Coarse, broad blades in an upright clump are a light green in summer and turn red and orange in fall, cream-colored in winter.
Hardiness: Zones 7 to 10
Height: To 10 feet, but usually 6 to 8 feet
Regions: South, Lower Midwest, wherever hardy
Landscape use: Back border, specimen
Culture: Moist to wet soil in full sun; cut back in late winter
Species: Narrow plume grass (*E. strictus*) grows to only 6 feet, is narrower but showy.
Propagation: Seed

*Sugarcane plume grass (*Erianthus giganteus*) plumes, far left and back right, mix with other grass flowers for a winter bouquet.*

FESTUCA CALIFORNICA California fescue
GRAMINEAE Grass family

A big little grass is how I think of California fescue. Just 30 inches tall, it manages to put on a big-grass show. Showy panicles on stiff flower spikes densely borne in spring and early summer enlarge the clump to nearly double its size. Then they begin to age to a warm almond color, giving the plant an attractive two-tone look.

Native plantsman Bart O'Brien of Rancho Santa Ana recommends the cultivar 'Serpentine Blue', a selection made by Roger Raich of the UC–Berkeley Botanical Garden. Its foliage is steel blue, stiff, and upright and grows from 2 to 4 feet. Flower panicles are open, attractive, stiff, and enduring, to about 5 feet tall.

Although California fescue does not thrive in dense shade, it becomes lush and lovely under deciduous trees, near the edge of a woodland, or under the margins of evergreen trees.

Origin: Meadows and open woodlands of California
Flower: Blue-green panicles in spring, aging in summer to warm almond
Foliage: Blue-green to light green clump
Hardiness: Probably Zones 7b to 10
Height: To 30-inch clump. Flowers rise 2 feet above clump.
Region: California
Landscape use: Meadow, accent, slopes
Culture: Sun to part shade, good drainage; drought-tolerant on the coast

California fescue (Festuca californica) *in a meadow of tidy tips at Strybing Arboretum, San Francisco* (Ron Lutsko Design)

Soft rush (Juncus effusus) *in a submerged container is a striking accent for a tiny pool.* (Rosa Finsley Design)

Cultivar: 'Serpentine Blue' (good foliage color, habit, flowers)
Propagation: Division

JUNCUS EFFUSUS Soft rush
JUNCACEAE Rush family

This is the beautiful bright green, spiky plant one often sees growing in wet mud at water's edge. Perfect for the edge of a natural pond, it can also be potted and set into a garden pool. It blooms early, and then its brown seeds are held on the plant for the rest of the growing season, adding interesting contrast.

Origin: Wet soil throughout eastern North America
Flower: Dainty, creamy white flowers, borne like a froth on the smooth, upright blades, are followed by light brown seeds in and among the blades.
Foliage: Bright green, very erect, cylindrical blades
Hardiness: Probably Zones 3 to 9
Height: To 3 feet
Region: Eastern North America
Landscape use: Pond edge, water garden, soil that is seasonally flooded
Culture: Very moist to wet soil in sun, part shade
Propagation: Division or seed

MILIUM EFFUSUM 'AUREUM' Golden grass
GRAMINEAE Grass family

Bright yellow-green and very showy in a moist, shady place, golden grass serves as a bright-colored accent or ground cover for climates with cool summers. In hot-summer climates, golden grass greens up very early in spring and grows vigorously while the weather stays cool, but it browns out in hot weather and, for me, eventually dies. A good golden grass substitute for hot, humid, and hazy southeastern gardens is *Carex austrocaroliniana*.

Origin: Quebec and Nova Scotia to Minnesota, Illinois, Maryland, Eurasia
Flower: Showy because they bloom en masse, flowers are small, fine, creamy yellow on 18-inch upright stems, in early summer.
Foliage: Bright yellow-green foliage greens up early in spring.
Hardiness: Zones 6 to 9

Golden grass (Milium effusum *'Aureum'*)

Height: 15-inch clump
Regions: Northeast, Midwest, Northwest, parts of Mountain
Landscape use: Ground cover, accent
Culture: Moist, well drained soil, light shade; needs cool weather
Propagation: Easy from seed

MUHLENBERGIA CAPILLARIS Muhly grass
GRAMINEAE Grass family

Muhly grass fills the need for a low clumping grass with attractive flowers and good winter color. Its densely packed blades are rather erect, but fan out under their own weight. Infrequently seen in landscaping in the North, it is popular with Florida designers because it tolerates salt, wind, and drought. Nancy Bissett of The Natives, a Florida nursery and design firm, reports that she has seen it in sand dunes and in the first swale behind the ocean line as well as in the Green Swamp, where, with seasonal flooding, it achieves twice its normal size. In gardens, it thrives under a great variety of conditions.

Origin: Eastern North America, west to Texas
Flower: Shimmering, filmy purple to pink panicles are held on 2- to 3-foot flower spikes in fall.
Foliage: Fine-textured, bright green blades, turning almond after frost
Hardiness: Zones 5 to 10
Height: 2-foot clump
Region: Eastern North America
Landscape use: Accent, ground cover, beach planting, poor soil
Culture: Good drainage, sun; tolerant of lime, poor soil, wind, salt, occasional flooding
Species: M. capillaris var. filiformis (Florida muhly) is slightly smaller
Propagation: Seed and division

MUHLENBERGIA DUMOSA Bamboo muhly
GRAMINEAE Grass family

From Arizona and Mexico comes bamboo muhly, a surprisingly tropical-looking plant that resembles bamboo. I first saw this plant at a native plant sale at the Desert Botanical Garden in Phoenix. It was so unusual that I bought one. All the other *Muhlenbergias* of my acquaintance were symmetrical grassy-looking grasses—different from this one. Unlike many of its relatives, bamboo muhly is distinctly vertical, with canes of varying height with lovely long, narrow, light green leaves. I could almost imagine a panda munching them. I assumed that it wasn't hardy enough to stand the cold or wet of my Zone 7 garden and gave it to friends in Sonoita, Arizona. Later, I learned that Niche Gardens in Chapel Hill, North Carolina (a warmer Zone 7 than my Zone 7), carries it. The jury is still out on bamboo muhly.

Origin: Southern Arizona, Mexico
Flower: Small purple flowers at the ends of the stems, turning tan
Foliage: Long, light green evergreen blades on wiry branches
Hardiness: Zones 7 (probably) to 10
Height: 5 feet
Regions: Southwest, California
Landscape use: Accent, pot plant, cutting garden, bamboo substitute
Culture: Good garden soil with excellent drainage. Bamboo muhly is drought-tolerant but can take summer water.
Propagation: Seed or division

MUHLENBERGIA RIGENS Deer grass
GRAMINEAE Grass family

Deer grass is one of the most popular California bunchgrasses sold at the Theodore Payne Foundation, named for an English-born nurseryman and California native plant enthusiast. Eliza Earle of the Foundation staff reports that the reason for brisk sales is in no small part because it looks so good in the entrance garden during all four seasons. Its slender-leaved fountain form stays green throughout the year with only occasional irrigation. The flowering stalks appear delicate and luminescent in the low sunlight of winter. These were

Bamboo muhly (Muhlenbergia dumosa)

Deer grass (Muhlenbergia rigens)

used in basket making by Californian Indian tribes. Deer grass is gaining fans for its carefree good looks. Recently, it was planted effectively as a good-looking but low-up keep accent in a school parking lot in Santa Monica.

Origin: Canyons and forests from southern California into Mexico and Texas

Flower: Delicate, gray panicles appear in summer and age to a tan color

Foliage: Slender, gray-green, evergreen blades

Hardiness: Zones 7 (to 7,000 feet) to 9

Height: 3 feet tall by 4 feet wide

Regions: California, Southwest

Landscape use: Meadows, mixed borders

Culture: Drought-tolerant, but best with moisture; will take overhead sprinklers; full sun to light shade

Propagation: Seed or division

NOLINA MICROCARPA Bear grass, sacahuista
AGAVACEAE Agave family

Bear grass looks like a cross between a yucca and a grass; its foliage is leathery and stiff but thin. A dry-climate plant, bear grass is evergreen and a member of the agave family. It has fine, stiff but flexible foliage that grows into a large, bushy clump. Small, cream-colored flowers are held on stout stems in May or June, depending upon local conditions.

Origin: New Mexico to Arizona and south

Flower: Small, cream-colored, clustered on tall stems, followed by seed husks

Foliage: Evergreen, fine, stiff but flexible

Hardiness: Probably Zones 5 (8,000 feet) to 10

Height: 3 feet

Regions: Southwest, southern California

Landscape use: "Shrub," accent

Culture: Sun, dry soil, good drainage; drought-tolerant.

Species: *N. texana* (shorter), *N. bigelovii* (6 feet)

ORYZOPSIS HYMENOIDES Indian rice grass
GRAMINEAE Grass family

Beautiful Indian rice grass is the most drought-tolerant of all the grasses listed here. The Plants of the Southwest catalog states that it can survive on only five inches of water per year—about what can be expected in Death Valley! Conversely and sadly, this is not a plant for moist climates. Of all the grasses I have seen that refuse to grow in my garden, this one is the one I most sorely regret. Not only is it exquisite, it is useful. Even in areas of great heat and drought, Indian rice grass earned its name by providing seed that Native Americans harvested for food. Quail and mourning doves love the seeds, too, so expect a good show if you are lucky enough to garden in a place where Indian rice grass will feel at home.

Origin: Widely distributed throughout the western states between 2,000 feet and 9,000 feet in elevation on ridges, rocky slopes, dry foothills, and sandy plains

Flower/seed: Light and airy seed heads on twisted, wiry stems in midspring, persisting into early autumn

Foliage: Very narrow, pale green leaves in summer, curing to pale blond in winter

Hardiness: Zones 4 (probably) to 10

Height: To 2 feet

Region: Dry climates of the West

Landscape use: As filler in dry beds, borders, and meadows; for textural interest, cut flowers

Culture: Full sun, fast-draining soil; very drought-tolerant

Cultivars: 'Nezpar' (may germinate easily), 'Paloma' (may be longer lived)

Propagation: Seed

Nolina *at the Arizona–Sonora Desert Museum*

Indian rice grass (Oryzopsis hymenoides)

PANICUM VIRGATUM Switch grass
GRAMINEAE Grass family

It's a bush! It's a flower! It's a field of wheat! And it will grow anywhere. Switch grass has an immense range and tolerates almost any set of garden conditions. Where moisture is plentiful and soil rich, the straight species grows taller than is generally useful, often flopping over its neighbors. After frost, it stands upright and turns a lovely shade of wheat that is spectacular contrasting with evergreens like holly or juniper.

Planted alone, it's a summer shrub. Planted in a border, it provides softness and changing color. In masses, switch grass can become a seamless, striking winter ground cover—a field of wheat—whose appearance is reason enough to endure its sometimes sloppy summer behavior. Unless there is a special reason to want height, however, the shorter and more upright cultivars work better for ground cover.

Origin: Nova Scotia to Florida, Mexico, and Central America, from the Atlantic Ocean to the Rockies and Arizona

Flower: Flowers that emerge maroon turn to tan, and are so delicate they appear as a haze over the plant.

Foliage: Light to medium green clumps increase in girth by rhizomes. Yellow fall color fades to cream.

Hardiness: Zones 5 to 9

Height: 3 to 7 feet, depending upon moisture available

Regions: North America where hardy, from the Atlantic to the Rockies and into Central America

Landscape use: Outstanding as a winter ground cover, switch grass is beautiful in a border, where its floppiness works to advantage; it weaves itself in among other ornamentals.

Culture: Not fussy. Prefers full sun, moisture, and good drainage, but tolerates almost anything but standing water.

Cultivars: 'Haense Herms' (3 feet, red fall color), 'Heavy Metal' (metallic blue, very upright, 3 feet), 'Cloud Nine' (7 feet, showy bloom, specimen, big-grass substitute with a cloud of seeds)

Propagation: Division or seed

PHALARIS ARUNDINACEA PICTA Ribbon grass, gardener's garters
GRAMINEAE Grass family

Ribbon grass has been grown in gardens for generations. Its clean green and white foliage works especially well with pastel flowers like shell pink roses or peonies. It is a vigorous plant that survives almost anywhere—sun, shade, standing water, or dry sites. Ribbon grass grows to about garter-height. Aggressive, it will quickly take over a flower bed, but its toughness makes it ideal for containers.

Origin: Circumboreal

Flower: White, held above the foliage in June

Foliage: Broad blades, striped green and white on decumbent stems, turning parchment in winter

Hardiness: Zone 4 (hardier with a snow cover) to 9

Height: To 3 feet

Region: North America

Landscape use: Erosion control, banks, ground cover in difficult areas, containers

Culture: Undemanding ribbon grass will grow just about anywhere in any kind of soil from standing water to moderately dry slopes; cut it back completely to renew foliage. If it is too dry, it will brown out in hot weather.

Cultivars: 'Fleesey' (very white variegation, pink in spring, fall), 'Tricolor' (white, pink, green)

Propagation: Division

Switch grass (Panicum virgatum) used as a shrubby softener with roses at Brookside Gardens

SCHIZACHYRIUM SCOPARIUM (ANDROPOGON SCOPARIUS) Little bluestem
GRAMINEAE Grass family

"Everywhere, as far as the eye could reach, there was nothing but rough, shaggy, red grass." Willa Cather's words perfectly capture the beauty of little bluestem on the prairie. Beloved as a symbol of the frontier, little bluestem's red late-season color makes it easily identifiable. A tough little grass with an immense distribution, little bluestem is dominant on the Great Plains today, but before extensive settlement, it grew nearly everywhere in North America.

In the garden, single plants in midborder will complement bronzy orange color schemes with mums and late sunflowers. It is probably best used as a transition planting—in a mass—between a wild and a cultivated area or as a stylized meadow, interplanted with black-eyed Susans and coreopsis.

Origin: Throughout most of the United States, southern Canada, and northern Mexico

Flower: After inconspicuous flowers, fluffy seed heads form in fall.

Foliage: Light to blue-green clumping grass with strong vertical lines

Hardiness: Zones 3 to 10

Height: 2 to 3 feet

Region: North America where hardy

Landscape use: As an accent in dry flower beds and borders, and in wildflower meadows

Culture: Because it self-sows readily in warm soil, in rainfall areas of 15 to 30 inches, it might become weedy in conventional flower beds; very adaptable.

Cultivars: 'Blaze' (deeper russet-red fall color), 'Aldous' (blue cast foliage)

Propagation: Fresh seed planted in fall in a cold frame

Gardener's garters (Phalaris arundinacea picta) *blends well with gray foliage and pastel flowers. (Mary Smith Design)*

Little bluestem (Schizachyrium scoparium) *in a field at Prairie Nursery, Westfield, Wisconsin*

SORGHASTRUM NUTANS (CHRYSOPOGON NUTANS) Indian grass
GRAMINEAE Grass family

A trio of Indian grasses have been agreeable fixtures in my garden for nearly a decade, beloved for their graceful copper-colored plumes and bright golden fall color. Nevertheless, I was unprepared for the dramatic sight of this grass en masse. In the 1930s, the conservationist Aldo Leopold had a hand in the restoration of the 60-acre Curtis Prairie at the University of Wisconsin's Arboretum. It was begun as pure science—to restore habitat and an extremely complex ecosystem—but it became a beloved monument to the exquisite beauty of the prairie. On the deck behind the McKay Center, which overlooks the prairie, I stood one August day, mesmerized by a stand of several acres of Indian grass, undulating copper in the late summer sunshine.

The unusual color and structure of a single plume of this grass always intrigue onlookers: strange little yellow flowers are borne on a muted coppery salmon plume with the sheen of fine embroidery silk. The plumes are carried on long, fine stems that bow gracefully under their weight. Clumps are rather upright, but not large as ornamental grasses go, so when used as an accent in a border, Indian grass ought to have companion plants that are lower and spreading, such as *Aster lateriflorous* or coreopsis or, to pick up the blue-green theme, santolina, and that do not compete.

Origin: From Quebec and Manitoba south and west to Florida, Arizona, Mexico

Flower: An elegant, drooping, satiny, pale copper plume, adorned for a time with yellow flowers, appears in July and is effective for up to two months.

Foliage: Upright clump of green to blue-green ½-inch

Indian grass (Sorghastrum nutans) *in a Wisconsin garden*

blades turns orange/yellow in fall. The clump grows outward slowly, thickening by short rhizomes.

Hardiness: Zones 4 to 9

Height: To 5 feet

Regions: Northeast, Midwest, Mid-Atlantic, South, Southwest

Landscape use: Wonderful massed, Indian grass also serves as a small specimen or accent

Culture: Full sun, medium to dry soil. Tolerates drought. Indian grass takes several years to establish.

Cultivars: 'Sioux Blue' (powder blue foliage, more upright), 'Osage' (typical prairie form)

Propagation: Division or seed

SPARTINA BAKERI Sand cordgrass
GRAMINEAE Grass family

A great transition plant, sand cordgrass is perfect between the flatness of lawn or paving and the height of taller shrubs and trees. It has been described as a "dense grass skirt." It can handle hot, full sun and low moisture, but is also good-natured about occasional flooding.

Origin: Coastal Southeast

Flower: Although sand cordgrass does produce seed, flowers are rather inconspicuous and it doesn't bloom every year.

Foliage: Dense, cascading foliage in a broad clump

Hardiness: Zones 8 to 10

Height: 3 to 4 feet

Region: South

Landscape use: Nice transition between planting and paving, accent, ground cover, berms

Culture: Sun, good drainage; salt- and drought-tolerant.

Propagation: Seed and division

SPOROBOLUS HETEROLEPIS Prairie dropseed
GRAMINEAE Grass family

One fine, late-August afternoon, I got out of my car at Prairie Nursery in Westfield, Wisconsin, and was treated to an olfactory experience: the air was filled with a lovely, cilantro-like aroma. Neil Diboll, who has planted hundreds of prairie dropseeds in a vast field at his nursery, explained that the "cilantro" was the scent of prairie dropseed flowers.

Prairie dropseed is lower growing and finer textured than many of its companions on the prairie, characteristics that work well in gardens. Add to this showy, dazzling, scented flowers and starchy foliage that turns orange in fall and relaxes into a creamy white swirl in winter, and it's no wonder this is a favorite of midwestern growers. As more people see it, it is only a matter of time until this grass

Sand cordgrass (Spartina bakeri) *(William Bissett Design)*

*Prairie dropseed (*Sporobolus heterolepis*)*

becomes a fixture in midwestern (and other) gardens.

If it has a fault, it is that prairie dropseed takes a long, long time (four to six years) to establish and grow to maturity, although it is otherwise undemanding of anything besides good drainage. A fully grown prairie dropseed is a wonderful addition to a border or a fine specimen on its own. When it blooms, dozens of fine flower stalks are held like jeweled pins in a pin cushion.

Origin: Prairies from Canada to the Gulf

Flower: Stiff, fragrant panicles appear in September on long, fine stems.

Foliage: Very fine, profuse, bright green blades arise from a symmetrical clump.

Hardiness: Zones 3 to 10

Height: 18 to 24 inches, slightly wider than tall

Region: Midwest

Landscape use: Accent, ground cover, naturalized in a prairie

Culture: Sun, good drainage, average to poor soil

Propagation: Seed

TRIPSACUM DACTYLOIDES Fakahatchee grass, eastern gamma grass

GRAMINEAE Grass family

"A hot item in Florida," says Palm Beach horticulturist and designer Joe Lawson, because Fakahatchee grass is well adapted to Florida and because it looks right with other hummock plants.

The truth is that Fakahatchee grass is plain, old eastern gamma grass with a fancy name, but in Florida, it stays evergreen and grows to perfection: a tall, broad, stoloniferous clumper with rather upright foliage that cascades from the midpoint. It has a coarse texture. Joe Lawson likes using it in a mass under palmetto trees with something of a finer texture in front, such as coral bean.

Origin: Eastern North America to Mexico

Flower: Flowers in rigid spikes, grainlike, at the end of arching stems, held above the foliage in summer

Foliage: Medium to blue-gray leaves are evergreen where there is no frost, but can look beaten up in winter. They color red with cooler fall weather and are killed with frost. Cut back for new growth. Sharp leaf margins!

Hardiness: Zones 5 to 10

Height: Taller in warm, moist climates. Fakahatchee grass can reach 9 feet, but is usually around 3 to 6 feet

Region: Eastern North America

Landscape use: Background, texture, ground cover, accent plant (in place of pampas grass), pond, streamside, boggy places

Culture: Sun to part shade; very adaptable; prefers moist soil but will tolerate a dryish place; cut back when foliage becomes disheveled

Species: Dwarf Fakahatchee (*T. floridanum*) is similar, smaller, less hardy (Zone 7).

Propagation: Seed or division

*Muhly grass (*Muhlenbergia capillaris*), foreground, with Fakahatchee grass (*Tripsacum dactyloides*)*

F e

rns

Cool

GREEN FERNS STAND APART FROM ALL
OTHER HERBACEOUS PLANTS, EVOKING AN ANCIENT AND
PRIMITIVE PAST. THE MYSTERY OF THEIR LACK OF FLOW-
ERS AND FRUITS PUZZLED OBSERVERS FROM THE ROMAN
NATURALIST PLINY THE ELDER ON, UNTIL IN THE 19TH
CENTURY, FREIDERICH HOFMEISTER DISCOVERED THAT
FERNS REPRODUCE BY MEANS OF SPORES.

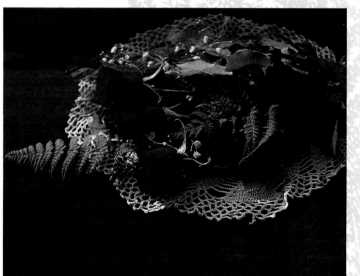

OVERLEAF: *Cool, green, mysterious,
and tough, ferns have been on the
earth since the days of the dinosaurs.*
ABOVE: *Florist's fern provides
lacy greens for romantic bouquets far
into winter.*

AFTER THE MUTINY HOLLYWOOD
LOVED SO MUCH, THE REAL-LIFE CAPTAIN
BLIGH SET SAIL AGAIN—THIS TIME FOR
THE WEST INDIES—AND RETURNED TO
ENGLAND AFTER AN UNDRAMATIC TRIP
WITH A CARGO OF FERNS. (MEANWHILE,
FLETCHER CHRISTIAN, WHO LED THE
MUTINY, TOOK THE *BOUNTY* TO ISOLATED PITCAIRN
ISLAND IN THE SOUTH SEAS WITH THE MUTINEERS AND
SOME TAHITIAN MEN AND WOMEN, WHERE TO ESCAPE
DETECTION AND CERTAIN HANGING, HE BURNED THE SHIP.
MANY YEARS LATER, A BRITISH VESSEL, CALLING AT
PITCAIRN, WAS AMAZED TO FIND THE DESCENDANTS OF

This tropical fern in the conservatory at Brookside Gardens in Wheaton, Maryland, recalls the Victorian passion for ferns in Wardian cases.

the mutineers and Tahitians, who spoke Pitcairnese, a mixture of Maori and 19th-century nautical English!) Bligh's new species added more fuel to what soon became a peaceful conflagration of interest in these seemingly demure plants. Wild for ferns, the Victorians indulged in a fern mania, second in intensity only to the tulip mania of 17th-century Europe, when a single tulip bulb sometimes commanded more than $1,000.

In the Victorian era, as today, the fern's power of suggestion—of primeval forests, of dewy glade and mountainside—lends it an aura of romance. In the garden, ferns are as useful as they are romantic. They are great softeners, filling in around shrubs and under trees with contrasting green texture that is useful in keeping the garden neat; the appearance of their cool, green, feathery fronds dovetails with and camouflages the passing of woodland ephemerals and bulbs. They also add drama. Like a dance in slow motion, unfurling fiddleheads open into great blades of fronds in early spring.

As if usefulness and romance were not enough, ferns are also tough. Not for nothing have ferns been around since the days of the dinosaurs. For all their feathery grace, they are adaptable landscape plants that need little care once established. While some thrive in bright sunlight so long as they have adequate moisture, most are plants for shady places, where the soil is loose, moist, slightly acid, and has been enriched with leaf mold. A position in high, bright shade is usually ideal.

ACROSTICHUM DANAEIFOLIUM Giant leather fern

POLYPODIACEAE Polypody family

A fern that can reach a distinct and bold-textured 12 feet, giant leather fern literally stands out wherever it is grown. As horticulturist and designer Joe Lawson says, "Just the size of it is impressive, and you couldn't have a better accent." Dramatic next to or in a pond, giant leather fern is also striking as ground cover in a low, moist spot.

Origin: Brackish and freshwater marshes of the New World tropics

Foliage: Broad, dark green, leathery upright fronds

Hardiness: Throughout Central Florida

Height: To 12 feet, but usually 4 to 6 feet

Regions: Caribbean, South, Central Florida

Landscape use: Bold, dramatic accent in a wet place—pond, marsh, pool

Culture: Constant moisture or standing water, sun to part shade, acid soil

Species: *A. aureum* is slightly smaller.

Propagation: Spores

Northern maidenhair (Adiantum pedatum)

ADIANTUM CAPILLUS-VENERIS
Maidenhair fern, southern maidenhair
POLYPODIACEAE Polypody family

Beautiful southern maidenhair is particular about its site, requiring not only moisture with good drainage but also a near-neutral soil. It spreads by underground rhizomes to form attractive colonies quickly.

In warm places (Zone 8 and southward), where southern maidenhair can be grown, the light green, lobed leaflets on fine, lustrous, ebony stems give it a flowing, lacy look. Give it room and let it spread. In colder climates, grow this choice fern indoors in a bright window.

Origin: Warm temperate and tropical regions around the world

Foliage: Lobed light green leaflets (pinnae) on dark, wiry stems; spreads by underground rhizomes

Hardiness: Zones 8 to 10

Height: To 2 feet

Regions: Southern United States, Mexico, Caribbean

Landscape use: Ground cover, rock garden, indoor pot plant

Culture: Well-drained, moist, neutral soil in part shade; houseplant in cold-winter areas

Propagation: Spores, division

ADIANTUM PEDATUM
Maidenhair fern, northern maidenhair, five-finger fern
POLYPODIACEAE Polypody family

At first sight, maidenhair fern's delicate leaflets and fine, ebony stems look too good to be true. For a long time, my mind automatically shelved this fern with beautiful but unattainable plants like pink lady slippers and ground pine.

Then my next-door neighbor called and said she had some ferns she wanted to get rid of. Between her house and some overgrown yews was a thriving colony of maidenhair fern. The surgery that followed was brutal. It was a difficult place in which to work and the fronds broke easily. (I once watched a little boy jump out of a tree directly onto a maidenhair and kill it utter-

Southern maidenhair (Adiantum capillus-veneris)

ly and instantly.) However, from the two pieces that were transplanted to a brightly lighted spot under a sycamore in my garden, a colony developed behind some wild ginger and in front of false Solomon's seal and some naturalized *Hesperis.* This site is humusy and shady, but a bit on the dry side in summer. The maidenhair fern has increased steadily from its creeping rootstock, lending a lacy finished look to this planting. Layers of its semicircular fronds add voluminous softness all summer.

Although maidenhair fern belongs in places near paths and patios, where it can be seen, it should nonetheless be sited out of the way of hoses and dogs and children. Maidenhair fern orients its frond layers toward light, so take care in siting.

Origin: Woodlands of North America and eastern Asia
Foliage: Small fronds composed of many leaflets (pinnae) hang down like fingers from a dark, wiry forked stem
Hardiness: Zones 4 to 8
Height: To 2 feet
Region: North America
Landscape use: Accent, softener in a woodland garden
Culture: Moist, humusy soil in part to full shade

Ferns growing in a wall in Jenny Fleming's garden include, left and right, five-finger ferns (Adiantum pedatum var. aleuticum); center, sword ferns (Polystichum munitum); and bottom, lady fern (Athyrium filix-femina).

Species: *A. p.* ssp. *subpumilum* (dwarf to 9 inches)
Propagation: Division, spores

ADIANTUM PEDATUM VAR. *ALEUTICUM* Five-finger fern
POLYPODIACEAE Polypody family

"It is heavenly," says Berkeley, California, gardener Jenny Fleming, "to walk up my driveway in midsummer and feel I am in a cool, moist glen." Five-finger ferns growing in a stone wall on the north side of the Fleming home add greatly to this illusion. Plant them in a wall or on a slope to show the fern off to best advantage; the finger fronds drape as gracefully as hands poised to touch a keyboard.

Origin: Redwood and mixed forests of the West Coast
Foliage: Bright green, airy, lacy pinnae (leaves) on black stems. Blades are divided into two equal parts with two to five pinnae each.
Hardiness: Zones 4 to 8
Height: 2 feet, plus or minus
Regions: Moist areas, waterfalls, seeps, shady slopes, by pond or pools in the Pacific Northwest, California
Landscape use: On slopes, in rock walls
Culture: It seems to love growing by concrete rails in the wall—perhaps for the lime. It needs shade, spreads relatively quickly, and volunteers occasionally.

ATHYRIUM FILIX-FEMINA Lady fern
POLYPODIACEAE Polypody family

Two forms of lady fern combine as uninhibited ground cover on a shady quarter-acre in my garden. One has reddish stems and the other light green ones. Otherwise, they seem identical and are identically vigorous. In moist, bright shade, they have made swift progress, steadily overcoming weeds and grass to form what is now a cool, green ground cover around deciduous azaleas.

Origin:: Temperate Northern Hemisphere
Foliage: Light green fronds in running clumps
Hardiness: Zones 4 to 8
Height: To 4 feet, but usually between 2 and 3 feet
Region: Virtually anywhere cultural requirements are met
Landscape use: Ground cover in shade
Culture: Moist, acid soil in part to full shade
Species: There are many varieties, including *A. f. rubra* (red stems). Some cultivars include 'Minutissimum' (small, to 8 inches), 'Vernoniae cristatum' (tiny, to 3 inches)
Propagation: Division, spores

Deer fern (Blechnum spicant) *with Pacific dogwood, starry Solomon's seal, and alum root*

BLECHNUM SPICANT Deer fern
POLYPODIACEAE Polypody family

Easily recognized as having two kinds of leafy fronds, deer fern is evergreen. Its fronds may be short with broad, divided leaves gathered at the base, surrounding (when fertile) the taller spore-bearing fronds with narrower leaflets that have the appearance of a ladder. Deer fern inhabits deep, moist conifer forests of the west side of the Cascades in the Pacific Northwest. It does best in the shade of woodland gardens, where it grows easily in acid soil.

Origin: Alaska to California, Europe, Asia
Foliage: Evergreen, to 2 feet. Two kinds of fronds: short with divided leaves gathered at base, and taller, narrower spore-bearing fronds.
Hardiness: Zones 4 to 8
Height: 2 feet
Regions: Very adaptable; Northwest, northern California
Landscape use: Woodland accent, ground cover
Culture: Moist, humusy shade
Propagation: Spores

DENNSTAEDTIA PUNCTILOBULA Hay-scented fern
POLYPODIACEAE Polypody family

I was always a little frightened of hay-scented fern and thought that perhaps the recommendations to use it as "ground cover" were only euphemisms for "spreads rapidly" and "has a mind of its own." Then I saw a great mass of it around a big stand of roseshell azaleas and I realized what a splendid and delicate composition its pale apple green fronds made with the new green and bubble-gum pink of the azaleas. What it really needs is the right place (some sunshine—either filtered or full—and even moisture) and plenty of room.

Origin: Eastern North America
Foliage: Roughly triangular, light green, soft fronds, fragrant when crushed
Hardiness: Zones 4 to 8
Height: To 3 feet, but usually around 18 inches
Region: Eastern North America
Landscape use: Ground cover in wild garden
Culture: Sun to filtered shade; spreads vigorously
Propagation: Division

DRYOPTERIS CARTHUSIANA (D. SPINULOSA) Florist's fern, toothed wood fern
POLYPODIACEAE Polypody family

Florist's fern is semi- or subevergreen, but in winter, it will bruise or rot where leaves and other debris rest on it. Handsome, lacy fronds frame flowers in arrangements, and the clumps are attractive in gardens as winter green accents.

Origin: North America, Europe, Asia
Foliage: Textured to the touch, medium green blade-

Hay-scented fern (Dennstaedtia punctilobula)

Florist's fern (Dryopteris carthusiana)

shaped fronds made up of roughly triangular leaflets (pinnae)

Hardiness: Zones 4 to 8
Height: To 2 feet
Region: Moist, humusy soils throughout North America
Landscape use: Accent, edger, cutting
Culture: Moist, rich soil in bright to full shade
Species: *Dryopteris* species cross in the wild; there are many similar and confusing forms.
Propagation: Division, spores

DRYOPTERIS FILIX-MAS Male fern
POLYPODIACEAE Polypody family

Male fern holds a special place in my heart because it is the only fern I have been able to grow from spores. Actually, it is the only one I have tried. Using peat pellets in a tray enclosed in a plastic bag and set in a north window, the spores gradually turned to a fuzzy green moss, then developed into queer little sporelings that resembled miniature lettuce leaves before becoming recognizable miniatures of the parent fern—a process that took about six or seven months. Mine is now over 2 feet and growing.

This almost evergreen fern (called "subevergreen" because its fertile fronds gradually decline over winter in mild climates) has been widely hybridized. The many forms add to the confusion one has trying to distinguish male fern from its look-alike relatives, marginal wood fern and Goldie's fern. Still, with plenty of rich soil and moisture, this fern becomes big and bold and spreads.

Origin: Western North America to west Siberia
Foliage: Long, leathery fronds taper at the end and slightly at the base. When new, they are a light, yellowish green; they deepen to dark green over the year. Subevergreen.
Hardiness: Zones 4 to 7
Height: To 4 feet
Region: Cool climates of North America
Landscape use: High, bold ground cover; accent
Culture: Cool, moist soil in part to full shade
Species/cultivars: Crested male fern, *D. f. cristata,* developed by English horticulturists, has little fingerlike forks at the ends of the leaflets; 'Barnesii' (ruffled pinnules); 'Grandiceps' (tasseled pinnules).
Propagation: Spores

DRYOPTERIS GOLDIANA Goldie's fern
POLYPODIACEAE Polypody family

Bold and impressive when well grown, Goldie's fern serves as a woodsy accent in shady gardens. Give it a place in very rich, moist, slightly acid soil and very bright shade and watch it grow to 4 feet, about the same size as an ostrich fern.

I always assumed its common name referred to the golden cast on its green fronds, but no, in the early 19th century, there was a man named John Goldie who found it growing in Canada. Later, the British botanist Sir William Hooker named it in honor of its finder.

Origin: Northeastern North America
Foliage: Broad, leathery, bright green fronds can be 18 inches across and taper abruptly to a point.
Hardiness: Zones 4 (probably) to 8
Height: To 5 feet
Regions: Northeast, Upper Midwest, Mid-Atlantic, mountains of the South
Landscape use: Accent, back of shady border
Culture: Cool, moist, slightly acid soil; very bright to full shade; surprisingly drought-tolerant when established
Propagation: Spores

F e r n s

DRYOPTERIS MARGINALIS Marginal wood fern, leather wood fern

POLYPODIACEAE Polypody family

Quintessentially ferny, leather wood fern is so classically fernlike that it strays from the stereotype only in that it is evergreen. Its fronds are blue-green, leathery, and broadly blade-shaped, tapering suddenly at the tip, and arise out of a central crown. The sori (spore cases on the underside of the leaflets) are located on the margins of the leaflets, giving rise to the common name "marginal shield fern."

Origin: Eastern North America

Foliage: Leathery evergreen fronds about 6 inches wide

Hardiness: Zones 4 to 7

Height: To 2 feet

Region: Eastern North America

Culture: Moist, acid, humusy soil in part to full shade; easy to grow

Propagation: Spores

MATTEUCCIA PENSYLVANICA Ostrich fern

POLYPODIACEAE Polypody family

Easy to grow, quick to spread, ostrich fern thrives anywhere—from seasonally wet soil to medium soil in sun. In spring, the fiddleheads can be harvested—perhaps two from a clump—and then cooked like asparagus. When the remaining ones unfurl, chartreuse fronds are held in an erect V-shape, presenting a dramatic spectacle for several weeks.

Place ostrich fern where it can spread: a shady slope, a ditch, in front of large shrubs. You'll soon have a cool, light green, feathery ground cover anywhere from 30 inches to 5 feet tall. Depending on the moisture and richness of your soil, a contented ostrich fern will send underground roots out two or more feet to send up new clumps.

In fall (or late summer in a very dry year), ostrich fern turns briefly yellow, then brown—not at all ornamentally. For up to a month, it is truly unattractive as a ground cover. At this time, it helps a lot if there's something pretty turning color nearby—a dogwood, a burning bush, asters—to draw the eye. Thereafter, fall rains usually beat down the foliage until only the attractive teddy-bear-brown fertile fronds remain for winter.

Origin: Cool, temperate North America

Foliage: Light green fronds, up to about 10 inches across and tapered at both ends, die back in fall.

Hardiness: Zones 3 to 7

Height: Up to 5 feet; varies with moisture and soil fertility

Regions: Northwest, Upper Midwest, Mountain, Northeast, Mid-Atlantic; not appropriate for hot climates

Landscape use: Ground cover in low, boggy ground

Culture: Moist, rich soil in shade to part sun; tolerates seasonally wet soil.

Propagation: Established plants send out runners to form new clumps; spores

ONOCLEA SENSIBILIS Sensitive fern, bead fern

POLYPODIACEAE Polypody family

Sensitive fern's pale green, simply cut fronds have a wonderful primitive look about them. Easy to grow and strongly rhizomatous, sensitive fern is best as ground cover with room to spread because it grows where it will. The loveliest stand I have ever seen was at Long Island artist Bob Dash's garden, where it grew under some tall privet that had been trimmed up to expose the trunks.

Garden litter such as fall leaves, layered thickly over the crowns in winter, will smother and kill this fern and can be a good way to control its growth.

Origin: Eastern North America

Foliage: Broad triangles of pale green turn rusty gold in autumn before dropping; fertile fronds appear first as green beads along the tips of upright stems, then turn dark brown and persist through winter. They are attractive in flower arrangements.

Ostrich fern (Matteuccia pensylvanica) *in a bed of sweet woodruff*

Sensitive fern (Onoclea sensibilis) under an overgrown but creatively up-trimmed hedge of privet in Bob Dash's garden

Hardiness: Zones 3 to 8
Height: To 2 feet
Region: Cool soils of eastern North America
Landscape use: Ground cover
Culture: Moist, rich soil; sun or shade; will tolerate boggy soil
Propagation: Division, spores

OSMUNDA CINNAMOMEA Cinnamon fern
POLYPODIACEAE Polypody family

Cinnamon fern's highly distinctive fertile fronds give it a stately appearance. Cinnamon-colored and woolly, the fertile fronds stand stiffly erect in the center of each crown, surrounded by a soft green nest of fronds.

Cinnamon fern will grow in ordinary soil that is moist, but it achieves perfection in form and size in sun and boggy ground or a place that is seasonally wet. Elsewhere, it requires shade. I have placed it in a low, wet place under a grove of river birch, where it mingles with Canada anemone and bee balm.

Origin: North America, West Indies, South America, Asia

Foliage: Pale green fronds narrow gradually at both ends; there is a tiny woolly tuft along the stem where leaflets (pinnae) attach.
Hardiness: Zones 4 to 10
Height: Depends upon richness of soil and amount of moisture: 3 to 6 feet
Region: Moist soils, North America
Landscape use: Bog garden ground cover; low, moist places; accent
Culture: Moist to wet, rich soil; best in full sun with soil that is constantly very moist
Propagation: Spores

OSMUNDA CLAYTONIA Interrupted fern
POLYPODIACEAE Polypody family

"Widely collected in the wild for the hardy fern mail-order trade," wrote Judith Jones about interrupted fern in the 1991 Fancy Fronds catalog. "It therefore seemed about time to take the pressure off of wild populations and produce this highly decorative species from spore." Her mail-order nursery sells only nursery-propagated ferns.

As is the case with other *Osmunda*s, interrupted fern's reproductive mechanism adds to its visual appeal. Just about midway along the fronds, small, spore-laden leaflets fall off by midsummer, leaving interruptions in the frond. Once it is established, interrupted fern seems better able to tolerate occasional drought than either cinnamon or royal fern, making it a good choice for those who don't have a wet spot.

Cinnamon fern (Osmunda cinnamomea) and false lily-of-the-valley

Interrupted fern (Osmunda claytonia)

Origin: Eastern North America, Asia

Foliage: Large crowns of woolly croziers unfurl to long, rather narrow, medium green fronds that are broken by orangy spore-covered leaflets.

Hardiness: Zones 3 to 7

Height: To 3 feet

Region: North America

Landscape use: Accent, ground cover

Culture: Moist, rich soil in part shade

Propagation: Spores

OSMUNDA REGALIS VAR. SPECTABILIS Royal fern

POLYPODIACEAE Polypody family

With a constant supply of moisture, royal fern will take either sun or shade and grow full and stately, befitting its name. A good mimic, at first glance royal fern might pass for a shrub; its fronds look more leaflike than those of other ferns and when the fertile fronds at the tips emerge, they resemble flower buds. Later they look like dried astilbe flowers. The whole plant has a rather upright, but asymmetric, irregular habit that is slightly bambooesque. In fall, royal fern's color rivals that of shrubs—a bright yellow-gold.

Origin: Newfoundland to Saskatchewan and south to Florida and Louisiana

Foliage: Fronds are composed of narrow, leaflike segments.

Hardiness: Zones 3 to 9

Height: To 6 feet

Regions: Northeast, Midwest, Mid-Atlantic, South, Mountain

Landscape use: Accent, ground cover at a pond's edge in saturated soil

Culture: Very moist to seasonally wet, rich, acid soil; light shade to full sun (with plentiful moisture)

Propagation: Fresh spores

POLYSTICHUM ACROSTICHOIDES Christmas fern

POLYPODIACEAE Polypody family

Some summers ago, in the great drought of 1989, my garden suffered over 45 days without rain. Except for what had been newly planted, nothing got watered. While deciduous ferns dropped their leaves, Christmas fern seemed to take the drought in stride. It didn't put on new growth, but it looked content to wait patiently for rain.

Royal fern (Osmunda regalis var. spectabilis)

(Jessie Harris photo)

Christmas fern (Polystichum acrostichoides) *with a ruffled collar of wild ginger*

Evergreen Christmas fern, still green at Christmas and throughout winter, serves as a good ground cover, especially as a foil or foreground to ephemerals like Virginia bluebells that go down in a state of gaudy dishevelment.

In late winter, just when wind has battered the old fronds and Christmas fern is really showing signs of wear, it puts on new growth right out of its center. Neatniks may mulch over the dead fronds; the more permissive simply wait for new growth to spread out and cover up.

Origin: Eastern North America

Foliage: Dark, leathery, evergreen fronds up to 5 inches across are long and narrow.

Hardiness: Zones 4 to 8

Height: To 30 inches

Regions: Northeast, Mid-Atlantic, South, Lower Midwest

Landscape use: Edger, accent, ground cover, cutting

Culture: Easy to grow; moist, rich, acid soil; part shade

Propagation: Division, spores

POLYSTICHUM MUNITUM Giant holly fern, sword fern

POLYPODIACEAE Polypody family

Like its eastern counterpart, the Christmas fern, sword fern is a well-adapted, evergreen plant. Native plant gardener Jenny Fleming calls sword fern a "workhorse." In her Berkeley garden, it grows in full sun, but she says it is better in partial to full shade.

Although sword fern is well adapted to the usual seven-month California summer drought, it will also take frequent watering. It stays crisp, upright, and evergreen in clumps that can get quite large. There are dozens—maybe hundreds—in Mrs. Fleming's yard because there are frequent volunteers.

Sword fern's large 2- to 3-foot-long fronds make it a striking accent. It inhabits the deep, moist conifer forests of the lowlands west of the Cascade Mountains. Best in the shade of woodland gardens, sword fern's fronds bear many finely toothed leaflets.

Origin: Moist woodland of Alaska to Montana and California

Foliage: Evergreen, large, 2- to 3-foot-long fronds of many finely toothed leaflets

Hardiness: Zones 7 to 8

Height: To 3 feet

Regions: Northwest, Mountain, northern California

Landscape use: Striking accent, ground cover, background understory, winter green. Beautiful on near-vertical stone walls, under California live oaks that may die with summer water.

Culture: Moist shade; thrives on neglect; takes clay or loam; can go dry all summer, but looks better with some water.

Propagation: Spores. Divisions okay, but may need an axe to separate; best to divide in fall; easy to transplant.

THELYPTERIS HEXAGONOPTERA Broad beech fern

POLYPODIACEAE Polypody family

Big, broad triangular fronds make broad beech fern distinctive. As much as 15 inches across at the base, the fronds taper to a point, forming perfect Christmas tree shapes. It spreads, but not rampantly, to form small, rather loosely organized colonies. It is low growing and nice company for woodland wildflowers such as trilliums, wood phlox, or Virginia bluebells because it waits to develop fully until after their show and then tactfully fills in when they fade away.

Origin: Eastern North America into Texas

Foliage: Broad triangular fronds are light green and deciduous, with winged leaflets along the stem.

Southern shield fern (Thelypteris kunthii) *and other natives surround this covered porch in Louisiana.*
(Natives Landscape Corporation Design)

Hardiness: Zones 4 to 8

Height: To 2 feet

Region: Eastern North America

Landscape use: Ground cover for small areas. Broad beech fern is especially nice with spring ephemerals.

Culture: Grow broad beech fern in part to full shade, in humusy, rich soil that is fairly moist. Spreads by rhizomes.

Species: *T. phegopteris,* the long beech fern, is very similar but doesn't have wings along the stem.

Propagation: Division, spores

THELYPTERIS KUNTHII Southern shield fern, maiden fern

POLYPODIACEAE Polypody family

Impressive as a ground cover, southern shield fern is distinctive, with very large, tropical-looking fronds. Spaces between the leaflets always remind me of the spaces between teeth that are left when children start losing their baby teeth. The combination of evenly spaced leaflets on very large fronds adds lightness to a mass of southern shield fern, and a mass is just what this spreader becomes. A whole bed of southern shield fern in the shade lends a cool note to the hottest day.

Origin: Coastal plain from Central America to Texas and South Carolina

Foliage: Long, broad fronds of widely spaced leaflets are deciduous, turning dark tan after frost.

Hardiness: Zones 7 to 10

Height: To 40 inches

Region: South

Landscape use: Bold ground cover, accent

Culture: Light to full shade; moist, neutral soil; spreads vigorously where conditions are right; established plants are somewhat drought-tolerant.

Propagation: Division, spores

THELYPTERIS NOVEBORACENSIS New York fern

POLYPODIACEAE Polypody family

Linnaeus named this fern in 1753, which ought to silence the wags who insist New York fern is so called because of its aggressive personality.

Spreading New York fern is another classic-looking ferny fern with narrow fronds that taper at both ends. Because it spreads swiftly, it is best sited away from your prize wildlings—perhaps as understory for shrubs in woodland gardens where wave upon wave of its soft fronds lend an immeasurable softness to a shady garden.

Origin: Eastern North America to Mississippi and Arkansas

Foliage: Pale green, delicate, deciduous fronds

Hardiness: Zones 3 to 8

Height: To 18 inches

Regions: Eastern North America to Mississippi and Arkansas

Landscape use: Ground cover in out-of-the-way areas

Culture: Easy to grow, hard to stop in moist, humusy soil; part to full shade

Species: Marsh fern, *Thelypteris palustris,* spreads quickly in boggy, wet places

Propagation: Division, spores

Netted chain fern (Woodwardia areolata)
(Larry Lowman Design)

WOODWARDIA AREOLATA Netted chain fern
POLYPODIACEAE Polypody family

Primitive looking, with broad, deeply cut light green fronds, netted chain fern resembles sensitive fern. Its leaflets, however, are alternate instead of vaguely opposite, and instead of beads clustered on an upright stalk, it has unique fertile fronds that look like frond skeletons.

This fern fits easily into odd corners—the shady little spaces that need a bit of dressing up—next to the house or between leggy shrubs. It teams well with impatiens.

Origin: Maine to Florida and Louisiana

Foliage: Deciduous, light green, roughly triangular

Hardiness: Zones 4 to 8

Height: To 15 inches

Region: Eastern United States

Landscape use: Ground cover

Culture: Easy; moist to wet; humus, part to full shade; spreads

Propagation: Division, spores

New York fern (Thelypteris noveboracensis)

Water

Plants

A WATER FEATURE DOES FOR A GARDEN WHAT A FIREPLACE DOES FOR A ROOM. IT DRAWS ATTENTION, CENTERS ACTION, AND ADDS AN ELEMENT OF MYSTERY. PEOPLE WANT TO BE CLOSE TO WATER. IF YOU ADD A POOL, BE SURE TO ADD SOME PAVING NEXT TO THE POOL TO ACCOMMODATE THE PEOPLE IT ATTRACTS.

WATER PLANTS ARE BEAUTIFUL AND EXOTIC, AND THEY ARE ALSO THE EASIEST OF PLANTS TO MAINTAIN. USUALLY, ALL THAT IS NECESSARY IS AN INSPECTION VERY EARLY EACH SPRING AND A REPOTTING IF A PLANT HAS OUT-GROWN ITS CONTAINER.

SALLY KURTZ, WHO OWNS AND OPERATES WATER WAYS NURSERY IN LOVETTSVILLE, VIRGINIA, SHARED HER VAST EXPERIENCE WITH WATER PLANTS TO HELP ME HONE THIS LIST TO A VERY SELECT GROUP OF AQUATICS, CHOSEN FROM AMONG THE MANY NATIVE WATER PLANTS FOR THEIR GOOD LOOKS AND THEIR ABILITY TO LIVE SUBMERGED THROUGHOUT THE

OVERLEAF: *A water feature, such as this garden pond at Wave Hill, never fails to draw the eye. Behind the variegated flag is a graceful clump of hardy water canna's shapely green leaves on dark stems. At far right is the fine-textured narrow-leaf cattail.*
ABOVE: *Although the native white water lily has been hybridized for over a century, records of crosses have been lost, and the origin of individual plants is not always known.*
(Sally Kurtz photo)

year. All are plants that, in the wild, can grow on the shallow edges of ponds, marshes, and lakes with their lower stems continuously submerged. They are called "emergents." Some—like *Iris versicolor*—may be able to survive in ordinary garden soil, but the ability to survive being submerged year-round is an all-important consideration in man-made pools of concrete or fiberglass. In these pools, the water level doesn't fluctuate as it will in an earth pond, but stays at a constant depth.

Although some of the most aggressive water plants—like the swiftly colonizing native lotus (*Nelumbo lutea*), the rampant primrose creeper (*Jussiaea repens*), or the unstoppable yellow floating heart (*Nymphoides peltata*)—have been excluded from this list, it is recommended that all aquatics be planted in containers before placing them in a garden pool or pond. This will help keep their growth under control and avoid the possibility of runaways.

Your choice of plants depends upon your water depth. Most emergents do not require more than six inches of water over their crowns, and some live happily in wet mud with only an inch or two of water overhead. You can vary the water depth by setting containers on plastic crates turned upside down, which displace very little water.

In nature, marshes, ponds, and lakes are open to the sky. It follows that water plants grow most vigorously and bloom best in full sun. However, many will accommodate light shade.

This New Orleans garden is all pool—fiberglass liners placed side by side and end to end. Decking leads over the water to a greenhouse and provides a way to get close to the water. (Christopher Friedrichs Design)

A general rule in designing a pool or pond is the rule of thirds. Plant one-third with water lilies and emergents, one-third in submerged plants such as *Elodea canadensis* and *Ceratophyllum demersum*—usually available by mail order—and allow the remaining third to remain open to the sky. You do, after all, want some water to look at along with your plants. The unplanted third of the pool is a window to the life within.

The rule of thirds keeps the pond clear. The water lilies provide just enough shade, and the submerged plants use up just enough nutrients, to discourage the growth of algae. You need both in order to have clear water and avoid the green pea-soup effect. Lined up along the edge of the pool, or situated at the bottom of a waterfall, submerged containers play a role in keeping the water clean, too: they act as water filters.

Once the pool is planted, all that remains is to add a snail or two, and some goldfish or rosy red minnows to keep down the mosquito population, before the pool becomes a self-sufficient little community that draws even more life: frogs and dragonflies.

The following list includes plants in a wide variety of shapes to contrast and complement water lilies, which should be on everybody's list!

Scouring rush (Equisetum hyemale) *with Rudbeckia*

EQUISETUM HYEMALE Scouring rush, horsetail
EQUISETACEAE Horsetail family

Scouring rush can live out of water easily. That's the problem. Once let loose in the garden, it's nearly impossible to stop. The primitive, jointed stems pop up everywhere. But when it's contained in a pot that is partly submerged, scouring rush is a dramatic vertical accent that stays put. Its marvelous green, jointed stems are great in bouquets.

Origin: Eurasia, North America, frequently in moist, boggy soils

Flower: Reproduces by spores

Foliage: Green unbranched stems are prominently jointed, not unlike bamboo.

Hardiness: Zones 4 to 9

Height: To 3 feet

Region: North America

Landscape use: Accent in a pool

Culture: Sun, part shade, moist to wet soil; contain this very aggressive plant.

Species: *E. scirpoides* (dwarf, to 8 inches)

Propagation: Division, spores

DECODON VERTICILLATUS Swamp loosestrife
LYTHRACEAE Loosestrife family

Although swamp loosestrife's deep pink flowers are similar in color to those of *Lythrum,* the comparison ends there. This plant has a graceful, cascading habit and it will look like a shrub growing in the water. It may be short lived. One of its nicest characteristics is its bright crimson foliage in fall.

Origin: Canada to Florida and Louisiana, west to Illinois

Flower: ½-inch bell-shaped, rose pink flower with five petals and protruding stamens in July/August

Foliage: Whorled willowlike leaves are opposite and 2 to 5 inches long.

Hardiness: Zones 4 to 9

Height: 2 to 3 feet

Region: Eastern North America

Landscape use: Pond accent, massing

Culture: Saturated soil with four inches of water overhead

Propagation: Fresh seed sown in saturate soil will germinate in April of the following year.

IRIS FULVA Red iris
IRIDACEAE Iris family

Outstanding for its unusual brick red flushed raspberry color, the red iris is beautiful in groups blooming at the edge of ponds. In the Mid-Atlantic area, it blooms later than *Iris versicolor* and, thus, extends the iris season. Possibly because it is at the northern end of its hardiness range in my garden, it is a

Red iris (**Iris fulva**) *(Sally Kurtz photo)*

Blue flag (Iris versicolor)

Origin: Northern United States from Maine to Minnesota and south to Virginia.
Flower: The violet blue flowers, unbearded, veined with yellow-based sepals, bloom in May and June.
Foliage: Thin, pale to bluish green, swordlike leaves rise from a basal cluster.
Hardiness: Zones 3 to 8
Height: 2 to 3 feet
Regions: Northeast, Mid-Atlantic, Midwest
Landscape use: Pond edger
Culture: Grow in containers under one or two inches of water or in moist soil.
Species: Western flag (*I. missouriensis*), southern flag (*I. virginiana*).
Propagation: Divide in spring or sow seed in autumn.

moderate to slow grower and does not multiply with the wild abandon of *Iris versicolor*.

Condition *Iris fulva* before using it in flower arrangements by cutting it in the afternoon and placing it in deep water in a cool place for several hours or overnight.
Origin: Lower Midwest south to Alabama and Louisiana
Flower: The reddish brown flower is 3 inches wide, is nonbearded with three recurved sepals and three narrower, recurved petals, in May/June.
Foliage: Swordlike leaves are a clean light green.
Hardiness: Zones 7 (possibly 6) to 9
Height: To 3 feet
Regions: Lower Midwest where hardy, South
Landscape use: Pond edge, massing
Culture: Grow in saturated soil under a half-inch of water.
Propagation: Divide roots, or sow seeds in shallow water.

IRIS VERSICOLOR Blue flag
IRIDACEAE Iris family

Blue flag carries several flowers on the ends of its sturdy stalks. It is a showy plant with foliage that remains attractive until hard frost. It grows lustily, but when contained in pots is easy to divide in spring. This is a good plant for any pond, but will even work in one as small as four square feet! In the last several years, I've seen miniature pools—just the right size for a deck or patio—that are a good way to get into water gardening by wetting just one toe at a time. Blue flag is a good plant with which to start.

MENYANTHES TRIFOLIATA Bog bean, buck bean
GENTIANACEAE Gentian family

Bog bean scrambles over the surface of the water, yet never loses its neat appearance and is great for hiding the edges of artificial ponds. Its apple green leaves add a bright note.
Origin: East Coast from Canada to central Colorado and the southern Sierra Nevada
Flower: Stout stalks as high as the leaves bear narrow (½- to ¾-inch) clusters of white or purple-tinged, starlike flowers.
Foliage: Beanlike leaves are apple green and borne three to a stem.

Bog bean (Menyanthes trifoliata) *(Sally Kurtz photo)*

Circular leaves and scent reveal Nymphaea odorata *blood.*

Hardiness: Probably zones 4 to 8
Height: 4 to 12 inches
Regions: Northeast, Mid-Atlantic, Midwest, Mountain
Landscape use: A low scrambler for the edges of ponds.
Culture: Under two to four inches of water.
Propagation: Divide the long rhizome. Underwater it has no leaves; in the air, it will produce leaves at every joint.

NYMPHAEA ODORATA Sweet-scented water lily
NYMPHAEACEAE Water lily family

This water lily is yet another example of a native American plant that went abroad as its own lovely but unsophisticated self and came back in many elegant forms. Hybrids developed from the species *Nymphaea odorata*—notably by Latour Marliac in Europe—usually have a telltale fragrance and circular leaves, and that is the only way of detecting American blood in a particular plant. Some hybridizers, jealous of their treasures, did not make the records of their crosses available, so there is no way of knowing the pedigree of many a water lily.

Anyone who has ever received a catalog of water lilies knows that each one is prettier than the last. Yet this simple, unimproved beauty in ponds and marshes of the East, is the most fragrant water lily of all. It needs full sun to bloom, but flowering is steady from late May to September. As with most water lilies, it performs best if fed once a month during the growing season.
Origin: Ponds, marshes, swamps, from Canada to Florida and Texas
Flower: White, about 4 inches in size, cup-shaped around a yellow center; it floats on the water; blooms from May to September. Very fragrant!
Foliage: Orbicular lily pads, green above, usually purplish below. Young leaves are purple.
Hardiness: Zones 4 (Quebec to Florida) to 9
Height: At least six inches of water to depth of two feet
Region: North America
Culture: Place in containers in man-made ponds. In mud-bottom ponds, start in six inches of water at the edge of the pond; it will grow into deeper water.
Propagation: By root division at growing points

ORONTIUM AQUATICUM Golden club
ARACEAE Arum family

Golden club is an emergent of striking beauty. Its leaves are dark green and elliptical, with the lovely depth of color and silvery sheen of good velvet. Like lotus foliage, they cause water to bead like pearls on velvet. In shallow water the leaves stand up, but in deeper water they float. Golden club blooms along with marsh marigold. Later on, the dark leaves are a welcome relief from and contrast to the midsummer green of other aquatics.
Origin: Slow-moving streams and marshes from Louisiana and Florida, north along the coastal plain to Massachusetts
Flower: Poker-plant spikes of yellow bloom for a month or more (April to June) on an upwardly thickened white stalk
Foliage: Dark green velvety blades are 5 to 12 inches long and have a silvery sheen.
Hardiness: Zones 6 to 9

*Golden club (*Orontium aquaticum*)*

Pickerelweed (Pontederia cordata)

Height: 12 to 18 inches (above water)
Regions: South, Mid-Atlantic, parts of Northeast where hardy.
Landscape use: Pond edge
Culture: Grow under 12 inches of water; not invasive.
Propagation: Propagate by fresh seed in late summer,

Arrow arum (Peltandra virginiana)

early fall. Plant in a planting crate in shallow water. Water should cover seed. Move to deeper water as golden club becomes established. Golden club is difficult to transplant because it has a deep root system.

PELTANDRA VIRGINIANA Arrow arum, tuckahoe
ARACEAE Arum family

Arrow arum's showy clumps of fleshy leaves are always handsome accents in a garden pool. Although the flower is not particularly showy, the leaves, with their prominent veining and arrowhead shape, are handsome and natural looking along the edges of pools. There is great variation within this species. Both the fruit and the rootstock, when thoroughly dried, are edible.

Origin: Coastal, fresh marshes from the Great Lakes and Maine south
Flower: An arumlike green flower in May–July is followed by clusters of green or amber berries.
Foliage: Arrow-shaped leaves with prominent veining grow in clumps.
Hardiness: Zones 5 (probably 4) to 9
Height: 12 to 18 inches

Lizard's tail (Saururus cernuus) *(Sally Kurtz photo)*

Regions: Northeast, Midwest, Mid-Atlantic, South
Landscape use: Pond edger
Culture: Grow under two to four inches of water.
Propagation: Fresh seed in shallow water

PONTEDERIA CORDATA Pickerelweed
PONTEDERIACEAE Pickerelweed family

Pickerelweed is easily grown and keeps its neat habit all season long. In summer, it is striking when blue flower spikes appear. These continue until autumn. Seeds can be eaten like nuts, and young leafstalks can be cooked as greens. The seeds were a Native American "starvation food." While they are nutritious, Sally Kurtz says they taste exactly like cardboard.

Origin: Nova Scotia and Ontario west to Minnesota and south to northern Florida, Missouri, and Oklahoma
Flower: Spikes of funnel-shaped, three-lobed, violet blue flowers are borne from June to November.
Foliage: Elongated, heart-shaped, 4- to 10-inch-long leaves are indented at the base and taper to a point.
Hardiness: Zones 4 (probably 3) to 9
Height: 2 to 4 feet

Region: North America from the Atlantic Coast west to Missouri and Oklahoma
Landscape use: Great pond edger
Culture: Grow in two to four inches of water.
Propagation: Division or fresh seed in saturate soil

SAURURUS CERNUUS Lizard's tail
SAURURACEAE Lizard's tail family

Lizard's tail grows from long, aromatic, creeping rhizomes, but I think the reason for its common name is not its root but its perky "tail" of a nodding white flower spike. It is fragrant and blooms over a long period. Heart-shaped leaves have a bushiness that is a nice change from the strappy look of irises and cattails.

Origin: North America from the Atlantic Coast west to Texas, Missouri, and Kansas
Flower: Long, white, nodding spikes are fragrant and appear from June to September.
Foliage: Heart-shaped leaves are 3 to 6 inches long and indented at the base.
Hardiness: Zones 4 (probably 3) to 9
Height: 2 to 5 feet

Region: North America, east of the deserts and Rockies
Landscape use: Pond edger
Culture: Grow under six inches of water.
Propagation: Division or cuttings

THALIA DEALBATA Hardy water canna
MARANTACEAE Arrowroot family

The hardy water canna is a tall, strong architectural feature for larger ponds and pools, with a long season of effectiveness. Leaves remain through most of winter. Because it is not invasive and maintains a neat habit, water canna can be planted directly in mud-bottom ponds. I can't really think of a place where it doesn't look good, but it is absolutely spectacular as an accent in a rectilinear pool, where its strong lines are set off by the angularity of the pool.

Origin: Warm-temperate North America
Flower: Small, bluish purple flowers in panicles
Foliage: Canna-shaped leaves to 12 inches long on long petioles
Hardiness: Zones 8 (move to pond bottom in Zone 7 over winter) to 10
Height: 6 to 8 feet

Hardy water canna (Thalia dealbata) *behind unopened pickerelweed* (Pontederia cordata) *(Rosa Finsley Design)*

Regions: Where hardy
Landscape use: Margins of mud-bottom ponds, containers
Culture: Grow in containers under two to six inches of water, or at pond margins. Water canna is a slow runner that reproduces moderately.
Species: *T. geniculata,* called arrowroot, is a bog plant.
Propagation: Root division, fresh seeds, sown in saturate soil

TYPHA ANGUSTIFOLIA Narrow-leaf cattail
TYPHACEAE Cattail family

Like its cousin the common cattail, the narrow-leaf cattail is extremely invasive. Compared with the common cattail, everything about the narrow-leaf cattail is smaller, narrower, and more graceful. Its flat, grassy leaves are very refined, making it a better choice for man-made ponds, and when planted in submerged containers, its pushy behavior turns civilized.

Origin: Commonest in the Northeast, but occurs in many places throughout the country.
Flower: Dark brown, pokerlike spikes are shorter than the leaves.
Foliage: Flat, gray-green, grasslike leaves, about the width of a pencil
Hardiness: Zones 3 (probably 2) to 10
Height: To 6 feet
Regions: Inland fresh and alkali marshes, coastal fresh and brackish marshes, throughout the country
Landscape use: Pot-contained in larger ponds
Culture: Never, never let *Typha angustifolia* loose. It takes water six feet deep to stop it once it is established.
Propagation: Division of rootstock in late winter

Vines

ARE THE MOST OBLIGING OF PLANTS. WHILE TREES GROW UPRIGHT AND DEVELOP HARD, UNCOMPROMISING TRUNKS, AND SHRUBS SPREAD OUTWARD INTO DISTINCT SHAPES, VINES ARE CHAMELEON PLANTS THAT CHANGE HEIGHT AND SHAPE ACCORDING TO THEIR SUPPORT. IS THERE A TELEPHONE POLE OR A TREE STUMP BLIGHTING YOUR GARDEN? PUT A VINE LIKE CLIMBING HYDRANGEA OR CLIMBING ASTER TO WORK CAMOUFLAGING IT. IS THE GARAGE WALL LESS THAN DECORATIVE? CONSIDER COVERING IT WITH VIRGINIA CREEPER.

WHEN THERE IS NO MORE ROOM TO SPREAD OUTWARD ON THE GROUND, VINES ALLOW YOU TO GARDEN UPWARD ON THE VERTICAL PLANES — WALLS, FENCES, TREE TRUNKS, AND PERGOLAS — A BOON TO SMALL GARDENS. VINES COVER DULL WALLS WITH LUSH FOLIAGE, ADDING FLOWERS AND COLOR FROM EYE LEVEL UP. UNLESS TRAINED OTHERWISE,

OVERLEAF: *Vines such as Carolina jessamine can turn the dross of a wooden fence into pure gold.*
ABOVE: *Cross vine (*Anisostichus capreolatus*) (Jessie Harris photo)*

they do all of this without shading out what grows around them, the way that even the smallest tree do.

Clinging vines hold on to their supports for dear life. Some, like Virginia creeper or trumpet vine, cling by means of little rootlets that stick to walls or with tiny, round plates that adhere like superglue. Others—clematis, cross vine—send out tendrils that grasp the supports. Twining vines circle their supports, moving from left to right (*Wisteria frutescens*) or from right to left (*Lonicera sempervirens*).

Like most other plants, vines grow best with some sun. A place where roots are cool and shady and the top of the plant receives sun is perfect—especially for flowering vines. Hardworking vines accomplish a lot in a little space.

ANISOSTICHUS CAPREOLATUS (BIGNONIA CAPREOLATA) Cross vine
BIGNONIACEAE Bignonia family

Spring-blooming cross vine produces large red and yellow, fat trumpet flowers that always attract hummingbirds. This evergreen vine clings by tendrils and can reach 60 feet, which means that at eye level, there is not likely to be much to see. John Bartram grew cross vine up one corner of his house in Philadelphia and subsequently commented that it would reach the "tops of buildings." It will always grow a little higher than its support, which makes it an ideal shade plant for a second-story deck or terrace. If you want to see the flowers, keep the support low.

Cross vine gets its common name from a cross shape that shows up in the wood when it is cut.

In my garden (Zone 7), where I am training it up to shade a second-story deck, the foliage doesn't drop but turns a very attractive dark purple in winter. In colder places, it may drop its leaves.

Origin: Thickets and alluvial forests of the southeastern United States, west to Illinois, Texas

Flower: 2-inch fat, red and yellow trumpet flowers in spring

Foliage: Lustrous, dark green, evergreen leaves turn purple in winter.

Hardiness: Zones 6 to 9

Height: To 60 feet

Regions: Eastern North America, Midwest

Landscape use: Vine for trellises, poles, fences, buildings; flowers face the sun.

*Climbing aster (*Aster carolinianis*) scrambles and leans, rather than climbing by twining or holdfasts.*

Culture: Sun to part shade, medium to moist soil

Variety/cultivar: *A. capreolatus* var. *atrosanguinea* (red flowers), 'Tangerine Beauty' (orange)

Propagation: Softwood cuttings, seed

ASTER CAROLINIANIS Climbing aster
COMPOSITAE Sunflower family

Unique as an aster that is both woody and vining, climbing aster produces, says Bob McCartney of Woodlanders Nursery, a wonderful display of flowers in fall. The same kind of generous bloom that characterizes other asters crowns this vine. A scrambler rather than a twiner or clinger, climbing aster is picturesque on a trellis or fence.

Origin: Swamp, water's edge, as well as dry, sandy woods, southeast coast, piedmont

Flower: Pink to purple in October, November

Foliage: Light green aster leaves, deciduous

Hardiness: Zones 6 to 10

Height: To 12 feet

Regions: South, Mid-Atlantic, Lower Midwest

Landscape use: Nice on trellis or fence

Culture: Easy; sun to part shade; not fussy about moisture; scrambles and leans without tendrils or hold-fasts; easy on a trellis

Propagation: Cuttings, seed

*Trumpet vine (*Campsis radicans*)*

CALYSTEGIA MACROSTEGIA 'ANACAPA'

CONVOLVULACEAE Bindweed family

This very vigorous, fast-growing vine that hails from Anacapa Island, California, is always showy, bearing 2-inch pink morning glory trumpets nearly year-round. Its leaves are roughly triangular and a bright, glossy green on vines that can quickly cover a small house—a drawback or a virtue, depending upon the house.

Origin: Selection from Anacapa Island, California

Flower: Pink, 2-inch-plus morning glory trumpets nearly year-round

Foliage: Leaves are 2 to 3 inches, bright glossy green, and roughly triangular.

Hardiness: Zones 9 (possibly 8) to 10

Region: California

Landscape use: Trellis, arbor

Culture: Full sun, partial shade; best with deep summer watering

Species: *C. purpurata* 'Bolinas', a selection from Bolinas, California, has pink-purple 1½-inch morning glory trumpets, triangular gray-green leaves; it twines to 8 feet or more, grows in full sun to part shade, and is best with deep summer watering; hardy in Zones 8 to 10.

Propagation: Cuttings

CAMPSIS RADICANS Trumpet vine

BIGNONIACEAE Bignonia family

In summer, one sometimes sees spots of scarlet along the edges of country fields. These are the flowers of trumpet vine, otherwise invisible in the tangle of life that crowds fencerows. When grown by itself, trumpet vine's foliage—large compound leaves—shows itself to be bold and dramatic and the flowers are profuse, showy, and often visited by hummingbirds. Grow this vigorous vine on a rustic rail fence or a stout pergola for summer shade.

Origin: Woodlands, road cuts, from Pennsylvania, Missouri, south to Florida and Texas

Flower: Orange/scarlet trumpets, 2 inches long, in July

Foliage: Clings by rootlike holdfasts; very leafy.

Hardiness: Zones 5 to 10

Height: To 30 feet

Region: Eastern North America

Landscape use: Covering fences, balconies; wildlife planting; erosion control on banks

Culture: Very adaptable; sun, part shade; suckers and roots where stems touch the ground; it holds by holdfasts that can damage brick or mortar.

Cultivars: 'Flava' (yellow); 'Madame Galen' (x *Tagliabuana,* an Asian species)

Propagation: Cuttings, seed

CLEMATIS VIORNA Leather flower

RANUNCULACEAE Buttercup family

Leather flower was one of the earliest vines sent from the New World to England. Peter Collinson, the avid 18th-century plant collector, grew one in his garden at Mill Hill outside London, only to have it stolen! The leather flower is one of about a dozen or so *Clematis* species native to eastern North America. Unlike the modern hybrids we think of as typical *Clematis,* leather flower has bell-shaped blooms, made up of four thick and leathery sepals that gave rise to the plant's common name. While the large-flowered hybrids are hard to miss in a garden, the leather flower is the sort of intimate plant that fascinates children. Richard E. Weaver, Jr., who propagates it at We-Du Nursery, says one has to approach closely to appreciate its charming flowers, "and perhaps to give them a gentle pinch to see if they are really as succulent as they appear." After each flower fades, a feathery, golden seed head takes its place.

This is an easy, carefree plant that will swiftly cover an unsightly post or stump. With no support, it will grow as a loose ground cover. Cut it back in the fall after it dies to the ground with hard frost.

Origin: Road banks and thickets in eastern United States, west to Illinois and Missouri

Flower: Bell shaped and nodding, with thick-textured, deep pink to reddish sepals, blooming in early summer

Foliage: Compound leaves; dies to the ground in winter

Hardiness: Zones 4 to 8

Height: Climbing to 6 feet

Region: Eastern North America

Landscape use: Good on a fence or stump, or climbing through shrubbery; also a loose ground cover

Culture: Full sun or partial shade; good drainage

Propagation: Seed, cuttings

DECUMARIA BARBARA Climbing hydrangea
SAXIFRAGACEAE Saxifrage family

There are two "climbing hydrangeas." One is a real hydrangea, exotic *H. petiolaris,* and the other is *Decumaria barbara,* an elegant vine that is

Leather flower (Clematis viorna)

Climbing hydrangea (Decumaria barbara) *is handsome as a ground cover, even when not in bloom.*

semievergreen in warm climates. It is called "hydrangea" for its small, creamy white flower clusters, but its foliage is handsome enough to stand alone. It is a clean, dark, glossy green. The stiff, reddish vine holds on to supports by little roots along the stems.

Climbing hydrangea adorns the brick walls of the Governor's Palace in Williamsburg, Virginia, where it blooms in early summer and always elicits admiring comments. People who have never seen it before want to know what it is and where they can buy it.

Origin: Low woods of the southeastern United States

Flower: 2-inch white flower clusters

Foliage: Dark green, semievergreen leaves climb by aerial rootlets, turn white in fall.

Hardiness: Zones 6 (probably 5; I have seen this at the Chicago Botanic Garden) to 8

Height: To 30 feet

Regions: Northeast, Midwest, Mid-Atlantic, South, Northwest

Landscape use: On trees, stone or brick walls

Culture: Sun to part shade, moist soil; if grown in sun, it needs a steady supply of moisture. Climbing hydrangea blooms on new wood.

Propagation: Cuttings, seed

*Trumpet honeysuckle (*Lonicera sempervirens*)
has a vast range.*

GELSEMIUM SEMPERVIRENS Carolina jessamine
LOGANIACEAE Logania family

To once have seen and smelled this vine in bloom is to want it and, despite logic, to have bought it. The state flower of South Carolina, Carolina jessamine blooms with wild abandon in North Carolina and parts of Virginia. When Jefferson grew it, he called it "Bignonia sempervirens." To my very great regret, it seems to lose vigor north of the Maryland line. A few miserable little branches of Carolina jessamine have clung to life and remained evergreen in my garden, but after four years, it is clear there will be no sheet of fragrant yellow bloom draping over a lattice fence this spring.

There is, however, a new hardy selection I plan to buy; it is available from Woodlanders and rated Zone 6. In addition to its other charms, Carolina jessamine is also a butterfly plant.

Origin: Woodlands, road cuts, from Virginia to Florida and west to Texas and Central America
Flower: Fragrant, yellow flowers in great abundance bloom in April in North Carolina, earlier farther south.
Foliage: Small, neat, dark green evergreen leaves on a twining vine
Hardiness: Zones 7 to 10
Height: 20 feet
Region: South
Landscape use: An evergreen vine good for hiding fences, covering porches, softening walls
Culture: Adaptable; sun, part shade; not fussy about soil
Species/cultivar: 'Pride of Augusta' (double); reputedly hardier (to Beltsville, Maryland) selections are available; swamp jessamine, *G. rankanii,* blooms both fall and spring on an evergreen plant.
Propagation: Cuttings

LONICERA SEMPERVIRENS Trumpet honeysuckle, coral honeysuckle
CAPRIFOLIACEAE Honeysuckle family

Many people have never seen the tough but well-behaved native trumpet honeysuckle (*Lonicera sempervirens*) and are understandably reluctant to try it because they associate it with an exotic invader. Japanese honeysuckle (*Lonicera japonica*) is truly a noxious weed. Deservedly infamous because it self-sows and spreads rampantly where it is hardy, Japanese honeysuckle is especially pernicious in woodlands, where its twining ropelike vines actually strangle trees.

Like Japanese honeysuckle, trumpet honeysuckle is a twiner—but there the comparison ends. Named for its clusters of long, narrow, scarlet trumpet flowers, trumpet honeysuckle blooms for two months or more in summer, attracting swarms of glittering hummingbirds. It will grow very high, but stops a foot or two above a support and is especially handsome at the top of a fence. Distinctive pairs of semievergreen leaves joined at the base are pierced by the vines.

Origin: Eastern North America to Texas
Flower: Clusters of narrow trumpet flowers attract hummingbirds and are followed by red berries, taken by other birds.
Foliage: Semievergreen, perfoliate leaves on a tall vine
Hardiness: Zones 4 to 8
Height: To 30-plus feet
Regions: Northeast, Mid-Atlantic, South, Midwest, Mountain
Landscape use: Great wildlife plant, attracts hummingbirds, pretty over a fence
Culture: Sun, part shade, moist to medium soil
Variety/cultivar: *L. sempervirens* var. *sulphurea* (yellow); red trumpet honeysuckle (*L.* x *heckrottii*) is a cross between (it is thought) *L. sempervirens* and another native.
Propagation: Hardwood cuttings

PARTHENOCISSUS QUINQUEFOLIA Virginia creeper, woodbine
VITACEAE Grape family

"Leaflets three, let it be. Leaflets five, let it thrive," warns against touching poison ivy but tells us that the similar Virginia creeper isn't harmful. Both occupy the same kinds of places: shady, acid woodland where birds are likely to have deposited seeds. Both climb high on fences, walls, and trees, and both flame scarlet in fall—particularly in sun.

Virginia creeper has been in cultivation since the

French botanist André Michaux introduced it as *Ampelopsis quinquefolia* in the last years of the 18th century. Its compound leaves are as familiar on college campuses as ivy. As both ground cover and climbing vine, Virginia creeper's vigorous nature makes swift progress in large areas.

Origin: Northeastern United States to Florida, Texas, and Mexico

Flower: Inconspicuous, followed by purple berries, beloved by birds

Foliage: Compound leaves of five leaflets are a lustrous dark green, turning scarlet in fall—the more sun, the more vibrant; Virginia creeper holds by little disks at the ends of short tendrils.

Hardiness: Zones 3 to 10

Height: 40 feet

Regions: Woods, rocky places of the Northeast, Midwest, Mid-Atlantic, parts of Southwest

Landscape use: Great for covering large areas

Culture: Sun, medium dry

Varieties/species: *P. quinquefolia* var. *englemannii* and *P. quinquefolia* var. *saint paulii* (smaller leaves); seven-leaf creeper, *P. heptaphylla,* is more tender (Zone 8)

Propagation: Cuttings

WISTERIA FRUTESCENS American wisteria
LEGUMINOSAE Pea family

Unlike the Asian wisterias, American wisteria doesn't have to be grafted to bloom early. Plants grown from cuttings will bloom when they are

Virginia creeper (Parthenocissus quinquefolia) *and its western relatives glow shades of scarlet to burgundy in fall.*

American wisteria (Wisteria frutescens) *blooms later in the season than its Asian relatives, but will bloom as a young plant. Sometimes it blooms twice during the growing season.* (Jan Midgley photo)

two years old, or sometimes even in the first year. And sometimes they bloom in June and again in September!

Later blooming than the Asian species, American wisteria flowers are unlikely to be bothered by frost. A combination of the Asian and American wisterias on a single (very strong) support would extend the showy season into May and June and confuse your neighbors. American wisteria's lavender flowers appear when the vine is in leaf, and are upright rather than hanging.

Origin: Lowland woods and streams from Virginia to Florida, west to Texas

Flower: Upright lavender, borne in May or June (depending upon locality) after the leaves have emerged.

Foliage: Ovate leaflets in compound leaves on a twining vine

Hardiness: Zones 5 to 9

Height: 10 to 30 feet

Regions: Southeast, Mid-Atlantic, Northeast, Midwest, Northwest

Landscape use: Nice on fences

Culture: Sun to part shade; moist, well-drained soil

Variety: Kentucky wisteria or Texas wisteria, *W. macrostachya,* once considered a separate species, now considered a variety, has more pendant flowers in June; *W. macrostachya* 'Clara Mack' (showy white, Zone 6).

Propagation: Cuttings; seed-grown plants may be much slower to bloom.

Shr

Shrubs

ARE THE BACKBONE OF THE GARDEN. THEY DELINEATE SPACE, CONTOUR THE GROUND, AND PROVIDE BACKGROUND AND STRUCTURE. WITHOUT THEM, GARDENS WOULD LOOK FLAT AND FEATURELESS.

HORTICULTURISTS CALL SHRUBS "WOODIES" TO SEPARATE THEM FROM PERENNIALS AND ANNUALS, THE HERBACEOUS PLANTS WITH FLESHY PARTS THAT DIE BACK TO THE ROOTS EACH YEAR. SHRUBS, TOO, HAVE SOFT, FLESHY PARTS—LEAVES, FLOWERS, BERRIES— BUT THESE GROW ON A WOODY STRUC- TURE THAT REMAINS ALL YEAR.

THIS COMBINATION MAKES SHRUBS PERMANENT GARDEN ELEMENTS THAT ARE ALSO DYNAMIC. THEY CHANGE WITH THE SEASONS: THEY BLOOM IN SPRING AND SUMMER; THEY GROW BERRIES AND CHANGE IN THE FALL; THEY ARE PRESENT THROUGHOUT THE WINTER. LARGER AND LONGER LIVED THAN PERENNIALS, SHRUBS PROVIDE LARGE-SCALE DRAMA AND LASTING PRESENCE ALL THROUGH THE YEAR.

OVERLEAF: *Fothergilla's scented bottlebrush flowers bloom in concert with Asian azaleas and viburnums.*
ABOVE: *Bottlebrush buckeye* (Aesculus parviflora *var.* serotina)

AESCULUS PARVIFLORA Bottlebrush buckeye

HIPPOCASTANACEAE Horse chestnut family

This is a shrub worth waiting for. When well grown and mature, it sends out suckers to nearly twice as wide as its ultimate 10-foot height—a generous mound of large, handsome, compound leaves studded in July with creamy flower spikes. While you're waiting, it will still look good. After a year or two in the garden, young shrubs develop a nice mounding habit that seems to flow into whatever space is given it. Allow both strong light for the best and fastest growth and plenty of room. This is an ideal shrub for an informal privacy hedge because of its ultimate size. It colors a golden yellow in fall, even in deep shade.

It is telling when nurserymen or horticulturists are high on a plant. And those who know the most about shrubs are enthusiastic about bottlebrush buckeye. Bob McCartney of Woodlanders Nursery recommends bottlebrush buckeye for the South, and horticulturist and author Fred Galle, formerly horticultural director of Callaway Gardens, calls it, in a word, "choice."

Origin: Georgia and Alabama

Flower: White flowers in erect bottlebrush clusters in early July

Foliage: Large, handsome compound leaves of five to seven leaflets, turning golden yellow in fall

Hardiness: Zones 5 (probably 4) to 8

Height: To 10 feet

Region: Eastern North America

Landscape use: Specimen, tall bank planting, massing

Culture: Sun to part shade; slightly acidic, moist soil

Species: California buckeye (*A. californica*), a tree from dry, sunny slopes in California, has foot-long cream flower spikes; with summer water, which it will tolerate with good drainage, it stays green in summer. Eastern *A. parviflora* var. *serotina* has unusual, narrow flower spikes.

Propagation: Seed (cool stratify)

AGARISTA POPULIFOLIA (LEUCOTHOE POPULIFOLIA) Florida leucothoe

ERICACEAE Heath family

"Toughest and hardiest of the leucothoes and much hardier than originally thought," is the way plantsman J. C. Raulston describes

Florida leucothoe (Agarista populifolia)

Florida leucothoe, a plant that was once thought to be extremely tender. Having seen it growing and thriving in both full sun and full shade in Memphis (rated Zone 7), where it is very popular with native plant enthusiasts, I planted one and promptly lost it over its first winter in my own more northern Zone 7 garden. This may have been just bad luck. So handsome an evergreen is certainly worth a second try.

Unlike other leucothoes, Florida leucothoe has very upright stems with an irregular, asymmetric branching habit that looks vaguely Oriental. It is handsome as a background to ferns and plants for half shade, such as amsonias, in a woodland border.

Origin: South Carolina to Florida

Flower: White

Foliage: Bright, medium green, smooth, lustrous, oval leaves taper to points.

Hardiness: Zones 6 to 10. Some individuals are probably hardier than others.

Height: To 10 feet

Regions: South, Lower Midwest, some parts of the Mid-Atlantic

Landscape use: Shrub border; also specimen with character

Culture: Sun, part to full shade, moist humus

Propagation: Cuttings of firm wood with hormone

AGAVE CHRYSANTHA Century plant
AGAVACEAE Agave family

Like a piece of living sculpture, century plant's blue-green, succulent, daggerlike leaves form a symmetrical rosette that looks something like a yucca. At maturity (which takes years, but not a century), a tall stalk emerges—like a gargantuan asparagus—from the plant's center. Eventually, the stalk expands into a candelabra shape, finally to be lit by glowing yellow clusters of flowers. The plant expends all its energy in flowering, then dies. The top of the dried flower stalk is used, I've heard, as a Christmas tree by folks in the tropics, where Christmas-card Christmas trees are hard to come by. Century plant is found on dry, rocky slopes in central Arizona. It is hardy to Zone 9, possibly 8. Nurseries with a good selection of cacti and succulents may carry it, or try botanical garden and arboretum plant sales.

Origin: Dry slopes of Arizona

Flower: Large yellow clusters held candelabra-fashion on an immense flower stalk (12 to 20 feet tall) once in the plant's life

Saskatoon Juneberry (Amelanchier alnifolia)

Foliage: A rosette of succulent, blue-green, stiff, narrow, pointed leaves

Hardiness: Zones 9 (possibly Zone 8) to 10

Height: 2 feet by 3 feet wide

Region: Desert Southwest

Landscape use: Accent

Culture: Sun; dry, well-drained soil. Agaves are dryland plants that store water in a rosette of succulent leaves.

Species: Octopus agave (*A. vilmoriniana*) tolerates shade and has unarmed leaf margins (no spines). There are some 300 species of agave in temperate and tropical America. Some species have become threatened due to commercial collecting. Buy only propagated plants.

Sotol, left, agave in flower, and saguaro in the background

AMELANCHIER ALNIFOLIA Serviceberry, Saskatoon berry, Juneberry, shadblow
ROSACEAE Rose family

Someone once told me a sad story about serviceberry. This common name, the story went, came from its use as a funeral flower in pioneer days, when the dead would have to wait for burial until spring, when the ground thawed—just about the time the serviceberry bloomed.

Leadplant (Amorpha canescens)

Serviceberry's snowy white flowers in early spring smother the tips of the many branches when the shad run. It also bears dark purple fruits that are great in preserves early—in June—and everywhere, even in Saskatoon! A tall, many-stemmed shrub, serviceberry's smallish oval leaves turn brilliant yellow before dropping in the fall.

Origin: Western Ontario to the Yukon, south to Nebraska, Colorado, Idaho, and Oregon

Flower: Pure white in April, followed by purple-black edible fruits, the "serviceable" berries, loved by birds

Foliage: Oval, medium green, toothed at the tips

Hardiness: Zones 4 to 8

Height: Usually 6 to 8 feet

Regions: Pacific Northwest, Great Basin, Southwest

Landscape use: Shrub border, massing

Culture: Sun; medium moist soil. It spreads by suckers to form thickets but may be pruned into tree shape.

Species/cultivars: 'Regent' (sweet fruits, red fall color); *A. stolonifera* (excellent fall color).

Propagation: Seed (cold stratify for four months); germination may be erratic.

AMORPHA CANESCENS Leadplant
LEGUMINOSAE Pea family

Difficult sites need tough plants. Members of the genus *Amorpha* may become undesirable weeds under optimal conditions in gentle climates, but where circumstances are trying, they succeed where most others fail. Taprooted, nitrogen-fixing plants, amorphas tolerate dry, infertile, sandy sites.

One of very few shrubs found on the prairie, leadplant produces mauve purple and orange flower spikes in May. Its small, gray, hairy leaves are held on short, stiff stems. In a garden, it might be teamed with artemisia and sedum 'Ruby Glow' to augment the silver/purple color scheme.

Origin: Manitoba to New Mexico and Louisiana

Flower: Purple and orange in spikes, in May

Foliage: Small, gray, hairy leaves on stiff stems

Hardiness: Zones 2 to 8 or 9

Height: To 3 feet

Regions: Upper Midwest, Lower Midwest, parts of Southwest (needs some water in dry areas)

Landscape use: Tough plant for difficult conditions

Culture: Adaptable; full sun to part shade; cold- and wind-tolerant

Species: Indigo bush, *A. fruticosa,* to 10 feet, has narrow spikes of deep purple flowers with gold-colored stamens that attract butterflies. Late spring, dry climate border, prune late winter. Zones 4 to 9.

Propagation: Seed in fall

ARALIA SPINOSA Devil's walkingstick
ARALIACEAE Ginseng family

Well named, devil's walkingstick is just the thing for the place near the hole in the fence where the neighbor's kids and dogs run through. It grows to a vast, impenetrable, suckering thicket of thorny, very upright, woody canes. In contrast, its foliage—large compound leaves—are held at right angles near the top of the canes. These attributes have earned devil's walkingstick the designation "tropical looking."

To me, its look is highly eccentric. When it blooms in late summer, it is striking in a bold rather than a pretty way. It would be a good plant to contrast with the wood, brick, or stone of a blank wall, especially if someone else would take care of it.

Origin: Pennsylvania to Florida and Texas

Flower: Cream-colored flowers in panicles at the tips of branches in July/August, followed by purple-black berries

Foliage: Stiff branches at right angles to canes bear huge compound leaves with yellow to red-orange fall color.

Hardiness: Zones 4 to 8

Height: To 20 feet

Regions: Midwest, Mid-Atlantic, South, Northeast

Landscape use: Unusual specimen

Devil's walkingstick (**Aralia spinosa**)

Culture: Very adaptable; sun or shade; medium to moist, well-drained soil. It suckers; don't let devil's walking-stick get away from you; control by diligent pruning.
Propagation: Seed (cool stratify)

ARCTOSTAPHYLOS Manzanita
ERICACEAE Heath family

One April morning while I was visiting a friend in the Napa Valley and was still on East Coast time, I awoke at five o'clock in the morning and decided to climb into the hills behind my friend's house. It was a walk I'll never forget. As the sun came up among the manzanitas, I was mesmerized by their sinewy, cinnamon-colored bark that was set off by the fragile new green of bunchgrasses growing around them. On that quiet hill, the vineyards and wineries, the smart shops and restaurants of the town below, vanished in a pouf and I could imagine myself seeing California with the eyes of one of the Spanish mission fathers. Forever after, manzanitas will always be a symbol of California to me.

Later, I learned there are dozens of manzanitas in all sizes and shapes, members of the genus *Arctostaphylos,* one of the most complex groups of woody plants in the United States. Among them are everything from ground covers to gigantic tree substitutes. Some are easy to grow; many are described by Bart O'Brien of Rancho Santa Ana in Claremont, California, a man who ought to know a thing or two about manzanitas, as "horticulturally challenging." He finds many other manzanitas to be garden gems.

The first thing that visitors from the East notice about the larger manzanitas is their gorgeous, sinuous stems and trunks. The smooth, matte bark on the elegant trunks looks as though it has been coated with cinnamon. The bark peels annually.

Most manzanitas have thick, leathery, evergreen leaves whose upper and lower surfaces look alike (*A. uva-ursi* is one notable exception to this). Nearly all manzanitas have clusters of white to pink, $\frac{1}{8}$- to $\frac{1}{4}$-inch lily-of-the-valley flowers that are followed by small fruits that resemble "little apples," or manzanitas.

In the garden, Bart O'Brien recommends that all manzanitas be planted higher than the surrounding soil to prevent crown rot. Overhead watering is not recommended, as this practice spreads various fungal diseases, which cause branch dieback and various leaf spot problems. Rock mulches are generally much more successful than organic mulches, and fertilizers are generally unnecessary. Pruning is necessary only to remove deadwood.

Manzanita (**Arctostaphylos**)

Bearberry (Arctostaphylos uva-ursi), *bottom, ceanothus, top*

In California, where most are native, manzanitas tolerate summer heat and drought, although, says California gardener Peggy Grier, "they look better with periodic water—perhaps once every four to six weeks." Even someone who hates to water can manage this.

"A bonus of all manzanitas," says Berkeley gardener Jenny Fleming, is that they are good for hummingbirds in the winter. Ms. Fleming favors the cultivar 'Warren Roberts' of the pajaro manzanita (*A. pajaroensis*). New growth, she says, is so bright red as to appear to be in flower from a distance. For her, the cultivar of *A. uva-ursi,* 'Point Reyes', does less well than the very handsome 'Radiant', whose large red berries are loved by birds.

California native plant gardeners are high on manzanitas. Bart O'Brien, Jenny Fleming, and Betsy Clebsch, who grow them in different parts of the state, helped to compose the *Arctostaphylos* chart (pages 238–239).

ARONIA ARBUTIFOLIA 'BRILLIANTISSIMA'
Chokeberry, red chokeberry
ROSACEAE Rose family

"I must confess," wrote Vita Sackville-West, "that the red chokeberry was unfamiliar until someone recently brought me a branch. It flamed bright as a cherry. I think it probably ought to be planted in a clump, say half a dozen, for it makes only a little bushy shrub, five to eight feet high, and a single specimen might not do it justice."

With all of chokeberry's positive traits, it is surprisingly underused as a midsized shrub. Its white flowers in May are perfectly respectable, and its fall color is spectacular. After the leaves drop, the berries are attractive far into winter. Well named, chokeberry holds its fruits until the birds have eaten everything else and are desperate. It is wonderfully free of insect predators and disease.

If chokeberry has a fault, it is its rather stiffly upright habit and legginess below the knees. Rather than bemoan this trait, think of it as more room to plant something else, or plant it in a clump, as the Honorable Vita Sackville-West proposed. Low ornamental grasses such as prairie dropseed would suit it well in a sunny, well-drained place; or tufted hairgrass, in a moist place, would be especially attractive in fall and winter when the shrub's brilliant red leaves and, later, berries contrast with the warm tan of the grass.

Origin: Nova Scotia and Ontario south to Florida and west to Michigan and Texas

Flower: Dense, white clusters with red stamens in May; abundant berries most noticeable in winter

Foliage: Glossy green leaves turn a rainbow of bright shades from deep salmon to brilliant scarlet in fall.

Red chokeberry (Aronia arbutifolia *'Brilliantissima'*)

Arctostaphylos

Name	Origin	Flower	Foliage	Zones	Height	Regions	Landscape Use
Arctostaphylos bakeri 'Louis Edmunds'	Sonoma County, California	Large pink panicles, spring	Gray green, to 1-in oval leaves	8, 7(?) to 10	6 to 8 ft by same	California	Specimen, hedge, background, screen
Arctostaphylos densiflora 'Howard McMinn'	Sonoma County, California	Profuse white, spring	Narrow, 1-in, smooth, bright green, glossy	8 to 10	4 to 8 ft, wider than tall	California	Specimen, informal or clipped hedge
Arctostaphylos densiflora 'James West'	Sonoma County, California	Pinkish, in spring	Narrow, smooth, bright green	8 to 10	3 ft, wider than tall	California	Specimen, rock garden, dry border
Arctostaphylos edmundsii var. *parvifolia*	Central coast, California	Pink, in spring	Glossy, green, small, dense	8 to 10	1 to 2 ft by 6 ft wide	California, Pacific Northwest	Ground cover, rock garden, bonsai
Arctostaphylos edmundsii var. *par-vifolia* 'Bert Johnson'	Monterey County, California	Shell pink, in spring	Pale gray-green, lightly hairy	8 to 10	1 to 2 ft tall, 5 to 6 ft wide	California	Rock garden, ground cover, dry border
Arctostaphylos glauca	Central California	White and pink, in spring	Rounded gray leaves	8 to 10	To 20 ft by 10 ft	California	Specimen
Arctostaphylos pajaroensis	Central coast, California	Pink, in spring	New foliage red, mature blue-green	8 to 10	4 to 5 ft by 7 to 8 ft wide	California	Dry shrub border
Arctostaphylos pajaroensis 'Paradise'	Monterey County, California	Rich pink, in spring	Glaucous gray-green leaves	8 to 10	6 to 10 ft tall by 10 to 15 ft	California	Specimen
Arctostaphylos uva-ursi 'Point Reyes'	Point Reyes, Marin County, California	Shell pink to white, in spring	Oval, medium green, dense leaves	8, 7(?) to 10	6 to 24 in by 6 to 10 ft	California, Pacific Northwest	Ground cover
Arctostaphylos 'Greensphere'	Garden seedling at Rancho Santa Ana Botanic Garden	Shell pink to white, in spring	Oval, medium green, dense leaves	8 to 10	5 ft by 6 to 8 ft wide	California	Specimen, dry border
Arctostaphylos 'John Dourly'	Garden seedling at Rancho Santa Ana Botanic Garden	Pink, in spring	Glaucous, gray-green leaves	8 to 10	3 ft tall by 4 to 6 ft	California	Specimen, ground cover (tall), rock garden, dry border
Arctostaphylos 'Pacific Mist'	Garden seedling at Rancho Santa Ana Botanic Garden	White, but rarely blooms, in spring	Long, narrow, gray, gray-green leaves long white hairs	8 to 10	2 ft tall by 8 ft	California	Ground cover

Hardiness: Zones 4 (possibly 3) to 8

Height: 6 to 8 feet (with competition for light, it can reach 10 feet)

Regions: Northeast, Midwest, Mid-Atlantic, South, Pacific Northwest

Landscape use: Naturalizing, shrub border, erosion control

Culture: Tolerates just about anything poor soils, wet or dry soil, sun or very light shade. It grows in a vase shape, often suckering at its base.

Culture	Propagate	Comment
Full sun to light shade, site in well-drained soil	Cuttings	Upright, upswept growth habit, rich mahogany-purple bark
Full sun to light shade, adaptable, drought-tolerant when established	Cuttings	Dense, twiggy, mounding habit, can be kept at 4 ft wide with prudent pruning; most adaptable, easiest, sturdiest of shrubby manzanitas; beautiful red-brown bark
Full sun to light shade; afternoon shade in hot climates; drought-tolerant when established	Cuttings	Good size, clean attractive plant, never outgrows its space in the garden
Full sun; drought-tolerant when established; good drainage, some water	Seeds, cuttings	Very handsome, creeping and crawling around rocks
Full sun to light shade; sturdy, adaptable, drought- and heat-tolerant when established	Cuttings	A remarkable plant, one of the best low manzanitas, dense mounding growth habit, never needs pruning or pinching
Full sun, drought-tolerant, good drainage	Seeds, cuttings	Dark mahogany trunk, limbs are slick, showy, produces many large berries
Full sun, good drainage, drought-tolerant when established	Seeds, cuttings	Fine foliage year-round
Full sun on the coast, afternoon shade where hot, good drainage, drought-tolerant	Cuttings	One of the few shaggy-barked manzanitas; outstanding foliage, flowers; generally requires a few years to settle in, perform
Full sun, drought-tolerant when established, no overhead water, well-drained soil	Cuttings	Easy and durable
Full sun, drought-tolerant when established, no overhead water, well-drained soil	Cuttings	Unusual dense, congested foliage gives this manzanita the most formal appearance of the genus; slow growth rate; always attractive, especially with age; rich brown bark
Full sun, drought-tolerant when established, no overhead water, well-drained soil	Cuttings	Dense growing, mounding with age; outstanding foliage, flowers; bronzy new growth
Full sun, drought-tolerant when established, no overhead water, well-drained soil	Cuttings	Widely sprawling ground cover, generally takes about two years to fill in; grown for foliage, growth habit; rarely flowers

Species: Purple chokeberry (*Aronia prunifolia*) grows to 12 feet; black chokeberry (*A. melanocarpa*), which has black berries, is much lower (3 to 5 feet) and forms thickets.

Propagation: Division, seed (cool stratify)

Red chokeberry (Aronia arbutifolia *'Brilliantissima'*)

ARTEMISIA FILIFOLIA Threadleaf sage, sand sage
COMPOSITAE Sunflower family

One of many sages that inhabit dry, windswept natural areas of the Southwest, the threadleaf sage is a graceful plant that is making the move from the wild into the garden. Low and pretty, its fragrant, silver-gray leaves are fine, lending the foliage a graceful, frothy quality. In winter, when grasses turn to tan, threadleaf sage's silvery green makes an especially effective contrast. Growing broader than tall at maturity, handsome, drought-tolerant, wind-tolerant, and cold-tolerant, threadleaf sage has a great future as a landscape plant in the Southwest.

Origin: Sandy plains, dunes, and slopes to 8,000 feet elevation, from the Black Hills to Utah and south into New Mexico, West Texas, and Mexico

Flower: Inconspicuous

Foliage: Semievergreen silver, aromatic, with textural interest

Hardiness: Zones 4 to 10

Height: To 4 feet

Region: Southwest

Landscape use: Mass planted as backdrop, tall ground cover and soil stabilizer on exposed sandy sites, mixed border, beds

Culture: Very drought- and heat-tolerant

Species: Fringed sage, *A. frigida* (mat-forming, very hardy, silver-gray)

Propagation: Seed

Sand sage (Artemisia filifolia) *(Charles Mann photo)*

ARTEMISIA TRIDENTATA Big sage
COMPOSITAE Sunflower family

Long lived, big sage has been known to survive for over a century. It is a character plant with a rugged, uneven habit and outstanding foliage color that is valuable as a color foil the year around. During the growing season, it contrasts with the greens of grasses and shrubs like mountain mahogany and sumac, and during winter with dark evergreens and tan grasses. Big sage serves as a rugged specimen that tolerates heat, cold, and drought in a watered or unwatered garden.

Origin: Canada south through the Rockies, Sierra Nevada, and Cascades; predominant in the Great Basin, where it covers hundreds of square miles, often in pure stands in areas with deep, well-drained soils at elevations from 1,500 to 10,000 feet

Flower: Inconspicuous flowers in August/September; seeds ripen in winter

Foliage: The silver, aromatic foliage is evergreen.

Hardiness: Zones 4 (probably 3) to 8

Height: To 6 feet, but typically 3 to 4 feet

Regions: Great Basin, Southwest, Mountain

Landscape use: Has a picturesque irregular form as an accent specimen when growing on rocky soil; mass planted in borders as background; color foil

Culture: Should be grown in full sun; overwatering in summer, particularly in clay soils, can kill plants; occasional pruning results in denser foliage and a neater appearance.

Propagation: Seed in fall or spring

BACCHARIS PILULARIS Baccharis, dwarf coyote bush
COMPOSITAE Sunflower family

Californian Peggy Grier gardens a dry, sunny hillside. She calls *Baccharis* a "stout character" whose primary virtue is its ability to cling attractively to the steep slopes in her garden, tying it to the hills beyond. She praises the strong, dense root system displayed in four- to five-year-old plants. She believes that although evergreen *Baccharis* will go without summer watering in coastal gardens, in a hotter inland garden, it looks much better with occasional summer water. In her garden, it is watered perhaps one time every four to six weeks.

Origin: Chaparral slopes, coastal bluffs, of California

Flower: Inconspicuous in fall, followed by a fairly inconspicuous fruit

Foliage: Very green year-round

Hardiness: Zones 8 to 10

Height: Mounding, 1 to 2 feet high in center and spreading to 6 to 7 feet across

Region: California

Landscape use: Ground cover, bank planting

Culture: Very fast growing. Mrs. Grier suggests planting 7 feet on center, because when it is crowded, it rises up in a woody fashion. Needs periodic pruning either every year or severely every few years, in early March. Occasional water keeps it looking good.

Cultivars: 'Twin Peaks' (male plant has no seeds)

CALLIANDRA ERIOPHYLLA Fairy duster
LEGUMINOSAE Pea family

Well named, ferny fairy duster's pink powderpuff flowers bring a feeling of elfin lightness to the garden. Fairy duster blooms copious-

Big sage (Artemisia tridentata) *(Charles Mann photo)*

Dwarf coyote bush (Baccharis pilularis) *covers the slope in the Grier garden. (Ron Lutsko Design)*

ly in spring, and on and off throughout summer, and often has a second spurt of flowering in the fall. The shrub occurs from southeastern California to western Texas and northern Mexico, typically growing along washes and on dry, gravelly slopes. Fairy duster is reliably hardy to Zone 8, possibly to Zone 7.

Origin: Washes, gravelly slopes from California east to Texas and south into Mexico

Flower: Pink powder-puff flowers bloom heavily in spring, again in fall, and sporadically through summer.

Foliage: Tiny acacia-like leaves have a ferny appearance.

Hardiness: Zones 8 (possibly 7) to 10

Height: 2 feet tall by 3 feet wide

Regions: Southwest, southern California

Landscape use: Dry shrub border, specimen

Culture: Sun, well-drained soil

CALLICARPA AMERICANA American beautyberry
VERBENACEAE Vervain family

Some find American beautyberry coarse when compared with the Asian beautyberry (*C. bodinieri*). I find it a bold and far more exciting plant. Its berries are the same color but twice the size, and the leaves are larger than those of the Asian beautyberry. Far from a dainty plant, it deserves a place in a shrub border or woodland garden, where its bold texture and loose habit dominate. Carolina wrens aren't the only ones who love beautyberry.

I have seen American beautyberry, a very adaptable shrub, growing in Memphis woodlands and sunny Florida gardens. Plants in Florida, whether from different genetic stock or more sun, were far more heavily berried. Sometimes, it looked as though the whole branch was ringed with the bright purple fruits instead of the more usual intermittent berry bracelets.

Origin: Often in pineland clearings or sandhills from Virginia west to Texas, south to the West Indies

Flower: Relatively inconspicuous pink flowers are followed by showy purple berries (loved and taken by Carolina wrens) that ring the stems on new wood.

Foliage: Large, medium green leaves are fuzzy white on the underside and turn yellow in fall.

Hardiness: Zones 7 to 10

Height: To 6 feet

Regions: Mid-Atlantic, Lower Midwest, South

Landscape use: Edge of woodland, especially with pines

Culture: Sun to part shade. Cut back each year to within inches of the ground.

Species: *C. a.* var. *lactea* (white berries that are said to be more attractive to birds)

Propagation: Seed (warm stratify) or cuttings

CALYCANTHUS FLORIDUS Carolina allspice, sweetshrub, strawberry shrub
CALYCANTHACEAE Calycanthus family

An old-fashioned favorite, Carolina allspice has been grown as an ornamental since Colonial days. People tell nostalgic stories about being children (in what must have been a vastly more innocent time) and carrying its aromatic flowers around wrapped in pocket handkerchiefs. Those of us who hail from the era of paper tissues, however, still remember the flowers as magical. Inexplicably dark, they appeared to be carved from wood—the kinds of cunning embellishments found on those German Christmas candelabras that are fixed with pinwheels that whirl above candle heat.

Fairy duster (Calliandra eriophylla) *(Charles Mann photo)*

Ceanothus

Name	Origin	Flower	Foliage	Zones	Height	Regions	Landscape Use
Ceanothus americanus New Jersey tea	Eastern North America	Creamy white in summer	Deeply veined leaves are deciduous	4 to 8	To 3 ft	Eastern North America	Border, cutting
Ceanothus foliosus x 'Centennial'	Selection	Many, bright blue, spring	Small, shiny flattish leaves	8(?) to 10	6 in by 5 ft(?) wide	California	Ground cover
Ceanothus griseus horizontalis 'Yankee Point'	Selection	Blue flowers, spring	Shiny green leaves	8(?) to 10	2 ft high by 8 to 10 ft wide	California	Ground cover
Ceanothus hearstiorum	Coastal bluffs of central California	Cobalt blue, spring	Shiny, dark green, warty leaves	8(?) to 10	6 to 10 in high by 6 ft wide	California	Ground cover
Ceanothus thyrsiflorus 'Snow Flurry'	Selection	White, spring	Shiny green leaves	8(?) to 10	6 to 12 ft high by 10 ft wide	California	Shrub, hedge
Ceanothus 'Concha'	Hybrid	Cobalt blue, spring	Rich green leaves	7b(?) to 10	5 to 8 ft high by 6 ft wide	California	Upright shrub
Ceanothus 'Dark Star'	Hybrid	Ultramarine with maroon buds, spring	Small, dense leaves	7b(?) to 10	6 ft high by 6 ft wide	California	Mounding shrub, dry border
Ceanothus 'Ray Hartman'	Hybrid	Deep blue, spring	Large, glossy leaves	8(?) to 10	8 to 15 ft high by 15 ft wide	California	Large shrub, small tree, specimen

Carolina allspice is a variable plant. Not only does its flower color vary from burgundy to dark copper, but there are marked differences in the fragrances of the twigs, foliage, and flowers of different plants. Because of its fragance and the subtle effect of its flowers, Carolina allspice ought to be grown near a patio.

Origin: Virginia to Florida

Flower: Stiff, almost woody, maroon to brown, can be highly fragrant but variable, flowering in May and June

Foliage: Handsome, broadly oval, glossy leaves on a broad, bushy plant turn a gorgeous golden yellow in fall.

Hardiness: Zones 4 to 9

Height: To 9 feet

Regions: Northeast, Midwest, Mid-Atlantic, South, Northeast

Landscape use: Shrub border, hedge

Culture: Light shade in the South, sun in colder areas; very easy, unfussy, trouble-free

Cultivars: 'Athens', 'Katherine' (yellow flowers)

Species: Spice bush or sweet shrub (*C. occidentalis*), from moist places in northern California, is taller with similar flowers and fragrance.

Propagation: Seed (cool stratify)

Beautyberry (Callicarpa americana)

CEANOTHUS Ceanothus, California lilac
RHAMNACEAE Buckthorn family

After seeing ceanothus at peak bloom in many of its forms—trees, large shrubs, and ground covers, flowering in shades of blue and white at Strybing Arboretum in April, I became fascinated with this plant and asked every California gardener I met

Culture	Propagate	Comment
Sun, light shade, dry to medium soil	Cool stratify seed	Not fussy, hummingbird and butterfly plant, tea substitute
Needs fast drainage, grows fast, sun, longevity unknown	Cuttings	Floriferous, grows rapidly, untested
Full sun, part shade	Cuttings	Wide climate tolerance, fast growing
Full sun, part shade easy, some summer water	Cuttings	Fast growing, may be short lived
Full sun, part shade, good drainage	Cuttings	Fast growing, heavy bloom, white!
Full sun, good drainage	Cuttings	Vigorous growth, "garden tolerant," best in background
Sun to part shade, drought-tolerant	Cuttings	Deerproof, attractive mounding habit
Full sun, good drainage, fast growing	Cuttings	Multi-stemmed, it is ideal to prune into a tree shape

'Snow Flurry' ceanothus (*Sidney Baumgartner Design*)

about it. I quickly learned that all you have to do is mention the word "ceanothus" to hear some deer tales. From what people said, I was sure that Strybing Arboretum hired night watchmen to keep the deer away, but Peggy Grier, of Lafayette, California, set me straight.

"There are many kinds of ceanothus and not all are deer candy," she said. Ceanothus foliage falls into three categories small, hard, dark, leathery leaves as seen in 'Dark Star', hard, toothed, holly-type leaves such as *C. hearstiorum,* and fleshy, succulent ones such as those of 'Snow Flurry' and 'Yankee Point'. Deer go for the fleshy, succulent-leaved plants and tend to leave the others alone.

"Rarely eaten by deer," says Berkeley gardener Jenny Fleming, *Ceanothus papillosus roweanus* is a species from mesas near Santa Barbara that is best in coastal climates. It has produced outstanding hybrids. Of these, one of her favorites is 'Dark Star', of which she says, "Although densely leaved, in March/April the flower clusters of deep, electric blue are so profuse that no leaves are visible. Grown with our native Douglas iris, with golden poppies around, it is a breathtaking sight. Just smashing!"

Next on her list of *Ceanothus papillosus roweanus* hybrids is the upright 'Julia Phelps', which is easy to find in nurseries, adaptable to some summer water, and a good specimen plant. Also choice is the hybrid 'Concha', with similar, but larger, more open flowers. It is a very vigorous plant—best in the background because of its larger size.

There is also great enthusiasm for a brand-new selection called 'Centennial', made by Roger Raiche of U.C. Botanical Garden from the species *Ceanothus foliosus* from Salt Point State Park in Sonoma County. "'Centennial' could be the best and most beautiful *Ceanothus* ground cover," says Mrs. Fleming. "Flowers nearly hide all the leaves in March/April. It makes rapid growth; mine was planted in April—too late, really—and is now

Sweetshrub (Calycanthus floridus)

243

[December] five feet across. And, so far, the deer have not shown any interest."

Besides deer, overzealous gardeners are a ceanothus's worst nightmare. Too much tender, loving care—forcing growth by watering in the dry, warm season or using fertilizers—is lethal. Because it has nitrogen-fixing bacteria in the roots, no fertilizer is best. Ceanothus develops root rot from water-borne molds when it is watered as frequently as lawn. To avoid problems with root crown rot, keep mulch away from the root crown and do not plant any Ceanothus deeper than it was in the container.

Pruning, a nasty job, full of jabs from sharp twigs, should be done in the dry season because ceanothus is prone to apricot canker, which is spread by splashing water onto open wounds. Once-a-summer pruning results in a shrub that is attractive all year.

"Good drainage," adds Jenny Fleming, "is a *must* for California lilac, along with full sun to very light shade. Often, they can survive without summer water, but periodic deep watering, once every four to six weeks—especially in warmer areas—keeps them looking good. Most species will take light frosts.

"Ceanothus are terrific," says Mrs. Grier, "because they are so useful. They come in every size—from ground covers to trees. And they can be pruned up like a tree. They bloom showily, and they are evergreen."

The chart on pages 242–243 also includes the single eastern species, New Jersey tea (*Ceanothus americanus*). Some people consider it a disappointing Plain Jane relation when compared with its stunning blue California cousins. New Jersey tea isn't dull, just conservative. Its flowers, not quite pure white, are moderately showy in a well-bred sort of way and last a long time on a neat, low shrub. New Jersey tea is also a butterfly and hummingbird plant, and more than once I've brought branches in

New Jersey tea (Ceanothus americanus)

for summer bouquets. After the Boston Tea Party, New Jersey tea's dried leaves were one of the substitutes for the real thing.

Adaptable New Jersey tea is a good plant for dry, sun-baked spots, but it will also grow in light shade with more moisture. Dick Bir writes that research is being undertaken to use New Jersey tea as rootstock for some of the exquisite California lilacs, thus creating the possibility of having both cousins in the same garden.

California gardeners Jenny Fleming, Peggy Grier, and Betsy Clebsch had a hard time limiting themselves to the outstanding cultivars and species in the chart.

CEPHALANTHUS OCCIDENTALIS Buttonbush
RUBIACEAE Madder family

Perfect for landscaping at water's edge, a low spot that doesn't drain, or in a place that is sometimes flooded, buttonbush needs very moist soil to standing water to thrive. Buttonbush gets its name from the perfect spheres of creamy white flowers that appear in July and August. Later, these darken to tannish green, remaining showy throughout. Leaves are long and bold.

Origin: North America
Flower: Balls of creamy white flowers darken to reddish brown in fall.
Foliage: Medium green, rough leaves turn yellow in fall.
Hardiness: Zones 5 to 10
Height: To 10 feet
Region: Wet places of North America

'Yankee Point' ceanothus (Sidney Baumgartner Design)

Landscape use: Marsh, pond, streamside
Culture: Choose plants of local stock. Sun; very moist to wet soil. Cut back to keep under control
Propagation: Seed

Buttonbush (Cephalanthus occidentalis)

CERCOCARPUS MONTANUS Mountain mahogany, palo duro
ROSACEAE Rose family

Mountain mahogany is the plant on rocky mountain slopes that dazzles the eye on sunny autumn days. Its seeds, showier than its flowers, capture sunlight, giving this otherwise dark shrub a luminous halo. The common names refer both to its reddish bark color and to its hard wood.

Mountain mahogany is grown for its upright vase shape and silver seed plumes in autumn, features that make it a stunning specimen. Site it in a sunny, well-drained place where it will be backlit by the rising and/or setting sun. Good companions are *Ceanothus* and *Arctostaphylos.* It can be pruned into a tree shape. Birds like it and it is tough drought- and wind-tolerant. Not all plants are completely evergreen.
Origin: Found in the foothills of most western mountain ranges from 5,500 to 8,000 feet on rocky slopes and along arroyos
Flower: Inconspicuous flowers give way to showy silver seed plumes in October.
Foliage: Often evergreen, small, dark green, round, fan-shaped leaves can turn a russet color in fall.
Hardiness: Zones 5 to 9
Height: 10 to 12 feet with a narrower spread
Regions: Mountains, foothills, Northwest, Southwest
Landscape use: Screen, windbreak, specimen; bird habitat; a good plant for defining space in foothills gar-

dens; soil stabilizer on slopes
Culture: Drought-tolerant once established. Plant where seed heads are backlit by rising or setting sun for best effect. Mountain mahogany is slow growing but very long lived; very hard wood requires sharp pruning shears.
Species: Mountain mahogany (*C. ledifolius*), an evergreen shrub, can be pruned into specimen tree. *C. breviflorus* is a broadleaf evergreen shrub or small tree. *C. montanus* becomes bonsai-like with age; hedge or specimen; low-water landscapes. *C. intricatus,* a twiggy, evergreen shrub, with airy, plumy seeds, is completely drought-tolerant.

CHRYSOTHAMNUS NAUSEOSUS Chamisa, rabbitbrush
COMPOSITAE Sunflower family

When it begins to bloom glowing yellow in fall, chamisa reminds me of reliable old forsythia, a familiar garden plant for which there is no replacement—except that chamisa is more restrained in growth and, to my eye, has a mounded form that is more attractive all year.

Combine this trouble-free western native with purple aster for riveting color. It will attract monarch butterflies when it flowers. Plants are variable depending upon available moisture and provenance.
Origin: Western North America, Canada to northern Mexico, east to Texas at elevations from 3,000 to 8,000 feet, usually along arroyos and in drainage basins where soils are gravelly
Flower: Brilliant yellow flowers that cover the new growth in September/October attract monarch butterflies.

Mountain mahogany (Cercocarpus montanus)

Chamisa (Chrysothamnus nauseosus) *(Charles Mann photo)*

Foliage: Silver-blue, narrow leaves are deciduous.
Hardiness: Zones 4 to 10
Height: 3 to 6 feet depending upon available moisture
Region: Southwest, Great Basin, Mountain
Landscape use: Mass planted on large sites; as backdrop for flower beds and borders; medium-height screens and unsheared hedges
Culture: Tolerates a wide range of growing conditions except waterlogged clay; requires full sun or becomes leggy; severe pruning in spring at budbreak can rejuvenate overgrown plants; form is best where it receives 8 to 15 inches of water per year.
Propagation: Seed

CLETHRA ACUMINATA Cinnamon clethra
CLETHRACEAE White alder family

Cinnamon clethra is the little-known cousin of the popular summersweet (*C. alnifolia*), described below. More upright than summersweet, cinnamon clethra's foliage is a rich, dark, textured, matte green. Racemes of white flowers are narrower, often with a curious squiggle as if, during growth, they changed directions more than once. They keep these twisted shapes from the time tight buds appear in late July, and open slowly from bottom to top, to well after leaves have fallen and the individual flowers have turned to round, tan seeds.

The common name refers to cinnamon clethra's peeling tan to brown bark that exposes a reddish trunk. It would be lovely uplighted by night in a dooryard garden in a ground cover of American pachysandra.
Origin: Southern Appalachians
Flower: White flowers in twisted racemes in June, followed by round, tan seeds
Foliage: Dark, matte green, turns yellow-gold in fall
Hardiness: Zones 6 to 8(?)
Height: To 25 feet
Region: Eastern North America where hardy
Landscape use: Shrub border, small tree
Culture: Sun to light shade in moist, well-drained soil
Propagation: Seed

CLETHRA ALNIFOLIA Summersweet, sweet pepperbush
CLETHRACEAE White alder family

Summersweet deserves its status as an old garden favorite. The spicy, intense fragrance of its many pinky white, bottlebrush flowers is one of the joys of sultry August evenings. A big, buxom shrub, summersweet is a good plant for a wet place, although it will grow well enough in ordinary garden soil.

Some years ago, a dwarf form of summersweet was discovered by Fred Galle in the Appalachians. Jim Plyler of

Chamisa (Chrysothamnus nauseosus) *in winter (Judith Phillips Design)*

Cinnamon clethra (Clethra acuminata)

Natural Landscapes Nursery in Pennsylvania popularized 'Hummingbird' and made it available to other nurserymen. If it will grow for you and you can find one, buy one. It is a terrific little shrub.

Origin: Maine to Florida
Flower: Fragrant, white, in racemes, open in July/August
Foliage: Glossy, green with yellow fall color
Hardiness: Zones 3 to 8(?)
Height: To 10 feet
Region: Eastern North America
Landscape use: Hedge, shrub border, massing
Culture: Moist, slightly acid soil; light shade. Will tolerate wet soil. Spreads by stolons. Sometimes gets mites if the soil is too dry.
Cultivars/variety: 'Hummingbird' (dwarf), 'Paniculata' (bigger white flowers), 'Pinkspire' (pink). *C. alnifolia tomentosa* has leaves with white undersides and is probably a better choice for the South.
Propagation: Cuttings of new wood with hormone in spring

CLINOPODIUM GEORGIANUM (SATUREJA)
Georgia savory, Georgia basil
LABIATAE Mint family

Georgia savory is a delightful, aromatic, mint-scented shrub that is perfect for the herb garden because it prefers the same dry-summer, sunny, well-drained spots favored by most herbs, and its 2-foot height and neat leaves make it a congenial neighbor to lavenders, sages, and rosemary. In fall, Georgia savory is covered with purple-pink blooms. An enlightened horticulturist has planted it at the Atlanta Botanic Garden, where it has grown to perfection.

Origin: North Carolina to Florida
Flower: Lavender-pink, in October
Foliage: Finely hirsute, elliptical, on a woody shrub
Hardiness: Zones 7 to 10(?)

'Hummingbird' clethra

Height: To 2 feet
Regions: South, Mid-Atlantic
Landscape use: Herb garden, edging, ground cover
Culture: Sun; dryish, poor, well-drained soil
Species: *C. coccineum* (red); there is also a yellow form.

COCCOLOBA UVIFERA Seagrape
POLYGONACEAE Buckwheat family

"You can't find a better seashore plant," says Palm Beach horticulturist and landscaper Joe Lawson. Tropical seagrape has been used as landscaping in Florida for generations because it is tolerant of salt, drought, and wind. And old-time Floridians wax poetic about seagrape wines and jellies.

Although seagrape can grow to tree size, along the coast it is shorn by the wind and remains at 8 to 10 feet. Its round, leathery leaves turn bronze, orange, and crimson in fall. Picking up after leaf and fruit drop is a small price to pay for this beautiful tropical native.

Origin: South Florida to South America
Flower: Spikes of small, ivory white flowers appearing in the spring through the summer are followed by grape-like clusters of edible fruits in fall.

*Seagrape (*Coccoloba uvifera)

Foliage: Round leaves up to 8 inches across have red veins; new foliage is bronze; with cool weather, light frosts, leaves turn gorgeous oranges and crimsons.

Hardiness: Zone 9b to tropics

Height: To 25 feet

Region: South, coastal Florida

Landscape use: Buffer, barrier, hedge, tree

Culture: Sun; sandy soil

Species: Pigeon plum (*C. diversifolia*) is more upright, can reach 40 feet

COMPTONIA PEREGRINA Sweet fern
MYRICACEAE Bayberry family

Not a fern at all, but a member of the bayberry family, sweet fern is so called because of its aromatic, ferny-looking foliage. Although it has been a common sight in New England and is known to spread vigorously in the wild, for a long time nurserymen had trouble propagating it. Transplants from the wild were difficult to keep alive and seeds simply would not germinate. Peter Tredici wrote of soaking seeds in gibberellic acid (*Horticulture,* March 1980) before finally achieving germination. Today, thanks to perseverance, sweet fern is available—especially in New England—in pots or sods started from root cuttings.

Because it fixes its own nitrogen, sweet fern grows happily in poor, infertile, sandy, acid soil. Its rapid spread by underground stems makes it a good plant for erosion control on banks and along highways. In gardens, I have seen it used as a path edge and understory plant in light shade at a wooded vacation property on Martha's Vineyard, where its sweet fragrance reaches anyone walking up the path and its trouble-free nature

is a boon to the owners, who are often away.

Origin: Nova Scotia to North Carolina and west to Indiana and Michigan

Flower: Small red flowers with long, thin, tousled petals like the spines of a sea anemone are fairly inconspicuous, followed by little brown burrs.

Foliage: Long green leaves with scalloped edges on floppy stems

Hardiness: Probably Zones 2 to 6

Height: 3 to 4 feet

Region: Eastern North America in acid soil

Landscape use: Bank planting, woodland edge, large-scale ground cover

Culture: Sun, part shade; well-drained acid soil—moist or dry; drought-tolerant when established.

CONRADINA VERTICILLATA Cumberland rosemary
LABIATAE Mint family

Cumberland rosemary is a perfect example of a native plant whose appearance in the wild does not reveal its great potential as a garden subject. With competition in nature, Cumberland rosemary

*Sweet fern (*Comptonia peregrina) *as a ground cover*
(*Michael Van Valkenburgh Design*)

Cumberland rosemary (Conradina verticillata)
(Jessie Harris photo)

sometimes appears irregular and unkempt, or it may not appear at all, but remain indistinguishable amidst a tangle of grasses and shrubs. But with room to grow and full sun in the garden, it becomes a handsome, low-growing, evergreen shrub with fragrant foliage that looks like a cross between prostrate rosemary and a dwarf conifer. Delicate flowers—like tiny, pink orchids upon close inspection—are borne in profusion in June.

Some members of the genus *Conradina* have been listed as federally endangered plants. Nurseries need a license to sell *C. verticillata*. Take care in buying only from reputable sources. Once obtained, *Conradina* is generally not difficult to propagate.

Origin: *Conradina verticillata* has a tiny native range sandy, stony riverbanks in the Cumberland Mountains of east Tennessee and Kentucky.

Flower: ½-inch lavender-pink with red spots

Foliage: Bunches of needles (to 1 inch) on shaggy, red-brown stems

Hardiness: Zones 5 to 6

Height: To 15 inches

Region: Eastern North America

Landscape use: Rock garden, herb garden, ground cover

Culture: Sun, good drainage; tolerates sandy soil, iffy in clay

Species: *C. canescens,* from coastal pinelands of Florida and Alabama, has gray foliage, is larger and more upright, and is one of the shrubs recommended for the South by nurseryman Bob McCartney.

Propagation: Easy from cuttings

CORNUS Dogwood
CORNACEAE Dogwood family

All the world loves flowering dogwood trees—the eastern *Cornus florida* and the western *Cornus Nuttallii*—though few know their shrubby relatives, a tribe of useful and handsome landscape subjects. Those who do know them are enthusiasts.

I know of a man who lives in Washington, D.C., who is so keen to have bunchberry (*C. canadensis*), a plant that dislikes heat and does well in Alaska, parts of New England, and other cool-summer climates, that he ices it mornings and evenings all summer long! This is not as insane as it seems. Beautiful bunchberry bears large, white dogwood flowers on a 4- to 8-inch plant. Without the ice treatment, it won't grow for everyone, but it is cherished as an exquisite, spreading ground cover plant wherever it can grow.

Pagoda dogwood (*C. alternifolia*) gets its botanical name from its alternate leaves and its common name from its habit, branches parallel to the ground and spaced to give it a layered look. In May, white flowers are borne in up-facing clusters, the effect not unlike that of some viburnums.

Silky dogwood (*C. amomum*) gets its name from silky hairs at the tips of branches; it becomes a dense, maroon-twigged shrub, wider than tall, with white flowers in June, followed by blue berries beloved by birds.

Gray dogwood (Cornus racemosa) in fruit

Shrubs

249

Cornus

Name	Origin	Flower	Foliage	Zones	Height	Regions	Landscape Use
Cornus alternifolia Pagoda dogwood	Nova Scotia to Minnesota, south to Georgia, Alabama, Missouri	White clusters, May, purple-black fruits	Medium green, turns maroon in fall	3	To 25 ft, broader than tall	Eastern North America	Shrub border, screening, specimen
Cornus amomum Silky dogwood	Newfoundland to Florida, Texas	Cream flowers, June, blue fruits	Medium green, turns mahogany; dark, hairy, red twigs	5	To 10 ft by 10 ft wide	North America	Shrub border, bird plant, massing
Cornus canadensis Bunchberry	Cool woodland, Labrador to Alaska, south to California, New Mexico	White flowers, June, red fruits	Lustrous green, turns wine	2	8 to 10 in	North America	Woodland garden, ground cover
Cornus racemosa Gray dogwood	Field edges from Georgia, Nebraska, north to Maine, Ontario	White flowers, May, white fruits	Green with gray cast, turns maroon	4	To 15 ft	North America	Shrub border, specimen
Cornus sericea Red-osier sogwood	North America	White flowers, May, white fruits	Medium green, turns mahogany, bright red stems	3	6 to 8 ft	North America	Shrub border, massing, tall ground cover

Yellow twigs of Cornus 'Silver and Gold' *with* Ilex 'Winter Red' *at Brookside Gardens, Wheaton, Maryland*

Gray dogwood (*C. racemosa*), another good bird plant, forms large suckering thickets. Its white, early-summer flowers are followed by white berries on attractive red stems.

Red-osier dogwood (*C. sericea,* formerly *C. stolonifera*) is grown as much for its red (sometimes yellow) winter twigs as for its flowers, summer foliage, and white fruits. Stems root where they touch the ground. A yellow-twigged cultivar with variegated leaves, *Cornus* 'Silver and Gold', took a Gold Medal Award from the Pennsylvania Horticultural Society in 1990. In winter, the yellow twigs of this shrub complement the distinct green twig color of such shrubs as hearts-a-bustin' or the orangy-red berries of possum haw. The red-twigged shrubs are splendid in combination with winterberry.

Depulp *Cornus* seeds before planting. Pagoda dogwood requires warm and cold stratification. Other species require cold stratification. (See *Cornus* chart, above.)

COTINUS OBOVATUS American smoke tree
ANACARDIACEAE Cashew family

Possibly because it is scarce in the wild after being used extensively during the Civil War as a dye plant, American smoke tree is little known. And that's a shame! Its scarlet-orange fall color alone is reason to grow it. It is a plant that is found in the wild on dryish, neutral to alkaline soil, says Woodlander's Bob McCartney, "but it doesn't require it in the garden." In

Culture	Propagate	Comment
Moist, cool, acid soil; good drainage; sun, part shade	Seeds, cuttings	Cool-climate plant, attractive habit, needs plenty of room, resistant to dogwood anthracnose
Part shade, sun with moisture; tolerates wet, dry soil	Seeds, easy from cuttings	Tolerates wet soil, prevents erosion on banks, dark maroon twigs add subtle winter color
Cool, moist, rich, acid soil in a cool-summer climate	Seeds, division	Needs a cool climate; cool, moist, rich, acid soil; a prize where it will grow
Sun to shade, average to moist soil; tough	Seeds, cuttings	Tough shrub for cold climates, good bird food and cover, attractive red panicles
Sun, moist soil, but very adaptable; cut out oldest stems	Cuttings	Great stem colors. Cultivars: 'Kelseyi' (dwarf, 18 in),'Silver and Gold' (green and white foliage, yellow twigs), stoloniferous.

Cliff rose (**Cowania**) *(Charles Mann photo)*

fall, American smoke tree's brilliant color would be splendid with the tawny orange of a field of prairie dropseed or little bluestem.

Larry Lowman, whose Ridgecrest Nursery in Arkansas carries American smoke tree, advises that it can be planted in full sun, and to keep it well drained, plant it high. In addition, he recommends "dolomitic limestone one time each year."

Origin: Found in limestone soil in Alabama, in the Ozarks, and in Texas

Flower: Purple-pink panicles in late spring

Foliage: Large dark to blue-green leaves are ovals, rounded at the tips, which turn bright colors in fall.

Hardiness: Zones 4 to 9

Height: To 25 feet

Region: Lower Midwest

Landscape use: Screen, shrub border, specimen

Culture: Good drainage, neutral soil, sun; seedlings are quite variable

COWANIA NEO-MEXICANA Cliff rose
ROSACEAE Rose family

"No place on earth can compare to the canyonlands of southern Utah for surrealistic landscape color and drama," says Gwen Kelaidis, author and owner of Rocky Mountain Rare Plants nursery. "The cliff rose, above all other plants, is the soul of the jubilant landscape." Cliff rose is a plant that is multiply blessed. This large shrub or small tree will eventually become picturesque and contorted. Its ashen, peeling bark and almost succulent evergreen leaves exude a rich, resiny aroma—the very fragrance of the desert. And it also has flowers. An inch across, they are unearthly roselike blossoms—white in some lights, soft moonlight yellow in others. Their scent is heavenly.

With all of these attributes, it's no wonder that Albuquerque designer/nurserywoman/author Judith Phillips uses cliff rose as a screen, as an accent, as a hedge, and even, pruned up, as a small tree.

Origin: Northern Arizona and Utah, western Colorado and western New Mexico

Flower: Fragrant, white, single rose flower with many yellow stamens in a burst of bloom in late spring, but sporadically from early spring to fall; ancient specimens may be half flower and half feathery fruit

Foliage: Dark green, thick, evergreen cut leaves

Hardiness: Zones 4 (but must not ever be too wet) to 8(?)

Height: To 10 feet

Region: Semiarid to arid and wherever fairly dry culture can be provided

Landscape use: Shear for a hedge, or a magnificent specimen shrub

Culture: Must be planted as a young specimen, but on dry, well-drained soil, it will grow quickly. Somewhat rangy; tip-prune for more density.

Species: Only *C. neo-mexicana* is cultivated, although several related species exist in Texas and Mexico.

Propagation: Seed

CYRILLA RACEMIFLORA Titi, leatherwood
CYRILLACEAE Cyrilla family

Pretty in summer, when its white flowers bloom in long, dangling sprays, titi is at its finest in places warm enough for it to grow lustily and cold enough (for example, Memphis) in late fall for its glossy, leathery leaves to take on mahogany, scarlet, and orange hues. This is a gradual affair; a few leaves begin to turn color, others stay dark green, and all contrast with the dark tan sprays of seeds still hanging on the plant.

Generally late to drop its leaves, titi is in some places partly to fully evergreen. I saw a fine specimen growing in a Memphis garden on the side of a house in an informal hedge with inkberries and holly. It was October, and the titi, hung with tan seeds, had begun to color in striking contrast to its green neighbors. The owner of that garden reported that the titi was nearly evergreen because of its protected site. It is a member of the heath family.

Origin: Coastal plain, Virginia to Texas, and into the West Indies and South America

Flower: 6-inch sprays of white flowers in June/July

Foliage: Dark green, narrow, glossy leaves are evergreen in very warm climates, take on orange to maroon fall color with cold.

Hardiness: Zones 5 to 9

Height: To 30 feet

Regions: Mid-Atlantic, South, Lower Midwest

Landscape use: Specimen, shrub, hedge, tree

Culture: Sun to part shade, moist soil; tolerates seasonal standing water

Propagation: Seed

DALEA GREGGII Trailing indigo bush
LEGUMINOSAE Pea family

Trailing indigo bush not only makes a carpet of delicate gray foliage but also holds the soil, as its stems root wherever they contact the ground. Purple ball-shaped flowers bloom in spring and summer. These are wonderful in contrast with desert marigold in either an informal ground cover or in a dryland border. Trailing indigo bush is reliably hardy to Zone 9 and to

Titi (Cyrilla racemiflora)

warmer parts of Zone 8. It occurs in western Texas and south through much of Mexico on rocky limestone hillsides. Plants are readily available.

Origin: Rocky limestone hillsides from West Texas through much of Mexico

Flower: Purple ball-shaped flowers in spring and summer

Foliage: Gray, hairy, on trailing stems

Hardiness: Zones 8b to 9

Height: 1 foot by 3 feet wide

Region: Desert Southwest

Landscape use: Ground cover

Species: Many dalea species are native to the Southwest, including bush dalea, *D. pulchra,* a rounded, evergreen accent plant to 4 feet, with purple flower clusters in March and April, from gravelly slopes of southeastern Arizona and northwestern Mexico. Warmer parts of Zone 8 to 10.

Culture: Sun; dry, well-drained soil

DASYLIRION WHEELERI Sotol, desert spoon
AGAVACEAE Agave family

Sotol can grow into a form so perfect that it has an almost manufactured look; each leaf appears to have been formed from the same mold and to be

Low-growing trailing indigo bush (Dalea greggii), right front, with agave and littleleaf sumac

attached to the center at precisely the same angle as every other leaf. The flower is another story. Like something from a Dr. Seuss landscape, a spike of creamy white flowers rises some 10 feet above the spiky bush—ever so slightly off center. It is dramatic all season long.

Origin: West Texas to Arizona and Mexico

Flower: Creamy white flowers in a spike on a stem, 8 to 12 feet, April–June. Male and female plants have slightly different flower spikes.

Foliage: Perfect ball of gray-green leaves that have thorns along the margins

Hardiness: Zones 8(?) to 10

Height: To 5 feet by 5 feet

Region: Desert Southwest

Landscape use: Accent

Culture: Full sun. In shady places, sotol may get mildew. No pruning! New leaves will eventually cover dead ones.

Species: Green desert spoon, *D. leiophylla,* is similar with green leaves.

Propagation: Seed

DENDROMECON HARFORDII Island bush poppy
PAPAVERACEAE Poppy family

Island bush poppy's big, yellow, buttercup flowers are beautiful in combination with the rich green foliage and blue flowers of *Ceanothus*—especially on a well-drained slope, where both will grow to perfection. Island bush poppy flowers year-round, although bloom is most profuse in April and May, when the plants are literally covered with flowers.

The plant has a dense hemispheric growth habit. It can be very difficult to transplant and establish because of its fragile root system, so buy containerized plants or plant seeds.

Origin: Channel Islands of southern California

Flower: Bright yellow, four-petaled, 2- to 3-inch poppies

Foliage: Evergreen, ovate, glaucous leaves are 2 to 4 inches long and 1 to 2 inches wide.

Hardiness: Zones 8 to 10

Height: 4 to 8 inches and equally wide

Region: Pacific states; it grows best and easiest in coastal climates

Landscape use: Specimen, mixed dry border

Culture: Full sun near the coast, light afternoon shade when grown in hot areas. Best in well-drained soil.

Species: Bush poppy (*D. rigida*) has similar flowers, but plants have a much shorter season of bloom and flowers are not as profuse. Foliage is blue-gray and willowlike. This plant has a much stiffer, upswept appearance.

ENCELIA FARINOSA Brittlebush, incienso
COMPOSITAE Sunflower family

The Spanish common name "incienso" comes from the practice, in Mexico, of burning this plant's resin as incense. Neat and compact, brittlebush's yellow, daisylike flowers wave gracefully above a flat-topped bush that fits nicely into the front of a dryland border with penstemons and lupines. After its flowers are spent, brittlebush's silvery foliage makes a good backdrop for other low-growing flowers such as Blackfoot daisy or desert four-o'clock.

Sotol (Dasylirion wheeleri)

Island bush poppy (Dendromecon harfordii)

Brittlebush (Encelia farinosa) *(Charles Mann photo)*

Brittlebushes welcome spring in warm desert areas from southern Nevada and southwestern Utah to northern Mexico. Plants are completely hardy in Zone 10; they may suffer mild damage in Zone 9.

Origin: Desert areas of southern California, northern Mexico, Arizona north into Nevada and Utah

Flower: Yellow daisy flower held above flat-topped foliage on leafless stems

Foliage: Broad oval leaves are very hairy, gray-green.

Hardiness: Zones 9 to 10

Height: 3 feet high by 4 feet wide

Region: Desert Southwest

Landscape use: Flower border, ground cover

Culture: Sun; dry, well-drained soil

EUGENIA FOETIDA Spanish stopper
MYRTACEAE Bayberry family

Palm beach designer and Florida native plant enthusiast Joe Lawson (a native Floridian himself) told me that stoppers got their name because people used the plants (in the olden days) for their antidiarrheal properties. It sounds plausible enough. Today, stoppers are grown because they are handsome, dark green, evergreen shrubs that bear small clusters of white flowers, followed by black fruits that attract birds and other wildlife. They are terrific in small gardens and perfectly adapted to Florida, the Gulf Coast, and the Caribbean Basin.

An excellent narrow hedge for small gardens, Spanish stopper also looks good pruned as a small tree, showing off its scaly bark. It is perfect for seaside gardens because it withstands poor soils, drought, and salt spray.

And Joe Lawson likes its "musky hammock smell."

Origin: South Florida, Florida Keys

Flower: Small, white, along branches in late summer, followed by black fruits

Foliage: Dark green evergreen leaves

Hardiness: Zones 9b to 10

Height: To 20 feet

Region: South Florida

Landscape use: Hedges, specimen, extra layer between upper canopy and low shrubs, good wildlife plant

Culture: Sun to dappled sunlight, good drainage, rich sandy loam, reasonably moist soil

Propagation: Seeds, cuttings

EUONYMUS AMERICANA Hearts-a-bustin', strawberry bush
CELASTRACEAE Staff-tree family

It is no wonder that hearts-a-bustin', a shrub gifted with an uncommonly winning common name, was one of the first New World plants introduced in England (1683). The funny, bumpy fruits are unforgettable and unique outside the tropics. "Hearts-a-bustin'" says it all raspberry red, plump berry "hearts" burst open to reveal what's inside—red-orange berries. Even more colorful than the fruit is the fall show this *Euonymus* puts on leaves begin to fade from dark green to a more and more pale yellow-green that contrasts with the raspberry-orange seeds and the stems, which stay a deep rhododen-

Hearts-a-bustin' (Euonymus americana)

dron green. This show is made all the more wonderful if it occurs in front of something very dark, say a rhododendron or a hedge of hemlock.

Origin: New York to Florida and Texas

Flower: Inconspicuous, creamy yellow, in May

Foliage: Medium green oval leaves on green branches fade to chartreuse and yellow in fall. Green stems in winter have the appearance of a dark, very upright broom.

Hardiness: Zones 6 to 9

Height: To 6 feet

Regions: Northeast, Mid-Atlantic, South, Lower Midwest, Northwest

Landscape use: Shrub border, woodland garden

Culture: Part shade; moist, humusy soil

Species: Western spindlebush, or wahoo, or burning bush (*E. occidentalis*), from Oregon, Washington, and northern California, has good yellow-red fall colors and red-purple berries.

Propagation: Cuttings of firm, new growth; seeds, planted in fall for spring germination

FALLUGIA PARADOXA Apache plume
ROSACEAE Rose family

When Apache plume's seed heads float like pink clouds over this broad-spreading shrub, it reminds me of a southwestern version of the exotic smoke tree. After the summer bloom, when a succession of white flowers is followed by feathery pink seeds, Apache plume goes on being showy. In fall, the oldest leaves turn red, and in winter, it is an evergreen all-season hedge or screen with silvery stems of the new growth contrasting with dark green foliage.

Plant Apache plume in a river of penstemon or chuparosa for early color.

Origin: California to Texas, Colorado south into Mexico,

at elevations from 3,500 to 8,000 feet, mostly along arroyos, but also found on slopes and in drainage basins

Flower: Single white flowers are followed by feathery pink seed heads from April (southern locations) through October on new growth.

Foliage: Dark evergreen foliage contrasts with the silver stems of new growth; old leaves color red in fall.

Hardiness: At least Zones 6a to 10

Height: 3 feet high by 5 feet wide

Regions: Southwest, southern California

Landscape use: Background, hedge, low screen, border shrub, accent plant, or mass planted as cover for wildlife and erosion control

Culture: Very adaptable to different sites and soils, especially hot, sunny locations; very drought-tolerant once established. Prune to maintain size and produce flowers and fruit.

FENDLERA RUPICOLA Cliff fendlerbush
SAXIFRAGACEAE Saxifrage family

Not easy to find, cliff fendlerbush is a heat-tolerant, erect shrub for southwestern gardens. Its pretty pink buds open to showy, big, sweet-smelling, white flowers in spring, not unlike those of mock orange. Both its common and botanical names describe its origin this "lover of rocks" (*rupicola*) hails from the dry, rocky slopes and canyons of the Southwest.

Pretty as well as drought-tolerant and hardy, cliff fendlerbush has small, glossy green leaves that blush red before dropping in fall. Combine it with taller, evergreen mountain mahogany in a dryland shrub border.

Apache plume (Fallugia paradoxa) *(Charles Mann photo)*

Origin: Steep rocky slopes from 3,000 to 7,000 feet in elevation in Colorado, Utah, New Mexico, and Arizona

Flower: Pink buds open to fragrant white flowers in April/May; small woody seed capsules in September–November.

Foliage: Deciduous, narrow, glossy green gives way to a tinge of red fall color.

Hardiness: Zones 5 to 9

Height: To 6 feet tall by 4 feet wide, with an upright vase shape

Regions: Southwest, Mountain

Landscape use: As a midheight unsheared hedge or screen; mass planted as backdrop; or singly for early interest in borders in sun or part shade

Culture: Deer browse on cliff fendlerbush. Full sun, good drainage; heat-tolerant.

Propagation: Seed: sow in fall or cold stratify.

Cliff fendlerbush (Fendlera rupicola) *(Charles Mann photo)*

FORESTIERA SEGREGATA Florida privet, wild olive

OLEACEAE Olive family

Along with lilacs and fringe trees, Florida privet is a member of the olive family. Fast growing with dense, twiggy branches and evergreen foliage that takes well to shearing, Florida privet is a good plant with which to begin a brand-new garden. Designer Joe Lawson considers it a far better choice than *Ligustrum* for Florida's alkaline soils, salt, and drought. It is an excellent plant for coastal gardens and can function as a hedge or a shrub or a small tree. It is hardy to central Florida and farther north on the coast.

Origin: South Florida

Flower: Very small, greenish yellow/white along branches in fall, followed by a black drupe

Foliage: 1 to 3 inches long, elliptical; evergreen to "facilitatively deciduous," meaning that leaves drop in response to moisture/dryness rather than cold (in dry winters, plants lose their leaves, a survival mechanism). They also drop old leaves as new ones appear.

Hardiness: Zones 9b to 10

Height: To 20 feet, but often grown as a hedge

Regions: South, central Florida

Landscape use: Very versatile; hedge, small tree, shrub

Culture: Low maintenance. Tolerant of drought, salt spray, low soil fertility, alkaline soils; sun or bright shade

Species: Swamp privet (*F. acuminata*) is hardier.

Propagation: Seeds, cuttings

FOTHERGILLA GARDENII Dwarf fothergilla

HAMAMELIDACEAE Witch hazel family

Blooming before the leaves emerge in early spring, dwarf fothergilla's flowers are creamy, short bottle-brushes with a sweet honey scent. In my garden, dwarf fothergillas share a border, backed by an ivy-covered wall, with variegated miscanthus that doesn't even put out new growth until well after fothergilla blooms. They look beautiful all by themselves against the dark green of the ivy. Of

Wild olive (Forestiera segregata) *trimmed into foundation plants*
(Charles Mann photo)

course, their bloom is part of the larger spring show going on in the rest of the garden, which includes serviceberries, wood phlox, trilliums, phacelia, and spring bulbs.

In summer, dark green, leathery, rather round leaves with fan-shaped veining cover this small, rather upright shrub with asymmetrically spreading branches. In full sun, its fall color is intense orange to scarlet. In shade, fothergilla turns a pretty pale pumpkin color.

Origin: Mountains of Tennessee, Georgia, and Alabama.
Flower: Creamy white, fragrant, short bottlebrush in early spring
Foliage: Rounded fan-shaped, dark, leathery green; intensity of fall color depends on the amount of sun
Hardiness: Zones 5 to 8
Height: To 3 feet
Regions: Eastern North America, Pacific Northwest
Landscape use: Good with azaleas and rhododendrons; small shrub, woodland garden
Culture: Needs moist acid soil, tolerates wet spots; sun to part shade.
Species/cultivars: *F. major* has blooms and leaves slightly larger than those of *F. gardenii,* 6 to 12 feet in height, red-orange in fall, Zone 4. *F. monticola* grows broader with larger flowers but is less hardy, Zone 6. *F. g.* 'Blue Mist', from the Morris Arboretum, has a powdery blue leaf and subtle to quite stunning blushed gold colors in fall, even in dense shade. It received a Gold Medal Plant Award from the Pennsylvania Horticultural Society in 1990.
Propagation: Seeds (warm and cool stratify), cuttings

Dwarf fothergilla (Fothergilla gardenii) *with foamflower*

FOUQUIERIA SPLENDENS Ocotillo
FOUQUIERIACEAE Candlewood family

Ocotillo is a ruggedly beautiful symbol of survival in the desert. In times of water stress, its thorny, branchless canes drop their leaves and go dormant. Gray and twisted, in the dormant state their looks belie their amazing powers of regeneration. Just a few days after rain, tiny, round, bright green leaves emerge up and down canes that are topped by scarlet flower spikes. And, out of nowhere, hummingbirds appear.

Because wood is scarce in the desert, ocotillo is cut to make fences. It is not unusual to see ocotillo fences sprout leaves or even flowers after a rain! The plant grows in all of the southwestern deserts, typically on desert flats, rocky slopes, and mesas. Ocotillo is readily available in bare-root form.

Like a piece of barometric sculpture that also attracts bird life, ocotillo is wonderful outside a window or rising out of a low ground cover such as penstemon or abronia next to a patio. A see-through plant, its transparent quality enhances perspective in a deep border or frames a view in a larger garden.

Origin: Southwestern deserts
Flower: Showy, coral red clusters of tubular flowers in spring
Foliage: Small, bright green, bluntly oval leaves appear after rain on one to several dozen thorny canes (mostly unbranched slender branches arising from the crown or base of the plant).
Hardiness: Zones 8 to 10
Height: To 15 feet high by 10 feet wide
Region: Desert Southwest
Landscape use: Wonderful accent
Culture: Sun; dry, well-drained soil

FREMONTODENDRON CALIFORNICUM Flannel bush, fremontia
STERCULACEAE Stercula family

"Any gardener seeing fremontia in its glorious yellow bloom, whether in the hills of southern California or in an English garden espaliered on a wall, would aspire to grow this unusual large shrub," says Eliza Earle of the Theodore Payne Foundation, where a magnificent pair of cultivars, 'Pacific Sunset' and 'San Gabriel', stand 15 feet tall and 30 feet across and bloom from March to June. Not until she tried growing fremontia in her own garden did Mrs. Earle discover this plant's drawbacks and difficulties. In

Ocotillo (Fouquieria splendens)

addition to being somewhat temperamental to propagate and establish (it succumbs quickly to root rot if the soil is too moist in warm weather), fremontia has irritating hairs all over (hence the common name "flannel bush"). To enjoy this plant, one must treat it with proper respect and give it a generous space and a dry out-of-the-way spot in the garden. As a background plant in a semiwild and certainly unirrigated part of the garden, fremontia's good points will shine and its ragged ends will be hidden. Its botanical name honors John Charles Frémont, who found it growing near the source of the Sacramento River in the Sierra Nevada.

Origin: California

Flower: Yellow, 5-petaled; large and showy.

Foliage: Leaves are lobed, dull green, and hairy.

Hardiness: Zones 8 to 10(?)

Height: 10 to 20 feet

Region: California

Landscape use: Dry gardens

Culture: Establish in cool weather; avoid water on the trunk and in hot weather; full sun

Species/cultivars: *F. mexicanum* is somewhat smaller, more southerly in range. Hybrids with *F. mexicanum* include 'California Glory' and 'Ken Taylor' (low, mounding habit).

Propagation: Seed and cuttings

GARRYA ELLIPTICA Silk-tassel bush
GARRYACEAE Silk-tassel family

When her silk-tassel bush begins to bloom in January, neighbors have come up to Peggy Grier's door to ask, "What *is* that plant?" Creamy, green-purple catkins—up to a foot in length—hang on the deep evergreen branches like tinsel on a Christmas tree. Ms. Grier calls silk-tassel "an absolutely sensational showstopper in midwinter, when the catkins do their thing." At other times of the year, she finds its evergreen foliage very satisfactory and points out further that it doesn't have to be a shrub. It can be trimmed up like a standard or an evergreen tree that will bloom as boldly as wisteria.

In a "hot garden" such as hers, as opposed to a coastal garden, she recommends planting silk-tassel bush in a place with morning sun, rather than a full western exposure, and giving periodic water—perhaps every two weeks.

Origin: Chaparral and mixed evergreen forests of outer coast ranges, Ventura County, California, to Oregon

Flower: Dioecious male catkins, tan-tinted greenish purple up to a foot long in January, February; female catkins are much shorter, stiffer.

Fremontia (Fremontodendron californicum)

Foliage: Dark evergreen, reminiscent of a live oak leaf, glossy above, white and tomentose below
Hardiness: Zones 7 to 10
Height: 8 to 20 feet
Region: Pacific states
Landscape use: Specimen with winter interest, trimmed up as a tree, hedge, screen
Culture: Full sun in northern and coastal gardens; tolerates dry, infertile soil, periodic water; takes well to pruning; avoid overhead watering in cooler, humid areas.
Cultivars/species: 'James Roof' (very long catkins), 'Evie'. *G. fremontii* is similar and tolerates more heat and drought; *G. buxifolia,* from California and Oregon, is smaller.

GAULTHERIA SHALLON Salal
ERICACEAE Heath family

This bold evergreen was once disdained because it was so common in the fairly moist to dryish conifer forests from northern California to southern British Columbia, where it spread by layering and underground stems into dense thickets. Dr. Arthur R. Kruckeberg of the University of Washington reports that it was once valued only for its lustrous, evergreen leaves, which provided the clean, green filler in florist's bouquets. Today, salal is coming into its own as a carefree evergreen garden plant. Its easy disposition makes it a natural for public plantings, and its ability to colonize makes it invaluable as ground cover under trees in a woodland garden or on a bank. Salal also works well as a companion shrub with taller rhododendrons or in the shrub border. Its copious white, goblet-shaped flowers are followed by edible fruits in late summer.
Origin: Conifer forests from southern Alaska and British Columbia to southern California
Flower: Pink to white urn-shaped flowers dangle upside down in late spring and are followed by fleshy purplish fruits that are sometimes used in jam.
Foliage: Evergreen, broad, oval leaves are lustrous.
Hardiness: Zones 6 to 10
Height: To 6 feet
Regions: Pacific Northwest, California
Landscape use: Mass plantings, large ground cover
Culture: Moist, well-drained soil; spreads aggressively by underground stolons and tips root; sun, part shade
Hybrids: A cross of a *Gaultheria* with Chilean *Pernettya mucronata* resulted in x *Gaulnettya* 'Wisley Pearl', with bright green, evergreen leaves and rose-colored stems.
Propagation: Cuttings

Silk-tassel bush (Garrya)

HESPERALOE PARVIFLORA Red hesperaloe
AGAVACEAE Agave family

I first set eyes upon red hesperaloe in a Phoenix garden at a time when, unschooled in the flora of the desert and dry places, all aloes were lumped together in my mind with the one I grow in a container at home. It was a big surprise to see large, loose clusters of deep pink flowers rise from red hesperaloe's thick, grasslike leaves and to learn that they adorned the garden from spring through fall. But it wasn't until hummingbirds visited the flowers that I became in awe of this charming plant. It looks splendid rising out of a ground cover of verbena. Red hesperaloe hails from central and western Texas and northern Mexico, where rocky slopes, prairies, and mesquite groves are typical habitat. It is hardy to the warmer portions of Zone 8. Plants are readily available.
Origin: Rocky slopes, prairies, mesquite groves of central and western Texas into northern Mexico
Flower: Deep pink flowers in clusters bloom from spring through fall.
Foliage: Grassy, thick leaves
Hardiness: Zones 8 to 10
Height: 18 inches high by 36 inches wide
Region: Southwest
Landscape use: Accent, dry border
Culture: Sun; dry, well-drained soil

Shrubs

Salal (Gaultheria shallon) (Jessie Harris photo)

HETEROMELES ARBUTIFOLIA Toyon, Christmas berry

ROSACEAE Rose family

Hollywood gardener and transplanted easterner Eliza Earle says that the toyon tree was her first love among the California native plants, as it provided Christmas cheer when she first moved to the state and missed the snowy scenes of home. Since then, she has learned that toyon is a plant for all seasons and all gardens. It can function as a small tree or large shrub in any setting, wild or urban. With its evergreen leaves, white flowers, and nice form, it takes to pruning well. Though propagated easily in the nursery, Eliza Earle welcomes the volunteers that self-sow in her steep Hollywood garden and also the flocks of robins that the berries lure in late winter and early spring.

Origin: California

Flower: White, in terminal clusters

Foliage: Evergreen, elliptical, and toothed

Hardiness: Zones 8b (possibly 8a) to 3,500 feet, to 10

Height: Up to 24 feet, but usually 10 to 15 feet

Region: Coast, valleys, and foothills of central and southern California

Landscape use: Specimen shrub, tree, hedge, or erosion control

Culture: Drought-tolerant, but takes extra water

Cultivars: 'Macrocarpa' has larger berries.

Propagation: Fresh seed

HOLODISCUS DISCOLOR Ocean spray

ROSACEAE Rose family

Aptly named, ocean spray blooms in foamy showers of creamy white flowers—each a tiny floret, but massed in large, pendant clusters. In the wild, it grows with serviceberry and mock orange on open sunny slopes in yellow pine country. In the garden, it is perfect at the edge of woodland, along a road or a driveway, where its masses of froth cover the shrub in spring. Severe pruning and deadheading the spent bouquets will keep it handsome in the garden.

Origin: British Columbia to Montana south to southern California, often in the company of madrone

Flower: Wonderful showy clusters like ocean spray, followed by dry fruit clusters

Foliage: Deeply lobed, toothed leaves turn light orange in fall.

Hardiness: Zones 5 to 10

Height: To 12 feet

Regions: Northwest, California, Mountain where hardy

Landscape use: Open woodland garden, slopes

Culture: Sun, medium to dry soil, good drainage

Species: Smaller (to 3 feet) desert ocean spray (*H. dumosus*) grows in rocky, gravelly soils of the high desert country from Wyoming and Utah to Arizona and New Mexico.

Propagation: Seed (sow in fall or cold stratify for four months)

Hesperaloe

*Toyon (*Heteromeles arbutifolia*) (Betsy Clebsch photo)*

HYDRANGEA ARBORESCENS Wild hydrangea, hills-of-snow hydrangea

SAXIFRAGACEAE Saxifrage family

Wild hydrangea can be just that: a little on the wild side as it colonizes woodsy gardens. But its good points make it ideal for the edge of woodland. There, its pretty white lace cap flowers light up part shade and its happy-go-lucky disposition springs up again after being cut to the quick—a real boon in northern gardens, where shrubs get frost damaged.

The cultivars of this plant are superior to the species. 'Annabelle' has a larger head of flowers (rather than the lace cap ring of them) and its posture is more erect, and 'Grandiflora' boasts very large flowers. Both are freely available from nurseries and have been for many years.

Origin: New York to Tennessee, Arkansas, to Florida

Flower: Creamy white in flat corymbs in June/July

Foliage: Large, toothed, rather coarse leaves on suckering, tan stems

Hardiness: Zones 3 to 9

Height: To 5 feet

Regions: Midwest, Northeast, Mid-Atlantic, South, Northwest

Landscape use: Shrub border; 'Annabelle' produces wonderful big flower heads for drying

Culture: Moist, humusy soil. Prune hard; flowers appear on new wood.

Cultivars: 'Annabelle' (large flowers), 'Grandiflora' (large flowers)

Propagation: Seed, cuttings

HYDRANGEA QUERCIFOLIA Oak leaf hydrangea

SAXIFRAGACEAE Saxifrage family

"If I had to pick one shrub for American gardens," said horticulturist John Elsley, speaking at the National Arboretum, "this would be it." The Asian hydrangeas—pee-gee hydrangea and bigleaf hydrangea—have been garden favorites forever, but native oak leaf hydrangea is not nearly as commonly grown—at least not yet! John Elsley favors the cultivar 'Snow Queen', with its large flowers held upright and in striking contrast with deep green leaves. I agree that this is a lovely cultivar, but I find the straight species

*Ocean spray (*Holodiscus discolor*)*

'Annabelle' hydrangea (Hydrangea arborescens *'Annabelle'*)

just as fine in other ways. The chief difference between them is the flower. 'Snow Queen' has a larger, more upright bloom than many seed-grown plants. Strange to say, the flowers of 'Snow Queen' sometimes strike me as a bit too large, too upright, too *too*. Perhaps flowers, like bosoms, can sometimes be too much of a good thing.

Both cultivar and species are handsome rather than pretty shrubs by reason of their large, bold, leathery leaves and huge flower heads. They draw attention in every season. In early spring, new leaves emerge a pale lettuce green before darkening to a matte green. In late May, great creamy white clusters of flowers bloom— even in shade. Over the summer, they turn (like those of pee-gee hydrangea) first to pink and then to tan. They are long lasting when dried and need no special attention. Oak leaf hydrangea holds on to its wine and orange and mahogany fall-colored leaves for a long time before dropping them to reveal cream-colored stems, streaked copper with exfoliating bark.

Several years ago, I began to grow oak leaf hydrangea from seed with surprisingly excellent results. The plants that I started three years ago are now three feet tall and are vigorously branching.

Origin: Moist woodlands of the Southeast

Flower: Very large, elongated white cluster in late May/June that remains on the plant, turning pink and, finally, tan

Foliage: Large, rough-textured oak-shaped leaves turn shades of wine and copper in fall.

Hardiness: Zones 5 to 9. Tops can be killed by extreme cold, but will grow back swiftly.

Height: To 6 feet, spreading to 8 feet wide

Regions: Northeast, Mid-Atlantic, South, Midwest where hardy, Northwest

Landscape use: Shrub border; screen; large, broad specimen

Culture: Moist, humusy soil in part to full shade; cut back to control growth and renew.

Cultivars: 'Snow Queen' (large, very white upright flowers, won Gold Medal Award), 'Snow Flake' (double hose-in-hose flowers, excellent for drying), 'Harmony 94' (large, creamy white flowers)

Propagation: Easy and fast from seed; cuttings of wood that is fairly firm (no hormone needed)

Oak leaf hydrangea (Hydrangea quercifolia) *in Joanna Reed's garden*

HYPERICUM FRONDOSUM Golden St. Johnswort
HYPERICACEAE Hypericum family

When it was named for John the Baptist, Christian missionaries were probably enlisting its reputation for magic to their cause. Teutonic tribes held St. Johnswort in high regard. Gathered on Midsummer's Night and hung over doorways and windows, it was a good all-around charm against imps, demons, evil spirits, witches, thunder, and lightning.

There are many St. Johnsworts, of which perhaps the exotic *H. calycinum,* frequently used as a ground cover, is the most popular. All are shrubs that bloom in summer, useful for sunny to lightly shaded, well-drained, dryish places. The flowers of this long-lived species are golden, with stamens so prominent they are showier than the petals.

The flowers of the venerable native *H. frondosum* cultivar 'Sunburst', a species introduced in 1747(!), raise the characteristic of showy stamens to an art form. Densely packed stamens radiate into a perfect globe shape, and almost hidden in their midst is a smooth pistil. This is an arresting plant that blooms all summer, but its inter-

est in the garden isn't confined to that season.

Golden St. Johnswort is a rounded, upright shrub that flowers in summer. Leaves are leathery green. In winter, a few tiny leaves blush maroon and remain on the plant (in my garden), semievergreen in fact but not in effect. Most prominent on my plant in the winter are seed heads that look like desiccated, brown rose buds. Golden St. Johnswort is more forgiving of wet clay than some other species—notably *H. buckleyi,* a beautiful little-leaved plant that dies regularly in my garden.

Origin: South Carolina, west to Tennessee and Texas
Flower: Golden yellow with prominent stamens, all summer
Foliage: Leathery dark green, narrow, sparsely evergreen
Hardiness: Zones 5 to 8
Height: To 3 feet
Regions: Midwest, Northeast, Mid-Atlantic, South, Mountain
Landscape use: Border, shrub
Culture: Sun to part shade, good drainage, soil that is on the dry side
Cultivars: 'Sunburst' (showy flowers)

'Sunburst' St. Johnswort (Hypericum frondosum *'Sunburst')*

ILEX Holly
AQUIFOLIACEAE Holly family

The stereotype of holly is English (*Ilex aquifolium*) or the American tree holly (*I. opaca*)—evergreen, with spiny leaves and red berries. In fact,

263

Ilex

Name	Origin	Flower	Foliage	Zones	Height	Regions	Landscape Use
Ilex amelanchier Sarvis holly	Southeastern Virginia to Georgia and Louisiana	Inconspicuous flowers, red-orange berry	Lustrous, light green leaves are deciduous	7 to 9	To 15 ft	South	Small tree, shrub
Ilex decidua Possum haw	West Virginia, Illinois to Florida, Texas	Inconspicuous flowers, red-orange berry	Lustrous, dark green, long elliptical leaves, deciduous	5 to 9	To 20 ft	South, Lower Midwest, Mid-Atlantic	Small tree, shrub
Ilex glabra Inkberry, gallberry	Coastal plain from Long Island to Florida, Texas	Inconspicuous flowers, black berries	Lustrous, small 1- to 2-in leaves, evergreen	6 to 9	6 to 10 ft	Eastern North America	Shrub border, foundation plant
Ilex verticillata Winterberry	States east of the Mississippi and Arizona, Idaho, Mexico, Missouri	Inconspicuous flower, scarlet berries	Dark green leaves turn chartreuse to yellow in fall	4 to 9	8 ft	Eastern North America, Northwest	Shrub border, masses, winter contrast
Ilex vomitoria Yaupon	Virginia to Florida, Mexico	Inconspicuous flower, red-orange berries	Small, elliptical leaves, evergreen	8 to 10	To 25 ft	South	Hedge, screen, small tree

of the shrubby native species, few have the spiny "holly" leaf, about half lose their leaves in winter, and not all of the berries are red. They are, however, each in its own way as handsome as their better-known relatives. Where it is warm enough and wet enough (at least 35 inches of rain annually, spread out over the year), hollies are outstanding landscape plants.

One of the first things one learns about hollies is that they are dioecious—they have two sexes. This means that to have berries, one needs both a female plant and a male pollinator. As with chickens, it isn't necessary to pair off each female; one male of each species generally suffices for the average yard.

Inkberry (*Ilex glabra*), named for its black berries, has been a workhorse plant in the nursery industry for generations. Although I have seen it in swampy thickets in Florida, where it is lanky and stoloniferous, in cultivation, it is a nurseryman's and a gardener's dream evergreen, very hardy, adaptable, and even tolerant of wet soil. With good light and pruning, its small, oval leaves become dense with an endearing uprightness that lends texture.

Unlike swamp dweller inkberry, yaupon (*Ilex vomitoria*), from dry, acid woodland, is drought-tolerant. It can grow to a small tree but is more often used as an evergreen shrub with neat, oval leaves and scarlet berries. It is

Inkberry (Ilex glabra) *hedge* (William Bissett Design)

Culture	Propagate	Comment
Well-drained, acid soil, sun to shade	Seeds, cuttings	Inhabits dry, sandy soil
Adaptable, sun to part shade, tolerates seasonally wet soil	Seeds, cuttings	Stunning trimmed as small tree; best berries in full sun. Cultivars: 'Warren's Red' (excellent foliage, berries), 'Pendula' (weeping), 'Council Fire' (6 ft tall). Attracts cedar waxwings in February, March.
Sun to shade, wet to moist soils, prune for legginess	Seeds, cuttings of firm new wood	Hardy, stoloniferous. Cultivars: 'Compacta' (compact), 'Ivory Queen' (white berries). Tolerates salt spray; stolons survive fire.
Sun, part shade, wet to medium soil	Seeds, cuttings	Tolerates wet soil; berried branches for cutting; late winter bird plant. Cultivars: 'Maryland Beauty', 'Red Sprite', Winter Red' (all have good berries, attractive leaves), 'Male' (pollinator), 'Carolina Cardinal' (bears heavily). Native hollies hardy where others cannot survive.
Sun, shade, adaptable, withstands drought, tolerates alkaline soil and salt spray	Seeds, cuttings	Takes pruning, dense, salt-tolerant. *I. opaca, I. decidua* may pollinate it. Cultivars: 'Virginia Dare' (orange fruit), 'Stokes, dwarf' (self-fertile), 'Will Fleming' (upright, male).

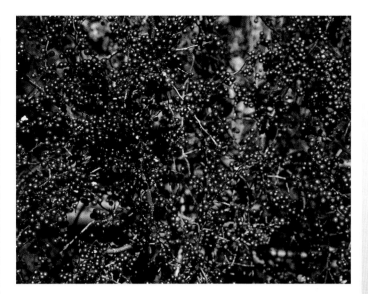

'Carolina Cardinal' winterberry (Ilex verticillata)
(Kim Hawks photo)

said that Native Americans used its leaves to brew a highly stimulating, caffeine-laced brew that also acted as an emetic for some. Hence the name. There are many cultivars, among which 'Nana', a dwarf, 'Jewel', with heavy fruit set, and 'Shelling', a berryless dwarf, are some.

Winterberry (*Ilex verticillata*) and possum haw (*Ilex decidua*) are both deciduous, losing their leaves in fall to reveal red and red-orange berries. These, being less tasty than others, are left on the plants all winter or until the birds have eaten everything else. In any case, you can always beat the birds to these branches for holiday decorations.

Winterberry, another sometime swamp dweller, is tolerant of wet places but grows well in ordinary garden soil. It becomes about 6 to 8 feet tall and is a nice, upright, but otherwise unremarkable shrub until fall. Then, in the presence of scarlet berries, its leaves bleed from medium green to light green and, finally, yellow-green before dropping. All winter long, its fruit-studded stems are a delight. Outside, they contrast with just about anything—evergreens, dried grasses, snow, or simply the earthy gray of an eastern winter. Inside, they are great in bouquets with evergreen boughs and bunches of baby's breath.

Possum haw is, in my opinion, best trimmed as a tree, although it gets no larger than a tall shrub (20 feet or so). It's a wonderful sight in winter—much like winterberry, with red-orange berries, only there is more of it. It tolerates seasonal wetness. I have planted a baby possum haw (and so cannot appreciate the way it will look just yet) on a hill that slopes away from my driveway so that only the bushy top will be visible in winter.

Sarvis holly or serviceberry holly (*Ilex amelanchier*) is a plant I have seen only twice, but read about and heard about wherever native plant enthusiasts gather. Woodlanders Nursery sells females. Their Fall 1992–Spring 1993 catalog says "Rare tall decid shrub w/red frt on long stems." The late Hal Bruce, a connoisseur of native plants, included it on a list of "choice natives" at a lecture he gave on the same subject. Memphis nurseryman Plato Touliatos thinks highly of it, remarking that it is a fast grower that will put on more than a foot a year. Found in the wild in the dry, sandy soils of open woodland, its deciduous foliage is lime green! (See *Ilex* chart, above.)

ILLICIUM FLORIDANUM Florida anise tree, Florida spice bush

ILLICIACEAE Illicium family

S ailing south of Lake George in Florida, probably in 1773, William Bartram came upon "a vast bason or little lake of crystal waters, half encircled by swelling hills, clad with Orange and odiferous Illicium groves."

The passage from *Travels of William Bartram,* describ-

Florida anise (Illicium floridanum*)*

ing *Illicium* in the company of *Citrus* (a genus I associate with vacations in very warm places), so struck me that I overreacted and planted Florida anise on the leeward side of the house for winter protection—whether or not it needed it. After three winters, both a red- and a white-flowered form are doing well. Although their growth cannot be described as fast, they are both becoming quite dense and have a nice, broad habit—better than many I've seen in the wild, where they are frequently tall and leggy from lack of strong light. One of mine thrives in summer dry shade near maple roots, even though experts recommend planting in moist soil.

Although the flowers are curious (the red, to my eye, is far more attractive than the white), the foliage is what makes this such a valuable plant. The flowers have been described as "malodorous," but I have never noticed this, and in any case, they do not overpower the scent of the foliage. Someday, I hope to have shrubs large enough to trim, so the fragrant evergreen leaves might be used in bouquets and arrangements.

Origin: Florida to Louisiana
Flower: Red star-shaped flower in May and, sporadically, later
Foliage: Leathery, elliptic leaves are wonderfully fragrant when brushed.
Hardiness: Zones 7 to 9
Height: To 10 feet
Regions: South, Mid-Atlantic, Lower Midwest
Landscape use: Shrub border, specimen
Culture: Light to full shade, humusy soil, medium to moist soil
Species: *I. parviflorum,* lighter green and more upright, does very well in the moist soils of the Memphis area.

Propagation: Cuttings of firm wood; roots easily with hormone; seed, gathered before it scatters

ISOMERIS ARBOREA (CLEOME ARBOREA)
Bladder-pod
CAPARACEAE Caper family

Eliza Earle, a California gardener, is enthusiastic about this little shrub for its adaptability to many situations, its unusual features, and its long season of bloom. Hummingbirds love its yellow flowers. Cursed with an ugly name that comes from its inflated fruit pods, bladderpod is frequently overlooked as a Xeriscape choice. Mrs. Earle, who gardens a steep, unirrigated slope, likes it for its gray-green leaves that tend to blue tones, its low, spreading habit of growth, and its drought-tolerance. At the Theodore Payne Foundation, where it has been grown in semishade, it intertwines becomingly with *Solanum xanti.* In full sun, with limited water, a grayer leaf and a stouter stature develop.

Origin: Coastal bluffs and desert, California
Flower: Yellow, borne in dense terminal clusters year-round, peaking in late fall to early summer
Foliage: Gray-green, evergreen leaves in three leaflets have a lacy look.
Hardiness: Zones 8b (above 15°F) to 10
Height: 3 to 5 feet
Region: California
Landscape use: Native plant gardens, slope planting, mixed Xeriscape borders

*Bladder-pod (*Isomeris arborea)*

Culture: Drought-tolerant but will take some summer water with good drainage; clay-tolerant
Propagation: Fresh seed

ITEA VIRGINICA 'HENRY'S GARNET' Virginia sweetspire
SAXIFRAGACEAE Saxifrage family

A low-growing juniper at Denver Botanic Garden

Winner of one of the first awards of merit from the Pennsylvania Horticultural Society, *Itea* 'Henry's Garnet' has many positive attributes—plenty of loose, dropping racemes of white flowers that contrast neatly with clean, green foliage in May, which turns gorgeous shades of crimson to mahogany in fall. For me, however, this has been a hard plant to site well. Five plants, grouped in light, moist shade, have proven themselves independent-minded, sending out runners every which way, and this trait, coupled with a lack of volume, lends a disorderly appearance to my planting. It is at its best in late fall, when the brilliant red of the leaves contrasts with dried, tan ornamental grasses nearby. In mild winters, a dwindling few leaves flash vivid crimson in an otherwise subdued landscape. While I like the winter look, in summer, I think they would look better in more light (so they would grow more densely) on a slope.

Very adaptable, *Itea* tolerates wet or dry soil and grows in sun or shade, although sun brings out the intense red fall color.
Origin: New Jersey to Florida and Louisiana
Flower: 4- to 5-inch drooping racemes of white flowers in May/June
Foliage: Medium green, oval leaves on arching stems

turn mahogany to bright red-orange in fall, are semievergreen in warm climates and protected places.
Hardiness: Zones 5 to 9
Height: To 5 feet
Regions: Northeast, Northwest, Midwest, Mid-Atlantic, South
Landscape use: Wet soil, banks, edge of woodland
Culture: Very adaptable, wet or dry soil, sun, shade
Cultivars: 'Henry's Garnet' is superior to the species
Propagation: Seed; cuttings of firm new wood with hormone

JUNIPERUS COMMUNIS SAXILATIS Mountain juniper
CUPRESSACEAE Cypress family

"With junipers," states horticulturist Michael Dirr, "we have reached a cultivar glut." There are dozens and dozens of cultivars—not only of the native junipers, but of *J. chinensis* and the Japanese shore juniper (*J. conferta*) and the Eurasian savin juniper (*J. sabina*), to name the most common of the exotic species. There is a reason for all of this—they are always dependable and presentable, with never an off-season.

Poor junipers have been overused in landscaping and put in places where they don't belong, and otherwise open-minded gardeners turn their noses up at them. But in their respective regions, native junipers are beautiful, useful signature plants—part of the distinctive spirit of the place.

Some grow to be tall trees: the Rocky Mountain juniper (*J. scopulorum*) and the eastern red cedar (*J. vir-*

'Henry's Garnet' sweetspire (Itea virginica)

Shrubs

giniana). Smaller natives useful for gardens include the dwarf juniper (*J. communis saxitalis*) from uplands in the West and the low-growing creeping juniper (*J. horizontalis*). The former, widely grown in California, is the more drought-tolerant and requires a place with good drainage and sun. The latter, from which dozens of cultivars have been derived, also prefers sun with good drainage. It is altogether more adaptable and survives in the humid East.

Mountain juniper is a low-growing, mat-forming plant that becomes very wide with age. There are dozens of selections.

Origin: Northern North America and Eurasia
Flower: Usually a blue-green berry
Foliage: Blue-green scaly needles
Hardiness: Zones 4 to 8
Height: To 1 foot, spreading wide
Regions: California, Pacific Northwest
Landscape use: Ground cover, rock garden
Culture: Sun, good drainage, occasional water
Species: *J. horizontalis* and cultivars 'Wiltonii' ('Blue Rug', 4 to 6 inches), 'Wisconsin' (good foliage, 8 inches), 'Bar Harbor' (good winter color, 1 foot), creeping, wide-spreading evergreens from the Northeast, Zones 3 to 9.

JUSTICIA CALIFORNICA Chuparosa, beloperone
ACANTHACEAE Acanthus family

Bird lovers of the Southwest, please note chuparosa is derived from the Spanish "chupar" (to suck) and refers to hummingbirds' fondness for this plant. The deep red, tubular flowers bloom nearly all year (although most heavily in spring), which makes for a jewellike, year-round show of flowers and birds.

I witnessed both copious bloom and attendant hummingbirds at the Desert Botanical Garden in Phoenix, where there was a big, cheerful ground cover of chuparosa under a palo verde tree. From southeastern California to southern Arizona and northern Mexico, chuparosa grows most commonly along washes and on rocky slopes. Fully hardy in Zone 10, it will suffer cold damage in Zone 9 but will survive. Chuparosa is available, but may take some tracking down.

Origin: Southern California, Arizona, and northern Mexico
Flower: Red tubular flower blooms nearly all year
Foliage: Small, widely spaced leaves growing on thick

Beloperone (Justicia californica)

stems are hairy and a dull green color.
Hardiness: Zone 10 (survives in Zone 9)
Height: 3 feet high by 4 feet wide
Region: Desert Southwest
Landscape use: Ground cover, flower border
Culture: Sun; dry, well-drained soil

KALMIA LATIFOLIA Mountain laurel
ERICACEAE Heath family

"Kalmia," says Woodlanders' Bob McCartney, "grows very well where it is happy, but it's not happy in many places." He recommends planting it high or, in heavy soils, on top of the ground with sandy, humusy soil mounded around it and a mulch of pine needles over the mound. It requires the difficult combination of ample moisture and perfect drainage.

Its botanical name honors Swedish botanist Peter Kalm, sent by Linnaeus to North America, where he saw the plant that had already been named for him growing on rocky hillsides in Pennsylvania. Today, we can see it growing gloriously along the Appalachian Trail in the mountains of Georgia, not far from the South Carolina border, on hillsides in Connecticut, and probably in a number of other places as well. In the wild, it seems, it always enjoys both moisture and excellent drainage.

Mountain laurel can become rather tall and spindly—even with good light. Cultivars offer tighter habit and a real choice of flower color from pure whites to red and banded forms. A Connecticut friend, whose rhododendrons are under siege by a herd of deer, adds that mountain laurel seems to get by unharmed.

Origin: Eastern North America, often on hillsides in association with beech and rhododendron

Flower: Pinky white, second week in June

Foliage: Lustrous, dark, evergreen

Hardiness: Zones 5 to 8

Height: To 8 feet

Regions: Northeast, Mid-Atlantic, higher elevations in the South, Midwest

Landscape use: Shrub border, specimen (with time)

Culture: Moist, acid, well-drained soil in light shade or morning sun

Species: Sheep laurel (*Kalmia angustifolia*), from dry, sunny places, has olive gray leaves on a 3-foot shrub with pale mauve flowers. Bog laurel (*K. polifolia*), very dwarf and very hardy (probably Zone 2), has rose-purple flowers and grows in cool, boggy soils.

Cultivars: 'Ostbo Red' (red buds, pink flowers), 'Sarah' (red buds, deep pinky red flowers), 'Elf' (dwarf, to 30 inches, typical flowers)

Propagation: Seed; cuttings of tender wood with no hormone

LARREA TRIDENTATA Creosote bush
ZYGOPHYLLACEAE Caltrop family

Evergreen creosote bush, a familiar sight in the desert Southwest, has bright green, glossy leaves on a low shrub whose open branching pattern lends it an Oriental feeling. Its characteristic "desert rain" fragrance is only one of its charms. Bright yellow flowers in bursts from April to October occur frequently

*Mountain laurel (*Kalmia latifolia*)*

*Creosote bush (*Larrea tridentata*)*

in the presence of fuzzy balls of seeds. At dawn and dusk, creosote bush's stems glow a lovely silver-gray that makes one want to plant it in thickets amidst a meadow of Indian rice grass.

Origin: Native in all the southwestern deserts on slopes and flats, particularly where gravelly surface soils are underlain with a hardpan; usually below 6,000 feet

Flower: Small yellow flowers followed by small fuzzy seed capsules appear sporadically throughout the growing season, April–October.

Foliage: Small, evergreen leaves on stems and branches that fan out broadly

Hardiness: Zones 7 to 10

Height: 4 to 8 feet

Region: Southwest

Landscape use: Mass planted, as backdrop; for light-textured screening; individually, as accent specimens

Culture: Very drought-tolerant

LEUCOTHOE FONTANESIANA Leucothoe, drooping leucothoe, doghobble, fetterbush
ERICACEAE Heath family

Some of leucothoe's common names—doghobble and fetterbush—are pithy mountain speech for the way it grows in the country, as a wild, dense thicket. One can almost see the dog and hunter, hot after deer, stopped short in their chase by its tangle of arching stems. But in the garden, with better light and room to grow, leucothoe behaves like a sophisticated city slicker. These plants grow dense and become extremely showy in May, when creamy flowers in long, drooping clusters hang from the arching stems.

Mahonia

Name	Origin	Flower	Foliage	Zones	Height	Regions	Landscape Use
Mahonia aquifolium Oregon grape holly	Northwest, west of the mountains	Yellow flowers in spring, blue-purple summer fruits	Shiny, spiney, dark green, evergreen	5 to 9	4 to 6 ft tall by 4 ft wide	North America	Shrub border, foundation plant
Mahonia fremontii Fremont mahonia	Utah, Colorado to New Mexico and California	Yellow flowers in spring, blue-black coating on rose-yellow fruit	Small, silvery, spiney, evergreen leaves	7(?) to 10	To 6 ft, but usually 4 to 5 ft	Southwest, southern California	Specimen, shrub border
Mahonia hamaetocarpa	Chihuahuan desert, Mexico, New Mexico	Yellow flowers in spring, red berries	Blue-green, spidery, evergreen leaves	5(?) to 10	6 to 8 ft tall, mounding, wide	Southwest, Mountain	Specimen, shrub border
Mahonia nevinii Nevin's barberry	Chaparral, desert edges	Yellow flowers in spring, red-orange fruit	Gray-green evergreen leaves	8 to 10	To 10 ft by 10 ft wide	Southwest, southern California	Specimen, shrub border, screen
Mahonia repens Creeping mahonia	Woods of the Northwest, east of the mountains	Small yellow flowers followed by edible blue fruits	Blue-green, spiney, evergreen leaves	4 to 8	1 ft tall by 3 to 4 ft wide	Western North America	Ground cover
Mahonia trifoliata Agarita	New Mexico, Texas, Mexico	Yellow flowers, sweet purple fruits	Silver-gray, starry, nearly succulent, evergreen leaves	6 to 10	5 to 7 ft tall, mounding	Southwest, parts of Mountain	Specimen, shrub border

Turning deep purple after frost with raspberry-colored buds, the evergreen foliage of leucothoe is handsome and understated. In summer, leaves are a lustrous dark green that contrasts with its red stems.

Origin: Moist woodland from Virginia to Georgia and Tennessee

Flower: Creamy white, tiny bells are densely packed in long, drooping clusters in May.

Foliage: Leathery, lustrous, evergreen, turns dark purple with frost

Hardiness: Zones 6 to 8

Drooping leucothoe (Leucothoe fontanesiana)

Height: To 6 feet

Regions: Mid-Atlantic, South, Lower Midwest

Landscape use: Woodland shrub, streamside ground cover, shady shrub border

Culture: Bright shade; moist, rich, acid (pH 4.5–6) soil

Species/cultivars: 'Girard's Rainbow', a cultivar of *L. fontanasiana,* is variegated pink, white, green. *L. axillaris,* a coastal species, is smaller (to 5 feet) and its cultivar, 'Greensprite', is more resistant to foliar diseases; it stays a clean, dark green. Florida leucothoe (*Agarista populifolia*) has a tall, upright habit and brighter green leaves.

Propagation: Seed, cuttings

MAHONIA (BERBERIS) Barberry, Oregon grape holly
BERBERIDACEAE Barberry family

From the mountains and deserts of the West come a tribe of ornamentals that have long graced gardens around the world. Most widely known and grown is Oregon grape holly (*M. aquifolium*), discovered by Lewis and Clark and named to honor their contemporary, nurseryman Bernard M'Mahon, author of *The American Gardener's Calendar* (1806).

Horticulturists seem never to have agreed upon a genus name. At one point, they were classified as *"Odostemon."* Then they were, I think, *"Mahonia,"* before someone differentiated the simple-leaved forms,

Culture	Propagate	Comment
Sun to part shade, good drainage	Cuttings, seed	Adaptable evergreen. Cultivars: 'Golden Abundance' (takes dry), 'King's Ransom' (takes sun, cold), 'Compacta' (3 to 4 ft).
Sun, good drainage	Cuttings, seed	Stunning leaves: blood red new, silver blue when dormant, razor sharp!
Sun, good drainage	Cuttings, seed	Very finely textured, delicate
Sun, good drainage	Cuttings, seed	Tolerates, heat, poor soil, drought; barrier plant, slow growing
Sun, part-shade, shade	Cuttings, seed	Bronze in winter, evergreen, tolerates dry shade
Sun, good drainage	Cuttings, seed	Deserves wider use; fruits make good jam

Nevin's barberry (Mahonia nevinii), at left, at the Arizona–Sonora Desert Museum with octopus agave and Blackfoot daisy

"Berberis," from those with compound leaves, "Mahonia." Today, all may sometimes be called by one name or the other. I have chosen "Mahonia."

Under any genus name, Oregon grape holly (*Mahonia aquifolium*) is as familiar on the East Coast as it is on the West, and has also been taken successfully abroad. In *The English Flower Garden,* William Robinson (who called it "Berberis"), thought it "useful both for the pleasure garden and as a cover plant in woods." A tough Oregon grape holly cultivar, 'Mahan', even survives (although sometimes stems die back) at the Longenecker Garden at the University of

Wisconsin Arboretum in Madison—evidence of its adaptability. At the northern limits of its range (Zone 5, possibly 4), it needs protection from both sun and wind.

Oregon grape holly becomes a 6- to 8-foot dense shrub of dark green, lustrous leaves that resemble those of holly. In spring, it produces very dense, butter yellow racemes of flowers followed by, to my eye, far more attractive, dusty blue-purple, egg-shaped berries.

The hybrid 'Golden Abundance', will tolerate watering only once or twice a month. Creeping mahonia (*Mahonia repens*) grows only a foot tall, but spreads to a matte (some say "dull") green ground cover 3 feet or more, sending out underground stems quickly.

Fremont mahonia (*Mahonia fremontii*), whose range is from Colorado to Mexico, "is an absolutely stunning plant," says Denver horticulturist Dermod Downes. Blood red new growth turns silvery and a striking silvery steel blue in dormancy. Its single drawback is razor-edged leaves.

Nevin's barberry (*Mahonia nevinii, Berberis nevinii*) comes from dry valleys in the chaparral country of California and the edges of the desert. Spiny leaflets are narrow, silvery gray above and light green below. (See *Mahonia* chart, above.)

MALOCOTHAMNUS ARCUATUS 'EDGEWOOD'
Bush mallow
MALVACEAE Mallow family

California gardener Betsy Clebsch combines this bush mallow with roses and other shrubs and likes it for its pink flowers and small, whitish gray, maplelike leaves.

'Golden Abundance' mahonia at Tree of Life Nursery, San Juan Capistrano, California

A striking evergreen shrub, *Malocothamnus* 'Edgewood's small pink flowers arranged in a spike are lovely next to its woolly white stem. 'Edgewood' blooms all summer and into the autumn. Pruning during this time is a necessity in order to keep the plant shapely.

Origin: This particular cultivar comes from a country park in San Mateo County, California.

Flower: Pink, about 1 inch deep and 1 inch across

Foliage: Whitish gray

Hardiness: Probably to 20°F for short periods (Zones 8b to 10)

Height: To 6 feet

Region: California where it is hardy

Landscape use: Combines well with roses and other shrubs

Culture: Fast drainage, full sun, no additional water once established

Propagation: Cuttings

MYRICA CALIFORNICA California wax myrtle
MYRICACEAE Bayberry family

Along the Pacific Coast, where California wax myrtle grows wild on the dunes, this shrub appreciates high shade and ocean fog, but it will do well in all but the hottest areas. California gardener Betsy Clebsch calls it a splendid evergreen shrub with a lustrous appearance, which grows rapidly to 10 feet and is excellent for hedges. Attractive bright-green foliage is its chief beauty. It is drought-tolerant.

Easterners, familiar with bayberry and inkberry, might see it as a cross between the two brighter green and more upright than inkberry, but with an inkberry's girth and depth.

Wax myrtle (Myrica cerifera) growing in a raised planter

Origin: Washington to Northern California along the dunes

Flower: Inconspicuous along stems, followed by purple, waxy berries

Foliage: Long, narrow, evergreen leaves

Hardiness: Zones 8 to 10

Height: To 15 feet

Regions: Pacific Northwest, northern California

Landscape use: Seaside garden, inland, shrub, hedge, screening

Culture: Sun; acid, well-drained soil; tolerant of salt spray

Propagation: Seeds, cuttings

MYRICA PENSYLVANICA Bayberry
MYRICACEAE Bayberry family

The scent of bayberries and pine needles baking in the sun always evokes memories of summers at the Delaware beaches. Along the Delmarva coast, bayberry is a familiar dune plant with waxy, aromatic berries that really are the source of those sage-colored candles, made since Colonial times. A plant of sandy, acid soils, bayberry thrives in exposed, dry, infertile sites like beach and seaside gardens. Because of its toughness, I have also seen it used in such hopelessly difficult places as a hotel parking lot in Rockville, Maryland.

Semievergreen at the southern end of its range, bayberry loses its aromatic, gray-olive leaves farther north. It takes shearing. Because the plant is dioecious (has male and female plants), both sexes are needed for good fruit set.

Origin: Sandy soils from Newfoundland to North Carolina

Flower: Inconspicuous green flowers are followed by blue-gray berries that are eaten by birds.

Foliage: Semievergreen to deciduous (depending upon climate) glaucous green leaves, bluntly tipped, turning bronze with cold

Hardiness: Zones 2 to 7

Height: To 9 feet

Regions: Sandy, acid soils of Northeast, Mid-Atlantic, Upper Midwest

Landscape use: Beach landscaping; dry, exposed places; wildlife planting

Culture: Adaptable; grows on poor, sandy soil; salt-tolerant

Species: Wax myrtle (*M. cerifera*), a suckering shrub that becomes a tree, is salt-tolerant, dense, evergreen; leaves used as flavoring. Atlantic coast from central Florida to New Jersey, where it overlaps with *M. pensylvanica*,

Bayberry (Myrica pensylvanica)
and tall ships, Mystic, Connecticut

Zones 7 to 9. Dwarf wax myrtle (*M. cerifera* var. *pumila*), grows to 3 feet. Sweet gale (*M. gale*), a circumpolar plant of northern North America and Eurasia, grows in wet soil in cold climates.

Propagation: Seed (cool stratify)

OPUNTIA Prickly pear, cholla cactus
CACTACEAE Cactus family

New Mexican designer and author Judith Phillips likes the fierce geometry of *Opuntia* species for year-round interest in the landscape and as an accent and filler in places too harsh for unarmed plants. Spines are a safety consideration if there are small, unruly children about, but where there are not, one can enjoy the showy spines, held long and singly or arranged in starlike clusters of silver, yellow, or russet brown.

Opuntia also bears large, waxy rose-pink, yellow, or gold flowers. Fleshy stems vary in form from flat "beaver-tail" pads lumped together as "prickly pears" to cylindrical canelike stems, called "cholla."

Mix them and soften with masses of penstemon, desert marigold, abronia, or verbena for no-touch tableaux against the walls of the house or set back from paths and patios.

Origin: On rocky slopes, hillsides, and prairies, as well as desert flatlands, throughout western North America at elevations between 3,000 and 7,000 feet

Flower: Large, waxy flowers in pink, yellow, or gold borne after rains in early and midspring. Flowering is followed by summer fruit, some quite delicious.

Foliage: Often light, gray-green foliage varies in form from flat pads to cylindrical, canelike stems, studded with single or clustered spines.

Hardiness: Many tolerate Zone 6a, although some are restricted to warm deserts (8b).

Height: Varies, up to 4 to 6 feet

Region: Southwest

Landscape use: Barrier plantings, accents, filler in harsh places

Culture: Planting away from high traffic areas and other plants that drop an abundance of leaves avoids the problem of having people or litter caught up in the spines. Sun; good drainage.

PAXISTIMA CANBYI Paxistima, mountain lover, rat stripper
CELASTRACEAE Staff tree family

Low-growing paxistima spreads outward (very slowly), rooting as it goes to form a neat, evergreen carpet as much as 5 feet in diameter. From a distance, it looks like a tiny conifer, but upon closer examination, the "needles" are really very dark green, narrow, toothed "holly" leaves. A great finishing plant for acid, well-drained soil in sun, paxistima is tough as nails once it is established.

Origin: Mountains of Virginia, West Virginia

Prickly pear (Opuntia)

Shrubs

Mountain lover (Paxistima canbyi)

Flower: Small, inconspicuous, chocolate brown, in spring, followed by white fruits

Foliage: Lustrous bright green in spring, darkening in summer and taking on a bronze cast with cold weather; evergreen

Hardiness: Zones 4 to 7

Height: To 12 inches; spreads laterally

Regions: Northeast, Midwest, Northwest, Mountain, Mid-Atlantic, higher elevations in the South

Landscape use: Front of shrub border, ground cover, rock garden

Culture: Acid, well-drained soil in sun, very light shade; needs a snow cover in very exposed sites; do not fertilize

Species: Oregon boxwood, *P. myrsinites* (taller, fragrant flowers, Zone 5)

PHILADELPHUS LEWISII Western mock orange

SAXIFRAGACEAE Saxifrage family

Old-fashioned mock oranges evoke memories of long-ago summers when people escaped to sleeping porches on airless nights and porch swings creaked rhythmically on hot, bee-buzzing afternoons. *That* mock orange was probably the sweetly scented European hybrid, *P. lemoinei* or, perhaps, *P. coronarius* or one of their many cultivars. This mock orange, *P. lewisii,* was introduced into England in 1825 by David Douglas,

who explored the flora of the Pacific Coast. It is probably better known in England than in its native land, but it deserves wider use at home. Dr. Arthur Kruckeberg of the University of Washington calls it the finest of its clan. It hails from rocky slopes from California to British Columbia. Like its European relatives, it displays lavishly its fragrant snow-white flowers, and its leaves, borne in opposite pairs, are broad, toothed ovals. It is taller and more upright than the European species. It would be lovely to see it growing next to the porch of a Victorian house or as the backdrop to an old-fashioned perennial border.

Origin: East and west of the Cascades on rocky slopes and talus from California to British Columbia

Flower: Fragrant, white, 1- to 2-inch flowers

Foliage: Oval, toothed leaves turning yellow in fall

Hardiness: Zones 5 to 9

Height: To 10 feet

Regions: Northwest, Great Basin, Mountain

Landscape use: Specimen, shrub border

Culture: Sun, medium moisture; prune out old wood

Species: *P. microphyllus:* delightful, slow-growing shrub to 3 feet with fine foliage and large mock orange flowers, from rocky cliffs of the Southwest and Rocky Mountains

Propagation: Cuttings, seeds

PIERIS FLORIBUNDA Fetterbush, mountain andromeda

ERICACEAE Heath family

"It gets sick and dies," joked Mt. Cuba Center director Dr. Richard Lighty when I asked him about fetterbush. He is right that it is tricky to

Fetterbush (Pieris floribunda)

Shrubby cinquefoil (Potentilla fruticosa)

Landscape use: Handsome shrub

Culture: Bright shade, moist with good drainage. I have read that fetterbush is lime-tolerant.

Propagation: Seeds

POTENTILLA FRUTICOSA Shrubby cinquefoil, bush cinquefoil

ROSACEAE Rose family

Shrubby cinquefoil is at home almost anywhere in the North Temperate Zone. Its common name refers to its compound leaves, usually in fives, but sometimes more or fewer. These are fine and ferny in appearance on a very dense, twiggy, rounded shrub. In summer, shrubby cinquefoil is covered with yellow flowers. I have seen it blooming cheerfully in early June at the Connecticut College Arboretum. It was used as high ground cover with an evergreen foreground of *Paxistima.*

Origin: North Temperate Zone, circumpolar

Flower: Yellow, from June until frost

Foliage: Green, small compound leaves have a ferny appearance.

Hardiness: Zones 3 to 7

Height: 3 to 4 feet

Region: Possibly because it is so hardy, I think of this as a northern plant; it probably does best where summers are moderate.

Landscape use: Nice summer color; shrub border; smaller forms in rock garden

Culture: Very adaptable; sun to part shade, medium to dry soil, good drainage, cold-tolerant

Cultivars: These are just a few of the many cultivars 'Primrose Beauty', 2 to 4 feet tall, has silvery foliage and pale yellow flowers. 'McKay's White', 2½ feet tall, with cream flowers, has yellow-green foliage. 'Goldfinger' has yellow-green foliage and yellow flowers. 'Yellow Gem', a prostrate plant, has ruffled yellow flowers. 'Yellowbird', from Canada, has semi- to fully double yellow flowers. 'Tangerine', a 2-foot dense mound, produces copper-colored flowers in cool weather and shade. 'Boskoop Red' produces red flowers that fade a bit in summer on a low plant.

grow this mountain plant in the Washington area, of course, but I took his words as a verbal gauntlet and determined to grow this native counterpart to the exotic *Pieris japonica.* And, anyway, I had seen a good specimen of fetterbush on the woodland trail at London Town Publik House and Gardens in Edgewater, Maryland. So I brought three little plants back from the Cullowhee Conference of 1990, and all three survived the summer. Two disappeared between then and now, but one is alive—thriving, bushy, evergreen, healthy. It's growing in part shade on an east-facing slope. I will never move it. In fact, I am afraid to touch it.

This broad evergreen with white lily-of-the-valley flowers is likely to remain a rarity for those who don't live in New England or on a mountainside, but for those who enjoy a challenge and believe in luck, this little shrub is a treasure worth trying.

Origin: Mountain slopes, Virginia to Georgia

Flower: White, upright clusters in April

Foliage: Lustrous, dark green, leathery, finely toothed leaves are evergreen.

Hardiness: Zones 5 to 7

Height: To 4 feet tall by 6 to 8 feet wide

Regions: Higher elevations in the South, Mid-Atlantic, Northeast

PRUNUS BESSEYI Western sand cherry

ROSACEAE Rose family

A shrub of many virtues, western sand cherry feeds birds and people with its berries. Beautiful in spring, when it is covered with clusters of pinkish white cherry blossoms, it is equally showy in fall, when

Western sand cherry (**Prunus besseyi**) *(Charles Mann photo)*

its gray-green leaves turn brilliant red. Drought-tolerant and very hardy, it is a fine addition to midwestern and western gardens and a good choice for a difficult site.

Origin: Manitoba to Wyoming, Minnesota, and Colorado

Flower: White to pink covering the shrub in April/May, followed by sweet, edible, black berries in July/August. Plant several varieties to ensure pollination.

Foliage: Gray-green leaves turn red in fall.

Hardiness: Zones 3 to 9

Height: 1 to 8 feet

Regions: Midwest, Southwest, Great Basin, Northwest east of the Cascades, Mountain

Landscape use: Shrub border, bird plant

Culture: Heat-, drought-, frost-, and cold-tolerant; sun; good drainage. Western sand cherry suckers.

Species/cultivars: 'Hansen's Bush Cherry' (seed-propagated form, sold by nurseries), 'Tom Thumb' (compact). Wild plum (*P. americana*), a suckering shrub to 10 feet with a range that extends from Massachusetts to New Mexico, is a good, hard-to-kill wildlife plant with pretty white flowers. Use beach plum (*P. maritima*), a suckering thicket (inland, a small tree), for beach landscaping; Zones 3 to 8.

Propagation: Seed (cold stratified or planted in fall) or division

PRUNUS LYONII Catalina cherry
ROSACEAE Rose family

Eliza Earle of the Theodore Payne Foundation in Sun Valley, California, is excited about Catalina cherry, a vigorous, evergreen plant that grows hedges and screens—fast. It comes from the fog-clothed Channel Islands, where high humidity teams with a Mediterranean climate to produce wonderful species for mainland southern Californian gardens. She says that *Prunus lyonii* is typical of one of these species in its abundant big leaves and rapid growth, compared with its mainland cousin, *Prunus ilicifolia.* A tidy green all year, Catalina cherry takes well to pruning. If left unpruned, it will eventually become a small- to medium-sized tree, more narrow and upright than many chaparral species. The marble-sized fruit can be a hazard on pavements, but is easily swept up, if wildlife doesn't get to it first.

Origin: Channel Islands, California

Flower: White, borne in racemes, 2 to 5 inches, May/June

Foliage: Bright green, evergreen

Hardiness: Zones 8b (15°F and above) to 10

Height: Up to 45 feet

Region: Throughout southern California

Landscape use: Specimen tree, screen, or hedge

Culture: Not particular, but will grow quickly with regular water. Resistant to oak root fungus.

Species/cultivars: Hybridizes freely with the hollyleaf cherry, *P. ilicifolia.* It is a survivor and will grow throughout California. The birds love its red fruit. Very drought-tolerant, this evergreen shrub or small tree grows anywhere, from 10 to 40 feet tall and about 10 feet wide.

Propagation: Seed

RHAMNUS CALIFORNICA 'EVE CASE' Coffeeberry
RHAMNACEAE Buckthorn family

Big, broad 'Eve Case' coffeeberry, a selection introduced by the Saratoga Horticultural Foundation, is just the thing to define the edge of a garden or

Catalina cherry (**Prunus lyonii***) *hedge*
(Sidney Baumgartner Design)

Coffeeberry (Rhamnus californica) *(Betsy Clebsch photo)*

to screen out an unwanted view graciously. If it is pinched frequently when it is young (do not shear!), it will become a full, dense evergreen shrub with insignificant clusters of green flowers but big, red berries like those of a holly. In hot, dry climates, this coffeeberry is best in partial shade, where it won't burn. It is not fussy about soil and is drought-tolerant, but will look its best with occasional summer water.

Origin: A selection introduced by Saratoga Horticultural Foundation

Flower: Insignificant clusters of small, greenish flowers followed by attractive ½-inch red berries in fall

Foliage: Evergreen, 3 to 5 inches long, 1 inch wide, dark grayish green, ovate leaves

Hardiness: Zones 7 to 10

Height: 6 to 8 feet, spreading about as wide

Region: Pacific states

Landscape use: Background shrub, informal hedge

Culture: Best in partial shade; frequently burns in hot, dry climates if grown in too much sun; looks best with some summer water

Propagation: Cuttings

RHAPIDOPHYLLUM HYSTRIX Needle palm
PALMAE Palm family

"The hardiest palm in the world," according to Bob McCartney of Woodlanders, "is probably only truly hardy as far north as Washington, D.C."

There are needle palms at the National Arboretum and at Brookside Gardens in Wheaton, Maryland, nice specimens at Williamsburg, and isolated successes with this palm as far north as Massachusetts. A stemless palm that doesn't form a trunk, needle palm sometimes has only one growing point, and, at other times, multiple heads. Its leaves are bright green and serve as bold, dramatic sculpture. It would be equally fine as part of a tropical tableau behind a swimming pool, where it can be seen but not brushed up against.

Origin: South Carolina to Mississippi

Flower: Inconspicuous, down in the crown, followed by seeds that are protected by sharp, black needles

Foliage: Bright green, fan-shaped

Hardiness: Zones 7b to 10

Height: 8 feet by 8 feet

Regions: South, protected places in Mid-Atlantic, Lower Midwest

Landscape use: Accent

Culture: Sun to part shade (it is shade-tolerant in the wild); good drainage; protection at its northern limits, such as a site on the southeast side of a building

Propagation: Seed (slow)

Needle palm (Rhapidophyllum hystrix)

RHODODENDRON Native azalea
ERICACEAE Heath family

No other native plant has been so undeservedly undervalued as the native azalea, or "wild honeysuckle." Perhaps the reason for the obscurity of natives is that the enormous popularity of the Asians has set a standard for what people think an azalea should be low, mounding, evergreen, spring blooming, and suitable for foundation planting. The natives are few if any of these things. Not evergreen, some bloom in March before the leaves are out, while others flower as late as August or September. In between, there is at least

Piedmont azalea (Rhododendron canescens) *and Florida azalea* (R. austrinum) *at Callaway Gardens, Pine Mountain, Georgia*

one native azalea in flower every month. Rather than low and dense, some grow to be quite tall and airy. Others are stoloniferous, forming uneven, irregular colonies that are most fitting in a wild garden.

In the woods, their bloom responds to sunlight, forming irregular tiers, not unlike those of dogwoods grown under similar conditions. They grow faster, flower more evenly and profusely, and become fuller plants where there are several hours' sun or filtered sun each day. Grow the late bloomers in light shade, especially in hot climates, to keep the plants evenly moist and their flowers fresh longer. High, dappled shade, plentiful moisture with excellent drainage, and, of course, a humus-rich, acid soil suits most native azaleas.

"Ball-trusses"—balls of distinctive tube flowers with flaring petals and long, showy stamens at the tips of branches of some species—grow bigger and fuller when the plants have had plenty of sunlight and water during the previous season. Generally speaking, the farther north an azalea is grown, the more sunlight and wind protection it needs.

Most native azaleas grow wild in limited areas, yet they frequently adapt in a far wider range. The coastal azalea (*R. atlanticum*), found along the coast from New Jersey to South Carolina, grows happily inland, and the Alabama azalea (*R. alabamense*), whose natural range is restricted to a small part of Alabama and Georgia, can be grown on Long Island. The pinkshell azalea (*R. vaseyi*), found only at high elevations, thrives in a far greater range in North Carolina.

Sometimes, one tries to stretch an azalea's limits too much. In this case, it responds by sulking, languishing, or dying. The western azalea (*R. occidentalis*), from the West Coast, sulks, languishes, and finally dies when transplanted to gardens east of the Rockies. Azaleas from the deep South, the Alabama (*R. alabamense*) and the hammocksweet (*R. serrulatum*), are not reliably hardy north of Philadelphia. Conversely, some northerners or mountain forms need a cool climate. One of these is the rhodora (*R. canadense*). Another northerner, the roseshell azalea (*R. prinophyllum*), one of the parents of some of the extremely hardy "Northern Lights" azaleas, fares beautifully in my hot-summer, Zone 7 garden.

The trick to designing with natives is to consider them in their own right as showy spring- and summer-flowering shrubs and not to consider them substitutes for the Asian azaleas. The earliest bloomers, like pinkshell azalea and Florida azalea, flower before they leaf out; they need a dark background a wall, a hedge, or a large evergreen to set off their blooms. Or they ought to be massed so that the pale flowers on leafless shrubs will have the effect of clouds. English garden writer William Robinson extolled this leafless lightness as "a relief from the heaviness of Rhododendrons."

One of the yellow- to red-flowering types—makes a spectacular specimen. The tall, golden Florida azalea (*R. austrinum*) or one of the boldly red- and orange-colored ones—the July-blooming firecracker red Cumberland azalea (*R. bakeri*), the famous flame azalea (*R. calendulaceum*), the salmon-colored Oconee azalea (*R. speciosum*), and the plumleaf azalea (*R. prunifolium*), which grows to 20 feet—definitely hold their own as specimen plants.

Pale white, yellow, and pink azaleas counter subtle coloration with intense fragrance. Native azaleas offer a delightful spectrum of aromas. Site a fragrant azalea—

Sweet azalea (Rhododendron arborescens)

Alabama, coastal, sweet, flame, swamp, western, roseshell, or hummocksweet—near a porch, deck, or window, where its sweet aroma can be savored. Superb in little groves where their lovely effect is magnified by massing, one wants to see a whole hillside of the pink popcorn flowers of the Piedmont azalea (*R. canescens*), or the coastal azalea (*R. atlanticum*) repeated like a leitmotiv throughout a low shrub border, a recurring cloud of pale, scented butterflies.

Propagate your own native azaleas by gathering seeds in the early fall before the pods turn completely brown. Sow immediately. Do not transplant until new growth starts the following spring. Cuttings are tricky because they have to be very, very tender. Once they wilt, it's hard to get them to stand up again. Use no rooting hormone or fertilizer in the cutting medium.

Rhododendron alabamense Alabama azalea

At the tender end of the azalea spectrum is the Alabama azalea. It can be quite low growing, but it spreads broadly by underground runners, becoming, with time, a thicket of lovely, large white flowers with a charming yellow spot that seems to indicate the distinct lemon scent. In the wild, it crosses with *R. canescens* and produces taller, pink forms. In the garden, the pure form (rarely found in the wild, but carried by nurseries), with its large, floppy, fragrant flowers, is exquisite cascading down a hill.

Origin: Alabama
Flower: White with a yellow blotch
Foliage: Medium green, rounded at the tips, on a stoloniferous plant
Hardiness: Zones 6b to 9a
Height: To 5 feet
Regions: South, Lower Midwest, Mid-Atlantic
Landscape use: High ground cover, shrub border
Culture: Sun to part shade; rich, moist, well-drained, acid soil
Varieties: There is a yellow form available.

Rhododendron arborescens Sweet azalea, smooth azalea

Beautiful, fragrant, white sweet azalea usually grows 10 feet tall, although there are shorter forms that spread into small thickets by underground runners in addition to early (May) and late (July) flowering kinds. Flowers of seedling sweet azaleas are sometimes pink, sometimes yellow, and often white with pink tubes and red stamens! This is an azalea you'll want to site under a window to enjoy its glorious heliotrope-scented flowers. When it is situated in good light, the flowers cover the whole plant and leaves color in the fall from bright orange to crimson.

Origin: Uplands, Pennsylvania to Georgia and Alabama
Flower: White, fragrant, often with red stamens and a reddish tube
Foliage: Light to blue-green with pleasant orangy red fall color
Hardiness: Zones 5a to 9a
Height: To 10 feet
Regions: Northeast, Midwest, Mid-Atlantic, South
Landscape use: Woodland's edge, shrub border
Culture: Sun to part shade; rich, moist, well-drained, acid soil
Cultivars: 'Georgiana' is a good, late-flowering cultivar available from nurseries. Also 'Hot Ginger and Dynamite' (intense fragrance), 'Summer Lyric' (cross with plumleaf azalea, coral/yellow throat).

Rhododendron atlanticum Coast azalea

May blooming, fragrant, and white, coast azalea is low and spreads by underground stolons, a characteristic that is enhanced in the sandy soils of its coastal range from South Carolina to New Jersey. Fred Galle, now retired as Callaway Gardens' director of horticulture, reported seeing a single coast azalea that covered over an acre in the pine barrens of Virginia. Clay soils will slow it down, but the coast azalea will grow into a big thicket from 18 inches to 5 feet tall. It tends to grow taller in shade.

In gardens, coast azalea is an excellent foreground plant in front of dark evergreens, with which it contrasts in color and form. It is also beautiful as a ground cover plant, especially in wooded gardens near the sea.

Coast azalea crosses in the wild with *R. canescens* at the southern end of its range and with *R. periclymenoides* at the northern end. Crosses with *R. periclymenoides,* found by Mrs. Julian Hill near the Choptank River in Maryland, have given rise to an outstanding group called the Choptank River hybrids. These include yellow, rose, and pink fragrant flowers. The exquisite 'Nacoochee' is widely available.

Origin: Coastal Delaware to South Carolina
Flower: White, spicy fragrance
Foliage: Light green
Hardiness: Zones 6 to 9
Height: To 6 feet
Regions: Mid-Atlantic, South, Northeast, Lower Midwest
Landscape use: Foreground of shrub border, beach planting

Shrubs

Florida azalea (Rhododendron austrinum)

Culture: Sun to part shade; rich, moist, well-drained, acid soil

Cultivars: Choptank hybrids (crosses with *R. periclymenoides*), 'Nacoochee' (orange buds, creamy white flowers)

Rhododendron austrinum Florida azalea

One fine April morning, while walking in Brookgreen Gardens in South Carolina, I caught a tantalizing scent on a puff of wind. Following my nose to the source of that sweet perfume, I came upon a Florida azalea at peak bloom. It may be that imagination has gilded memory, but this one azalea stands out as more splendid than all the other shrubs of my experience. Years later, it still dazzles in my mind's eye an 8-foot mound of flowers, almost as wide as it was tall, glowing golden orange in a shaft of sunlight. Its gracefully arching stamens protruded from clustered flowers that resembled orchid bouquets of enchanting fragrance. I resolved instantly to spend every springtime for the rest of my years downwind from such a plant and rushed forward to learn its name. I was devastated to read "Florida azalea," thinking this plant could never live in my cooler garden. But no. The word "Florida" in the common name seemed to suggest a tender shrub for gardens of the Deep South. However, like the dogwood *Cornus florida,* the Florida azalea has a far greater range and in fact does poorly, if at all, in South Florida.

Blooming in May, it not only thrives in my Zone 7 Maryland garden, but it also can grow as far north as Zone 6—into Ohio, southern Michigan, and Long Island.

Origin: Florida, Georgia, and Alabama

Flower: Yellow to gold/orange with prominent stamens, in April/May

Foliage: Medium green leaves, may have fine hairs

Hardiness: Zones 6b to 10a

Height: To 12 feet

Regions: South, Mid-Atlantic, Lower Midwest

Landscape use: Specimen, shrub border, woodland garden

Culture: Rich, moist, well-drained, acid soil

Cultivars: 'Millie Mac' (yellow/white margin), 'Escatawpa' (golden yellow, fragrant), 'Austrinum Gold' (hardy, fragrant)

Rhododendron bakeri Cumberland azalea

Not fragrant, but brilliant in color, the Cumberland azalea comes from open woodland on the high Cumberland Plateau from Kentucky to Tennessee to the mountains of Georgia, Alabama, and North Carolina. Similar to the flame azalea, the Cumberland tends to be more orange, with slightly smaller, later flowers. Like all late-blooming azaleas, in the garden, it needs protection from the hot summer sun.

Origin: Uplands of Kentucky and West Virginia to North Carolina, Georgia, and Alabama

Flower: Usually orange, in a ball truss, in July

Foliage: Medium green

Hardiness: Zones 5b to 8b

Height: To 6 feet

Cumberland azalea (Rhododendron bakeri)

Regions: Northeast, Mid-Atlantic, South, Upper and Lower Midwest

Landscape use: Specimen, shrub border, woodland garden

Culture: Part to high shade in summer; rich, moist, well-drained, acid soil

Varieties: Deep orange forms are available.

Rhododendron calendulaceum Flame azalea

The flame azalea has been admired since Colonial times, when William Bartram, after traveling through the hills of Georgia in the summer of 1776, came upon it in bloom and wrote: "The clusters of the blossoms cover the shrubs in such incredible profusion of the hill sides, that suddenly opening to view from dark shades, we are alarmed with the apprehension of the hill being set on fire. This is certainly the most gay and brilliant flowering shrub yet known."

When one comes upon a flame azalea blooming in the wild, the grandeur of this shrub and the brilliance of its flowers still have the power to astound (even to one who has known the likes of the Asian azaleas 'Christmas Cheer' or 'Girard's Hot Shot'). One of the most memorable plant excursions of my life was a rainy ramble in the Georgia mountains with Mary, Jeff, and Lisa Beasley, who specialize in azaleas at Transplant Nursery. It was not, as in Bartram's time, a hillside of solid flame, but rather a hillside of sentry fires, glowing from deep red to bright orange to golds. In the gray light, the azaleas' colors were vivid and true.

Introduced into England in the early 19th century, the flame azalea was one of the parents of the Ghent hybrids and of the Knapp Hill hybrids. An upland plant, the flame azalea can be slow to start in gardens that are hot in summer (Zone 7 and below). Give it a cool place in high shade and plenty of water until it is established. It is not fragrant.

Origin: Uplands from Pennsylvania to Georgia

Flower: Large red, orange, yellow, gold flowers in late May (mid-June in the mountains), not fragrant

Foliage: Medium to dark green leaves, may color slightly in fall

Hardiness: Zones 5b to 8b

Height: To 8 feet

Regions: Northeast, Midwest, Mid-Atlantic, parts of the South

Landscape use: Flowering shrub, summer bloom

Culture: Light to full shade in summer; rich, moist, well-drained, acid soil

Cultivars: 'Chatooga' (4 to 6 feet, ruffled pink turning soft yellow with maturity), 'Cherokee' (4 to 6 feet, soft apricot/bright red stamens), 'Richard Bielski' (8 feet, bright yellow with dark yellow blotch)

Rhododendron canadense Rhodora

The hardiest species of all is the rhodora (*R. canadense*). *Hortus* lists its range as from Newfoundland to Pennsylvania and its hardiness as Zone 3. It can be found growing along the Maine coast in the crevices of rocks, where, windblown, it seldom grows over a foot tall and blooms in early June. It is also found in bogs, where it grows taller, to 3 feet. Its flowers, usually a pale pinky lavender but sometimes much darker, are freckled. They are different from those of many other azaleas, being more bell-shaped by virtue of fused upper petals without the long tube.

This is not a plant for southern or even Mid-Atlantic gardens, but as landscaping in cold climates or on the sea, rhodora is perfect.

Origin: Bogs, granite crags from Newfoundland, along the coast of Maine, to Pennsylvania

Flower: Lavender pink to magenta, tubeless flower (sometimes white) with freckles, in May/June, lightly fragrant

Foliage: Light to gray-green on a low, stoloniferous shrub

Hardiness: Zones 3 to 7

Height: To 3 to 4 feet

Regions: Northeast, Upper Midwest

Landscape use: Northern seaside garden, collector's garden

Culture: Sun to part shade; rich, acid soil; needs constant moisture; very hardy but intolerant of hot summer climates

Rhododendron canescens Piedmont azalea, southern pinxter

Of the pinks, the Piedmont azalea is not only the earliest, flowering in late March in upper Florida, but it is also the most abundant. It is found all over the lower South. Scattered through the woods at Callaway Gardens in Pine Mountain, Georgia, Piedmont azaleas send up a sweet cloud of perfume that hovers over the garden. In the wild, Piedmont azaleas occur frequently under tall pines. I learned this not from observation on the site, but from photos I had taken of them. A tinsel of pine needles caught in the flowers belonged so integrally to the gestalt of this plant that I had trouble recognizing the pine needles for what they were.

Origin: Acid woodlands from upper Florida through Georgia and west to East Texas

Piedmont azalea (Rhododendron canescens)

Flower: Two-tone pink to white, strongly scented flowers in early spring
Foliage: Light green
Hardiness: Zones 6b to 10a
Height: To 10 to 12 feet
Regions: South, Mid-Atlantic, Lower Midwest
Landscape use: Woodland garden, shrub border, specimen
Culture: Sun to part shade; rich, moist, well-drained, acid soil

Rhododendron flammeum (R. speciosum) Oconee azalea

It is thought that the first Oconee azaleas reached England before 1789, and that it was William Bartram who sent them. It is an early bloomer with typically deeper color, sometimes salmon (but also yellow to pink to red), and varies in habit as well as color. Some plants are low and mounding, others will be tall and open. It blooms in mid-April, after the Florida azalea. Because it comes from low elevations of the South, it is heat-tolerant.

Origin: South Carolina, Georgia
Flower: Orange, in ball truss, in April
Foliage: Medium green
Hardiness: Zones 6b to 9a
Height: To 6 feet
Regions: South, Lower Midwest
Landscape use: Specimen, shrub border, woodland garden
Culture: Sun to part shade; rich, moist, well-drained, acid soil
Cultivars: 'Harry's Speciosum' (red, stoloniferous)

Rhododendron occidentalis Western azalea

The legendary western azalea is an exceptional azalea for a special place. Easterners lament the fact that this gorgeous plant simply will not adapt to the East. Even in the West, western azalea is finicky. It needs adequate moisture at all times, bright light—but not full sun— for excellent flowers, and good air circulation to avoid mildew problems. It is best in acid soils that are rich in organic materials. Such a site and a good place to see western azaleas is at Stagecoach Hill, a natural area south of Dry Lagoon Beach State Park in California, often shrouded in fogs from the Pacific.

Bart O'Brien of Rancho Santa Ana Botanic Garden says that while western azalea is not the easiest plant to grow, for those who succeed with it, exquisite white flowers are the reward. They appear in late May and June after most other azaleas have flowered and are remarkable not only for their beauty, but also for a strong, spicy scent. Like all native azaleas, western azalea is quite variable in nature. There are pink, rose, and nearly reddish flowers. Late flowering and fragrance have made western azalea a frequent choice for hybridizing. *R. occidentalis* was a parent in the Knapp Hill strain of hybrid azaleas.

Origin: Streamsides, moist areas, southwestern Oregon, California, into Mexico
Flower: Variable; to 4 inches, typically white with yellow-orange flares on upper two petals (often petals are frilled along the margins); also cream, pink, deep pink, or red; fragrant
Foliage: Varies from oval to nearly round; thick, light green, deciduous
Hardiness: Zones 7(?) to 10
Height: 4 to 10 feet tall and upright or equally wide
Region: Pacific states (does not succeed in the East).

Oconee azalea (Rhododendron flammeum)

Western azalea (Rhododendron occidentalis)

Flower: Small cotton-candy pink flower with a very long tube, prominent stamens blooming in May, before the leaves are out. Some are fragrant.
Foliage: Light to glaucous green, bronze to orange in fall
Hardiness: Zones 5 to 8
Height: To 10 feet
Regions: Northeast, Midwest, Mid-Atlantic
Landscape use: Woodland garden, shrub border
Culture: Sun to part shade; rich, moist, well-drained, acid soil
Species: *R. canescens* is very similar, but fragrant.

Pinxterbloom (Rhododendron periclymenoides)

Landscape use: Specimen, edges of woodland
Culture: Good air circulation; best in light shade, but bright light for good flowering; requires adequate moisture at all times; rich, acid soil
Propagation: Seed, cuttings

Rhododendron periclymenoides (formerly *R. nudiflorum*) Pinxter azalea, pinxterbloom

The northern counterpart to *R. canescens* is the pinxterbloom, or pinxter. The common name refers not to the color (which would be apt) but to the German (or Dutch) for Pentecost, the seventh Sunday after Easter, which is its approximate bloom time in May. The pinxterbloom is widely variable, with some flowers almost lavender and others nearly white and the flower tube and filaments in matching or contrasting colors. Its habit ranges from a low shrub to a large, airy tree form.

For a sight that will lift your spirits and inspire you to grow this lovely plant, go see a good display of pinxters when they are in bloom. There are great banks of it along woodland openings at Bowmans Hill Preserve in Washington Crossing, Pennsylvania, and there are also excellent plantings of it at the Connecticut College Arboretum in New London.

Origin: Woodland from Maine to South Carolina, Tennessee, and Ohio

Rhododendron prinophyllum (R. roseum) Roseshell azalea, mountain pink azalea

R. prinophyllum was not always *R. prinophyllum*. It used to be called *R. roseum* and continues to be (with vehemence!) by those who think it still ought to be. Recently, it was again reclassified as a variety of *R. periclymenoides* (which is the new name for the pinxterbloom azalea, formerly called *R. nudiflorum*). Botanical nomenclature can be confusing.

By any name, roseshell azalea is an outstanding ornamental. "Clove-scented" is a fair description of the aroma produced by its two-tone pink flowers on large shrubs. The combination of this deepening pink and the freshest of new greens is unforgettable. Wandering around the Connecticut College Arboretum in mid-May, when it blooms with a ground cover of apple green hay-scented fern, is a good time to sample both its fragrance and its grace. Very hardy, roseshell azalea occurs in the wild from southern Quebec to Oklahoma.

Fortunately for those who live in climates with severe winters, crosses have yielded hybrids of extreme cold-

shrubs

Roseshell azalea (Rhododendron prinophyllum)

hardiness. Dr. Harold Pellett of the University of Minnesota's Landscape Arboretum has continued work begun by Al Johnson on the "Northern Lights" series of azaleas.

Origin: Southern Quebec and Maine, west to Illinois and Ohio and southwest to Arkansas and Oklahoma and southwestern Virginia

Flower: Two-tone pink, fragrant, tube flowers in May

Foliage: Medium green

Hardiness: Zones 4 to 8 (to −25°F)

Height: To 8 feet

Regions: Northeast, Mid-Atlantic, Midwest

Landscape use: Shrub border, specimen, woodland garden

Culture: Sun to part shade; rich, moist, well-drained, acid soil

Cultivars: 'Pink Lights' and 'Rosy Lights' (7 to 8 feet, almost equally broad, fragrant, flower bud hardy to −45°F), 'Marie Hoffman' (very hardy, clear pink, 8 feet by 8 feet), 'Spicy Lights' (a *R. prinophyllum* cross with an Exbury azalea, flower bud hardy to −35°F, good resistance to mildew [a problem in areas with cool, wet summers]).

Rhododendron prunifolium Plumleaf azalea

Scarlet plumleaf (*R. prunifolium*) is the flower that appears on the logo of Georgia's Callaway Gardens. It hails from a small area of southwestern Georgia and eastern Alabama near Callaway Gardens. Like many brilliantly colored native azaleas, it is not fragrant. Its flower color is striking, varying from a bright orange to the deepest red of all.

The Beasley family, who run Transplant Nursery in Lavonia, Georgia, have crossed plumleaf azalea with *R.*

arborescens and *R. serrulatum* and created pink-flowered plants that are sometimes fragrant.

A very late bloomer (July to August and sometimes even into September), the plumleaf azalea requires a cool, shady place in the garden, where it can reach 20 feet and will attract hummingbirds.

Origin: Mountains of southwestern Georgia and eastern Alabama

Flower: Scarlet, tube flower

Foliage: Good green, complements flowers

Hardiness: Zones 7 to 9

Height: To 20 feet, commonly 8 to 10 feet

Regions: Uplands of the South, Mid-Atlantic, Lower Midwest

Landscape use: Specimen, woodland garden, shrub border

Culture: Part to full shade in summer; rich, moist, well-drained, acid soil

Cultivars: 'Pine Prunifolium' (bright red flowers)

Rhododendron serrulatum Hammocksweet azalea

Hammocksweet azalea hails from the Deep South. In the wild, it is found from the palmetto country of Florida up the coast to Georgia and west to Mississippi. Its fragrant white flowers appear and contrast with lustrous leaves from July to September, depending upon where it is grown.

Plumleaf azalea (Rhododendron prunifolium)
(Sylvia Martin photo)

Pinkshell azalea (Rhododendron vaseyi)

Origin: Hammocks of Georgia and Florida to Louisiana
Flower: White, fragrant, in late summer
Foliage: Nice lustrous green; remain for a long time
Hardiness: Zones 7 to 9
Height: To 20 feet
Regions: South, coastal areas of Mid-Atlantic
Landscape use: Specimen, shrub border
Culture: Sun to part shade; rich, moist, well-drained, acid soil; prune lightly and routinely

Rhododendron vaseyi Pinkshell azalea

Even though it is native to a rather small area in the mountains of North Carolina, the pinkshell azalea's tolerance for low temperatures grants it a far greater range. It grows happily at Mt. Cuba in Delaware and at Garden in the Woods in Massachusetts. Shell pink flowers appear before the leaves, making the bare branches look as if they are being visited by butterflies.

Appearing in April/May, the flowers of pinkshell azalea are shaped differently from most native azaleas, having no corolla tube and with the three upper petals grouped together. Orange freckles dot the base of the pink petals. Not fragrant like other native azaleas, the pinkshell does well in filtered sun and rich, moist, acid soil. Unlike most other azaleas, this one adapts well to very moist soils. *R. vaseyi* does not hybridize.

Origin: Mountains of North Carolina
Flower: Soft pink fades to white with freckles on a tubeless flower
Foliage: Medium green
Hardiness: Zones 5 to 9 (there are reports of it thriving in Minneapolis, Zone 4)

Height: To 6 feet
Regions: Northeast, Mid-Atlantic, Midwest, South
Landscape use: Specimen, woodland garden, shrub border
Culture: Sun to part shade (the hotter the climate, the shadier the site); rich, moist, well-drained, acid soil
Cultivars: 'White Find' is a cultivar whose snow white petals are peppered with green dots at the base.

Rhododendron viscosum Swamp azalea

Swamp azalea blooms after its leaves are out, typically from June into July, but earlier or later depending upon location. While the white flowers are pretty up close, the abundant foliage sometimes obscures them. They are also sticky. However, the swamp azalea has two characteristics that compensate for any drawbacks It is intensely fragrant and it is adaptable to almost any situation, growing from swamp to upland and tolerating heat to extreme cold—hardy to Zone 3b. This means it will adapt anywhere from Maine to southern Louisiana. It reaches about 9 feet with an equal spread and can form thickets where conditions are ideal. There are some good pink forms.

Origin: Swamps from Maine to South Carolina
Flower: Very fragrant, white, in June (just before flame azalea)
Foliage: Green foliage, turns bronze in fall
Hardiness: Zones 4b to 9a
Height: To 6 feet
Regions: Northeast, Midwest, Mid-Atlantic, South
Landscape use: Pond edge, streamside, shrub border
Culture: Tolerates soils that are seasonally wet. Sun to

Swamp azalea (Rhododendron viscosum)

Shrubs

CARE OF AZALEAS

Fred C. Galle is the author of several books on azaleas and a retired former director of horticulture at Callaway Gardens, where he developed one of the country's largest plantings of azaleas. He offers the following advice for growing native azaleas.

1. Choose azaleas that are hardy in your area.

2. Site azaleas in light shade with good drainage. Azaleas need sunshine to bloom well, but a hot, dry spot is as bad as a dark place with no sunlight. A position with morning sun and protection from the wind is best. Late-blooming azaleas, especially, need protection from the afternoon sun.

3. Choose a site where the azaleas will not have to compete with shallow-rooted trees such as maples and elms.

4. Provide acid soil with a pH between 5 and 6. Dig a planting hole twice as deep and wide as the container, and add plenty of organic matter such as peat, leaf mold, and ground or shredded pine bark.

5. If the plant has been grown in a container, use a sharp stick to loosen its roots from the soil ball before planting. Otherwise, they will grow back into the ball rather than out into the soil. This will eventually cause the plant to be stunted or even to die.

6. Spring is the best time to plant or transplant azaleas, but, with care, it can be done in fall. Take care never to set azaleas too deep. The top of the root ball should be at the surface of the ground, or slightly higher if planting in heavy clay soil. Leave plenty of space around the plant so it won't be overshadowed by larger or faster-growing plants.

7. Mulch azaleas to preserve moisture and discourage weeds. Use about three inches of airy mulch—pine or hardwood bark, pecan or peanut hulls, or wood chips.

8. Water azaleas at least once each week if it doesn't rain.

9. Feed azaleas twice each year—once immediately after bloom and once about a month later. Use a fertilizer packaged especially for azaleas.

10. Although very little pruning is necessary beyond removing deadwood and, possibly, to shape the shrub, prune after flowering and before flower buds form in summer to fall.

NATIVE AZALEAS FROM SEED

Seed from native azaleas germinates readily, but plants started in spring may be insufficiently mature to make it through a first winter. For this reason, plants from seed that is collected in fall and sown in late winter have the best chance of survival.

---

part shade; rich, moist, acid soil. Tends to form thickets with age.

Species: June-blooming Texas azalea (*R. oblongifolium*) is very similar. Where it grows wild—Texas, Arkansas, and Oklahoma—it should be used; elsewhere, the swamp azalea is a better, hardier choice. *R. viscosum* var. *montanum* is a low-growing form.

Cultivars: 'Lemon Drop Viscosum' (rare yellow), 'Pink Mist' (pink)

RHODODENDRON Evergreen rhododendrons
ERICACEAE Heath family

In old stories in which the hero is secretly a prince, it is his regal bearing and his noble character that give him away. And so it is with the evergreen rhododendrons. They are aristocrats no matter where they grow, as noble on a mountainside as they are standing as sentinels at the gates of a grand estate.

Some of the first American shrubs sent to Europe, they gained instant acceptance. And, unlike many other natives, they also found acceptance at home. In the 18th century, John Bartram grew them in Philadelphia and it was probably he who sent *R. maximum* to the English Quaker Peter Collinson, the most acquisitive plant collector of his day. George Washington grew them at Mount Vernon. Thomas Jefferson grew them at Monticello and included "Dwarf Rose Bay" in the list of Virginia's plants in his *Notes on the State of Virginia.*

In the wild, native rhododendrons favor cool, well-drained sites on hillsides or in the mountains. Near the summit of Mount Laconte on the North Carolina–Tennessee border, hikers are rewarded with a fantastic sight Carolina rhododendrons as far as the eye can see. Far more accessible are the Catawba rhododendrons that dot the slopes of the Alleghenies. You can see their deep green against the tawny forest floor from the Pennsylvania Turnpike.

The five rhododendrons included here range from the rosebay, which grows to the height of a medium tree, to the 5-foot-tall, heat-loving Chapman's rhododendron. In between are two very similar six-footers, the Carolina and Piedmont rhododendrons, and the Catawba, which grows to about 10 feet high and wide.

Rhododendron carolinianum Carolina rhododendron

May at Garden in the Woods in Framingham, Massachusetts, presents a celebration of bloom and scent that looks like the last scene

Carolina rhododendron (Rhododendron carolinianum)

of a Disney fairy tale; you can almost see Cinderella and the Prince driving off in their golden carriage while all the trees and flowers bloom their heads off in vicarious joy. The tidy, deep green Carolina rhododendrons, which lend structure to plantings along the paths, cover themselves with neat, 3-inch flower balls in shades of white to rose to mauve-purple in the midst of foamflowers, roseshell and pinkshell azaleas, and woodland phloxes. Compared with its relatives, Carolina rhododendron is neater, finer in texture, and more compact in habit. In gardens, it is lovely in a shrub border with deciduous azaleas and fothergillas.

Origin: Slopes of the Blue Ridge Mountains and Smoky Mountains of North Carolina and Tennessee
Flower: Usually pink or purplish rose and sometimes white; individually look like those of an Asian azalea but are borne in ball trusses, 3 to 4 inches in diameter. They bloom in May.
Foliage: Nice dark, matte green, leathery, elliptical leaves
Hardiness: Zones 5 to 8 (possibly hardier)
Height: To 6 feet
Regions: Northeast, Midwest, Northwest, Mid-Atlantic, higher elevations in the South
Landscape use: Shrub border, specimen
Culture: Moist, rich, acid soil with good drainage; bright shade or filtered sunlight
Varieties: R. *carolinianum* var. *album* (white)
Cultivars: R. *carolinianum* is one of the parents of the P.J.M. hybrids.
Propagation: Seed

Rhododendron catawbiense Catawba rhododendron

Big Catawba rhododendron has lustrous, leathery, dark evergreen leaves and bold flower heads of a kind of lilac-purple-pink it shares with garden phlox, *Geranium maculatum,* and other unimproved plants of lusty disposition. Perhaps because it is so common, people complain about this color, but I find it attractive as long as it does not clash with the plants growing around it. There are plenty of cultivars, and a white variety for those who disdain this mother-of-all-pinks.

Origin: Mountain slopes from West Virginia to Alabama
Flower: Big ball truss of lilac purple flowers in May
Foliage: Lustrous, leathery, dark green leaves
Hardiness: Zones 4 to 8
Height: To 10 feet by 10 feet
Regions: Parts of the Northeast, Mid-Atlantic, parts of the South, Lower Midwest, Northwest
Landscape use: Shrub border, screen, informal hedge, specimen
Culture: High, bright shade or dappled sun; moist, rich, acid soil that is well drained
Varieties: R. *catawbiense* var. *album* (white)
Cultivars: Many, many cultivars, including 'Roseum Elegans' (large, rosy purple) and 'America' (large, red)
Propagation: Seed, cuttings

Rhododendron chapmanii Chapman's rhododendron

Chapman's rhododendron looks like a cross between a wild azalea and a rhododendron. Medium green, lustrous, wavy leaves, the size of tablespoons, are evergreen on an upright shrub. In May (in Maryland), pink, freckled flowers on short tubes are

Catawba rhododendron (Rhododendron catawbiense)

Chapman's rhododendron (Rhododendron chapmanii)

borne in 4-inch balls. From a small area of the piney woods of North Florida, Chapman's rhododendron stands apart as a rhodie that can take the heat of the South. It thrives in my Zone 7 garden as well. Its name honors Alvan Wentworth Chapman (1809–1899), who introduced the pale grass pink and the sedge *Cyperus retrorsus,* both found in northern Florida. Rare Chapman's rhododendron has been placed on the list of federally endangered plants. To ensure that the plant you buy has been nursery-propagated, nurseries need a permit, so check your sources carefully.

Origin: Coastal northern Florida

Flower: Pink flowers with short tubes

Foliage: Small, leathery, lustrous, wavy evergreen leaves

Hardiness: Zones 7 (with protection) to 9

Height: To 5 feet

Regions: South, Lower Midwest, parts of Mid-Atlantic, Northwest

Landscape use: Fine-textured, heat-tolerant rhododendron for southern gardens; shrub border, woodland garden

Culture: High, bright shade; acid, well-drained soil

Cultivar: 'Chapmanii Wonder' (x *R. dauricum,* heat-tolerant)

Propagation: Seeds; cuttings from tender wood with no hormone, no fertilizer

Rhododendron maximum Rosebay rhododendron

Once, hiking on Tray Mountain in northern Georgia in mid-June, I came upon a rosebay rhododendron so huge that from a distance, I mistook it for a bull bay magnolia. It was probably 30 feet tall and bore a discreet few balls of white flowers—possibly because it grew in deep shade. Shade had not thinned the foliage but probably had discouraged the production of more flowers.

Of rosebay rhododendron, Hal Bruce wrote that it was once "collected by the millions for estate planting." It is easy to imagine one of these great, dark, stately shrubs at the gate of a Gatsbyesque mansion in the Hamptons. Leaves are deep green and have a satiny sheen, like a flapper's party dress.

Rosebays have a reputation for great shade tolerance, cold-hardiness, and for patiently enduring other unpleasant extremes of weather. Judging from a pair of very young plants growing on a north slope in my garden, they are slow growers.

Origin: Mountain slopes from New England to Georgia and Alabama

Flower: A ball of white flowers, lightly freckled green, in June

Foliage: Long, to 8 to 10 inches, dark, satiny green

Hardiness: Zones 3 to 7

Height: To 30 feet, but usually 15 feet

Regions: Northeast, Mid-Atlantic, South, Midwest

Landscape use: Large shrub, evergreen tree

Culture: Light to full shade; rich, moist, well-drained, acid soil

Form: There is a purple-flowered form.

Cultivars: 'Summer Glow' (red buds, pink flowers), 'Red River' (bright red), and 'Summer Solace' (large white flowers) are derived in part from *R. maximum.*

Propagation: Seed, cuttings

Rhododendron minus Piedmont rhododendron

In a family of large, rather weighty relatives, Piedmont rhododendron is small in stature and leaf and quick in growth. Seedlings planted three years ago now measure 15 to 18 inches high, while seedlings of giant rosebay rhododendron, which eventually reaches 35 feet, planted at the same time, measure a mere 3 to 5 inches tall.

Piedmont rhododendron's relatively small, leathery, almost olive green leaves resemble those of *Kalmia.* Its open habit reveals reddish stems that bring out the pure pink of the flowers, which appear in small clusters in June.

Origin: Mountain slopes of Tennessee, North Carolina to Alabama

Flower: 2- to 3-inch balls of small, magenta pink flowers in June

Foliage: Leathery; green tinges maroon with cold weather

Hardiness: Zones 6 to 8

Height: To 6 feet

*Piedmont rhododendron (*Rhododendron minus*)*

Regions: South, Mid-Atlantic, Northwest, parts of Northeast, Midwest
Landscape use: Shrub border, woodland garden
Culture: Bright shade to dappled sun; moist, acid, well-drained soil
Propagation: Seeds, cuttings

RHUS Sumac

ANACARDIACEAE Cashew family

"In my mind," wrote horticulturist Michael Dirr about *Rhus aromatica,* "this shrub is something of a second class citizen but I have bumped into hundreds over the years and cannot remember any that were offensive." The same may be said for other species of the genus *Rhus.* In many of our minds, the sumacs are not quite up to snuff—mainly because they grow too easily everywhere and especially because they sucker vigorously. Ubiquitous along highways, the deciduous sumacs—staghorn, shining, and smooth—are familiar sights from the East Coast as far west as British Columbia and Arizona. And like a great, unruly mob, they are hard to tell apart unless one takes the time to examine them closely—their leaves and stems. Shining sumac has "wings" along the stem connecting the compound leaves; staghorn sumac's young stems are fuzzy, and those of smooth sumac are smooth.

Absolutely spectacular in large plantings, in fall all three blaze scarlet and crimson, an effect that is stunning in contrast with tan native grasses. In winter, their bare limbs are like sculpture with a rhythmic logic that is pleasing to pass by. Seen at first at a distance as a dense

and complex whole, close up, they are composed of independent plants that grow bent and stretched and never crossing or touching to accommodate neighbors politely. Eventually, a thicket of sumacs fits together like a three-dimensional puzzle.

Sometimes, one sees what appear to be dwarf forms, but these were probably mowed earlier in the season along with the grass. It always makes me wonder what an annual bush hogging would do to a large planting, because they are so bright and attractive as low shrubs peeking out from amidst the grasses. The cultivar 'Laciniata', with exquisitely cut leaves, makes a splendid specimen. Its fall color is bright orange.

The fragrant sumac (*R. aromatica*) always strikes me as well groomed, perhaps because of its vague aroma of mouthwash, but also because it is a much smaller plant than the staghorn, shining, or smooth sumac, although, like them, it too, will eventually sucker into masses. The fragrant sumac is one of the shrubs recommended for the Upper Midwest by Professor Hasselkus of the University of Wisconsin. However, it lacks the spatial cooperation that gives the other sumac colonies their sculptural quality and grows more shrubbily, with stems interlocked and crossed. Its leaves resemble slightly those of poison ivy (long classified as *Rhus taxodium,* now *Toxicodendron radicans*) and are a whimsical addition to a bouquet, especially in fall, when they turn orange. There is, I have read, a cultivar 'Green Globe' that is said to become a round shrub, and another, 'Grow Low', which is a ground cover in my garden.

Two western sumacs, littleleaf or desert sumac (*R. microphylla*) and threeleaf sumac, squawbush, or

*Cutleaf sumac (*Rhus typhina *'Laciniata') at Wave Hill*

Rhus

Name	Origin	Flower	Foliage	Zones	Height	Regions	Landscape Use
Rhus aromatica Fragrant sumac	Ontario to Minnesota, Florida, Texas	Yellow catkin, March	Medium green; turns orange in fall	3 to 9	To 6 ft	North America	Massing, banks, sunny shrub border
Rhus copallina Shining sumac	Eastern U.S.	Chartreuse panicles, July, red fall fruit	Lustrous, dark green, compound leaves, winged on leaf stem in fall	4 to 9	To 25 ft	Eastern North America	Highways, large-scale plantings, banks
Rhus glabra Smooth sumac	Atlantic Coast to British Columbia, south to Florida, Arizona	Chartreuse, June, red fall fruit	Matte green on smooth stem, scarlet in fall	2 to 9	To 15 ft	North America	Highways, large-scale plantings, banks
Rhus integrifolia Lemonade berry	Coastal southern California	White to pink, February/March	Evergreen, thick, leathery	8b to 10	3 to 9 ft	Southern California, mild, not too dry California	Screening, hillside erosion control, inland gardens
Rhus microphylla Littleleaf sumac, desert sumac	Southwest, northern Mexico	Yellow clusters, March/April, orange clusters	Tiny compound leaves emerge red in fall	6 to 7	To 8 ft	Southwest, Mountain	Massing, dry banks
Rhus ovata Sugarbush	Santa Barbara County to northern Baja	Dense spikes of cream and pink flowers	Simple, leathery, cool gray-green, folded into "taco shell"	Below 4,000 ft, 8b to 10	8 to 15 ft	Southern California	Hedge, screen, specimen
Rhus trilobata Threeleaf sumac, lemita, squawbush, skunkbush	Missouri, Texas, west to Washington, California	Yellow clusters, orange-red berries	Dark green, lobed, aromatic, turn orange-red in fall	5(?) to 9	To 8 ft	Western North America, Midwest	Shrub border, specimen, banks, screen
Rhus typhina Staghorn sumac	Eastern North America	Chartreuse panicles, red fall fruit	Medium green, compound leaves turn scarlet in fall, fuzzy stems	3 to 9	To 25 ft	Eastern North America	Highways, large-scale plantings, banks

skunkbush (*R. trilobata*), are drought-tolerant and used in Xeriscaping. Littleleaf sumac's very tiny leaflets are an adaptation that helps this species resist drought. Leaves

Bright orange fall color of sumac (Rhus)

and small yellow blooms in March/April give littleleaf sumac a very fine texture.

The threeleaf sumac's lobed, dark green leaves, says New Mexico designer, author, and nurserywoman Judith Phillips, "have a clean, crisp look; the plant is aromatic but one of the common names, 'skunkbush,' is a gross exaggeration." In summer, threeleaf sumac bears showy orange berries that are sometimes crushed and mixed with water and sugar to make a lemonade-type drink. In fall, the leaves turn bright red. Different plants and conditions result in a height range from 4 to 10 feet with equal or greater spread, adds Ms. Phillips.

Of the evergreen species of *Rhus,* the most coastal, characteristically dotting the southern California hills, is the lemonade berry (*Rhus integrifolia*). Typically darker green than the rest, with reddish stems, this medium- to large-sized shrub takes pruning well to become a specimen shrub or hedge. Eliza Earle at the Theodore Payne Foundation says there are three lemonade berries in a mass planting 20 feet across and 7 feet tall. Recently, it took the groundskeeper a full week to thin and shape this

Culture	Propagate	Comment
Adaptable; sun to part shade, suckers	Seed, cuttings	Leaves resemble poison ivy, good fall color. Cultivars: 'Gro-Low' (prostrate), 'Green Globe' (rounded habit).
Adaptable; sun, light shade	Seed, cuttings	Handsome foliage, vigorous spreader
Adaptable; sun, light shade	Seed, cuttings	Hardy, excellent fall color, interesting growth habit in colonies. Cultivar: 'Laciniata' (cut leaf, scarlet fall color).
Full sun to part shade, occasional water (once a month)	Seeds, cuttings	Great screen, naturalizes
Adaptable; sun, drought-tolerant, give occasional deep watering	Seed, cuttings	Suckers to broad thickets, fine texture
Full sun to part shade, drought-tolerant, needs good drainage, takes occasional water	Seed	Easy! Good for dry gardens, erosion control
Adaptable; sun, drought-tolerant	Seed, cuttings	Height varies with water, great fall color. Cultivars: 'Big Horn' (large), 'Autumn Amber' (prostrate).
Adaptable; sun, light shade	Seed, cuttings	Excellent fall color, interesting growth habit in colonies. Cultivar: 'Laciniata' (cut leaves, orange fall color).

exuberent mass of foliage. It was worth it. Now these lemonade berries form a magnificent screen and backdrop for a partially shaded spot in the entrance garden.

Sugarbush (*Rhus ovata*) is a familiar component of the chaparral community, seen on the hillsides of southern California along with its cousin laurel sumac. Eliza Earle, a passionate and experienced California gardener, cherishes it all the more because it belongs in that landscape. Typical of many members of this plant community, sugarbush, she says, is drought-tolerant, fire adapted, and deep rooted. On her property, a large self-sown volunteer has clung to the edge of the hillside for 20 years in a spot so steep she'd need a ladder to reach it! Nevertheless, she finds that this "wild one" has handsome and civilized features that one can welcome into the garden. She says that it maintains a good rounded shape and pleasing branch structure, and the gray-green leaves and dusty pink clusters of flowers from a distance give a wonderful Impressionist view of light, texture, and color.

Eliza Earle and Judith Phillips helped make up the chart above.

*Lemonade berry hedge (*Rhus integrifolia*) and sugarbush (*Rhus ovata*) at Santa Barbara Botanic Garden*

RIBES AUREUM Golden currant
SAXIFRAGACEAE Saxifrage family

"These currants (when dried) become the best raisins ever eaten," says Gail Haggard of Plants of the Southwest, "if the birds don't beat you to them." Pretty golden currant bears fragrant, golden flowers in spring, followed by purple-black currants that can be left on the shrub to dry. Small, three-lobed leaves turn bright shades of scarlet in fall.

In nature golden currant is often found on streamsides. In the garden, it thrives with regular water. Described by horticulturist Hal Bruce as "softer and better than forsythia," golden currant is the prettiest kind of edible landscaping, whether you feed the birds or net off the fruits for yourself.

Origin: Washington and Montana to California
Flower: Racemes of fragrant, yellow flowers in spring, followed by purple-black fruits
Foliage: Small, bright green, three-lobed leaves turn scarlet in fall.
Hardiness: Probably Zones 3 to 8
Height: To 6 feet
Regions: Northwest, Mountain, Southwest, California
Landscape use: Shrub border
Culture: Sun, shade, good drainage, tolerates summer drought but looks better with irrigation
Varieties: *R. aureum* var. *gracillimum,* from central and southern California, is far more tolerant of drought. Buffalo currant, *R. odoratum,* from the Plains, is similar in appearance to *R. aureum* but has larger flowers.

Shrubs

RIBES SANGUINEUM Red-flowering currant
SAXIFRAGACEAE Saxifrage family

This elegant deciduous shrub, first introduced to England in the 19th century, is now widely used in cool temperate gardens around the world. In early spring, the reddish purple flowers emerge before the leaves in graceful, pendant clusters at the ends of the branches; the dusty gray fruits persist through fall.

Several cultivars are in the trade; best known are the deep red ones such as 'Atrorubens' or the pure whites 'Albidum' and 'Iceberg'. In the garden, they do well in partial shade. They are especially attractive as espaliers. In the wild, they are found in open woods, mostly on the west side of the Cascades. This elegant currant does get over the mountains into Douglas fir–grand fir forests in Washington and Oregon, adding its cheerful deep pink to their evergreens.

Origin: Open woods from British Columbia to California

Flower: Rose red flower clusters in April, before leaves, followed by black fruit

Foliage: Three-lobed round leaves are downy, textured.

Hardiness: Zones 6 to 8

Height: To 10 feet

Regions: Pacific Northwest, northern California

Landscape use: Shrub border, good espalier plant

Culture: Adaptable; tolerant of sun and shade but leggier without good light; tolerant of summer water

Species: Pink flowering currant (*R. sanguineum* var. *glutinosum*), from Del Norte to San Luis Obispo, is more drought-tolerant, better suited to warmer, interior parts of California. Chaparral currant (*Ribes malvaceum*) tolerates much more sun, heat, and drought than *R. sanguineum*. The foliage is somewhat grayer, stickier, more aromatic. The plants flower earlier—usually November/December—and have pendulous racemes of pink- to rose-colored flowers.

Cultivars: 'Pulborough Scarlet' (deep red flowers), 'Spring Snow' (white flowers), 'White Icicle' (white)

RIBES VIBURNIFOLIUM Evergreen currant, Catalina perfume
SAXIFRAGACEAE Saxifrage family

Good-looking the year around, evergreen currant is outstanding for use as an evergreen ground cover under mature oaks that require summer drought. Easy to care for, it needs pruning only to keep it trim by removing the odd long, arching stem. On the coast, evergreen currant grows in either sun or part

Red-flowering currant (Ribes sanguineum)

shade, but inland the foliage will burn in full sun. It is easy to grow in most gardens.

Origin: Coastal sage scrub from Santa Catalina Island, San Diego County, to northern Baja California

Flower: Pink-maroon flowers in upright clusters in January and February (in southern California), followed by interesting but subtle red fruits

Foliage: Shiny, roundish, dark green, 2-inch evergreen leaves, aromatic

Hardiness: Zones 8 to 10

Height: Mounding, 3 to 4 feet high by 8 feet wide

Region: Pacific states

Landscape use: Ground cover, and one of the few plants that thrive under coast live oaks, which die from overwatering; it can also tolerate one- to two-times-a-month irrigation.

Culture: Part to full shade, drought-tolerant, tolerates occasional water.

Propagation: Cuttings, rooted stems, seed

ROSA Rose
ROSACEAE Rose family

The most-grown flower in the country, the rose is probably also the best-known flower in the world; it is native to all parts of the North Temperate Zone and has figured significantly and beautifully throughout history. The rose was known to the ancient Minoans (c. 2500 B.C.), and to Confucius (551 to 479 B.C.), and the Romans cultivated roses in their greenhouses. Thousands of years of cultivation have brought hybrids to a high art. They are elegant and sophisticated.

Compared with high-strung hybrid teas, native roses

Evergreen currant (Ribes viburnifolium) *at Rancho Santa Ana, Claremont, California*

are like wild ponies. Generally tough, always fascinating, they will suceed pretty much on their own. Endearingly simple, these are the floppy-petaled roses of country fields. One of these shrubs is the perfect accent on a picket fence.

There are probably more than 100 species of wild roses in North America, not counting the naturalized ones tomato rose (*R. rugosa*) and memorial rose (*R. wichuraiana*), which are often taken for natives but are not. All of those listed here are single and usually pink, although white forms exist. Showy rose hips and fall color add to their appeal. Except for the swamp rose, which tolerates wet soil, all do best in sun with medium-moist soil.

As a further boon to those who love roses but cherish relaxation, native roses thrive without the sprays and supports needed to keep hybrid teas happy. (See *Rosa* chart, pages 294–295.)

SAMBUCUS CANADENSIS Elderberry
CAPRIFOLIACEAE Honeysuckle family

Elderberry wine and jelly belong to an American tradition that was already becoming old-fashioned when we were young. In addition to producing berries, elderberry is lovely to look upon in early summer, when large, creamy flower heads, looking very like oversized viburnum blossoms, adorn this generous shrub. (People have been known to make elderberry flower fritters.) It is no wonder this shrub helped fill larders all over the country. It has a huge range—from Nova Scotia west to Manitoba and south to Florida and Texas. And where it ends, blue elderberry (*S. caerulea*) takes over. It is always prudent, when plants have a vast range, to seek out local material that performs well under local conditions. Some elderberries are tolerant of wet soils, and some are hardier or more heat-tolerant than others.

Not tame little landscape shrubs, fast-growing elderberries are best in naturalized areas, at the edges of meadows and woodland. Fast growing, very hardy, and relatively pest-free, elderberries can be rejuvenated by cutting them to the ground. When growing them for berry harvest, the only real problem is the birds, who love them too.

Origin: Nova Scotia to Manitoba and south to Florida and Texas

Flower: White, flat clusters in June/July, followed by edible purple-black berries in August/September

Foliage: Dense, coarse, compound leaves are bright green when they emerge, turn fleeting yellow in fall.

Hardiness: Zones 3 to 9

Height: To 12 feet

Regions: Northeast, Midwest, Mid-Atlantic, South, parts of Mountain

*Pasture rose (*Rosa carolina*)*

*Prairie rose (*Rosa setigera*)*

Rosa

Name	Origin	Flower	Foliage	Zones	Height	Regions	Landscape Use
Rosa arkansana Arkansas rose	New York to Alberta, south to Texas, Colorado	1 in, pink to red	Small, toothed leaves in leaflets	Probably 4 to 8	3 ft	North America	Ground cover
Rosa carolina Pasture rose	Nova Scotia to Minnesota, south to Florida, Nebraska, Texas	2 in, rich pink, in summer, red hips in fall, fragrant	Small, toothed leaves in leaflets	5 to 9	3 ft	Eastern North America	Borders
Rosa nutkana Nutka rose, Sitka rose	California to Arkansas and Rockies	2 to 3 in, pink to rose, red hips	Shrubby, medium green	6 to 9	3 to 6 ft	Western North America	Borders
Rosa palustris Swamp rose	Nova Scotia to Minnesota, south to Florida, Arkansas	2 in, dark pink, in summer, red hips in fall	Toothed leaves in leaflets	4 to 8	To 8 ft	Moist soils of North America	Pond side, border
Rosa setigera Prairie rose	Ontario to Kansas, south to Texas, Florida	2 in, fragrant, pink, late summer, red hips	Oval, toothed leaves	4 to 8	To 15 ft	North America	Leaner/climber, border
Rosa virginiana Virginia rose	Newfoundland to Delaware	2 in, pale pink, in summer, scarlet hips	Neat, dark green, toothed leaves	4 to 7	To 6 ft	Northeastern North America	Border, informal hedge

Landscape use: Berry gardening, naturalized areas

Culture: Sun to part shade, medium to wet soil, very adaptable. Cut down to rejuvenate; forms thickets; grows fast!

Species: Blue elderberry (*S. caerulea*), from the West Coast, is taller, with dark blue, edible berries; it tolerates a medium to dry place. Red elderberry (*S. callicarpa*) is a tall shrub with red berries.

Cultivars: Many, including 'Adonis' (large fruits)

Propagation: Seed (warm/cool stratify), cuttings

SERENOA REPENS Saw palmetto
PALMAE Palm family

"This plant," says Florida native plant enthusiast Joe Lawson, "is making a leap in popularity, even though cattle ranchers will laugh at you for growing what they see as worthless 'scrub.'" Saw palmetto is being grown as slow-growing sculpture by gardeners who savor its multiple charms in their hot southern gardens, despite a few sideways glances. Part of its popularity stems from a renewed appreciation of Florida's native plants and, perhaps, nostalgia for the way Florida used to look when bright green saw palmettos poked up like stars in tawny rivers of wire grass.

Extremely slow growing, saw palmetto can gain tree form, but its big, round spokes-of-a-wheel leaves are most often seen close to the ground—either because an area has been burned off, because the trunk has not developed aboveground, or because it is twisted and recumbent along the ground. The huge leaves can measure over a yard across. They are "armed." In botanical parlance, this means they have spines along the edges. Hence their name.

Especially when the stem is recumbent, hard-edged saw palmetto contrasts with a soft, billowing plant such as Muhly grass or beach sunflower, which relaxes along the ground.

Elderberry (Sambucus canadensis)

Culture	Propagate	Comment
Sun, spreads	Seed, cuttings	Adaptable
Sun, well-drained soil	Seed, cuttings	Delicate, forms thicket, fall color
Sun, good drainage	Seed, cuttings	Very showy flowers, fruits
Sun, moist soil	Seed, cuttings	Tall, tough, needs constant moisture
Sun, moderate moisture	Seed, cuttings	Needs plenty of room, suckers
Sun, moderate moisture	Seed, cuttings	Glossy foliage, fall color, red stems, adaptable

Saw palmetto (Serenoa repens)

Origin: Piney woods of the southeastern United States, Florida Keys to South Carolina

Flower: Very attractive ivory white flowers in late spring and early summer, fragrant, from 1 to 3 feet long

Foliage: Green to yellow-green, spined, nearly circular leaves, fan-shaped, slender 4- to 5-foot stems

Hardiness: Zones 8 to 10

Height: To 10 feet, but not often because trunk reclines

Regions: Coastal South Carolina, Florida

Landscape use: Accent, shrub mass

Culture: Prefers sandy, well-drained soil, but tolerates a range of habitats dunes (salt-tolerant), hammocks, scrub, flat woods

Propagation: Seed (very slow), rhizomes (very tricky)

SOPHORA TOMENTOSA Necklace pod
LEGUMINOSAE Pea family

It is possible to have both flowers and fruits of the necklace pod at the same time. Sulphur yellow flowers are sweet pea–shaped and open from bottom to top on spikes at the tips of the branches during warm weather at any time of the year. The flowers are lovely, but the really intriguing part of this tree is the way the wonderful long, showy pods drape the branches like necklaces.

Its height varies. Florida designer Joe Lawson says, "Along the beach, with the wind whipping it, the necklace pod might remain at three or four feet. With shelter, it can grow to ten or fifteen feet."

Origin: Florida, Florida Keys, West Indies, a plant of warm coastal areas

Flower: Sulphur yellow pea flowers on 4- to 16-inch spikes at branch tips develop long, very showy pods containing very hard, poisonous seeds.

Foliage: There is much variation. Twelve-inch compound leaves are composed of elliptic to oval leaflets—often covered with a silvery pubescence.

Hardiness: Zones 9(?) to 10

Height: 3 to 15 feet

Region: Warm coastal areas

Landscape use: Specimen, shrub masses, hedge

Culture: Well-drained soil and sun (it may get a sooty mold if grown in shade); flowers on new growth

Propagation: Seed

Necklace pod (Sophora tomentosa)

Silky camellia (Stewartia malacodendron)
(Jessie Harris photo)

STEWARTIA MALACODENDRON Silky camellia
THEACEAE Tea family

Discovered near Williamsburg and sent to Linneaus by Virginian John Clayton (who was immortalized by Linnaeus for another botanical discovery, *Claytonia*), the silky camellia is rare in the wild and is almost, but not quite, impossible to find in nurseries. Yet, silky camellia remains a connoisseur's plant that truly deserves wider popularity. Horticulturist Dick Bir reports that silky camellia's seeds need both warm and cool stratification for success and that cuttings are problematical—both traits that make its propagation troublesome for growers.

Having heard of its hard-to-get reputation, I was astonished to see silky camellias treated like ordinary, mortal ornamentals at the Dabney Nursery outside Memphis. I bought two and put one into full shade and the other in a shady place that receives morning sun. This it shares with phacelias in the spring and scutellarias later on. Predictably, the one with morning sun and blue floral company has grown to twice the size of the other in two years.

These plants draw attention even in winter, when their zigzagging growth pattern and lightly striped cinnamon-colored bark are distinctive. Mine finally bloomed, in rows of big, waxy, white cups that open out flat each morning around a fancy center of long, dark purple stamens.

Origin: Coastal plain from Delmarva to Florida and Louisiana

Flower: 4 inches, waxy, white (sometimes streaked with cherry red), opening flat to reveal a prominent dark purple center, in May/June

Foliage: Nice clean green, deciduous leaves

Hardiness: Zones 7 to 9

Height: To 12 feet

Regions: South, Mid-Atlantic

Landscape use: Specimen, shrub border

Culture: Moist, part shade; slightly acid (pH 5.0–6.0) soil

Species: Mountain camellia (*S. ovata*), with slightly smaller, later flowers, is hardier (Zone 5).

Propagation: Seed (warm/cold stratified); tender wood cuttings in early spring with no hormone, no fertilizer

TAGETES LEMMONI Mountain marigold
COMPOSITAE Sunflower family

Mountain marigold is a medium-sized shrub that grows wider than tall, with finely divided, smooth, soft green foliage. Tiny glands on the underside of the leaves release a pungent citrus aroma when they are rubbed, making pruning an exercise in aroma therapy.

Twice a year—in spring and again in late fall—mountain marigold literally covers itself with 1-inch golden yellow daisy flowers that attract butterflies. In fact, when it blooms, it announces butterfly season.

Origin: Arizona

Flower: 1-inch yellow gold daisy flowers in masses, spring and fall

Foliage: Glabrous, finely divided, soft green foliage, very aromatic

Hardiness: Zones 8b to 10

Height: 24 to 30 inches high by 48 inches wide

Regions: Southwest, southern California

Landscape use: Cascading wall plant, edging, rock garden

Culture: When it looks ragged, let it go to seed or prune it one-half to two-thirds back. It volunteers from seed but is not a nuisance.

Species: It is closely related to Tarahumara anise (*T. lucida*).

Propagation: Seed

TRICHOSTEMA LANATUM Woolly blue-curls
LABIATAE Mint family

Woolly blue-curls, with its striking flower spikes that positively glow purple and raspberry, stands as a rather erect, 4-foot-tall, evergreen, well-branched shrub. Its foliage releases a minty scent when brushed. The densely set woolly flower spikes appear in summer; their conspicuous arching stamens add to the beauty of the flowers.

It is a lovely, long-lived, and long-flowering addition

Woolly blue-curls (Trichostema lanatum)

to a dryland border and can share a bed with St. Catherine's lace or penstemons.

Origin: Dry coast ranges in California, from Monterey County to San Diego County

Flower: Spikes of densely set woolly flowers in glowing violet and blue

Foliage: Rosemary-like, yellowish green

Hardiness: Zones 8 (possibly 7) to 10

Height: 4 feet

Regions: California, Southwest

Landscape use: Beautiful specimen plants; hillsides, banks

Culture: Full sun, good drainage, no additional water once established

Propagation: Cuttings

VACCINIUM OVATUM Evergreen huckleberry, California huckleberry

ERICACEAE Heath family

Evergreen huckleberry's rich, dark foliage and edible fruits make it a double-duty ground cover. Like salal, it hails from western open forest habitats, from redwood country north, mostly along the coast to the Olympic Peninsula. Its smallish evergreen leaves are often bronzy red when new, reminding one a bit of common boxwood but for their deeper, more lustrous green. Twigs are tipped with clusters of white flowers followed by many edible, purplish black fruits.

Evergreen huckleberry thrives in cool, moist, well-drained, acid soil. It is slow growing.

Origin: British Columbia to California

Flower: Waxy, pinkish white flowers in April/May are followed by edible fruits, long used in pies, jams.

Foliage: Handsome, toothed, dark green oval leaves are evergreen and used by florists.

Hardiness: Zones 7 to 9

Height: To 8 feet

Regions: Pacific Northwest, coastal and northern California; mountains and areas with summer moisture, coastal fog

Landscape use: Shrub border with other ericaceous plants

Culture: Moist, well-drained, acid soil in part shade

VIBURNUM

CAPRIFOLIACEAE Honeysuckle family

Of the more than 200 species of viburnum worldwide, at least 11 from the American continent bear attractive white to cream flower clusters on the ends of their branches in spring. These are followed in summer by red, blue, purple, or black fruits, unfortunately or fortunately—depending upon your point of view—eaten rather quickly by birds.

All deciduous native viburnums have some fall color, though it varies from the scarlet of American cranberry to the dusky rose-purple of the maple leaf viburnum. In the slow turning to their final colors, the berries, too, can put on a show. It is not unusual to see, for example, a possum haw viburnum with both rose pink and dusty blue berries.

Viburnums range in size from medium to large shrubs to small trees that are just the right size for gardens. When correctly sited, they are remarkably pest-free and healthy. Cross-pollination improves fruiting. (See *Viburnum* chart, on pages 298–299.)

American cranberry bush (Viburnum trilobum)

Shrubs

297

Viburnum

Name	Origin	Flower	Foliage	Zones	Height	Regions	Landscape Use
Viburnum acerifolium Mapleleaf viburnum, dockmackie	New Brunswick to Minnesota, south to North Carolina	Yellow-white, flat head in mid-June, blue-black berries	Light green, maple leaf turns pink-purple	4(3?), to 7	5 to 6 ft	Eastern North America	Woodland, deep shade
Viburnum alnifolium Hobblebush, moose ears, wayfaring tree	New Brunswick to Michigan, south to North Carolina	White, flat cluster in May, red to black berries	Very large, green heart-shaped leaves, downy beneath	3 to 7	To 10 ft	Eastern North America	Woodland, shady garden
Viburnum cassinoides Witherod viburnum	Newfoundland, Minnesota, south to North Carolina	Creamy, flat clusters, June, blue-black berries	Lustrous oval leaves turn wine red, nice gray stems	3 to 8	To 8 ft	Eastern North America	Shrub border, specimen
Viburnum dentatum Arrowwood viburnum	New Brunswick to Florida, Texas	Showy white flower in June, blue berries	Round, toothed leaves turn crimson	4 to 8	To 10 ft	North America	Shrub border
Viburnum ellipticum Oregon viburnum	Open woods from Washington to California	Small white flowers, red berries	Toothed, oval leaves	6 to 8	To 8 ft	Northwest	Woodland garden
Viburnum lentago Nannyberry	New Brunswick to Mississippi, Georgia	White, flat clusters, May, black berries	Small, lustrous, oval leaves turn purple-red	3 to 8	To 20 ft	Eastern North America	Woodland edge, wildlife planting
Viburnum nudum Possum haw	Connecticut to Florida, Louisiana	Creamy clusters in June, purple-black berries	Lustrous, oval leaves turn mahogany	6 to 9	To 15 ft	Eastern North America	Shrub border, specimen
Viburnum obovatum Walter viburnum	Hammocks, swamps, of Florida, South Carolina	Heavy white bloom, in spring; red fruits turn black in fall	Neat, evergreen	7b, 8 to 10	To 12 ft	South	Hedge, specimen
Viburnum prunifolium Blackhaw	Connecticut to Wisconsin, Florida, Texas	White clusters in May; large blue black fruits are edible	Lustrous, oval leaves on stiff branches turn red in fall	4 to 9	To 15 ft	North America	Shrub border, small tree with training, large shrub
Viburnum rufidulum Blackhaw	Virginia to Florida	Flat, creamy clusters, dark blue berries	Glossy green leaves on stiff branches, turn bright red in fall	6 to 9	To 30 ft	South	Small tree, large shrub
Viburnum trilobum American cranberry	Northern North America	Creamy white clusters in late May, edible red berries	Maple leaves, turn orange-mahogany in fall	2 to 7	To 12 ft	Northern North America to Zone 7	Shrub border, screen, understory

Arrowwood viburnum (Viburnum dentatum)

VIGUIERA STENOLOBA Skeletonleaf goldeneye
COMPOSITAE Sunflower family

Skeletonleaf goldeneye, a mouthful of a common name, paints an accurate picture of this plant's yellow daisylike flowers, carried above the linear, lacy, bright green foliage throughout warm weather, making this an ideal plant for both small and large gardens. Arizona landscape architect Judy Mielke likes to group several plants in a flower garden, along a patio, or near the pool. Specialty nurseries will carry this plant, but as skeletonleaf goldeneye's charms become more widely known, it will be more freely available.

Origin: Texas into Mexico on desert plains, rocky slopes
Flower: Bright yellow daisy flowers in warm weather

Culture	Propagate	Comment
Medium to dry, part to deep shade	Cuttings	Bird plant, colors in shade, good understory plant, a northern plant
Moist, humusy, acid soil; shade; drooping stems root at tips	Cuttings	Thicket forming, understory plant with showy flowers, interesting leaves
Full sun, shade, very hardy, moist to wet soil	Cuttings	Excellent wildlife, butterfly plant; handsome foliage, very hardy, scented flower
Very adaptable, will take dry soil, grows fast, suckers	Cuttings	Showy flowers, good fall color, manageable size. Cultivars: 'Moonglow' (later, larger flowers), 'Chicago Lustre' (good foliage).
Sun to part shade; medium to moist, well-drained soil	Cuttings	Rare in trade, but worth growing for fruit and flowers
Very adaptable, seek local stock, thicket forming	Cuttings	Thicket forming, good wildlife plant, very hardy
Sun to part shade, well-drained to wet soil, adaptable	Cuttings	Southern counterpart of *V. cassinoides*, grows in wet or dry soil. Cultivar: 'Winterthur' (compact, superior).
Sun, shade, well-drained soil, adaptable	Cuttings	Good plant for the South, the only evergreen native
Sun to part shade, medium to dry soil, slow, tall growing	Cuttings	Edible "currant," takes dry soil, good crabapple substitute, a tree in the South, a shrub in the North
Sun to part shade, medium to dry soil, grows tall	Cuttings	Southern counterpart to *V. prunifolium,* good autumn color, some find its odor disagreeable
Thrives in sun, shade, in moist to boggy soil	Cuttings	Handsome combined with grasses. Cultivar: 'Phillips' (good-tasting berries), dwarf form (2 ft).

Foliage: Bright green, lacy foliage

Hardiness: Zones 8 to 10

Height: 3 feet tall by 3 feet wide

Region: Desert Southwest

Landscape use: Ground cover, flower garden

Culture: Sun; dry, well-drained soil

YUCCA

AGAVACEAE Agave family

" I would have great groups of Yucca standing up against the sky and others in the rock-face, and some bushes of this great Euphorbia and only a few other plants, all of rather large grey effect," wrote

*Blackhaw (*Viburnum rufidulum*)*

Gertrude Jekyll of her unfulfilled desire for a precipitous, rocky hillside in full sun. Never achieving her precipice, Miss Jekyll nonetheless combined yucca in the border with gray plants—stachys, santolina, lyme grass—and in the white garden with lilies and baby's breath.

Even with Gertrude Jekyll's stamp of approval, and even though *Yucca filamentosa* and *Yucca smalliana* are native to the Southeast, it took me years to warm to the idea of this genus in any landscape other than the Southwest. What finally did the trick was seeing Wolfgang Oehme's inspired use of Adam's needle with sedum 'Autumn Joy' and *Hypericum* at the Federal Reserve Garden in Washington, D.C. You either love or hate the flower stalk. To me it is distracting, but the presence of the sculptural evergreen leaves in the winter garden is wonderful. They are flat and stiffly held and look particularly nice in snow.

In the garden, yuccas are best combined with low-growing plants of contrasting density and texture.

Yucca

Name	Origin	Flower	Foliage	Zones	Height	Regions	Landscape Use
Yucca filamentosa Adam's needle	North Carolina to Florida and Mississippi	Waxy, cream-colored bells on tall 5-ft stalks	Stiff, green blades with hairy edges	4 to 9	To 3 ft	Eastern North America	Accent, massing
Yucca glauca Soapweed	South Dakota to New Mexico	Slender spike of white flowers in summer	Narrow, ¾-in gray leaves	3 to 8	To 30 in	Southwest, Mountain	Accent, massing
Yucca rupicola Twisted-leaf yucca	Texas	White to green on a 3-ft stalk	Blue-green old leaves twist	6 to 8(?)	To 2 ft	Southwest	Accent
Yucca smalliana Adam's needle	South Carolina to Florida and Mississippi	Creamy white flowers on 3-ft stalk	Evergreen, very stiff, upright leaves	5 to 9	To 4 ft	Eastern North America	Accent, massing, bank planting

Yucca *with 'Autumn Joy' sedums* (Wolfgang Oehme Design)

Erigeron, low-growing cultivars of threadleaf coreopsis, or evening primroses might be good companions.

The reproductive life of yuccas is as interesting as they are. Yuccas are pollinated by moths that fly from flower to flower, taking pollen from one, rolling it into a ball, then flying on to another flower to deposit both eggs and pollen ball. In this symbiotic relationship of insect and plant, moths do the work of pollinating flowers and yuccas provide food for the young moths to feed upon as seeds develop.

Of the many, many yuccas in North America, some garden-worthy species may be found in the chart above.

ZAMIA PUMILA (Z. FLORIDANA) Coontie, Florida arrowroot
ZAMIACEAE Cycad family

Very primitive plants with thick underground stems, coonties are fascinating evergreen shrubs for the lucky gardeners who live in climates warm enough to grow them. "Arrowroot" in one of the common names recalls their use as a starch by Native Americans. Coontie's leaves are leathery, evergreen, and fernlike and grow to about 3 feet long around a central crown, which holds the reproductive structures a slender green cone in males and a conelike fruiting organ in females, which looks like a cross between an orange and a giant squash but is called a megasporophyte.

Very adaptable, coonties grow from full sun all the way to deep shade. They are very drought-tolerant, but when stressed will drop all their leaves and then revive. Coonties are excellent as a ground cover for well-drained sites, as accent plants, and as low shrubs.

Palm Beach designer Joe Lawson says coonties are on the threatened plant list because the young plants are quicker to transplant from the wild than to grow from spores. Query your sources on this point before buying.
Origin: Florida pinelands and hammocks
Flower: Not a true flower, coontie has "megasporophytes" on dioecious plants.
Foliage: Dark, leathery, evergreen, frondlike leaves
Hardiness: Zones 9 to 10
Height: To 2 to 3 feet
Regions: Florida, West Indies
Landscape use: Accent, low shrub, ground cover
Culture: Sun to shade, well-drained soil, very drought-tolerant
Propagation: Seeds, division

Culture	Propagate	Comment
Sun, medium to dry soil with good drainage	Seeds, cuttings	Great winter presence, wide leaves
Sun, medium to dry soil, good drainage, cold-tolerant	Seeds, cuttings	Hardiest yucca, with very narrow, glaucous leaves, state flower of New Mexico
Sun, medium to dry soil, good drainage	Seeds, cuttings	Small, with interesting foliage
Sun, medium to dry soil, good drainage	Seeds, cuttings	Cultivar: 'Variegata' (creamy white stripes on leaf margins)

Variegated yucca (Yucca smalliana 'Variegata')

ZENOBIA PULVERULENTA Dusty zenobia
ERICACEAE Heath family

Recommended for the South by Bob McCartney, dusty zenobia, a member of the heath family, will also grow farther north. "Glaucous," the horticultural word used for gray-blue leaved plants, does not adequately describe the foliage of this striking little shrub. If you were to mix paint to color dusty zenobia's neat, oval leaves, you might begin with chartreuse and hints of pale turquoise, then lighten and mute the whole with white. "Dusty" in the common name refers to a matte, luminescent quality in the color. This makes the leaves look as though they were down-covered. In fact, they are smooth and almost leathery. The foliage contrasts with cinnamon-colored stems. In summer, fragrant bells the color of bridal satin hang from ends of the branches.

Origin: Pine barrens and moist, acid soils from Florida to the Carolinas along the coastal plain

Flower: Clusters of small, bell flowers, cream with pale turquoise stems, in June

Foliage: Smooth, bluntly serrated, oval leaves, which are a unique luminescent blue-green that in fall turns to creamy golden yellow dusted with raspberry; very late to drop. In warm climates, the foliage is semievergreen.

Hardiness: Zones 6 to 9

Height: Usually 3 to 4 feet, but rumored to reach 6 feet

Regions: South, Mid-Atlantic, Lower Midwest

Landscape use: Great small shrub for contrast; cutting; low, informal hedge

Culture: Moderate to moist, slightly acid soil (pH 5.0–6.0), good drainage. I have mine growing in dry full sun (where it prospers). Prune lightly to keep shapely.

Propagation: Seeds (gather pods in early fall and mash to extract seeds; sow on milled sphagnum), or very tender cuttings (choose plants with good leaf color)

Coontie (Zamia pumila), left, with wild olive, right

Tr

Over A GARDENING LIFETIME, YOU MAY BUY A FAIR NUMBER OF SHRUBS AND ALSO PURCHASE MANY, MANY HERBACEOUS PLANTS—PERENNIALS, ANNUALS, FERNS, AND GRASSES. BY COMPARISON, THE NUMBER OF TREES YOU ACTUALLY PLANT WILL BE VERY SMALL. AND YET NO OTHER PLANT WILL EXERT AS MUCH INFLUENCE ON THE DESIGN AND WELFARE OF A GARDEN.

THERE ARE REALLY TWO KINDS OF TREES: THOSE YOU PLANT AND THOSE YOU INHERIT WITH THE HOUSE. VERY LARGE TREES—OFTEN THE ONES ALREADY GROWING IN YOUR GARDEN—CAST SHADE OVER A LARGE AREA, AND THEIR MASSIVE ROOTS TAKE MOISTURE

OVERLEAF: *The slender leaves of honey mesquite cast dappled, but welcome, shade.*
ABOVE: *Diminutive fringe tree is large enough to shade a garden bench.*

AND NUTRIENTS FROM THE SOIL BELOW. THEY ARE WONDERFUL IF YOU HAVE THEM, BUT ALONG WITH THEIR VERY WELCOME SHADE, THEY IMPOSE RESTRICTIONS, AND YOU'LL HAVE TO GARDEN ACCORDINGLY.

THE TREES AND LARGE TREELIKE SHRUBS IN THIS CHAPTER HAVE BEEN CHOSEN FOR THEIR (MOSTLY SMALL) SIZE.

Paradoxically, a small tree plays a larger role in the garden because you will be able to see more of it (besides its trunk). Its size will also help to marry house and garden as it occupies a step in the progression from the mass of a house to details as fine as the flowers in a perennial garden.

Small- to medium-sized trees are big enough to frame houses, gardens, and views. When properly placed, they can enhance perspective or direct traffic. And even a small tree will provide some shade.

North America is so rich in trees that books about a single genus could fill a library. And this is a short chapter, a small token to the great wealth of American species. I started out with the notion that very few trees would be included and that each one that was had to prove itself to me. Those that survived all the cuts and culls did so because they were truly outstanding or because one of the regional experts insisted it be included or because I couldn't bear to leave it out.

At eye level, the expressive trunks of palo verde, rising from a bed of chuparosa, intrigue.

Vine maple (Acer circinatum), Grier residence

ACER CIRCINATUM Vine maple
ACERACEAE Maple family

This slender, elegant tree is one of the few West Coast trees small enough for consideration in small gardens. In the wild, it is found on cool, moist slopes and forests and along streams, where it can appear as a shrubby thicket. In the garden, vine maple needs a cool spot—in the shade or with an eastern exposure—and it needs year-round moisture.

California gardener Peggy Grier grows vine maple on the shady side of her house in Lafayette, where its graceful silhouette is set off by a large wall. She recommends purchasing vine maple in fall because the leaf color varies from pinkish to orange. If you buy by mail, specify your fall color choice. It can't hurt.

Origin: Mixed conifer forests on moist, humusy slopes, woods, stream banks, from British Columbia to northern California

Flower: Small white flowers with maroon centers in April, before leaves, followed by winged maple seeds

Foliage: Round, lobed leaves are a light green on reddish

Red shanks (Adenostoma sparsifolium*)*
at Rancho Santa Ana

green stems; in fall, they turn shades of pink, yellow, and orange.

Hardiness: Zones 6 to 8

Height: To about 20 feet

Regions: Pacific Northwest, northern and coastal California

Landscape use: Small, multistemmed tree or shrub

Culture: Moist, humusy soil, shade; Dr. Arthur Kruckeberg warns that clumps taken from the wild are doomed. Buy nursery-propagated plants.

Species: Rocky Mountain or Douglas maple (*Acer glabrum*), a fine small tree, is a hardier substitute for colder places. Common and elegant from central Washington to Montana and the Great Basin.

Propagation: Seed

ACER LEUCODERME Chalk maple
ACERACEAE Maple family

Do you want a sugar maple color without the size? Then chalk maple is the tree for you. Its common name refers to its bark color. In fall, the leaves turn the brilliant hue of a sugar maple on a tree that usually grows only about 20 feet tall. Once considered a subspecies of the sugar maple, chalk maple is one of the trees recommended for the South by Bob McCartney, whose Woodlanders Nursery carries this hard-to-find plant.

Origin: Southeastern United States

Flower: Inconspicuous, followed by maple seeds

Foliage: Yellow-green foliage turns red-orange in fall on a small, multistemmed tree with whitish bark

Hardiness: Zones 5 to 9

Height: To 20 to 25 feet

Regions: South, Mid-Atlantic, Lower Midwest

Landscape use: Small tree

Culture: Tolerant of dry soils; sun to part shade; acid soil ("chalk" refers to trunk color, not soil composition)

Propagation: Seed (cool stratify)

ADENOSTOMA SPARSIFOLIUM Red shanks, ribbon bush
ROSACEAE Rose family

There are red shanks at Rancho Santa Ana in Claremont, California, that horticulturist Bart O'Brien showed me when I visited there. Dramatic in a grove, red shanks has shaggy, peeling bark and wispy, evergreen, needlelike foliage. A large shrub or small tree, it is excellent for a hot, dry place. In fact, red shanks performs best in poor, rocky, gravelly, well-drained soil where other plants fail. In rich, heavy soil, it will develop too quickly and, frequently, will not become an asset to the garden.

It would be striking underplanted with poverty weed or California buckwheat, especially when the flower heads dry to a rust color.

*Red buckeye (*Aesculus pavia*)*

Serviceberry grove (Amelanchier laevis)

Origin: San Luis Obispo County, California, south to northern Baja California.

Flower: Tiny white flowers appear in small, terminal panicles in early summer. Spent flowers turn an ochre-rust color.

Foliage: Evergreen foliage is about ½ inch long, bright to midgreen and needlelike.

Hardiness: Zones 8 to 10

Height: 8 to 20 feet

Regions: Southern California, Southwest

Landscape use: Specimen tree or shrub, informal landscape divider, hedge, grove

Culture: Full sun, likes heat, best in well-drained soils

AESCULUS PAVIA Red buckeye
HIPPOCASTANACEAE Horse chestnut family

Perhaps the best place to see red buckeye is in the woods at Callaway Gardens in Pine Mountain, Georgia. These small trees flourish as understory and along the edges of woodland, their terminal racemes of coral red flowering in concert with the scented bloom of the sweet and Florida azaleas (*R. canescens* and *R. austrinum*). I have seen this lovely small tree serve as a focal point at the curve of a path in a garden in Jackson, Mississippi, where it blended beautifully with native and exotic azaleas and wildflowers. Red buckeye has a more natural, asymmetric habit than the big-flowered but rigidly symmetrical European horse chestnut.

Red buckeye flowers best with good light, but the whole tree can look pained and uncomfortable when planted in full, dry sun.

Origin: Virginia to Texas and Florida

Flower: Coral red tubular flowers, held in upright racemes

Foliage: Textured, medium green, five to seven leaflets in a palmate

Hardiness: Zones 4 to 9

Height: Usually to 15 feet

Regions: South, Mid-Atlantic

Landscape use: Understory small tree, shrub

Culture: Moist, acid, well-drained soil; semishade; pollinated by ruby-throated hummingbirds

Varieties: *A. p.* var. *flavescens* has yellow flowers, is bee pollinated.

Propagation: Seed; it will bloom in three years from seed.

AMELANCHIER Serviceberry, shadblow
ROSACEAE Rose family

The botanical names of serviceberries are so mixed up, I don't even want to write this (and yet I must, because serviceberries bloom and berry beautifully, feed folks and fauna, and tolerate tough territory). The biggest problem is that even if all the taxonomists agreed on the names (and they don't, and probably won't in our lifetime), it would still take a lot of doing before nurseries complied and assigned trees their "correct" names. So knowing the right name will probably not do you a great deal of good.

A man I know and trust, Dick Bir, says that really tall trees (the ones I and others think of as *A. arborea*—after all, doesn't "arborea" signify "tree"?) are *A. arborea* var. *laevis*. And the ones I and many others think of as *A. laevis*—the small, multitrunked, gray-barked ones—are in truth *A. arborea* var. *arborea*. Furthermore, because the nomenclature is so confusing, some hybrids are called *A. grandiflora* just to get around the whole sticky name problem. That leaves the shadbush, or shadblow (thank heavens!), still *A. canadensis*. And the western *A. alnifolia* is a shrub.

Amelanchier laevis (or *A. arborea* var. *arborea*)
Serviceberry, Allegheny serviceberry

An upright, small, multistemmed tree that grows slowly to 25 feet, serviceberry produces clouds of small white flowers in April. They remain for anywhere from a week to two, depending upon the weather. For an absolutely heart-stopping effect (and if you have a very large garden), plant a grove of these and walk among them when they bloom!

As with any plant, hot weather accelerates the demise of the flowers. After the flowers fade, finely toothed leaves that have a mauve cast unfold to a clean, matte medium green. Next, edible berries appear and turn from green to magenta to blueberry purple in June. These the birds strip as soon as they are ripe, but if you manage to harvest them, they make a "serviceable" jam or jelly very early in the season—a fact that must have been a great boon to early settlers.

Origin: Edges of woodland, open moist areas, from Newfoundland to Ontario, south to Ohio, Georgia, and Iowa

Flower: White, starry flowers in April

Foliage: Finely toothed leaves emerge maroon, then turn matte green and yellow in fall.

Hardiness: Zones 4 to 9

Height: To 30 feet

Regions: Northwest, Mid-Atlantic, Midwest, South

Landscape use: Small tree

Culture: Sun (part shade in hot climates), moist soil; very adaptable

Species: Shadblow or shadbush (*Amelanchier canadensis*) is so called because this large shrub / small tree flowers at the time shad once ran up northeastern rivers. Hardy to Zone 3.

Amelanchier x *grandiflora* 'Forest Prince' (a confused group taxonomically), is a good grower with nice form, heavy bloom, and fruit with excellent fall color; more selections are in the wings. 'Cumulus' has outstanding flowers and orange-scarlet fall foliage.

Propagation: Depulp seeds

Madrone (Arbutus menziesii)

ARBUTUS MENZIESII Madrone
ERICACEAE Heath family

Madrones, says Prof. Arthur Kruckeberg, thrive on neglect. And that may be why they grow so beautifully in the wild. Evergreen madrones inhabit dry, sunny slopes from California north into Oregon. As one travels north along the coast, the madrones grow larger. To keep them as healthy as they are in the wild, Dr. Kruckeberg counsels "studied neglect." Too much TLC in the garden invites fungal disease.

Madrone is being propagated by some West Coast nurseries—among them Yerba Buena in California—in an effort to get these beautiful natives into home landscapes. Plants are often difficult to establish and have to be planted small and watered carefully. Because it is best to plant the progeny of local plants, as this species varies considerably over its great range, nurseries growing them seek out the seeds of promising locals. Once established, madrones grow fairly quickly and generally need no pruning.

The mahogany-red, smooth bark is outstanding at all seasons, and the attractive yellow, orange, or red fruits ripen in the fall and winter and can be strung for Christmas decorations like cranberries. The trees are very effective when strung with lights and viewed at night. The glaucous nature of the underside of the leaves reflects light.

Origin: Dry, open woods west of the Cascade Mountains, British Columbia to Baja California

Flower: White, small, urn-shaped, honey-scented panicles of flowers in spring, followed by red, yellow, orange fruits

Foliage: Evergreen, ovate, 3 to 6 inches long, 1 to 2 inches wide, bright glossy green above, glaucous below

Hardiness: Zones 8 (possibly 7) to 10

Height: 20 to 150 feet

Region: Pacific states

Landscape use: Specimen tree

Culture: Full sun to light shade; good drainage; careful watering

Species: There are about 20 species worldwide. Of these, Texas madrone (*A. xalapensis*) is one that is being propagated.

Propagation: Seed

ASIMINA TRILOBA Pawpaw
ANNONACEAE Annona family

Pawpaws look like tropical trees mysteriously translocated into temperate forests. In the wild in Maryland, where the piedmont meets the coastal plain, pawpaws flourish—and they continue to do so farther north into New York, Michigan, and Ontario! The leaves are distinctive: big, pointedly pear-shaped, and drooping. They can measure up to a foot long and turn a nice banana yellow in fall.

Some of the common names—"Hoosier banana" and "Michigan banana"—refer not to fall color but to the taste of the pawpaws, yellow mango-shaped fruits that ripen in fall. Once cultivated by Native Americans, the fruits are favored by wildlife. I've never eaten one, something I hope to change soon if I can beat the raccoons and possums to them.

Origin: Ontario to Georgia, west to Texas and Nebraska
Flower: An interesting, inconspicuous, small dark maroon flower in spring, followed by edible pawpaws in fall
Foliage: Large, pointed, pear-shaped leaves that hang straight down
Hardiness: Zones 5 to 8
Height: To 30 feet
Regions: North America west to Nebraska and Texas
Landscape use: Small tree, edible landscaping
Culture: Sun, moist soil; adaptable
Species/cultivars: 'Davis' (commercially produced for fruit), 'Sunflower' (fruit), *A. parviflora* (dwarf pawpaw)

BETULA NIGRA 'HERITAGE' White river birch
BETULACEAE Birch family

'Heritage' river birch is a vigorous white cultivar of the usually salmon- to pink-barked river birch that grows along creek beds. It sheds its outer bark in shaggy strips to reveal the white bark beneath. In 1990, this cultivar won a Gold Medal Plant Award from the Pennsylvania Horticultural

'Heritage' river birch (Betula nigra) *grove, underplanted with bee balm and grasses*

Society. River birches are especially useful in the South, the Mid-Atlantic region, the Lower Midwest, and wherever else the European and canoe birches, suffering from heat and humidity, often fall prey to bronze birch borers and other pests. (Most birches are susceptible to borer injury when stressed, so it's a good idea to choose a birch well suited to your region to keep it healthy.)

'Heritage' is a fast-growing tree that responds to plentiful moisture and sunshine. In my garden, a group of 6-foot trees planted in a sunny, moist swale grew to 20 feet tall by 10 feet wide in three years. A single-stemmed tree, cut back at planting time, quickly developed into a clump. Trees planted 25 feet uphill of the swale and in half shade were markedly younger-looking and smaller—12 feet tall and only 6 feet wide. Two that were shaded out eventually died.

Pawpaw (Asimina triloba) *glows banana yellow along the C&O canal.*

A see-through screen of birches (Betula)
(Michael Van Valkenburgh Design)

Foliage is a medium green that turns yellow in fall, when the tree resembles an aspen. It is a good foil for a background of evergreens.

Origin: The species inhabits stream banks from Massachusetts to Florida and west to Kansas

Foliage: Small, light green, turning golden yellow in fall. *Betula nigra* has a pinkish exfoliating bark. 'Heritage' is a cultivar with white bark.

Hardiness: Zones 4 to 9

Height: To 70 feet

Regions: Northeast, Upper and Lower Midwest, Mid-Atlantic, South

Landscape use: Fast-growing tree for damp places

Culture: River birch will sulk, and perhaps die, without sun and moisture. It grows very fast.

Cultivars: 'Heritage'.

Species: *B. fontinalis* is a graceful, small to medium-sized tree, usually with three to ten trunks of shimmering, cinnamon peeling bark of great beauty. Deeply serrated leaves are finely textured and the branches have a semi-weeping habit. *B. papyrifera,* the classic white canoe birch, is a plant for northern gardens, hardy to Zone 3. It is the state tree of New Hampshire.

CEANOTHUS ARBOREUS Feltleaf ceanothus
RHAMNACEAE Buckthorn family

April in California is *Ceanothus* time. Then, it seems that the many species of this beautiful genus fill every cultural niche—from ground cover, to large shrub, to tree—blooming in shades of blue, lavender, pink, and white. Among the many species and cultivars is the feltleaf ceanothus, a true tree, one of the plants suggested for California by horticulturist Bart O'Brien. At the California meadow restoration at Strybing Arboretum, the feltleaf ceanothus is a focal point at the edge of a meadow that includes irises, *Calamagrostis foliosa,* tidy tips, California fescue, and hundreds of California poppies.

C. thyrsiflorus, a very large shrub, can be pruned to shrub or tree form.

Origin: Catalina Island, California

Flower: Fragrant, deep blue to pale lavender blue in April

Foliage: Oval, evergreen leaves, downy white beneath

Hardiness: Zones 8 to 10

Height: 20 feet

Region: California

Landscape use: A fine, broad, spring-blooming tree

Culture: Very drought-tolerant once established, ceanothus is susceptible to root rot when it is watered in summer.

CERCIDIUM FLORIDUM Blue palo verde
LEGUMINOSAE Pea family

Although this tree boasts blue-green foliage and spectacular lemon yellow flowers in late spring, what fascinates a visitor from the East is palo verde's green bark. Desert plants cope with drought in many ways; young palo verdes drop their leaves, but continue the process of photosynthesis through their branches and trunks! An outstanding accent tree, palo verde's lower branches can be pruned up to create a shade tree, or you can utilize the naturally shrubby form for

Feltleaf ceanothus (Ceanothus arboreus)   *Palo verde* (Cercidium floridum)

screening. Plant desert marigold nearby for a bright mix of yellow and gold.

Origin: Blue palo verde grows along dry washes and on desert grassland in southeastern California, southern Arizona, and northwestern Mexico

Flower: A mass of yellow flowers in late March or April, depending upon altitude. The beanlike seedpods were used by Native Americans for food.

Foliage: Blue-green, small leaves with a spine at each node

Hardiness: Zones 8 to 10

Height: 20 feet high by 25 feet wide

Region: Southwest

Landscape use: Specimen tree, hedge, screen

Culture: Provide excellent drainage. Blue palo verde is drought-tolerant when established.

Species/cultivars: The foothill palo verde, *C. microphyllum,* common on the Arizona desert in association with saguaro and ocotillo, has yellow-green leaves and, later, pale yellow flowers.

CERCIS Redbud, Judas tree
LEGUMINOSAE Pea family

Legend holds that Judas hung himself from a redbud, but rest easy! It was surely an exotic, not one of the natives that are the delights of spring from one end of the country to the other. The eastern redbud (*C. canadensis*) overlaps in bloom with dogwoods and grows along with them at the edges of woodland. Eastern redbuds grow broad and fast—to perhaps 15 feet by 15 feet in six years. That means that in gardens, redbuds establish quickly and therefore are good trees for a new house, but need plenty of room and a ground cover beneath their drip line. Christmas ferns or *Pachysandra procumbens* would do nicely.

Eastern redbud's range extends westward through Texas, where smaller, climate-adapted varieties (*C.c.* var. *texensis, C.c.* var. *mexicanis*) appear and, probably, hybridize. These have smaller, rounder, shinier leaves. On the other side of the Sierras, the western redbud (*C. occidentalis*) inhabits hillsides in the California chaparral and oak woodlands. All of this is to say that wherever you live, there's a redbud for you.

Cercis canadensis Eastern redbud

Fast growing and broadly vase-shaped, eastern redbud, the state tree of Oklahoma, is lovely spreading over a patio. To see its bright magenta flowers and yellow heart-shaped leaves (in fall) close up, plant it near a deck or second-story window.

Texas redbud (Cercis canadensis *var.* texensis)

Origin: Eastern to south-central United States

Flower: Little clusters of magenta pink flowers held on ½-inch stems along the branches, provide deep shade

Foliage: Heart-shaped leaves, turning bright yellow in fall

Hardiness: Zones 4 to 9

Height: To 40 feet

Regions: Eastern to south-central United States

Landscape use: Small tree, edge of woodland

Culture: Sun to part shade, moist soil

Varieties: Texas redbud (*C. canadensis* var. *texensis*) is smaller, with smaller, rounder, shiny leaves. Far more drought-tolerant, less hardy (Zone 7), it blooms rose pink and produces attractive red seedpods. Mexican redbud (*C. canadensis* var. *mexicanis*) has shiny, wavy-edged leaves and is more tender (Zone 8?); *C. reniformis* 'Oklahoma' has very dark flowers.

Cultivars: 'Forest Pansy' (red foliage, scarlet fall color), 'Alba' (white flowers), 'Wither's Pink Charm' (pink)

Propagation: Seed (scarify and cool stratify)

Eastern redbud (Cercis canadensis)

Cercis occidentalis Western redbud

Trim shrubby western redbud up to expose its stems for a small-scale, multistemmed tree that blooms bright magenta in April. The blues of *Ceanothus* make good companions to this small tree's stunning spring flowers.

Origin: Hillsides in chaparral and oak woodland in California and along streams into the Mohave and Arizona deserts

Flower: Magenta flowers on short stems held along branches, followed by fruits that turn red-purple

Foliage: Kidney-shaped leaves, matte green, deciduous

Hardiness: Zones 9 (to 15°) to 10

Height: To 20 feet

Region: California

Landscape use: Large shrub, small tree

Culture: Full sun, part shade, good drainage; drought-tolerant, clay-tolerant. Water once or twice per month; it is resistant to oak root fungus.

Varieties: *Cercis occidentalis* var. *arizonica* occurs in Arizona around the Grand Canyon; *C. occidentalis* var. *orbiculata* occurs in southern Utah.

CHILOPSIS LINEARIS Desert willow
BIGNONIACEAE Bignonia family

The minute desert willow's showy lavender flowers appear, so do the hummingbirds, and they stay throughout summer, feasting on the profuse flowers. This thornless, frost-hardy tree's twisted trunks lend character to a planting. Albuquerque designer Judith Phillips, who uses it in her water-saving designs, says it is very cold-sensitive and should be hardened off (by withholding water) in fall to discourage new growth. Its bright green, willowlike leaves wait until late spring to reappear. When established, desert willow's deep roots make it extremely drought-tolerant. Underplant it with Blackfoot daisy, bush penstemon, and low junipers.

Origin: South-central Texas to the West Coast, central New Mexico into Mexico; usually in dry arroyos from 1,500 to 5,000 feet

Flower: Rose pink tubular flowers attract hummingbirds from June through September. Pencil-sized seedpods in late summer persist into winter.

Foliage: Very narrow, bright green leaves, deciduous

Hardiness: Zones 7 (borderline in 6b) to 10

Height: To 25 feet

Regions: Southwest, southern California

Landscape use: Light shade for patios and sun screen for windows; mass planted for wind protection; as accent specimens singly or in groves

Culture: Will grow in porous, sandy soil or any that is well drained. It is probably root-hardy to 15°F. Plants continue to grow as long as moisture is available in fall, so it should be hardened off early in autumn to reduce winter damage in Zones 6b through 8a.

Cultivars: 'Barranco', 'Hope' (white), 'Marfa Lace' (double)

Desert willow (Chilopsis linearis), *late to leaf out, has a fine, spidery silhouette.*

Fringe tree (Chionanthus virginicus)

CHIONANTHUS VIRGINICUS Fringe tree, old man's beard

OLEACEAE Olive family

Perhaps one of the reasons this absolutely spectacular large shrub or small tree isn't more frequently seen is that it is slow to propagate. The seeds need a double dormancy period (basically two winters) to sprout, and then the seedlings take several years to bloom. Of the seedlings, roughly half will be male and produce marginally showier flowers, and the other, slightly less showy, half will be female and produce dangling deep purple berries.

"Because of [difficulties in propagation] many plants sold are produced by grafting onto a seedling of ash," states the cutting-edge garden bulletin *Avant Gardener.* "So it is worth keeping an eye on the base of your fringe-tree so you can remove any shoots arising from the ash before they take over the plant."

Any reasonable person who sees this plant bloom and smells its sweet perfume is smitten. Thomas Jefferson was, and planted it at Monticello. Typically broader than high, with loose, arching branches, fringe tree's flowers have petals so long and narrow they look like twisted fringe. Blossoming in May, just as the leaves emerge, they lend the tree a cloudlike appearance until the leaves take over.

If fringe tree has a fault, it is that its rather rough, gray branches bear neither flowers nor leaves until May, and one always frets that the plant might be dead, when in truth, it's probably hard to kill because it grows well in urban environments.

Origin: Well-drained but moist acid soil from Pennsylvania to Florida and west to Texas

Flower: A fragrant fringe of white or ivory petals in late spring, showier in male trees

Foliage: Broadly oval, medium green leaves, late to emerge in spring

Hardiness: Zone 5 (Dick Bir reports that fringe tree is grown in Canada, Zone 3) to 9

Height: To 25 feet

Region: Eastern North America where hardy

Landscape use: Shrub border, specimen tree

Culture: Sun, light shade; acid, moist, well-drained soil. Needs pruning to grow as a tree. Grows well in urban environments

Propagation: Seeds need double dormancy; warm and cool stratification

x *CHITALPA TASHKENTENSIS* Chitalpa

BIGNONIACEAE Bignonia family

The chitalpa is a man-made hybrid between seemingly highly unlikely partners, the eastern *Catalpa bignonioides* and the southwestern *Chilopsis linearis.* It was first bred at the Uzbek Academy of Sciences Botanical Garden in Tashkent, Uzbekistan. Then director of the National Arboretum Tom Elias and Walter Wisura of Rancho Santa Ana Botanic Garden named the cross and developed the cultivars 'Pink Dawn' and 'Morning Cloud', with pink and pale pink to white flowers respectively.

Chitalpa (x Chitalpa tashkentensis) (Tom Elias photo)

Trees

Chitalpa seems to have inherited its desert forebear's preference for climate: it is drought-tolerant like the desert willow and subject to mold during humid weather in the Southeast. The leaves are narrower than those of the catalpa and the flowers stay on the tree until they wither, a characteristic that didn't seem especially desirable until I learned from Tom Elias that people have been known to slip on the gooey litter of still-moist, fallen blossoms.

Origin: Hybrid

Flower: Big trusses of 20 to 40 1-inch, tubular flowers of white to pink are born from May to November in warm climates like southern California.

Foliage: The deciduous leaves are broader than the willow-shaped leaves of the desert willow, but render something of the same airy effect.

Hardiness: Zones 6 to 10

Height: 20 to 25 feet high and 25 feet wide

Region: Southwest

Landscape use: Specimen tree

Culture: Sun, good drainage; drought-tolerant when established

Propagation: Cuttings

CLADRASTIS KENTUKEYA (C. LUTEA) Yellowwood

LEGUMINOSAE Pea family

Never mind that yellowwood grows slowly or that it doesn't flower every year. When it does, the white, wisteria-like clusters are so beautiful and fragrant that they are worth waiting for.

If grown in woodland, as it is on the close of the National Cathedral, it gets very tall and narrow. Only its gray trunk and scented flowers give it away. With full

Yellowwood (Cladrastis kentukeya)

sun and plenty of room, yellowwood develops a symmetrical, broad crown that casts dense shade. Its gray trunk has been compared with that of the American beech.

Origin: Isolated places in the Southeast and Lower Midwest

Flower: 1-foot-long, pendulous cluster of white, fragrant flowers in May, seedpods in fall

Foliage: Bright green, compound leaves, turning yellow in fall

Hardiness: Zones 4 to 8

Height: Yellowwood grows slowly to 50 feet, with a crown nearly as broad as the tree is high.

Regions: Midwest, South, Mid-Atlantic

Landscape use: Street tree, specimen

Culture: Very adaptable; sun, well-drained soil (tolerates both acid and alkaline soils)

Cultivars: 'Rosea' (pink flowers)

Propagation: Seed (scarify and cool stratify)

CORNUS Dogwood

CORNACEAE Dogwood family

In 1915 and again in 1917, as a reciprocal gesture for the gift of the flowering cherry trees, the United States sent several hundred dogwood trees and a large quantity of seed to Japan. There, dogwoods flower prettily, as does the Japanese native *Cornus kousa,* but I was surprised to learn that in England, they do not usually flower at all. William Robinson wrote in *The English Flower Garden* (1883): "We do not obtain sufficient summer heat . . . and so the flowering of this species in Britain is not common, although it was one of the earliest amongst N. American shrubs to find its way to British gardens."

This is one of the few instances in which I have felt sorry for English gardeners! I cannot imagine a spring without dogwoods. Their May bloom (in the Washington, D.C., area) is the crest of the year's greatest wave of bloom which has been swelling since March with the first little bulbs. Azaleas, redbuds, phloxes, Virginia bluebells, dogtooth violets, Dutchman's breeches, trillium, *Tiarella,* tulips, daffodils, fothergilla, all join in the extravaganza. When it occurs, all of the trite phrases that people use to try to describe the phenomenal effect are operative: "a fairyland," "too beautiful for words," "absolutely gorgeous," but all fall short of doing justice.

After the dogwood's white flowers fall, the time of lightness and floral celebration is over and the trees, shrubs, and herbaceous plants get down to the business of growing dense and green. In fall, however, the dogwood

Eastern dogwoods (Cornus florida)

leaves put on another grand show, turning first shades of pink and then deepening to crimson and copper.

Probably the most popular tree in the country, the dogwood is threatened by disease; in the wild, populations of both the Pacific dogwood (*C. nuttallii*) and the eastern dogwood (*C. florida*) have been hard hit by dogwood anthracnose. A fungus called Discula, which thrives in cool, moist areas, has been implicated in what is primarily a disease of the forest that began in Washington State and New York and spread to other states. Nursery-grown trees and those in gardens are less at risk. The symptoms of the disease include spots on the leaves, the dying back of twigs and branches, the appearance of water sprouts, and annual cankers. The disease is progressive and fatal.

Some trees in wild areas have escaped the disease and may have natural immunity. In the future, perhaps material from these trees will provide disease-resistant cultivars. 'Spring Grove', a new cultivar of *Cornus florida* from a tree found in Cincinnati's Spring Grove Cemetery, a great American arboretum, is said to be resistant to anthracnose in addition to having precocious bloom with three or four flowers, instead of one, at the end of each branch.

My garden must be the epicenter of the *Cornus florida* range because little trees are my number-one volunteer. Seedlings grow quickly into trees. Dogwoods bloom wherever sun or strong light filters through to them, a trait that can be used effectively in the garden. Neighbors across the street have a driveway edged with a string of dogwoods on the south side of a wood. In spring, these trees present a solid wall of bloom; in fall, it is a wall of brilliant red foliage.

Unlike the fairly adaptable eastern dogwood, the Pacific dogwood is more demanding. It can be hard to please. Berkeley, California, gardener Jenny Fleming accepts that some trees die and delights in those that survive: "A very difficult tree, but one I love too much to quit trying is our western native dogwood," she says.

Cornus florida Eastern dogwood

This dogwood, the state tree of Missouri and Virginia, is multiply blessed; it has showy white flowers in spring, a short, broadly spreading crown in summer, and brilliant red berries and fall color. Versatile, it looks lovely espaliered, as a specimen, or grown along the edge of woodland where it is covered with flowers from the ground up.

Origin: Woodland edges and understories, Maine to Florida and west to Kansas and Texas

Flower: Large white petals (bracts) in May, followed by attractive red fruits that are swiftly taken by birds

Foliage: Oval green leaves, turning a magnificent red in fall

Hardiness: Zones 5 to 9

Height: To 30 feet

KEEPING DOGWOODS HEALTHY

The Horticultural Research Institute of Washington, D.C., and the United States Department of Agriculture have prepared pamphlets detailing suggestions for keeping dogwoods healthy. The following is based upon these pamphlets.

Since the forest is the source of the disease, never transplant from the wild; buy only nursery-grown, disease-free trees. Site them in places that are well drained and enjoy good air circulation. The HRI suggests "at least 6 hours of direct sun on an average day"—a lot for an understory tree! Mulch to prevent drought stress, and to prevent mechanical injury from mowers and string trimmers, keep them three to four inches from the trunk of the tree. Avoid high-nitrogen fertilizers that cause succulent branching, which is prone to trunk canker formation. Prune out deadwood and water sprouts, dispose of litter, and use a fungicide (chlorothalonil, mancozeb, or benomyl) at 10- to 14-day intervals during leaf expansion in spring.

Region: Eastern United States

Landscape use: Small flowering tree, sometimes espaliered

Culture: Before anthracnose, people were criticized for growing dogwood in full sun, where, anthracnose or not, it looks miserable and often gets borers. An understory woodland tree, it is still best in part shade, in moist, well-drained, humusy soil.

Cultivars: Many! 'Spring Grove' (floriferous, disease-resistant), 'Pen-dula' (weeping), 'Autumn Sunset' (coral branches), 'Cherokee Princess' (disease-resistant), 'Autumn Gold' (gold in fall), 'Wonder Berry' (silver-dollar-sized clusters)

Propagation: Seed (depulp and cool stratify)

Cornus nuttallii Pacific dogwood, mountain dogwood

The snowy white flowers, which in botanical terms are accurately called "bracts," are largest of all in the Pacific dogwoods, measuring 5 to 6 inches across. And there are hybrids such as 'Corigo Giant' with even larger flowers—up to 8 inches across. Pacific dogwood has an upright habit, red-orange fruits, and wonderful red fall color. Its botanical name honors English naturalist Thomas Nuttall, who was commissioned to seek plants in the Northwest for the sum of $8 per month in the early years of the 19th century.

Origin: Moist, cool soils from British Columbia to southern California

Flower: Large, white bracts (four or more) in late spring and early summer, followed by red fruits; may rebloom in fall

Foliage: Green leaves, glaucous beneath, turning red in fall

Hardiness: Zones 7 to 8

Height: To 75 feet

Regions: Cool, moist places in California, Pacific Northwest

Landscape use: Tree

Culture: Moist soil, part to full shade

Cultivars: 'Goldspot' (leaves spotted yellow), 'Corigo Giant' (large flowers)

CRATAEGUS Hawthorn
ROSACEAE Rose family

According to legend, the Glastonbury Thorn took root and bloomed when Joseph of Arimathea thrust his staff into the ground as he preached in Glastonbury, England. It was on Christmas Day in the first century A.D. Now an English hawthorn, grown from a cutting of the Glastonbury Thorn, stands in front of St. Albans School on the cathedral close on Mt. Saint Alban, the highest point in Washington, D.C. It has become gnarled with age and treasured.

Hawthorns are that kind of tree; they conjure up times past. Before they were associated with Christianity, they were used by the Romans as bridal decorations. Their very name echoes down the centuries with associations.

Perhaps two-thirds of the world's hawthorns are native to North America. (It was a native hawthorn branch, too, that Paul Bunyan used as a back scratcher.) Characteristics shared by many include very dense, thorny, bushlike foliage on smallish trees that are almost (or indeed) as wide as they are tall. Think of them as the kind of broad, dense shrubs on trunks, the kinds of plants favored by nesting birds, and you will have the picture. In spring, they produce apple blossom clusters of white (sometimes pink) flowers followed by red fruits, called "pomes" or "haws," that can be made into jellies, something I've seen advocated but haven't tried.

Some trees have foliage that turns scarlet in fall, but the fruits that hang on the trees for much of the winter are what the show is about. The cultivar 'Winter King', winner of the Gold Medal Plant Award of the Pennsylvania Horticultural Society, has a very wide range, avoids many of the fungal rust problems to which hawthorns are prone, tolerates a wide range of soils, and has outstanding fruits. Other hawthorns are listed under "Species."

Hawthorn (Crataegus)

Crataegus viridis 'WINTER KING' Green hawthorn

Attractive year-round, 'Winter King' is an outstanding small tree that eventually grows as wide as it does tall (30 feet by 30 feet). Its orange-red fruits, stunning against silver-gray bark, appear after the white flowers. The fruits remain on the tree into winter, when they are taken by migrating cedar waxwings.

Origin: Sunny places with rich, sometimes limy, soil from Florida to Texas and north to Missouri, Illinois, and Virginia

Flower: Small white (to pink) flowers in clusters in May are followed by bright red-orange fruits that persist, often throughout winter, until taken by birds.

Foliage: Glossy green leaves sometimes color yellow or red in fall, but generally fruits create the show.

Hardiness: Zones 5 to 8

Height: To 30 feet high by 30 feet wide

Regions: Midwest, Upper South, Mid-Atlantic, Northeast

Landscape use: Specimen tree, wildlife planting

Culture: Sun, rich soil; very adaptable

Species: Parsley haw, *C. marshalli,* propagated from fresh seed, a small (to 25 feet) southern tree with parsleylike leaves, attractive exfoliating bark, and red fruit, even grows in the white clay around Chapel Hill, North Carolina. Western black hawthorn, *C. douglasii,* is a small tree with good fall color and black fruits. Tracy hawthorn, *C. tracyi,* a small (to 20 feet) tree from Texas, tolerates both igneous and limestone soils and turns bright red in fall.

Cultivars: 'Winter King', a winner of the Gold Medal Plant Award of the Pennsylvania Horticultural Society, tolerates a wide range of soils, is somewhat resistant to fungal rust problems, and has outstanding fruits.

FORESTIERA NEOMEXICANA Desert olive, palo blanco, New Mexico privet, mountain ash

OLEACEAE Olive family

Desert olive is a versatile plant that will serve either as a shrub or as a tree. If you remove its lower branches, you'll have a small tree with smooth gray bark and an upright, angular branch pattern. If you leave it unpruned, you'll have a shrub that is bushy enough to serve as a hedge or windbreak. Its bright, apple green leaves are a good contrast for the many gray-green desert plants such as fringed sage or santolina that might be grown in front of it.

Origin: Along arroyos, in cottonwood bosques or canyon bottoms of Texas, New Mexico, and Colorado

Desert olive (Forestiera neomexicana)*, trimmed into tree form (Charles Mann photo)*

Flower: Small, fragrant, cream-colored flowers in spring, producing blue fruits on female plants in midsummer

Foliage: Bright apple green leaves contrast with the very dark color of new growth on stems. Dense when moisture is available, foliage drops in drought; turns yellow in fall.

Hardiness: At least Zones 5b to 8

Height: To 15 feet

Region: Southwest

Landscape use: The desert olive serves as an accent or small shade tree. It can also be planted as a screen, barrier, hedge, or low windbreak.

Culture: Once established, plants become quite drought-tolerant, but they drop their leaves in response to moisture stress, so it is best to deep-water them occasionally.

FRANKLINIA ALATAMAHA Franklinia, Franklin tree
THEACEAE Tea family

This is the tree found in the 18th century by Colonial botanist John Bartram on the shores of the Altamaha River (the species name somehow acquired an extra "a") and named for his friend Benjamin Franklin. It was never again found in the wild. All of the plants today come from the specimens collected in Bartram's day.

It wasn't until seeing a mature, multi-stemmed small tree at Winterthur that it struck me that I had wrongly thought of this plant as a shrub. Its leggy, open, upright habit is definitely treelike, yet its small stature makes it an outstanding garden-sized specimen.

Franklinia bears very showy white flowers that are teasingly slow to open. They arrive not so much in one grand event as in small numbers and over a long period

*Franklinia (*Franklinia alatamaha*)*

*Silverbell (*Halesia diptera*)*

of time in the manner of bull bay magnolia, from summer into fall. Franklinia's foliage turns pretty shades of orange, red, and mahogany in fall, often overlapping with dazzling white bloom.

Origin: Banks of the Altamaha River, Georgia

Flower: White, resembling a single camellia around a large yellow center, summer into fall

Foliage: Glossy, dark green foliage turning shades of orange, red, and mahogany in fall

Hardiness: Zones 6 to 8

Height: To 30 feet

Regions: Northeast, Mid-Atlantic, South, Lower Midwest

Landscape use: Small specimen tree, shrub border

Culture: Sun to part shade, with moist but very well-drained, acid, humusy soil. Franklinia is susceptible to the wilt of phytophora, which lives in soil where cotton has been grown. It doesn't transplant easily; start with a small, container-grown plant.

Propagation: Seed

HALESIA DIPTERA Silverbell, snowdrop tree
STYRACACEAE Styrax family

The best place to site a silverbell is very close to where you'll see its blooms in spring—next to the door, over a patio, outside the window of a child's room. Then you'll enjoy its week to 10 days of delicate bloom, when snowdrop flowers dangle from the stems like thousands of tiny fairy bells.

Where it can be grown (Zone 6 and southward), and *if* it can be found, *Halesia diptera* is the stunningest of a stunning genus, with the largest flowers on the smallest plant. At last checking, Salter Tree Farm in

Madison, Florida, carried it. Actually a large shrub, it is lovely pruned up as a tree that grows to 15 feet in an ordinary garden situation. The foliage, a clean green, is seldom troubled by insects or disease. White, bell-shaped flowers arranged along the branches bloom for a week to 10 days in May and are followed by winged green seeds that ripen and serve as wildlife food. Although the bloom time is relatively short, this tree makes up for the brevity by the sheer number and delicacy of its flowers.

Origin: Woodland edges from South Carolina to Florida, Tennessee, and Texas

Flower: White bell flowers along the branches, in May

Foliage: Green, small, elliptical leaves

Hardiness: Zones 6 (possibly 5) to 9

Height: To 15 feet

Regions: South, Mid-Atlantic, parts of Northeast

Landscape use: Small specimen tree

Culture: Sun to part shade in rich, moist, very slightly acid soil

Varieties/species: 'Magniflora' (very large flowers); Carolina silverbell (*H. carolina*) grows to 30 feet; mountain silverbell (*H. monticola*) grows to 90 feet.

Propagation: Plant fresh seed in fall (dry seeds may take years to germinate); cuttings of firm new wood

HAMAMELIS VIRGINIANA Witch hazel
HAMAMELIDACEAE Witch hazel family

Other people are so enthusiastic about this small tree—the last of all flowering trees to bloom—that my experience with a single, very healthy 10-foot specimen in my yard must be grossly aberrant.

*Witch hazel (*Hamamelis virginiana*) (Jessie Harris photo)*

In an enviable site—sun morning to midday and moist soil—this obviously healthy tree is a disappointment.

In no way does my witch hazel's behavior support the glowing testimonials. "Its tardy yellow flowers and 4 twisted ribbonlike petals are revealed as the leaves drop in late October and November," wrote Sally Smith in *American Nurseryman.* "Spidery flowers remind us that the natural world is not asleep when leaves have fallen," writes Dick Bir in *Growing and Propagating Showy Native Woody Plants.* The leaves on my witch hazel are brown, and it is late January and they still haven't dropped. I have seen photos in which leaves and flowers glowed yellow together—a very nice effect. This did not happen, although surely this is what William Robinson must have been thinking when he wrote (in *The English Flower Garden*), "The Virginian Witch Hazel is really a beautiful hardy tree, and charming in October even in poor stiff soil."

"A wonderful shrub especially in fall as the leaves turn a gorgeous yellow and the fragrance of the flowers permeates the cool autumn air," writes Michael Dirr in *Manual of Woody Landscape Plants.* Flowers from my tree at 2 inches from the nose had no detectable fragrance. In only one way does my witch hazel conform: its seeds pop out of the capsules as if shot from guns, a phenomenon that fascinates children, large and small.

Here are my conclusions: there must be great differences in flowers, scent, and leaves in *Hamamelis* populations. Perhaps mine is indeed a poor specimen and better, more dependable selections will be made in the future. Also, plant performance must vary according to place. A disproportionate number of glowing testimonials come from cold places. There is altogether too much written and said about this small tree's beauty to regard my experience as typical. Or perhaps my tree comes from the practical but plain side of the witch hazel family and its ancestors were those whose twigs were cut for distilling the astringent witch hazel or whose forked branches were used by diviners to witch for water.

Origin: Moist woods of eastern North America

Flower: Yellow, with four ribbonlike petals; some are fragrant

Foliage: Coarse leaves turning yellow and then orangy brown

Hardiness: Zones 3 to 8

Height: To 20 feet

Region: Eastern North America

Landscape use: Small specimen tree

Culture: Sun to shade, moist soil. Choose a plant in fall for good leaf color and fragrance.

Species: *H. microphylla* (probably a geographic race that is better for the South) is similar, blooms in December. *H. vernalis* is shrubby, to 9 feet, with orange-red flowers in midwinter to early spring; some have maroon-purple new growth; tolerates moist soil and shade.

Propagation: Seed (warm and cool stratify)

ILEX Holly

AQUIFOLIACEAE Holly family

"Of all the trees in the greenwood, the Holly wears the crown," goes an ancient Christmas carol. This carol and its haunting refrain, "Oh the rising of the sun, and the running of the deer . . . ," call to mind medieval England, a wild, wooded island where people lived close to nature. In that world, holly (*Ilex aquifolium*) had not lost the magical significance it acquired along with mistletoe and oak in pagan times. "Holly" is a word laden with the associations of millennia. This heritage crossed the Atlantic with English settlers and attached itself to the similar native hollies they found in the New World: *Ilex opaca* and *Ilex cassine.* A cross of these two species, *Ilex* x *attenuata,* is hardy to Zone 7 and has yielded 'Foster #2', an excellent, self-fertile, narrow, swift-growing, conical tree.

Ilex cassine Dahoon holly

Large, evergreen Dahoon holly, like its northern counterpart, American holly, grows to a broad cone shape in good light, but it has a more southerly range and will not tolerate extreme cold. It takes well to shearing and makes a good hedge. Its small fruits are abundant.

Origin: Southeastern United States, Florida Keys, Cuba

Juniperus

Name	Origin	Fruit	Foliage	Zones	Height	Regions	Landscape Use
Juniperus ashei Ashe juniper	Limestone soils, Missouri, Arkansas, Texas, Mexico	Dark blue	Dark green, scaly; shaggy bark	6 to 9	To 20 ft	Lower Midwest, Southwest	Small tree
Juniperus californica California juniper, desert white cedar	Dry slopes, desert, from Colorado to southern California	Reddish cone	Dark green, scaly foliage, upright, broadly conical, open with age	7 to 10	To 35 ft	Southwest, southern California	Dry hillside planting, screening
Juniperus deppeana Alligator juniper	Texas to Arizona, Mexico	Reddish tan	Blue-gray, silvery, broad crown; patterned bark	7 to 8	To 40 ft	Southwest	Specimen, character tree
Juniperus flaccida Weeping juniper	Chisos Mountains, Texas	Reddish tan	Weeping, blue-green foliage on drooping branches	7 to 10	To 40 ft	Southwest	Specimen, character tree
Juniperus monosperma One-seed juniper	High plains of Colorado, Texas, New Mexico, Mexico	Blue	Yellow-green	5(?) to 9	To 15 ft	Southwest, Mountain	Specimen, wild garden
Juniperus scopulorum Rocky Mountain juniper	Rocky Mountain foothills, from Alberta, Washington to Texas, Arizona	Frosted blue	Gray green/silver on broadly conical tree	3 to 7	To 30 ft	Southwest, Mountain, Northwest	Specimen, hedge, background plant
Juniperus virginiana Eastern red cedar	Eastern North America to Texas	Blue	Blue to yellow green, conical tree, shaggy bark	2 to 9	To 40 ft	Eastern North America	Screening, hedge, specimen

Dahoon holly (Ilex cassine)

Flower: Inconspicuous, in February, followed by orange-red berries

Foliage: Mostly spineless, elliptical, 2- to 4-inch-long leaves, slightly toothed on the ends, evergreen

Hardiness: Zones 8 to 10

Height: To 30 feet

Region: South

Landscape use: Hedges, large shrub, unpruned; eventually, an evergreen tree

Culture: Sun to part shade; tolerates seasonal wetness; takes more alkaline soil than other hollies; finicky

Cultivars: I. x *attenuta* 'East Palatka' is a cross between *I. opaca* and *I. cassine*.

Propagation: Seed or cuttings

Ilex opaca American holly

One of the trees recommended for the South by Bob McCartney, American holly, the hardiest broadleaf evergreen in eastern North America, has a huge range. My garden, central in that range, functions as a holly nursery, encouraging, with help from the birds, baby hollies to pop up wherever there is moist shade. Although the most seedlings can be found in fairly dense shade, American holly grows better, thicker, and faster (relatively) with more sun. Growth is very, very slow.

Culture	Propagate	Comment
Sun, well-drained soil	Seed	Tolerant of lime, disease-resistant, killed by fire
Sun, good drainage	Seed	Requires excellent drainage, drought-resistant
Sun, good drainage	Seed	Very hardy, drought-resistant, beautiful blue-green foliage
Sun, good drainage	Seed	Striking, drought-tolerant ornamental
Sun, good drainage	Seed	Rugged; grows fast with irrigation; tolerates lime, drought, cold; wildlife plant
Sun, well-drained soil	Seed, grafts	Hardy, tolerates poor soil. Cultivars: 'Skyrocket' (narrow), 'Moonglow' (silvery, pyramidal), 'Wichita Blue' (bright blue).
Sun, well-drained soil	Seed, grafts	Extremely variable, adaptable; cold-, heat-tolerant. Many cultivars: 'Nova' (small, good habit), 'Glauca' (columnar), 'Grey Owl' (like Pfitzer).

'Skyrocket' juniper (Juniperus) *with roses, Brookside Gardens, Wheaton, Maryland*

The finest specimens I have ever seen, a 30-foot pair (male and female), grow next door to my house in a moist meadow surrounded at some 30 feet or so by tall trees. They are broadly cone-shaped, clothed in foliage all the way to the ground. In the woods, one frequently sees them bare in places where light does not penetrate. Leaves are leathery but not glossy, and medium green with serious spines that are most treacherous when they are dry. American holly is the state tree of Delaware.

Shorn American holly (Ilex opaca), *William Paca Garden, Annapolis, Maryland*

Origin: Massachusetts to Florida, west to Texas and Missouri

Flower: Inconspicuous, in early spring, followed by a red berry

Foliage: Evergreen, spined, leathery, dull green. Sometimes deer browse on it.

Hardiness: Zones 5 to 9

Height: 30 to 40 feet

Regions: Northeast, Mid-Atlantic, South, Lower Midwest

Landscape use: Shrub when young, evergreen tree

Culture: Acid, well-drained, moist soil; sun to part shade; salt-tolerant

Cultivars: Some of its more than 1,000 cultivars include 'Greenleaf' (faster growing), 'Fallow' (yellow berries), 'Leatherleaf' (male, also pollinates *I. decidua*), 'William Hawkins' (narrow leaves)

Propagation: Seed or cuttings

JUNIPERUS Juniper
CUPRESSACEAE Cedar family

Large junipers do not ask to be grown in front of houses and hacked back constantly because they obscure windows and doors. Nor do they crave situations in deep shade, where their foliage grows mangily.

People put them there because they fail to inform themselves of a particular juniper's ultimate size and its preferred growing conditions. It is grossly unfair to loathe poor junipers for the evil men do to them. By rights, we ought to elect a minister of plants whose job it would be to oversee tasteful landscapes (no tricolor dogwoods) and eliminate cruelty to plants—particularly junipers, so often mutilated and neglected. Rather than revile these plants, we ought to celebrate their outstanding qualities.

Junipers, or "cedars," from a tough and durable genus, *Juniperus,* have evolved to inhabit some of the most rigorous climates on the continent. There is a juniper for every region, for every situation, for every garden.

The Rocky Mountain juniper (*Juniperus scopulorum*) is found in the wild from British Columbia to Arizona and Texas. It is slow growing to about 30 feet, with blue-green, scaly foliage. However, there are some magnificent, ancient, 100-foot specimens of this hardy and moderately drought-resistant tree in Texas's Palo Duro Canyon. Many, many cultivars have been developed from *J. scopulorum,* including the very narrow, 15-foot-tall 'Skyrocket', popular in perennial borders as an evergreen vertical accent.

Eastern red cedar (*Juniperus virginiana*), an eastern counterpart to the Rocky Mountain juniper, grows from the Eastern seaboard into Texas. It often pops up along fencerows and in road cuts. In northern Virginia, one frequently sees columnar specimens with gray-green scale-like needles—in old fields in the company of broom sedge (*Andropogon virginicus*). In the garden, it serves as a stately tall hedge, a dense background plant, or a specimen. 'Nova', a narrow, symmetrical, and very hardy cultivar, grows to only 12 feet tall.

Eastern red cedar is immensely variable. The evergreen foliage can be anything from light green to blue. In win-

Alligator juniper (Juniperus deppeana) *(Charles Mann photo)*

ter, some trees frequently turn a rich brown. This is the result of the color mixture of the male's yellow pollen and the green foliage. Female plants often appear bluish, because the female's blue fruits blend with the foliage.

One-seed juniper (*J. monosperma*) grows into a highly picturesque, twisted tree. Its gnarled trunks and wind-blown aspect suit its wild High Plains settings from Colorado to Texas, New Mexico, and Mexico. Gray-green with blue fruits, one-seed juniper is hardy and drought-tolerant.

Ashe juniper (*J. ashei*) is found in limestone soils from Missouri and Arkansas through Oklahoma into Texas and Mexico.

Alligator juniper (*J. deppeana*) gets its name from the squares on old bark that look like alligator skin. Very drought- and cold-tolerant, hardy to 6,000 feet and reaches 40 feet. It grows in several mountain ranges in the Trans-Pecos region of Texas and is superb as a character tree in high, dry gardens because it endures both drought and cold.

Weeping juniper (*J. flaccida*), to 40 feet, a beautiful tree with drooping branches and branchlets, is not as cold-hardy as some of its cousins. There are some fine

'Nova' juniper at Brookside Gardens, Wheaton, Maryland

Bull bay magnolia (Magnolia grandiflora)*, Callaway Gardens, Pine Mountain, Georgia*

Bull bay magnolia (M. grandiflora)

specimens in Big Bend National Park in Texas. It is hardy in Zone 7. (See *Juniperus* chart, pages 320–321.)

MAGNOLIA

MAGNOLIACEAE Magnolia family

I remember, a long time ago, taking picnics to the Sarah P. Duke Gardens at Duke University and making straight for some behemoth bull bay magnolias that lined a field. Beneath their great, spreading branches one could sit, eat, and even stand in what felt like a large, cool, private cave. Very soon afterwards I moved north to Maryland and learned that while *Magnolia grandiflora* grows and flowers just fine here, it will never achieve the splendid proportions of those North Carolina trees. In Maryland, every 20 years or so, severe temperatures cause many of the trees to drop their evergreen leaves and die back.

Yet, some of bull bay's more than 100 cultivars are extremely hardy: 'Edith Bogue', a winner of the Pennsylvania Horticultural Society's Gold Medal Plant Award in 1992, shows the greatest leaf and stem hardiness ($-22°F$). It will grow to about 40 feet in the Philadelphia area. Two more cold-tolerant trees are 'Spring Grove #16', from Cincinnati's Olmsted-designed horticultural treasure trove, Spring Grove Cemetery, and 'Bracken's Brown Beauty', with leaves smaller than the average, which are a lovely orange-brown on the underside.

Bull bay magnolias grow quickly. In my garden, a one-foot volunteer seedling a friend transplanted from beneath her own tree 13 years ago is now 15 feet tall. Every December, I cut off a branch or two from the bull bay for holiday decorations and am always amazed at how what seemed like a small branch outside becomes more than enough greenery to decorate the whole house.

The bull bay is a heat- and sun-loving tree. "Best treated as a wall plant," wrote William Robinson in *The English Flower Garden,* "under these conditions it thrives well and flowers freely." Otherwise, in the cool, misty climate of England, the bull bay will not get enough sun to bring forth its huge, creamy white, fragrant flowers in summer. Its large, oval, glossy evergreen leaves—often fuzzy rust color on the underside—are handsome enough to make you forget all about the flowers and want this plant as an elegant screen or giant hedge.

The bull bay magnolia has a number of handsome relatives—wonderfully primitive-looking trees—found in the wild in the South, but often able to tolerate colder temperatures than those in their place of origin. Some

Bull bay magnolia (M. grandiflora) *espalier, Memphis*

Magnolia

Name	Origin	Flower	Foliage	Zones	Height	Regions	Landscape Use
Magnolia ashei Ashe magnolia	Florida, Texas	White flower, 6 in across in spring	Large, oblong, deciduous leaves with white undersides	6 to 9	To 15 ft	South, Mid-Atlantic, Lower Midwest	Small tree
Magnolia cordata Yellow cucumber magnolia	North Carolina, South Carolina, Georgia	Yellow, May; cucumber fruit opens to red seeds	Long, 10-in leaves, hairy beneath, deciduous	6 to 9	35 ft	South, Mid-Atlantic	Tree
Magnolia grandiflora Southern magnolia, bull bay magnolia	North Carolina, Florida, Texas	8-in fragrant flower, May–August, red fruits	Thick, dark green, leathery, evergreen	6 to 9	To 100 ft	South, Mid-Atlantic, Lower Midwest	Large hedge, specimen, espalier
Magnolia macrophylla Bigleaf magnolia, cucumber tree	Kentucky to Florida, Louisiana	Giant flower, May/June	Leaves to 3 ft long, light green, deciduous	5 to 8	To 50 ft	South, Mid-Atlantic, Midwest, Northeast	Large unusual specimen tree
Magnolia tripetala Umbrella magnolia	Pennsylvania to Alabama, Mississippi	Beautiful, malodorous flower, May	Large leaves at ends of branches give umbrella effect, deciduous	5 to 8	To 40 ft	South, Mid-Atlantic, Midwest, Northeast	Tree
Magnolia virginiana Sweet bay magnolia, swamp magnolia	Coastal areas of eastern U.S.	Fragrant, creamy white, 3 to 5 in, May, red fruits	Leathery, green, glaucous beneath, evergreen in South	6 to 9	To 60 ft, usually 20 to 30 ft	South, Mid-Atlantic, Lower Midwest	Small tree

theorize that they were originally northern plants that seeded themselves ahead of advancing glaciers and survived at the glacier's southern limit with some of their northern genotypes intact. Most are on the too-large side for an average garden, but their tropical-looking leaves and creamy, fragrant flowers are good reasons to bend the rules. Their generous size puts them in scale with nonresidential buildings such as schools, office buildings, churches, and apartment buildings.

Umbrella magnolia (Magnolia tripetela)

Two of the hardiest magnolias are the yellow cucumber tree (*M. cordata*), which will survive in Zone 5, and umbrella magnolia (*M. tripetela*), which survives in some places in Zone 4. Both grow to about 40 feet and are deciduous.

Called "the most spectacular flowering tree in the Temperate Zone" (by someone important, I cannot remember who), bigleaf magnolia (*M. macrophylla*) is the most primitive- and tropical-looking of all. Leaves that measure up to 30 inches long by 12 inches wide, a matte, medium green with a fine yellow midrib above, reverse to an icy gray-green below. In early summer (here, the third week in May), cream-colored flowers, up to 16 inches across, nestle in the whorls of these giant leaves.

Bigleaf magnolia grows quickly and will reach 40 feet. The outlandish size of its leaves and flowers makes it a unique specimen. Most books say that it ought to be sited out of the wind because the big leaves shred, but some people who grow these trees contend that they become stronger if grown in the open.

For those who want the bigleaf look in a small garden, the Ashe magnolia (*M. ashei*) is the answer. Similar in appearance to the bigleaf magnolia, with leaves almost as big and flowers up to 8 inches across, it is a much smaller plant. In addition to its large flowers and its leaves and

Culture	Propagate	Comment
Moist, rich soil, sun	Seed	Small size puts flowers at eye level; immense leaves, flowers; blooms early; has been grown in Chicago!
Moist, rich soil, sun	Seed, cuttings	Yellow flowers, cucumber fruits are exotic. Cultivar: 'Miss Honeybee' (pale yellow flowers). Similar: *M. acuminata* (larger leaves, taller).
Rich, moist soil, pH 5–6, plenty of space, sun	Seed, cuttings	Grows fast, needs space. Many good good cultivars: 'Edith Bogue' (hardy), 'Little Gem' (dwarf), 'Symmes Select' (nice shape). State tree of Louisiana, Mississippi.
Medium soil, not too wet, not too dry, sun or very good light	Seed	Dramatic, tropical, grows fast. Shield from wind. Species: *M. fraseri* (smaller leaves, flowers).
Sun, part shade, moist, well-drained, slightly acid soil	Seed	Dramatic flowers, handsome foliage, nice landscape tree
Moist, acid (pH 4–5) soil; tolerates wet soil; sun to very light shade	Seed, cuttings	Large range, hardiness varies with origin, found in swamps, tolerates wet soil, flowers after last frost. Varieties: *australis* (evergreen, upright, one stem), *pumila* (blooms early, deciduous).

Ironwood (Olneya tesota) *(Marcus Bollinger Design, Charles Mann photo)*

small size, it has the advantage of blooming while it is still quite young. Precocious flowers appear on 18-inch plants. Of bushy habit, ashe magnolia grows only about 15 feet tall. Horticulturist J. C. Raulston has called Ashe magnolia "one of the great plants of the world." And he is absolutely right. If you can grow one of these, buy one immediately!

Sweet bay magnolia (*M. virginiana*), a small tree suitable for small gardens, can replace exotic Asian magnolias, whose flowers are so often ruined by late frosts. It blooms in May/June, when all danger of frost is past. Usually multistemmed, it is nearly evergreen in warm climates but drops almost all of its leaves here (Zone 7). The taller, more upright *M.v.* var. *australis* is said to be evergreen. Sweet bay magnolia is sometimes called "swamp magnolia" and is tolerant of wet soils. (See *Magnolia* chart, above.)

OLNEYA TESOTA Ironwood, desert ironwood
LEGUMINOSAE Pea family

Ironwood got its name from its wood, so heavy, hard, and dense it sinks in water, something I would love to test. Native Americans used it for arrowheads and tool handles. They also roasted its seeds for food and ground them into pinole. In more recent times, the presence of ironwood in the wild has been used as an indicator of places that will support citrus, since their cold-tolerance is similar.

Similar to those of the palo verde tree, ironwood's small leaves are blue-green, but its trunk and larger branches are gray. Arizona landscape architect Judy Mielke likes to use ironwood in her residential designs. She says that although it has thorns, if placed carefully, it can be an excellent poolside tree, as it produces mini-

'Miss Honeybee' (Magnolia acuminata)

mal litter. Growing gnarled with age, the trunk of an older tree lends a great deal of character and is a powerful symbol of the desert landscape.

Origin: Ironwood grows naturally along washes and low hills in southeastern California, southern Arizona, and northwestern Mexico.

Flower: Pink to lavender pea-shaped flowers, borne in racemes, in spring

Foliage: Leaflets in 2 to 10 pairs, blue-green

Hardiness: Zones 9 to 10

Height: 25 feet high by 30 feet wide

Region: Southwest

Landscape use: Specimen tree

Culture: Ironwood needs good drainage and is drought-tolerant when established.

Propagation: Seeds

OXYDENDRUM ARBOREUM Sourwood, sorrel tree
ERICACEAE Heath family

Sourwood has so many good qualities that one wonders why there isn't a sourwood in every garden. A slow-growing tree, packed with talent, it stays small for a long time; it blooms showily in summer—sprays of lily-of-the-valley white, fragrant bells. After the flowers fade, the seeds and panicles turn tan and stay on the tree, contrasting with the fall foliage of flaming

Sourwood (Oxydendrum arboreum)*, fall color*

red-orange. Even in winter, the pretty bark is striking. The classic combination of sourwood with oak leaf hydrangea is showy the year around, but especially in fall, when their tan flowers and seeds blend and their scarlet and mahogany leaves contrast.

Possibly due to air pollution, there are few decent specimens in the Washington, D.C., area, but I've seen wonderful examples of sourwood in the Smokies and in Memphis (where, it seems, all trees grow to magnificence).

Origin: A member of the heath family that occurs on acid, well-drained soil from southern Illinois and Pennsylvania south to Louisiana and Florida

Flower: Sprays of fragrant white flowers to 10 inches in June/July. These fade to an attractive tan color and remain on the tree into winter.

Foliage: Long, medium green, turning brilliant red in fall

Hardiness: Zones 4 to 9

Height: Slow growing to 50 feet or more

Region: Eastern United States

Landscape use: Specimen tree

Culture: Acid, moist, well-drained soil; sun

Cultivar: 'Chameleon' (abundant flowers and variable fall color)

PICEA ENGELMANNII Engelmann spruce
PINACEAE Pine family

A bold symbol of the Mountain West, Engelmann spruce colors low, moist slopes and valleys a deep, rich green. Sharp-pointed needles and a shallow flaky bark on old trunks separate lovely Engelmann spruce from its look-alike, grand fir. In the garden, Engelmann spruce grows into a majestic specimen. The steel blue–needled cultivar 'Glauca' is a favorite in cold midwestern gardens. The species name honors St. Louis physician and botanist George Engelmann, whose name appears in a number of southwestern species, as does that of his partner in medicine and in botanizing, Dr. Frederick Adolphus Wislizenus.

Origin: Low, moist slopes and valley bottoms from British Columbia to New Mexico

Cone: To 3 inches, scaled

Foliage: Short, dark green, evergreen needles clothe the stems densely.

Hardiness: Probably Zones 2 to 5 or 6

Height: To 150 feet

Regions: Pacific Northwest, Mountain, moist slopes of Southwest

Landscape use: Specimen

Culture: Sun, moist soil

Longleaf pine (Pinus palustris) *in the "grass" stage*

Cultivar: 'Glauca' has steel blue foliage and eventually reaches up to 60 feet.
Propagation: Seed, cuttings

PINUS PALUSTRIS Longleaf pine
PINACEAE Pine family

Once the longleaf pine, one of Alabama's state trees, covered thousands and thousands of acres in the Southeast. Eighteenth-century plant explorer William Bartram described a "vast plain" that was covered with "grass, interspersed with an infinite variety of herbaceous plants . . . and a forest of the great long-leaved pine." The savannah community to which the longleaf pine belongs is as unique botanically as the prairie communities of the Midwest. Both are rich in species and have existed over millennia, honed by intermittent fires that determined what grew and prospered. Today, although it may not be vanishing with the same speed as the prairie did, the longleaf pine community is in dangerous decline. The commercial raking of pine straw for garden use further endangers existing communities by removing nutrients, damaging the layer of grass and herbaceous plants under the trees, and supplanting controlled burning programs.

Growing a longleaf pine in your front yard won't bring back the past, but it does provide a dramatic tree that slowly—at the rate of perhaps one foot each year—grows to 100 feet tall. Longleaf pine stays in its distinctive "grass stage" for the five years or so it takes to develop a root system. During this time, it is a trunkless spray of needles more than 12 inches long that looks like an evergreen clump of bright green grass. Position it in a spot where you can watch it develop.

A stand of these at the edge of a vacation house garden near the sea would be a lovely way to keep track of the summers spent there. And it would send forth the nostalgia-inducing aroma of pine needles baking in the sun.
Origin: Southeastern United States from Virginia to Texas
Foliage: Very long (more than 1-foot) needles in bunches of three, evergreen
Hardiness: Zones 7 to 10
Height: To 100 feet
Region: South
Culture: Sun, good drainage
Species: *P. edulis* is a deep green, neatly mounded evergreen from 10 to 40 feet high at maturity, depending upon moisture. It develops a rugged, bonsailike shape with time. It has finely textured needles and small cones that only rarely produce seed in cultivation.

P. monophylla: This silvery-needled piñon from the Great Basin has somewhat larger cones and needles than common piñon, but just as elegant a mature shape. Both are extraordinarily useful in small-scale landscapes.
Propagation: Seed (cool stratified)

PITHECELLOBIUM FLEXICAULE Texas ebony
LEGUMINOSAE Pea family

A small, handsome evergreen tree, Texas ebony is named for its dark mahogany (but not black) wood. A lovely addition to a desert garden, Texas ebony has refreshing dark green leaves. When pruned, its lacy evergreen leaves on multiple trunks make it a stunning specimen plant. Allowed to grow naturally, it serves as a flowering hedge. Its fragrant cream-colored feathery flower spikes bloom in spring

Mature longleaf pines (P. palustris) *landscape,*
Palm Beach County Schools

Trees

and sometimes more than once again in summer. Slow growing, Texas ebony is worth the wait.

Origin: South Texas and northeastern Mexico

Flower: Creamy white spikes blooming intermittently from May through November, followed by brown bean-like pods and red seeds

Foliage: Dark, evergreen leaflets

Hardiness: Zones 9 to 10

Height: To 30 feet

Region: Southwest

Landscape use: A pruned tree with multistemmed trunks has character as a specimen. Unpruned, it can serve as a hedge.

Culture: Well-drained soil; is frost-tender and may die back to the roots. Texas ebony is drought-tolerant when established.

POPULUS FREMONTII Valley cottonwood
SALICACEAE Willow family

Once common along the West's permanent rivers, the valley cottonwood is disappearing today, due to encroachment by development

Valley cottonwood (Populus fremontii) *(Charles Mann photo)*

and competition from weedy introduced species. Albuquerque designer Judith Phillips uses cottonwoods in combination with golden currant and creeping mahonia for a beautiful effect in spring and summer and bright color in the fall. Fast growing and handsome, these trees are ideal for large gardens.

Origin: Along streams or in places where groundwater is shallow, to 6,500 feet in southern Colorado and Utah, New Mexico, West Texas, and northern Mexico

Flower: Conspicuous red male catkins in spring before budbreak; females produce the cottony vehicle for seed dispersal in early summer.

Foliage: Glossy, large yellow green leaves, turning bright yellow in fall

Hardiness: Zones 4 to 9

Height: To 80 feet

Region: Southwest

Landscape use: Very large shade tree

Culture: Needs moisture

Species/cultivars: *P. sargentii,* the rugged sentinel poplar of the plains, attains heroic proportions with time; plant accordingly. One of the most statuesque park trees, the heavy limbs can shed large branches in storms; site it away from windows and delicate structures. Suckers prolifically.

P. acuminata, the narrowleaf cottonwood, gives quick shade to new suburbs. Somewhat more slender but even faster growing than *P. sargentii.*

POPULUS TREMULOIDES Quaking aspen
SALICACEAE Willow family

In nature, one never sees a single quaking aspen. These stunning trees grow in colonies, the straight gray-white trunks forming patterns and the trembling leaves making their own distinct sound. "Aspen is gregarious," writes Dr. Arthur Kruckeberg, "forming clumps of bold green stems . . . all from a single seed!"

A steep, sloping yard is the ideal setting for a grove of aspen, underplanted with grasses and wildflowers for spring and summer color and dark, evergreen *Mahonia repens* for winter contrast with the glorious gray trunks. But it would be in fall, when these trees shimmer yellow-gold, that the gardener would thank his lucky stars for a yard too steep for an ordinary garden. Otherwise, a clump of aspen as an accent behind a shrub border or marking an entrance or walk provides the same effect on a smaller scale.

Origin: Moist sites from Alaska east to Labrador, south to Virginia; Rocky Mountains south into New Mexico and Arizona. Often "in sagebrush–yellow pine country and

Aspen grove (Populus tremuloides)*, Strybing Arboretum, San Francisco*

upwards to nearly timberline," writes Dr. Kruckeberg.

Flower: Brownish catkins

Foliage: Attractive all year, it turns a shimmering gold in autumn.

Hardiness: Zones 3 to 6

Height: To 30 feet

Regions: Southwest, high country in most of North America

Landscape use: Accent plants in clumps

Culture: Quaking aspen is poorly adapted to low elevations partly because it doesn't tolerate heat and will suffer leaf scorch below its normal range. It is relatively short lived.

Species: Black cottonwood (*P. trichocaroa*) is a much larger tree (50 to 100 feet).

PROSOPIS GLANDULOSA VAR. GLANDULOSA Honey mesquite
LEGUMINOSAE Pea family

After seeing a honey mesquite in bloom at San Antonio Botanic Garden in Texas, it is easy to understand why native plant research scientist and author Benny J. Simpson of the Texas Agricultural Experiment Station feels that it should be the state tree. Honey mesquite is handsome, carefree, and attracts creatures great and small. Honeybees come for pollen, and birds and small animals forage for the flat, long seedpods.

People use the rootwood to barbecue. Older trees are picturesque, with gnarled trunks that contrast with the fine, lacy foliage. Just one on a buffalo grass lawn is like a piece of living sculpture. When left unpruned, honey mesquite's foliage acts as a screen.

Origin: Found along streams and arroyos and on adjacent alluvial hills of Kansas southwest over Texas into Arizona and Mexico

Flower: White-gold flower spikes, late March through May, followed by beans through summer

Foliage: Fine-textured, lacy foliage on thorny branches

Hardiness: Borderline in 6b, best adapted to Zones 7b (and warmer) to 10

Height: To 30 feet

Region: Southwest

Landscape use: In warmer areas, a deciduous specimen tree or an effective hedge or barrier

Culture: Deep, well-drained soil. Establish deep-rooted honey mesquite with generous, intermittent waterings.

Species/cultivars: *P. pubescens* is similar (with pollen that is toxic to honeybees), has screw-bean-shaped seedpods. *P. velutina,* the velvet mesquite, from farther west, has edible beans, narrower leaves, and is available in thornless hybrids.

QUERCUS AGRIFOLIA Coast live oak
FAGACEAE Beech family

A very large coast live oak, like a spectacular view, is something that comes along with a piece of property—if one is very, very lucky. Traditional landscape practices—particularly lawns that require irrigation—are lethal to these beautiful giants. For those fortunate West Coast gardeners who already own a coast

Mesquite (Prosopis)*, southern California*

Trees

Fawn-colored leaf litter and rocks are all the ground cover needed under this coast live oak (Quercus agrifolia).
(Thomas Church Design)

live oak, Bart O'Brien has listed some dos and don'ts for living and dealing with it (see box, opposite).

QUERCUS CHRYSOLEPIS Canyon live oak, golden cup oak
FAGACEAE Beech family

The best evergreen oak for the garden, canyon live oak feels at home in a wide variety of situations from sun to part shade, from dry to moderately moist. Native on open slopes and wooded canyons throughout California and north to southern Oregon, it is drought-tolerant. Gardeners trim its hollylike evergreen leaves into dense hedges or allow a single plant to grow into a fine, evergreen tree. Leaves are usually a lustrous green above and blue-gray beneath, but can vary to yellow-green.

Dr. Arthur R. Kruckeberg of the University of Washington reports fine specimens in Seattle at the Government Locks and on the University of Washington campus.

Origin: Open slopes and wooded canyons from Oregon to Baja California.

Fruit: Nut

Foliage: Leathery, evergreen leaves, variable from elliptical to those with hollylike spines

Hardiness: Zones 8 and 9

Height: Variable, from a shrub to a 100-foot tree

Regions: Pacific Northwest, California

Landscape use: Specimen, hedge, shrub (responds to trimming)

Culture: Adaptable; it is best to use local plants. Avoid deep shade or wet spots.
Propagation: Fresh acorns

QUERCUS GAMBELII Gambel's oak
FAGACEAE Beech family

Possibly the most widespread and certainly the most winter-hardy of western upland oaks, says nursery owner Gwen Kelaidis, is Gambel's oak, which grows on millions of acres of the Rocky Mountain and Intermountain West. She recommends planting it as a young plant or seedling, but says it grows surprisingly quickly. In nature, it forms extensive colonies by underground rhizomes—but in cultivation, it appears to be a solitary specimen. In the garden with light irrigation, it will form taller (to 12-foot) and larger specimens than in the wild. In fall, it colors brilliantly red-orange and looks terrific with little bluestem and chamisa. Tough, versatile, and compact, Gambel's oak is an excellent selection for home landscapes.

Origin: Rocky Mountain and Intermountain West: Nevada and Utah to Colorado and south to central New Mexico and Arizona

Flower: Not showy

Foliage: Typically white oak leaf shape

Hardiness: Zones 4 to 8

Height: To 12 feet

Region: Semiarid, cold temperate climates

Landscape use: Screening, background plantings

Grove of Gambel's oak (Quercus gambelii) *(Charles Mann photo)*

Culture: Semiarid to lightly irrigated, well-drained slopes and beds

Species: *Q. turbinella:* a powdery gray, holly-leaved oak forming billowy mounds a yard or two tall (sometimes forming a small tree). Leaves persist through winter, only turning brown before the new leaves emerge—an exciting alternative for dry gardens.

Q. undulata: this diminutive tree usually stays below 20 feet, forming heavy trunks and graceful, almost Japanese shapes with maturity. Fantastically varied leaf shape and plant form. Most turn deep orange before frost.

Propagation: Seed, young plants

QUERCUS VIRGINIANA Live oak
FAGACEAE Beech family

Hung with Spanish Moss, live oak, a dreamy symbol of the Old South, is the queen of all southern shade trees. A giant of a tree that eventually spreads wider than tall, live oak is a tree to plant for posterity because it will not reach its majestic potential in a single lifetime. But even a young tree is very attractive, with fine, evergreen leaves (it may become deciduous in the northernmost part of its range) and a nice broad habit. With grandchildren in mind, give live oak plenty of room to spread.

Magnificent examples of live oaks grow at Magnolia Gardens in Charleston, where they line the entrance drive, and at Middleton Place, also in Charleston, where people make pilgrimages to the 900-year-old Middleton Oak. But there are hundreds of less-celebrated live oaks throughout the South, including northern Florida and the lower parishes in Louisiana, where they spring up in

Live oak (Quercus virginiana), *Magnolia Gardens, Charleston*

HOW TO NURTURE A LIVE OAK

Do leave oak leaf duff under the tree intact.

Do make sure to keep the crown of the plant dry.

Do plant lightly beneath existing oaks with appropriate drought-tolerant plants that will need no summer water (once they are established). Use a drip irrigation system (not sprinklers) to establish these plants:

Dryopteris arguta

Heuchera maxima and hybrids

Iris douglasiana and hybrids

Mahonia aquifolium, M. pinnata, M. repens

Rhamnus californica

Ribes sanguineum var. *glutinosum, R. viburnifolium*

Rosa californica, R. gymnocarpa

Symphoricarpos albus

Do use decking under oaks if it is very carefully constructed, and if plenty of space will be left free for future expansion of the trunk; potted plants (which drain to the ground) must not be used on this deck.

Do thin out dead and diseased growth.

DON'T grade beneath the tree's canopy.

DON'T allow soil compaction activities beneath the tree's drip line: vehicle parking, storage of construction materials.

DON'T pave with impermeable surfaces.

DON'T use supplemental irrigation—except during winter (coolest) months in drought years.

DON'T plant a lawn under the tree—ever!

AVOID trenching activities and running utilities beneath the tree's drip line.

---

fencerows. At St. Martinville, in the heart of Cajun country in southern Louisiana, Evangeline's Oak towers over the bayou next to St. Martin of Tours Catholic church.

Origin: Southern Virginia along the coast to Florida, Louisiana, and Texas

Fruit: Acorn

Foliage: Small, evergreen, oval leaves, will drop with cold at the northern limits of their range

Hardiness: Zones 8 (7b) to 10

Height: Grows slowly to 40 to 60 feet tall by over 100 feet wide.

Regions: Lower South

Landscape use: Specimen shade tree

Culture: Sun, moderately moist soil

Propagation: Fresh acorns

Cabbage palm (Sabal palmetto)

SABAL PALMETTO Cabbage palm, sabal palm, palmetto

PALMAE Palm family

Cabbage palm is the state tree both of Florida and of South Carolina. Eventually reaching 50 to 60 feet, it seems to pass through its shrub stage slowly. For this reason, and because it self-sows abundantly, it is frequently seen in gardens in its young, shrubby stage.

What is very distinct about cabbage palm, says horticulturist and designer Joe Lawson, is that the places where the old leaf stalks were attached look a little like the markings on a pineapple and give this tree's trunk character. Because cabbage palm tolerates salt spray, Joe Lawson uses it in seaside gardens, where its shrubby stage can be enjoyed and where the tree that ultimately results will be welcomed.

Origin: North Carolina to Florida, Bahamas, and West Indies

Flower: Large spikes of fragrant, greenish white flowers on a very long inflorescence

Foliage: Palmate, fan-shaped leaves, 6 feet long, glossy gray above with hairy filaments and a hard, smooth stem

Hardiness: Zones 8 to 10

Height: To 60 feet

Regions: Coastal South, Florida

Landscape use: Framing trees, clumps

Culture: Sun; easy; little problem of disease; tolerates salt spray but not saltwater in soil, although it tolerates occasional flooding. Trim off seeds to discourage self-sowing; trimming off fronds is optional. Sabals need much care after transplanting because they have to grow what is basically a new root system.

Propagation: Seed

SOPHORA SECUNDIFLORA Mescal bean, Texas mountain laurel

LEGUMINOSAE Pea family

Recommended for the Rio Grande plains of Texas by Benny J. Simpson and for parts of the South by Bob McCartney, mescal bean is a small evergreen tree (or called by some large shrub). Its gorgeous drooping clusters of pale purple, intensely fragrant pealike flowers are reminiscent of wisteria—except for one thing: the flowers smell exactly like grape Kool-Aid.

Children of all ages (those who can be trusted not to eat the poisonous red beans that follow the flowers) love this tree for its beauty and its evocative scent.

Origin: Texas, New Mexico, Mexico

Flower: Drooping clusters of purple/white pea flowers that look like shortened wisteria flowers, followed by a poisonous, very hard, bright red bean that has been used in jewelry making

Mescal bean (Sophora secundiflora), right, at San Antonio Botanical Center

Foliage: Dense, evergreen compound leaves on multi-stemmed shrubs

Hardiness: Zones 8 to 10

Height: To 20 feet, but usually 10 feet

Regions: South, Lower Midwest

Landscape use: Specimen, shrub border, small tree

Culture: Full sun to light shade, neutral to alkaline soil; tolerates drought and heat

Propagation: Seed (scarify very hard beans by filing or nicking), cuttings

TAXODIUM DISTICHUM Bald cypress
TAXODIACEAE Bald cypress family

The same ghostly, moss-draped bald cypress that breaks the black waters of southern swamps with its cypress "knees" can be grown in Illinois fields. But don't expect the knees or the stalagmite growths that arise from the roots in Illinois, unless bald cypress is grown in standing water or saturated soil. Though bald cypress does grow in water, the tree thrives in ordinary garden soil and, when well established, it will even tolerate drought. Its seed always needs stagnant water in order to germinate.

The "bald" in the common name refers to the fact that although this is a conifer, it drops its needles annually. Bald cypress and its somewhat smaller, narrower near relative, the pond cypress (*T. distichum* var. *nutans* or *T. ascendens*), are the only native conifers that do so, turning a beautiful rusty brown in the fall before becoming "bald." After the leaves drop, bald cypress's rough, textured bark and distinct descending branch structure serve as winter sculpture.

In habit, the bald cypress resembles a tall, narrow Christmas tree, but its reddish brown trunk is "buttressed"—flaring out at the base like an elephant's foot—especially in wet situations.

Interestingly, says Illinois nurseryman Earl Cully, who grows many varieties, the cypresses "have tremendous potential as a street tree. They do well in Chicago, for example. They are tough and appear to be tolerant of pollution."

Origin: Delaware south to Florida and as far west as southern Illinois, Texas, and Arkansas

Foliage: Deciduous, feathery bright green needles appear in spring and turn a copper orange color in fall before dropping.

Hardiness: Zones 4 to 9. It will grow north of its range into Zone 4. Michael Dirr writes of 75-year-old specimens in southern Canada, Minnesota, and in Syracuse,

*Bald cypress (*Taxodium distichum*)
turns a lovely rust color before dropping its needles.*

New York, and Donald Wyman mentions an 80-foot specimen in Boston "in perfect condition." To be sure of a bald cypress's hardiness, locate local sources.

Height: Varies with the individual or cultivar, from 45 to 100 feet or more

Regions: Northeast, Mid-Atlantic, South, Midwest

Landscape use: Specimen tree, grove, pondside

Culture: Ordinary to saturated soil, sun. Once established in an ordinary garden situation, a tree will grow two to three feet per year without extra care. Pest-free.

Species/cultivars: 'Monarch of Illinois' (regally spreading), 'Shawnee Brave' (perfectly pyramidal, narrow habit).

Pond cypress, *Taxodium ascendens,* narrower, with scalelike foliage, slower growing, Zone 5. A cultivar, *T. ascendens* 'Prairie Sentinel' (very narrow, upright). *Taxodium ascendens* var. *nutans,* extremely hardy (having withstood −26°F), excellent foliage, vigorous.

Montezuma cypress (*Taxodium mucronatum*), a Mexican species, nearly evergreen.

Propagation: Seed (sown in standing water)

Appe

ndix

Appendix 1

CONSIDER THE SOURCE

While it is ridiculously easy to buy azaleas from faraway Asia or primroses from the Himalayas, it can be surprisingly difficult to buy goldenrods native to the next county. The hunt for native plants suitable to your region and the microclimate of your own garden can be a challenge, but it is one that adds spice to gardening. While the local garden center may stock a few tried and true, superpopular natives—dogwood, asters, phlox—unless you are lucky enough to live near a good retail native plant nursery, you'll have to track down others from more specialized sources—usually through the mail. This involves that most delightful of winter gardening chores: browsing through catalogs until they are dog-eared, the only gardening that can be done in bed.

The list in this chapter includes a source for every plant described in this book and, to the best of my knowledge, includes only those nurseries that propagate their own plants. While nursery propagation is the best and most efficient means of producing most natives, in the past wild collection has been the principal means of acquiring others—particularly bulbs and woodland ephemerals such as lilies, trilliums, and dogtooth violets, which take years to go from seed to flowering size.

A sense of being at the eleventh hour in terms of preserving species has made some native plant societies take a firm stand on the issue of wild collection. The New

England Wild Flower Society's pamphlet *From the Garden* states: "The collection of wild plants by nurserymen and gardeners has seriously diminished or even eliminated local colonies of native wildflowers from their natural habitats. In particular, wild orchids, trilliums, and some fern species have been badly victimized by this practice . . . purchasing wild-collected wildflowers generally equates with paying for their removal from the wild!"

The New England Wild Flower Society encourages nurseries to undertake the long process of propagating difficult natives, and it encourages gardeners to purchase from these nurseries. This is conservation through propagation. "Propagated" means that the plant has been started from a cutting, seed, or tissue culture. It means the plant was not collected from the wild. Today, in an age of vanishing habitats and endangered species, buying only nursery-propagated plants is one way to protect our wild heritage.

Most people heartily agree and do their best to avoid buying collected plants, but labeling can be confusing. At the time of this writing, the term "nursery grown" can be applied legally to any plant that has spent a single growing season in a nursery. This means that wild-collected plants can be potted up and spend only months in a nursery to be called "nursery grown."

If you're buying from a walk-in retail nursery, you can usually tell something about a plant's origin by

the way it looks. There are some obvious signs that a plant is nursery propagated. It is likely to be young rather than mature and will be growing in a grow mix with a neat, centered-in-its-pot position. You won't find other wildlings in its pot. If you look around, you'll probably see row upon row of the same species in the uniform sizes of plants started at the same time.

If you buy from a catalog, you may find a statement that the nursery propagates its own natives. If not, there are other indicators. Price is one, because it reflects the time and work that has gone into nurturing. For example, the price of a white trillium (*Trillium grandiflorum*), a plant that is easily propagated but requires five to seven years to go from seed to flowering size, should be, at the very least, the going rate for a perennial plant. Expect to pay two or more times as much for a blooming-size plant. Be wary when the prices of trilliums as well as other woodland ephemerals (*Goodyera, Cypripedium, Erythronium,* and ferns) are just too good to be true. They are probably wild collected.

Perhaps the biggest red alert is the presence of the pink lady slipper (*Cypripedium acaule*). The fall 1989 issue of *Native Notes* quoted from an Eastern Native Plant Alliance "Plant Alert" bulletin by Bill Brumback and Richard Lighty. "No nursery in the world is propagating [pink lady slipper] *Cypripedium acaule*."

Until tissue-cultured plants became available, the very act of offering the pink lady slipper speaks volumes. Not only is the origin of the plant suspect, its survival rate in the average garden is next to zero because few gardens enjoy the conditions and contain the specific mycorrhiza required to keep it alive. To me, the act of selling pink lady slipper says that the nursery doesn't know or want to know or care where it came from and, worse, doesn't care that most pink lady slippers die within a year or two out of their habitat.

Beyond ethical considerations, there is the simple fact that other collected plants, too, do not travel, transplant, or fare as well in your garden as nursery-grown plants whose roots haven't been disturbed but are safely contained. Nor do collected plants always have the neat, tight, even growth of plants that have never had to compete for light. Finally, collected plants were often collected too far from your region to make an easy transition.

Most natives do best if they remain close to home. The same logic that supports growing natives because they are environmentally suited to a region can be carried a little further. Although there are numerous plants that are widely adaptable, finicky ones perform best in your garden's microclimate if their provenance is local.

"Provenance"—the place within a plant's native range from which it originated—is a word that comes up again and again when horticulturists speak of native plants. They know that there is much variation within a species and that little pockets of differentiated populations exist within the range. Like Darwin's sparrows, plants of the same species will have evolved slightly different characteristics that are advantageous under the condi-

tions of their special microclimates.

A plant with a huge range—such as redbud, found in the wild from New Jersey all the way to Florida and west to Missouri and Mexico—looks a little different in Texas than it does in Virginia. Differences might be a darker shade of flower, shorter stature, or a smaller spread. And there are also important differences that can't be seen. Trees from Illinois might be hardier than those from around Jacksonville. And the ones from Jacksonville, while more tender, might be more resistant to disease.

Dr. Richard Lighty of the Mt. Cuba Center for the Study of Piedmont Flora stresses the importance of provenance. "What we're finding," he says, "is that this kind of variation is true of all plants."

The very nature of natives—plants appropriate only to a particular region—means that knowledge about them will be limited to a particular region. Big national firms tend to market only those plants with a very large range. The ephemerals of the eastern woodland that they designate as "wildflowers" are not everybody's wildflowers, but the ones that have become our stereotype.

A native plant nursery concentrates on a specific region or habitat. It can be small and intimate enough to allow the personality and idiosyncrasies of the owner to shine through, adding to the pleasure of purchase. The delightful list from Las Pilatas Nursery in Santa Margarita, California, codes its California natives from 1 to 10 in degrees of difficulty of culture. A #1 encoded plant, advises their list, "will become a weed." As for the #10 plants, the list states, "you will lose 50% while praying, doing all things right and planting

in the perfect spot."

The sometimes quirky route to finding the natives that will flourish in your garden makes the hunt for them an adventure. Acquiring an elusive, longed-for plant becomes a great victory, watching it take off in your garden a deep satisfaction.

The following list of nurseries that carry native plants is compiled from regional publications listing native growers, information made available by the New England Wild Flower Society and distributed at native plant conferences and seminars, catalogs I have used, and, in some cases, site visits. Not all nurseries are mail order. Although it was impossible to list all walk-in retail nurseries, I have tried to include outstanding ones in each region. Your local native plant society is another place to find information about places to buy nursery-propagated native plants and may also conduct sales of natives from members' own gardens.

Because botanical clubs and native plant societies often change addresses from year to year (with the election of new secretaries or membership chairs), it's a good idea to obtain (for a nominal cost) a current list of these organizations, published by the New England Wild Flower Society, 180 Hemenway Road, Framingham, MA 01701-2699, (508) 877-7630, (617) 237-4924.

Another wonderful source of information about native plants is the National Wildflower Research Center, 2600 FM 973 North, Austin, TX 78725, (512) 929-3600. This nonprofit organization provides lists of growers and nurseries in addition to other helpful information.

Nurseries That Sell Native Plants

Abundant Life Seed Foundation, P.O. Box 772, Port Townsend, WA 98368. Seeds for native perennials, trees, shrubs, and books, mail order, catalog $1.

Amenity Plant Products, RD #5, Box 265, Mt. Pleasant, PA 15666. Native seeds, rootstocks, ferns, shrubs, trees, grasses, catalog $1, mail order.

American Ornamental Perennials, P.O. Box 385, Gresham, OR 97030-0054, (503) 661-4836. A few hard-to-find West Coast natives among exotic ornamental grasses, catalog, mail order.

Appalachian Wildflower Nursery, Route 1, Box 275A, Reedsville, PA 17084, (717) 667-6998. Native and exotic perennials, trees and shrubs, catalog $1.25, mail order.

Barber Nursery, 23561 Vaughn Road, Veneta, OR 97487, (503) 935-7701. Retail and wholesale bare-root, liners, mail order.

Barfod's Hardy Ferns, 23622 Bothell Way, Bothell, WA 98021, (206) 483-0205. Retail and wholesale container, B&B, mail order.

Bernardo Beach Native Plant Farm, 1 Sanchez Road, Veguita, NM 87062. 520 Montaño N.W., Albuquerque, NM, (505) 345-6248. Retail nursery, sells desert four-o'clock, buffalo grass, Indian grass, and sages.

Blue Oak Nursery, 2731 Mountain Oak Lane, Rescue, CA 95672, (916) 677-2111. Retail and wholesale bare-root, liners, cuttings, mail order.

Boehlke's Woodland Gardens, W. 140 N. 10829 Country Aire Road, Germantown, WI 53022. Perennials and ferns, wholesale and retail, fall mail order, catalog $1.

Boothe Hill Wildflower Seeds, 23B Boothe Hill, Chapel Hill, NC 27514, (919) 967-4091. Mostly native seeds, some perennials, free catalog, mail order.

Botanic Garden Seed Co., Inc., 9 Wyckoff Street, Brooklyn, NY 11201, (718) 624-8839. Seeds, retail and wholesale, free catalog, mail order.

Broken Arrow Nursery, 13 Broken Arrow Road, Hamden, CT 06518, (203) 288-1026. Great list of Mt. Laurel cultivars, some other woody natives, SASE, mail order.

Brookside Wildflowers, Route 3, Box 740, Boone, NC 28607. Catalog gives excellent descriptions of native perennials for woodland and sunny gardens listed in order of bloom, mail order.

Burnt Ridge Nursery, 432 Burnt Ridge Road, Onalaska, WA 98570, (206) 985-2873. Retail and wholesale bare-root, containers, B&B, liners, mail order.

Callahan Seed, 6045 Foley Lane, Central Point, OR 97502, (503) 855-1164. Retail and wholesale seeds, mail order.

Carlson's Gardens, Box 305, South Salem, NY 10590. Native azaleas and rhododendrons, mail order, catalog $2.

Cherrymont Farm Nursery, Box 387, Shiloh Road, RD #1, Morgantown, PA 19543, (215) 286-9601. Many natives in a long list of perennials, very reasonable retail and mail order with $50 minimum.

Clyde Robin Seed Co., P.O. Box 2366, Castro Valley, CA 94546, (415) 785-0425. Seeds of native and exotic species, retail and wholesale, free catalog, mail order.

Colvos Creek Farm, 1931 2nd Avenue, #215, Seattle, WA 98101, (206) 441-1509. Retail and wholesale containers, B&B, liners, mail order.

County Wetlands Nursery, Ltd. Box 126, Muskego, WI 53150, (414) 679-1268. Native grasses and forbs of wetland and prairie communities, seeds, plants, consultation, catalog, mail order.

Crownsville Nursery, P.O. Box 797, Crownsville, MD 21032. Catalog $2, mail order.

Dabney Nursery, 5576 Hacks Cross Road, Memphis, TN 38125. Complete retail and wholesale nursery with some hard-to-find natives, including *Stewartia malacodendron.*

DeGiorgi Seed Company, 6011 N Street, Omaha, NE 68117, (402) 731-3901. Seeds of many wildflowers and wildflower mixes along with exotics, catalog $2, mail order.

Eco-Gardens, P.O. Box 1227, Decatur, GA 30031, (404) 294-6468. One-third of offerings native in eastern United States, rare, retail and wholesale, catalog $1, mail order.

Elixer Farm Botanicals, Brixey, MO 65618, (417) 261-2393. Ozark native seeds and roots that are used medicinally, *Echinacea,* books, mail order catalog $1 (refundable with order).

Fancy Fronds, 1911 4th Avenue West, Seattle, WA 98119. Excellent selection of native and exotic ferns, mail order, catalog $1. Fancy Fronds grows interrupted fern, among others, from spores.

Fern Valley Farms, US 421 Service Road East, Route 4, Box 235, Yadkinville, NC 27055, (919) 463-2412. Specializes in native trees and shrubs including *Stewartia malacodendron.* Call first.

Henry Field's Seed & Nursery Co., 415 North Burnett, Shenandoah, IA 51602. Some interesting native shrubs, perennials, and trees mixed in with exotics, catalog, mail order.

Flowerplace Plant Farm, P.O. Box 4865, Meridian, MS 39304, (601) 482-5686. A nice selection of native perennials and woody plants, mail order, catalog $2.

Forest Farm, 990 Tetherow Road, Williams, OR 97544-9599. Many native plants: trees, shrubs, perennials. Retail, mail order, catalog $3, includes *Magnolia ashei*!

Forest Seeds of California, 1100 Indian Hill Road, Placerville, CA 95667, (916) 621-1551. Retail and wholesale seeds, mail order.

Frosty Hollow Nursery, P.O. Box 53, Langley, WA 98260, (206) 221-2332. Retail and wholesale seeds, does site-specific seed collection, mail order.

Garden Place, P.O. Box 388, 6780 Heisley Road, Mentor, OH 44061-0388, (216) 255-3705. Field-grown natives and exotics, mail order, catalog $1.

Goodness Grows, Inc., 550 Athens Road, Winterville, GA 30683.

Gossler Farms Nursery, 1200 Weaver Road, Springfield, OR 97478-9663, (503) 746-3922. Selected native trees, shrubs, perennials among exotics, mail order, catalog $1.

Great Lakes Wildflowers, Box 1923, Milwaukee, WI 53201.

Greenlee Nursery, 301 E. Franklin Avenue, Pomona, CA 91766, (714) 629-9045. Mail order.

Greens Creek Nursery, Route 2, Box 113-A, Sylva, NC 28779, (704) 586-2726. Native woody plants, contract-grown ginseng and an evergreen native azalea.

Greer Gardens, 1280 Goodpasture Island Road, Eugene, OR 97401-1794. Some natives among exotic trees, shrubs, retail, mail order, catalog $3.

Hidden Hill Nursery, 8700 Snouffer School Road, Gaithersburg, MD 20879, (301) 869-1618. By appointment only.

High Altitude Gardens, P.O. Box 4619, Ketchum, ID 83340, (800) 874-7333. Seeds for native grasses and some perennials, mail order.

Holbrook Farm and Nursery, Route 2, Box 223B, Fletcher, NC 28732. Native perennials, grasses, shrubs, ferns, mixed in with exotics, well-illustrated catalog, mail order. Holbrook Farm sells Stokes' aster 'Klaus Jelitto'.

Holland Wildflower Farm, 290 O'Neal Lane, Elkins, AR 72727, (800) 752-5079. Perennial plants and seeds, wholesale, retail, shop, mail-order catalog $1.50.

Holley's Hobbies, Route 4, Box 130, Warrenton, VA 22186. By appointment only.

Homeplace Garden, Harden Bridge Road, Commerce, GA 30529. Native azaleas, mail order, catalog $2.

Hungry Plants, 1216 Cooper Drive, Raleigh, NC 27607, (919) 851-6521. Perennials, wholesale and retail, mail order, catalog $1.

Intermountain Cactus, 2344 South Redwood Road, Salt Lake City, UT 84119, (801) 972-5149. Winter-hardy cacti, mail order, SASE for list.

Kester's Wild Game Food Nurseries, Inc., P.O. Box 516, Omro, WI 54963. Seeds of aquatics and plants that attract wildlife, mail order.

Kline Nursery Company, P.O. Box 23161, Tigard, OR 97223-0021, (503) 244-3910. Retail and wholesale bare-root, mail order.

LaFayette Home Nursery, Inc., LaFayette, IL 61449, (909) 995-3311. Seeds of native grasses, forbs, shrubs, and trees listed by community, mail order.

Lamtree Farm, Route 1, Box 162, Warrensville, NC 28693, (919) 385-6144. Native azaleas, hard-to-find shrubs and trees, mail-order catalog $2. Lamtree carries Turk's cap lilies as well as franklinia.

Larner Seeds, P.O. Box 407, 235 Fern Road, Bolinas, CA 94924. Seeds of California native perennials, grasses, shrubs, trees, and books, mail order, catalog $1.

Las Pilatas Nursery, Star Route, Box 23X, Santa Margarita, CA 93453, (805) 438-5992. California natives, some seeds, most in containers, ship to some states, nursery open Saturdays, SASE for list, catalog $4.

Limerock Ornamental Grasses, R.D. 1, Box 111-C, Port Matilda, PA 16870. Mail order, catalog $2, sells broom sedge and turkeyfoot.

Little Valley Farm, Route 3, Box 544, Snead Creek Road, Spring Green, WI 53588, (608) 935-3324. Books, plants, and seeds of native perennials, shrubs, and vines, with emphasis on prairie plants, catalog, mail order.

Midwest Wildflowers, Box 64, Roackton, IL 61072. Wildflower seed, mail order, catalog $1.

Missouri Wildflowers Nursery, Route 2, Box 373, Jefferson City, MO 65101, (314) 496-3492. Seeds and plants of only native perennials, grasses, and some shrubs, mail order.

Moon Mountain, P.O. Box 34, Morro Bay, CA 93443. Water-saver seeds of mostly western native annuals and perennials, mail-order catalog $2.

Native Gardens, Route 1, Box 464, Greenback, TN 37742, (615) 856-3350. Perennials, trees, vines, and shrubs, seeds and plants, mail order catalog $1. Native Gardens carries white bear sedge.

Native Nurseries, 1661 Centerville Road, Tallahassee, FL 32308, (904) 386-8882.

Rows of Cornus florida *at the Don Shadow Nursery in Winchester, Tennessee*

The Natives, 2929 Carter Road, Davenport, FL 33837, (813) 422-6664. Muhly grass is one of the Florida natives carried.

Native Seed Foundation, Star Route, Moyie Springs, ID 83845, (208) 267-7938. Retail and wholesale seeds, mail order.

Native Seeds, Inc., 14590 Triadelphia Mill Road, Dayton, MD 21036, (301) 596-9818. Seeds of perennials and regional mixes, mail order, catalog.

The Natural Garden, 38W443 Highway 64, Street Charles, IL 60175, (708) 584-0150. Seeds and plants of prairie natives, mail order, catalog SASE.

Nature's Garden, P.O. Box 574, Scio, OR 97374-0574, (503) 394-3217. Retail and wholesale bare-root, container, B&B, mail order.

New England Wild Flower Society, Garden in the Woods, 180 Hemenway Road, Framingham, MA 01701. Mail order for seeds, container plants at the garden, catalog $1, plus SASE. The nursery at Garden in the Woods sells trilliums—both single and double.

Niche Gardens, 1111 Dawson Road, Chapel Hill, NC 27516, (919) 967-0078. Nice selection of mostly native perennials, shrubs, trees, retail, mail order catalog $3. Niche carries skullcap, dog fennel, purple love grass, and bamboo muhly.

North Carolina Botanical Garden, Totten Center 457-A, UNC-CH, Chapel Hill, NC 27514 (919) 967-2246. Seed list.

Northplan Seed Producers, P.O. Box 9107, Moscow, ID 83843-1607, (208) 882-8040. Retail and wholesale seeds, mail order.

G. W. Park Seed Co., Inc., Highway 254 N., Greenwood, SC 29647, (803) 223-7333. Seeds of a few native plants, mail order, free catalog.

Piccadilly Farm, 1917 Whippoorwill Road, Bishop, GA 60621.

Plant Delights Nursery at Juniper Level Botanic Gardens, 9241 Sauls Road, Raleigh, NC 27603. A very unusual collection of natives and exotic perennials, mail order, catalog $2.

Plants of the Southwest, 930 Baca Street, Santa Fe, NM 87501, (505) 983-1548. A beautiful and well-written catalog of seeds and plants, trees, shrubs, perennials, vegetables, books, retail, mail order. Plants of the Southwest carries Indian rice grass, plains zinnia, and golden currant.

Plants of the Wild, P.O. Box 866, Tekoa, WA 99033, (509) 284-2848. An excellent list of container-grown West Coast native plants, retail and wholesale, plants shipped.

Portable Acres, 2087 Curtis Drive, Penngrove, CA 94951, and 4036 Trinity Drive, Santa Rosa, CA 95405. Pacific Coast irises, mail order.

Prairie Moon Nursery, Route 3, Box 163, Winona, MN 55987, (507) 452-1362. Wetland, prairie, and woodland plants and seeds, mail order, very informative catalog $1.

Prairie Nursery, P.O. Box 306, Westfield, WI 53964, (608) 296-3679. Perennial plants and seeds; very informative, well-illustrated catalog, 2 years/$3; mail order. Prairie dropseed, shooting star, and silphiums are among their offerings.

Prairie Restorations, Inc., P.O. Box 327, Princeton, MN 55371, (612) 389-4342. Wholesale and retail, seeds and plants of midwestern flora, mail order for seeds only, free catalog.

Prairie Ridge Nursery, CRM Ecosystems, RR 2, 9738 Overland Road, Mt. Horeb, WI 53572-2832, (608) 437-5245. Retail and wholesale, native woodland, wetland, and prairie plants, consulting, mail order, catalog $1.

Primrose Path, R.D. 2, Box 110, Scottsdale, PA 15683, (412) 887-6756. Native and exotic perennials and a few woody plants, mail order, catalog $2.

Ridgecrest Nursery, U.S. Highway 64 East, Route 3, Box 241, Wynne, AK 72396, (501) 238-3763. Many natives including American smoke tree and false indigos, retail, no mail order.

Robinett Bulb Farm, P.O. Box 1306, Sebastapol, CA 95473-1306. West Coast native bulbs, publishes a new list each August, ships from September 1 through November 1 only, SASE, mail order.

Rocky Mountain Rare Plants, P.O. Box 200483, Denver, CO 80220-0483. Specializes in "seed of plants native to the Rocky Mountains and to similar regions, alpine to xeric, around the world," mail order, catalog.

Salter Tree Farm, Route 2, Box 1332, Madison, FL.

F. W. Schumacher Co., Inc., 36 Spring Hill Road, Sandwich, MA 02563, (508) 888-0659. Retail and wholesale, seeds for trees and shrubs, mail order, free catalog.

Shooting Star Nursery, 444 Bates Road, Frankfork, KY 40601, (502) 223-1679. Native perennials, shrubs, trees, mail order catalog $2.

Silver Springs Nursery, HCR 62, Box 86, Moyie Springs, ID 83845, (208) 267-5753. Retail and wholesale, northwestern natives for ground covers, SASE, mail order.

Siskiyou Rare Plant Nursery, 2825 Cummings Road, Medford, OR 97501, (503) 772-6846. Many natives in a long list of perennials and woody plants, specializes in alpines and dwarf plants for rock gardens, mail order, catalog $2.

Solar Gardens, 14400 New Hampshire Avenue, Silver Spring, MD 20904.

Southern Perennials & Herbs, 98 Bridges Road, Tylertown, MS 39667, (601) 684-1769. Catalog $3.

Southwestern Native Seeds, Box 50503, Tucson, AZ 85703. Seed for desert and mountain trees, shrubs, and perennials identified by state of origin!, mail order, catalog $1.

Stock Seed Farms, Inc., RR1, Box 112, Murdock, NE 68407, (800) 759-1520. Seed of midwestern forbs and grasses, mail order, free catalog.

Suncoast Native Plants, P.O. Box 248, Palm View Road, Palmetto FL 34220, (813) 729-5015.

Sunlight Gardens, Route 1, Box 600-A, Hillvale Road, Andersonville, TN 37705. Choice, well-described perennials, vines, shrubs, and ferns, mail-order catalog $3.

Sunshine Farm & Gardens, Rt. 5-N, Renick, WV 24966 (304) 497-2698, great selection of unusual natives; send SASE for native list.

Transplant Nursery, Parkertown Road, Lavonia, GA 30553. Outstanding selection of species and named native azalea cultivars, wholesale, retail at the nursery between March 15 and May 15, mail order. Transplant sells the flame azalea and the Choptank hybrids.

Tripple Brook Farm, 37 Middle Road, Southampton, MA 01073. Some hard-to-find native perennials, shrubs, ferns, and grasses, mail order.

The springhouse at Water Ways Nursery in Lovettsville, Virginia

Valley Nursery, Box 8545, Helena, MT 59601, (406) 442-8460. Retail and wholesale native and exotic perennials and woody plants, hardy for Montana area, mail order, catalog 25 cents.

Vans Pines, Inc., 7550 144th Avenue, West Olive, MI 49460, (616) 399-1620. Retail and wholesale, seeds and plants of native and exotic trees and shrubs, a few perennials, mail order, catalog 30 cents.

Vermont Wildflower Farm, Route 7, Box 5, Charlotte, VT 05445-0005, (802) 425-3931. Retail and wholesale, seeds of wildflowers and meadow mixtures, mail order, free catalog.

Andre Viette Farm and Nursery, Route 1, Box 16, Fishersville, VA 22939, (703) 943-2315. Some natives in a long list of perennials, wholesale, retail, mail-order catalog $2.

Virginia Natives, Wildside Farm, P.O. Box 18, Hume, VA 22639, (703) 364-1001. 101 natives, 85 native to eastern United States, toughies, no mail order.

Water Ways Nursery, Route 2, Box 247, Lovettsville, VA 22080, (703) 822-5994. Offers a selection of native and exotic water plants and native perennials. All of the water plants listed in this book are available from Water Ways.

Wavering Place Gardens and Nursery, Route 2, Box 269, Eastover, SC 29044, (803) 783-1682. Native woody plants, no mail order.

We-Du Nurseries, Route 5, Box 724, Marion, NC 28752, (704) 738-8300. Very long list of rare perennials, some shrubs, catalog $2. We-Du's excellent catalog lists many violets, creeping mint, *Carex austrocaroliniana,* and skullcap.

Wetlands Northwest, 8414 280th Street East, Graham, WA 98338, (206) 846-2774 and 1514 Muirhead, Olympia, WA 98502, (206) 943-0217. No mail order.

Wildflower, 234 Oak Tree Trail, Wilsonville, AK 35186, (205) 669-4097. Native plants, no mail order.

Wildginger Woodlands, P.O. Box 1091, Webster, NY 14580. Seeds and plants of wildflowers and ferns, mail order, catalog $1.

Wildlife Nurseries, Inc., P.O. Box 2724, Oshkosh, WI 54903-2724, (414) 231-3780. Roots and seeds of native grasses, grains, marsh plants, mail order.

Wildseed Farms, 1101 Campo Rosa Road, P.O. Box 308, Eagle Lake, TX 77434, (800) 848-0078. Seeds of *individual* native perennials by the packet, ounce, and pound as well as mixes, mail order, catalog $2.

Wild Wood Farms, 5231 Seven Islands Road, Madison, GA 30650, (404) 342-4912. Trees, shrubs, perennials, retail, wholesale, contract growing, open selected weekends, mail order, catalog $3.

The Wildwood Flower, Route 3, Box 165, Pittsboro, NC 37312, (919) 542-4344. Specializes in interesting hybrid lobelias, athyrium ferns, SASE for list.

Willamette Prairie Seed, 434 N.W. 6th Avenue, Suite 304, Portland, OR 97209, (503) 224-0333. Seed, retail and wholesale, mail order.

Woodlanders, 1128 Colleton Avenue, Aiken, SC 29801, (803) 648-7522. A good selection of hard-to-find native trees, shrubs, perennials, ferns, mail order, catalog $1. Georgia savory, needle palm, and climbing hydrangea are a few of their rare plants.

Wood's Native Plants, 5740 Berry Drive, Parkdale, OR 97041, (503) 352-7497. Retail and wholesale, containers, B&B, liners, cuttings, mail order.

Yerba Buena Nursery, 19500 Skyline Boulevard, Woodside, CA 94062, (415) 851-1668. Excellent selection of California native plants, retail at the nursery, including madrone and manzanitas.

Yucca Do Nursery at Peckerwood Gardens, P.O. Box 655, Waller, TX 77484. Offers Texas and southeastern native and exotic perennials, shrubs, and trees, mail order and by appointment, catalog.

WHOLESALE SELLERS

American Ornamental Perennials, P.O. Box 385, Gresham, OR 97030-0054. Bareroot, container, B&B, Northwest native grasses and perennials, mail order.

Apalachee Nursery, Turtletown, TN 37391.

Appalachian Trees, P.O. Box 92, Glendale Springs, NC 28629. Seedlings of native and exotic trees.

Applewood Seed Co., Inc., 5380 Vivian Street, Arvada, CO 80002, (303) 431-6283. Native and exotic seed mixes, free catalog.

Argura Nurseries, Inc., Route 68, Box 200, Tuckasegee, NC 28783. Native and exotic conifers, trees, shrubs.

Babikow Greenhouses, 7838 Babikow Road, Baltimore, MD 21237. Perennials, grasses, ferns.

Bluemount Nurseries, Inc., 2103 Blue Mount Road, Monkton, MD 21111. Perennials, grasses, ferns.

Bluff Mountain Nursery, 340 Bluff Road, Hot Springs, NC 28743. Azaleas, woody ornamentals.

Cedar Lane Farm, Inc., 3790 Sandy Creek Road, Madison, GA 30650, (404) 342-2626. Difficult-to-find native species and plants adaptable to the Southeast, selected for hardiness, fragrance, unusual flower color, or texture.

Cornflower Farms, Inc., P.O. Box 896, Elk Grove, CA 95759, (916) 689-1015. Containers, B&B, liners, mail order.

Tom Dodd Nurseries, Inc., P.O. Drawer 45, Semmes, AL 36575. Rare natives.

Eccles Nurseries, Inc., Drawer Y, Rimersburg, PA 16248, (814) 473-6265. Native and exotic evergreen seedlings and transplants, free catalog.

Environmental Seed Producers, P.O. Box 2709, Lompoc, CA 93438, (805) 735-8888. Large selection of native and exotic seed, free catalog.

Fern Valley Farms, Route 4, Yadkinville, NC 27055, call first: (919) 463-2412. Nice selection of native shrubs, vines, azaleas, and trees, container and B&B.

Forrest Keeling Nursery, P.O. Box 135, Elsberry, MO 63343, (314) 898-5571. Native and exotic trees and shrubs, free catalog.

Fox Hill Nursery, Route 1, Box 133-B, Turtletown, TN 37391.

Greenlee Nursery, 301 E. Franklin Avenue, Pomona, CA 91766, (714) 629-9045. Some native grasses, mail order and by appointment, including purple three-awn.

Hess Nurseries, Inc., Box 326, Cedarville, NJ 08311.

Hurricane Gap Nursery, P.O. Box 361, Flat Rock, NC 28731.

Johnston Nurseries, R.D. 1, Box 100, Creekside, PA 15732, (412) 463-8456. Native and exotic conifer and hardwood seedlings, free catalog.

Lawyer Nursery, Inc., 950 Highway 200 West, Plains, MT 59859-9706, (406) 826-3881. Bare-root, container, B&B, liners, cuttings, seeds.

Nature's Garden, 372 Welch Road, Bryson City, NC 28713.

North Creek Nurseries, Inc., RR #2, Box 33, Landenberg, PA 19350, (215) 255-0100. Mostly native perennials, shrubs, and grass liners, contract growing of such treasures as *Heuchera* 'Dale's Strain'.

North Temperate Wildflowers, RFD 1, Box 317A, New Castle, ME 04553, (207) 563-1713. Comprehensive list of herbaceous plants, catalog $1.50.

Pinelands Nursery, RR 1, Box 12, Island Road, Columbus, NJ 08022, (609) 291-9486. Native trees, shrubs, perennials, specializing in wetland species.

Salter Tree Farm, Route 2, Box 1332, Madison, FL 32340. Sells *Halesia diptera* 'Magniflora'.

Shadow Nursery, Inc., Winchester, TN 37398. Large selection, many good cultivars of native plants.

Stonecrop Gardens, 2037 S.W. 16th Avenue, Albany, OR 97321-1835, (503) 928-8652. Bare-root, containers, B&B, mail order.

Sunshine Seed Co., RR 2, Box 176, Wyoming, IL 61491, (309) 286-7356. Seed from North American habitats.

Tree of Life Nursery, P.O. Box 736, San Juan Capistrano, CA 92693, (714) 728-0685. California native plants, contract growing, has lovely specimens of *Mahonia aquifolium*.

Turner Seed Co., Route 1, Box 292, Breckenridge, TX 76024, (800) 722-8616. Native and improved grass seed climatized for Lower Midwest and Southwest.

Weston Nurseries, Inc., Route 135, P.O. Box 186, Hopkinton, MA 01748, (508) 435-3414. Among many other natives and exotics are hybrids of native azaleas.

Appendix 2

WHERE TO SEE NATIVE PLANTS

The following list includes some of the larger, better-known gardens that are devoted to native plants or contain native plant collections, as well as one or two smaller gardens.

The South

Armand Bayou Nature Center, P.O. Box 58828, Houston, TX 77258, (713) 474-2551. Includes wetland natives.

Atlanta Botanical Garden, P.O. Box 77246, Atlanta, GA 30357, (404) 876-5858. Georgia savory thrives in the herb garden.

Birmingham Botanical Garden, 2612 Lane Park Road, Birmingham, AL 35223, (205) 879-1227. Features wildflowers and ferns.

Bok Tower Gardens, P.O. Drawer 3810, Lake Wales, FL 33859, (813) 676-1408. There is a savannah restoration with wire grass and longleaf pine, as well as formal gardens that integrate natives and exotics.

Brookgreen Gardens, U.S. 17, Murrells Inlet, SC 29576, (803) 237-4218. A magnificent Florida azalea and a live oak allée are two splendid features of this garden.

Callaway Gardens, Pine Mountain, GA 31822, (404) 663-2281. Florida azaleas, sweet azaleas, wild ginger, and red buckeyes light up the woods in April.

Hilltop Arboretum, P.O. Box 82608, 11855 Highland Road, Baton Rouge, LA 70884, (504) 767-6916. Displays many natives.

Houston Arboretum & Nature Center, 4501 Woodway, Houston, TX 77024, (713) 681-8433. Has many natives.

Magnolia Plantation and Gardens, Route 4, Highway 61, Charleston, SC 29407, (803) 571-1266. Splendid live oaks, cypresses, hung with Spanish moss make this riverfront garden unforgettable.

Marie Selby Botanical Gardens, 800 South Palm Avenue, Sarasota, FL 33577, (813) 366-5730. Butterfly weeds and climbing aster bloom together in the native section.

Middleton Place, Ashley River Road, Charleston, SC 29407, (803) 556-6020. The 900-year-old Middleton live oak dominates the azalea garden.

Monticello, P.O. Box 316, Charlottesville, VA 22902, (804) 295-2657. American beautyberry, fringe tree, pineapple sage, and dogwoods grace this stunning hilltop garden.

North Carolina State University Arboretum, NC State University, Raleigh, NC 27695. Among its many attractions is the great perennial border that features dog fennel.

Pinecote, The Crosby Arboretum, 1801 Goodyear Boulevard, Picayune, MS 39466, (601) 798-6961. Feathery cypresses and natives of the Pearl River Basin are featured in this garden.

Sarah P. Duke Gardens, Duke University, Durham, NC 27706, (919) 684-5579. Magnificent bull bay magnolias tower over part of the garden.

The State Botanical Garden of Georgia, 2450 South Milledge Avenue, Athens, GA 30605. Sturdy natives—coreopsis, salvias, helianthus—mingle with exotics in the perennial garden.

The Southwest

The Arboretum at Flagstaff, Woody Mountain Road, four miles south of old U.S. 66, Flagstaff, AZ 86002, (602) 774-1441. Is devoted to propagating native plants.

In Lafayette, Louisiana, a sign points the way to a native plants conference, a satellite of the Cullowhee Conference in North Carolina, a hotbed of native plant interest in the Southeast begun as the brainchild of Dr. Leo Collins of the Tenessee Valley Authority, editor of **Native Plant News.**

Arizona-Sonora Desert Museum, 2021 North Kinney Road, Tucson, AZ 85743. A striking, formal display of natives including octopus agave, Blackfoot daisy, and hops.

Boyce Thompson Southwestern Arboretum, Box AB, Superior, AZ 85273, (602) 689-2723. Look out for rattlesnakes among the yuccas, agaves, cacti, and aloes!

Desert Botanical Garden, 1201 N. Galvin Parkway, Phoenix, AZ 85008, (602) 941-1225. Plan to visit in the spring, when *Penstemon parryi* paints the desert bright pink. Creosote bush, cacti, desert willow, sotol, palo verdes, and chuparosa are only a small part of this excellent collection.

National Wildflower Research Center, 2600 FM 973 North, Austin, TX 78725-4201. Displays of Texas wildflowers including lupine and wine-cups.

San Antonio Botanical Center, 555 Funston Place, San Antonio, TX 78209, (512) 821-5115. Mesquite trees are part of this large garden's charm.

California

The Arthur L. Menzies Memorial Garden of Native Plants, Strybing Arboretum and Botanical Gardens, Ninth Avenue at Lincoln Way, San Francisco, CA 94122, (415) 558-3622. Look for *Ceanothus,* Pacific reedgrass, and manzanitas in the magnificent California meadow restoration.

Rancho Santa Ana Botanic Garden, 1500 North College Avenue, Claremont, CA 91711, (714) 625-8767. Many different communities of California natives grow here. *Ceanothus, Chrysopsis villosa* 'San Bruno', *Artemisia* 'David's Choice', Pacific reedgrass, giant wild rye, California fescue, and a grove of red shanks are some of the highlights.

Regional Parks Botanic Garden, Tilden Regional Park, Berkeley, CA 94708, (415) 841-8732. Ceanothus, western redbud, and sword ferns are some of the many natives in this lovely hillside garden.

Santa Barbara Botanic Garden, 1212 Mission Canyon Road, Santa Barbara, CA 93105, (805) 682-4726. There's a wonderful California meadow with California poppies, ceanothus, California fescues, edged by coast live oaks, as well as a hillside of eriogonums, manzanitas, giant coreopsis, and many other California treasures. SBBG maintains a small nursery of California natives!

Stagecoach Hill, McKinleyville, CA. An area immediately south of Dry Lagoon Beach

State Park on U.S. Highway 101, the place to see the western azalea.

The Theodore Payne Foundation for Wild Flowers and Native Plants, Inc., 10459 Tuxford Street, Sun Valley, CA 91352, (818) 768-1802. The Theodore Payne Foundation sells, among others, Matilija poppy, deer grass, and many cultivars and species of ceanothus.

University of California Botanical Garden, Centennial Drive, Berkeley, CA 94720, (415) 642-3343. One could spend days here, wandering from one part of the California native plant garden to another—especially in spring, when *Fremontodendron, Ceanothus, Sisyrichium bellum,* madrone, and manzanita all compete for attention.

The Pacific Northwest

The Berry Botanic Garden, 11505 S.W. Summerville Avenue, Portland, OR 97219, (503) 636-4112. This garden works to restore the rare and endangered plant species of the Pacific Northwest. Common and uncommon natives, including lilies, rhododendrons, and alpines, grace its woodland walks and rock garden.

Leach Botanical Garden, 6704 S.E. 122nd Avenue, Portland, OR 97236, (503) 761-9503. A lovely acreage of native woodland is home to ferns, western dogwood, vine maples, mahonias, ocean spray, *Iris innominata,* rock and bog gardens.

The Mountain Region

Denver Botanic Gardens, 909 York Street, Denver, CO 80206, (303) 575-2547. Don't miss the splendid rock garden, the short grass prairie, zauschnerias, eriogonums, cacti, and the sumacs, especially colorful in fall.

Garden of the Gods, Colorado Springs, CO. This garden was planted by God and is a spectacular place to see chamisa, mountain mahogany, Gambrel oak, and little bluestem.

The Midwest

Cemetery of Spring Grove, 4521 Spring Grove Avenue, Cincinnati, OH 45232, (513) 681-6680. This Olmsted-designed cemetery is a treasure trove of trees, including swamp cypress and *Cornus florida* 'Spring Grove'.

Chicago Botanic Garden, Lake Cook Road, East of Edens Highway, P.O. Box 400, Glencoe, IL 60022, (312) 835-5440. Natives and exotics mix in the new walled garden, and there's a native area with prairie grasses and native perennials, and a pretty wildlife garden with *Chelone,* obedient plant, and native honeysuckle.

Lichterman Nature Center, 5992 Quince Road, Memphis, TN 38119. Lichterman sells natives including *Aster lateriflorus* 'Horizontalis' and American beautyberry.

Lincoln Memorial Garden and Nature Center, 2301 East Lake Drive, Springfield, IL 62707. There are Jens Jensen–designed "council rings" and trails lined with the trees, shrubs, and wildflowers of Illinois.

Memphis Botanic Garden, 750 Cherry Road, Memphis, TN 38117, (901) 685-1566. Has a lovely azalea and dogwood trail and many natives.

Minnesota Landscape Arboretum and Horticultural Research Center, University of Minnesota, 3675 Arboretum Drive, P.O. Box 39, Chanhassen, MN 55317, (612) 443-2460. Displays the Northern Lights series of native azaleas.

Morton Arboretum, Route 53, Lisle, IL 60532, (708) 968-0074. Visit the prairie restoration and communities of North American plants.

The Robert Starbird Dorney Ecology Garden, University of Waterloo, Waterloo, Ontario. Visitors can see native vines of Ontario, as well as prairie plants and native roses.

Shaw Arboretum, P.O. Box 38, Gray Summit, MO 63039, (314) 577-5138. A 74-acre prairie restoration and trails lined with Ozark wildflowers are don't-miss features of this arboretum.

Tennessee Botanical Gardens and Fine Arts Center at Cheekwood, Forest Park Drive, Nashville, TN 37205, features "Wildings," a wildflower garden.

The University of Wisconsin Arboretum, Madison, WI 53711. August is the time to see silphiums in bloom as well as Indian grass and prairie baby's breath.

The Northeast

Bowman's Hill State Wildflower Preserve, Washington Crossing Historic Park, Washington Crossing, PA 18977. Camas blooms with unfurling ostrich and sensitive ferns in spring.

Connecticut College Arboretum, entrance on Williams Street (Route 32), New London, CT 06320. This garden has an exquisite collection of native azaleas of which the fragrant roseshell is well represented.

Garden in the Woods, 180 Hemenway Road, Framingham, MA 01701-2699, (508) 877-6574. *Trillium grandiflorum, Zizia aptera,* rhododendrons, pinkshell azaleas, and amsonia are a beautiful part of the explosion of May bloom.

Longview Farm, Bodine Road, Box 76, Malvern, PA 19355, (215) 827-7614. Oak leaf hydrangea, false Solomon's seal, and many other natives mix with exotics in this private garden that is open to the public on Thursday, Friday, and Saturday afternoons.

Longwood Gardens, P.O. Box 501, Kennett Square, PA 19348, (215) 388-6741. *Erianthus contortus* is one of the native grasses in the grass display. Longwood has everything!

New York Botanical Garden, Southern (Kazimiroff) Boulevard, Bronx, NY 10458, (212) 220-8700. A well-endowed native plant garden with fringe tree, yellowwood, and cut-leaf sumac and the home of the F. Gordon Foster Hardy Fern Collection.

Wave Hill, 252nd Street and Independence Avenue, New York, NY 10025, (212) 678-6886. Among the hundreds of native trees is a drop-dead specimen of *Rhus* 'Laciniata'.

The Mid-Atlantic

Bartholdi Park, Independence Avenue at First Street, S.W., Washington, D.C. A part of the United States Botanic Garden, has devoted a garden to ornamental natives.

Brookside Gardens, 1500 Glenallen Avenue, Wheaton, MD 20902, (301) 949-8230. The perennial garden is a fine mixture of natives and exotics, including queen-of-the-prairie, American beautyberrry, and *Panicum* 'Heavy Metal', and a needle palm. Gama grass and roses team in the Rose Garden.

Green Spring Garden Park, 4603 Greenspring Road, Alexandria, VA 22312, (703) 642-5174. Walk the Virginia Native Plant Trail of perennials and shrubs, including clethras, Joe-Pye weeds, winterberries, and asters among hundreds of other plants.

Hillwood, 4155 Linnean Avenue, N.W., Washington, D.C. 20008, (202) 686-8500. Features a native plant garden around the Indian Building that includes fringe cups.

London Town Publik House & Gardens, 839 Londontown Road, Edgewater, MD 21037, (301) 956-4900. Among the many treasures of this creek-side garden is a large specimen of *Pieris floribunda.*

Mt. Cuba Center for Study of the Piedmont Flora, Box 3570, Barley Mill Road, Greenville, DE 19807-0570, (302) 239-4244. 'Miss Honeybee' magnolia, leucothoes, great merrybells, and thousands of other wildflowers.

National Arboretum, 3501 New York Avenue, N.E., Washington, D.C. 20002, (202) 475-4815. Dutchman's breeches, Oconee bells, and Mayapples are part of the spring carpet in Fern Valley. Look for the needle palm.

William Paca Garden, c/o Historic Annapolis, Inc., King George Street at Marin Street, Annapolis, MD 21401, (301) 267-6656. Magnificent specimens of American holly.

Winterthur, Route 52, Winterthur, DE 19735, (302) 654-1548. A well-grown Franklin tree graces the edge of Coach House Road, and American witch hazels on Oak Hill.

A p p e n d i x   3

SPECIALIZED PLANTS

BIRD PLANTS

Swamp milkweed, *Asclepius incarnata*
Butterfly weed, *A. tuberosa*
Purple aster, *Aster bigelovii*
New England aster, *A. novae-angliae*

The following plants are tried and true producers of nectar, seeds, or fruits taken by birds.

Perennials and Annuals

New York aster, *A. novi-belgii*
False indigo, *Baptisia australis*
Chocolate flower, *Berlandiera* spp.
Wild senna, *Cassia* spp.
Eared coreopsis, *Coreopsis auriculata*
Threadleaf coreopsis, *C. verticillata* and
cultivars
Prairie clover, *Dalea* spp.
Wild bleeding heart, *Dicentra eximia*
Pale purple coneflower, *Echinacea pallida*
Purple coneflower, *E. purpurea*
Dog fennel, *Eupatorium capillifolium*
Sunflower, *Helianthus* spp.
Blazing star, *Liatris* spp.
Cardinal flower, *Lobelia cardinalis*
Great blue lobelia, *L. siphilitica*
Penstemon spp.
Creeping phlox, *Phlox stolonifera*
Black-eyed Susan, *Rudbeckia* spp.
Salvia guaranitica
Goldenrod, *Solidago canadensis*
Golden crownbeard, *Verbesina encelioides*

Grasses

Most grasses produce seeds taken by birds; the following have been observed.
Big bluestem, *Andropogon gerardii*
Bushy bluestem, *A. glomeratus*
Splitbeard bluestem, *A. ternarius*
Broom sedge, *A. virginicus*
Sideoats grama, *Bouteloua curtipenula*
Lovegrass, *Eragrostis spectabilis*
Indian rice grass, *Oryzopsis hymenoides*
Switch grass, *Panicum virgatum*

This garden at the Chicago Botanic Garden was designed with hummingbirds, birds, and butterflies in mind. Trumpet honeysuckle, like cross vine and trumpet vine, attracts hummers.

Little bluestem, *Schizachrium scoparium*
Prairie dropseed, *Sporobolus heterolepis*

Shrubs and Vines

Chokeberry, *Aronia arbutifolia, A. melanocarpa*
Buttonbush, *Cephalanthus occidentales*
Silky dogwood, *Cornus amomum*
Gray dogwood, *C. racemosa*
Red-osier dogwood, *C. sericea*
Ilex spp.
Virginia sweetspire, *Itea virginica*
Mahonia spp.
Virginia creeper, *Parthenocissus quinquefolia*
Prunus spp.
Sumac, *Rhus* spp.
Currant, *Ribes* spp.
Rose, *Rosa carolina, R. virginiana*
Elderberry, *Sambucus candensis*
Silver buffaloberry, *Shepardia argentea*
Viburnum spp.

Trees

Maple, *Acer* spp.
Serviceberry, *Amalanchier* spp.
Birch, *Betula* spp.
Dogwood, *Cornus* spp.
Hawthorn, *Crataegus* spp.
Holly, *Ilex* spp.

The following plants tolerate drought. There are, of course, degrees of drought. Plants from the West or from desert regions can go for weeks without water. "Drought" for an eastern plant might mean a fast-draining, hot, exposed site. Check the origin of a plant first to make sure it is suitable for your garden.

Perennials and Annuals

Leadplant, *Amorpha canescens*
Anemone, *Anemone cylindrica*
Artemisia, *Artemisia*
Butterfly weed, *Asclepias tuberosa*
Sky blue aster, *Aster azureus*
Purple aster, *A. bigelovii*
Wood aster, *A. divaricatus* (dry shade)
Heath aster, *A. ericoides*
Smooth aster, *A. laevis*
Stiff aster, *A. linarifolius*
Silky aster, *A. sericeus*
Tahoka daisy, *A. tanacetifolius*
Wine-cups, *Callirhoë* spp.
Sweet fern, *Comptonia peregrina*
Threadleaf coreopsis, *Coreopsis verticillata*
Pale purple coneflower, *Echinacea pallida*
Fireweed, *Epilobium angustifolium*
Flowering spurge, *Euphorbia corollata*
Prairie smoke, *Geum triflorum*

Albuquerque designer Judith Phillips uses native plants such as cactus, chamisa, and Indian rice grass to create a tableau like this one—as appealing in winter's silvers and tans as it is during the growing season.

Maximilian's sunflower, *Helianthus maximiliani*
Downy sunflower, *Helianthus mollis*
Western sunflower, *H. occidentalis*
Ox eye daisy, *Helopsis helianthoides*
Rough blazing star, *Liatris aspera*
Dwarf blazing star, *L. cylindracea*
Spotted gayfeather, *L. punctata*
Flax, *Linum perenne*
Lupine, *Lupinus* spp.
Evening primroses, *Oenethera* spp.
Sedum, *Sedum* spp.
Goldenrod, *Solidago spathulata*
Zauschneria, *Zauschneria* spp.

Grasses

Big bluestem, *Andropogon gerardii*
Purple three-awn, *Aristida purpurea*
Grama grass, *Bouteloua gracilis*
Sideoats grama, *B. curtipendula*
Buffalo grass, *Buchloë dactyloides*
Reed grass, *Calamagrostis foliosa*
River oats, *Chasmanthium latifolium*
Giant wild rye, *Elymus condensatus*
Lovegrasses, *Eragrostis* spp.
California fescue, *Festuca californica*
Bamboo muhly, *Muhlenbergia dumosa*
Deer grass, *M. rigens*
Bear grasses, *Nolina* spp.
Indian rice grass, *Oryzopsis hymenoides*
Switch grass, *Panicum virgatum*
Little bluestem, *Schizachrium scoparium*
Indian grass, *Sorghastrum nutans*
Prairie dropseed, *Sporobolus heterolepis*

Shrubs

Agave, *Agave* spp.
Indigo bush, *Amorpha fruticosa*
Manzanita, *Arcotstaphylos* spp.
Sage, *Artemesia* spp.
Red bird of paradise, *Caesalpinia pulcherrima*
Fairy duster, *Calliandra eriophylla*
Ceanothus spp.
Mahogany, *Cercocarpus* spp.
Chamisa, *Chrysothamnus nauseosus*
Cliff rose, *Cowania neomexicana*
Dalea spp.
Sotol, *Dasylirion wheeleri*
Bush poppy, *Dendromecon* spp.
Hop bush, *Dodonaea viscosa*
Brittlebush, *Encelia farinosa*
Apache plume, *Fallugia paradoxa*
Cliff fendlerbush, *Fendlera ripicola*

Many prairie plants, like this North Carolina switch grass, thrive in clay soil.

Florida privet, *Forestiera segregata*
Ocotillo, *Fouquieria splendens*
Fremontia, *Fremontodendron* spp.
Toyon, *Heteromeles arbutifolia*
Bladderpod, *Isomeris arborea*
Chuparosa, *Justicia californica*
Creosote bush, *Larrea tridentata*
Nevin's barberry, *Mahonia nevinii*
Bush mallow, *Malocothamnus arcuatus*
Bayberry, *Myrica pensylvanica*
Prickly pear, cholla, *Opuntia*
Western sand cherry, *Prunus besseyi*
Beach plum, *P. maritima*
Littleleaf sumac, *Rhus microphylla*
Sugarbush, *R. ovata*
Squawbush, *R. trilobata*
Chaparral currant, *Ribes malvaceum*
Evergreen currant, *R. viburnifolium*
Silver buffaloberry, *Shepardia argentea*
Mountain marigold, *Tagetes lemmoni*
Woolly blue-curls, *Trichostema lanatum*
Skeletonleaf goldeneye, *Viguiera stenoloba*
Yucca spp.
Coontie, *Zamia pumila*

Trees

Chalk maple, *Acer leucoderme*
Red shanks, *Adenostoma sparsifolium*
Madrone, *Arbutus menziesii*
Feltleaf ceanothus, *Ceanothus arboreus*
Palo verde, *Cercidium floridum*
Desert willow, *Chilopsis linearis*
New Mexico privet, *Forestiera neomexicana*
Ironwood, *Olneya tesota*
Longleaf pine, *Pinus palustris*
Texas ebony, *Pithecellobium flexicaule*

Honey mesquite, *Prosopis glandulosa* var. *glandulosa*
Coast live oak, *Quercus agrifolia*
Mescal bean, *Sophora secundiflora*

CLAY-TOLERANT PLANTS

Perennials and Annuals

Heath aster, *Aster ericoides*
New England aster, *A. novae-angliae*
White false indigo, *Baptisia alba*
Wild senna, *Cassia* spp.
Purple coneflower, *Echinacea purpurea*
Bergamot, *Monarda fistulosa*
Yellow coneflower, *Ratibida pinnata*
Silphium spp.
Stiff goldenrod, *Solidago rigida*
Ironweed, *Vernonia noveboracensis*

Grasses

Big bluestem, *Andropogon gerardii*
Switchgrass, *Panicum virgatum*
Indian grass, *Sorghastrum nutans*

SALT-TOLERANT PLANTS

Perennials

Narrow-leaved sunflower, *Helianthus angustifolius*
Seashore mallow, *Kosteletzkya virginica*
Seaside goldenrod, *Solidago sempervirens*

Grasses

Muhly grass, *Muhlenbergia capillaris*

Shrubs

Groundsel, *Baccharis halimifolia*
Seagrape, *Coccoloba* spp.
Florida privet, *Forestiera segregata*
California wax myrtle, *Myrica californica*
Bayberry, *M. pensylvanica*
Simpson stopper, *Myricanthes fragrens*
Beach plum, *Prunus maritima*
Saw palmetto, *Serenoa repens*

Trees

Cabbage palm, *Sabal palmetto*

HUMMINGBIRD PLANTS

Cross vine, *Anistochus capreolatus*
Columbine, *Aquilegia* spp.
Butterfly weed, *Asclepius tuberosa*

Trumpet vine, *Campsis radicans*
Indian paintbrush, *Castilleja* spp.
New Jersey tea, *Ceanothus americanus*
Fireweed, *Epilobium angustifolium*
Standing cypress, *Ipomopsis rubra*
Iris spp.
Chuparosa, *Justicia californica* & spp.
Blazing star, *Liatris* spp.
Cardinal flower, *Lobelia cardinalis*
Coral honeysuckle, *Lonicera sempervirens*
Lupine, *Lupinus* spp.
Bee balm, *Monarda didyma*
Penstemon spp.
Wild petunia, *Ruellia* spp.
Cup plant, *Silphium perfoliatum*

BUTTERFLY PLANTS

Some of the same people who love the notion of butterflies circling their summer gardens are uncomfortable with the idea of caterpillars.

Perennials and Annuals

Leadplant, *Amorpha canescens*
Columbine, *Aquilegia* spp.
Swamp milkweed, *Asclepius incarnata*
Butterfly weed, *A. tuberosa*
Aster, *Aster* spp.
Turtlehead, *Chelone* spp.
Bugbane, *Cimicifuga racemosa*
Eared coreopsis, *Coreopsis auriculata*
Threadleaf coreopsis, *C. verticillata* and
    cultivars
Prairie clover, *Dalea purpurea*
    (*Petelostemum*)
Pale purple coneflower, *Echinacea pallida*
Yellow purple coneflower, *E. paradoxa*
Purple coneflower, *E. purpurea*
Fleabane, *Erigeron* spp.
Dog fennel, *Eupatorium capillifolium*
Wild ageratum, *E. coelestinum*

Seagrape serves as salt- and wind-defiant landscaping on the Florida coast.

A butterfly alights on chamisa.

Joe-Pye weed, *E. dubium, E. fistulosum,*
    E. maculatum, E. purpureum
Boneset, *E. perfoliatum*
Sneezeweed, *Helenium autumnale*
Mallow, *Hibiscus* spp.
Marsh mallow, *Kosteletzkya virginica*
Blazing star, *Liatris* spp.
Cardinal flower, *Lobelia cardinalis*
Bee balm, *Monarda didyma*
Bergamot, *M. fistulosa*
Beardtongue, *Penstemon* spp.
Wood phlox, *Phlox divaricata*
Creeping phlox, *P. stolonifera*
Goldenrod, *Solidago* spp.
Ironweed, *Vernonia* spp.

Shrubs and Vines

New Jersey tea, *Ceanothus americanus*
Buttonbush, *Cephalanthus occidentalis*
Carolina jessamine, *Gelsemium sempervirens*
Mountain laurel, *Kalmia latifolia*
Pinxter azalea, *Rhododendron periclymenoides*
Elderberry, *Sambucus canadensis*

Trees

Birch, *Betula* spp.
Redbud, *Cercis* spp.
Fringe tree, *Chionanthus virginicus*
Hawthorn, *Crataegus* spp.

SHADE-TOLERANT PLANTS

Perennials

Canada anemone, *Anemone canadensis*
Columbine, *Aquilegia* spp.
Turtlehead, *Chelone* spp.
Shooting star, *Dodecatheon* spp.
Bottle gentian, *Gentiana andrewsii*
Alum root, *Heuchera* spp.
Turk's cap lily, *Lilium superbum*
Monarda, bergamot, *Monarda* spp.
Meadowrue, *Thalictrum* spp.

Spiderwort, *Tradescantia* spp.

Grasses

White bear sedge, *Carex albursina*
    C. austrocaroliniana
Palm sedge, *C. muskingumensis*
Pennsylvania sedge, *C. pensylvanica*
River oats, *Chasmanthium latifolium*
Hairgrass, *Deschampsia caespitosa*
Bottlebrush grass, *Hystrix patula*
Golden grass, *Milium effusum* 'Aureum'
Ribbon grass, *Phalaris arundinacea picta*

Ferns

All ferns

Shrubs

Bottlebrush buckeye, *Aesculus parviflora*
Florida leucothoe, *Agarista populifolia*
Devil's walkingstick, *Aralia spinosa*
Chokeberry, *Aronia arbutifolia*
Clethra spp.
Hearts-a-bustin', *Euonymous americana*
Fothergilla spp.
Wild hydrangea, *Hydrangea arborescens*
Oak leaf hydrangea, *H. quercifolia*
Ilex spp.
Florida anise tree, *Illicium floridanum*
Virginia sweetspire, *Itea virginica*
Mountain laurel, *Kalmia latifolia*
Drooping leucothoe, *Leucothoe fontanesiana*
Fetterbush, *Pieris floribunda*
Azaleas, *Rhododendron* spp.
Evergreen rhododendrons, *Rhododendron*
    spp.
Evergreen currant, *Ribes viburnifolium*
Viburnum spp.

Trees

Vine maple, *Acer circinatum*

After a morning's weeding, a garden bench in a shady spot is just the place to bask in a well-earned sense of achievement.

Bald cypress tolerates a wide range of conditions—from well drained to standing water.

PLANTS THAT TOLERATE OCCASIONAL FLOODING

The plants described in the chapter Water Plants are emergents, those that can live in water all year round. In the list that follows are plants that will happily survive seasonal flooding, but need a drier period. They also adapt to continually moist sites—low places or the edge of wetlands. Some will also grow in drier gardens.

Perennials and Annuals

Canada anemone, *Anemone canadensis*
Jack-in-the-pulpit, *Arisaema triphyllum*
Swamp milkweed, *Asclepius incarnata*

New England aster, *Aster novae-angliae*
Turtlehead, *Chelone* spp.
Shooting star, *Dodecatheon meadia*
Joe-Pye weed, *Eupatorium maculatum*
Boneset, *E. perfoliatum*
Queen-of-the-prairie, *Filipendula rubra*
Bottle gentian, *Gentiana andrewsii*
Alum root, *Heuchera richardsonii*
Swamp hibiscus, *Hibiscus coccinea*
Blue flag, *Iris versicolor*
Louisiana iris, *Iris* spp.
Blazing star, *Liatris pycnostachya*
Turk's cap lily, *Lilium superbum*
Cardinal flower, *Lobelia cardinalis*
Great blue lobelia, *L. siphilitica*
Meadowbeauty, *Rhexia virginica*
Greenheaded coneflower, *Rudbeckia laciniata*
Sweet black-eyed Susan, *R. subtomentosa*
Rosinweed, *Silphium integrifolium*
Cup plant, *S. perfoliatum*
Prairie dock, *S. terebinthinaceum*
Ironweed, *Vernonia* spp.
Culver's root, *Veronicastrum virginicum*

Grasses

Big bluestem, *Andropogon gerardii*
Lurid sedge, *Carex lurida* (wet site)
Palm sedge, *C. muskingumensis*
River oats, *Chasmanthium latifolium*
Sugarcane plume grass, *Erianthus giganteus*
Soft rush, *Juncus effusus* (wet site)
Muhly grass, *Muhlenbergia capillaris*
Ribbon grass, *Phalaris arundinacea picta*
Sand cordgrass, *Spartina bakeri*
Fakahatchee, eastern gama grass, *Tripsacum dactyloides*

Ferns

Giant leather fern, *Acrostichum danaeifolium*
Ostrich fern, *Matteuccia struthiopteris*

Sensitive fern, *Onoclea sensibilis*
Cinnamon fern, *Osmunda cinnamomea*
Royal fern, *O. regalis* var. *spectabilis*
Chain fern, *Woodwardia areolata*

Vines

Virginia creeper, *Parthenocissus quinquefolia*

Shrubs

Chokeberry, *Aronia arbutifolia, A. melanocarpa*
Groundsel, *Baccharis halimifolia*
Buttonbush, *Cephalanthus occidentalis*
Summersweet, *Clethra alnifolia*
Silky dogwood, *Cornus amomum*
Gray dogwood, *C. racemosa*
Red-osier dogwood, *C. sericea*
Titi, *Cyrilla racemiflora*
Hearts-a-bustin', *Euonymus americanus*
Fothergilla, *Fothergilla gardenii, F. major*
Possum haw, *Ilex decidua*
Inkberry, *I. glabra*
Winterberry, *I. verticillata*
Virginia sweetspire, *Itea virginica* 'Henry's Garnet'
Sweet gale, *Myrica gale*
Bayberry, *M. pensylvanica*
Swamp azalea, *Rhododedron viscosum*
Swamp rose, *Rosa palustris*
Elderberry, *Sambucus candensis*
Witherod, *Viburnum cassinoides, V. nudum*
Blackhaw, *V. prunifolium*

Trees

Pawpaw, *Asimina triloba*
River birch, *Betula nigra*
Dahoon holly, *Ilex cassine*
Witch hazel, *Hamamelis virginiana*
Sweet bay magnolia, *Magnolia virginiana*
Cypress, *Taxodium* spp. (wet)

BIBLIOGRAPHY

Abbey, Edward. *Desert Solitaire*. New York: Ballantine Books, 1971.

Baldwin, John L. *Climates of the United States*. United States Department of Commerce, U.S. Government Printing Office.

Bartram, William. *Travels of William Bartram*, ed. Mark Van Doren. New York: Dover Books, 1928.

Bell, C. Ritchie, and Bryan J. Taylor. *Florida Wild Flowers*. Chapel Hill, North Carolina: Laurel Hill Press, 1982.

Benson, Lyman, and Robert A. Darrow. *Trees and Shrubs of the Southwestern Deserts*. Tucson: The University of Arizona Press, 1945.

Bir, Richard E. *Growing and Propagating Showy Native Woody Plants*. Chapel Hill and London: University of North Carolina Press, 1992.

Connelly, Kevin. *Gardener's Guide to California Wildflowers*. Sun Valley, California: Theodore Payne Foundation, 1991.

Diboll, Neil. "Prairie Plants and Their Use in the Landscape," ed. Steven M. Still. *Proceedings of the 1987 Perennial Plant Symposium*, August 1987.

Dirr, Michael A. *Manual of Woody Landscape Plants*. Champaign, Illinois: Stipes Publishing Co., 1975.

Dirr, Michael A. "Southern Magnolia Introduces Beauty, Hardiness to Landscape." *Nursery Manager*, July 1991.

Dirr, Michael A. "Testing the Limits of the Southern Magnolia." *Horticulture*, March 1992.

Dorman, Caroline. *Natives Preferred*. Baton Rouge: Claitor's Book Store, 1965.

"The Fringetrees." *Avant Gardener*, vol. 23, no. 11, September 1991.

Fukuoka, Masanobu. *The One-Straw Revolution*. Emmaus, Pennsylvania: Rodale Press, 1978.

"Gaultheria shallon." *Berry Botanic Garden* (bulletin), vol. 4, no. 1, Winter 1991.

Grazzini, Rick. "On the Origin of *Gaillardia* x *grandiflora*." *Bulletin of the Perennial Plant Society*, 1991.

Haddrill, Marilyn. "Taming the Texas Madrone." *American Horticulturist*, August 1992.

Hasselkus, E. R., *A Guide to Selecting Landscape Plants for Wisconsin*. Madison: University of Wisconsin Extension Bulletin, n.d.

Holden, Mark. "The Greening of the Desert." *American Nurseryman*, April 15, 1992.

Johnson, Fran Holman. *"The Gift of the Wild Things:" The Life of Caroline Dormon*. Lafayette, Louisiana: The University of Louisiana, 1990.

Kruckeberg, Arthur R. *Gardening with Native Plants of the Pacific Northwest*. Seattle and London: University of Washington Press, 1982.

Leopold, Aldo. *A Sand County Almanac*. New York: Ballantine Books, 1970.

Meerow, Alan W. *Native Shrubs for South Florida*. Florida Cooperative Extension Service, University of Florida, 1989.

Mielke, Manfred E., and Margery L. Daughtrey. *How to Identify and Control Dogwood Anthracnose*. USDA Forest Service, Northeastern Area, NA-GR-18, 1989.

Native Plants for Landscape Use in Dallas and Fort Worth. Native Plant Society of Texas, NPSOT, Box 891, Georgetown, TX 78626.

Newmann, Erik A. "The Viburnums," *Garden Journal*, National Arboretum, November–December 1966.

Niering, William A., and Richard H. Goodwin. eds. *Energy Conservation on the Home Grounds*. Connecticut Arboretum, 1975.

Niering, William A., and Richard H. Goodwin. eds. *Inland Wetland Plants of Connecticut*. Connecticut Arboretum, 1973.

Ogburn, Charlton. *The Southern Appalachians, A Wilderness Quest*. New York: William Morrow and Company, 1975.

Phillips, Judith. *Southwestern Landscaping with Native Plants*. Santa Fe: Museum of New Mexico Press, 1987.

Price, Martha. "Our Native Azaleas." *Azalean*, vol. 5, September 1983.

Roberts, Edith A., and Elsa Rehmann. *American Plants for American Gardens*. New York: Macmillan Company, 1929.

Rushing, Felder, and Steven E. Newman. *Wildflowers for Mississippi Meadows and Gardens*. Cooperative Extension Service, Mississippi State University, n.d.

Sawyers, Claire. "From Nature's Backyard, Small Natives for Your Garden." Philadelphia Flower Show exhibit catalog, 1989.

Schmidt, Marjorie G. *Growing California Native Plants*. Berkeley: University of California Press, 1980.

Sharples, Ada White. *Alaska Wild Flowers*. Stanford, California: Stanford University Press, 1938.

Stokes, Donald W. "Native Dogwoods." *Horticulture*, February 1977.

Taylor, Sally L., Glenn D. Dreyer, and William A. Niering. *Native Shrubs for Landscaping*. Connecticut Arboretum, 1987.

Tenenbaum, Frances. *Gardening with Wild Flowers*. New York: Ballantine Books, 1973.

There's Hope for Dogwoods. An HRI Information Release pamphlet, Horticultural Research Institute, Washington, D.C. 20005.

Wasowski, Sally, with Andy Wasowski. *Native Texas Plants*. Austin: Texas Monthly Press, 1988.

INDEX

Index

Calliandra eriophylla, 240–41
Callicarpa americana, 241, *242*
Callirhoë involucrata, 85–86
Calycanthus floridus, 241–42, *243*
Calystegia macrostegia, 226
Camas, 86, 87
Camassia quamash, 86, 87
Camellia, silky, 296
Campion, 144–45, *146–47*
Campsis radicans, 226
Canada anemone, 72
Canyon live oak, 330
Cardinal flower, 120
Carex albursina, 185
Carex austrocaroliniana, 186
Carex muskingumensis, 186–87
Carex pensylvanica, 187
Carolina allspice, 241–42, *243*
Carolina bush pea, 153–54, *156*
Carolina jessamine, *222–23,* 228
Carolina rhododendron, *56,* 286–87
Cassia hebecarpa, 86–87
Castilleja integra, 87, 88
Catalina cherry, 276
Catalina perfume, 292, *293*
Catawba rhododendron, 287
Catchfly, 144–45, *146–47*
Cattail, narrow-leaf, *212–13,* 221
Caulophyllum thalictroides, 87–88
Ceanothus, 25, 237, 242–44
Ceanothus, feltleaf, *25,* 310
Ceanothus arboreus, 310
Celandine poppy, 150–51, *154*
Century plant, 234
Cephalanthus occidentalis, 244–45
Cercidium floridum, 310–11
Cercis, 311–12
Cercocarpus montanus, 245
Chain fern, netted, 211
Chalk maple, 306
Chamisa, *20, 37,* 245–46, *344, 346*
Chapman's rhododendron, 287–88
Chasmanthium latifolium (Uniola latifolia), 187
Chelone, 88–89, *135*
Cherry, Catalina, 276
Chihuahuan paintbrush, 87, *88*
Chilopsis linearis, 312
Chionanthus virginicus, 313
Chitalpa, 313–14
Chitalpa tashkentensis, 313–14
Chocolate flower, 84
Chokeberry, 237–39
Cholla cactus, 273
Christmas berry, 260, *261*
Christmas fern, *186,* 208–9

Chrysogonum virginianum, 89
Chrysopsis mariana (Heterotheca mariana), 90
Chrysopsis villosa, 90
Chrysothamnus nauseosus, 245–46
Chuparosa, 268
Cimicifuga racemosa, 90–91
Cinnamon clethra, 246, *247*
Cinnamon fern, 207
Cinquefoil, bush, 275
Cinquefoil, shrubby, 275
Cladrastis kentukeya (C. lutea), 314
Clarkia, 170–71
Clarkia pulchella, 170–71
Clay-tolerant plants, list of, 345
Clematis viorna, 226–27
Cleome serrulata, 170, 171
Clethra, cinnamon, 246, *247*
Clethra acuminata, 246, *247*
Clethra alnifolia, 246–47
Cliff fendlerbush, 255–56
Cliff rose, 251–52
Climbing aster, 225–26
Climbing hydrangea, 227
Clinopodium georgianum (Satureja), 247
Clover, purple prairie, 91–92, *93*
Clover, stinking, *170,* 171
Club, golden, 218–19
Coast azalea, 279–80
Coast live oak, 329–30
Coccoloba uvifera, 247–48
Coffeeberry, 276–77
Cohosh, blue, 87–88
Columbine, *17,* 73–74, *75*
Compass plant, 145, *148, 149*
Comptonia peregrina, 248
Coneflower, *43,* 95–96, *97*
Coneflower, prairie, 136, *137*
Conradina verticillata, 248–49
Coontie, 300, *301*
Coral bells, 109–10, *111*
Coral honeysuckle, 228
Cordgrass, sand, 196
Coreopsis, 91, *92–93*
Coreopsis, plains, 171–72
Coreopsis tinctoria, 171–72
Cornus, 249–50, *251,* 314–16
Cotinus obovatus, 250–51
Cottonwood, valley, 328
Cowania neo-mexicana, 251–52
Coyote bush, dwarf, *27,* 240, *241*
Cranberry bush, American, *297*
Crataegus, 316–17
Cream false indigo, 84
Creeping mint, *122,* 123
Creosote bush, 269
Cross vine, *224,* 225
Culver's root, *104,* 160, *162*
Cumberland azalea, 280–81

Cumberland rosemary, 248–49
Cup plant, 145, *148–49*
Currant, evergreen, 292, *293*
Currant, golden, 291
Currant, red-flowering, *31,* 292
Cutleaf daisy, 96–97
Cymophyllus fraseri, 187–88
Cypress, bald, 333, *347*
Cypress, standing, 174–75
Cyrilla racemiflora, 252

D

Dahoon holly, 319–20
Daisy, beach, 97–99
Daisy, blackfoot, 123, *271*
Daisy, cutleaf, 96–97
Daisy, Engelmann, 96–97
Daisy, Michaelmas, 80–81
Daisy, seaside, 97–99
Daisy, Tahoka, 170
Dalea greggii, 252, *253*
Dalea purpurea (Petalostemum purpureum), 91–92, *93*
Dasylirion wheeleri, 252–53
'David's Choice', 76–77
Decodon verticillatus, 216
Decumaria barbara, 227
Deer fern, 204
Deer grass (*Muhlenbergia dumosa*), 192–93
Deer grass (*Rhexia virginica*), 136–37, *138*
Delphinium cardinale, 93–94
Dendromecon harfordii, 253, *254*
Dennstaedtia punctilobula, 204
Deschampsia caespitosa, 188
Desert ironweed, 325–26
Desert marigold, 170
Desert olive, 317
Desert spoon, 252–53
Desert willow, 312
Desert zinnia, 163–64, *165*
Devil's walkingstick, 235–36
Dicentra, 94–95
Dicentra cucullaria, 94, *95*
Dicentra eximia, 94
Dicentra formosa, 94, *95*
Dodecatheon meadia, 95, *96*
Dog fennel, 101, *102*
Doghobble, 269–70
Dogtooth violet, *8,* 100–101
Dogwood, *59,* 249–50, *251,* 314–16
Doll's eyes, *45,* 70
Dragonhead, false, 133, *135*
Dragonroot, 74–75
Drooping leucothoe, 269–70
Dropseed, prairie, 196–97
Drought-tolerant plants, list of, 344–45
Drummond's phlox, *176,* 177
Dryopteris carthusiana (D. spinulosa), 204–5

Dryopteris filix-mas, 205
Dryopteris goldiana, 205
Dryopteris marginalis, 206
Dusty zenobia, 301
Dutchman's breeches, 94, *95*
Dwarf coyote bush, *27,* 240, *241*
Dwarf fothergilla, 256–57

E

Eastern dogwood, 315–16
Eastern gamma grass, 197
Eastern redbud, 311, *312*
Eastern wild bleeding heart, 94
Ebony, Texas, 327–28
Echinacea, 95–96, *97*
'Edgewood', 271–72
Elderberry, *45,* 293–94
Elymus condensatus, 188–89
Encelia farinosa, 253–54
Engelmann daisy, 96–97
Engelmannia pinnatifida, 96–97
Engelmann spruce, 326–27
Epilobium angustifolium, 97, *98*
Equisetum hyemale, 216
Eragrostis spectabilis, 189
Eragrostis trichoides, 189
Erianthus contortus, 189–90
Erianthus giganteus, 190
Erigeron glaucus, 97–99
Eriogonum, 98, 99, *100*
Eryngium yuccifolium, 99–100, *101*
Erythronium, 100–101
Eschscholzia californica, 172
Eugenia foetida, 254
Euonymus americana, 254–55
Eupatorium, 101–2, *103*
Euphorbia corollata, 102–3, *104*
'Eve Case' coffeeberry, 276–77
Evening primrose, *19,* 126–27, *128–29*
Evergreen currant, 292, *293*
Evergreen huckleberry, 297
Evergreen rhododendrons, 286

F

Fairy duster, 240–41
Fakahatchee grass, 197
Fallugia paradoxa, 255
False dragonhead, 133, *135*
False indigo, 83–84
False indigo, cream, 84
False indigo, white, 82–83
False lily-of-the-valley, 121–23, *207*
False lupine, 153–54, *156*
False Solomon's seal, 147–48, *151*
Fawn lily, 100–101
Feltleaf ceanothus, *25,* 310
Fendlera rupicola, 255–56